THE DARTNELL

PERSONNEL

DIRECTOR'S

HANDBOOK

Third Printing, 1971
Second Printing (revised), 1970

Copyright 1969
in the United States, Canada, and Great Britain by
THE DARTNELL CORPORATION
All rights reserved

Library of Congress Catalog Card Number 76-77249
International Standard Book Number 85013-028-X

Printed in the United States of America by Dartnell Press, Inc., Chicago, Illinois 60640

THE DARTNELL

PERSONNEL DIRECTOR'S HANDBOOK

by
Wilbert E. Scheer

THE DARTNELL CORPORATION
CHICAGO and LONDON

ACKNOWLEDGMENTS

Author and publisher are grateful to the following for their valuable contributions to this handbook:

ROBERT E. ANDERSON, Director, Administrative Services, Honeywell EDP.

LAWRENCE A. APPLEY, President, American Management Association.

WALTER E. BAER, Corporate Labor Relations Representative, Brunswick Corporation.

FRANK H. CASELL, Former Director, United States Employment Service.

PHILIP B. CROSBY, Director, Quality Control, International Telephone & Telegraph Corp.

RALPH A. DREKMANN, Manpower Development Division, The Equitable Life Assurance Society of the United States.

JOHN ELLIOTT, Vice-President, Behavioral Sciences, Fry Consultants, Inc.

ROBERT M. EVANS, Professional Recruitment Manager, Cummins Engine Company.

SYDNEY J. HARRIS, Chicago *Daily News.*

FRANK G. HOFFMAN, Principal Partner, Practical Management Association.

RALPH D. HULTGREN, Engineering Division, The Procter & Gamble Company.

HERMAN C. KRANNERT, Board Chairman, Inland Container Corporation.

LEWIS E. LACHTER, Managing Editor, *Administrative Management Magazine.*

JOAN R. MCALLISTER, Eastern Airlines.

PHILIP L. MORGAN, Vice-President, Personnel Data System, Information Science, Inc.

DEWITT O'KIEFFE, Senior Vice-President, Leo Burnett Company, Inc.

PAUL C. SHEDD, JR., Engineering Division, Unarco Industries, Inc.

WILLIAM SLEITH, President, Iona Manufacturing Company.

COLONEL JOHN SLEZAK, Board Chairman, Kable Printing Company.

WALLACE R. SNYDER, Manpower Resources and Development, Blue Cross Association.

ERIC WEBSTER, Creative Director, Pemberton's of London.

CONTENTS

DEDICATION

To my wife, who has to contend with my peregrinations into the writing field, I dedicate this book. Thank you, ERNA, for your unending patience with a husband who spends so many weekends married to a typewriter.

And to the many people and their companies who have contributed so much in the way of ideas, illustrations, and case histories to this personnel handbook, my grateful appreciation. You will find your names throughout its pages—I wish they could be in neon lights.

And to the people who use this personnel handbook, in search for guidance in specific situations, my hope that it will prove helpful.

WILBERT E. SCHEER

INTRODUCTION

A PHILOSOPHY FOR A PERSONNEL EXECUTIVE

By Edwin B. Gilroy
Assistant to the President, VSI Corporation
Pasadena, California

What's this book all about? And why are you, a personnel "pro," reading it and learning from it?

Do you hope to find some answers to some puzzling problems? Well, that is a fair reason. The boss has a burr under you because some action is needed to complete a project? Another good reason. Or maybe you need an exchange of ideas, like your own with the author's and editor's? Very worthy.

I would like to recommend you read it, learn from it, and use it for several other reasons. What are they? Here are some samples:

First of all, because it is *different*. Personnel administration needs another handbook or casebook like you need a third elbow. There are a number of good, reliable, readable handbooks a lot cheaper— and a lot easier to read.

This book is different. It touches on the horizons of personnel administration. That is where its secret of success resides, that is its beauty, and that is one of the reasons you should be able to enjoy and use it. It will help you to gain stature in the profession and strengthen your company to serve your customer better.

Then there's another reason, more important than the first. That is the spirit that motivated the book in the first place and forms the cohesion throughout the various chapters. It's a spirit of adventure and excellence. If there is a message in the book, it is this: time, company's money, and possibly your future to innovate, initiate, and even inspire your colleagues, your subordinates and your superiors to exploit imagination and ingenuity. And to do so with all the abilities and acumen you possess.

Why is this so important? Why should you, probably with a pretty decent job with a fair-to-middling company and a secure future risk all you have worked for by (1) reading the book and (2) tackling something new?

I believe the answer lies at the heart of why you are on the payroll. Why you have chosen "personnel" as a career. And why your company needs your services more than ever.

Business is people! Business is people bringing together ideas, money, and facilities to satisfy needs of other people. Today this task is difficult because of the fantastic social, technological, political, and cultural changes we are encountering.

If the leadership for accommodating change—or even stimulating it—does not emanate with the "people pro," where else can business look? Certainly not to the money, engineering, and production pros. Chances are they see business in terms of things. Not all, of course, but the leadership for an organization must be people-oriented.

The Values Are Different

Perhaps you can default the marketing and sales pros. They spend their lives analyzing and creating products to satisfy people's needs. And in many cases they are very good. But oftentimes they look at their "people universe" in terms of economics and status, not in terms of individuals with emotions, aspirations, ideals, or even in some cases with intelligence.

That leaves you, Mr. Personnel Pro, with the responsibility for wheel-horsing some of the new ideas in people-management through your own organization. I believe this is necessary, and I believe it is good. Here's why:

In my explanation I'd like to touch on two fundamental points. The first having to do with where we (American industry) find ourselves roaring through the second half of the twentieth century. In other words, our environment and what lies ahead for us. The second having to do with you, your career, your company, your family, your neighborhood, and your community and country.

This whole business of people is of crucial importance right now, and from all I can put together will continue to grow in importance. Leadership will determine whether this business of people as we know it will survive, and whether free men will continue to have an opportunity to join together "voluntarily" to sustain themselves through their own efforts. Or whether the "voluntary" efforts will be in response to laws, edicts, directives and influences from a central authority.

The Challenge Ahead

Life in the United States is about one-half highly satisfactory. Our abilities to produce and consume are great, and improving. By continuous research new products are emerging to permit us to assert a greater degree of control over our lives. Education is improving. Along a broad technological and social front we are encouraging a better and fuller life. But what about the second half, the half having to do with world tensions (now in Vietnam; yesterday in Berlin, Korea, and Greece), racial unrest, and concern about individual freedom?

The two go together in the mid-twentieth century. They will continue until well into the twenty-first century. The business community will be one of the élites which helps America and the world toward a better century.

Look at it this way: America is only a little more than 175 years old as an organized form of federalism, yet in this incredibly short period of time finds itself as one of the world's leading powers. Fortuitous circumstances occasioned this almost unbelievable leap from a wilderness to an industrial, economic, social, political, and cultural complex incomparable on this planet.

The forces of freedom were ranging strongly in Europe when the constitution was debated, cussed, and discussed. The assertion of man over his government instead of the power of government over man gained the most significant momentum in history in the late eighteenth century. The impact and influence of freedom and federalism throughout the old world came loud and clear.

Almost simultaneously the ability to navigate, move raw materials from continent to continent and trade across oceans sustained the new country. Her energetic citizens were moving toward opportunity and they pushed the frontiers of the West and began to build a broad producing base of agriculture, production, and distribution.

The country survived the crises of a bitter civil war. Though the enmity ran deep and, indeed, bad feeling still remains, the country was forced to look intently at her political institutions, her philosophy toward all men and, just as importantly, build a stronger productive base.

When the great war of 1914-1918 began in Europe, the country had recovered and was able to become for the first time an arsenal for a great portion of a contending side. She was able to send a citizen army to force capitulation of an already spent enemy.

Then the country survived the worldwide economic crises of the thirties. At the same time it began experiments to minimize the wild fluctuations in our economic system. These experiments are continuing, and are one of the reasons this business of people is important. But this is an aside, let's return to the environment.

The Tests of World Leadership

World War II catapulted the United States into a position of power and prominence. We are today, and will continue for a long time to come, contending with the opportunities and problems of world power.

The industrial base of the North plus her superiority of manpower caused the South to forcefully rejoin the Union. In World War II the allied powers soaked up supplies, material and food provided by the factories, mills, mines, forests and farms of America.

So, too, did the United States become the productive base for the struggle in World War II. Again, and even more than before, the farms, mills, mines, and plants poured forth the material needed to defend Western Europe and the Pacific from aggression. Even more importantly, while a tired, war-weary world was recovering from the ravage of conflict, the country produced and distributed goods and materials not only for her own people but also for a sizable portion of the world.

Now we come closer to today. Granted that after extending ourselves as we did in World War II we would like to rest on our efforts, take a furlough from our hard work. But that's not in the cards.

Greece was the first test. Then came the supplying of Berlin. America was back in the front lines. And then Korea. We seemed to go from one crisis to another. Even today there's contention about our involvement in Southeast Asia. Yet there will be little respite. If you would like to forget Vietnam, there's another crisis brewing for the 1970s or the 1980s. That's the way it is with a world power. That's the way it has been since the dawn of recorded history. And that's the way it looks today.

This is the environment you are in now, and the environment in which you will be working. There will be international tension. There will be conflict. There will be contention.

The Hunger for Better Things

Now, why are you—Mr. Personnel Pro—so important? Why are you reading this book in the first place? Did you notice something throughout the last 150 years? I hope so.

It is simply this. The industrial base of America has served as the foundation for freedom or, at least, as the strength opposing aggression. Your role to maintain this strength is highly important.

By your actions and decisions the people running your machines, mining your ore, distributing your products and managing your enterprise will determine the ability of America to continue her role as a defender of the aggressed. Our spirit of independence, philosophy of individualism is meaningless without the support of a viable, energetic, highly productive complex exerting every effort to satisfy the needs of both an affluent economy and a hunger for better things elsewhere in the world.

If you do not work to improve the technology, the productive capacity of your company, the spirit of your enterprise from a people point of view, who will? Whether you realize it or not, the

13

gold ring—not the brass ring—is ready for you to grab. Let's look at this in some detail.

The character of your company can be determined by you. How? By doing what you do best, and doing it regularly. You can improve the overall competence of your company. One of the major functions of a personnel pro is the acquisition, selection, and induction of people into his organization. The caliber and lasting attitudes of new people coming into a company can be improved by the personnel pro using all his resources from a multichanneled approach in recruiting, multiple interviewing, appropriate testing, depth referencing, and final mental, physical and emotional evaluating. Implied here is the crucial importance of all the employment tasks. Unfortunately these tasks are looked upon with some disdain and the employment office merely as a jumping-off spot to the more exotic functions of training, salary administration, or labor relations. This is unfortunate, because the employment function determines the personnel strength of a company. It is no place for an amateur.

The Induction Opportunity

In many companies the employment people introduce new employees to their jobs, bosses, working neighbors, and the company generally. This is a golden opportunity to spark a spirit of energy and communicate information when motivation and receptivity are high. How well is this opportunity being seized and exploited? If your induction philosophy and techniques do not sparkle, you are not doing all you can for the new employee or the company. If they do not create a favorable impression or get a new employee working at a productive pace, a redesign is in order.

Then there's the ever-present responsibility of constantly working on a company's environment: physical, policy, and attitudinal. They are all important. The work to improve must be relentless. For many companies, working conditions and personnel policy are fairly good. If not, every effort should be made to bring the company into the twentieth century. But it probably is in the attitudinal area that the personnel pro can make his most significant contribution.

This brings me to the second of my reasons for you, Mr. Personnel Pro, to espouse "Business is People" in your company. On this feature you can accelerate the progress of your career. It will have great influence on your status within the company, your professional advancement, your salary, and your family's standard of living.

Premium on Ideas

Be willing to initiate new ideas. Be willing to thrust into new and unexplored ventures. Particularly when and where the ideas and ventures will improve the efficacy of your organization.

Fortune favors the bold! The entrepreneur has always been richly rewarded. You can be a personnel entrepreneur. In fact, I prefer to describe the type of man who will make his mark in the personnel field as an entrepreneur rather than a pro. This book contains the ideas and germs of ideas from many sources. Use them. Adapt them to your own needs, of course, since the mere act of adoption will not satisfy your organization.

Of greater import, use your own ideas. We are fortunate in personnel work to attract, generally, high-caliber people. I know there are many men and women who only need encouragement to try new ideas. The ideas are good, but what is lacking is the spirit or courage to take a chance. The country and the personnel field need more men and women who can take risks of a new venture and see it through.

So that is what this book is all about. It is, first of all, a call to adventure in personnel work. It offers exciting ideas—proven ideas —which can be used by you to advance the cause of your company and your career. It is even more. It is a chart, map, outline of some of the best thinking of how to do things well in our growing, dynamic work.

How the book will be used is up to you. If you need it, refer to it, and rely on it in the same spirit it was written, the book will serve you well.

PART 1

PERSONNEL MANAGEMENT

The functions of personnel
Organizational charts
Personnel relationships
Philosophy of management
The social climate of business
Personnel administration
Turnover research
Testing procedures
Generalities vs. specifics
Personnel periodicals

THE FUNCTIONS OF PERSONNEL

To guide them in their planning and operating, many companies have organization charts. Similarly, divisions within a company often have sections of an overall chart developed into greater detail to help them in planning.

Personnel, too, could utilize such a chart. Personnel activities within an organization ought to be clearly set forth. But the personnel chart should show functions, not staff. Functions are usually permanent; interests and abilities of individuals tend to change with time.

There are two methods by which the personnel chart may be developed. The popular way is to list all the separate items which are being performed and arrange these into natural groupings. This type of chart shows what *is* done; there is no indication of what *should be* done.

Too often, personnel programs grow without any real plan of organization. Sometimes they include items which do not belong. Some phases of a personnel program are often done by other departments, or possibly not done at all.

How to Begin

Therefore a better way to design a personnel chart is to forget for the moment the program as it is presently in practice. Consider what a comprehensive personnel program ought to include. Start with a purely academic approach to find this answer.

Such standard version of an organization chart for the personnel program will classify all activities into logical subdivisions. The number of such subdivisions is not important so long as it is reasonable—not too few nor too many. For this discussion let us suggest these breakdowns: (1) Research and Standards, (2) Employment, (3) Education and Training, (4) Safety and Health, (5) Employee Activities, (6) Wages and Salaries, (7) Benefit Administration. Labor Relations could be a separate category if this is a serious and troublesome area; otherwise its involvements should rightfully be included in the above groupings since it is usually concerned with wages and benefits.

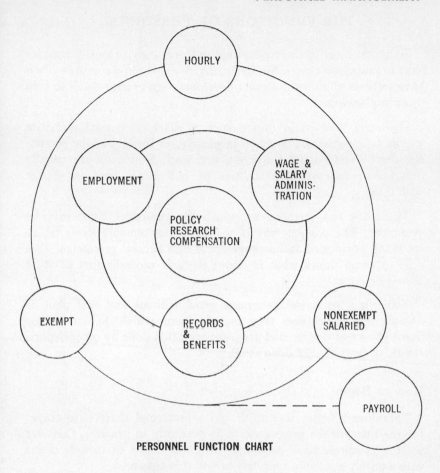

PERSONNEL FUNCTION CHART

Starting with these separate section headings, the chart is then expanded into greater detail by arranging the individual personnel practices appropriately until all activities of a comprehensive program are properly listed.

This standard, or one similar to it, is applicable to all industry. It fits a two-man butcher shop, small business establishment, large corporation, and far-flung international organization. The difference between personnel programs in various companies is not in basic functions but in the degree to which these functions are formalized, and the size of the staff necessary to carry them out.

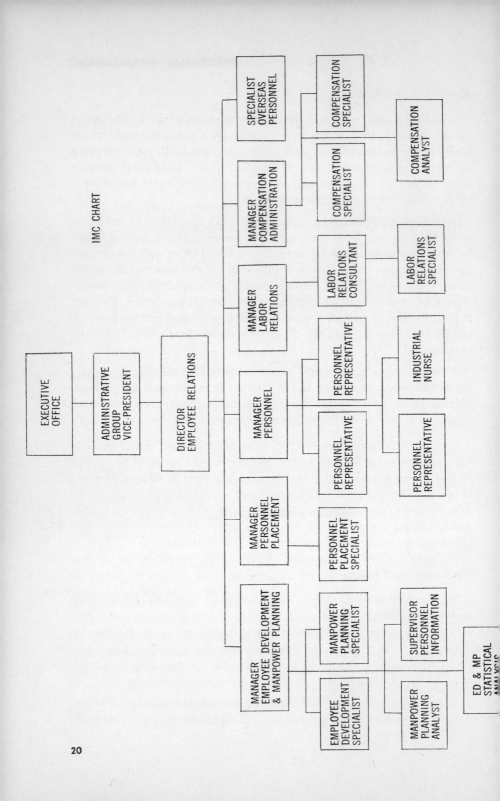

IMC CHART

20

Keep Things Flexible

Dividing a total program into a specific number of logical areas does not mean that in an average-size firm the personnel officer needs that same number of staff assistants. In a small company, two or more functions could well be handled by the same employee. In large industrial establishments each one of these areas could be a large section requiring many employees.

After this chart has been understood it can be applied to any company by adapting it to the particular needs. This is accomplished by making a comparison between the standard chart and the present or existing chart. At a glance it will point up two areas of disagreement. First, it will reveal items presently performed which probably should be transferred elsewhere or possibly discontinued. Second, it will disclose phases of a comprehensive personnel program which should be initiated or which, if performed elsewhere, should perhaps be absorbed.

This tailor-made personnel chart incorporates all the characteristics which are necessary and desirable. It is obtained by philosophizing as to what the relationship of the many separate personnel functions should be to the company's overall objectives.

It must be remembered that there can never be any "pure" personnel program regardless of how attractive it may be made to appear on the drawing board. In actual practice the ideal is seldom, if ever, obtained. The personal influence of top executives, financial situation, nature of the industry, competition, location, bargaining agreement, and the status quo will have their effect. In many respects this effect can be wholesome, not necessarily detrimental.

Be Ready to Change

No matter how much time and energy are expended developing and refining the personnel chart, the real effort comes in maintaining it. Like any other organization chart it cannot be static. It must be dynamic, to keep apace of change which is inevitable. Even the standard should be restudied constantly, since a standard is defined as: *The best known today, which is to be improved tomorrow.*

A good organization chart does not ensure a good organization, nor does it insure good management. It does reflect good planning.

This, however, is at best only a beginning. The implementation of a good personnel program depends upon many factors, the most important of which is the leadership provided by the personnel executive who directs it.

THE PERSONNEL DIRECTOR AS
THE PHILOSOPHER OF MANAGEMENT

There is much more to personnel management than the necessary day-to-day administrative duties involving people. Applying scientific, or at least systematic procedures to the area of human relations calls for a different understanding from that used in the materialistic realm. Here we are dealing with human values, blood-bought souls, divinely created and eternally destined beings. We are not dealing with human machines.

If man were an animal it would be efficient to use him, depreciate him, consume him, and discard him; but man is a human being. When we think of the human element in our business we must think in terms and values that are different from those we apply to the technical side of our jobs.

In our employee relations programs we need more than methods and devices, no matter how good they are. We need also the leaven of compassion and the understanding of human relations. What the soul is to the body, that is what human relations is to personnel administration. Employee programs which are made up of techniques but not understanding have a shell for a body and an ache for a soul.

Prestige Is Not Enough

Anyone, by whatever title he may be known, who is entrusted with anything as vital as the human relations activities in his company, must be a unique person. On the one hand he cannot be dictatorial, for the success of his endeavors is not determined by prestige nor by his position on the official organization chart. No matter where or how he ranks he cannot be effective by imposing his will upon people.

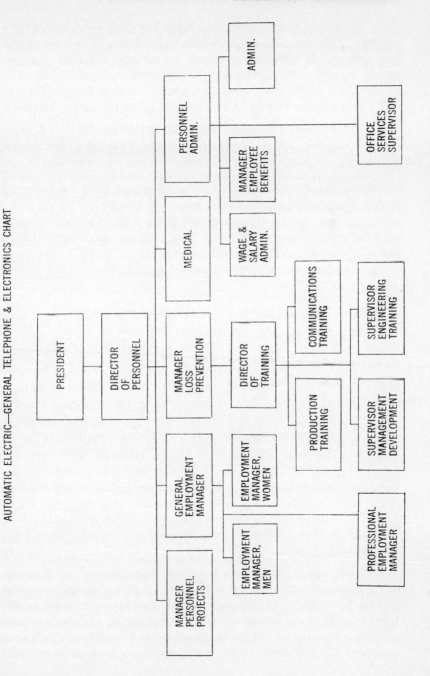

AUTOMATIC ELECTRIC—GENERAL TELEPHONE & ELECTRONICS CHART

On the other hand he has to be more than the instrument of management. He must recognize that he has a responsibility to people, not just to top officials who seek to maintain control over his activities. To fulfill his obligation he cannot be just the administrator of everybody else's ideas, some sound, some untried. He must also be an influence in the human relations functions of company operations.

Let me use one of his many duties to explain this. Let's talk about his involvement in writing policies to make this point. Our policies are merely the outgrowth of practice, they are an expression of our management philosophy. For a personnel man to write policies he should be careful that he does not copy from a book. His written policy statements must reflect the philosophy of the company and serve the interests of the people. While he cannot dictate, he has a twofold obligation: (1) he has to be certain that these official policies are not based on prejudice, tradition, sentiment, or personal whims; (2) they must fit the work force or they are useless.

It's More Than a Job

This puts the personnel executive in the singular position of becoming the philosopher of management. While other officials are preoccupied with specific functions he must, in addition to his day-to-day duties, also theorize on what is happening. He becomes concerned about the immediate decision but he cannot stop there. He must look at the current action in terms of its long-range implications. Besides being practical he should also be studying, probing, thinking, talking, listening, asking penetrating questions—all the while testing his theories as I am doing here.

At any rate, he doesn't have a job; personnel administration should never be thought of as a job. This is not an occupation that young people are encouraged to enter for a good livelihood. The man who wants to get into personnel work because it is better than driving a truck belongs on a truck.

For this reason I have mixed feelings about those companies that use the position of personnel director as a training ground for other management work. The danger lies in performing the day-to-day functions of personnel administration intelligently, perhaps, but with cold efficiency, the way a tradesman "lays bricks instead of building a cathedral." A church organist who plays flawlessly with his head

PERSONNEL RELATIONSHIPS

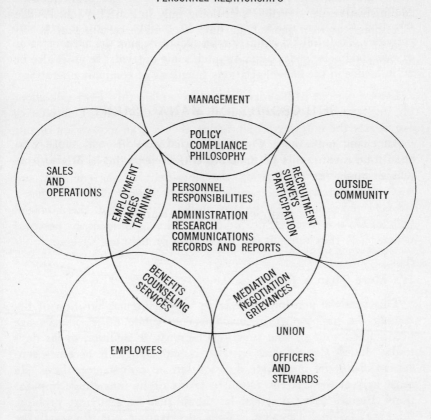

and his hands may be a polished musician, but if he expects to inspire the congregation into spirited singing he must play from his heart.

Conscience of the Company

Remember, personnel administration is never a job; it is a vocation. No one has a right to be in the explosive area of human relations who has only the brain for the occupation and not the conscience of the vocationalist. For a vocation is truly a "calling," and this classic definition carries with it divine overtones.

Any job in the field of human relations is at once the most precious and the most dangerous duty entrusted by mankind to men.

In the final analysis, the personnel executive who performs his own administrative work well is still doing only half of his job. As the philosopher of management, he must also make certain that in the area of human relations the entire company performs well. This is his opportunity and his obligation.

PHILOSOPHY OF MANAGEMENT

An example of those who need technical skills and those who need the human skills of management, or how this skill shifts as jobs go up, is illustrated in this diagram.

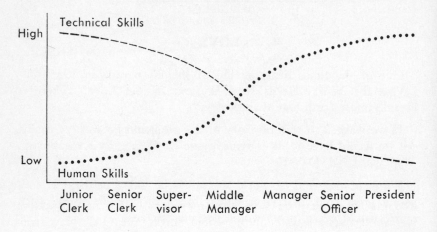

PHILOSOPHY OF MANAGEMENT

Note that technical skills are high at the clerical level and drop slowly but definitely until the officers, although they may have technical skills, no longer use them as much. On the other hand, the human skills are low at the clerical level and rise steadily until the officers must have a real degree of skill in this area.

As one man expressed it: The higher a man goes in his company the less he is the technician and the more he becomes the politician. Or put another way: as an executive advances in his company, his perspective changes. It is like looking at a painting, as he steps back he sees less detail but is more aware of the total picture.

HUMAN RELATIONS

You as the boss should know your people personally, we're told. Do you? Of course you do, you say . . . and you demonstrate it by walking around and talking with them. You ask the employee how he is, what problems he has, about his wife and children, and so on. In all those man-hours of contact, asking the employee about his problems, how many times has the employee asked about your wife and your problems? If you talk to your employee and he does not feel free to ask you about your problems, as you feel free to ask him about his, you are increasing rather than decreasing the distance that already exists between you as employer and employee.

LOVE

One of the tunes near the top of the hit parade in 1966 was, "What the World Needs Now Is Love, Sweet Love." There is literally more truth here than poetry.

If we wanted to ruin our way of life we could do so very easily. All we would have to do is remove one word from our vocabulary. That word is L-O-V-E.

Think of the kind of world we would be living in then. Homes would grow cold, marriages would break up, friends would part, music would cease, poets would become bitter.

Sometimes in our existence we wonder whether the world has grown somewhat cold toward love. Many groups and many individuals have become inhuman toward each other.

The Price of Hate

When love is lost, the price of hate is staggering. Men spend much more to destroy one another than to help one another. World War II alone was recounted by a late congressman as having cost four hundred billion dollars in property. Think how much good could have been done with this money. This amount would have

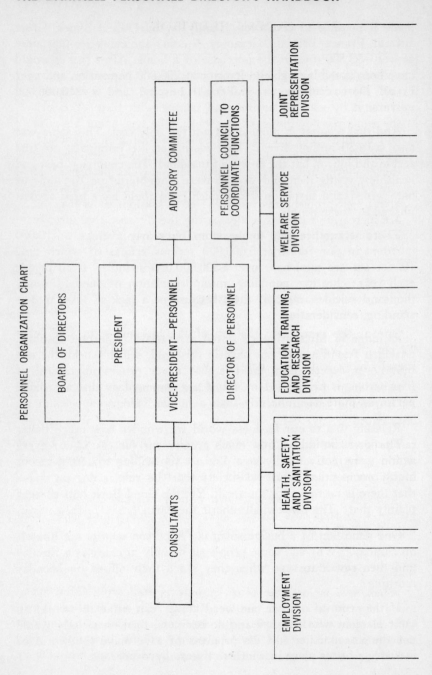

PERSONNEL ORGANIZATION CHART

BOARD OF DIRECTORS

PRESIDENT

VICE-PRESIDENT—PERSONNEL

CONSULTANTS

ADVISORY COMMITTEE

PERSONNEL COUNCIL TO COORDINATE FUNCTIONS

DIRECTOR OF PERSONNEL

EMPLOYMENT DIVISION

HEALTH, SAFETY, AND SANITATION DIVISION

EDUCATION, TRAINING, AND RESEARCH DIVISION

WELFARE SERVICE DIVISION

JOINT REPRESENTATION DIVISION

made it possible to give every family in the United States, Great Britain, France, Belgium, Germany, Russia—the countries that were at war—$3,500 toward the purchase of a home. After that it would have been possible to give every city of 200,000 population and over in all these countries a $5,000,000 hospital and a $10,000,000 university.

And that amount in money was not the only cost. This same war also cost 30 million lives. These were not the criminals, nor the feeble and infirm, but the flower of mankind. The countries' best and healthiest young men and women were slaughtered on the altar of hate, greed, and suspicion. How much good could have been accomplished by these people.

There is another side to the story. A yearly average of 10,000 murders in our country; 5,000,000 serious crimes of which only 10 percent are punished; over $500,000,000 swindled from people each year; cheating, gambling, misappropriation of funds. Twenty thousand suicides, most of them because of a lack of love, understanding, consideration.

A judge in Missouri once stated at a trial: "The one absolute, unselfish friend a man can have in this cold, selfish world, the one that never deserts him, the one that never proves ungrateful or treacherous, is his dog." Isn't this a sad commentary that an animal performs more magnificently than a human being?

Relating this to our business world we wonder how much better our progress would be, how much greater our success, if our every action were motivated by love. We are too willing to accept in our highly competitive industrial society that the rule is dog-eat-dog—that there is no room for the weak. Yet the Good Book tells us very plainly that "The meek shall inherit the earth."

One definition of a businessman is "A person who is not himself on Sunday." Why can some people sit humbly in church on Sunday and then revert to type when they reach their offices on Monday morning?

If the removal of that one word "love" can make the world an unfit place in which to live and do business, then conversely would not the introduction and development of love make the world of industry a better place in which to live and prosper?

The Power of Morality

This is also the only answer to our international relations difficulties. Nothing will ever be settled permanently by force. Wars do not prove who is right, they merely show who is left; but both sides lose. The answer to atomic power is not hydrogen power; the answer is moral power.

Fortunately there is a lot of love in people. There is also a lot of sentiment in business. Otherwise life would really be a mess. But we are not talking about the good part of life—which costs us nothing and brings us tremendous benefits—we should concentrate on the other part of life, the dark and troublesome areas which cost so much in money, restrictions, heartaches.

Oh, yes, we are developing and applying many techniques, but most of them are offsetting devices not corrective measures. Let's use tolerance as the oil to take the friction out of life. Let's try to neutralize our bad habits and practices; those we cannot eliminate let's dilute, and lessen their influence on our lives.

In short, for success in life and business let's not put our trust in man-made laws and our destinies in technical textbook procedures. Let's go back to the original set of standards or rules of conduct— so simple they were carved on two stone tablets, so comprehensive that they have stood the test of time:

1. Thou shalt love thy neighbor as thyself . . .

2. Thou shalt love thy God above all things . . .

Therein lies the formula we are seeking as we try to motivate ourselves and others toward better performances. By comparison all other approaches to the problem pale into insignificance.

First, let's motivate ourselves. Then surely we shall motivate others. For to be a leader we must have people willing to follow us.

BUSINESS WIDOWS AND ORPHANS

Business in today's competitive economy is a severe taskmaster. Many executives are unaware of the toll which their dedication to work exacts. Many times they do not find out until too late.

How many men do we know who are literally married to their jobs? With some men the company takes the place of the "other woman." And business is a demanding mistress. This is an industrial version of the eternal triangle.

Companies absorb too much time, energy, and devotion as industry squeezes all the mileage possible out of executives. The heavy corporate demands, coupled with an individual's driving ambition, are affecting the lives of businessmen and their families.

Many families cannot adjust to the demands of business life. Pressures are a major contributing factor. The jet age has increased the time away from home. Frequent transfers keep families from rooting down.

Preoccupied husbands may be unaware of what is happening to their marriage and family lives. Frustrated wives, with feelings of insecurity or inadequacy, may become tipplers or gamblers as they seek surcease from loneliness. The marriage erosion often leads to marital infidelity. Neglected children become troubled and confused.

Business even dictates our mode of living. Families are going from homes to high-rise apartments. These new apartments are dehumanizing forms of dwellings. They reduce human beings to ciphers. They are a manifestation of the regimentation of business life.

A cartoon depicted business as a rat race and showed the president's door identified as "No. 1 Rat." This is, of course, an exaggeration, but it does remind us of what is happening. Maybe we should step off the dizzy merry-go-round long enough to reflect on the trend. Like the richest man in the cemetery, we might discover one day that we are going down in the graveyard of history as executives with full business success but empty lives.

THE DANGER IS NOT IN MACHINES THINKING LIKE MEN BUT IN MEN THINKING LIKE MACHINES

Personnel administration, to be effective, should be personal. But the trend seems to be the other way. In a materialistic age we substitute impersonal procedures for personal considerations. We worry about automation, then try to apply automation principles to human values. We in industry have too much automation, not in machines and methods but in the minds of men.

For some reason it is difficult to be personal and still remain objective. This difficulty, however, is in keeping with a weakness inherent in all aspects of management. It is impossible under our method of doing business to measure success, progress, sales or profit in anything but numbers. We show improved reports to stockholders, better statements to boards of directors, impressive charts to top management—all expressed in figures, generally dollars—which is all that we seem to be able to comprehend. We have had no way of measuring results in intangibles which, in the final analysis, are the important factors since they govern the figures we put down on paper. Until such a time as our presidents and comptrollers can grasp the significance of human resources as readily as they understand trends and summaries in figure comparisons, we will have to continue to coat our personnel activities with an artificial frosting of numbers.

"By the Numbers"

Everything in business seems to be measurable in numbers. This is also true of personnel management. When we devise a job-evaluation method we let the influence of the industrial engineer, who is mathematically trained, govern the system. In merit rating, or performance rating, we reduce factors and degrees to rating scales and end up considering scores, not performance at all. In testing procedures we establish a norm, or percentage, and less than a passing grade eliminates an applicant. This happens because the line managers we are trying to assist "get the message" of a personnel technique easier when we reduce it to numbers.

Too often we are inclined to forget that business fulfills a function that transcends the concept of profit. We become so enmeshed in talk of dollars and cents that we forget these are only symbols of the true role of business.

Business does not exist merely to produce more goods or better services, though that is no small part of its obligation. Business, especially in today's enlightened era, affords the principal means whereby individuals may gain the satisfaction of accomplishing something more than merely sustaining their own lives.

It is too bad that personnel management, in its efforts to appear scientific, has fallen into this pit of conformity. For in the area of human relations it is well to remember that "the things that count most cannot be counted."

A BLIND SPOT IN THE CRYSTAL BALL

By Sydney J. Harris
Chicago *Daily News*

Whenever people say, "I wonder what life will be like 30 years from now?" or whenever some journalistic visionary draws a portrait of life in 1990, it is always the material conditions of mankind that intrigue them.

We listen to speculations about our buildings, our highways, our merchandising, our scientific and technological changes. The portraits are attractive, if a little frightening—but none of them considers the most important thing.

Nobody asks, "What will people be like 30 years from now?" or "How will we behave with one another and toward one another in 1990?" We fail to ask this because most of us believe (mistakenly) that human conduct remains substantially the same, that "human nature doesn't change."

But while the basic nature doesn't change, different social orders bring out different traits and patterns of conduct in people. We do not behave like the ancient Romans or the medieval French or the Elizabethan English or even the nineteenth-century New Englanders. For better and for worse, our attitudes and relations are vastly different today.

It seems plain to me that the essential question we must ask about the future is: "What sort of people is this society bound to produce?"

As our society becomes more urbanized, more mechanized, more militarized, more specialized, there can be no doubt that what is called the *ethos* of the American people will change along with our ways of physical living. Certain traits will be encouraged, and others will be repressed; certain kinds of knowledge will be highly rewarded, and others will be ignored or even frowned upon.

And this is why most speculation about the future strikes me as trivial and marginal. At the root of all our problems is always the *human personality;* and this is the last field of inquiry we seem interested in. Or, at most, we want to "adjust" the personality to fit the technical and social changes, rather than shape the culture to fit what we think a full human being ought to be.

We don't even think in terms of a full human being, as the old Greek philosophers understood it. We think of "economic man" and "psychological man" and "man the citizen" and "man the maker." Our pragmatic society is concerned with *functions,* not with *goals,* with "Will it work?" not with "Is it worth the human effort?"

What kind of children are we turning out? What attitudes and ideals and sentiments are we encouraging and discouraging? These are the proper questions for the future, and not space travel or electronic kitchens.

NOTE: Sydney J. Harris, as millions of newspaper readers know, is the author of "Strictly Personal," a daily column originating on the editorial page of the Chicago *Daily News* and syndicated to a hundred newspapers throughout the United States, Canada, and South America.

The above essay is reprinted, with the author's permission, from his book, *On the Contrary.*

BUSINESS IN A SOCIAL CLIMATE

It is impossible to separate the industrial society from the rest of the world in which we live. There are forces in our social and spiritual lives which affect the way in which we behave in business.

In what we call our modern society are many factors which appear to be out of tune with purely business objectives. To say, for instance, that there is no sentiment in business is nonsense. Yet how can kindness, consideration and understanding be reconciled with the competitive demands of our impersonal business operations? Can the businessman be ethical and still be prosperous?

There are many different strands of tradition and belief which are woven into the fabric of modern living. Imbedded in the culture which conditions us for life are influences which are handed down from generation to generation. Their roots can be traced back to a form of existence quite different from what we enjoy in our industrial existence today. We cling to these values since they give meaning and substance to living in a world which would otherwise be cruel and confusing.

Bend the Golden Rule?

Many of these influences are moral principles which have stood the test of time. Without relaxing them in precept we try to adapt them to changing conditions. But do they, collectively, become an impossible ideal which meets head-on with practical business requirements? In that case, which standards should be adjusted or abandoned?

Must the Golden Rule be bent a bit to keep from interfering with the normal course of business? Is the old, distinct difference between good and bad now warped into shadings of good and shadings of bad? Does trust in ethics become altruistic in a materialistic world? Compromising principles in business, as in other walks of life, is neither good nor necessary.

The spread of scientific application to business operations need not precipitate a conflict with the higher values which play such an important part in individual and business lives. It is quite possible that the doctrine of moral right and the principles of industrial might can be coalesced into a power of unknown potency for the greater benefit of mankind.

To do this the social influences in our lives must be recognized in business. Actually they have become so thoroughly ingrained in our pattern of everyday living that they can hardly be ignored without serious consequences. They exert a powerful force on the way we, as individuals, conduct ourselves in business. In fact, the whole structure of our business prosperity is built upon the foundation of a great national and religious heritage which oftentimes runs counter to the materialistic ambitions of a profitminded industrial society.

Managements are wise who do not let these social mores develop into a problem. Instead of fighting them, which could create an untenable situation, it would be better to stand up to them, admit their existence, and put them to use.

How? The basic desires of human beings are a tremendous

motivating force. They account for all our actions. Business should not resist these personal and social motivations. Commonsense tells us that the better business activity can be dovetailed into the natural drives of its people the smoother will be its operation. In today's concept of living, business is the focal point around which we build our personal and family lives. In strengthening the fiber of our industrial society we must take into account all the many varied and seemingly unrelated contributions made by the social climate within which business functions.

Relationships in business are of three orders: (1) to things, which we must dominate; (2) to people, whom we must respect as equals; (3) to a higher authority, to whom we must be willing to submit. These are the materialistic, humanistic, and divinistic relationships that exist in our day-to-day operation of business. These three forces exist; we cannot hope to be successful by ignoring any one of them.

It is quite obvious that no one of us succeeds alone. We are all interdependent upon each other. It was Tennyson who said, "I am a part of all I have met." While this is truly a potent observation, there is more to success than that. Let me remind you that in life all of us have met more than each other.

Throughout our lives there is an invisible means of support which guides and directs our individual and national destinies. That this influence is a factor in our personal success is evidenced by the fact that many problem situations in life, which may not conform to the obvious laws of nature or man, often find easy solution in the spiritual laws, which also exert an impelling force in the universe.

The lesson is a simple one, but by its simplicity it leaves a profound message. If we want to be successful in business we must first come to a full and final realization that business does not operate in a vacuum. The fact remains that our cold, competitive, calculating business operates in many situations in what is anything but a businesslike climate.

ETHICS

It is strange that here in the United States where average wages are the highest in the world, vast numbers of people display a cynical attitude toward their daily work. In our expanding service industries, for instance, surliness and irresponsibility among workers who deal with the public have become almost legendary.

The purchaser of a high-priced automobile finally traced the persistent rattle in his new car to an empty Coke bottle inside the door assembly and found a note addressed to "You Capitalist!" This typifies the resentment and hostility of many overly pampered production workers. The indifferent quality of the workmanship in some American factories has caused the manufacture of certain technical equipment to be lost to European facilities.

Among people employed in offices and factories we can discern two basic types: The intensely involved minority and an extremely bored majority. The minority is made up of senior executives with a substantial personal stake in the enterprise; junior executives hoping for promotion; salesmen on commission; new employees who are not yet disillusioned; and a few exceptions to every rule, sometimes called "wheelhorses," who do a good job in spite of management's abject disinterest in them as human beings. The wheelhorses seem to be regarded by the bored majority with a sort of pity, as neurotics who bury themselves in work to escape from personal frustrations.

A quote from Winston Churchill's book, *Amid These Storms:* "Rational, industrious, useful human beings are divided into two classes: first, those whose work is work and whose pleasure is pleasure; and secondly, those whose work and pleasure are one. Of these the former are the majority."

Clearly, many Americans are far from enthusiastic about their jobs—at a time when wages are at an all-time high, fringe benefits run an average of 25 percent of payroll, and the coddling of workers includes such non-job-related gimmicks as paid time off for shopping, no docking for coming in late, tuition refunds, picnics, haircuts on company time, free coffee—you name it!

Impersonal Relations

Why is all this? Why don't decent wages reduce costly turnover? Why don't welfare benefits motivate more than they do? Why don't employees appreciate all we do *for* them? I'll tell you why.

Because in the administration of our personnel programs we've become impersonal. In the process of developing personnel programs we've appealed to the worker's pocketbook and not to his heart. In our efforts to simplify and standardize work, to reduce training time, we have destroyed the very soul of personal job satisfaction and pride of accomplishment. We have made human machines out of people.

Somehow in our modern materialistic world we've got to figure out how to improve the worker, not the machine or the method. We've got to appeal to the better instincts of man so he will produce more and produce better because he wants to, not because he is expected to.

Like so many other industries, business needs a code of ethics. Many employers criticize the attitude of their workers which, in reality, is little different from that of the company. The father who flagrantly violates the speed laws is hardly in a position to preach personal integrity to his son.

Many employers are not averse to a little hanky-panky, corner-cutting, playing fast and loose with the trust reposed in them, engaging in shady but not illegal deals, taking unfair advantage of situations, treating people shabbily. Because of pressure they bend a little, go with the tide. And their employees see this.

But this seems to be the pattern of life. Whenever there is an embarrassing investigation in the House of Representatives or Senate a hue and cry goes up for a new code of ethics for members. But once the clamor subsides, Congress moves with less-than-deliberate speed in devising the code. Most of the time the reform movement is lost in hearings confined to generalities. After a flurry of activity to impress the general public, everybody goes home.

Movie and television people have established their own code; but judging from some of the trash which is permitted to escape the censors, nobody pays much attention to the self-imposed restrictions. The code is little more than salad dressing to placate the public while fattening the pocketbook.

There are other examples: The price-fixing scandals make news headlines every once in a while. Graft and bribes are accepted as everyday practices in many places. We could mention ticket fixing, payola and other payoffs, loan rackets, phony insurance schemes. It is only wrong, apparently, if a person gets caught; until then, anything goes.

Morality Does Pay

Yet, a moral man *can* be successful in business. There are many respectable companies where ethical behavior influences the conduct. Many executives, managers, and supervisors are able to reconcile personal beliefs with commercial interests. They can preserve their devotion to fundamentals and not compromise with truth.

We are a Judeo-Christian-oriented society and religion plays a part. Whether or not a man is a participant, i.e., a churchgoer, he cannot escape the influence. He should not rationalize that the principles of right or wrong, which he accepts in his personal and family life, are not applicable in the cold, calculating, dog-eat-dog business existence. The laws of morality are just as implacable as the laws of nature.

Just as parents are usually held accountable for the delinquency of their children, so may our society, including the industrial society, be breeding the kind of work attitude that business abhors.

It is not what the boss says or does that counts, but what he believes. People will trust us if we first trust them. Workers will willingly help management reach its goals if in the process management helps them realize their own hopes and ambitions. Employees will give an honest performance when they recognize that the company's every policy and manner of operating are motivated by honesty and integrity for fair dealing and a respect for the dignity of man.

Business ethics and moral principles are not the same in precept. Business ethics is not something that is preached by people who are not in business.

Businessmen ought to be their own ethicians. Ethics has to do with what is right and what is wrong. Each decision should not conflict with the laws of God, of nature, and of the land.

There is a difference between making a profit and profiteering. Charging a fair price is not the same as charging as much as the traffic will bear.

The unscrupulous businessman can "get away with it" because he operates in a scrupulous society. If every other businessman would be similarly unscrupulous, then he would lose his ill-gotten advantage.

39

Unrestricted greediness ultimately leads to control, usually by governmental agencies. Industries often establish a "code of correct conduct" to avoid outside restrictions. Otherwise when a company or an industry fails to recognize its responsibility to the community it serves, and subverts the public interest in favor of "gain at any price," it follows that civic, church, and possibly national reaction will exert a pull in the other direction.

PERSONNEL ADMINISTRATION—
THE RESPONSIBILITY OF ALL

Ours is an era of specialization. Throughout our personal and family lives we encounter professional and business people who devote their full time to one activity. The lawyer, schoolteacher, merchant are illustrations. Even the good old family doctor has given way to medical specialists—the pediatrician, eye-ear-nose-and-throat specialist, and the like.

In business, too, this holds true. Everywhere in our factories and offices are staff experts who handle one specific type of duty, generally off to the side away from the main stream of production. They are in all divisions of the company working on legal matters, budgets, real estate, market analysis, and so on. Usually the operating supervisor has no clear picture of exactly what they do or how they fit into the organization.

To most line operators the personnel function is also an activity of staff specialists. It is located up front in a central office, conveniently tied to the top executives. It is a friendly office, a place where the manager or foreman can take his problem. There a staff expert (who oftentimes looks like the night-school-bright-boy type) refers to a policy manual for the answer. The line operator then goes back and tries to put into effect what he considers is someone else's solution, not his. This is the picture in many companies.

Where such a condition exists the personnel officer is probably to blame. When the personnel man succumbs to the temptation to take over management responsibilities that should remain within the line manager's scope of control, he finds it difficult to help line managers on a consultative basis.

Managers and supervisors often feel that the personnel man thinks he knows all about handling employees; actually, many foremen and supervisors know a lot about their workers, how to get along with them and how to get them to produce. Sometimes they feel that personnel people overrate the value of meetings that only take time away from more important duties. Again they may feel that the personnel man accepts every complaint from an employee as fact, that he is too quick to sympathize with the employee; to the line supervisor the personnel office is an escape, a place of last resort which the employee is encouraged to use to go over the manager's head. Finally the manager or supervisor often feels that personnel interferes too much with the way he runs his department. When the personnel manager offers panaceas without thoroughly understanding the situation, managers tend to wash their hands of problem employees, saying, in effect, "You're the expert—you straighten them out!"

The Ideal Picture

This type of relationship between the line organization and personnel office is not conducive to mutual trust and cooperation, both of which are paramount to the success of a company's employee relations program. This is not the way the picture should look, nor is it the way the dedicated personnel executive wants it to be.

In an ideal situation the staff personnel director endeavors to build his employee program by building the supervisor, not himself. For all practical purposes he prefers to stay out of the act. He tries to make the line supervisor the personnel practitioner in his particular area. He does not do things *for* the supervisor but *through* the supervisor.

And this is for a reason, a selfish reason: The front-line supervisor is the key man in management. He alone can relate workers' needs accurately for top-management decisions. He alone can interpret management's needs to the workers for the personal good of employees and the overall good of the firm. He alone stands between a good performance and a mediocre performance.

It stands to reason, therefore, that a company's employee relations program is more effective when as much of it as possible is handled by front-line supervisors and managers. Personnel problems should

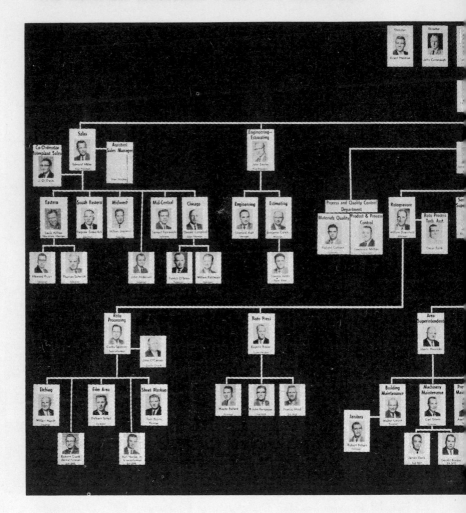

be met at the operational level. These problems cannot be isolated and transplanted to a central staff which is removed from the scene of action.

Personnel administration is not the responsibility of a few specialists, but of all people in management. It is just as effective as the trained personnel staff guides and directs it; and as line supervisors understand, accept, and apply it. The central personnel staff members are expected to be experienced and competent, but they should not be visionaries who have lost the common touch.

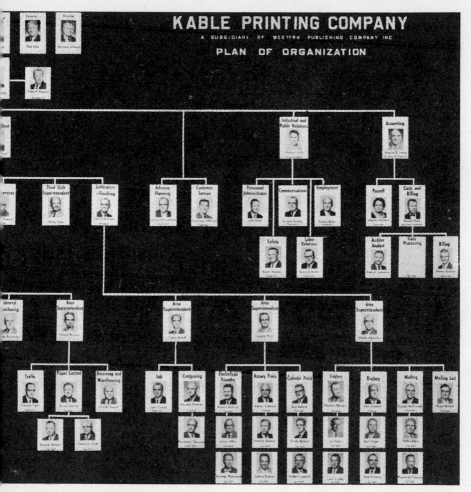

This pictorial organization chart is displayed in the entrance lobby of the main office and plant of the Kable Printing Company at Mount Morris, Illinois. Callers can identify a man they want to see as to his correct name and position, also can recognize him when they meet.

On the other hand, the supervisor responsible for results will attain those results better if he also recognizes his responsibility to the workers through whom he accomplishes his mission. It is important that the supervisor recognizes this, for he is involved in every phase of the employee relations program. It is the supervisor in his day-to-day activities who deals directly with the workers.

Members of the central personnel office concern themselves with the factors affecting people.

This dual relationship in a common program is confusing to many people. To clarify it the following outline of the complete employment procedure has been prepared. It covers the program from the time the new worker is hired until he leaves. Each separate step is listed. The work of the line organization is indicated by an (L) and the work of the personnel staff is marked with a (P).

THE LINE MANAGER'S ROLE IN EMPLOYMENT PROCEDURE

1. (L) In regular day-to-day conduct of work, help create reputation that will attract applicants.

2. (P) Develop sources of qualified applicants from local labor market. This requires carefully planned community relations, advertisements, employee referrals, and active high school, college, and technical school recruiting, including participation in career programs.

3. (L) When vacancy occurs, or new job opens, prepare requisition outlining specific qualifications necessary to fill particular position.

4. (P) Conduct skilled interviews, give appropriate tests, and make thorough reference checks, etc., using requisition and job description as guides. Screening must meet company standards and conform with employment laws.

5. (P) Refer best candidates to manager, after physical examinations and qualifications for the position available have been carefully evaluated.

6. (L) Interview and select from candidates screened by personnel. Make specific job placement that will utilize new employee's highest skills to promote maximum production and job satisfaction.

7. (P) Give new employee preliminary indoctrination about the company, its policies, benefits, and necessary regulations.

8. (L) Give new employee local indoctrination with specific details regarding assigned job, explain "our customs," and introduce to associates.

9. (L) Instruct and train on the job according to procedure which has proved effective.

10. (P) Schedule orientation classes for new employees in order to impart company information, such as history, background, and philosophy.

11. (L) Follow up, develop, and rate employee job performance; decide on raises, promotion, transfer, layoff, or discharge.

12. (P) Maintain record of current performance and future potential of each employee.

13. (P) Administer and counsel on separate aspects of welfare or benefit program.

14. (L) Hold separation interview when employee leaves—determine causes. Make internal department adjustments to minimize turnover.

15. (P) Conduct exit interview with terminating employee, to verify reason given or to uncover underlying cause. Explain checkout package: rights under benefit program, unemployment compensation, etc.

16. (P) Diagnose information given in separation interviews, analyze causes, and take positive steps to correct.

17. (P) Maintain for some period the files of terminated employees for purpose of answering reference inquiries, unemployment claims, etc.

KEEPING THEM HAPPY ISN'T YOUR JOB

By Frank O. Hoffman
Principal Partner, Practical Management Associates

If keeping employees happy isn't the job of the personnel director, what is his job?

For the past several semesters, participants in a U.C.L.A. extension course on personnel management have attempted to seek answers to this question by interviewing personnel directors. They have consistently found that well over 70 percent of today's personnel directors feel that their major role, their major contribution, and the major justification for their existence lies in one or several of the following areas:

Administration of personnel plans, policies, programs, procedures.

Promoting sound labor relations.

Improving the company's relations with employees.

On the surface, these seem like reasonable areas of activity for any progressive personnel director. But, the fact that better than 70 percent of our top people see their jobs this way accounts for most of the problems personnel people face in achieving professional status and recognition in the eyes of line management! To understand this last statement, we must look at what lies beneath the surface—we must look at what personnel directors actually do.

We find that the lofty statement, "My major role is to administer personnel plans, policies and procedures," really means that the personnel man signs forms in multiple copies, writes an occasional employee-information pamphlet, and spends much of his time keeping records.

"My primary contribution to the company is promoting sound labor relations" turns out to mean that the personnel director has taken on his own shoulders the direct responsibility for preserving labor peace. We find him engrossed in seniority lists, playing "oracle" to interpret contract clauses to some department manager's subordinate supervisors, and acting as go-between among employees and their immediate supervisors.

Trivia vs. Significance

If we look at what many personnel directors actually devote their attention to, "Improving the company's relations with employees" really means trying to do just what this article says the personnel job is not: keeping them happy.

We find many personnel men running around bothering management with a lot of nonsensical prattling about "morale"—without ever having defined what it means, nor having tested whether it has any connection with increased productivity.

We find others engrossed in such critical management problems as parking lots, coffee machines, cafeteria menus and prices, and recreation programs. (I guess if you really want to stimulate employee relations, there's nothing like a nice recreation program such as a mixed bowling league.)

Or, they may have their collar on backwards, playing chaplain to all comers, dispensing the crying towel for some unsuspecting manager's employees, or otherwise carrying out their stated function of "protecting the employee from the company." (Can you really imagine a manager hiring someone to protect his people from himself?)

Why do these activities of a majority of personnel directors hurt the progress of the profession? For two reasons: (1) Personnel people have come to accept the inconsequential as the significant. (2) Personnel people are attempting to do someone else's job.

Both of these faults are drawbacks to professional growth. Let's look at each of them in detail.

Accepting the Inconsequential as the Significant

Because they have not been allowed to participate as active members of management, many personnel men attempt to gain status and job security by building up the inconsequential aspects of their jobs into activities of apparently major import. For example, too many personnel directors give too much misplaced emphasis to such "tail of the dog" activities as:

1. Maintaining vacation, sick-pay, and group insurance accrual records (which are undoubtedly duplicated in payroll, and could be done better on EDP, anyway).

2. Checking for accuracy and approving: wage requests, promotion recommendations, retirement sign-ups, and other forms (usually in multiple copies, and which in no way contribute to the decisions made by—or to the productivity problems faced by—the originating supervisors).

3. Processing employment, and recruiting. (Instead of counseling with managers on matters of manpower planning, allocation, and utilization. Typical is the personnel department which is trying to fill a requisition for 200 engineers, but which has never shown the engineering manager ways of analyzing his workload to determine if some of the 200 spots could be filled by lower-skilled people.)

4. Setting up recreation programs, service-award dinners, newsletters and other delightfully inconsequential drivel, about which a profit-problem-centered management could hardly care less. (And we waste college-trained M.B.A.'s on this kind of nonsense because the status-seeking personnel director won't admit that an average clerk can handle it.)

The clerically oriented, detail-minded personnel director will never recognize the high calling he could embrace as a participating member of management—as a strong influence upon business-management decisions and the underlying management thinking from the top down.

Doing Someone Else's Job

It is always a dangerous state of affairs when you try to do someone else's job for him. He resents it. You can never do it as effectively as he could if he did it right. And it separates him from his responsibilities, thereby assuring that he will never learn to do it right.

Whose job do personnel directors often attempt to do? Well, who is responsible for seeing that the workers in any unit get to work on time, or meet production deadlines and schedules, or follow proper work methods, or do any other thing they are charged with? Obviously, the supervisor. It is the supervisor's job that personnel people try to do when they:

1. Set themselves up as employee counselors and accept as their major charter the job of trying to keep individual employees satisfied—thereby actually driving a wedge between the supervisor and his employees. (Instead of advising managers on how to improve rapport between their subordinate supervisors and employees.)

2. Attempt to glorify their existence by making a big show of personally "staving off the union," or magnify their importance by keeping contract interpretation information unto themselves and only parceling it out piecemeal. (Instead of showing managers how to insure that their subordinate supervisors understand and observe the contract.)

3. Attempt to take the responsibility for stimulating employee participation in suggestion plans or safety programs; often by sponsoring posters, envelope stuffers, letters to employees, or "inspirational" meetings. (Instead of counseling with managers on what the managers can do to get supervisors to undertake activities to motivate their employees.)

Of course, several of the personnel directors surveyed claim, "We can't really try to do the supervisor's job for him. We're staff. All we do is advise." But let's look at that "advice." In most companies, the personnel "staff": Gives final approval to raises and promotions, signs off on tuition refunds, authorizes in-hire offers, approves safety procedures, approves suggestion awards, decides the content of supervisory training, etc.

This is not staff advice, but staff control. (Really "direction," but commonly misused as "control.") Yet, control is a managerial function, and should be carried out by managers over the groups they supervise. Therefore, by exercising staff "control," the personnel director is doing the line manager's job—thereby practically insuring that line managers will never become truly proficient in their personnel management judgments.

A Mistaken Role

Why is it that personnel directors feel they must "control" the personnel activities of line managers and supervisors? Probably because of a mistaken belief that their job is to "run the personnel programs"; whereas, actually their job is to "contribute to the 'mission' of the business."

And it is not the "mission" of most companies to exist for the purpose of maintaining a nice, neat personnel program—although we sometimes act as if it were. We coerce supervisors into following exactly our carefully prepared personnel procedures (as if that is what supervisors were put into the company to do); yet often those procedures are for our own administrative convenience rather than to prevent abuses.

The personnel job should be to give guidance to managers in the accomplishment of their departments' missions—not to get in their way with programs, procedures and administrative entanglements. Occasionally, it might be better for a supervisor to violate a procedure or miss a submittal deadline in order that he might devote his attention to "mission" problems—yet we tie his hands with having to obtain multiple before-the-fact approvals which rob him of the right to use his judgment, *which is really what he is paid for!*

In companies where it is the pattern to allow personnel, accounting, quality control, or other staff groups, functional authority over line managers, we find that line people are often diverted into serving staff purposes rather than the other way around. For example, line people are forced to take time to document records, to "support" staff programs, to satisfy and get the concurrence of staff officials, and to prepare reports for staff analysis—all this to the point that it must often appear that the company is in business to provide accounting data, to maintain personnel files, or to keep workers engaged in safety and training sessions.

Even though the personnel director, controller, quality control manager, etc., undoubtedly feel safer with "control" in their own hands, it should be obvious that each of these departments cannot be given delaying or punitive authority without some conflict with, and sacrifice of, line objectives. For the sake of having staff procedures followed to the letter, the line manager is deprived of the right to exercise judgment in balancing the many demands which must be satisfied in order to produce, transport or sell the product at a profit.

Programs Work Better if Controlled by Line

Where personnel has approval authority over the decisions of line supervisors, or takes over the responsibility for policing and motivating people in other departments of the company, confusion, resentment, friction, and poor manager-development will result. Approval authorities rightfully belong with the higher levels of line management—and if they don't want to be bothered, the authority should be delegated to their line subordinates. Otherwise, if personnel has to "sell" programs, and then has to both administer and "control" them, personnel can well end up being the only ones who care whether the programs continue or not. An example of this can be found in the performance appraisal programs of many companies.

Further, it is a fact that any program depending upon the performance of line managers, supervisors, or employees works better if properly placed in the hands of line managers, with control exercised by their line superiors. In my experience this has been true of: Stimulating employee suggestions; adherence to wage policies; training of employees and supervisors; cost reduction; work simplification; observing labor contracts; enforcing time-off, vacation, and sick-pay policies; control of absenteeism; performance appraisal; accident-prevention.

When the meaning and purposes of policies are made clear to supervisors, and enforced by their supervisors, fewer staff controls and staff reviews are needed to prevent abuses, and the results of the programs are far superior.

The personnel director contributes by recommending practical processes by which managers and supervisors can arrive at objective decisions on personnel matters; and by suggesting to higher management the means by which it can insure that those practical processes are followed by subordinate levels of management. For example:

Instead of reviewing Charlie's background to see if the personnel department agrees that he should be the one chosen for a particular promotion, the personnel manager might be a far better contributor to the success of the business if he develops, and gets managers to use, a system which will insure that factors of job requirements vs. personal qualifications are objectively considered. He will be even more effective if he can encourage line managers to exercise the controls (i.e., ask the appropriate questions of their subordinates) necessary to insure that the system has indeed been applied by those subordinates in shaping their promotion decision or recommendation.

The role of the personnel department would be to spot-check the system, not in order to control individual cases, but to uncover flaws or desirable improvements in the system, and to advise managers on how to make the system work best in their organization. In short, both the personnel department and higher management would be concerned primarily about the existence and use of a sound system of selection, and would accept any name which comes forth as a result of lower-level managers' application of the system.

Proper Role of Personnel

As we have already said, the primary job of the personnel director should be to contribute to the "mission" of his company. He can best do this by improving the ability of managers to manage. In other words, he should be judged by his overall educational effectiveness, not by how many programs he has instituted, nor by the direction the accident and turnover rates are taking, nor by how well he is doing part of the managers' job for them. The personnel director should be judged by how much better line managers perform on their own authority as a result of his influence.

He can achieve this influence with managers only if he divests himself of his overriding involvement in insignificant activities and "control" activities. He must prepare himself as a professional in organization, worker motivation and work-force productivity, and manager development—and be equipped to contribute to management's thinking in these areas during the "thinking out" stages of arriving at decisions.

When top management recognizes the personnel director as a sound, practical advisor on the thought processes which go into the making of decisions, he is more likely to be:

Called in to discuss the organizational pros and cons of establishing a new top-level marketing position (instead of being told to go out and find a good man for a spot management wants to create— or, even worse, being directed to complete the necessary employment forms after the man has already been hired by top management).

Asked to consult with top management on the pros and cons—

WESTERN ELECTRIC INDUSTRIAL AND LABOR RELATIONS DEPARTMENT
(HAWTHORNE WORKS)

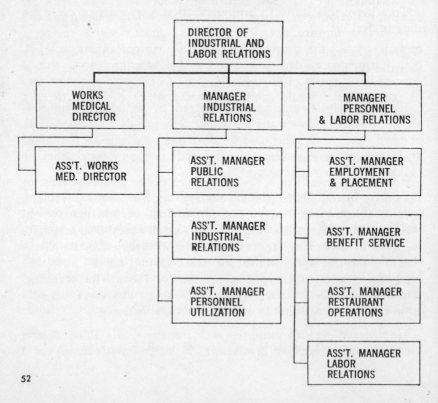

with relation to availability of labor and impact upon productivity of current work force—of new-plant location (instead of being told, after the fact, to whip up a household moving program which will be palatable to the union).

Consulted by department managers for advice on how to improve the productivity of their work force (instead of merely being asked to process job changes and transfers after industrial engineering has completed installation of a new-methods improvement).

Asked for his expert research-based advice on work-force motivation during the design of a cost-reduction program (instead of merely being asked to have someone post the new cost-reduction posters).

Consulted for his advice on the probable impact of various organization-structure designs upon the motivation and performance of managers (instead of merely being told to develop new job descriptions to suit the latest reshuffle).

To achieve this status in an organization, personnel people must start to deal in:

Trends instead of individual cases (e.g., "What is the pattern of absenteeism through the company, and why?"—rather than, "How many days' sick-leave has Suzie Glutz used to date?").

Factual analysis and research instead of moralistic platitudes about "morale." (How many personnel departments are now staffed, or have their work scheduled to allow even as little as 5 percent or 10 percent time available for research into new approaches or evaluation of current programs?)

Profit affecting needs instead of fads. (How many personnel programs are based on thorough evaluation of whether certain human behaviors are affecting company profits adversely; and, if so, whether these human behaviors can reasonably be expected to change so as to affect profits favorably? On the other hand we have lots of programs which have been instituted on no more evidence than "They're doing it over at Acme": Appraisal programs, brainstorming, suggestion plans and, more recently, sensitivity training and management games.)

We can see that the personnel director qualifies as a professional

TYPICAL TURNOVER REPORT

DIVISION	TABLE OF ORGANIZATION				TERMINATIONS		PERCENT TURNOVER		
	June 1 Previous Year	May 1 This Year	June 1 This Year	Year Average	Month	Last 12 Months	Month	Year	Year Ago
Executive	27	26	25	26	-	4	-	15	8
Sales	166	168	168	167	6	23	4	14	6
Research	12	12	13	12	-	3	-	25	25
Financial	71	89	91	83	5	38	5	46	21
Manufacturing—A	276	334	338	313	8	112	2	36	26
Manufacturing—B	207	227	229	217	6	117	3	54	38
Manufacturing—C	177	361	367	306	16	154	4	50	3
Companywide	936	1217	1231	1124	41	451	3	40	24

member of management only through being able to give useful advice to those managers who must effectively utilize, manage and develop people in the course of discharging the company's obligations to the stockholders.

If he continues to bury his attention in "controlling" the decisions of supervision, "selling" programs he wishes to carry out in other people's departments, and "forcing" adherence to procedures set up for administrative convenience, he is doomed to the role of after-the-fact irritant in the minds of managers.

With permission of the American Society for Personnel Administration. From *The Personnel Administrator.*

TURNOVER RESEARCH

A turnover report is a good barometer of what is happening in the employment picture. A rise in the turnover rate is a signal that something is changing. It could also be a warning of danger ahead.

An increase in the turnover percentage is often an indication that the salary level has fallen below the community average. Benefits may be inadequate and consequently a company might be losing employees to competitors whose programs are more attractive. A bad turnover report might also point up poor supervision.

It is unwise to ignore the message which a good turnover study delivers. But in addition to soft spots in a company's employee program, a turnover report also reflects the times. Even when salaries, benefits, and working conditions check out well, the turnover rate might still climb simply because the employment market is unstable and making employees restless.

In that event a study of turnover may reveal hiring practices which need to be reviewed. The employment situation may have become bad enough—through a shortage of qualified applicants or a rapid expansion of company business—to force the personnel office in its referrals and the managers in their acceptance to relax the standards somewhat. If this leads to higher turnover, an analysis of terminations will point up those areas where changes may be called for.

In such a study all terminations for a given period of time—say, six or 12 months back—are tallied. They are broken into those categories which should be examined. These could well be: age, sex, job classification, salary, length of service, referral source, etc.

Generally, turnover occurs during the first six or 12 months of employment. If this is the problem then steps need to be taken to stay closer to new employees, to make them feel welcome, to help them over problems; in short, to give them that feeling of belonging so they will not quit so readily.

If the turnover study shows a high percentage of newly married women, then interviewers should be less inclined to hire their counterparts knowing the chances are not too good in getting a long-term employee. If people on lower classified or lower paid jobs are quitting, this group should be carefully watched to see where an improvement may be worked out.

A turnover analysis will reveal the weak spots in either the employee program or in hiring practices. These then are the problems over which management should be concerned.

DEVELOPING COMPANY TEST NORMS

In a program of selection testing there are advantages to building your own company norm tables. By compiling your own data you can obtain a comprehensive picture of the company's applicant supply. In addition, you can accurately assess each applicant in relation to the type of person who usually applies to your company for employment. National norms are useful in the absence of other guidelines; but since you probably operate in a specific locale with unique labor-supply characteristics, building your own norms will increase the value of your selection and placement instruments.

A Formal Procedure

The following procedure was prepared by the Test Division Staff of Science Research Associates, Inc., a leading publisher of industrial tests, Chicago. It is taken from *Developing Company Test Norms*, © 1967, Science Research Associates, Inc., and reprinted by permission of the publisher.

Step I—Accumulating Scores

Gathering Data

Accumulation of data is the first step in a norm study. You must keep a record of each applicant's score. One quick way is simply to store all the test booklets in one place. A more thorough method is to keep a ledger (Example One) with date the test was administered; applicant's age, sex, number of years of education, and whether or not he was hired. At the time of testing, this information can be entered in a ledger in a few seconds.

Example One: Ledger for Scores

Test Title..

Date	Name	Score	Age	Sex	Years of Education	Position Applied For	Hired
1/10/67	William, John	45	27	M	16	Supervisory	Yes
1/15/67	Jones, Theodore	40	30	M	10	Machinist	Yes
1/15/67	Smith, David	30	38	M	12	Machinist	No
1/17/67	Anderson, Jane	42	22	F	14	Secretary	Yes

Separate norm ledgers should be developed for each job category, because applicants for positions at different levels will have widely divergent scores on the same test. In order to save time in accumulating scores it is frequently advisable to set up several ledgers, grouping jobs with similar prerequisites. For example job categories such as clerk, typist, and clerk-typist often can be combined. In addition, many jobs have characteristics common to the category of supervisor; these also can be grouped together. Further breakdowns of norms by age or sex may be pertinent to your personnel operation.

Amount of Data

It is necessary to accumulate enough scores to obtain a representative sample of your applicant population. There is no ideal number of scores; the more you obtain the better your sample will be. As a minimum, you should have 40 to 50 scores on which to base a set of percentile norms.

Step II—Tabulating Data

When you have accumulated a sufficient number of scores you can proceed to set up a worksheet (refer to Example Two).

Example Two: Worksheet for Percentiles

(1) Raw Scores	(2) Frequency Tabulation	(3) Cumulative Frequency	(4) Cumulative Proportion*	(5) Percentile
43	/	52	.99996	100
42		51	.98073	98
41		51	.98073	98
40	/	51	.98073	98
39		50	.96150	96
38		50	.96150	96
37	///	50	.96150	96
36		47	.90381	90
35		47	.90381	90
34		47	.90381	90
33	/	47	.90381	90
32	/	46	.88458	89
31	//	45	.86535	87
30	/////	43	.82689	83
29	////	38	.73074	73
28	////	34	.65382	65
27	////	30	.57690	58
26	//	26	.49998	50
25	//	24	.46152	46
24	////	22	.42306	42
23		18	.34614	35
22	/	18	.34614	35
21	//	17	.32691	33
20	/////	15	.28845	29
19	//	10	.19230	19
18	///	8	.15384	15
17	//	5	.09615	10
16	/	3	.05769	6
15		2	.03846	4
14		2	.03846	4
13		2	.03846	4
12		2	.03846	4
11		2	.03846	4
10	/	2	.03846	4
9		1	.01923	2
8		1	.01923	2
7	/	1	.01923	2
6 or less				

Legend: Maximum score on test = 46. Number of persons in sample = 52.

*The cumulative proportion is the cumulative frequency multiplied by the reciprocal:
$$\left(\frac{1}{\text{total in sample}} = \frac{1}{52} = .01923 \right)$$

1. List the entire range of possible scores from the top down on the left-hand side of the worksheet as in Column 1.

2. Tabulate each score obtained by any person in the group in Column 2 beside its corresponding number in Column 1.

3. Find the cumulative frequencies (Column 3). To do this, begin at the bottom of the page and work upward, cumulating the tab marks for each raw score. For example:

a. The lowest score obtained was 7. One person got 7, and this one frequency is added to the total number of frequency tabulations below it. Thus the cumulative frequency for score is 1.

b. No one received a raw score of 8, so zero is added to the frequency immediately below and 1 is placed in the Cumulative Frequency column for the raw score 8.

c. For the raw score 10, the 1 in the Frequency Tabulation column is added to the cumulative frequency for all the raw scores below it, and the total 2 is placed in the Cumulative Frequency column for the raw score 10.

d. As a last example, 5 persons received a raw score of 20 and 10 persons had scores below 20, so the cumulative frequency is 15 at this point. Each raw score is treated in this manner.

4. As a check, be sure the number in the Cumulative Frequency column opposite the top score equals the total number of scores tabulated in Column 2.

5. Next, divide the total number of scores into 1 to obtain the reciprocal. Then multiply the reciprocal by each cumulative frequency to obtain the cumulative proportion for Column 4.

6. To get the approximate percentile score, move the decimal two places to the right, and round to the nearest whole number.

Smoothing the Percentiles

If you had 100 or more scores to tabulate, the above procedure is adequate. However, if you initially had only 40 to 100 scores, you should smooth your percentages to eliminate some of the (assumed) random variations. See Example Three (following) for a worksheet providing smoothed percentiles.

Example Three: Worksheet for Smoothed Percentiles

(1) Raw Score	(2) Frequency Tabulation	(3) Smoothed Frequency	(4) Cumulative Frequency	(5) Cumulative Proportion	(6) Percentile (Smoothed)
46		0			
45		0			
44		.25	52.00	.99996	100
43	/	.50	51.75	.99515	100
42		.25	51.25	.98554	99
41		.25	51.00	.98073	98
40	/	.50	50.75	.97592	98
39		.25	50.25	.96631	97
38		.75	50.00	.96150	96
37	///	1.50	49.25	.94708	95
36		.75	47.75	.91823	92
35		0	47.00	.90381	90
34		.25	47.00	.90381	90
33	/	.75	46.75	.89900	90
32	/	1.25	46.00	.88458	89
31	//	2.50	44.75	.86054	86
30	/////	4.00	42.25	.81247	81
29	////	4.25	38.25	.73555	74
28	////	4.00	34.00	.65382	65
27	////	3.50	30.00	.57690	58
26	//	2.50	26.50	.50960	51
25	//	2.50	24.00	.46152	46
24	////	2.50	21.50	.41345	41
23		1.25	19.00	.36537	37
22	/	1.00	17.75	.34133	34
21	//	2.50	16.75	.32210	32
20	/////	3.50	14.25	.27403	27
19	//	3.00	10.75	.20672	21
18	///	2.50	7.75	.14903	15
17	//	2.00	5.25	.10096	10
16	/	1.00	3.25	.06250	6
15		.25	2.25	.0433	4
14		0	2.00	.0385	4
13		0	2.00	.0385	4
12		0	2.00	.0385	4
11		.25	2.00	.0385	4
10	/	.50	1.75	.0337	3
9		.25	1.25	.0240	2
8		.25	1.00	.0192	2
7	/	.50	.75	.0144	1
6		.25	.25	.0048	.5
5		0	0		0
4		0	0		0
3		0	0		0
2		0	0		0
1		0	0		0

1. To smooth the percentile, manipulate the Frequency Tabulation column (Column 2) before proceeding. Multiply each frequency by 2, add the frequencies immediately above and immediately below, and divide the sum by 4. This is illustrated in Example Three, Worksheet for Smoother Percentiles. Always begin with the raw score below the one for which your first tabulation occurs.

2. For example:

a. In the row containing the raw score 6 (which is the score just below the bottom tabulation), you multiply your frequency by 2 (the frequency for raw score 6 to 0) and add the sum of the frequencies for the raw scores immediately above and below (0 for raw score 5 and 1 for raw score 7). Take this sum, divide it by 4 (to average), and enter the result to the right of the raw score that you were smoothing. Thus, for the raw score 6 your calculations appear as $\dfrac{(0 \times 2) + 0 + 1}{4} = .25$, and your smoothed frequency for 6 is .25.

b. Similarly, if you were to proceed to the next number above, the smoothed frequency for a raw score of 7 would be $\dfrac{(1 \times 2) + 0 + 0}{4} = .50$.

c. Last, for a raw score of 18, 3 X 2 (twice the frequency) is added to the frequencies below (+2) and above (+2), equaling 10. Ten divided by 4 equals 2.50, which is entered in Column 3.

3. Proceed in this manner, smoothing each raw score unit in turn. Remember to extend your figuring to include the raw score just above the highest one having a tabulation.

4. Be sure to include each raw score unit in your calculations, even though there may be some raw scores that no one received. As a check on your computations, add the numbers together in the Smoothed Frequency column. This total should equal the number of scores originally tabulated.

5. Follow steps 3, 4, 5, and 6 as you did previously in Step II to obtain the percentile (smoothed) scores associated with each raw score.

Step III—Updating the Norms

The simple procedure outlined should be repeated every year, or any time you have accumulated enough cases to ensure a good sample. Norms become outdated; it is possible that over a period of time and as the labor market changes, your company will attract a different caliber of applicant for a given job.

PERSONNEL RESEARCH

All personnel offices engage in some form of research activity. It is impossible to run a personnel program without some preplanning and post-reviewing.

Unfortunately most of this is done out of necessity, not out of foresight. Once the minimum results have been accomplished the study is over. Much more could be contributed to a sound personnel program if "research and standards" were made an integral part of the personnel activity, as are other aspects such as employment, wages, and benefits.

In a good research approach the object is to get facts and information about personnel specifics in order to develop and maintain a program that works. Don't just hire applicants, as is so often the case. Explore the market, use the best aids to reach the goal of hiring not the first but the best available applicants. Who knows what the ideal combination might be unless he does a bit of research?

Every salary survey is, in a sense, research. Most of the time this consists of gathering outside data to support a recommendation for an upward revision of existing wage scales. Perhaps there are other possibilities to consider. What are the trends in the community or in the industry? What is best for the particular makeup of the company's work force? Who knows without doing some research?

For that matter, any survey on personnel policy or practice is good research. How many companies analyze their turnover? It has long been recognized that turnover is an excellent barometer of wages, benefits, and other aspects of an employee program. When wages fall below the community average, turnover will increase to reflect this.

How about classifying terminations? Most terminations occur in the first year of employment. Why merely accept this as a fact of personnel life? Why not try to do something about it? Are the terminations among men or women, married people or single, young or old, lower-rated jobs or higher classifications? Once the source of the problem can be pinpointed, perhaps employment patterns can be altered to alleviate the expensive problem of turnover.

Research certainly applies to employment. Before any new worker can be hired the job must be analyzed, described, specifications spelled out, an evaluation made, the job classified, a rate set. This is obvious, and to some extent these steps are taken. How much better would the placement be if this helpful information were arrived at by objective means.

What about the sources of applicants? The costs of acquisition? Where are the *most* applicants coming from? Where are the *best* applicants coming from? Which of the referrals are the more skilled, stay the longest, become promotable, and work out the best? Research here can provide answers which in turn can reduce employment costs.

Tests and Training

Research is also required in the building of an adequate testing program, and certainly in its validation within a specific company. The universities and other agencies create these tests on the basis of their research findings. But a local research application should be made before any tests, developed in outside locations, are used to aid in solving company problems. What tests to use, what combination of tests to put together into a test battery, what different tests or batteries to consider for different jobs, what norms to be guided by, how to challenge these norms in a tightening employment market, and how to apply the whole concept of tests in a changing social climate are questions that must be answered long after the printed test is completed and made ready for industry use.

In a tight labor market while business is expanding, the need to forecast employment requirements is always a matter of corporate life and death. This begins with an inventory of existing jobs and people; their qualifications and potential; and a planned effort to recruit, train, and build people at all levels to maintain the lifeblood of the organization. A personnel audit should be made periodically as a basis upon which to plan, and the amount and depth of research to accomplish all this will determine the effectiveness of the employment effort for years to come.

Speaking of training, how much is planned and how much is hit and miss? A bit of research will help identify those areas where training would be useful. In too many instances men are sent off to meetings or seminars for no justifiable reason. In-house courses are sometimes offered to employees not because the need has expressed itself but simply because a promoter sold the boss on the idea. Education and training are too important to be left to chance; research of the need, the programs, and the results will aid a company in getting more value for the time, money, and effort expended.

The whole area of welfare benefits leads itself to research. What elements should be included in a comprehensive program, how extensive should the coverages be, which of several available insurance contracts would best fit the particular work group, how should the entire program be administered, how much red tape is involved, and what are the trends in this field—all these aspects need constant study.

Reading Employee Morale

A delicate attempt at research is a morale reading. Through a well-designed attitude survey, employee opinions are asked on wages, promotions, working conditions, opportunities, job security, leadership, management, and the like. It is easy enough to ask questions of employees; it is more difficult to take the actions their answers suggest, and downright dangerous to ignore their well-intentioned advice.

Policies should not be put into effect without being researched. Practices should be checked out and never based solely on whim or personal prejudice. The same logic applies to personnel reports which are often requested for incidental use, only to be perpetuated long afterward. Research should test the practical value of such reports, as well as other statistical data, much of which may be compiled for no better reason than an almost automatic machine print-out. Publishing periodic reports on tardiness and absences is worthless if nothing is done to try to correct the problems. The forms used in personnel to gather information or to dispense information ought to be researched to determine how well they may be fulfilling the original purpose for which they were designed. Conditions change and personnel paperwork should keep in step.

There are many other opportunities for research in personnel administration. One important concern is that of the organization structure and organization planning. And there are always requests for special studies. By and large, research is no one-time duty. Like safety education, it must be continuous not sporadic.

In most companies, research is the most neglected area because the personnel people are too busy putting out fires. Research is not done to put out fires but to prevent them. It could well be the most meaningful aspect of personnel management, worth so much more than it costs that neglecting it becomes a tragic waste too expensive to tolerate.

RESEARCH ON ADS AND AD WRITING

Most help-wanted advertisements are rather matter of fact. They tell the story of a job opportunity in convincing terms. Since there is really very little difference in basic salaries, fringe benefits, and working conditions, all ads begin to sound alike.

The help-wanted pages of the big metropolitan newspapers look more like a directory of corporations in trouble than a list of career opportunities.

The big, screaming ads actually sound more like a cry of despair than job openings. In an effort to evoke a response, some ads attempt to be different. When ads do not pull, new approaches are tried.

One employer told why his secretarial position was open. "My girl couldn't put up with my temper and unreasonableness." He was honest and said he was a tough boss. He filled the job opening while other, sterile, ads which boasted about "convenient location, excellent benefits, good opportunity for the right person" (whatever all that means) went unanswered.

Another ad asked for "a girl smart enough to be worth $100 a week but dumb enough to start for less." It brought in sufficient replies to give the employer a choice of candidates.

Why? Why do some ads appeal to job hunters while others fall on deaf ears? There are many reasons, some of which, such as a tight labor market, we have no control over.

Ads should be studied to see how well they serve their purpose. A good check is to keep a record of telephone, mail, or walk-in responses; how many who inquire are invited in for interviews; how many show up; how many are considered at all; how many listen to the job offer; how many accept; how many are hired.

Look for the Reasons

There is no rule of thumb which tells when an advertisement is effective. A newspaper ad for middle-aged housewives to do un-skilled office or factory work will pull better than an ad for secretaries. But any ad which does not bring in a fair response should be reviewed and revised before it is re-run.

Maybe the medium is wrong. A newspaper which brings in responses from women may not be the medium to use for actuaries and engineers. The time of year makes a difference. High-school students may be reached in June but not at other times.

Most of the time, help-wanted advertisements are placed because a problem exists. If the job opening is filled, the problem is forgotten and the employment interviewers concentrate on a new problem. If the job opening is not filled, the strategy is repeated, possibly changed. Somehow, through trial and error, results are attained.

Help-wanted advertising, like other recruiting efforts, is costly. How can we know whether or not we are getting our money's worth? How can we know if results are the best possible under existing circumstances?

Research helps. A simple record of results, as indicated earlier, will be helpful as a guide for future ads. Costing out acquisition expense per new worker hired may serve as an eye-opener. Followup on applicants hired to see how well they worked out, how long they stayed, may indicate the type of applicant attracted through one medium as against another.

It is not recommended that endless paperwork should be undertaken. The effort must be on getting the jobs filled, but a studied effort will produce a better result.

PERSONNEL GENERALITIES VS. SPECIFICS

One of the functions of personnel research is to discover new and better ways of doing things. The old, comfortable paths could easily become deep ruts. The personnel executive should pause occasionally to reflect on what is happening. He must be able to depart from the traditional, be willing to experiment with a different approach.

For the personnel director who is satisfied with his procedures but unhappy with the results, here are a few ideas. They are presented not as a comprehensive list of problem areas but as "teasers" or "thought starters."

Recruiting

We are still using the old standbys of recruiting methods that were originated years ago to meet emergency situations. These methods are rapidly reaching the point of no return as, for example, the uselessness of help-wanted ads for typists, stenos, and secretaries. In one Sunday newspaper I counted 152 ads calling for shorthand; I wondered how any likely applicant would ever find our company ad calling attention to (what we must have felt) was the best offer in the bunch. Ads no longer give the public a notion of expansion but, rather, of desperation. We are in a recruiting stalemate; we need new and better recruiting approaches.

Shortage of Skills

With machines taking over increasing amounts of clerical as well as factory work, a careful inventory of human resources needs to be made. We may have plenty of people—loyal, dedicated workers at that. But do we still have plenty of necessary skills? The shortage is not in hands, the shortage is in skills; and this becomes more acute as the demand for talent and ability increases. Typists are scarcer than file clerks, secretaries harder to hire than typists, and so on.

The shortage, however, doesn't stop "along the line" but goes right on up. The real shortage, the one companies ought to worry about, is the executive shortage.

Testing

Most companies use employment tests to determine learning ability, aptitudes, interests, and personality traits. But how many realize that these tests, most of which were developed decades ago and validated under conditions existing then, cannot predict attitude, fortitude, and other ingredients of success? Using present-day testing devices, Horatio Alger would not have had a chance; Benjamin Franklin would have flunked; Leonardo da Vinci would not have made it past the reception desk; Nellie Fox would not have been signed by the White Sox, but he went on to be named the American League's Most Valuable Player in 1959 because of two traits that tests cannot measure—desire and determination. The questions are: Have tests lost their usefulness? and, What new tests are being created?

Selection

We use the word "selection," but are we really selecting from a list of applicants? Or has the selection process become a series of eliminations? The number of candidates for a job is reduced by tests, physical exams, references, interviews, and such devices, until there is no selection; we merely hire the one who is left. A very well-known group of 12 applicants would have been turned away, for by our standards they would have been declared unfit because of age, lack of education, inexperience; 11 of the 12 were unmarried, all were unqualified for saleswork; yet these are the 12 Apostles who become the best sales force the world has ever known.

Employment Requirements

At a time when skilled office workers are in short supply, we turn down qualified applicants simply because we are unwilling or unable to bend our rigid nine-to-five, five-day-a-week, 50-week-a-year routine, which is geared more to cherished past practices than to modern business needs. There are thousands of secretaries, stenos, typists, bookkeepers, and other experienced white-collar workers who are "out of reach" because we don't know how to fit these odd-hour, on-again-off-again workers in with the regimented regular staff. Consequently we tell them to take their job needs to some of the temporary-help agencies from whom we then hire them anyway.

Policies

This reminds us that policies in general are made in terms of the total work force and not the individuals. Is this good, or does it create more problems than it solves? Work hours, for instance, are different for computer personnel than for clerical workers. Employees who work by the job should not be required to fit the mold of employees who work by the clock. Imposing sameness upon people who are different leads to difficulties. Policies should relate to the classes, not the masses.

Vacations

The usual policy is to schedule a worker's vacation on the basis of: (1) seniority and (2) convenience to the company. This idea goes back to early days and was designed for primary wage earners—the chief worker, more than likely the only worker, in a household. Today our offices are full of secondary wage earners whose vacation choice is dictated by the husband's requirements, not by company convenience. In such conflicting circumstances how flexible can we afford to be?

Holidays

We will probably never see a less number of holidays. Even now when Memorial Day or Fourth of July fall on a Saturday we have been pressured into closing the preceding Friday. If you are considering the number of holidays from the standard six, how far do you dare to innovate? Can you add a "floating" holiday or two? How about a "personal" holiday, observed at the discretion of the employee? Today's restless workers like to vary the pattern.

Training

We have always accepted training as part of the personnel activity and as necessary for increasing the productivity and efficiency of the work force. But training is not enough now. This is the first generation in which a man's earlier training is no longer sufficient to carry him through life. So the new problem is retraining, which few companies are doing much about. The government has picked up the challenge and has agencies and funds ready for this purpose. Are we going to accept retraining as the responsibility of industry or are we going to leave the door of opportunity wide open for unwanted government intervention?

Retirement

Retirement is many things to many people. To some it is freedom from a lifetime of work; to others a dreaded point of no return, a "ringing down of the curtain." Like it or not, many who work for someone else are routinely forced into retirement at the arbitrary age of 65. The age of 65 was chosen because for government and industry it makes for uniform and easy administration. While it may be true that "all people are created equal" it soon becomes obvious that by the time they reach age 65 they are anything but equal. Should we try to devise a retirement system that suits the individual's age and abilities instead of taking the easy way out and using one that fits the convenience of the company? Would not the company benefit in most instances?

Promotion

There are two main routes to business promotion: (1) The passive route and (2) The active route. It is entirely possible to get to the top in business by being passive. It is possible to rise to eminence from humble beginnings by doing practically nothing, but looking good while doing it. Given a well-developed instinct for survival, it is possible in some businesses to get ahead simply by being available—by being the handiest person to fall heir to the promotion as smarter men move up or out, or otherwise clear the way. The logical way, however, calls for careful selection of successor prospects. And this task of selecting the one right person need not be difficult as long as we are honest with ourselves, our companies, and our candidates. We confound the issue by interjecting seniority, loyalty, or sentimental personal qualities, thereby making the problem complicated.

Discrimination

Maybe you think you don't discriminate, but you do. To check, just look at your management group, or even your supervisors and administrators, and see how many members of minority groups are in influential positions. Firms which do not discriminate against race, color or creed, might be guilty of discriminating against age which, incidentally, is far more serious. And industry discriminates generally against women; the Illinois eight-hour law for women, which was passed under the guise of safeguarding the fragility of womanhood, is in reality discrimination against women since it prevents them from competing with men for many jobs. Discrimination in any form is a luxury that is too expensive to tolerate.

In addition to asking questions, as we have just done, let's make a few suggestions. Here are 10 thoughts which we hope will make your employee relations programs better and more effective.

1. Can we treat applicants as guests instead of strangers? How about simplifying the processing procedure with less cumbersome application forms, more respect for the applicant's time, more interest in each one as a person. How about following up with replies to all responses, not just a selected few? And how about reducing the indecision annoyances of unsure interviewers?

2. In hiring workers, let's not try merely to fill a vacancy; let's try at the same time to help the applicant solve a problem by finding a job to his liking. Ideally, every placement should be a happy job marriage in which *both* sides are satisfied.

3. When we want to transfer or promote a worker we should not think only of solving our problem. People should not be looked upon as a load of cinders moved around to fill a hole. We should be big enough to respect the worker's feelings about the new job for which he is being considered.

4. Can we arrange to give our people, through training, a chance to increase their skills or add new ones to help them qualify for better job opportunities? This would enhance their earning power for themselves and increase their value to the company.

5. If we are going to establish a recognition program, for something like length of service, let's honor each worker individually on

his anniversary date—the day which means something to him—rather than lumping recognitions all together, once a year, for the easy planning of a group dinner or party.

6. Let's develop a better "hearing aid" for business. You say you practice the open-door policy. But who walks in? Why don't you walk around among the workers, preferably in shirt sleeves. You will be surprised at what you will learn.

7. Why wait until you have to announce something before you write a "memo to all employees"? Why not write when nothing is at stake and tell your associates what a good job they are doing?

8. Instead of passing out your expensive but dull annual statement, accompanied by a mass-produced letter full of lifeless statistics, what would be wrong with a personal letter from the president telling each worker, at home where his wife may also read it, that the company is making good progress and his job is secure?

9. There should be a Golden Rule in business. Man is a sacred personality made in the image of God. If man were a machine, then it would be appropriate to use him, depreciate him, consume him, discard him. But man is not a machine. No one, no company, no employer, no supervisor can trample with impunity upon the human personality.

10. If respecting the dignity of man in our fellow blood-bought souls sounds altruistic, then for selfish reasons let's recognize how important other people are to us in the accomplishment of our own goals. Our employees are the people through whom we do our work and through whom we attain our purpose. They are the ones who, in reality, make us look good. Let's make our personnel programs "people programs."

FRINGE BENEFITS SURVEY

Fringe benefit growth during recent years has substantially improved employee well-being, and has also increased business costs.

Payments for vacations, holidays, rest periods, etc., constitute almost one-half of total fringe benefits. These payments are included in most government wage reports as a portion of employee wages. Such payments give employees increased compensation for each hour actually on the job. Thus, they also increase the employer's cost for each hour of productive labor.

Pension, Social Security, and other employer payments for employee benefits are not part of the payroll, and are not reflected in current income or wages of employees. Such benefits, however, greatly improve employee security and well-being, and also increase the cost of doing business.

About two decades ago the United States Chamber of Commerce noted the scarcity of statistical information regarding the scope and nature of fringe benefits, and conducted the first comprehensive fringe benefit study for a cross section of American industry. This study was widely and favorably received. At the request of employers it has been repeated biennially with extended coverage and in greater detail.

The survey is conducted in the Chamber's Economic Analysis and Study Group. Its questionnaire is available from the Chamber of Commerce of the United States, 1615 H Street, N.W., Washington, D. C. 20006.

FRINGE BENEFITS QUESTIONNAIRE

The following sample fringe benefits questionnaire may be used by companies that want to figure their own fringe benefits cost. It may also be used to make comparisons with other companies which use this same form.

Total company cost for the year 19..........

A. Legally required payments (company share only)

1. Old Age and Survivors Insurance $..........

2. Unemployment compensation

   a. Tax to Federal Government ....

   b. State tax (net) ....

3. Workmen's compensation (actual cost of insurance or estimated cost if self-insured) ....

4. State sickness benefit insurance (if any) ....

5. Other (specify) ....

Subtotal $..........

Total company cost
for the year 19..........

B. Pension and other agreed-upon payments

1. Retirement program premiums (company share only) $..

2. Life insurance premiums (company share only)   ....

3. Accident and health insurance protection   ....

4. Hospitalization and medical-surgical fees (company share only)   ....

5. Accumulated severance pay at time of termination (not "2 weeks' pay in lieu of notice" at time of dismissal)   ....

6. Other (specify) ....

Subtotal $..

C. Payments for time not worked

1. Rest periods a.m. and p.m. $..

2. Vacations   ....

   a. Wages during vacation time   ....

   b. Payment for unused vacation (as at time of termination)   ....

3. Sick leave pay   ....

4. Payment for holidays not worked (actual amount of time off—including possible double days such as Thanksgiving, etc.)   ....

5. Jury duty and/or court witness pay allowances (any amount over and above salary)   ....

6. Voting time off allowances   ....

7. Temporary military leave or guard duty (include time off for military physical exam, etc.)   ....

8. Payment for time off lost due to death in family   ....

9. Marriage leave   ....

10. Payments for time off for personal reasons   ....

11. Check cashing time   ....

12. Merit or attendance bonus days, or unused bank time   ....

13. Other (specify) ....

Subtotal $..

Total company cost
for the year 19............

D. Contributions toward employee program

1. Cafeteria subsidy (toward food and labor; *not* equipment, rent, etc.) $............................

2. Canteen or other lunchroom allowances   ....

3. Cost of maintaining health and hygiene clinic (supplies and equipment, but *not* salaries, rent, etc.)   ....

4. Cost of medical services (such as flu shots, polio shots, X-rays, etc.)   ....

5. Company cost of employee credit union (salary of clerk, adding machine, and other items which company furnishes)   ....

6. Cost of company-sponsored employee functions   ....

    a. Christmas or other party   ....

    b. Plcnic   ....

    c. Service recognition dinner or party   ....

    d. Other (specify) ....

7. Contribution toward employee-sponsored activities   ....

    a. Bowling league   ....

    b. Golf tournament   ....

    c. Baseball or basketball team   ....

    d. Employee clubs   ....

    e. Other (specify) ....

8. Company contribution toward gift or flower fund   ....

9. Tuition refund program   ....

10. Other (specify) ....

                  Subtotal $............................

E. Supplemental compensation, special awards, etc.

1. Supplemental compensation $............................

2. Suggestion awards   ....

3. Service awards   ....

4. Any personal club membership (not business or trade associations)   ....

5. Other (specify) ....

                  Subtotal $............................

                  Grand Total $............................

THE PERSONNEL DIRECTOR

The personnel director is generally regarded as a specialist in his field. But in the eyes of Amy K. Hartman, director of personnel at St. Vincent's Hospital, Jacksonville, Florida, the personnel man may be looked upon as a general practitioner because he must possess many of the specialties associated with the medical environment.

He must be—

A radiologist: to be able to read people's minds like a fluoroscope, to deduce who the "introverts" and the "extroverts" are.

A psychologist: to be able to understand not only what the employee said and what he meant, but what he should have said; and, what's more important, what he did not say.

An orthopedist: to be able to understand and cope with those employees who have chips on their shoulders, look upon change as a fractured way of life, and refuse to be anything but hardheaded.

An allergist: to be able to handle all types of allergies and to stimulate self-improvement for those employees who suddenly are allergic to work and to almost everything else, except payday.

A dermatologist: to be able to handle the thin-skinned ones.

A rhinologist: to straighten out the ones who get their "noses out of joint."

A dietitian: to be able to cook up appetizing policies, rules and regulations, that can be easily digested and well-flavored with enthusiasm.

An otologist: to be an expert in the "art of listening"—to complaints, to personal problems, to "lonely conversation."

A diagnostician: not only to listen to problems but to make suggestions, to advise, to inform.

The personnel director must be alert to all the "ills" which can affect the job satisfaction of the individual, efficiency of a department, or the general attitude within the company.

AND WHAT OF THE HUMAN ELEMENT?

By Joan R. McAllister, Eastern Airlines

In this, the day of the computer, electronic equipment, and the jet age, we have a tendency to think we live in a gigantic impersonal world where the individual is being replaced by machines and is thought of as a number.

We have a social security number, a telephone number, a bank account number—numbers *ad infinitum.* Are we just a number amidst a great many numbers or are we individuals and human beings, each with his own wants, needs, and desires? Does anyone look at us as individuals?

We live in the age of the computer: A machine with a fantastic memory and the ability to come up with answers at an amazing rate of speed. Our "friend" the computer *never* makes a mistake, unless with the help of some human's faulty "input."

Eastern Airlines Systems Control Center in Charlotte, North Carolina, has a complex Univac installation. Reservations information and aircraft routing information all are programmed into the computer. An answer to any engineering, routing, or service problem is no more than a fraction of a second away. Radioactive isotopes help look inside jet engines, and a new method of X-raying fuselages finds wear almost before it happens.

500 Corporate Giants

In his book, *The Industrial State,* John Kenneth Galbraith talks of a consortium of 500 corporate giants controlling the destiny of the United States with a concern only for profits.

There were times when a corporate president knew every individual in his company. Nowadays a manager is lucky if he knows everyone who works in his department.

A recent issue of *Parade* magazine pointed out that the man in the street is no longer familiar with names of the presidents of large corporations. The day of dynamic individuals like the Rockefellers or the Morgans is in the past. According to this thesis, corporations don't want creative, thinking individuals. The heads of our giant companies are merely good organization men. They are bland, nondistinctive men, who are competent at their jobs and whose main claim to fame is that they have never rocked the boat.

Some companies don't seem to be interested in even publicizing their names. They want to be identified by letters. We have TWA, A.T. & T., P & G, GM, GE, and, of course, let us not forget, IBM.

The United States Government employs over 15 million people. This is almost 15 percent of the total work force of this country. As individuals, we frequently feel that we have no contact with the people who supposedly represent us. There are 12 Cabinet Departments in our government. Each is divided into many bureaus, divisions, offices, and services so that all the work that needs to be done can be carried out. On the basis of size alone, these great bureaucratic mazes have become impersonal.

As the government continues to grow, it tends to keep a closer look on all citizens' activities. Since every working individual has a social security number, the IRS (please note letters) and the computers keep a very close watch on the income we receive from the companies we work for, the places at which we bank, and the places at which we invest. The Census Bureau is collecting more and more personal data about us. All of this is fed into the government's computer. It is no wonder that Uncle Sam is IBM's largest customer. Uncle Sam is more than likely everybody's largest customer.

Do our Congressmen and Senators reflect their constituents' opinions or do they vote for what is politically expedient? Do our representatives vote on issues based on a sound philosophy or are they just concerned with voting in a manner which will get them reelected? It is interesting to note how many government officials feel the need to discover culture abroad in such places of note as the Parthenon, the Louvre, St. Peter's, and the Lido de Paris.

Viewpoints Are Changing

Communism with its strong central control and belief that the State is more important than the individual is having a slight change of outlook. After decades of putting all their emphasis on the development of capital goods, they are just now beginning to give the little man a few of the frills such as shoes, suits, dresses, etc.

There is a great hue and cry about the hippies. NBC recently did a study and seemed to conclude their major preoccupation is with drugs. If so, how can most of these hippies come from a middle-class suburban society? It seems that a great deal of their protestations stem from their dissatisfaction with society and their treatment as part of an insignificant conglomorate rather than a significant individual. They may not be totally correct, but are they totally incorrect?

It has been said that the Protestant ethic has been the single greatest contributing factor to man's emergence from the Dark Ages into the Society of the Western World as we know it today. The Protestant ethic was the greatest initial stimulus to the development of our capitalist society, but, does not this philosophy, as well as the entire Judeo-Christian philosophy, emphasize the love of one's neighbor? It means the love for, respect for, and the importance of the individual.

We frequently categorize corporations for being monolithic, impersonal giants. Corporations and countries may be successful, but they are only successful because of the individuals who comprise these entities.

For example: In the airline industry, as well as in many others, the important difference between companies is people and their concern for fellow human beings. Rarely a day passes when we cannot cite an instance of an individual caring for another's welfare.

A Way Can Be Found

A recent illustration involved an Eastern Airlines sales representative in Chicago who received a call asking for assistance for the wife of a young wounded Vietnam veteran. The vet had been blinded and had not been with his wife for two years. Since they had limited funds they inquired whether Eastern could offer free transportation. The easy and obvious answer would have been, "I wish we could help, but the Government will not allow us to give free transportation under any circumstances." Because of this representative's concern for another human being, the effort was made to collect sufficient funds to purchase transportation. Over a hundred people contributed, everything from quarters to dollars. In less than two hours enough money was collected to purchase a ticket. These people contributed because they cared. True, Eastern reaped a great deal of benefit because of the news coverage, but the important thing is that whatever benefit all the parties involved received, it was due directly to one individual and her concern for another individual.

The Key Is People

There are many examples of people taking the time, the effort, and the money to do something for others. All young children are thrilled by airports and the sight of airplanes. Taking a large group of orphans through Eastern's facilities at O'Hare Field in Chicago, and seeing the excitement and joy in their eyes, is a reward in itself.

The examples go on and on.

In all instances, success in business or in government is the direct result of the initiative, imagination, and diligence of individuals. The degree of success is in direct proportion to the credit given individuals for these characteristics.

Mr. Arthur D. Lewis, president of Eastern Airlines, in a speech before the New York Society of Security Analysts, summed up our thoughts when he said: "In the last analysis—we come back to people. Our ultimate problem in the airline industry is not principally technology, for technology can be made to serve our needs, to solve the problems it has brought us, and the growth it has engendered and will continue to engender. The greatest challenge to airline management is to develop and motivate the people who put technology to work."

PERSONNEL RESEARCH

The Toronto, Ontario, chapter of the Administrative Management Society made a study of hitherto unavailable up-to-date information on personnel practices. The 25-page report covered 193 firms in the Toronto metropolitan area. Some of the findings follow.

In a majority of instances employees are hired by both supervisor and personnel. The supervisor alone has this function in twice as many instances as personnel only.

The three most effective sources used in recruiting, shown in order of greatest frequency, were newspaper ads, employment agencies, and government employment service. Other sources included friends of employees, voluntary applications, high schools, universities, and business schools.

A very large majority use office service organizations for temporary help. Such service is for emergencies, occasionally, peak periods, and regularly. Less than half the respondents reported having employees who regularly work less than standard hours.

Very few post vacancies on the bulletin board for clerical positions and fewer still for supervisory positions. Only eight offer a tangible reward to employees for recruiting new applicants.

Most Use Tests

Preemployment tests are used by 62 percent. Such tests are based (in numerical frequency) on clerical ability, mechanical performance, intelligence, personality, and aptitude. Aptitude testing is applied by less than 10 percent of the respondents.

Checking up of background and previous records is dominated by the easy method of phoning previous employers. School records and character references are checked much less frequently and then usually by telephone. A majority of new employees are on probation up to and including three months.

Only about 25 percent conduct formal induction programs or orientation courses. A majority of this minority include a tour of the office or buildings and the supervisor is generally involved. Use of movies, filmstrips, visual aids, and top management speakers is still quite limited.

When the employee is leaving, on the other hand, he or she is given considerable attention. Some 121 respondents conduct exit interviews. Fifty-three consider them helpful in saving employees, 109 consider them valuable in correcting causes for terminations. Personnel most often conducts the exit interview, the supervisor is also interviewed in about half such cases.

More than two-thirds of the firms have a stated policy covering sick leave. Sick leave is cumulative from year to year in 44 instances and not so in 90 of the companies.

Attendance and Tardiness

Only 13 firms reward good attendance—10 with cash and three with time off. Lateness is recorded by 114 respondents and 100 of these terminate employment for frequent lateness. Only seven reported rewards for good punctuality records.

As for salary administration, 133 respondents pay their office employees by check, 42 by bank deposit, 11 in cash. Employee benefits such as pension and retirement plans, group life insurance, supplementary group hospitalization and other medical plans are promisingly considered in most instances.

Thirty-two respondents have libraries. Service clubs exist for employees with long service. The awards rate service pins as tops, with watches or clocks a close second. However, only about half of the respondents do anything at all on this point.

Office staffs are unionized in only about 3 percent of the 193 firms. Music is provided in about 20 percent of the offices. Lunchrooms are almost unanimously available in most groups.

ANALYSIS OF FORMS, PROCEDURES, PRACTICES, REPORTS

As personnel administration becomes more complex and involved, it seems that personnel people are so busy "doing" that they cannot find time for "thinking." As the familiar accusation puts it, they spend so much time putting out fires that they cannot work on fire prevention.

What began as a simple report form is now more detailed. What was a routine procedure is today more cumbersome. Reports are getting wider distribution and evoking more comments, some of which lead to localized or interim reports. All sorts of influences are exerting a pull on personnel practices.

All of this seems understandable at the time it happens. The extra involvement comes in small doses, insignificant in each request, and hardly worth resisting at the time. Yet the cumulative effect over a period of time throws the best designed personnel program out of kilter.

The line of least resistance calls for adding more people to the personnel staff. The number of people in the personnel office should increase as the total work force grows or as new functions are added. But it is unprofitable to add people because of red tape. Maybe some of the red tape that has been sneaking in is no longer necessary.

It is better to analyze forms, procedures, practices, and reports periodically if not regularly. Put each on trial to determine whether it can be simplified, combined, mechanized, or possibly even eliminated. The results may well be surprising.

ORGANIZATION PLANNING
(As Related to Personnel)

The personnel officer plays an increasingly important role in organization planning. In most current organization charts the personnel officer reports to a top executive, quite often the president. This puts him in a responsible position of becoming involved in overall planning—provided, of course, he is qualified in this area.

The day of the "personnel department" concerned mainly with "doing"—similar to other operating departments—is over. In addition to day-to-day administrative duties, the personnel office must also plan for the future, not just the future of the personnel program but how this relates to and serves corporate planning. This makes the personnel officer a part of the corporate "think" team.

Planning Outranks Doing

In fact, in medium and large companies where personnel has been accepted for the contribution it can make, the planning and doing functions of personnel administration are often separated. One may not even be accountable to the other. The "planning" aspect, known as "Management Development" or "Corporate Personnel" or "Manpower Resources," is accountable to the president. The "doing" function, headed by "Manager of Personnel" or "Personnel Director," may report to the works manager or the vice-president of manufacturing or the vice-president of administration—executives responsible for day-to-day operations.

In all these cases, the planning job rates higher than the doing job. Its duties include manpower resources, management development, policy, and compensation. Its main responsibility is to assist top management in overall corporate planning, especially as related to human resources.

This development places a unique responsibility upon the personnel officer. It moves his opportunity from the periphery of company operations to the very center of management activities where the hard decisions are made.

PERSONNEL PERIODICALS

Members of the personnel staff may wish to subscribe to publications to aid them in their work. Listed below are magazines in the field of personnel administration as well as others of a specialized or technical nature.

Administrative Management
51 Madison Avenue
New York, New York 10010

Association Management
2000 K Street N.W.
Washington, D.C. 20006

Bankers Monthly
162 Fourth Avenue, North
Nashville, Tennessee 37229

Banking
90 Park Avenue
New York, New York 10016

Best's Insurance News
Columbia Turnpike
Box 232
Rensselaer, New York 12144

Broadcasting
1735 DeSales Street, N.W.
Washington, D.C. 20036

Buildings
427 Sixth Avenue, S.E.
Cedar Rapids, Iowa 52406

Business Automation
288 Park Avenue, West
Elmhurst, Illinois 60126

Business Education World
330 West 42nd Street
New York, New York 10036

Business Management
22 West Putnam Avenue
Greenwich, Connecticut 06830

Datamation
1830 West Olympic Boulevard
Los Angeles, California 90006

Data Processing
134 North 13th Street
Philadelphia, Pennsylvania 19107

Drug & Cosmetic Industry
101 West 31st Street
New York, New York 10001

Dun's Review
P.O. Box 3088
Grand Central Station
New York, New York 10017

Editor & Publisher
850 Third Avenue
New York, New York 10022

The Education Digest
416 Longshore Drive
Ann Arbor, Michigan 48107

Engineering and Mining Journal
330 West 42nd Street
New York, New York 10036

Engineering News-Record
330 West 42nd Street
New York, New York 10036

Factory
330 West 42nd Street
New York, New York 10036

Finance
25 East 73rd Street
New York, New York 10021

Food Engineering
Chestnut and 56th Streets
Philadelphia, Pennsylvania 19139

Food Management
Ojibway Building
Duluth, Minnesota 55802

Food Processing-Marketing
111 East Delaware Place
Chicago, Illinois 60611

Forest Industries
731 S.W. Oak Street
Portland, Oregon 97205

Fuel Oil & Oil Heat
447 Orange Road
Montclair, New Jersey 07042

Gas Age
Ojibway Building
Duluth, Minnesota 55802

Graphic Arts Monthly
7373 North Lincoln Avenue
Chicago, Illinois 60646

Harvard Business Review
Cambridge, Massachusetts

Hotel & Motel Management
105 West Adams Street
Chicago, Illinois 60603

Industrial and Labor Relations Review
Cornell University
Ithaca, New York 14850

Industrial Marketing
740 Rush Street
Chicago, Illinois 60611

Industrial Relations
University of California
Berkeley, California 94720

Insurance
232 Madison Avenue
New York, New York 10016

Iron Age
Chestnut and 56th Street
Philadelphia, Pennsylvania 19139

Journal of Data Management
505 Busse Highway
Park Ridge, Illinois 60068

Management of Personnel Quarterly
University of Michigan
Ann Arbor, Michigan 48104

Management Review
135 West 50th Street
New York, New York 10020

Mill & Factory
205 East 42nd Street
New York, New York 10017

Modern Materials Handling
221 Columbus Avenue
Boston, Massachusetts 02116

Modern Office Procedures
812 Huron Road
Cleveland, Ohio 44115

Modern Packaging
330 West 42nd Street
New York, New York 10036

Modern Plastics
330 West 42nd Street
New York, New York 10036

Nargus Bulletin
360 North Michigan Avenue
Chicago, Illinois 60601

National Petroleum News
330 West 42nd Street
New York, New York 10036

The Office
73 Southfield Avenue
Stamford, Connecticut 06904

Office Administration
1450 Don Mills Road
Toronto, Ontario, Canada

Office Appliances
288 Park Avenue, West
Elmhurst, Illinois 60126

The Office Economist
Art Metal, Inc.
Jamestown, New York 14701

Oil and Gas Journal
211 South Cheyenne
Tulsa, Oklahoma 74101

Paper Trade Journal
551 Fifth Avenue
New York, New York 10017

Personnel
135 West 50th Street
New York, New York 10020

The Personnel Administrator
Amer. Society for Personnel Admin.
52 East Bridge Street
Berea, Ohio

Personnel and Guidance Journal
1605 New Hampshire Avenue, N.W.
Washington, D.C. 20009

Personnel Journal
100 Park Avenue
Swarthmore, Pennsylvania 19081

Savings and Loan
221 North LaSalle Street
Chicago, Illlnois 60601

Steel, the Metalworking Weekly
Penton Building
Cleveland, Ohio 44113

Stores (Retailing)
100 West 31st Street
New York, New York 10001

Supervisory Management
135 West 50th Street
New York, New York 10020

Systems
200 Madison Avenue
New York, New York 10016

Systems & Procedures Journal
24587 Bagley Road
Cleveland, Ohio 44138

Tea & Coffee
79 Wall Street
New York, New York 10005

Television Age
1270 Avenue of the Americas
New York, New York 10020

Textile World
330 West 42nd Street
New York, New York 10036

Think
I B M
Armonk, New York 10504

Today's Secretary
330 West 42nd Street
New York, New York 10036

Training in Business and Industry
31 West 60th Street
New York, New York 10023

Transport Topics
1616 P Street, N.W.
Washington, D.C. 20036

Transportation & Distribution Management
Washington Building
Washington, D.C. 20005

plus

**Publications of the
    United States Department of Labor**
Washington, D.C. 20402

FROM THE RANKS of black businessmen themselves comes expertise in the recruiting and training of minority workers.

FRANK W. ROSELLE (left) is manager of recruitment projects for Mattel, Inc., a responsibility which includes training of professional and technical personnel at all levels. He formerly held personnel posts with the Boy Scouts of America and the New York Times Company.

DAVID S. CUNNINGHAM (above) is a West Coast leader in minority community and personnel relations. He has been community relations manager for Hughes Aircraft Company and West African manager for Dukane Products.

TED SHORT (right) has held personnel administration posts at the Whittaker Corp., North American Rockwell, and the Home Savings and Loan Management Program.

EMPLOYMENT

TABLE OF ORGANIZATION

How many employees does a company need? How should they be divided among the several organizational units? How can the number be kept from increasing unnecessarily?

One effective control is a "Table of Organization." This is a device to aid in the efficient operation of a company through establishing and controlling manpower requirements.

The T/O is a simple statement of the total manpower needs of a company. It is a listing, arranged along structural or functional lines, of the number and classification of positions in a total organization, broken down into divisions, departments, or other operational units.

The tabulation shows each separate job title, the salary grade or position classification, and the number of such jobs in the unit. It would not list all 10 secretarial jobs in the firm in one place but rather show one such position in each department where it belongs. The order follows that of the budget, using the same code numbers. If, for instance, the Executive Division has its departments in budget series 10, it will be listed ahead of the Marketing Division whose budget series is in the 20's; Finance Division, budget 30, would precede Manufacturing if its budgets were in the 40's.

To illustrate, that portion of a company's total T/O which covers the personnel and public relations functions, each with its separate budget, might look like this:

Budget	Job Title	Grade	Number
50	Personnel director	X	1
	Secretary I	8	1
	Assistant personnel director	VIII	1
	Secretary II	6	1
51	Employment manager	VI	1
	Interviewer	10	2
	Employment clerk	5	1
	Receptionist	3	1
52	Wage administrator	V	1
	Clerk, etc.	4	1
60	Public relations director	X	1
	Secretary I	8	1
61	Artist	IX	1
62	Copywriter	VII	2
	Typist, etc.	5	3

In this hypothetical example, the jobs are further differentiated in that the salary grade of exempt positions (using one job system) is shown in Roman numerals, while wage-and-hour jobs (evaluated under another system) are designated in Arabic numeral classifications.

The orderly listing of all jobs in a company by title, grade, and number would of itself make the T/O a convenient instrument for management. But that is not its purpose. It serves as a control if a proper procedure for maintaining it is followed. This could be something like the following typical policy.

As soon as any job is vacated, either because the employee terminates or transfers, personnel is given a requisition for a replacement. This protects the job. The requisition is signed by the manager and approved by his immediate superior, who may have his own opinion whether the job should be continued, changed, or dropped.

Some Have Time Limit

A job may be abolished at any time simply by written notice from the manager to the personnel office, or whoever is in charge of the T/O, asking that it be removed from his list. Some companies go so far as to automatically delete any job which remains unfilled for a reasonable period of time (maybe 90 days or six months) on the theory that if the manager was able to get along without someone in that job maybe he doesn't need the person.

By observing the foregoing procedure the T/O will remain intact or possibly be reduced. If management's objective is to be satisfied with the status quo, no further control may be necessary. If the work volume or operating cost fluctuates, it may be advisable to have the comptroller or budget administrator countersign all replacement requisitions.

In all cases it is recommended that a tighter control be installed for additions to the T/O. These could be either new jobs or extra personnel for existing jobs. This control can be accomplished by having the president approve all requests for additions to the T/O. Usually the manager completes a requisition for an additional job or person, has his superior concur with his request then, supported with substantial documentation, pleads his case before the chief executive.

Any job so approved becomes a permanent addition to the T/O. A similar procedure may be followed for temporary jobs except that it is suggested these be authorized for a short duration, possibly 30 days, so that the need can be reviewed periodically.

A table of organization, if properly drawn up and carefully administered, can indeed be an effective control mechanism over the manpower requirements, not only of an entire company but also for each of its separate operating units.

ARMY TABLE OF ORGANIZATION AND EQUIPMENT

Since the table of organization, as used in industry, is an adaptation of the Table of Organization and Equipment of military days, a look at Army Regulations seems appropriate.

A fixed TOE is defined as a table prescribing a standard unit composition with its organic personnel and equipment. In addition, there are Cellular TOE (composed of separate teams, each of which prescribes personnel and equipment required for performance of a specific function) and Flexible TOE (two or more variations in organizations, each fixed in composition).

Further definitions cover Team, Squad, Section, Platoon, Detachment, Company (battery, troop), Battalion (squadron), Group, Regiment, Division Brigade, Nondivisional Brigade, Division, Logistical Command, Intersectional Command, Corps, Field Army.

Guidance is furnished in relation to: Multiple shift operations, Layering of organizational echelons, Additional duties, Administrative services in tactical headquarters, Overhead positions, Supervisory positions, Manpower authorization criteria and standards, Combat arms positions, Combat support and service support positions, Staff and technical inspector positions, WAC personnel positions.

Categories of personnel, from the highest-level commissioned officer and warrant officer to enlisted personnel, are designated. MOS (military occupational specialty) codes and grades are prescribed.

Provisions are made for reduced strength, the minimum required for extended periods of noncombat and limited periods of combat.

The army also has a type "B" TOE. Its purpose is to conserve U.S. military manpower. It is a table containing only the minimum of U.S. military command, supervisory, technical, and necessary maintenance personnel positions, and constitutes the method for utilizing non-U.S. personnel for the support of the army outside the continental United States.

Certain terms peculiar to TOE Manpower Authorization Criteria are defined:

Function. All the work activities devoted to fulfillment of a work area.

Work Activity. A group of closely related work processes within a specific functional area.

Work Unit. An item of work selected to express quantitatively the work to be accomplished.

Work Load. The amount of work in terms of predetermined work units which organizations or individuals perform or are responsible for performing.

Performance Standard. An established number of man-hours for the accomplishment of a unit of work.

Manpower Authorization Criteria. The minimum number of direct workers required to effectively perform a specified work activity.

Nonproductive Time. That portion of total time available which is consumed in other than primary MOS duties required in the performance of the function.

HELP-WANTED REQUISITIONS

Some type of control system for keeping track of all jobs, filled and unfilled, is recommended. This need be little more than a record of all authorized jobs by title, type, division or department, and classification. Postings are made as jobs are added, dropped, vacated, or filled.

The number of jobs filled and unfilled is known at all times. Jobs that remain open for a while should be investigated for possibly they are not needed. Additional jobs should carry the approval of a top officer, preferably the president or comptroller. This prevents divisions or departments from creating jobs without proper justification.

The control should rest with personnel, where the responsibility for keeping jobs filled rests. In auditing an action, personnel can make certain that jobs are filled by new hires, transfers or promotions, in accordance with policy.

The control device is a help-wanted requisition. A requisition is filled out, signed, and authenticated whenever a job is vacant— either by being added or when it is vacated by a termination. This requisition lists the job title, location, classification, starting salary, qualifications, description of duties, date to be filled, and other information which is needed to fill the job.

It is advisable to have a different requisition, or the regular one in a different color, for jobs which are temporary, emergency, summer vacation, or otherwise short term. Filling one of these jobs does not cancel out a regular requisition.

There follows a sample of "Permanent Help Requisition" and "Temporary Help Requisition."

```
TO PERSONNEL
                            PERMANENT HELP REQUISITION
                                                            DATE_____

      JOB CLASSIFICATION_____ DEPARTMENT
Recommended Weekly Salary to Start From $_____to $_____
Duties (Including machines to be operated):_____
                                _____

Replacement For:_____
If Addition To T/O, Explain Fully:_____

Age Range:_____to_____ Education_____ Experience_____

Requested By_____ Approved_____ Approved_____
              Manager                    Vice President        President
                            TO BE COMPLETED BY PERSONNEL

Job Filled By_____ From_____
```

REQUISITION FOR TEMPORARY PERSONNEL

IMMEDIATE SERVICE REQUIRED — ☐ Yes   ☐ No

TO	DATE
FROM	DEPT.
REPORT TO	DEPT.

JOB DESCRIPTION	NO. OF TEMPS.

HOURS FROM TO	STARTING DATE	ESTIMATED DURATION TO DATE

KIND OF MACHINE	MODEL NUMBER

SPECIAL CONSIDERATIONS

REASON FOR NEED

☐ EMERGENCY REPLACEMENT   ☐ PEAK PERIOD
☐ SPECIAL PROJECT   ☐ UNIQUE JOB
☐ FILL IN WHILE RECRUITING   ☐ PART-TIME JOB

☐ OTHER_____

APPLY TO (PROJECT OR JOB, IF ANY)

REQUISITION APPROVED BY	DATE

TEMPORARY SERVICE CONTACTED

☐ STAFF BUILDERS
☐ OTHER_____

ORDER CONFIRMED   BY   ☐ STAFF BUILDERS

DATE _____ TIME _____   ☐ Other_____

FORM NO. P–102

MANAGEMENT INVENTORY

The Canadian National Railways has established a program called "Management Inventory and Assessment of Potential."

By way of introduction, the Woods, Gordon & Company Report (1963) recommended that management development should be expanded and that every effort be made to ensure that the work of headquarters, regions, and areas be integrated into one overall, well coordinated program. A Personnel and Labour Relations Functional Conference, with representatives from headquarters and all regions and levels of the employee relations function was held in Winnipeg. This conference emphasized the need for an integrated and common approach which would provide all functions and levels of management with more meaningful information about the human resources in the company. Further discussions with line and staff officers at headquarters, regions, and areas supported this requirement.

As a start toward overall coordinated management development, a middle-management inventory program was designed. Its purpose is to secure information to assist management at all levels in staff planning; it is not to replace performance appraisals where used as a basis for communication with employees regarding on-the-job performance.

The various consultations, during the personnel functional conference and since then, indicated the logical place to start was with middle-management, especially with the increased attention to selection, training, and succession planning at lower grades where the middle-management population is largest and where the need to identify potential is perhaps greatest.

The objectives of the program may be stated as follows:

1. To identify employees who possess potential for promotion, including an assessment of individual readiness to advance and suitability for present and other jobs.

2. To identify specific training and staff development requirements.

3. To provide management with the information required for staff succession and development planning.

4. To identify overall strengths and weaknesses within functions and levels of management.

The program consists of three phases and involves two basic inventory forms: (1) The Master Inventory and Development Record, and (2) The Management Assessment of Potential Record.

The Master Inventory and Development Record, which is nonconfidential, has rather wide distribution. The Assessment Form is confidential and is centrally held at each level but readily available. By having systemwide use of these two forms and by striving for quality and common standards between headquarters, regions, and areas, a common currency for the exchange of data about people for day-to-day appointments, job rotation, and succession planning can be achieved.

Three Phases of Program

The section on career and development interests is of value in taking into consideration training and development needs when making appointments or working out successions.

The three phases are as follows:

Phase I—The Master Inventory and Development Record. This consists of completion of the biographical-historical information recorded on a standard form (CN-80) for each employee in grades 7 to 14 or comparable salary ranges.

Phase II—The Management Assessment of Potential. Included here are assessment of potential for each employee embracing readiness for advancement, jobs which those with potential are considered to be qualified for, and training and development needs. This information is documented on form (CN-81) and distributed as indicated.

Phase III—A Summary and Analysis of Phases I and II. A summary and analysis of data is produced in cooperation with headquarters' departments and regions and this is made available to management. The data are analyzed and at least some items or factors transferred to machines in order to make it more readily available and usable. This information is consolidated in such a way that it is of assistance to management for use in staff and succession

CN

MASTER INVENTORY AND DEVELOPMENT RECORD

REGION OR HEADQUARTERS DEPARTMENT	AREA OR SUB-DEPARTMENT	BRANCH OR SECTION	DATE (DAY – MONTH – YEAR)
SERVICE DATE (DAY-MONTH-YEAR)	BIRTH DATE (DAY-MONTH-YEAR)	MARITAL STATUS	PRESENT POSITION	LOCATION

EDUCATION

GRADE SCHOOL				HIGH SCHOOL			
6	7	8	9	10	11	12	13
UNIVERSITY							
1	2	3	4	5			

DEGREE OR CERTIFICATE, YEAR OBTAINED, UNIVERSITY, AND MAJOR FIELD OF STUDY

COURSES

TYPE OF COURSE	SUBJECT OR COURSE NAME	YEAR

CN SPONSORED AND OTHERS (STAFF COLLEGE, WORK STUDY, EXTENSION, CORRESPONDENCE, ETC.)

TYPE OF COURSE	SUBJECT OR COURSE NAME	YEAR

CAREER AND DEVELOPMENT INTERESTS

ARE YOU INTERESTED IN ALTERNATIVE TYPE OF CN WORK?   YES*   NO

WOULD YOU ACCEPT TRANSFER TO ANOTHER LOCATION?   YES   NO

WOULD YOU ACCEPT LATERAL MOVES FOR FURTHER DEVELOPMENT?   YES   NO

*IF YES, SPECIFICALLY WHAT TYPE?

COMMENT ON ANY QUALIFYING CIRCUMSTANCES,

WHAT TYPE OF TRAINING DO YOU BELIEVE YOU REQUIRE TO:–

(A) IMPROVE YOUR SKILLS AND PERFORMANCE IN YOUR PRESENT POSITION?

(B) IMPROVE YOUR EXPERIENCE AND ABILITIES FOR ADVANCEMENT?

WHAT OTHER POSITIONS DO YOU BELIEVE YOU ARE QUALIFIED TO PERFORM NOW?

LANGUAGES

WRITTEN
FRENCH   ENGLISH   OTHER-SPECIFY

SPOKEN
ENGLISH   FRENCH   OTHER-SPECIFY

PHOTO NO.

| LAST NAME |
| FIRST NAME |
| MIDDLE NAME |
| S.R.B. NUMBER |

... WHEN LAST HELD (YEAR), INDICATE NAME OF ASSOCIATION AND OFFICE HELD, IF ANY.

WORK HISTORY CN

SIGNIFICANT WORK EXPERIENCE. (OMIT REPETITIVE EXPERIENCES)

POSITION	LOCATION	FROM YR	TO YR

OTHER EMPLOYMENT

SIGNIFICANT WORK EXPERIENCE, AND OR MILITARY SERVICE. (OMIT REPETITIVE EXPERIENCES)

POSITION	LOCATION	FROM YR	TO YR

COMMENTS:

OTHER SIGNIFICANT EXPERIENCE, RECREATIONAL ACTIVITIES, HOBBIES, INTERESTS, OR PERSONAL DATA.

CN-80 (3-65)

CN   MANAGEMENT ASSESSMENT OF POTENTIAL

CN-81(3-65).

PRESENT POSITION	GRADE	S.R.B.	NAME
REGION OR H.Q. DEPT.	AREA OR SUB DEPT.	BRANCH OR SECTION	LOCATION

READINESS FOR PROMOTION

RETAIN ON PRESENT POSITION ☐	RETAIN ON PRESENT POSITION FOR MORE EXPERIENCE ☐	MOVE TO LATERAL OR SIMILAR POSITION TO BROADEN EXPERIENCE ☐	READY FOR PROMOTION NOW ☐

REASONS FOR ABOVE ASSESSMENT: (INDICATE ANY RESTRICTING FACTORS SUCH AS ILL HEALTH, AGE, INABILITY TO MOVE, ETC.- STRENGTHS AND/OR WEAKNESSES- SUPERVISORY, TECHNICAL, PERSONAL, JOB SKILLS, ETC.)

IMMEDIATE	**POTENTIAL**	LONG RANGE
PROMOTABLE TO: NEXT POSITION(S)		POSITION OR LEVEL IF LONG RANGE POTENTIAL CAN BE ESTIMATED:

TRAINING AND DEVELOPMENT NEEDS

SPECIFIC TRAINING, COURSES, ASSIGNMENTS, OR DUTIES WHICH WOULD PROVIDE FOR EMPLOYEE DEVELOPMENT:

ASSESSED BY:	DAY	MONTH	YEAR

planning, and establishing training programs to meet the essential needs indicated through this program.

Form CN 81 is above; CN 80 is on pages 98-99. Further information may be obtained from A. T. Mathews, Staff Planning Officer, Canadian National Railways, Personnel & Labour Relations, P.O. Box 8100, Montreal 3, Quebec, Canada.

MANPOWER INVENTORY

By Wallace R. Snyder
Senior Director, Manpower Planning
Blue Cross Association, Chicago, Illinois

A recent survey of 31 of the independent companies that make up the Blue Cross system reveals that the number one concern of the chief executives of these companies was their need to recruit, select, and retain manpower capable of meeting the increasingly complex management demands of the health care industry.

But this problem is not limited to Blue Cross or the health care industry. Any organization to survive must have the right kind of manpower. It is fairly well accepted that future organizational survival, regardless of industry, hinges on the acquisition, development, and retention of talented people.

What makes this such a critical problem? We have only to look at a few facts about *today's* labor market and its implications for the future to see the answer:

1. *The low birth rate of the 1930's.* Figures from the United States Bureau of Census reveal there will be a decline of one million men in the 35 to 45 age group between 1963 and 1974. This age group has traditionally made up the bulk of middle management in most organizations. It is this "pool" of middle management from which organizations draw their top management and leadership talent.

2. *There has been unprecedented growth in the size of most private business, governmental, and educational organizations in recent years.* One has only to look at *Fortune* magazine's annual listing of the 500 largest U.S. corporations to note this burgeoning growth in the private sector alone. The U.S. Bureau of Census reports in the period from 1954 to 1964 the number of employees in the "executive" classification of federal government service jumped from 163,000 to 258,000. Regardless of industry, such growth is also characteristic of most institutions and corporations in this country. Such growth adds to the critical demand for executive talent.

3. *The art of management in today's large organization has become increasingly complex.* Again, one has only to look at the tremendous impact on the art of management by data processing and computers, or the continuing impact on all types of business by government. These are only two factors well known to everyone. Some experts predict the amount of knowledge available in most fields of endeavor is doubling every eight years. This simply means that keeping up with the latest knowledge that has significant influence on a business could be almost a full-time job for most managers.

The above facts contribute to the continuing and increasing demand in both the quantity and quality of executive, managerial, and technical employees in this country. This has led to a vast amount of monies being poured into the recruitment, selection, and development of manpower. Look at the personnel divisions of most well-managed, sophisticated companies today and we find the most "experts" and the largest "budgets" are in the functions devoted to the recruitment, selection, and development systems of these organizations. One has only to review the help-wanted sections of the New York *Times,* the Chicago *Tribune,* and the *Wall Street Journal* to note the growing emphasis in these media on the recruitment of executive, management, and technical manpower.

Two Systems That Work

Unfortunately, too many organizations fail to completely capitalize on two personnel systems that can help them better spot and develop manpower talent already in their organization as well as better plan their external recruitment and selection efforts.

Two fundamental questions any personnel or manpower manager should periodically ask himself: (1) What do we *now* have in manpower? (2) What are we going to need in the future? Answers to these two personnel questions permit the organization to take stock of what it has in talent at a given point in time and then to effectively estimate what it needs for the future. Only when the organization builds its recruitment, selection, and development programs can it really proceed on an efficient and effective basis in tapping external sources of manpower and in planning the training and development effort for manpower it currently has "on board."

These key questions can be answered by the implementation of two personnel systems:

1. A sound and continuing manpower inventory process.

2. An effective system of manpower forecasting.

The essential principles of these systems can be enumerated by recognizing the organization must reappraise on a continual basis what it has in manpower strengths and at the same time estimate what it needs to fulfill its organizational objectives and purposes. Without undertaking this appraisal of current manpower and then estimating future needs the organization is reduced to "guessing" about its manpower; this is not a very sound management technique.

Another important advantage in periodically undertaking a manpower inventory and forecast is the opportunity they offer to evaluate recruitment, selection, placement, and training and development activities. How do we effectively evaluate these activities? The answer is deceptively simple. Do we have the right man, at the right time, and in the right spot who can fulfill an organizational manpower need when that need arises? An inventory and forecast system can help in this evaluation.

In Blue Cross we believe it is essential these systems complement each other. An inventory of what we have is not very meaningful unless we analyze it in terms of what we need, both currently and in the future. At the same time, a forecast of future manpower needs is not very meaningful unless we analyze such a forecast against what we currently have on hand or what we can adequately internally develop during the period covered by the forecast. Why spend the money on an elaborate recruitment effort if we already have employed the talent that could fulfill needs?

It is essential that the manpower inventory and forecasting process be "married" if it is to be of maximum value.

An organization must also carefully determine specific techniques that are most appropriate to fully develop the information sought. It would not be practical to develop a highly sophisticated and complex system of inventory and forecasting if the organization using it numbered only 200 employees with a management and supervisory structure of 10 or 15 people. At the same time, a diversified organization of several thousand employees with a management and supervisory structure that numbers into the hundreds may require a highly sophisticated effort to assure obtaining sound data. It would seem the inventory and forecasting systems should be developed only after clearly determining the goals or results expected. Only then can specific mechanics be designed which are appropriate to the organization.

What are some essential goals of a manpower inventory and forecast system?

The Blue Cross Criteria

In Blue Cross we believe it very important to determine what it was we needed to know about our current manpower that would permit us some judgment of individual potential for larger responsibility. To accomplish this it seemed to us there were several basic questions that first had to be answered:

1. Whom do we include in the inventory?

2. What do we need to know about those included?

3. How do we obtain data about these individuals?

4. What is the most effective way to record the data obtained?

5. How do we report the inventory results to top management?

6. How often do we update the inventory?

Answering the above questions led us to some basic principles, fundamental to the design and implementation of the inventory process.

1. The inventory had to concentrate on individuals and not jobs.

   a. Indicate *what* the individual is doing.

   b. Indicate *how* the individual is doing.

   c. Estimate *what* the individual is capable of doing.

   d. Indicate *how* to further assist the individual to better performance.

2. Have line management involvement.

3. Be kept as *simple* as possible particularly as to the paperwork required.

4. Be *updated* when required.

The above principles permitted the design of an inventory system that involves four basic steps:

Step I—A review by each individual with his supervisor about the duties and responsibilities of his job.

Step II—An appraisal of performance and estimate of potential on each individual included in the inventory.

Step III—The design of a development and training program for the individual based upon the performance and potential appraisal.

Step IV—Development of a personal data record that would permit us to record and update the information about the individual.

Understanding what the man is currently doing is essential because we cannot appraise performance or make an estimate of potential unless there is clear understanding (between the individual and his supervisor) of the job dimensions and responsibilities held by the individual.

Once this has been completed an *appraisal of performance* and an *estimate of potential* can realistically be accomplished. The steps of performance and appraisal analysis flow from the *results* of job accomplishment. But it is very important that this analysis not be exclusively on job performance factors such as *how many* widgets *sold,* how much he *overspent* or *underspent* his budget, etc. It must also pinpoint those *leadership qualities* that he demonstrated in accomplishing the sale of the widgets or the meeting of his budget.

Help and Guidance Offered

Performance and potential analysis serve no useful *inventory purpose* unless they pinpoint management qualities already demonstrated or that can be fostered through development and training within or without the organization. For example, if a man is weak in his ability to give direction to subordinates, then there certainly must be consideration of training that will assist him in overcoming such weakness. If a man is strong in handling administrative detail but weak in his ability to delegate, then training must be made available to him that will assist him in correcting these weaknesses.

The specific tools or processes that are used to identify what the man is doing, assess his performance as a means to estimate his potential for more significant responsibility, and develop a training program to realize this, must be designed in a manner appropriate to that organization. The inventory system as to forms and mechanics need not be elaborate if it is a small organization where top management already knows a great deal about individuals included in the inventory. What is important is that the forms and procedures obtain the information necessary to the goals of the inventory.

All of this—the manpower inventory—is preparation for the next personnel system, that of manpower forecasting.

MANPOWER FORECASTING

By Wallace R. Snyder
Senior Director, Manpower Planning
Blue Cross Association, Chicago, Illinois

As indicated earlier, it is not enough to assess our current manpower strengths unless we also estimate what our needs will be in the future. How can we plan a sound recruiting effort, or thoughtfully develop executive or management training programs, if we concentrate only on the *strengths* and *weaknesses* of our current manpower? If we gear our recruitment and development efforts simply on *today's* needs we can very conceivably short-change ourselves for the future. Today's management trainee is tomorrow's executive candidate. Is the *number* of management trainees needed to staff the business today appropriate to staff the executive organization needed tomorrow?

These questions lead us to the need for manpower forecasting.

What are the essential steps to a manpower forecast? Dr. Eric

Vetter, associate professor of management, Graduate School of Business, Tulane University, cites the following three steps:

1. *Start with the corporate objectives.* Manpower forecasting must be tied to a base point and this base point is corporate objectives. Because of this it is essential the forecast begin by familiarity with the long-range goals of the firm and the reasoning behind these goals. The firm's basic profit objectives, sales and financial forecasts, their implication for capital resources, and funds available for manpower and technological change must be known by the forecaster or he is wasting his time.

2. *Review your manpower in the light of labor productivity.* Employment trends, turnover rates, and the current composition of the managerial and professional work force by age, level, experience, and potential are essential to the success of a forecast. Good manpower forecasting requires data from past labor productivity, employment, occupational trends, and the managerial work force data and composition.

Perhaps most basic in these informational needs is the determination of labor productivity. A useful approach is the input-output model used by many economists. The relationship between the outputs produced and the inputs required tells the productivity of the factors of production. As a production process is made more efficient, productivity rises.

3. *Make a forecast of manpower needs.* Using the data from points 1 and 2, you now have the framework that permits the development of a forecast.

How Blue Cross Does It

Let's look at some of the concepts of manpower forecasting that we use as a base for our efforts in Blue Cross.

1. What are the likely *changes* in business activity that will occur during the period of the forecast?

2. What are the likely *new* types of activities the organization will undertake during the period of the forecast?

3. What departments, divisions, and functions are likely to grow

most rapidly during this period; i.e., where will our greatest needs be if our business objectives are met?

4. What possible impact will future changes in automation and data processing have on our work force?

5. What is the adequacy of our current staffing in view of the answers to the above four questions. Where are we weak? Where are we strong?

6. What existing manpower skills are likely to grow obsolete during this period?

7. What new manpower skills are likely to be needed?

It is rather obvious from the above that a meaningful forecast must refer to the past to provide a base for projection into the future. A simple and basic forecasting methodology that can be followed within this framework is as follows:

1. Determine past output per employee. This output may be revenue, customers obtained, production, or whatever is appropriate as the most significant output factor for the organization. The decision as to what is the output factor is determined by the nature of the organization and the purpose of its existence. The number of employees should be based on the average work force during the years used as the base to determine historical output. For example, if you were developing a forecast for the next five years, you would then review the average work force for the past five years computing this on a 13-month average for each of the past five years.

2. Determine past ratios of major manpower groups to total manpower. The determination of major manpower groups in an organization may include, for example, exempt management, non-exempt management, staff, line, female, male—whatever is appropriate to pinpoint the major manpower groups in your organization.

3. Project a *future* ratio of major manpower groups to the total manpower for the period of the forecast. At this point, we can use the knowledge from the past as obtained in steps 1 and 2 plus information about the future as determined from the answers to such questions as long-range plans, projected sales on revenue objectives, etc., to estimate these ratios.

4. Project future output per employee. Again using the knowledge from the past and the information about the future we can make this estimate.

5. Project future manpower. Divide the estimate of future output per employee (from step 4) into an estimate of future output as the means to determine future total manpower.

6. Project future manpower by major manpower groups. Apply the projection of ratios of major manpower groups (from step 3) to the estimate of total future manpower (from step 5).

The Margin of Error

Obviously the compilation, analysis, and application of the above methodology clearly indicate the need for some basic assumptions determined from historical performance. Because of this it would be a rare manpower forecast that would be 100 percent accurate. Assumptions, even though fed into the most sophisticated computer, are still assumptions subject to variation and error. Because of this it is important that each suborganizational group also project its own manpower needs for the period of the forecast. In this way the sum of the separate suborganizational forecasts can be compared with the overall corporate forecast as a possible means to reduce the margin of error that could occur if you were to simply develop a corporate manpower forecast on the above methodology.

The above is intended simply as a basic exploration of some of the fundamental concepts necessary to project manpower needs. Experienced manpower forecasters work on 5- to 10-year projections and with much more sophisticated data. But they also do annual revisions whenever information is obtained that alter the basic assumptions on which the forecast was developed. Revisions become necessary because of changes that occur in any organization that were not anticipated or recognized at the time of the original forecast.

What are some of the other guidelines essential to the success of a forecasting effort?

1. *Top management must be behind the program.* This is axiomatic to any manpower program, but of extreme importance in a manpower forecast. Unless we have endorsement of top management,

the possibility of simply undergoing an academic exercise is very strong. Sources of basic data, such as corporate objectives, long-range plans, labor productivity, and managerial and professional work force data can generally be obtained only through line management. Seeking the cooperation of these key executives is more readily attained when they endorse the goals of the program.

2. *All major departments and operating units must be involved.* It is extremely doubtful that any forecaster has at his fingertips all the necessary data and knowledge essential to a corporate forecast. He must rely upon assistance from personnel in each of the operating units.

3. *A well-designed forecast must exist to serve the entire company.* We cannot concentrate on single divisions or suborganizations and expect a reasonable forecast of total corporate manpower needs. This means forecasting for staff activities as well as line operating functions. It does very little good, from a total corporate picture, to concentrate on forecasting manpower for line functions and exclude the staff activities essential to the overall performance of line functions.

Back to the Inventory

Once the manpower forecast has been completed we must then "marry" it to the inventory for the most complete picture of strengths and needs in the organization.

The following exhibit is one procedure that can be followed. The illustration given is an example of a completed report that blends inventory and forecast data. Supplemental information essential to the data on the report would include identification of manpower needs by position title resulting from the analyzation of the forecast and inventory information. For the completion of this process, the forecaster lays out on one or two sheets of paper the basic information and facts necessary to planning future recruitment, selection, and development efforts.

To quote Ralph Besse of Cleveland Electric Company, "There is nothing we can do about the performance of past management, or the qualifications of today's management. But tomorrow's management can be as good as today's managers care to make it."

CORPORATE MANPOWER STATUS REPORT

Management Level	INVENTORY—FORECAST DATA					FUTURE STAFFING SOURCES			
	Current Manpower	Attrition	Available Manpower	Available Promotable Manpower	Forecasted Manpower	Incumbents	Promotions	Total	Deficiency
Top	5	1	10	—	6	4	2	6	0
Middle	12	2	4	3	15	8	5	13	2
Lower	23	6	17	5	29	12	—	12	17*
Total	40	9	31	8	50	24	7	31	19

*Ten lower management positions to be filled by promotions from existing nonmanagement force.

DISCUSSION:

This set of illustrative data shows the overall manpower situation in a mythical company. The future management growth is expected to be 10 positions, raising management staffing to 50. One new top management, three middle management, and six lower management positions are expected to be created. A total of nine managers are expected to leave the organization for various reasons. This leaves 31 managers currently employed for future staffing. Of these, eight are considered promotable.

Future staffing of top management will include four incumbents and two men promoted from middle management. The 15 middle management positions will include the eight managers now in middle management who will not be lost to the company nor promoted to top management. Five men from lower management rated promotable will raise the total known staffing at middle management to 13. This leaves a deficiency of two positions that we expect to need to fill but for which we currently lack manpower.

We may do several things to meet this deficiency. They include developing some lower managers so they become promotable, recruiting middle managers from the outside, trying to prevent the loss of two managers via attrition, or filling our top management from outside sources and thus not promoting two middle managers. Or we might try to reorganize so we won't need 15 middle management positions and attempt to get by with 13 managers.

Lower management staffing indicates we will have 12 incumbents available after promoting the five promotable lower managers. The deficiency of 17 positions is expected to be filled in part (10 positions) through promotions from nonmanagement ranks. This is based on a survey of nonmanagers and their promotion potential. The other seven positions will be filled by college recruiting or other outside sources.

MANPOWER DEVELOPMENT

Management trainees for replacement and expansion are recruited and developed for the future. Locating them, convincing them they should accept your opportunity, and fitting them into the company are real problems. But the biggest problem is keeping them.

Anyone good enough to qualify for special management training consideration is certainly going to be attractive to a competitive employer. All it takes in some cases is an offer of more money or a better opportunity.

No one keeps tab nationally on turnover among people in this group, but there are surveys made on college graduates from whose ranks most of the trainees come. There is a rapidly growing group of recent college graduates who are finding it more profitable and easier than ever to switch jobs.

Hanging on to management trainees poses a mounting problem at many firms. Studies indicate that more than 50 percent of college graduates change jobs at least once during their first five years.

For one thing, there seems to be a lot of unrest in these young people. They are eager and impatient. They don't know what they want; they know only that what they find is often not what they'd hoped to make a career of. Many young men want to settle down, with college and their military obligation behind them; and they expect to move up fast.

Money is a big concern, but money alone won't solve the problem. These people need to be challenged. Many companies try to keep their recent college graduates satisfied by assigning them more difficult and meaningful work.

Faced with the threat of losing promising potentials, in technical fields as well as in management, companies are coming up with new ways to keep these people happy. Conventional attractions such as tuition reimbursement are expanded to cover postgraduate study. Time off with pay for special study and exams is granted liberally. The eligibility requirements for profit sharing are lowered so that they may participate immediately. Research projects are encouraged. Training programs are shortened drastically to give them earlier on-the-job responsibilities. Chances for travel are increased. But the biggest single item is frequent evaluation and review sessions where they can air their complaints to supervisors and vice-presidents.

SECRETARY

Since the private secretary is such an important part of every company, and a good one is so hard to find, we felt a few words on her behalf might be appropriate.

Maybe we should begin with a definition of "secretary." The word comes from the Latin word for secret and its original meaning was a confidant. Literally it means "keeper of secrets." In its original concept it has nothing whatever to do with the skills we ascribe to the job today. Modern usage of the word "secretary" refers to a confidential employee having responsibilities to an executive—a clerical administrative assistant to a busy boss.

The executive secretary is a manager. She must manage her time and often the time of her employer so that the necessary work gets out on schedule. The efficient secretary can attend to many demands with such ease that they seem to be part of a single activity. She must demonstrate, in addition to the basic skills of typing and shorthand, the ability to take care of a multitude of details which fall in other fields. She must also possess a personality and a versatility such as is required by few other occupations.

A secretary becomes worthy of the title only when she has assumed some of the responsibilities of an executive—responsibilities that call for the exercise of initiative, judgment, imagination, and tact.

The best description of the secretary's job is simply, "My job is to make my boss' job easier."

Please pardon this addendum, coming as it does from a man. In this electronic age the position of the secretary is not in danger. There is little likelihood that men will ever want to discontinue the use of women secretaries. When the old upper-class, mid-Victorian homes vanished, where man dominated his wife and family, he set about recreating, in his office, this lost paradise. Women secretaries supply the sense of comfort and importance men formerly had in their homes.

WHAT IS A SECRETARY?

Secretaries are human . . . just like the rest of us. They come in both sexes, mostly female. They are available in a variety of shapes, sizes, ages, and dispositions. Generally speaking, there are three kinds: prizes, surprises, and consolation prizes.

They are found everywhere—in offices, on committees, and in coffee shops. They are always on hand and never busy when we don't need them, and usually in the mailroom, print shop, or stockroom when we're desperate. The best place to find them is in Pollyanna's Dress Shop. The hardest place to find them is in employment agencies.

Secretaries like three-day weekends, lunch invitations, erasers, single men, low-calorie salads, boss away at conventions, late TV movies, and the Panama Beaver salesman. They don't like cigar-chewing dictators, corrections written on letters, old jokes, and cleaning out files. They don't like bosses who boss.

They prepare letters, reports, and cover-up excuses for their bosses. They are required to have the patience of Job, the wisdom of Solomon, the memory of an elephant, the disposition of a lamb, the experience of a travel agent, and the poise and personality of a Powers model. They are expected to produce, on a moment's notice, papers that were filed in briefcases, glove compartments, and yesterday's coat pocket. Instinctively they are supposed to see things that never happen, and also to conveniently overlook other things that go on.

On television secretaries are glamorous girls who save their bosses from one predicament after another. In real life they are girls whose spelling, punctuation, and paragraphing seldom agree with those of their bosses.

When they do something good, that's their job. When they do something wrong, that's what we have to put up with these days. Secretaries dream about homes covered with ivy; the few who don't live in apartments have homes covered with mortgages. If they enjoy the luxury of driving cars to the company parking lots they're well fixed and don't need a raise, but if they ride the bus and arrive late they are part of the common herd and not worth promoting.

Because of their devoted dedication to duty, they deserve to be executaries in their own right. But until they realize this ambition they will continue to serve as their bosses right arm. They will continue to make us look good, and we will go right on neglecting to tell them how important they are to us . . . a fact we discover, but never admit, every time they go on vacation.

May we forever bless that first day when some overworked boss invented that immortal labor-saving phrase, "Miss Smith, will you bring in your book!"

The tribute, "What Is a Secretary?" was written by the author of this Handbook especially for meetings of the National Secretaries Association. It is not copyrighted and may be reproduced, or adapted, to suit any local situation.

NATIONAL SECRETARIES DAY

The last week in April is usually set aside as Secretaries Week, and Wednesday of that week is designated as Secretaries Day.

Executives who wish to recognize their secretaries may be interested in the following "Proclamation to My Secretary." It was composed by Eugene P. Foley, Assistant Secretary of Commerce for Economic Development, Washington, D.C. Mr. Foley was selected as International Boss of the Year for 1965 by the National Secretaries Association (International), and appropriately honored at a luncheon.

Proclamation
To My Secretary

A secretary should be her boss's right hand, but the good secretary is even more.

She is a creative, thinking individual who continuously finds better ways to do her job and to help her boss do his.

As a recognized expert in many fields, she must coordinate, negotiate, delegate and meditate—but not too long for more work is waiting.

Every day she must accomplish a harder task. She does hundreds of useful things her boss never knows.

Those of us who have secretaries meeting these qualifications are lucky...and I am fortunate to be one of these persons.

Signed

THE CERTIFIED PROFESSIONAL SECRETARY

The Institute for Certifying Secretaries, 1103 Grand Avenue, Kansas City, Missouri, has been conducting certification examinations since 1951. Over 3,000 secretaries, including seven men, have been authorized to use the CPS designation, having successfully passed the six-part examination.

The program was designed to raise the standards of the secretarial profession. The CPS examination is management oriented to:

- Insure a higher level of understanding and performance by secretaries.

- Provide a practical criterion in evaluating and selecting personnel for executive secretarial and administrative positions.

The exam, offered annually, takes two days and covers six subjects:

1. Personal adjustment and human relations.

2. Business administration.

3. Business law.

4. Secretarial accounting.

5. Secretarial procedures.

6. Secretarial skills.

The exam is offered simultaneously in widely distributed test centers in the United States, Canada, and Puerto Rico, and is administered by colleges and universities. Approximately 38 percent of those who sat for the exams have passed to date.

A few are able to pass the test without outside study, because they have had job experience in all the fields it covers. But most find it necessary to go back to school, take brushup courses, and do a great deal of home study.

Secretaries who pass feel that the money, time, and effort were well spent. Their companies generally reacted favorably. To almost one-half, being certified meant a raise, a promotion, or other special benefits. The intangible results include a gain in self-confidence and assurance, encouragement to continue self-development, a reawakening or intensification of their interest in education.

ACQUISITION COST

The employment function is a continuing one in every company, regardless of whether or not the procedure is formalized. The selection and retention of efficient workers is one of the most important operations of any company. In a tightening labor market this is also one of the greatest problems.

The reason this becomes a problem of dimensions is not simply to keep jobs in the company filled. The problem is concerned with cost. The cost of hiring applicants has been variously estimated in different companies and in different parts of the country. For female clerical workers, for instance, the employment agency fee itself, often paid by the employer, is sizable. For this fee the agency does little more than refer applicants; there is no testing and very little screening.

For certain types of jobs newspaper advertising is effective; for other jobs it is of little value today. For instance, an advertisement in a local newspaper for housewives to do typing for a few hours each day will bring in an avalanche of inquiries. On the other hand, an advertisement in a big city daily for a secretary will bring in little response, especially when such notice is included among hundreds of other similar ads for stenos and secretaries. In such case the few referrals and the limited selection resulting from the advertisement make newspaper classified or display ads quite expensive. It is not sufficient to think of the cost of the ad itself; the number of ads and the amount of work in connection with replies must be considered in relation to results obtained.

Many companies have found it profitable to reward employees who refer their friends or relatives for employment. This payment may take any of many forms, such as cash, government bonds, time off, and the like. This practice has two distinct advantages. First, it is the cheapest form in use, for surely a government bond or two is less in cost than an advertisement and all the screening work this entails, or an agency fee. Second, it tends to bring in the same type of person who has already been found acceptable to the company. There is another intangible benefit which many companies recognize as valuable: The employee who recommends his company to another person not only sells the company and its favorable working conditions to the friend but in so doing also resells this to himself.

ACQUISITION COST ANALYSIS

Newspaper	Telephone Responses						Mail Responses						Personal Interviews						Acceptances					
	M	T	W	Th	F	Total	M	T	W	Th	F	Total	M	T	W	Th	F	Total	M	T	W	Th	F	Total
1.																								
2.																								
3.																								
4.																								
5.																								

Newspaper	Cost of Ad	Total Leads	Cost per Lead	Total Acceptances	Cost per Acceptance
1.					
2.					
3.					
4.					
5.					

Whatever method is used, we can be almost certain that the cost of each new worker is high, much higher than we realize. Add to this the expense of interviewing, low production during the beginning or training period, the time of the person who does the training, and all the many other obvious as well as hidden costs, and we get some idea of the cost of employment.

EMPLOYMENT COSTS OUTLINE

1. ACQUISITION

  1.1 Advertisements
    1.11 Preparation of advertisement (writing it)
    1.12 Blind advertisement
      1.121 Writing the advertisement
      1.122 Screening replies
      1.123 Contact applicant by telephone or letter
  1.2 Agency (free or fee)
    1.21 Preparation of job orders
    1.22 Time and cost of phone orders
    1.23 Those interviewed who are rejected at once
  1.3 Bonus payment for employee referral
  1.4 Recruitment
    1.41 Membership in organizations for applicant contact
    1.42 Visiting high schools and colleges
    1.43 Participation in career days
    1.44 Expenses of entertaining
    1.45 Work study or work experience program costs

2. EMPLOYEE PROCESSING

  2.1 Receptionist
    2.11 Supplies
      2.111 Application blanks
      2.112 Other forms
    2.12 Interviewer
      2.121 Time of interviewing
      2.122 Education to improve oneself
      2.123 Cost of tests

RECRUITMENT

The employment of workers begins with the act of recruiting. Recruitment, as this is often called, is like the outstretched arms in the employment picture. Ideally it should gather in enough applicants from whom the final selection can then be made.

The problem of recruiting varies by type of job, industry, location, and current labor market. The company must: (1) establish and maintain the most productive sources of supply, and (2) devise the most effective and efficient means of reaching applicants. Then it must succeed in encouraging them to inquire about the job opportunities offered.

There are two sources of applicants to fill vacant positions: internal and external. The internal source is inside the company for lateral transfer and promotion. This rewards faithful and loyal workers with more remunerative positions or with work that is more to their liking. But it could have the disadvantage of inbreeding.

For some jobs it might be better to go outside. Most job vacancies, especially beginner positions, are filled from the external source. This consists of many aspects. Sources of external applicants are among the following:

1. Employment agencies
   a. Private—or fee
   b. Government—or free

2. Advertisements
   a. Metropolitan newspapers
   b. Neighborhood weeklies
   c. Trade publications

3. Schools
   a. High schools
      (1) City public
      (2) Suburban
      (3) Parochial

b. Junior colleges
c. Universities
d. Business colleges
e. Trade schools

4. Employee referrals

5. Miscellaneous sources
   a. Churches
   b. Clubs
   c. Fraternal organizations
   d. Minority group headquarters
   e. Handicapped
   f. Business associations

6. Unsolicited applications
   a. Walk-ins
   b. Write-ins
   c. Job-shoppers

UNITED STATES POST OFFICE

An Important Message From Your Postmaster

Your Post Office is seeking applicants for Clerk and Carrier positions. Starting salary is $2.57 per hour, with periodic increases to $3.50 per hour. Ten percent extra will be paid for work performed between 6:00 p.m. and 6:00 a.m. These career Civil Service positions offer excellent job security, good working conditions, and opportunities for advancement. Postal employees enjoy 2½ to 5 weeks vacation yearly, liberal sick leave with pay, low cost life insurance and health and hospitalization benefits, and participate in an excellent retirement system.

ALL QUALIFIED APPLICANTS WILL RECEIVE CONSIDERATION FOR EMPLOYMENT WITHOUT REGARD TO RACE, CREED, COLOR, SEX, OR NATIONAL ORIGIN

Complete and return this form if you are interested in a postal career; or, you may wish to pass it on to some other qualified person. The form must be completed and returned by the applicant. Thank you for your help.

REQUIREMENTS.—The minimum age for Clerk-Carrier positions is 18. This age limit is waived for high school graduates who may be appointed after they have reached their 16th birthday. The age limit is waived for veterans. There is no maximum age restriction. Applicants must be U.S. citizens and must reside within the appropriate postal area. Applicants must qualify on a Civil Service examination to be eligible for employment.

INSTRUCTIONS.—Full name and address should be *PRINTED* in the box below. Hand the form to your letter carrier, or take or mail it to your Post Office.

FIRST NAME	MIDDLE INITIAL	LAST NAME
HOUSE NUMBER	STREET	
CITY	STATE	ZIP CODE

GPO 822-698

Success stories of some employees

JUDY LEEK graduated from Hughes High School in 1962 . . . Hired as a records clerk in June . . . Promoted to stenographer and in 1965 to secretary.

ROBERTA WILLIAMS graduated from Seton High School in 1964 . . . Hired in 1965 as a junior clerk . . . Promoted in 10 months to approve hospital bills.

MARTY CONNELLY graduated from Perry High School, Fayetteville, in 1965 . . . Hired in December as a junior clerk . . . Promoted in two months to transcriber.

DIANNE HARMON graduated from Dayton (Ky.) High in 1964 . . . Hired in June as a records clerk . . . Promoted in seven months to an auditor trainee.

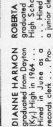

PHYL WAGGONER was graduated from Withrow High School and hired in 1957 as a file clerk . . . Promoted recently to HCC's first woman programmer.

JIM WEBSTER graduated from Grant County (Ky.) High in 1962 . . . Hired as a junior approver in 1964 . . . Promoted to approver in 1965 and senior approver in 1966.

KAREN EAVES graduated from Aiken High School in 1965 . . . Hired in June as a file clerk . . . Promoted to addressograph operator in seven months.

MIKE STEELE graduated from Purcell in 1962 . . . Hired in 1964 as a mail boy . . . Promoted in three months to addressograph clerk and in nine months to billing clerk.

looking for that first job?

consider these benefits . . .

- full-time, permanent employment
- 37½-hour week
- congenial atmosphere
- regular salary review
- opportunity for advancement
- convenient bus transportation
- equal opportunity for everyone

and these . . .

- college tuition refund program (for job-related courses)
- employee social club
- paid vacation (two weeks after one year)
- nine paid holidays (including your birthday)
- pension program (for career people)
- free company parking lot
- cafeteria serving nutritious meals at half cost
- free medical programs (blood bank, flu shots, chest X-rays)
- complete health care protection (at no cost to you)
- life insurance program

Recruitment brochure of Blue Cross/Blue Shield of Virginia lists employee benefits and pictures some of its satisfied workers as "success stories."

RECRUITMENT FOLLOWUP

Blue Cross and Blue Shield of Virginia, engage in a summer-help employment program each year. High school and college students are invited to work during their vacations.

These young people are added to the payroll in order to help out while regular employees are away on their vacations. But, more important, these potential employees are given firsthand experience in various types of office work. It is the hope of the companies that these prospects will enjoy their work and return for permanent employment after graduation.

This in itself is not a unique approach to the employment problem. What is different is the followup. Not too long after these people return to school they receive an attractive brochure which tells them, "We're glad you worked with Blue Cross and Blue Shield this summer."

The booklet contains individually identified pictures of all the summer employees, showing each individual at his own desk or work station. In addition to a "thank you" message from the executive director, the publication includes a few short statements of an educational nature about the meaning of Blue Cross and Blue Shield and the services both plans provide for the community.

There is no obvious recruiting effort, but it is apparent that through this device the companies hope to interest the temporary worker into coming back. It is also obvious that the program pays off for it is continued year after year in a successful effort to maintain the flow of qualified applicants, offer practical work experience to students, and cooperate in a worthwhile project.

SOURCES OF APPLICANTS

Throughout history there always seemed to be an inexhaustible supply of workers. There was no shortage of applicants for jobs until World War II. Then the tremendous defense effort, combined with the transfer of millions of able-bodied young men and women to the armed services, caused a severe crisis. The problem was eased somewhat after 1945, when the war ended, but the help situation remained critical.

A review of industrial history shows that whenever the supply of labor became a problem, there was a solution nearby. For years the boatloads of immigrants brought a continuing supply of skilled and unskilled workers to American companies. When this source dried up, another developed.

Farm labor moved from rural areas to the big factories in the urban communities. Small towns saw their workers attracted to the cities. Schools graduated an endless supply of trained and educated workers until finally this source was no longer sufficient to meet industries' growing demands.

What saved the war effort was the widespread acceptance of women into the nation's work force. After the war the women stayed on. It wasn't long until this source was exhausted. There are today no women left who can be hired.

Still the labor shortage remained critical. So business turned to the migrants, people who were previously hopelessly out of consideration. These are the Negroes, Puerto Ricans, and Appalachian whites. Now they've been used up. There are no qualified minority group members overlooked anymore.

During all this time some relief was provided by the moonlighters, workers who accept a second job in another firm. But their number is shrinking as these people are able to increase their earnings through overtime on their primary jobs. Nor is there any hope left trying to recruit workers away from other geographical areas since the problem there is usually no less acute.

There appears to be no hope. The supply of qualified workers shows no promise of meeting the demand forecast for the years ahead.

The only untapped source is that of the unskilled workers. Government, trade associations, and social agencies are making serious efforts to interest business in these people. As long as there are thousands of men and women unemployed, there are potential workers available if only they can be made employable.

It appears that companies have a choice—either to continue indefinitely short-handed or cooperate in programs to utilize these people who, on their own, are unqualified and unprepared to enter the labor force. It is, at least, worth a try.

HELP-WANTED ADVERTISING

How do you get best results from help-wanted advertising? Two little words hold the key: "Be natural."

What to say is a simple thing, and yet can be a problem.

The following helpful ideas and suggestions are taken from a booklet, *The Secret of Writing Productive Help Wanted Advertising*, published by *The Chicago Tribune* and reprinted here with special permission.

* * *

You have a job to fill and you want to find the best qualified man or woman who is available for that kind of job. So you start to write an ad, and because you are busy you say: "Order Fillers, Stock Men—good pay, see today, 622-0745."

Or, if you are looking for a girl, perhaps you word your ad something like this: "Switchboard-Typist—some experience pref., 22-28, Gump Co., 536 Blank Street."

Well, that's that. The ad is written and all you have to do is call a pleasant-voiced adtaker. But haven't you forgotten something? You're not advertising for wooden Indians—or are you? You're supposed to be advertising for people—people with feelings, desires, hopes, and aspirations.

"Then you think our ad is a dud?" you say. No, not a dud. You may get replies and you may fill the job, but the odds are against you. Naturally you want the best class of applicants; the most efficient workman; a speedy and personable typist; a future department head. If a better ad will bring in better applicants it would be well worth while, wouldn't it?

Let's see, then, how those ads could have been worded:

ORDER FILLERS—STOCK MEN

A good spot. Ten of our present executives started in this department. We like to see men get ahead. Good pay to begin and better if you do a good job. Permanent. Five-day week. Many benefits. Mr. Henry will interview all day.

3527 E. CENTRAL STREET
(½ Blk from Main Street car line)

Switchboard-Typist

GIRLS SAY THEY LIKE
TO WORK HERE

Anyway we think it's a nice place and we believe you'll think so, too. A good position with top pay is open to you if you've had some experience and don't mind a "peak load" now and then. All basic benefits. Forty-hour week; 2 weeks' vacation after first year. Save money on many food items which we process. Bus stops almost at door. Ask for Mr. John Smith, right on main floor. 236 N. Broad St.

There is no doubt about it—stilted, stereotyped ads do not get the best applicants. When you tell people what *you* want (and often very little of that) and nothing about what *they* want, the desirable applicants you seek may skip over your ad and look for those that are more interesting.

You, of course, will do the selecting and hiring, but after all it is a two-way proposition. Both employer and applicant have to be satisfied. When you run an ad, you are *seeking* somebody—so why not put your best foot forward? Why not tell them why yours is a good place to work? Why not offer a friendly handshake? Why not give them the kind of facts and ideas that interest them?

When they look at an ad they see only type printed on paper. From this they must form an opinion and decide which ads to answer.

Suppose you were the applicant. What would you see in the want ads? Here's one that makes you feel that the employer is a cold, calculating fellow sitting behind an armored desk and peering through a peephole. You cringe. Certainly no employer means to give that kind of an impression, but some do nevertheless.

Then there is the in-between ad. While not belligerent it is definitely impersonal and says, in effect, "This organization thinks strictly in terms of figures rather than people. So take it or leave it as you see fit." Such ads are not natural and they will not appeal to the best employee regardless of whether you are seeking a stenographer, a ding man, die caster, or merchandising manager.

The "Partnership" Approach

The last and preferred type of help-wanted advertisement is one which takes the reader into partnership. It tells something about the company; possibly even something about the product, and at the same time recognizes the human desires of the applicant by telling about conveniences, benefits, compensation, associates, future, and other employee dividends. That type of approach will always get the *best* results at the *lowest cost.*

Granted there are many good ways to write the same help-wanted ad. But try not to write it like all the others in the paper. It can be a very sincere advertisement, it can be a very informal advertisement, or it may even be a little on the breezy side for some specific situations.

One manufacturing plant, employing a great many women, conceived the idea of heading its advertisements with the first name of the personnel manager. The familiar words, "Molly Says," or "See Molly," appearing regularly in the want-ad columns produced exceptional results in a period when employment problems were next to unsolvable for many firms. Another company desiring people for an early morning shift had excellent results with the human-interest term "early bird." These approaches appeal to people because they talk like people and not like automatons.

Obviously, pay is always a prime motivator. If you are in a position to feature actual salaries or commissions along with human-interest factors and natural wording, your ad can be a top-flight producer. But featuring pay is not always expedient. The *natural* approach then becomes the perfect substitute.

Perhaps the brawny boilermaker is not appealed to by the same points that will interest the petite stenographer, but both are alike in that they have human problems, likes and dislikes and some aspirations. The boilermaker may be interested primarily in permanency, locations, and a pay check coming in regularly for the wife and six youngsters. The little stenographer, on the other hand, may prefer the large office where she can make new friends or perhaps a location near a shopping district where it will be easy for her to buy necessary things during her lunch hour. These and a thousand other factors enter into the question, "Which ad shall I answer?"

Remember it's the human factor that does the trick! Use your own ideas but think of the other fellow, too—then word your ad *naturally.*

CHECKLIST

A well-written help-wanted advertisement contains the following information:

1. *Hours*
2. *Remuneration*
3. *Distinguishing features of work or product*
4. *Benefits*
5. *Transportation and location*
6. *Requirements and references*
7. *How to apply*

To WRITE AN AD THAT WILL BE READ

I. Attract their attention.

A good opening line or phrase—a catchy head in big type helps to get an audience.

II. Hold their interest.

A. *Be natural.* A few lines in informal, friendly style will attract more readers than a hundred lines of dull print.

B. *Be specific.* Tell exactly what type of person you want to hire, to avoid excessive screening of misfit applicants.

C. *Be different.* To attract high-quality applicants, appeal to the imagination with attention-getting phrases.

D. *Be explanatory.* Don't leave out important facts that will cause the person you want to hire to pass over the ad. The sin of omission is a costly one.

E. *Tell them what they want to know.* What business are you in? What conveniences do you have? What hours do you require? What experience is necessary? Where are you located? What salary range are you planning? What will your job *do* for the applicant? What are the opportunities for advancement? What are the qualities you are seeking?

III. Invite action.

A. Tell them how to apply or whom to call.

B. Tell them to *do it now.*

C. Give them a specific person to contact (they'll feel more confident, more inclined to apply for the job).

D. Make them feel welcome.

"The NATURAL way makes want ads pay"

RADIO-TELEVISION ADS AID IN RECRUITING

In a tight labor market, the Cedar Rapids, Iowa, area became the base of operations for a full-scale radio and television recruiting campaign for Collins Radio Company.

The company found this type of program most effective. It both compensated for normal labor attrition and increased the production force, in a city where at the time the unemployment rate was one of the lowest in the country. The big appeal was for local housewives—not in the labor market—to come to work. It worked well enough to aid in supplying a new labor force of more than 1,000 people in slightly over three months.

The industrial relations director, Elmer Stambaugh, said: "We found radio and TV a very important factor in the success of our recruiting program. We could regulate the number of applicants by varying the intensity of the advertising."

EXECUTIVE SEARCH

In certain types of recruiting, especially for top-level or high executive positions, it may be advisable to engage an executive search firm. For many corporations the professional search is literally the executive marketplace. Such a firm is not only better equipped as search specialists for management talent but also better qualified than the customary recruiting efforts.

By using experienced search consultants, a company is relieved of the time-consuming tasks of recruiting, screening, and interviewing all candidates who make themselves available, most of whom turn out to be underqualified or otherwise unacceptable. Besides, there is no way of knowing whether the right candidates have been reached by the company offer.

A search outfit, by concentrating on this type of executive recruitment, has access to many applicants and also to fields of specialization in which the proper kind of candidate may be located. In addition, the search consultants are impartial and neutral, are not handicapped by the built-in bias that many companies may have toward an individual or his former employer.

What the Experts Do

Once the search firm is engaged, the consultants assigned to the task familiarize themselves with the company and the position to be filled. They review the qualifications asked for, experience needed, and the personality desired as they endeavor to find someone who comes closest to meeting the precise requirements.

The search outfit scans its files of registered applicants, discusses the need with companies, associations, and other acquaintances in the hopes of getting referrals, obtains clearance to contact likely prospects.

The company name is held confidential by the search consultants. They identify and contact candidates without jeopardizing the client's position. They present each applicant's resumé or abstract of qualifications. The company screens a paper instead of a person as the first step toward selection.

The first report to the client company is a list of screened candidates and a preliminary appraisal of one or more possibilities secured from these outside references and investigations. Candidates in which the company expresses interest are then approached confidentially on a personal basis. On the results of their depth interviews they make recommendations of those candidates who should be considered further.

The objective is to present to the client company one or more of the best prospects, considering qualifications, interest, and availability. Throughout the negotiations they stay close to candidates and the client company.

How They Charge

Naturally, they charge for this service. This can be a fixed amount or other contract. One arrangement calls for a fee of 25 percent of the annual starting salary. As the search progresses they bill per-diem time charges monthly. These per-diem charges are automatically credited to the placement fee billing at the completion of the project.

To this they add normal and reasonable out-of-pocket expenses, such as telephoning, travel, field interviewing, promoting, and other incidentals incurred during the conduct of the search.

The company may cancel the search and entire agreement at any time, with the liability limited to the original advance payment or per-diem charges plus out-of-pocket expenses accumulated to that time.

There is no guarantee of completing a successful placement. The search firm can reasonably assure a client company of qualified referrals, otherwise they should not accept the assignment. But the final decision to select or reject any of their referrals is with the client company, and over this they have no authority or control and possibly little influence.

THE UNITED STATES EMPLOYMENT SERVICE

By Frank H. Cassell, Former Director

The United States Employment Service is identifiable as the "Manpower Services Center for Our Nation." It was created by the Wagner-Peyser Act of 1933 and is a Federal-State system which now services workers, employers, and all concerned with manpower problems. The Office of the Director is in the Department of Labor Building, 14th Street and Constitution Avenue, Washington, D. C. More than 2,000 other offices are in all 50 states, the District of Columbia, Puerto Rico, Guam, and the Virgin Islands.

The local offices are operated by the states under the guidance of the United States Employment Service within the Bureau of Employment Security in the Department of Labor's Manpower Administration. Established originally to serve the unemployed millions during the great depression, over the years the public employment service has been assigned additional manpower responsibilities. It has adapted and strengthened its operations to meet the changing needs of the times, and has evolved from a labor exchange to a manpower services center devoted to greater development and utilization of human resources as indicated by these goals:

1. Reduction of poverty and unemployment.

2. Elimination of denial of access to jobs because of racial discrimination.

3. Improvement of employability.

Many Facets to Program

Multiple activities fall within the scope of the United States Employment Service. USES might be likened to a diamond with many facets:

Job Placement

Human Development

Building Employer Relations

Training Disadvantaged Youth

Mobile Services to Urban-Rural Areas

Occupational Information Programs

Gains in Unskilled Job Professional Placement

Job-Finding Technique Classes

New Skills for Americans

Service to Veterans

Job Vacancy Studies

Testing for Unemployment Benefits

Recruitment of Farm Workers

Service to Older Workers

Human Resource Planning

Employment Counseling and Testing

Creating Outreach to Those Who by Reason of Personal Characteristics, Backgrounds, Educational Deficiencies, Lack of Skills, Cultural Deprivation, or Economic Denial Are Disadvantaged in the Job Market

Development Dissemination of Labor Market Information

Advance Planning to Combat Mass Layoffs

Outreach to Employers

Fostering of Interarea Recruitment

Administration of Federal Immigration Laws
—and more.

Major USES efforts are being focused upon the Human Resources Development Program comprised of four major functions:

1. Outreach.

2. Improving Employability.

3. Developing Job Opportunities and Pleasant Services.

4. Providing Job Market Information.

These efforts are concentrated in Opportunity Centers throughout the country.

What Is Outreach?

Outreach in the Employment Service is designed to search out those people who will not otherwise seek needed assistance. This includes persons who do not know that services are available, who do not have the means to go to centralized offices, who have problems that blind them to their own needs, who are so closely tied to their immediate environments that they have no idea of what lies outside them. Ours is an active, not a passive role.

The next basic function of our Human Resources Development Program, and also reflective of the new posture, is human development itself. Some call it the employability function; certainly, increasing the number of people who are more employable is the purpose. It provides a diagnostic service which is designed to aid the individual to plan better for his future, to provide him with the information and the insights with which he can make better decisions about his job and his career. This comprehensive function also includes referral to and often performance of services which enhance the employability of the individual. He may be referred to a job, to a training program, to preparatory programs preceding training, to the Neighborhood Youth Corps, to the Job Corps, or to some form of work experience in whatever combination of programs or activities will provide the appropriate sequence of growth and preparation.

The outreach-development sequence is incomplete, tragically so, if there is no job at the end of the rainbow. Just as we need integrated outreach to those who need help, we also must have an integrated, equally unified outreach to employers. We are engaged in a long-range program of showing employers that we know how to organize and carry out the function of job development and placement.

The final stage of the sequence is providing job market information to all people engaged in the intermediary process, whether it be outreach, human development, or the development of job openings. One can hardly operate at peak effectiveness without information about jobs, where they are, what is required in the job, where they are emerging or declining, both long- and short-run jobs. Job market information is an integral part of every employment office and opportunity center.

The Mission: To Serve

The Employment Service has had over 30 years to become part of thousands of communities across the land. At various levels, federal and regional, state and local, there are innumerable capable and dedicated people who have demonstrated great resourcefulness helping to solve the nation's manpower needs. It has become increasingly clear that our mission is to serve all who want and need service and aid to find work or become qualified for competitive employment. With the decision of our nation to include everybody in the opportunity orbit, the USES Human Development Program is helping people of all ages break out of the straitjacket of hopelessness and participate in the freedom that comes with finding and holding a job.

COLLEGE RECRUITING

In college recruiting, how does a basic materials company, whose customers are other industries, compete against those companies whose names are household words all over the country? One way is to recruit outstanding youngsters the year *before* they graduate. This is the method followed by American Metal Climax, Inc., New York, in a summer training program launched recently.*

Amax, with current sales running in excess of $500 million and extensive interests in metals manufacturing, mining, chemicals, and oil, has been expanding rapidly in recent years, and its accelerated

*This report was adapted from *Employee Relations Bulletin*, published by the Bureau of Business Practice, Waterford, Connecticut.

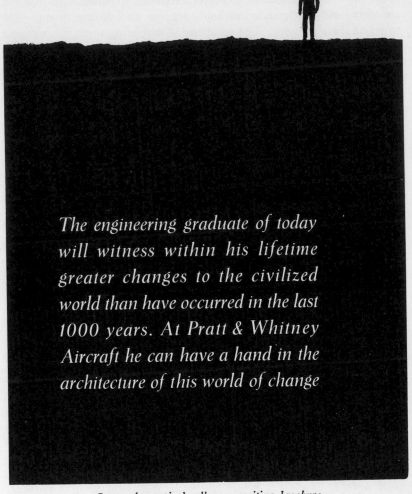

Pratt & Whitney Aircraft

The engineering graduate of today will witness within his lifetime greater changes to the civilized world than have occurred in the last 1000 years. At Pratt & Whitney Aircraft he can have a hand in the architecture of this world of change

Cover of a typical college recruiting brochure.

needs strain its management manpower resources. Its need for talented young managers was greater than that of the average company.

The company recognized a disadvantage in recruiting because it is not as well known as many other companies that are seeking technically trained graduates. But it was not at a disadvantage when it came to offering summer jobs. These are not easy for students to get.

So they decided to hire capable, outstanding young men for the summer—men with undergraduate degrees and men with one year to go on their masters'. The company would bring them in and get a look at them. The students could get a look at the company. Then they hoped to get first crack at the best ones upon graduation a year later. Amax set a goal of 10 students for the first summer. There remained the problem of recruiting them, and, more important, planning a program that would show which ones had management potential.

Contacts With Colleges

Six schools were chosen: Carnegie Tech, Columbia, Harvard, New York University, the University of Pennsylvania (Wharton School of Finance and Commerce), and the University of Virginia. David Neill, employment manager, who took charge of the new activity, got in touch with the placement officer at each college and explained the special program. He visited the campuses along with other Amax executives, and set up a management group at headquarters to screen candidates. About 20 were screened, each one interviewed by three or four Amax people. As it turned out, 14 were chosen.

Although they were looking mainly for technical people, NYU sent some financial students who were too good to turn down. So the company wound up with four more students than anticipated.

Meanwhile, Amax executives had been debating whether to assign their summer recruits to special projects or routine jobs. Both suggestions seemed to have drawbacks. Special projects often smack of "make work," and routine jobs frequently lack the opportunity for planning needed to evaluate a program of this kind. The decision was to assign one-time projects, but to go all out to make them meaningful.

The divisions were asked what studies they had been intending to do—and really needed—but hadn't gotten around to because of the press of business. There was a good response because the company had been growing so fast. Among the studies lined up were marketing surveys in copper and aluminum; a financial study of the molybdenum mining activity at Climax, Colorado, and research on the worldwide use of cadmium sulphide.

Immediate Assignments

The students arrived at headquarters the first week in June, and no time was lost in putting them to work. So they could get started on their projects right away, orientation was crowded into one week with two additional sessions on the next two Mondays.

Orientation consisted of talks by key executives and films on company operations. The students were immediately exposed to top management through a luncheon with Ian MacGregor, Amax president, and the division presidents. Throughout the summer the support of top management was very much in evidence.

In assigning projects, the company attempted to match them up with the interests and background of each man. For the most part they were able to do this, although some arbitrary assignments had to be made. Since the program had been geared for only 10 participants some of the NYU men did not receive formal project assignments, but worked in the financial department.

Each man received a free rein to accomplish his project in his own way. Goals were set without dictating methods, and all students worked at a high management level. Their supervisors were usually division-level executives.

Many of the projects called for travel. One NYU business student traveled throughout the Northeast to study the copper tubing market and its potential. Incidentally, the study was similar to one he had done in Germany the previous summer under a student exchange program.

A Carnegie Tech student traveled to Colorado to study the Climax operations. A Columbia student did the cadmium sulphide study, a lengthy document detailing current production levels and markets, current supply and demand factors and potential markets.

Two Appraisals

Each participant's immediate supervisor evaluated him twice, once in midsummer and once at the end of the session. The double evaluation was instituted because several of the students had been assigned two short projects instead of one major study. The supervisor used a flexible form in his evaluation, writing out his appraisal in essay style. Some mentioned specific weak and strong points of the student; others were more general.

The key question to be answered was whether the man had the potential to become a manager within a few years. The company wanted to get people with the capability of being trained quickly— even though many would have to take time out for military service.

Amax paid the students out of the management payroll as regular employees. Most worked until the beginning of September, when there was a final dinner meeting, again with the company president. Each student spoke for five or 10 minutes about his project and the results, thus exchanging information between various divisions.

How many of the 14 proved out? About a dozen were offered permanent jobs. The letters outlined the initial training the man would have to undergo, and described in some detail what was proposed as his first assignment.

Although there were the usual problems of selling a program such as this to managers throughout the divisions, the reaction at the end of the summer was just about unanimous: "Great." Amax expects to conduct these programs each summer from now on, though the number of students recruited may vary. The only major concern at the moment is whether the company can come up with enough genuine projects each year, since Amax is determined to avoid "make work."

The company hopes that all of these students will return and accept permanent jobs—they all expressed interest. Three of the NYU students, in fact, are still working part time. Ideally, the company would like to meet each year's quota for new managers from the previous year's group.

Potential Draftees

There remains the big question of military obligations. For a time Amax officials considered applying for deferments for the men it would hire. Its technical operations would probably provide the necessary grounds. But the company decided that this would be poor corporate citizenship. On the other hand, no prospect was to be excluded because he might have to go into service. The feeling is that the company will always need good men.

President Ian MacGregor summarized the program: "A major goal is to prepare now for management skills we need in the future. We believe the selection and development of future managers should have the same care and attention that is devoted to our engineering and research and development activities."

COLLEGE RECRUITING

By Robert M. Evans
Professional Recruitment Manager
Cummins Engine Company, Inc.
Columbus, Indiana

This presentation is not intended to be a case history in the classical sense. It is simply intended to portray the approach we took to the broad-based problem of how to attract the outstanding graduate under an extremely adverse, from industry's viewpoint, supply-and-demand condition.

Cummins began searching for managerial talent on the college campus in 1949—hiring five men. In 1966 we recruited 125 graduates, the majority with graduate degrees, from universities all across the country. During this same period, our sales grew from $23 million to a figure that exceeded $320 million. To us, these figures dramatically illustrated that college recruiting is an essential ingredient in our growth. We now conduct a continuing effort to attract outstanding young men.

How Techniques Developed

The techniques used in college recruiting will vary from company to company, but the basic mechanics remain fairly standardized. Every young man who found a job through his college placement office is an expert on the mechanics of college recruiting. This statement is not intended to be facetious, for most of our on-campus and in-plant activities do follow certain well-established paths. What is significant, however, are a number of emerging philosophies being used successfully by innovating companies. Certainly there are organizational idiosyncrasies that make adoption of certain techniques difficult for a particular company; however, the majority of companies recruiting on the college campus today could, and in many cases have, adopted these techniques with great success.

The only limiting factor in a company's ability to innovate in the competition for college graduates is the recruiting climate within the organization. This is often expressed as top management's acceptance of college recruiting as one of the company's primary functions. If the chief executive officer of a company embraces this philosophy and his management team understands his feelings, then the company is well along the way toward success in college recruiting.

College recruiting at Cummins is not viewed as a personnel function *per se,* although traditionally this has been the case throughout industry. Each member of our management group and, in fact, each of our salaried employees has developed a strong sense of responsibility in attracting new talent to the organization. The personnel function plans and coordinates this effort, but without the total commitment of the management group results can only be mediocre.

There are a number of ingredients, in addition to managerial support, which are essential to the success of our program. As previously mentioned I will not discuss mechanics, but simply describe some of the unique techniques which have been responsible for our success in recent years.

The School Sponsor Program

Each of the 56 universities we will visit has been "adopted" by one or more members of our management group. These persons are designated as "sponsors." In most cases, these people are alumni of their sponsor schools and have strong faculty contacts at these schools. Their function is twofold:

- To maintain a year-round relationship with the faculty and staff to ensure they understand the Cummins organization—what we do, where we are going, and what kind of young men we are seeking.

- To identify potential candidates for employment.

This requires an aggressive approach on the part of each sponsor. He must visit his school several times each year to fulfill these objectives, and these visits are in addition to our regularly scheduled interviewing dates. Along with simply reestablishing relationships with old friends, meeting new faculty members, dropping in on the placement staff and generally playing the "hail fellow well met," he will volunteer his time and the time of other Cummins executives to serve as guest lecturers, as speakers at professional meetings, and to make company time and facilities available for student and faculty research. He may also organize a trip to the plant for a faculty group to better acquaint them with Cummins, and industry in general.

Our success at a particular school is the direct responsibility of the school sponsor. We have been very fortunate in having people who readily accept this responsibility and attack it with considerable zeal.

Utilizing this approach, we have found that we can actually *reduce* the total number of universities on our recruiting schedule and still meet our constantly increasing requirements for college graduates. We have simply made each school infinitely more productive than it was before we initiated the sponsor program. We are now able to concentrate our effort and achieve a much bigger payoff.

As a point of interest school sponsors do no actual interviewing, even at their assigned schools. Trained interviewers are utilized to evaluate the prospects that the school sponsor has identified. The sponsor usually accompanies the recruiters to his school to provide continuity to his efforts.

Recruiter Selection and Utilization

Historically, Cummins felt that it was advantageous to use as many people as possible to recruit on the college campus. It allowed us to have all our divisions and departments represented on campus, and our managers looked upon it as an enjoyable break in the normal routine.

Our position has changed rather radically, since we now use only 18 men to cover our entire schedule. We use middle-management personnel, give them extensive training, and assign each of them to recruit from eight to 10 schools a year. There are several advantages in using fewer recruiters:

- It is easier to train a smaller group.

- It makes it possible to use the very best people.

- With the increased recruiting load, a recruiter develops his skills more fully and produces more consistent results.

The primary objective of this switch in our recruiter selection philosophy is to invite to the plant only those candidates who will eventually receive job offers. We are not so naive as to believe we won't have any misses, but these misses cost money.

Perhaps I should mention the criteria we use in selecting campus recruiters. Put yourself in the graduate's seat when evaluating recruiter candidates. Make sure the recruiter is the right type to represent you on the college campus. Ideally he should be young enough to enable a student to identify with easily, experienced enough to know your company and its opportunities thoroughly, be blessed with great intuition, and naturally be as impressive as possible.

Identification of Requirements

Obviously this is the initial step in any program, and one that usually receives far too little thought. Do we actually have positions which will challenge today's graduate? Are we willing to give him the responsibility he is seeking, and indeed must have? We have to be able to answer these questions affirmatively before we start scheduling schools. Cummins has just been through one of these periods of introspection, and it's a healthy process.

We feel very strongly that each young man we hire from the college campus must be given a specific responsibility—a well-defined and accepted position—rather than be designated a "trainee" with few obligations other than to "watch and learn." This is particularly true when considering master's level people. Today's MS or MBA doesn't want anything that even remotely resembles a training program. A BS-level candidate may feel he needs a training program to get him started, but after 90 days we have found that he is eager for a specific job. Psychologically, he wants to be accepted as a regular member of the company.

There are some major problems in using a college graduate in a position below his ability or level of initial aspiration. When we put a man in a clerical or repetitious job in which his capacity for sharp and incisive managerial thinking is dulled, we obviously do neither the individual nor the company a service.

More specifically, we recognize there are a number of salaried positions in our company that are simply not suitable for a college graduate. We utilize the following criteria in determining the positions to be filled from the college campus:

- The position should be a highly analytical or thinking-type position to which a man can contribute through specialized skills.

- A supervisory position.

Since the main purpose of our college recruiting is to ensure the company a supply of managers in the future, it therefore makes sense that we commence his managerial training immediately. Additionally, we feel: (1) persons hired should have the potential to reach the managerial level, and (2) we should have some rather firm ideas as to the steps necessary for him to reach this level.

We go to the heads of our operating divisions and ask them to describe positions within the organization which meet these criteria (a copy of the form upon which this information is transcribed follows). A screening committee of our top management-development people reviews each position thoroughly to determine the advisability of its inclusion in our program.

This committee traditionally accepts only about 40 percent of the positions that are submitted by the divisions. The divisions are then notified as to what positions have been accepted and what positions do not meet the basic criteria. They can then restructure the jobs or utilize other recruiting sources to fill them. These other sources include associate degree schools, professional recruiting (the experienced market), or an internal program whereby people are promoted from the hourly ranks to salaried positions.

Literature

This seems to be an integral part of any discussion on college recruiting these days, but this is certainly not the keystone that

POSITION DESCRIPTION
COLLEGE RECRUITING

Division:...

Department name:

Title of position:

Reports to (name and title):

Has position been evaluated?

If so, salary grade:

Number of persons required in this position:

Desired qualifications (age, degrees, etc.):

Progression from this position and approximate time scale:

Duties, responsibilities, contribution that can be made (list four in order of importance):

supports the entire program as some writers would suggest. You should be concerned if you have no specific on-campus literature designed solely for recruiting use. An attractive, creative, well-told story is one of the basic requisites for a successful program. But it's more like the price of admission—it won't get the job done by itself, but without it the odds against success rise significantly. Today's graduate expects a good, strong piece of recruiting literature from a company. Again, however, we cannot rely on this to do the job, just as we cannot rely on the classic "sign-up process" to get the top men on our schedule.

Assimilation of the New Graduate

This is one of the most critical problems that any company faces in the college recruiting area. Cummins is no exception. Like so many authorities in this field we recognize the problems, but the solutions are still a little hazy. The problem boils down to how we start an untrained but highly motivated young man in a job almost completely foreign to him, and maintain his high level of motivation while he learns the job. On-the-job supervisory coaching is about the best training mechanism we have, and we rely heavily on this. The key to this approach is to ensure that the new man is assigned to a supervisor who we know will devote the time to develop our newly acquired resource.

In addition to job-oriented training, we use two formal programs:

- The nature of our product dictates that the new employee must undergo rather extensive product indoctrination. This requires two weeks of full-time study.

- We have an obligation to provide the new employee with some general company orientation.

The general company orientation is done in a formal environment where each major division of the company puts on a two-hour presentation for the new graduates. As much innovation and theatrics as possible are encouraged in these presentations. A group of sharp young college men will get very bored listening to a department head talk for 20 minutes about the functions of his operation. We are constantly challenged to maintain a high interest level and at the same time get our message across.

Assimilation is a *continuous* process. For at least his first year with the company we must carefully monitor the new employee's progress. We provide and encourage the use of our psychological counseling facilities to treat individual problems. We also hold a series of unstructured bull sessions every 60 days for the first six months of employment. In these sessions, consisting of groups of from 10 to 12 people working in the same functional area, the new employee discusses his progress with a trained psychologist. These sessions are surprisingly frank and quite beneficial. It's helpful just to get something off your chest and to know others are encountering some of the same assimilation problems that you are. Naturally, we provide feedback to the operating divisions when undesirable situations are uncovered. One lasting benefit of this approach is that the employee starts out with the assurance that the company cares about his development; it also gives him someone to turn to should future troubles arise.

Conclusion

With a strong top management commitment generating a total corporate effort and the immediate implementation of programs such as those I have just discussed, Cummins has been able to stay quite competitive in the college recruiting market. Continued success, however, will be determined by our ability to continue innovating and to adapt to the volatile nature of this market.

REIMBURSEMENT FOR MOVING AND RELOCATION EXPENSE

One characteristic of our modern industrial society may be described as "people on the move." It is not uncommon for executive, managerial, professional, and sales personnel to transfer from one location to another.

At some stage of his life every man must make a decision, either to remain bound to a geographical location or to stake his future with the corporation and move around as opportunities for growth present themselves.

In this day of multiplant operations it is easy to shift a needed man from one installation to another. The same situation obtains when a man finds he wants to change jobs and accepts employment with a new firm in a different state. Advertisements are placed in national magazines and in metropolitan newspapers in the large population centers, but the positions that are offered are often not in the vicinity of the applicant's place of residence.

What is the policy as it relates to easing the financial burden and personal inconvenience of an employee who is transferred or for an applicant who is hired from another area?

Patterns of Policy

Usually if the action is initiated by the company, or is for the convenience of the company, the employee is reimbursed. In cases where an applicant decides, for reasons of his own, to move to another city and then to look for a job there he is not reimbursed.

The common practice seems to be to pay the bill for moving a man and his family from their present location to their new one. This means door-to-door moving of furniture and personal possessions, and includes crating and packing at one end, transporting by insured carrier, and delivery to the new address. If the family is moved by air or train, with luggage, the fare is paid for. If the family moves by private automobile, usually no travel allowance is made; although this could vary, depending upon circumstances and any agreement made.

When the man and his family relocate in another city additional expenses are encountered because of reestablishing their living in a different home or apartment. Carpets, drapes, and other furnishings must be purchased anew. Many companies make an allowance or concession toward the additional expense incurred in a relocation. Here, again, much depends on individual circumstances.

There is at least one other item to consider. This is the maintenance of two places of residence if the moving and the start of employment in the new job do not coincide. Often a man starts the new job while his family remains behind to complete the sale of property, to dispose of personal or household belongings, to let children complete school terms, and the like. In such cases the man lives on an expense account for a specified period of time, after which he is expected to have his family affairs in order. The company may also pay his fare traveling home periodically or on weekends until everything is settled.

Usually when a company wants a man it will make whatever arrangements are necessary. No man who takes a new job for the good of the company should be expected to pay a price for it. At the very least, he ought to break even.

MOVING EXPENSES

The following is the policy of United Air Lines as it relates to moving expenses of new and transferred employees.

At times it is necessary to transfer employees from one domicile to another in keeping with the needs of the service. When transfers are made at company request the employee should ask for a copy of the "Transfer and Moving Expense" booklet. He should thoroughly discuss it with his supervisor and the personnel office prior to the move, so there is a definite understanding as to what is allowed. Generally speaking the following limits will govern.

Transfer at Company Request

Personnel transferred at company request are eligible for moving expense allowance as follows: Normal packing, insurance, shipping, and unpacking charges of personal and household effects up to a maximum of 10,000 pounds including weight of crating; transportation of employee and family to the new domicile, either by plane or personal auto. If employee elects to drive his automobile, he will be allowed 4 cents per mile for the most direct AAA mileage from the point of origin to the destination, he will be allowed toll road charges and car storage for overnight stops. No other automobile expenses will be allowed. See regulations regarding mileage allowance for a second automobile.

Actual and necessary expenses for meals, hotel, etc., will be allowed for the employee and his dependents for a period not to exceed seven days after arrival at the new location. If living quarters are not secured, an above cost of living per diem agreement for a period not to exceed 30 days may be approved. The employee and his supervisor will prepare a per diem allowance on the basis of normal living expenses, which ordinarily are the cost of meals, housing and utilities at the old station compared with the expenses at the new location.

For an employee to submit a claim covering such expenses, he should complete an expense report form covering all expenses except transportation of household furnishings.

All items on the claim, except meals, must be supported by receipts.

Transfers Requested by Employees

Employees transferred at their own request, or making mutual transfers with the approval of the company, will not be permitted any expense allowance for the move. If space is available the company will furnish transportation for employees and immediate families over company routes, to the extent permitted by law.

New Employees

New employees hired at one point but who report for duty at another point will be allowed to ship 300 pounds of personal belongings via company planes. They will not be reimbursed for any other expenses.

HIRING THE HANDICAPPED

In hiring the handicapped, keep in mind that companies, as a cardinal rule of survival, should hire no one who for any reason is incapable of doing the work. When the incapability is the result of physical or mental limitations, the first bugaboo to remove from our minds is one that implies we are seriously considering employing someone who cannot do the work.

But this does not mean we should unthinkingly close the door to any and all applicants who have obvious limitations. A physically handicapped person may not be industrially handicapped. He regularly performs many services for himself; he might be able to do certain types of work if given a chance, training, and encouragement.

For many jobs, poor eyesight is a definite liability. By the use of corrective lenses, however, many individuals are quite capable of performing most jobs, including tasks which would otherwise be dangerous. Driving an automobile is a good illustration. Even professional athletes remain competitive by wearing glasses or contact lenses.

A hard-of-hearing person could be disqualified for many jobs, but a hearing aid may be all he needs to restore him to full usefulness.

These are obvious examples of handicapped persons becoming employable. Other workers with some degree of physical limitations include men and women recovering from recent illnesses, some who have a "controlled" condition, and others with minor deformities. Perhaps the day will come when a crutch or artificial limb will be equally acceptable in offices and factories.

Sometimes the corrective measures are as simple as a cushion on a chair or a raised platform. A person who cannot bend his arms enough to reach back to comb his own hair may, nonetheless, be able to do telephone work if the receiver can be mounted on the wall or desk; a speaker phone could eliminate any problem completely.

The key is to understand the content of the job and the skills required to perform it. A man crippled in his legs may be able to do desk work, and a man crippled in his arms may be able to do messenger work.

Blind workers can be trained for many occupations. Blind typists have been known to be successful, and blind musicians are familiar to all of us. One company had a very good experience with deaf-and-dumb keypunch operators; once the supervisor learned to communicate with them, they became proficient because they were not distracted.

Agencies Will Help

Rehabilitation agencies cooperate with employers who are willing to consider hiring the handicapped for work for which they are suited. These workers receive counseling and are referred to a school or medical service for guidance and help, therapy, and psychotherapy.

State and federal funds are available with no economic need requirement for tuition. These services are available for deaf, blind or otherwise visually handicapped, and others with cardiac, arthritic, and rheumatic conditions.

The handicapped want no more than an opportunity to work. They have learned to lead productive lives, and usually ask for no special consideration or concession. They are appreciative of their jobs and are therefore loyal and dedicated in return. Employers of handicapped persons claim that once they are properly placed there is less turnover, less absenteeism, less tardiness.

Companies should realize that many people who are physically handicapped may not be vocationally handicapped. Given a job within their limitations, in a company with an understanding climate, these people can indeed be good employees.

Some Case Histories

The Credit Bureau of Cook County, Inc., has over the years employed physically handicapped workers in its office at 425 North Michigan Avenue, Chicago, Illinois. The motivation, according to Ray Babiarz, personnel manager, is not sympathetic but practical. The people are employed for work for which they qualify and are expected to produce.

Included in the work force are men and women amputees, others with deformed limbs, birth defects, epilepsy, etc. They also have a number of deaf mutes; these people present no serious communications problem since they read lips, give audible responses, use sign language, or write notes.

Any credit for the humanitarian aspects of the program go to Gilbert Hamblet, general manager. He hired the physically handicapped as a necessity but found they worked well. The rewards are in loyalty and attendance.

Globe Weaving Service has hired deaf mutes for the past 20 years in its plant at 210 West Van Buren Street, Chicago. Norman Appelman explains that his partner is a deaf mute. This eases the problem of communications. But with 20 years of experience he and other employees have learned to communicate with their deaf mute coworkers.

The State of Illinois Vocational Rehabilitation program assists in the training of some of these people for hand reweaving work. The crux of quality reweaving is concentration; deaf mutes, possibly because they are not distracted by sounds and needless conversation, are good at this painstaking work. As workers, however, they are no different from others; some are good, some are not.

Some years ago this firm received a Presidential citation for its fine rehabilitation program.

HIRING THE MENTALLY HANDICAPPED

By William Sleith
President, Iona Manufacturing Company
Manchester, Connecticut

A few years ago it would never have occurred to me to deliberately select a mentally retarded person to fill a vacancy in my plant. That was before I was exposed—quite accidentally—to the potential in this reservoir of skills.

It happened in the pre-Christmas rush, when a shipment of defective motors was returned for repair. I needed some men to unpack and break down the motors and then repack the parts. And I needed them fast.

I put in a call to the nearby State Training School for the Retarded. They sent me two men—retarded youths who had never worked before. Working together, the two did the job in less than four hours—half the time previously required for a similar job.

I now have about 35 retarded men and women among my 600 employees. Their flying fingers, devotion to the job, and their even dispositions more than compensate for their lack of intellect. Some of them are doing work which normal employees wouldn't want to do—and they are taking pride in doing it well. I couldn't ask for more satisfactory employees.

Gain Speed Quickly

Generally speaking it takes only a little longer to train a retarded worker for a routine task than it does a person of normal intelligence. And once he learns what is required, he develops speed quickly. For example, three of ten women on a soldering line in my plant are mentally retarded. In fact, they are still residents of the State Training School. But their slow mental processes do not affect their manual dexterity. After only three months on the job, one of those retarded girls was outproducing her lead lady, who has been doing this work for 12 years.

I have had similar results elsewhere in the plant. One man, put to work packing electric blenders, was working so fast after only two weeks that the line couldn't keep up with him. We transferred him to the warehouse where he can set his own pace.

That's the only problem we've had with retarded employees—they work *too* fast. I think it is because of their complete concentration. It takes all their mental ability to perform even a simple task; thus they are forced to keep their minds on the job.

Other businessmen have asked me how these workers fit in with my other employees. I would say it works out very well. Far from shying away from them, our employees have, by and large, been solicitous of their welfare. For example, one Christmas one of our lead ladies took her retarded charges for a drive to see the Christmas lights. Others have taken them shopping or bought them gifts. I frankly think that having these people with them has been a morale-booster for my staff.

Pride and Dedication

One thing we have noticed about the retarded is the unusual, personal pride they take in their work. They get upset if they are told they've made a mistake. And they are dedicated workers—sometimes more so than we would wish. For instance, they insist on coming to work regardless of how they feel. Problems that beset the normal worker in terms of colds, headaches, etc., do not deter the mentally retarded from appearing at their workplaces. Absenteeism is absolutely no problem with these people.

The list of other contented employers is growing and includes both large companies and small. The biggest employer of retarded workers is the United States Government. Less than two years after the establishment of regulations permitting the hiring of retardates without Civil Service examinations, the government had

---

MENTALLY RETARDED DOES NOT MEAN MENTALLY ILL

It is a mistake to lump together the mentally retarded and the mentally ill. The mentally retarded are men and women of limited intellectual ability. Generally they enjoy performing routine, repetitive tasks—the kind of work that a normal worker would consider boring.

Mental illness, on the other hand, does not affect basic intellectual ability. When recovered from their illness, former mental patients are capable of holding virtually any job for which their training and experience has qualified them.

Supervisory Management (American Management Association).

---

over 700 mentally retarded at work. They include building maintenance workers, janitors, elevator operators, and warehousemen, as well as clerks, messengers, and office machine operators. The great majority are performing their duties satisfactorily, with a few rated by their superiors as outstanding employees. Only 5 percent have failed to make the grade.

None of the government jobs filled by the mentally retarded was created especially for that purpose. They are established jobs which happen to fall within the capabilities of a retarded individual. The retardates come to the government already trained by a sheltered workshop or other agency and fully prepared for work.

The success of these experiments bodes well for the future of the retarded in American business and industry. We have been slow in overcoming the prejudice that stems from lack of knowledge. But once we've employed retarded persons and have seen what they can do for us, we cannot help but be convinced of their worth.

The retarded do have skills that business and industry are constantly seeking. I think we should give them a chance to prove it.

WHEN YOU HIRE A MENTAL RETARDATE

Supervising a mentally retarded worker is no more difficult than supervising a normal one. But you will feel more self-assured about dealing with a retarded employee if you learn the following guidelines:

1. Talk to the retarded employee on a person-to-person level, as you would to anyone else. Only try to be more specific, more precise and crystal-clear—as if

you were speaking to someone in the upper levels of grade school. Don't talk down to him as though he were a small child. He's not.

2. Speak in concrete terms, not abstractions. If, for example, you want him to put the pail away show him exactly where "away" is.

3. Demonstrate what you want him to do; don't just tell him.

4. Show him where things are—time clocks, lockers, restrooms, cafeteria or lunch area, drinking fountain, supply room—as you would for any new employee. But take your time, don't rush, and be sure he understands.

5. Take extra care to explain about working hours, proper clothes on the job, his work station, whom he reports to, what his pay will be, where the bus stops. It is important for him to know these points.

6. Ask a question now and then to make sure he is keeping up with you: "Now show me your work station," or "Where does the bus stop?"

7. Introduce him to his fellow employees and supervisors. He may seem a bit withdrawn at first, but he will warm up once he gets to know the people. He'll warm up faster if he can find one co-worker at first with whom he can feel free and easy; someone to answer questions and listen to problems.

8. Let him know he is one of the workaday family. He may learn to mix with others at work, but tend to be by himself after work. After-hour friendships should not be forced; he may be vocationally ready but not quite socially ready.

9. Be ready to help him in new situations and new problems.

10. Make note of his on-the-job points. When he turns out to be a good employee, pass the word on to other employers that it can be good business to hire qualified, mentally retarded workers.

TEMPORARY HELP

The temporary-help industry, which started when Sam Workman began offering temporary service in Chicago in 1935, has mushroomed into a quarter of a billion dollars a year business. It currently employs a million wage earners. Under its arrangements workers are hired by the temporary-help agency (which does not charge them any fee), then leased to industrial and professional firms on a short-term basis.

The company pays a flat hourly rate, depending upon the skill. The employee is on the payroll of the agency, not the company where the work is performed. The agency assumes obligations for Social Security payments and records, insurance, vacation, and other benefits. The big item, of course, is that the agency recruits, interviews, tests, selects, and hires the employees and either finds them qualified in a specialty skill or trains them. The employing company gets a fully trained worker.

A Special Breed

Temporary workers are mostly women, especially married women. These are often well-trained and skilled workers who for reasons of their own are unable or unwilling to accept full-time employment.

The temporary-help industry is a blessing for wives who want extra money. But it may also be the answer for career girls who like to travel, students working their way through college, actresses between engagements, athletes during the off-season, and older people who need new jobs. Job arrangements can be tailored to the worker, who can work those weeks when he or she is available, certain days of the week, and occasionally even limited hours of the day. Mothers can take the summer months off to be at home with school-age children simply by making themselves unavailable during that period.

Travel for single girls can be more than saving money while working for a vacation trip. Companies which have offices in different cities have been known to certify girls in their home city and then assign them out of offices in other cities. An example is the British secretaries recruited and hired in London for six or 12 months' work, then assigned to companies in various cities in the United States.

Many workers like the variety which this kind of service offers. Creative types may find working for the same company somewhat stifling. As temporary workers they can move about, actually pick and choose the kind of work they prefer.

What Do You Want?

Temporary workers are mostly typists and secretaries. But there are also many other types of office skills—comptometer operators, clerks, bookkeepers, file clerks, key punch operators. Some are trained in computer programming, as receptionists, demonstrators, convention registrars, pollsters, survey interviewers, etc.

A few agencies are now specializing in men for temporary jobs. Some of these supply laborers, freight handlers, watchmen—hired and paid by the day. Others are office and factory workers, product demonstrators, booth attendants, sample distributors, and so on.

Olsten's Temporary Personnel, Inc., is unique in that it also

Olsten's, a typical professional temporary help service, displays its wares.

offers temporary executives, technicians, and specialists—such as managers, supervisors, CPA's, statisticians, chemists, buyers, artists, EDP and systems analysts, proofreaders, editors, interpreters, and the like. Other agencies have available ushers, models, hostesses, security guards, narrators, and Santa Clauses who can be supplied for a day, a week, or longer. These later developments in the field, however, represent a very small part of the total market.

While there are many advantages from the employee point of view, there are equally as many benefits accruing to employers.

Temporary workers are used for work overloads caused by peak loads, cyclical conditions, inventories, vacations, sickness, and job openings.

For companies there is no red tape, recruiting, interviewing, selection, union rules, payroll deductions, fringe benefits, training, supervision, or age limit.

Companies save since they pay only for the number of hours worked, do not have the cost of employment, have no fringe-benefit costs, and pay on weekly invoice in place of the usual amount of payroll work and recordkeeping.

Temporary personnel is a new industrial cost-saving tool. Apart from the savings in recordkeeping, payroll taxes, workmen's compensation, and fringe benefits, the big item is direct-labor cost savings. Temporary workers are used only when there is work for them. Whereas regular employees remain on the payroll even when the volume of work decreases, temporary workers are released. No work, no direct labor cost.

The use of temporary personnel has introduced a new cost-control concept of flexible planning. Companies retain a minimum hard-core permanent staff, and supplement this with temporary workers who are used only as needed.

There are hundreds of temporary-help offices in all major cities in the United States and Canada. Some of the largest and best-known companies are Olsten's, Manpower, Kelly Service, Office Overloads, and Western Girl. There are many other firms, some with offices in more than one location, others which are strictly local. A company interested in using temporary help will most likely go where it gets the best service and satisfaction.

HOW TO PREPARE FOR TEMPORARY HELP

When temporary help is needed either in office or plant, there are certains steps that can be taken to facilitate matters for both the company and the temporary worker.

1. *Prepare a work station manual.* This can be simple—samples of the kind of work to be done, information about the company and the department where the work is to be done. This should be readied before the temporary worker arrives.

2. *Check the equipment.* Have the supervisor to whom the temporary worker will report check in advance to see that the machine or equipment is working properly, that supplies are adequate and handy.

3. *Welcome the temporary worker.* Upon arrival, the temporary worker should be shown around and introduced to co-workers in the unit. The temporary worker should be made to feel at home, free to ask questions, and join in with the group.

4. *Provide good supervision.* Make it clear to whom the temporary worker reports. Explain the problem which necessitated the temporary help, and outline thoroughly the significance of the work. Understanding leads to better productivity and efficiency.

5. *Discuss local routines.* The temporary worker will feel more at ease if the customs, such as coffee breaks, lunch hours, and any other rules and regulations of the firm are explained.

6. *Explain the company style.* Every firm has its own peculiarities. These may be a distinctive letter form, a unique way of packaging, stylized telephone answering, etc. The temporary worker should be adequately instructed in these matters.

7. *Arrange for a contact.* Assign a regular employee to act as sponsor to the temporary worker. This will make the temporary worker more comfortable since the fellow worker will be a source of immediate information and help should problems arise.

8. *Be friendly.* Make the temporary worker feel needed and wanted. Try to create a favorable rapport with permanent employees. Don't make the temporary worker feel like an outsider.

9. *Explain the function to the permanent staff.* Discuss the need for temporary help with the regular employees who will be involved. Make it clear that this is a special case, that the temporary worker is in no way competing with them and is not a threat to their job security.

10. *Keep in touch with the referral source.* Let the agency know that the temporary worker arrived, report on progress whether good or bad, keep the lines open in case a replacement or addition may be needed, and upon completion of the assignment give a fair and honest report of the performance.

APPLICATION BLANK

The Application for Employment form is used to gather information. By the use of a standard form, the information is always in the same place and the interviewer is spared the time and annoyance of having to hunt for the specifics he needs to know. The form may be professionally prepared and widely used, or individually developed by any one company through its own experience.

The information asked for depends upon company requirements and job demands. In all cases certain necessary data are required. But questions to a sales applicant will vary considerably from those of a shop worker.

The sections of an application blank are usually these:

1. *Personal data*—name, home address, telephone number, social security number, age and/or birth date, height, weight, sex, marital status, dependents, citizenship.

2. *Helpful information*—type of work sought, salary desired, when available to start work, reason for wanting to change jobs, and from what source the applicant was referred.

3. *Education*—chronological education history, highest level attained with everything below that detailed by names and locations of grammar school, high school, trade or business college, correspondence school, college or university, night school: years attended, whether graduated, courses specialized in.

SELECTIVE SERVICE CLASSIFICATIONS

CLASS I

Class I-A: Available for military service.

Class I-A-O: Conscientious objector available for noncombatant military service only.

Class I-C: Member of the Armed Forces of the United States, the Coast and Geodetic Survey, or the Public Health Service.

Class I-D: Qualified member of reserve component, or student taking military training, including ROTC and accepted aviation cadet applicant.

Class I-O: Conscientious objector available for civilian work contributing to the maintenance of the national health, safety, or interest.

Class I-S: Student deferred by law until graduation from high school or attainment of age of 20, or until end of his academic year at a college or university.

Class I-W: Conscientious objector performing civilian work contributing to the maintenance of the national health, safety, or interest, or who has completed such work.

Class I-Y: Registrant qualified for military service only in time of war or national emergency.

CLASS II

Class II-A: Occupational deferment (other than agricultural and student).

Class II-C: Agricultural deferment.

Class II-S: Student deferment.

CLASS III

Class III-A: Extreme hardship deferment, or registrant with a child or children.

CLASS IV

Class IV-A: Registrant with sufficient prior military service or who is a sole surviving son.

Class IV-B: Official deferred by law.

Class IV-C: Alien not currently liable for military service.

Class IV-D: Minister of religion or divinity student.

Class IV-F: Registrant not qualified for any military service.

CLASS V

Class V-A: Registrant over the age of liability for military service.

4. *Work experience*—work history in inverse order, names and addresses of companies worked for (listing most recent one first and working back), dates of employment, earnings, types of work done, progress made, name of supervisor who may be contacted for reference.

Other information requested may pertain to:

1. *Military record*—for ex-service personnel: branch of service, years of service, military specialty, work done, specialized training, progress in rank, nature of discharge, present Reserve status. For young men: draft status and explanation of any deferment.

2. *Machines*—types of office or factory equipment operated, and how long; whether these skills were obtained in school or on the job.

3. *References*—personal acquaintances who may be contacted. This is not used much now because it has little value.

Provision should be made for the applicant to supply additional data which he feels would be pertinent to his qualifications. Usually, the bigger the job the more information requested.

It is advisable to have the applicant sign the form. Above the space for his signature enter a "clearance" statement which guarantees all information to be accurate and gives the prospective employer the right to investigate any of it. Quite often, however, the interviewer will be asked not to check with the present employer; this request, of course, should be respected.

Different application blanks may be used for office personnel, factory workers, salesmen, technicians, supervisors and managers, and executives.

Since different information is often needed for higher positions, the specialized application blanks are more detailed. They provide for information about an applicant's family background, extracurricular activities, scholastic honors and leadership positions, military accomplishments, civic responsibilities, hobbies, and the like.

Two Schools of Thought

On the general subject of application blanks there are two schools of thought. Some companies feel the blank should ask only those

APPLICATION FOR POSITION

Date_____

Name (print)_____   Home Tel. No._____

Present address_____   How long have you lived there?_____
No.   Street   City   State

Previous address_____   How long did you live there?_____
No.   Street   City   State

Position applied for?_____   Earnings expected $_____

PERSONAL

Sex: ☐ M, ☐ F; Date of birth_____19____   ☐ Single, ☐ Married, ☐ Separated   No. children____Their ages____
Check your State law as to discrimination because of age.
Height____ft____in. Weight_____lbs.   ☐ Engaged, ☐ Widowed, ☐ Divorced   No. other dependents____Ages____
Are you a U. S. citizen? ☐ Yes, ☐ No   Date of marriage____   Soc. Sec. No.____

Do you: ☐ Own your home? ☐ Rent? ☐ Live with relatives? ☐ Board? ☐ Stay with friends? Other____

(If you rent) What monthly rent do you pay? $_____Do you own your furniture? ☐ Yes, ☐ No

Is your wife employed? ☐ No, ☐ Yes, part time, ☐ Yes, full time; What kind of work?_____Her earnings $____per____

Do you carry life insurance? ☐ No, ☐ Yes; Amount $_____

What physical defects do you have?_____

In case of emergency, notify_____
Name   Address   Phone

EDUCATION

Type of School	Name and Address of School	Courses Majored in	Check Last Year Completed				Graduate? Give Degrees	Last Year Attended
Elementary			5	6	7	8	☐ Yes, ☐ No	19
High School			1	2	3	4	☐ Yes, ☐ No	19
College			1	2	3	4		19
College			1	2	3	4		19
Graduate School			1	2	3	4		19
Business or Trade School			1	2	3	4		19
Corresp. or Night School			1	2	3	4		19

Scholastic standing in H. S.?_____In College?_____

EXTRACURRICULAR ACTIVITIES (athletics, clubs, etc.)
(Do not include military, racial, religious, or nationality groups)

In high school_____   In college_____

Offices held_____   Offices held_____

SERVICE IN U. S. ARMED FORCES

Have you served in the U. S. Armed Forces? ☐ Yes, ☐ No; (If yes) Date active duty started_____19____

Which Service?_____What branch of that Service?_____Starting Rank_____

Date of discharge_____19____Rank at discharge_____

Form No. OA-201

Application blank used by many large companies which may be obtained in quantity from The Dartnell Corporation. Well organized, it provides a good profile of the job applicant while taking up a minimum of file space.

WORK HISTORY

List below the names of all your employers, beginning with the most recent:
a. Employer's Name
b. Address and Telephone Number

	Kind of Business	Time Employed				Nature of Work	Starting Salary	Salary at Leaving	Reasons for Leaving	Name of Immediate Superior
		From		To						
		Mo.	Yr.	Mo.	Yr.					
1. a. b.										Name Title
2. a. b.										Name Title
3. a. b.										Name Title
4. a. b.										Name Title
5. a. b.										Name Title
6. a. b.										Name Title
7. a. b.										Name Title
8. a. b.										Name Title

Indicate by number————any of the above employers whom you do not wish us to contact.   Ever bonded? ☐ No, ☐ Yes; On what jobs?

References (Not former employers or relatives)

	Address	Phone Number
1.		
2.		
3.		

Are there any other experiences, skills, or qualifications which you feel would especially fit you for work with this Company?

If your application is considered favorably, on what date will you be available for work?

19____ Signature _____

APPLICANT SHOULD NOT WRITE BELOW THIS LINE

1 2 3 4: Comments _____

Interviewer: _____

Reverse side of the application blank available from The Dartnell Corporation, providing a complete work history of the applicant, including tenure of former positions, salaries at start and at termination, reasons for leaving, and other data pertinent to the prospective new employer.

questions which are pertinent to employment in the company; their application form lists only minimum questions. Others believe there is value to interspersing necessary questions with general and possibly irrelevant questions on the theory that everybody likes to talk about himself. While the applicant is concentrating on harmless questions, he is unaware of the importance attached to some of the less obvious but more meaningful statements he makes.

Be Careful of Questions

Because of the tight labor market as well as the pressure to hire marginal applicants, some companies are purposely expanding their application blanks to ask for more personal information. As protection for the company that does not want to hire any bad risks, and also to protect the applicants from being hired for work for which they are unsuited, these firms now ask more in-depth questions about the health record and medical history, family and marital situation, financial status, police record, and preparation for work. Care must be exercised in not asking for data which conflicts with legislation. It is unlawful to ask questions about:

1. *Name:*

   Original name if name has been changed.

   If he ever worked under another name.

   However, a married woman may be asked to give her maiden name.

2. *Birth:*

   Birthplace of applicant.

   Birthplace of applicant's parents, spouse, or other relatives.

   Birth certificate, baptismal record, or naturalization or first papers.

3. *Citizenship:*

   Citizen of what country.

   Where applicant was naturalized.

   Whether parents or spouse were naturalized.

4. *National Origin:*

Lineage, ancestry, descent, parentage, nationality.

What is the mother tongue?

Language commonly used at home or with parents.

How applicant learned to read, write, or speak foreign language.

5. *Race:*

Complexion or color of skin.

Require applicant to affix photograph.

6. *Religion:*

Religious affiliation.

Religious holidays observed.

7. *Organizations:*

Membership in clubs, societies, or lodge to which applicant belongs.

The Application for Employment blank is one of the chief tools in the selection procedure. It is important that it be properly designed and correctly used.

INTERVIEWING IS "INNER VIEWING"

Interviewing is a big part of every manager's or supervisor's job. His other involvements with the personnel program—such as recruiting, testing, selection, orientation, training—can easily be shared with the central personnel staff. But interviewing is his "tool of the trade" upon which he relies more than he realizes. He uses it in hiring new workers and in other functions of the employee relations program.

Since interviewing is usually associated with the hiring process, let's begin there. Let's start by classifying employment interviews— not by the book but rather by type. Just as interviewers become adept, so do interviewees; we have all seen applicants who appeared to know all the angles.

An interesting commentary could be developed under the title, "Interviewers I Have Met." Included would be:

- The test-happy type.

- The big brother who can't say "no" but insists upon being helpful.

- The decision-maker who tells the applicant what to do.

- The familiar type who gets chummy to the point of disarming the applicant.

- The up-from-the-ranks man who relates his personal progress.

- The fringe-benefit type who tells about pensions rather than opportunities.

When we get right down to it, few managers or supervisors know exactly what they want to discover or are looking for in an interview. Not one in a thousand has consciously prepared questions which will indicate those characteristics for which he might be looking. Consequently, the questions asked are the conventional ones which might or might not have much bearing on what the interviewer really needs to find out in order to make a decision.

"I'll Take the Blonde"

All of us are familiar with the hiring of secretaries, so let's use this as an example. Ask any group of managers for their personal comments about the kind of individual they are looking for when they want to hire a secretary, and we will get all the usual adjectives: neat, accurate, conscientious, good judgment, optimistic, natural, sincere, tolerant, honest, persistent, punctual, cooperative, conservative, fast, steady, energetic, vivacious, pleasant, logical, diligent, competent, emotionally stable, one with initiative, one who loves work. Now if the applicant met all these qualifications she could trade places with the interviewer. In the majority of cases the boss might as well take one look, eliminate the too-old, the too-young, see who recognizes a typewriter and steno notebook, flip a coin, and then announce in a decisive voice, "I'll take the blonde."

Most interviews are confused bluffing sessions; no one knows for sure who is trying to impress whom. Both interviewers and interviewees try so hard to cover up weaknesses that they don't get around to letting their good qualities show through. Is it any wonder that the interview becomes a conglomeration of disconnected questions and confused answers?

It's too bad that the interview is bungled so much. After all is said and done, the interview is the determining factor in the employment procedure. From the time the first worker was hired, the personal interview technique has been used. All of the later aids that have been developed have not minimized the importance of the interview. It is safe to say that more than 99 percent of all workers are hired as the result of interviews.

There are two specific types of employment interviews: the planned or patterned interview—aimed at getting directly to specific data; the informal interview—aimed at getting indirectly at general impressions as well as necessary facts.

Both types of interviews have advantages and disadvantages. The common practice is to use the informal type; it is informal not because of training, but because of lack of training. It is too informal and too often misses the point; it consists of too much talking and too little listening.

In employment we generally recommend that the line manager also interview the applicant since he is the one responsible for the final decision to hire. But in some companies where this procedure is used the sequence of interviews is somewhat like an obstacle course. What is designed as a multiple interview, a recommended approach if properly done, too often becomes a chain interview—a practice in which an applicant is passed along from the personnel manager, to the department head, down to the supervisor. And the supervisor is so busy and so far behind schedule he routinely accepts the applicant that the more skilled interviewers have been sparring with. No wonder our interviews are ineffective and costly.

Interviewing is different from other management skills since it involves the attitudes and behavior of people. No two interviews can be alike. The success of an interview depends upon the extent to which the interviewer can create a feeling of mutual confidence and cooperation between himself and the applicant.

The Art of Predicting

The purpose of an employment interview is to collect information, combine and classify it, to help predict the likelihood of the applicant being able to perform the job successfully. The personal interview provides the opportunity of meeting the applicant and observing his appearance, verbal ability, general personality, and attitude toward life. While the applicant is on his best behavior—dressed in his best, polite, and cooperative—the interviewer must cleverly disarm him so as to get a picture of the applicant's natural self, how he will appear later on the job.

In each case, the objective is to appraise the individual's qualifications and personal traits in terms of his chances for success on a specific job. Sometimes the job to be filled can be adjusted to meet the qualifications of an applicant. Particularly in specialty types of positions, the kind of person on the job often influences the way the job shapes up and the various duties that are included.

The reason many interviews fail is that many people, when they get written or oral information, are unable to analyze their impressions objectively. Many interviews are affected by personal subjective traits which unconsciously result in some bias or prejudice which colors the decision. Companies are realizing that ability knows no restrictions, that unfounded prejudices create artificial barriers to success which are too costly to tolerate. Unfortunately some interviewers have not learned this lesson yet; they must be told how to be objective.

To improve the interview, skilled and unskilled interviewers alike often resort to different types of aids. The use of prepared lists of questions can point up what is really being sought. Rating charts for the evaluation of answers are helpful. On a scale from low to high, opinions are recorded on such factors as experience, sincerity, general knowledge, personality, self-expression, enthusiasm, initiative, and judgment. Some people use checklists on which items like appearance, character, attitude, physique, and ability are rated from "very poor" to "excellent." Often a set of trade questions can serve as a guide. The written job description can be used to get better understanding of the nature of the job and the separate tasks that make up the job.

Interview Essentials

Some necessary essentials for all interviews include:

1. *Privacy*. A private office or booth is recommended in many situations, on the theory that both parties may speak without restraint. Sometimes clear-glass partitions give an impression that the candidate is being given the "once over" to the viewers outside. Therefore, just any area that lends itself to privacy may suffice. Many successful interviewers prefer to visit with applicants out in an open office, since no particularly confidential discussion takes place. The applicant is given a practical view of the environment instead of being sheltered in some ideal but unreal climate.

2. *Comfort*. Certainly the interviewee should be at ease, to permit a free exchange of information. On the other hand, letting him smoke in the waiting room or during the interview may lead to an erroneous impression of working conditions if this same privilege is not granted at the work station.

3. *Understanding*. The interview should not be attempted, nor should any decision be made, unless and until mutual understanding is reached. It often takes time, patience, and some innovation to get through to the other person. A good practice is to turn the applicant—especially the beginner or one who is nervous—over to another employee with whom he or she may have something in common. A high school senior will be more comfortable in the hands of a recent graduate from the same school. The applicant will ask such a clerical worker many casual (though significant) questions which he would be afraid to broach with a more formidable interviewer. An applicant with a transportation problem will get more helpful answers from a worker living in the same locality.

4. *Attitude*. Much more important than the fine furniture, modern environment, and other visible appurtenances is the attitude of the interviewer and company toward the applicant. The best physical facilities will not offset insincerity, annoyance, or "going through the motions" which soon become apparent to the applicant. The interviewer's interest must be in both applicant and job, and it must be equally divided. The best applicant will not fit the job unless at the same time the job fits the applicant. The interviewer's concern

APPLICANT
SCREENING PROFILE

Name _____ Date _____

Address _____ Telephone _____

Applying For Job As _____ Date Available _____

Present Job _____ Education _____

PERSONAL GROOMING	Unkempt; noticeable lack of neatness	No special care in dress or appearance	Neat and clean	Pays special attention to personal details	Immaculately dressed and groomed
	1	2	3	4	5
VOICE QUALITY	Harsh, irritating	Indistinct, difficult to understand	Pleasant tone and voice	Clear, understandable; good tone quality	Unusually expressive; excellent voice
	1	2	3	4	5
PHYSICAL APPEARANCE	Unpleasant, unhealthy appearance	Appears to lack energy, listless	Good physical condition; pleasant appearance	Appears fit, alert, energetic	Especially energetic, good carriage; appears in excellent condition
	1	2	3	4	5
PERSONAL MANNER	Nervous, embarrassed; compulsive mannerisms	Stiff, uncomfortable; ill at ease	No unusual tension, comfortable, at ease	Appears alert, free of tension	Unusually self-possessed and composed
	1	2	3	4	5
CONFIDENCE	Shy, retiring; arrogant, "cocky"	Submissive; argumentative	Reasonably self-assured; forthright	Shows self-confidence	Unusually self-assured; inspires confidence
	1	2	3	4	5
EXPRESSION OF IDEAS	Unclear, illogical; speaks without thinking	Dwells on non-essentials; thoughts not well defined or expressed	Thoughts clearly expressed; words convey meaning	Convincing; thoughts developed logically	Unusual ability to express ideas logically
	1	2	3	4	5
MENTAL ALERTNESS	Dull, slow to grasp ideas	Comprehends ideas but contributes little to discussion	Fairly attentive; expresses own thoughts	Quick-witted, alert; asks intelligent questions	Unusually quick thinker, keen mind; grasps complex ideas
	1	2	3	4	5
MOTIVATION AND AMBITION	No drive, ambition limited	Little interest in development; seems satisfied	Interest and ambition fair; reasonable desire to work and develop	Definite future goals; wants to succeed and grow	Ambitions high, future well planned; evidence of personal development
	1	2	3	4	5
EXPERIENCE AND EDUCATION	Education and experience unsuitable for the job	Education and experience not directly applicable, but helpful	Good educational and work background; experience fair	Education and experience fit job; above average qualifications	Background especially well suited; continues to study
	1	2	3	4	5
PERSONALITY	Immature, impulsive; indecisive, unstable	Opinionated; difficulty in accepting others' ideas	Reasonable stability and maturity.	Stable, cooperative; accepts responsibilities	Very mature, a "self-starter"; outstanding personality
	1	2	3	4	5
				TOTAL	

Remarks: _____

Recommended For Further Consideration: _____ Not Recommended: _____

_____

Signature of Interviewer

FORM NO. 7
EMPLOYER'S SERVICES CORP.
BOX 314 — BRISTOL, TENN. 37621

Screening profile developed for job applicants by the Employer's Service Corp. of Bristol, Tennessee, makes it easier for interviewers to judge personal qualities of applicants.

over filling the job for the company rather than filling the need of the applicant is one of the weaknesses of interviews.

Some do's and don'ts of interviewing are:

Do:

1. Use a quiet, comfortable place.
2. Put the interviewee at ease.
3. Be interested in the person as well as the job.
4. Outline clearly the requirements of the job.
5. Explain fully the conditions of employment.
6. Tell about benefits, promotions, opportunities.
7. Encourage the applicant to ask questions.
8. Guide the interview.
9. Listen; let him talk freely.
10. Be natural; use a conversational tone.
11. Know when and how to close the interview.
12. Announce your decision or explain your next step.

Don't:

1. Keep the applicant waiting.
2. Build false hopes.
3. Oversell the job.
4. Interrupt the applicant or the interview.
5. Rush through the interview.
6. Repeat questions already answered on the application form.
7. Develop a "canned" interview approach.
8. Give opinions; just answers.
9. Pry into his personal life needlessly.
10. Prejudge and reflect prejudices.
11. Use a phony excuse for turning him down.
12. Send him away with a bad taste in his mouth.

These are general suggestions, of course, and must be individualized to fit each particular situation.

Questions asked by the employer pertain to such items as the applicant's physical characteristics, health and record of illness, abilities and training, education qualifications, work experience, personal aspirations, and family and living conditions. Other questions cover dependents, handicaps and limitations, outside activities and hobbies, financial stability, habits (good and bad), social interests, citizenship, references, and the like. His attitude toward many of these things is reflected in the reasons he gives for doing something or for not doing it. Debts, problems, time lapses, or a bad record should be scrutinized critically.

The applicant must understand such things as:

- The job for which he is being considered.

- The reason the position is open.

- Why he would want to work in the company.

- Wages, hours, conditions of employment.

- Promotions and opportunity for growth.

- Benefits.

- Stability of employment in the company.

- The philosophy of the company toward its workers.

Finding the right person for any job is, however, only half the task. The applicant must feel that he too has found a job opportunity which meets or exceeds his expectations. Only when there is a happy job marriage, in which both sides are satisfied, does the placement stand a chance of being successful. In that case the company will provide the worker with the job satisfaction he needs in order to be happy; and he, in turn, will have that built-in motivation a company looks for in order to make his employment pay off.

Other Uses of the Interview

But the interview is more than an employment technique. It is widely used in business for seeking credit information, making loans, selling, adjusting complaints, and diagnosing ailments. In the company's personnel program it is used in discipline cases, counseling, testing, transfer, promotion, layoff, salary adjustments and rejections, merit rating, appraisals, separations, as well as employment. It is used in every interpersonal relationship between manager and worker. It is in this broader context that I would like to offer a suggestion.

The suggestion concerns the word "interview" itself. We have become so accustomed to this word in the parlance of the trade that we don't realize that to many people, applicants and workers alike, it may be a foreboding word. If I were to visit with you in your home, you would ask me to sit beside you on the davenport or nearby in a comfortable chair. You would treat me as a guest and make me feel welcome. Yet when I come to your office to discuss our mutual business relationship (which may be much more significant to both of us than a friendly visit at your home) you unintentionally place a barrier between us. This barrier may be real in the form of a desk; an involved procedure; or a cold, efficient approach. Or the barrier may be mental and imagined by the applicant. In either case it is there and has a direct bearing on the result.

In any situation, whether it be for employment, counseling, or otherwise, if we would think of the word "interview" as "inner view" we would get through to the other person much easier. Let's try not to look at the situation, whatever it may be, from our own viewpoint; but instead let's try to see it from his side. Let's get his "inner view" and we will understand him much better.

I would like to suggest that we discard the word "interview" entirely. Then, for want of a better word, we would simply go back to holding "face-to-face conversations" with applicants and workers. How much better it would be for the other person, and how much easier for us, if we merely visited with each other—sat alongside him instead of across the desk. I'm sure you would find the experience more enjoyable and the results surprisingly better.

The purpose of any such face-to-face conversation, commonly referred to as the interview, is twofold:

1. To exchange information.
2. To make a friend.

So much depends upon the interview, so let's make it a good one. Let's not be concerned with the technique but rather with the purpose; not with the cost but with the results.

THE PATTERNED INTERVIEW

Many companies have established some sort of standards for the interview in selecting and placing personnel. But the interviewing technique has three weaknesses:

1. Many interviewers do not get complete or relevant information necessary in making a decision. Many interviewers do not know what information should be sought.

2. Experienced interviewers may be able to determine from the information obtained what an applicant *can* do, but they lack a means of judging what he *will* do on the job.

3. Personal feelings enter into the interview; the interviewer is influenced by promises and general rationalizations of the applicant rather than unbiased, objective, factual information.

The Patterned Interview, developed by Dr. Robert N. McMurry and published by The Dartnell Corporation, has been designed to overcome the limitations and faults of ordinary ineffective interviewing. It has many advantages of which these are most important:

1. It guides the interviewer in getting the facts and discovering valuable information about the applicant.

2. It makes possible a systematic coverage of necessary information upon which to predict the applicant's probable chances for success.

3. It provides a set of principles for use in interpreting the facts obtained for the purpose of judging what the applicant will do besides what he obviously can do.

4. It provides a means for minimizing the interviewer's personal biases and prejudices.

A sampling of the McMurry patterned interview form is shown nearby.

PATTERNED INTERVIEW FORM

S U M M A R Y	Rating: 1 [✓] 3 4 Interviewer _QGB_ Date _10/1/65_

Comments (List both favorable and unfavorable points) _Stability is good; industry is excellent; perseverance is_
In making final rating, be sure to consider not only the man's ability and experience
good; ability to get along with others is good; loyalty is very good; self-reliance is only reason-
but also his stability, industry, perseverance, ability to get along with others, loyalty, self-reliance, and leadership. Is he mature and realistic?
ally good; leadership is reasonably good; maturity is very good; he is strongly motivated. His living
Is he well motivated for this work? Are his living standards, finances, his domestic situation, and the family influence favorable to this work?
standards, finances, domestic situation & health are all favorable. He appears to be a very
Does he have sufficient health and physical reserve?
well qualified applicant for this position as Vice President of a medium sized manu-
facturing company.
Position Considered for _Factory Manager_

Name _Louis B. Alton_

Present Address _642 S.E. Alberto Street_ City _Chicago_ State _Illinois_
Will this location affect his attendance? Is this a desirable neighborhood? Does it appear consistent with income?

Telephone Number _BR 7-4343_ Is it your phone? _yes_

Date of your birth _9/9/16_ Age _49_ Have you served in the Armed Services of the United States? ☐ Yes, ☒ No
In some States, legislation forbids discrimination because of age.

(If yes) What were the dates? ___19___ to ___19___ If rejected or exempted, what were the reasons? _essential industry_
Discuss military service as a job in chronological order with other jobs. Will this affect his performance on our job?

Why are you applying for this position? _improvement in security_
Are his underlying reasons practical? Does he have a definite goal?

Are you employed now? ☒ Yes, ☐ No; (If yes) how soon available? _one month_
What are relationships with present employer?

WORK HISTORY: LAST OR PRESENT POSITION

Company _H-J Company_ Division _Exec._ Dates from _9/8_ 1959 to _still employed_ 19___
If out of work—how long?
Address _Chicago, Illinois_
Does this check with application?

How did you get this job? _agency - had been looking for 9 months_
Did he show self-reliance in getting this job? Stability of interests? Perseverance?

Nature of work at start _assisted factory manager - 4 mos._ Earnings at start _$10,000_
Did this work require energy and industry? Close attention? Cooperation?

How did the job change? _Factory Manager - Jan. 61 V-P of Manufacture_ Earnings at leaving _rate $18,000 bonus $3000_
Was progress made? Any indications of strong motivation? Is this in line with what he can earn here? _factory eng_

What were your duties and responsibilities at time of leaving? _supervise 400 people - production, inventory control, purchasing,_
Did he accept them? Indications of industry? Self-reliance? Perseverance? Leadership?

Superior _O.A. Anderson_ Title _President_ How was he to work with? _reasonably good - no leadership_
Was this close supervision? Are there indications of loyalty? Hostility?

What did you especially like about the position? _working with foremen & key people - handling all problems_
Has he been happy and content in his work? Indications of loyalty, ability to get along with others?

What did you especially dislike? _reorganization after Pres.'s illness = new Pres & reorganization not sound_
Did he get along well with people? Is he inclined to be critical? Were his dislikes justified?

How much time have you lost from work? _3 weeks_ Reasons _appendectomy - 1964_
Is he regular in attendance on the job? Are there other interests?

Reasons for leaving _Chairman of Board hired him - died 2 mos. ago_ Why right then? _questions security of company_
Are his reasons for leaving reasonable and consistent? Do they check with records?

Part-time jobs during this employment _none_
Does this indicate industry? Ambition? Lack of loyalty? Lack of interest in duties of position?

NEXT TO LAST POSITION

Company _Trans-Vex_ Division _Production_ Dates from _1/8_ 1956 to _9/6_ 1959
Any time between this and last job?
Address _Barnsville, Illinois_
Does this check with application?

How did you get this job? _contacted by them_
Did he show self-reliance in getting this job? Stability of interests? Perseverance?

Nature of work at start _Super. methods & time study, tool room maintenance and_ Earnings at start _$7800_
Did this work require energy and industry? Close attention? Cooperation?
buildings & equipment

How did the job change? _remained largely the same_ Earnings at leaving _$10,500_
Was progress made? Any indications of strong motivation? Is this in line with what he can earn here?

What were your duties and responsibilities at time of leaving? _remained largely the same_
Did he accept them? Indications of industry? Self-reliance? Perseverance? Leadership?

Superior _D.E. Castle_ Title _V-P Production_ How was he to work with? _good_
Was this close supervision? Are there indications of loyalty? Hostility?

Form No. EP-812

Unusual patterned interview form developed by Dr. Robert N. McMurry and distributed by The Dartnell Corporation. Form is printed in two colors, and questions are posed the interviewer in the second color, keeping interviewer alert to the real purpose of the interviewing process.

SELECTION

The employment function is a continuing one in every company, regardless of whether or not the procedure is formalized or the job centralized. The selection and retention of efficient workers is one of the most important operations of any company. In any kind of labor market the proper selection of applicants for jobs poses one of industry's greatest problems.

A big concern is that of cost. There are statistics available to tell us how many dollars were lost last year because of fires, termites, floods, and hurricanes. Unfortunately not even an estimate exists for the loss due to incompetent employees, the result of poor hiring practices and improper placement. But if such a survey could be made, the total would undoubtedly be in the billions of dollars. Add to this staggering cost the waste of human capacities and the countless cases of tragic frustration, and the significance of proper selection and placement becomes apparent.

Many Unrealized Costs

This cost item is many things. Acquisition costs are more than agency fees, newspaper ads, or employee referral bonds. The cost of interviewing and screening applicants, including the many who are rejected, must be taken into account. Medical examinations, if given for new employees, will add substantially to the cost. Whatever method is used and whatever steps are taken we can be certain that the cost of each new worker is higher, much higher, than we realize.

Add to this the expense of low production during the beginning or training period, the time of the person who does the training, and the many other obvious as well as hidden costs, and we get some idea of the cost of employment and the importance of good selection. Poor selection, hurried placement, and such considerations add even more to this hidden cost. The employment of incompetent, unstable, and nonproductive workers can be a costly item in terms of direct expense.

Then think of the less desirable employees who get into the

work force who are not released for any of many reasons. Sometimes a contract complicates the firing of such employees. In other instances seniority or company policy keeps these people on the payroll. And don't think for a minute that there is no sentiment in business; otherwise, how can we justify the retention of workers who obviously have lost their usefulness?

The Investment Is Heavy

Add all these factors together and we begin to understand the investment that companies have in their people. An investment decision of this magnitude in other departments would be given close scrutiny and consideration. Yet, investments of this amount are made in newly hired employees every day with very little caution. Employment is the one item that is governed by little objective decision. There are those who hire new workers who like to think of themselves as amateur psychologists, and a certain measure of subjective opinion influences their decision to hire or not to hire an applicant.

One of the consequences of ineffective selection of employees is a drag on efficiency, low production, poor morale. The hope that these people will somehow fit into the work scheme is wishful thinking. Unsatisfactory work habits in people are usually a result of long-established practices and character traits that are difficult, if not impossible to change.

The selection procedure covers the entire period from initial contact with the applicant to his final acceptance or rejection. The screening out of the unqualified should be accomplished in the shortest time consistent with good community relations since the procedure is costly and, of course, nonproductive.

A Series of Rejections

Selection begins as soon as an applicant makes himself available for employment, either in person or by mail. Sight screening eliminates the obviously unqualified. Knock-out questions eliminate those who cannot meet specific job requirements. Interviewing is done to reduce the number of candidates. Sensible testing programs eliminate some applicants and serve as aids in interviewing the

SELECTION AND EVALUATION SUMMARY

Applicant's Name _____ Date _____ 19____

Position Applied for _____ Job Class _____

	Check Each Factor	Above Requirements	Meets Requirements	Marginal	Unacceptable
CAN-DO FACTORS	Appearance, manner......................................				
	Availability..				
	Education...				
	Intelligence (as measured by test)........................				
	Experience in this field (if applicable).......................				
	Knowledge of the product (if applicable)....................				
	Physical condition, health.................................				

	CHARACTER TRAITS (Basic Habits)	A Lot	Some	Not Much	Almost None
WILL-DO FACTORS	STABILITY; maintaining same jobs and interests............				
	INDUSTRY; willingness to work...........................				
	PERSEVERANCE; finishing what he starts...................				
	ABILITY TO GET ALONG WITH OTHERS................				
	LOYALTY; identifying with employer......................				
	SELF-RELIANCE; standing on own feet, making own decisions				
	LEADERSHIP...				

JOB MOTIVATIONS (not already satisfied off the job)

NEED FOR INCOME or desire for money..................					
NEED FOR SECURITY....................................					
NEED FOR STATUS......................................					
NEED FOR POWER.......................................					
NEED TO INVESTIGATE.................................					
NEED TO EXCEL (to compete)..........................					
NEED FOR PERFECTION.................................					
NEED TO SERVE...					

BASIC ENERGY LEVEL (vigor, initiative, drive, enthusiasm)

DEGREE OF EMOTIONAL MATURITY

Dependence					
Disregard for consequences..............................					
Incapacity for self-discipline............................					
Selfishness...					
Show-off tendencies.....................................					
Pleasure-mindedness					
Destructive tendencies					
Wishful thinking					
Unwillingness to accept responsibility.....................					

Important: Do not add or average these factors in making the Over-all Rating. Match the qualifications of the applicant against the requirements of the *particular position* for which he is being considered, and consider the importance of each mismatch.

Strong Points for This Position _____

Weak Points for This Position _____

Over-all Rating: [1] [2] [3] [4]   Recommendation to Employ: [ ] Yes [ ] No   Rating by _____

Form No. ES-404R-2

Copyright, 1964, The Dartnell Corporation, Chicago, Ill. 60640. Printed in U. S. A. Developed by The McMurry Company

This selection and evaluation form divides an applicant's personal traits into "Can-Do" and "Will-Do" factors. Method was developed by the McMurry Corporation and is distributed by The Dartnell Corporation.

others. Reference inquiries, physical examinations, and multiple interviews are additional devices used in the selection procedure.

Selection actually is a normal process of a series of rejections:

a. Preliminary interview................if not rejected, then ...

b. Application blank............................if not rejected, then ...

c. Interview..if not rejected, then ...

d. Check on references........................if not rejected, then ...

e. Physical examinations..................if not rejected, then ...

f. Mental tests..if not rejected, then ...

g. Multiple interviews........................if not rejected, then ...

h. What is left..make final selection.

The sequence might be slightly rearranged in some companies or under some circumstances, but the use of a series of rejection steps remains unchanged.

Six Appraisal Factors

For better selection, and a corresponding reduction in the size and cost of the problem of selection, it is well to know just what we are looking for. There are six appraisal factors involved in the selection and employment of applicants:

Informational:	abilities and personal data.
Motivational:	drives and personal goals.
Emotional:	maturity and business outlook.
Attitudinal:	sense of values.
Behavioral:	habit patterns and conduct.
Physical:	health and peace of mind.

In selecting employees to work with us, these are the qualities we try to identify and evaluate. It is necessary, therefore, that the interviewer understand what is involved.

A selection and evaluation summary published by The Dartnell Corporation is shown on page 180.

TESTING

Psychological testing of students, workers, and others has been going on in one form or another for more than a half century. With some people it is almost an academic or industrial religion. Many large corporations process candidates for employment or promotion through a ritual of testing that must be passed satisfactorily in order to even be considered. Still there are others who are skeptical and, while they might not be openly against testing, they are far from enthusiastic.

In a broad sense it is the purpose of testing to help predict future performance in various fields of endeavor, to diagnose personal characteristics, and to research for understanding of individual and group behavior. It is the purpose of personnel tests in business to assist in getting the best available person on the job, and the best available job for that person. The most effective test of a person's ability to handle a particular job is an actual trial of that person on the job. This, however, is costly. So various methods and tools are utilized to help in this process.

Not a Cure-all

Testing is *one tool* used in determining the suitability of an individual for a particular position. Tests by themselves should not be thought of as giving all the answers to placement problems but, used in conjunction with the other tools, they can indicate a person's strengths and weaknesses. Test scores interpreted in terms of specific needs, combined with the personal interview, references, and general work background should provide a reliable guide to an applicant's or worker's potential.

Testing has come a long way since Alfred Binet, working at the Sorbonne in Paris, began intelligence quizzing of schoolchildren in 1905. Spurred by World War II experience, businessmen and schools have come to embrace tests. This has created a new industry and spawned an army of psychologists who specialize in this area.

Tests are used in schools and colleges for admissions, ability groupings, scholarship awards, career planning. The military uses them to find specific aptitudes for skill training, such as radar operators. Business firms use tests to aid in the selection of people they hire or promote, probably in a negative sense by screening out the less competent and unqualified candidates. Tests are also used to uncover hidden talent among the "sleepers" in the work force, to bring to the surface abilities which might otherwise go unnoticed.

About three out of five companies use tests of one kind or another in selecting office and factory employees. Tests are used more for white-collar workers than for blue-collar workers. The responsibility for developing and administering the testing program is with the personnel staff. The personnel specialists explain the use of tests and interpret the individual results to line supervisors, foremen, and managers with whom the responsibility for final selection rests.

Old-fashioned virtues of plodding, ambition, and perseverance are giving way to measurable characteristics which now become the determining factors in employment, promotion, and assignment.

There is some criticism against pigeonholing people into convenient slots by machine-manipulated cards. There is resentment against prying into the skulls of people, calibrating of capabilities, mechanized packaging of talents, shaping of human's destinies. Since tests as used today tend to become elimination devices, they have been accused of preventing deserving youngsters from entering certain professions.

Yet the results seem to be better than the old ways of depending upon a boss' intuition and shrewd appraisal—possibly because these were not as good in the boss as he wanted to make himself and others believe they were. Testing is more objective, albeit limited. The old-time boss made more mistakes in judgment than he cared to admit. As time went on these mistakes became more costly as employment, training, dismissal, or retention proved to be costly.

Five Test Categories

Tests may be classified in five categories:

1. The *Learning Ability Test,* sometimes referred to as an intelligence test. This type of test measures the more fundamental factors of the mind. It gives a good indication of the approximate level at which a person can operate by establishing the extent of ability to learn in a variety of situations. A typical test of this design consists

of three kinds of questions: arithmetical, vocabulary, and block-counting.

Good examples are—

   a. Tiffin Adaptability.

   b. Otis Employment.

   c. Thurstone Test of Mental Alertness.

2. The *Skill Test,* which measures the specific clerical or mechanical skills needed. These include the achievement exercises to see how much a person has learned. Among them are tests of arithmetic computation, error location, alphabetizing, coding, spelling, reading comprehension, and grammar. Familiar are tests in typing and shorthand, and performance on standard office machines or shop equipment.

Good examples are—

   a. Arithmetical Reasoning.

   b. Typing and Shorthand Tests.

   c. Manual Dexterity Exercises.

   d. Trade Tests.

3. The *Aptitude Test* attempts to determine the inborn suitability, or the degree of natural endowment in a particular field. It measures the proclivity, or built-in readiness, for specified types of work. Generally, aptitude tests are simple for they take a narrow range of intellectual measurement.

Good examples are—

   a. Psychological Corporation's General Clerical Booklet A and B.

   b. Minnesota Clerical.

   c. How Supervise?

4. The *Interest Inventory Test* measures the job preference of the employee by drawing out opinions about work, home, life. It should be noted here that a decided interest in a category does not mean an aptitude for it. These tests definitely aid in careful selection.

Good example is—

   a. Kuder Preference Test.

5. The *Personality Inventory Test* determines a person's reactions to different types of situations from which general conclusions can be drawn within the limits of measured personality characteristics. This type of test attempts to uncover drives and ambitions, or the lack of them, plus traits of temperament such as stability, frankness, persistence, etc. Personality (nonintellectual) tests are subject to factor analysis and result interpretation.

Good examples are—

a. Personal Audit.

b. Thurstone Temperament Schedule.

The "Test Battery"

A test battery is a group of carefully chosen different tests, assembled to fit a situation. The choices and combinations of tests are varied according to the function: sales, clerical, trade, executive, secretarial, etc.

The criteria of a good test are: (1) to be reliable, (2) to have validity, and (3) to provide statistical norms for interpretation purposes. These terms should be defined.

Reliability is a measure of the test's consistency of performance over a group of people. Will the results be about the same if the tests are given to the same group later on, or to a similar group?

Validity refers to how well the test measures what it is supposed to measure. In the less complex work assignments, such as where typing skill, number checking or inspection for minor defects or mechanical assembly are the main duties, validity is more readily discoverable and attainable. Aptitude tests do not have as high validities as those known as intelligence tests. The tests of personality have even less validity. This validity is often expressed in the form of a coefficient of correlation between the test and a criterion of success.

Norms are the bases, usually expressed in terms of an average or median score, against which any individual's score is compared. How much better or worse is a person than the average or middle person, is the question to be answered. A test may have one or more

TEST PROFILE

NAME

		DATE	LOW	BELOW AVERAGE			AVERAGE			ABOVE AVERAGE
L E A R N I N G A B I L I T Y	**TIFFIN ADAPTABILITY:**									
	A									
	B									
	OTIS EMPLOYMENT:									
	THURSTONE PMA:									
	Space									
	Number									
	Reasoning									
	Word Fluency									
	Verbal Meaning									
A P T I T U D E S	**GENERAL CLERICAL:**									
	Filing									
	Grammatical									
	Arithmetical									
	MINNESOTA CLERICAL:									
	Names									
	Numbers									
	HOW SUPERVISE:									
	A									
	B									
	M									
	PRACTICAL JUDGMENT:			10	20 25 30	40	50	60	70 75 80	90

		DATE	
I N T E R E S T S	**KUDER PREFERENCE:**		
	Mechanical		Personnel will analyze and interpret the test re‐
	Computational		and prepare a report to be discussed with
	Scientific		manager.
	Persuasive		
	Artistic		
	Literary		
	Musical		
	Social Service		
	Clerical		
P E R S O N A L I T Y	**PERSONAL AUDIT:**		
	Seriousness - Impulsiveness		Personnel will analyze and interpret the test re‐
	Firmness - Indecision		and prepare a report to be discussed with
	Tranquility - Irritability		manager.
	Frankness - Evasion		
	Stability - Instability		
	Tolerance - Intolerance		
	Steadiness - Emotionality		
	Persistence - Fluctuality		
	Contentment - Worry............		
	THURSTONE TEMPERAMENT:		
	Active		
	Vigorous		
	Impulsive		
	Dominant		
	Stable		
	Sociable		
	Reflective		

SKILLS: Typing_____W.P.M.   Shorthand_____W.P.M.

RB-12 1-60   Blue Cross Plan for Hospital Ca:e of Hospital Service Corporation; Blue Shield Medical-Surgical Plan of Illinois Medical Service

Test Profile used by Blue Cross/Blue Shield of Illinois.

sets of statistical norms derived from samplings of people of different backgrounds or levels of qualifications.

The test scores are meaningless out of context. These raw scores must be converted to the norms. It is the interpretation of these norms, the analysis of the composite test scores, and the resolution of confusing or even conflicting test evidence that is compiled into a test profile. It is this finding, not the specifics of each test, that is reported to supervisors or management. Only generalized information should be revealed to the testee. There is a certain ethics in testing that requires careful safeguarding of confidential test data and results, as well as the material itself.

Tests serve best when kept secret. They reveal personal information which should be treated impersonally. Good testing procedures are effective because they are objective; unfortunately, some managers are not, and for that reason tests can fail.

Psychological tests have limitations. They are good tools to assess certain abilities, traits, and aptitudes. But they are much less accurate in judging motivation, creative capacity, or other complexities of human nature. They cannot judge moral charcter or detect larceny in a man's heart.

Tests are not yet very successful in predicting such characteristics as initiative, imagination, loyalty, because these are hard to measure. Too much depends upon environmental influences in the situation at the time.

Tests may tell what a man *can* do but not yet what he *will* do. The critical will-do factors are affected more by personality and social relations on and off the job. In selection and placement the problem is determining not what a worker can do but what he will do.

Fads and Fancies

Occasionally testing is undertaken because it is regarded as fashionable or up-to-date. A company executive hears of a competitor's use of tests and instructs the employment office to "get on the ball" at once. Some companies use quickie tests because they are a relatively inexpensive adjunct to the employment procedure, easy to administer by a clerk, and simple to score by a receptionist—as though they have universal application. Testing is growing in popularity but in many cases it is getting a patent medicine approach.

Nor should tests be used to eliminate, or even reduce, the importance of interviews, reference checks, careful screening, and thorough selection. Other factors must be weighed to estimate the potential development of an individual. Education opportunities, stimulation from home environment, societal background, appropriate habits of work, and attitudes toward self and life are all involved in any man's chances for success and satisfaction on a job.

But the danger is not only in relying too heavily upon tests. There are dangers inherent in the use of tests. One source of difficulty lies in inappropriate test choices, indifferent administration, and inconclusive interpretation. Tests that measure the wrong abilities, that are too easy or too difficult, or that place a premium on certain types of experience and training will give inadequate results. Careless test administration leads to performance which is not typical of the applicant. Improper test interpretation permits incorrect standards and erroneous conclusions.

Another important thing to remember is that tests measure individuality. They relate to the applicant, not to his co-workers or supervisor. Nor do they take into account the company climate as an influence upon the applicant's development. These considerations can have more effect upon his chances for success in a job than any series of test results.

Finally, psychological tests are not infallible. They can occasionally be wrong. Yet, it would be unfair to condemn the whole notion of testing because of a few disappointing experiences with it. As with any other new procedure, the concern over testing should not be whether it achieves perfection, but whether it results in some improvement over earlier methods. It seems only fair to evaluate a testing program in terms of averages rather than in terms of specifics, either good or bad.

The "Cons" of Testing

Proponents of testing can advance many convincing arguments and can point to all kinds of impressive results. But opponents of testing also want to be heard.

They maintain, for example, that there are many people who are successful in their chosen occupations who would not be able to pass the qualification tests. They believe it is one thing to test a prospective machine operator for manual dexterity but another to determine whether he will "make a go of it" once on the job. They point out that 90 percent of workers who lose or leave their jobs do so not because they are unqualified to perform the work but because of other reasons which are "out of reach" of tests.

At a time when top management is looking for leaders, the testing program scrupulously weeds out likely candidates by coming up with the standardized, supinely-adjusted, well-conformed personality that fits the norm. Their biggest argument is that testing in all forms has become too much of a cult and that the corporate world places too much reliance and blind faith on tests.

Testing is undoubtedly useful in getting people into jobs but opponents find comfort in the thought that farmers, housewives, bartenders, and elected public officials are not asked to pass tests to get their jobs.

Well, where does this leave us? Maybe two observations would be in order.

1. Proponents of testing should understand that while tests can be helpful, they alone cannot be expected to predict success or satisfaction in a job. Testing is one tool in the selection procedure and used that way can be useful.

2. Opponents of testing might consider some of the advantages that are available to them. Certainly doing something ought to be better than doing nothing.

TESTS AS TOOLS OF THE PERSONNEL MANAGER

Test use is increasing at a much faster pace than is test understanding. A look at tests as tools of the personnel manager would therefore be in order.

Tests are becoming an increasingly important tool in the personnel manager's kit, to be used in conjunction with other techniques (interview, application form, reference check, records of past performance) for gathering the most complete set of information possible about an applicant or employee.

But, tests are only a tool. Personnel decisions can only be made by managers and supervisors. Analogy: Tests have a "staff" function (provide information), not a "line" function (make decisions on the basis of evidence).

Critical analysis of recent publications condemning tests indicates major objections arise from improper test use, rather than the tests *per se*. An evaluation of the technique of testing should be clearly separated from the application of the technique. Analogy: The saw should not be eliminated from the carpenter's kit because a building cannot be erected with it alone.

Available tests are not, and never will be, perfect measurement devices. They must be used with their limitations clearly understood.

However, in the literature there is sufficient evidence on the potential effectiveness of testing, as a methodology, to warrant increased efforts to: (1) develop more and better instruments, and (2) determine the situations in which they can be effectively utilized.

Definition of a Test

L. J. Cronbach, in *Essentials of Psychological Testing*, defines a test as ". . . a systematic procedure for comparing the behavior of two or more persons."

The words "systematic procedure" may be further defined as a "standardized sample of behavior." That is, the items or tasks included in a test are a sample of a very large number of questions or tasks. In a test, every person is asked to respond to the *same* set of items or tasks in the *same* manner, and the results are observed, or scored, in the *same* way. Thus, the test is a *standardized* or *systematic* procedure.

Observations (scores) that are standard for all persons can be *compared* and evaluated in a measurement sense. Thus, we can say that individual A is better or poorer in a skill than most people in a reference group, or has more or less aptitude or interest than another individual. When we can quantify behavior we can *diagnose* strengths and weaknesses, or *predict* other behavior, for example, success on a job.

A test may take various forms. It may be a performance or job sample test involving apparatus (e.g., typing). Or it may be a set of questions presented in a paper-and-pencil format. Also, a test may measure any of a variety of characteristics. It may measure a mental ability, knowledge, attitude, or personality trait.

Test Use in Industry

There are some characteristics that can be evaluated (measured) more reliably by means of a test than by other personnel evaluation techniques. That is, assessments of an individual through interview will vary more from interviewer to interviewer, or from day to day by the same interviewer, than with the individual's scores on a well-developed test.

However, tests are not perfectly reliable either. The stringent interpretation of a test score (accepting applicants scoring 50, but rejecting those scoring 49) is one very common misuse of tests.

Reliable and valid tests are not available to measure all human behaviors or characteristics. Thus, more subjective techniques must necessarily be used to evaluate many factors about an applicant.

A test may not measure the same characteristics for all people. Using a test developed on one group with persons from a different kind of group is probably the most frequently found test misuse. For example, the widely used short intelligence test (Wonderlic, Otis, TMA) may indeed estimate the general mental ability level of persons who have had the average high school education, but may measure something quite different if given to a person with an inferior educational background. In general, a test may be expected to measure what it purports to measure only when it is given to persons similar to the group on which it was developed.

Purposes for which tests are used are twofold—

1. *Diagnosis,* or description of an individual's characteristics— his strengths and weaknesses, his knowledges and deficiencies. In the past, this purpose has been more associated with testing in schools, vocational guidance programs, and psychological clinics. Now being found more and more in industry as companies are initiating employee development programs and long range organizational planning, including the planning for future human resources.

2. *Prediction* of future success on a job. This use can be further divided into:

    a. *Selection.* The traditional purpose for which tests have been used in industry. Every decision to hire, promote, or transfer one person but not another infers the *prediction* that the person selected will have the greater probability of success. In the process of selection, some persons are rejected.

    b. *Placement.* The process by which all available persons are utilized, but are placed in different jobs or training programs to optimize individual and/or group output. This use is becoming increasingly important in business and industry as more and more companies

- Recruit and hire inexperienced personnel to relieve tight labor market conditions.

- Become equal opportunity employers and assume responsibility for training, upgrading, and maximizing the efficiency of persons who would not have been selected previously.

- Change their methods of business and manufacturing operations in keeping with technological advances (computers, automation) and face the problems of transferring and retraining displaced employees.

Installing a Testing Program

When installing a testing program, keep in mind that a sound testing program is based on four critical steps.

1. Analysis of job tasks and employee requirements.

This should not be done cursorily by someone sitting in the personnel office. It should be done systematically and thoroughly for each job classification coming under the proposed testing program. The analyst must talk with both supervisors and employees, observe the job being done, and break it down into its task components. Each task component should be rated (or ranked) on two scales: time spent, and criticalness (cost to company when task is not performed properly).

2. Selecting tests for experimental program.

For most jobs certain of the important applicant requirements can be evaluated most reliably and validly through test instruments. This procedure leads to testing batteries that are job specific—that simulate each job space—because they are based on an analysis of the attributes required by the tasks in specific jobs. Jobs differ within a company and even jobs with the same classification title will differ from company to company. Predictions of later job success can have little hope of success unless the requirements of that job are reflected in the evaluation of applicants for it. Thus, general testing programs for all office workers, or all plant employees, are usually not as effective as job specific programs. The selection of tests to be administered should be viewed as "experimental" at the outset.

3. Testing the tests.

The experimental testing program for each job should be subjected to research at the local level.

a. Local norms. Administering the tests to currently employed persons in the job will provide preliminary information about standards that might be expected from applicants. Norms based on test scores of applicants provide a statistical description of the talent in the labor pool of the company's locale.

b. Local validation. Whether the tests are being used for the purposes of selection or placement, their validity (relationship of scores to successful performance on the job) should be established. Such research can be conducted by either

• Testing current employees and relating scores to job performance evaluations (concurrent validity), or

• Testing applicants, filing test records, and later correlating test scores with job performance criteria (longitudinal validity).

4. Interpreting results from validity studies.

Test-performance correlations based on data obtained by testing current employees are likely to be lower than correlations obtained in a longitudinal study. This is because current employees are usually a rather selected group, with a restricted range on both test scores and performance ratings. Even though the criterion might be arbitrarily extended to include an "unsuccessful" category, these employees are not truly "unsuccessful." They are simply the least successful of the group retained in the job and are at least adequate.

The Operational Testing Program

Tests can be administered by clerical people in the personnel office. However, such persons should be thoroughly trained in the methods of administering each test. It is essential that each test be given in exactly the same way each time if it is to be used as a "standardized" measurement technique. Similarly, interviewers and other personnel staff members using test scores in their evaluations must be thoroughly familiar with the test research studies and the results so that their interpretations, or comparisons, are standard from day to day.

Testing programs provide partial information about an applicant. Interpretation must be guided by prudence. Since tests are not perfectly reliable, the use of an absolute test standard is not the best practice. A "cut-off" score might be established, but applicants scoring within a range of this score should be considered, particularly if information obtained through other employment techniques appears to be favorable.

People tend to view test scores as absolutes and to put undue importance on small differences. For this reason, test scores should not be given to applicants or supervisors who do not understand their proper interpretation. The best procedure is to provide supervisors test score information in terms of probability of success, or in terms of qualitative descriptions (very high, high, average, below average, poor).

From an administrative standpoint, establishing a multiplicity of testing programs, each specific to a job classification, is more complex for the personnel office, but this is the most effective and professional approach to test use.

Procedures should be established to collect test score and criterion information on a continuous basis. Periodically the collected data should be analyzed to ascertain that the operational testing programs are still effective. Jobs change with time; available talent in the company's labor market fluctuates. It is particularly important to conduct a second validity (cross-validation) study on a testing program, utilizing applicants, as soon as possible after the first study. A validation study is based on a *sample* of employees or applicants, and this sample may be biased in some unknown way so that individual test validities are affected. The results are used to predict behavior of future samples. If these results hold up for a second group, the chances of the program being effective for future applicants is greatly enhanced.

Special Problems

There are problems created by the changing environment.

1. Technological advances, rapid changes in methods and processes, and the increasing national productivity are already straining industry's human resources. This trend is destined to continue and accelerate. A company's greatest potential for strengthening its competitive position lies in its personnel—in their talents, skills, and potential. Forward-looking companies are creating departments for long-range organizational planning which must involve action programs for the recruitment, hiring, training, and development of personnel today against tomorrow's needs.

In the past companies have tended to "overselect" at entry-level jobs so that in some haphazard way the talent required for higher level jobs was usually available. But, when labor markets are tight, such an abundance of well-qualified applicants is not available.

The potential of new hires and older employees must be identified and developed. The time may well arrive soon when companies must assume a very major role in the training and education field. The shortage of qualified people in the labor market—the rate at which skills become obsolete—the high degree of specialization in many occupational families—all these will increase the need for company-sponsored training and employee-development programs.

Such an investment in training should be backed up with better records and more complete information in the personnel files—or an inventory of the potential human resources available among the employee group, an inventory that includes not only developed skills, but complete aptitude, ability, and interest information. For such purposes, testing programs would be extended to present employees and would be used in much the same way they are used today in the school vocational counseling program.

2. The influx of minority group members into the labor force puts a strain on present employment and testing programs.

The following is taken from a recent publication of the Federal Equal Employment Opportunities Commission:

> *Title VII of the Civil Rights Act of 1964 provides that an employer may give and act upon the results of "any professionally developed ability test provided that such test . . . is not designed, intended or used to discriminate because of race . . . "(Sec. 703 (h)).*

The language of this statute and its legislative history make it clear that tests may not be used as a device to exclude prospective employees on the basis of race.

This publication recognizes that many companies may be inadvertently discriminating because the tests used in employment programs do not measure equally well for all groups. Many things may influence a test score, quite apart from the attribute being measured.

For example, Science Research Associates, a leading developer, publisher, and distributor of tests, has recently published a new test titled *Pictorial Reasoning*. In its development representatives from seven subcultures were utilized, one of these being a middle-class-white control group. It was found that test scores across subcultures varied very little when the test items were administered under an untimed condition, but cultural differences were increased when an arbitrary condition of speed was introduced into the measurement situation. Thus, for groups less accustomed to taking tests a bias was introduced into the measurement of reasoning ability.

As an immediate step in utilizing available standardized tests for evaluating persons from different cultural groups, or with limited educational experience, the EEOC and other writers have stressed the need for establishing different cultural validities and norms. This involves considerable research, but is nevertheless necessary. The potential of such persons for succeeding in training and on the job must be evaluated, and tests are probably the most adequate technique for doing so. For example, assumptions about ability that employers have traditionally made on the basis of formal educational achievement do not hold for these groups.

In addition to the development of local validity information and special normative standards for minority groups, professional test developers might be expected to provide more appropriate instruments over time.

It should be noted that suggestions to adjust test score standards do not include the implication that job performance standards should be changed. These suggestions simply recognize the possibility that on Test A a raw score of 25 for a minority member may be related to the same level of job performance as is a raw score of 40 for a member of a different group.

3. Limited local research capabilities cause problems. The preceding paragraphs repeatedly point up the necessity for test research at the local level. However, there are relatively few companies with sufficient manpower to adequately validate assessment tools for all job classifications. There are even fewer capable of studying the problems associated with predicting success in training—or the problems of assessing minority group members.

Need For More Data

But, the local company can do much more than it has done previously, particularly in establishing the general validity of tests and other assessment techniques for predicting job performance. The data published in the typical test manual can serve as guidelines for estimating validity and for making general interpretations until better data can be obtained locally. If test score information is systematically accumulated, eventually there will be a sufficient amount to conduct validation studies, even for low-employment job classifications.

Test research directed toward problems of placement, predicting trainability, and assessment of minority groups probably require a broader base than the local company. In the future, more data and guidance might be expected from test publisher sources.

For example, SRA is sponsoring a systematic test validation project of national scope that calls for the cooperation of not only hundreds of companies, but educational institutions as well. Under this project, a wide variety of tests (intelligence, special aptitude, achievement in basic skills, interest, attitude) are being studied to determine their potential for predicting success in vocational training and in later performance of some 35 skilled and semiskilled jobs. The project will include analyses of sub-breakdowns of the data by geographical area, by cultural group, by sex, etc. Such information will provide a good base from which the individual company can pursue its studies aimed at refining the general results to make them more effective locally.

TESTING DISADVANTAGED APPLICANTS*

Companies have been accused of using tests as a means of maintaining unfair discrimination against groups which have already suffered from many forms of discrimination. Such practices are a distortion of the proper function of tests and deserve condemnation. It does not follow, however, that tests themselves merit condemnation. Most users in industry expect the tests to help them identify the people best suited for the jobs to be filled.

From the standpoint of corporate management, the employment function can legitimately be viewed as a type of purchasing operation. It then is the duty of the employment manager to hire those candidates who offer the best promise of contributing to the success of the enterprise. The reason that tests have been used for many years by many employers is that, in management's opinion, the information furnished by tests is valuable in making hiring decisions. If the employer sets his minimum scores too high he does not fill the available jobs. If he sets his minimum scores too low he hires persons difficult to train, low in productivity, and high in liability to error. Sophisticated personnel officers realize that predictors such as interviews, reference investigations, and tests are part of a total evaluation problem, that of obtaining better workers or of matching workers and jobs more precisely.

Whenever the number of applicants exceeds the number of job openings, some applicants will be rejected. This is one of the hard facts of life. It is not surprising that those who are rejected sometimes attack the selection procedures on the grounds that these are invalid or unfair. Although testing is not free from defect or beyond criticism, appropriately chosen and properly administered ability tests are superior to most available alternatives.

Some of the problems which stem from the testing of disadvantaged groups are of a technical nature and are not related to the issue of discrimination. Reduced reliability is often due to the fact that score distributions obtained from disadvantaged groups are compressed. The same compression(and reduced reliability) is also found when only highly capable individuals are being tested. These problems require technical study and, in some instances, may call for the use of different measures or the development of new and more appropriate tests. The basic issue is not necessarily one of discrimination against a particular subgroup.

Fear, Hostility Aroused

Many of the issues in the testing of disadvantaged groups have both psychometric and social aspects. Some of the current testing procedures should be changed to reduce the fear and hostility that may be engendered by materials felt to be biased or unfair. More attention must be devoted to research with actual score and performance data in order to improve the predictive efficiency of tests.

Discrimination against disadvantaged groups, which is at the root of the concern of many who attack tests, will not be resolved by improved psychometrics alone. Discrimination in the world of work is a social ailment. Although poor showings on tests may be a symptom of the ailment, the use of tests in employee selection is inherently a friendly rather than a hostile act to those who come to the job market from backgrounds of limited opportunity. Society may well have the responsibility of providing effective remedial instruction for those who have been culturally deprived. The rejection of measuring instruments which register the consequence of such deprivation is merely a modern version of killing the messenger who brings bad news.

---

*The above is taken from the *Test Service Bulletin No. 57* of The Psychological Corporation. It was written by Jerome E. Doppelt and George K. Bennett.

REFERENCE INQUIRIES

Reference inquiries, or checking references, is a very important part of the employment procedure. Inquiries are made about prior work experience, character, education, and whatever else may be considered necessary to help arrive at a decision to hire and not to hire an applicant. Inquiries are chiefly addressed to former employers, schools, and personal acquaintances of the applicant.

The names and addresses of the individuals, schools, or firms are taken from the information supplied by the applicant on the application blank.

Former employers are queried about the applicant's dates of employment, the nature of his job, quality of performance, any strong or weak points that stand out and can be remembered, the reason for leaving, and so on. A key question is "Would you rehire?"

Schools are asked about levels of academic achievement, such as completion of courses, graduation, degrees, and majors or concentration of study. They can also report on the former student's attendance record. One of the useful services schools can furnish is that of checking ages of people. School records are kept indefinitely and reveal the age of an individual accurately as a student, before the person may have been tempted to lie about the age and try to change the year of birth.

Form Letters Not Advised

As a suggestion, do not send schools a form letter listing a string of questions. Some details of a former student's record may no longer be accessible in the front office, and a clerk might have to spend hours in the archives hunting for an answer to a question that really does not deserve this much time and trouble. Usually the information that is readily available in the school office is more than sufficient.

Personal references are not used much anymore since their usefulness is questionable. Friends, relatives, acquaintances, and clergymen are likely to give favorable reports. The only value might be to specific questions such as, "How long did the applicant work for his last company?" or "Where did he reside before you met him?"

Police records are worth checking for certain jobs. Local and national bureaus of information could come up with information not obtained in routine inquiries.

Military service records provide data which is useful. Discharge papers tell about the length of service, duty performed, advancement, and type of release from service. It might be well to ask to see such papers, especially for a veteran whose military service is not too far in the past.

Reference inquiries are made by mail, telephone, and personal visit.

Key Question: Would You Rehire?

Most references are checked by mail because this can be done in an easy routine procedure. The signed replies form a permanent record, easily filed for possible future use. But written references also have disadvantages. Most people are reluctant to tell the truth if they think it will hurt someone. They tend to minimize adverse comments. Besides, once the former employee is gone and forgotten, and the sting of his termination no longer felt, a manager is inclined to brush off a written request with a response that has little substance. The tip-off comes when he answers "No" to your question, "Would you rehire?" He is trying to tell something without running the risk of putting his remarks on paper. In effect he is hinting, "Why don't you phone me and I'll tell you why."

The telephone is used because it is faster and more intimate. A direct two-way conversation can clear up questions. The telephone brings two people close together immediately, whereas it is usually total strangers who exchange letters in a routine mail inquiry. For the more important jobs telephone reference checking may be better. In these cases it is advisable to make a written report of the call, documenting the answers received.

The personal visit to a former employer or school is used infrequently since it is time consuming. It is done when the job is unusual or highly important, or when some questionable record needs to be looked into.

There are credit agencies that will check out an individual and report in writing their findings. Their detailed reports tell about the person's family, neighborhood, education, age, employment history, character, reputation, financial stability, and anything else that may be requested. In the process of checking the individual they will uncover any lawsuits, bankruptcies, or criminal record.

It takes time and talent to get useful answers to reference inquiries. It is safe to say that the value of any reference reply is worth very little unless the answer is negative. If it tells nothing new then it merely confirms what is already known. It verifies the information supplied by the applicant. This makes it safer to assume that other information may likewise be taken at face value.

A negative reply, on the other hand, alerts the employer to be on guard and suspect all the information given. If prior dates of employment, for example, are not correct as shown, perhaps the applicant is deliberately trying to gloss over an employment gap. Who knows but what he might be trying to conceal a prison term. A negative reply should be followed up immediately by a telephone call, possibly a personal visit, or a report from an outside agency.

Impress Or Inform

Letter inquiries are usually done by form letter. The one standard letter for all applicants contains vacant spaces which are filled in from data taken off the application blank. The former employer is asked to verify this information. Usually this is followed by a few questions the new employer would like to have answered.

It is amazing how many form letters are designed to impress rather than inform the manager who is considering the applicant. Many ask too many questions which often are difficult or impossible to answer. My personal pet peeve is the letter which contains, among other things, something like this:

	Sup.	Exc.	Good	Fair	Poor
Integrity	☐	☐	☐	☐	☐
Honesty	☐	☐	☐	☐	☐
Personality	☐	☐	☐	☐	☐
Appearance	☐	☐	☐	☐	☐
Attendance	☐	☐	☐	☐	☐
Attitude	☐	☐	☐	☐	☐

Imagine trying to answer these questions conscientiously about a former employee who left five years ago. In the first place, companies do not keep such records. The supervisor may no longer be on the job and the successor is unfamiliar with the former employee. If the supervisor is still around, how good is his memory and is his recollection colored by the circumstances of the termination? Anyway, isn't it possible that the former employee might today be different from what his former employment record reveals? Additional education, work experience, military service, changed marital status, travel, maturity, and the like could make him into a changed person and render the comparison almost useless.

Much to be preferred is a simple and direct request along these lines, as illustrated by the request form reproduced on the following page.

TELEPHONE CHECK

The telephone check is the quickest means of getting outside information about an applicant. It saves time and often saves money as well.

It can be used to verify statements made by the applicant. It can also be used advantageously in advance of a second or followup interview to give the interviewer something to check against as he talks with the applicant.

Dr. Robert N. McMurry, long an advocate of the Patterned Interview, has developed forms for this reference inquiry. The following are offered as samples:

Telephone Check

Telephone Check with Schools

Telephone Check on Sales Applicant

Telephone Check on Executive Applicant

These forms, and others like them, are copyrighted and may be obtained from The Dartnell Corporation, 4660 Ravenswood Avenue, Chicago, Illinois 60640.

Date:_____

May we verify the following information given to us by one of your former employees who has applied to us for a position?

Name_____

Position Held_____

Employment Dates_____

Earnings_____

Reason for leaving your firm_____

Is the above information correct?_____

Would you care to give us additional information on the following questions:

Were services satisfactory?_____

Would you rehire if you had an opening?_____

Do you know of any reason why we should not employ?_____

Is there anything outstanding about this employee that you would like to tell us?_____

Do you suggest we contact you by telephone?_____

Thank you for your cooperation.

Signature_____

_____
Employment Manager

Title_____

FIDELITY BONDS

Embezzlement has reached the proportions of a national scandal, with thievery by employees estimated as totaling over $1 billion annually. To protect themselves, employers purchase fidelity bonds.

Fidelity bonds are explained by John F. Beardsley, secretary of the Hartford Group, and author of Chapter 54 of *Property and Liability Insurance Handbook* by Long and Gregg, published by Richard D. Irwin, Inc. The following is an adaptation of this chapter.

The individual fidelity bond is evidence of an undertaking wherein the surety (insurance company) agrees, subject to stated conditions, to indemnify the obligee (employer) against loss resulting from dishonesty or default of the principal (employee) occupying a position of trust in the service of the company.

Such bond typifies the true surety relationship with two parties (principal-employee and surety) joining to guarantee the third party (obligee-employer) to the specific obligation that the employee will handle with fidelity the property entrusted to him by his employer.

There is also a further identity with suretyship in the inherent concept of no loss ultimately accruing to the surety, because the principal (employee) is required under an extensive body of law to repay the surety for whatever loss the latter might have sustained through employee misdeed.

Blanket Protection Now

Because of turnover, individual bonds, restricted as they are to designated employees and positions, have virtually disappeared from the present business scene, except in such specialized cases as treasurers of clubs, fraternal orders, church groups, and the like, where the sole exposure rests with one or two readily identifiable people. The manager or proprietor of the usual business establishment has to measure an exposure involving many people, and he cannot guess which of these employees will succumb to embezzlement. Recognition of this fact led the surety companies to the development of true "blanket" types of bonds.

FIDELITY DEPARTMENT

APPLICATION FOR FIDELITY BOND
Short Form

Company

Amount, $...................................   Agency...

Premium, $......................................   ....

I hereby make application to the   COMPANY,
cut, to become or continue as my surety on such bond or obligation as may be agreed upon by said
COMPANY and..., my employer,
covering my position as...at...
or any other position to which I may be assigned, from...............................19.........for $.........................or such other
amount as my employer may require; and I hereby affirm that in the following declarations made, and answers given
I state the truth without reservation and for the purpose of inducing the
COMPANY to become or continue my surety.

1. PRINT name in full...Age..........................years.

2. Residence..
                 (Street and number)   (City and State)

3. Business address...
                 (Street and number)   (City and State)

4. Social Security Number..Date of Birth.....................................

5. Name of father..{ Occupation.................................
                                                        { Address.....................................

6. Name of mother...Address....................................
                             (If parents are dead, give below names and addresses of two nearest relatives)

    Name....................................Address...Relationship...................

    Name....................................Address...Relationship...................

7. Full name and address of your wife..

8. How long have you been in the service of above employer?...

9. If under bond, by whom was it furnished?..

10. Has your application for a bond ever been declined?....................If so, by whom?.................................

11. Give amount of your debts other than liens on property...

12. What salary or compensation will you receive?..

13. Give source and amount of income other than salary..

    For Good and Valuable Considerations, I bind myself, my heirs, executors, and administrators, to hold the
COMPANY harmless against, and on demand to pay it, any and all loss,
costs, damages, charges, counsel fees, and expenses which it may sustain or incur, or for which it may become liable,
by reason of having executed said bond, or any renewal, continuation, or transfer thereof; and also against, and on
demand to pay it, any and all loss, costs, damages, charges, counsel fees, and expenses incurred by it in consequence of
executing any other bond or obligation for me, or any renewal or continuation thereof. I do also agree that said Company
may decline to become surety for me upon the bond hereinbefore applied for, or any other bond or obligation, and that it
may cancel or withdraw from such bond, if executed, or any other bond or obligation it may execute for me, or any renewal
or continuation thereof; and I do also expressly relieve said Company and all others from disclosing or furnishing any
information it may have obtained concerning me or my affairs, and do also relieve said Company from any compliance
with any provisions of any laws concerning the disclosure of any knowledge or information which may have been obtained
concerning me or my affairs, and do release and discharge said Company, and every person, association, firm, or corporation furnishing it with any information concerning me or my affairs, from any and all liability or responsibility under or
by reason of any of the provisions of any said laws, and from any and all claims, demands, causes of action, and damages
that may have or purport to have arisen by reason of any such laws, or any amendments thereof, or supplements thereto.

    In Witness Whereof, I have hereunto set my hand and affixed my seal, this..

day of...19.........

Signed in the presence of...   ....
                                                                  (Applicant sign here)

The underwriting for fidelity bonds customarily commences with
an application completed and signed by the employee. A typical
application blank is reproduced above.

Under terms of the blanket bond, the surety agrees to indemnify the employer against loss of money or other property sustained through any fraudulent or dishonest act committed by an employee during the period the bond is in force. This agreement merely means that there has to be a *loss* to the insured, such loss be due to *dishonesty*, and that such dishonesty was on the part of an *employee*.

The bonds cover each and every employee on the insured's payroll, without selection and without designation beyond the definition of "employees" as contained in the contract. New employees are automatically included.

Recent years have seen the development and widespread acceptance of "Combined Crime Coverage" in a package policy to provide fidelity, forgery, and broad-form disappearance and destruction insurance in a single policy for mercantile risks.

LOYALTY PLEDGE

For a while some employees were asked to sign a loyalty pledge, but this practice has fallen into disuse. The requirement is looked upon as an infringement of an individual's rights, and there is speculation that it would not hold up in the courts. In the military, and in certain types of federal employment, a loyalty oath is necessary for security purposes in the handling of classified information.

CONFLICT OF INTEREST

It is customary in many companies to get signed conflict of interest statements from board members, officers, and others in responsible positions. Such a request does not violate a person's constitutional rights.

Where higher level managerial people are placed under contract, it is not unusual to include a clause forbidding the employee from taking a position with a competitor soon after his contract is terminated or expires. To hold up in court such restriction should be reasonable in geographic scope and time.

JOB POSTING

Job posting, or open posting, is a method of publicizing to employees, possibly on bulletin boards, the jobs which are open in the company. The purpose is to fill as many jobs as possible from within the company and also to aid in the promotion of employees who are ready to be rewarded.

This can be a time-consuming procedure since many workers could apply for the same job and all have to be dealt with. Everyone who responds must be interviewed. During the interview the duties are explained and the requirements outlined. The applicant's training and experience are reviewed. Every qualified employee who expresses interest must then be considered to be "in the running" for the job. When the final selection is made the decision must be reported individually to each remaining candidate in such a way as to get his understanding and also to maintain his willingness to apply again when another job appeals to him.

When job vacancies are made known to the workforce, good and bad results may follow.

Good—

Keeps employees informed.

Present employees bring in applicants.

They apply themselves, thereby making their interests known.

They reveal feelings in present placement.

Lets jobs and salary grades for jobs be known.

Bad—

May encourage job hoppers.

May let disgruntled employee "run away" instead of meeting problem in present job.

May attract applicants who are more interested in money than in using their skills.

Results in a long chain reaction at times, with bumping involved.

Sometimes hard to select if ability is the criterion; usually it becomes seniority, especially where a union contract is involved.

It is easier to turn away an outsider than a co-worker.

Rules—

Use a definite posting period and close it, after which accept no more bids.

Announce in a definite place, openly, to avoid suspicion.

Must be controlled by some neutral agency, like personnel, not by a line department.

TRANSFERS

Transfers and promotions should not be confused. They are not the same and the two terms are not interchangeable.

A transfer is a lateral move, within the same labor grade, or from one job to another job of like value and importance. A transfer is a movement from one job to another, with changes in duties, supervision, work conditions, but not necessarily salary. A promotion, on the other hand, is an upgrading from one job level to a higher one, and should carry with it an increase in salary.

Transfers are made for the convenience of the company, the convenience of the worker, or to increase the flexibility of the workforce.

Transfers are made for negative or positive reasons:

Negative—

A worker is not suited for his present job.

His present job is eliminated.

Friction exists.

There is a physical handicap.

Positive—

Improving environment.

Changing to more prestige duties.

Building morale.

Adding experience.

A transfer, while it does not carry with it any automatic consideration for more money, has other advantages. It could offer the employee any of the following:

- A chance for broader experience.

- More suitable work.

- More interesting duties.

- More congenial work group.

- Better supervisor.

- Better hours.

- Location closer to home.

Quite often a manager or foreman is reluctant to suggest a transfer because he is unable to include a wage increase in the deal. This would be unfair to the employee who might eagerly accept the move for any of the above reasons, or others which are understandable to him.

A company may wish to transfer an employee who is worth keeping but who is obviously misassigned. A misfit in one type of work, provided his habits and attitude are good, might find his niche in another line of work. For example: A clerk who goes home tired every night might be better off at the next desk where less math is required.

Beware, however, of the person who seeks transfer as a means of running away from a situation he refuses to correct. Instead of admitting his shortcoming and agreeing with his supervisor to change a bad habit, such as excessive tardiness, he moves out, taking his unsolved problem with him. Before anyone is transferred his performance should be carefully checked. Is his record clear? Is he worth transferring?

Temporary transfers are a stopgap measure for an emergency situation. One or more employees may be transferred temporarily because another part of the company is shorthanded or overloaded and extra people are needed until the problem can be solved. In such cases, the employees may be moved bodily but not on paper; that is, no actual reassignment is effected. If their wages for this interim period are to be charged to the new department, this becomes an accounting transaction. Should the duration of the temporary transfer be more than just a short time, it might be advisable to keep the records straight by issuing the necessary transfer papers when the first move is made and again when the people return to their regular jobs. In all these cases, employees transferred for company convenience to a lower rated job should not be penalized in the paycheck. Should they be working in their temporary duty at jobs which rate higher, some consideration might be given to paying them accordingly.

Transfers are part of the "bumping" process that goes on during a cutback in the workforce. Rather than lay off a worker whose job has been eliminated, a company may permit an employee to bump another worker with less seniority or tenure.

Seniority generally accompanies a worker when he moves. This could be a deterrent since the new department, in addition to getting a loyal and experienced worker, also inherits all that goes with seniority—longer vacation with possibly an early choice, rate of pay possibly higher than others in the same job, etc. Seniority is company-wide and refers to length of service in the total organization. In those few cases where seniority is not plant-wide but departmental, or worse yet, job-line, the terms better be clearly spelled out and understood by all concerned.

PROMOTIONS

The best practice for filling any job vacancy is to select the best qualified candidate available, whether he comes from outside or inside the company. When he comes from within, he is moved into his new job by either transfer or promotion. There is a difference.

A horizontal promotion is really not a promotion but a lateral transfer. This results in a change of duties and opportunities but not in degree of responsibility, of job value, and therefore at no change in salary. (See Transfers.)

A true promotion is an upgrading of a worker's job from one level to a higher one with a correspondingly higher rate of pay.

A vertical promotion is an upgrading in the same area or type of work. Example: a stenographer to secretary.

A prestige promotion or transfer takes a worker to a less strenuous or more attractive job, sometimes at the same pay, but with certain more desirable features. Example: a typist clerk to receptionist.

A systemic promotion is one step in a sequence of jobs planned for workers to enlarge or broaden their understanding of overall operations. In management jobs this could be called job rotation, when the movement is made more in the employee's interest and not only for company convenience. Systematic promotion is a device of getting workers out of blind alley jobs.

Practically every employer boasts of having a promotion-from-within policy. But if a check were made, it could well be that the employees think otherwise.

Avoid Blanket Policies

A blanket statement of promotion-from-within in an employee handbook is not only erroneous but also foolish. No company today fills all its higher job openings from within. Some jobs require background and experience which cannot be found in the present work force. As soon as the first outsider is hired for one of these jobs, the employees know the blasé promotion policy mentioned in the handbook is untrue, and they could be expected to distrust similar statements about other aspects of the employee program.

When an employee is ready for a bigger challenge, and an opportunity for promotion presents itself, it is well to consider the employee. This not only makes it easy for the company to fill the job, but it also offers more responsibility and a better earnings opportunity to a deserving worker. If he is bypassed, there is the likelihood of losing him as he acquires a "what's the use" attitude.

This does not mean that all or most jobs should be filled from within the organization. Promote from within is good policy but should not be a rigid rule to close the door to qualified outsiders. Nor should better jobs be offered to outsiders and denied to present employees. Too much promotion from within results in inbreeding of ideas and experience, and does not take advantage of ideas from outside. An outsider's different viewpoint may be invaluable in some situations.

On the other hand, filling all or most of the job vacancies from the outside does not take advantage of valuable experience gained by employees. In many cases there is no substitute for on-the-job training and know-how. It should also be realized that too little promotion from within results in low morale and high turnover because of lack of opportunity.

Anyhow, jobs ought not to be filled by any company policy that says blindly that one course or the other must be followed. The most practical company policy is the one which says simply that jobs should be given to the best-qualified and best-suited applicant, whether from within the company or outside of it. Anything less, no matter how altruistic it may sound, shortchanges both the company and the workers.

What usually happens is that two types of jobs are filled from within: Those which are in the same field but are heavier or carry more responsibility, and those which call for general training and not for a peculiar skill or special talent.

The better secretarial jobs can often be filled by up-and-coming stenographers who have improved their skill through practice and increased their knowledge of company operations through experience to the point where they are ready for something bigger. A company is fortunate when it has enough movement in its work force to be able to offer bigger job opportunities to employees who have outgrown their present assignments.

Similarly, a job as order checker in a jobbing warehouse can usually be filled by an experienced order filler. Here knowledge of the company and its products is more important than a unique skill of checking. It is easier to teach a loyal company employee the new checking procedures than to acquaint a stranger with thousands of products in the line.

It is for specialty jobs that companies have to go outside. A retail drug or food chain, needing a real estate manager, would be unlikely to find the necessary background among its regular workers. An advertising agency would be hard pressed to promote even the best clerk into the position of commercial artist. A life insurance company would certainly have to bring in a physician from the medical community and not offer the position to any loyal and long-service nonprofessional employee.

There are two avenues which lead to a successful promotion-from-within program:

1. Training programs, to help employees develop beyond present duties. Without this the better jobs will, of necessity, be filled from the outside.

2. A system for recognizing and rewarding growth in individuals. Without this, promotable employees will leave to take their chances elsewhere.

One value of promotion from within lies in its chain reaction. To fill one higher job, which in turn creates a vacancy lower down, at least two persons, and oftentimes more, are involved. Movement in jobs is generally desirable, especially when boredom may be a factor. It is not desirable in all cases as, for instance, a worker who is peculiarly adapted for a certain type of work, or a skilled worker who would have to abandon the one talent that sets him apart from co-workers.

Some jobs never change; some people do not change. But in those cases where jobs grow bigger, we can be grateful that some people grow bigger too, so that these jobs can be filled. One of the basic job satisfactions a worker requires is to enjoy his work and be interested in what he is doing. Work which challenged a worker at first but bores him once he has mastered it does not provide this satisfaction. Ideally, every employee ought to have a job that is just a bit "over his head." This would keep him "on his toes."

Promotion is the answer.

SUPERVISION AND MANAGEMENT PROMOTIONS

There are two main routes to business success, the passive route and the active route. It is entirely possible to get to the top in business by being passive.

A social climber can rise to eminence from humble beginnings by doing practically nothing, but looking good while doing it. Given a well-developed instinct for survival, it is possible in some businesses to get ahead simply by being available, and by being the handiest person to fall heir to the promotion as smarter men move up or out, or otherwise clear the way.

The logical way, however, calls for careful selection of successor prospects. And this task of selecting the one right person need not be difficult as long as we are honest with ourselves, our companies, and our candidates. It is only when we confound the issue by interjecting seniority, loyalty, or sentimental personal qualities that we make the problem complicated.

In the process of selection we should spell out the requirements of the position and then look for people who approximate, or show promise of approximating, the standards. An executive and an automobile may be compared. A man without judgment is like a car without brakes; a man without enthusiasm is like a car without a motor; a man without initiative is like a car without a starter; a man without vision is like a car without lights. We know what specifications we want when we get an automobile; why should it be any different when we get a man?

Some Selection Fallacies

The following list of "Selection Don'ts" indicates some of the fallacies in executive thinking that must be avoided if proper selection of candidates for management is to be achieved:

1. Don't arbitrarily pick the top producer in any area for a bigger job where the demands are quite different.

2. Don't rely too heavily on tests. They are useful in determining intelligence, certain skills or knowledge, even emotional stability or lack of it. But they cannot measure attitude or predict success in applying measurable skills or knowledge. You can't use test results as a crutch against a poor decision on your part.

3. Don't let seniority be a heavy influence lest you select a faithful veteran for a job he is simply not qualified to handle.

4. Don't kid yourself that training is the answer. A candidate who lacks courage, desire, judgment, intelligence, or determination

won't be helped by management training. Such training may fill his notebook but not his heart; it may move his pen but not his spirit. A man has to have it "inside" to be a leader.

5. Don't go overboard on intelligence. I once heard a Phi Beta Kappa described as a man with a key on his watch chain . . . but no watch. Leaders must be intelligent, certainly, but intelligence without stability or character, self-control, or discretion is dangerous. A man's weaknesses must not be overlooked in favor of any outstanding strength.

6. Don't be overimpressed by any college degree. This country is mass-producing college graduates. Some are capable, some are not. Furthermore, today it is possible to get a degree in a wide variety ,of fields, some of which require very little in the way of hard disciplines such as mathematics, science, and languages. An honor student with a degree in "supervised recreation" probably doesn't qualify for management. So instead of looking for a degree, examine the credentials carefully.

7. Don't be misled by popularity. A man who goes out of his way to be liked, who is proud to be known as "one of the boys," may find it difficult, even impossible, to criticize or to reprimand because he doesn't want to run the risk of offending. A manager is often lonesome and by robbing a man of his biggest asset, that of popularity, we destroy the one trait which attracted us to him in the first place.

8. Don't close the door of opportunity to anyone. Selecting only the fair-haired boys is the best way to overlook or discourage some of the untapped talent which is just ripe for development. The crown prince theory would have closed the door to Abraham Lincoln, wouldn't it? Bright prospects should be encouraged, but room must be allowed for the surprise candidate who is not in the spotlight.

The Positive Side

These are some of the "don'ts" that we should avoid. On the other side of the ledger are positive aspects of selection for management promotion. There are three broad groups of factors to consider for an objective, honest, and reliable selection of a man for a management position:

1. The first is talent for the job ahead. A review of his background, skills, prior training, and general knowledge will provide this kind of information. In this area much can be learned from the use of appropriate tests.

2. The second is personality. Now he will be doing his work through others. A leader has to be someone others are "impelled" not "compelled" to follow.

3. The third factor is health, including emotional stability. Good health means more than physical fitness. It also includes peace of mind. Outside interests and relaxations are part of a balanced way of life. Lopsided living is a common cause of executive ill health.

In any selection process for promotion remember that the man or men singled out for management positions must "want" the job. Not everybody, you know, aspires to become an officer in the industrial army. Be happy, not annoyed, by the man who dares to be contrary, who sees challenges instead of problems, who can discard tradition, who doesn't think in stereotypes. Watch for the man who is presently not sufficiently occupied by his job duties; if he has to find extracurricular activities to round out his pattern of job satisfactions this is the signal that you are not channeling his abilities toward company objectives.

Beware of the man who is patient, willing to go along, satisfied that "the system" will take care of him. Loyal and unimaginative people do not make good managers, where creativity is an essential requirement.

The Marks of an Executive

When we make the final selection we will recognize it as the one right choice when we see in the man these three executive traits:

1. Willingness to discipline himself: To manage himself, his time, and his energies toward reaching realistic goals he has established as his objective.

2. Courage to seek change and face risks: With the right to success goes the right to failure. The man who is afraid to take risks does neither—fail or succeed.

3. Capacity for dedication: The extent of being able to be bigger than himself, to lose himself in the cause he espouses.

This last point is worth another comment. Achieving the result, not the credit for doing it, should be the motivation. The salt loses its own identity in order to preserve; the oil is entirely consumed to give light; the yeast is completely absorbed in the dough it transforms. Each sacrifices itself so the function may be fulfilled.

Give me that outlook in a man and I'll give you an executive.

DEMOTIONS

A promotion is easy to make; it is always pleasant to give out good news. A transfer is usually not difficult; at least the employee who is moved is not hurt in earnings. But a demotion is more delicate, even when such move is in the employee's best interest.

A demotion is made for one of two reasons:

1. The employee is unable to meet the performance requirements of his present assignment and is moved to another job which is more in keeping with his talent and ability.

2. An employee whose job is eliminated may be worth keeping and is "parked" on a lower job which is available until another opening comes up which is comparable in level to the one he had.

Demotions in industry should never be used as punishment or other disciplinary action. This practice is followed in the military service where, for example, a sergeant may be "busted" to private for misconduct or an infraction of the rules.

An employee who consistently receives a poor performance rating is obviously misassigned. Where counseling or training cannot bring about an improvement, the only choice may be to demote him to an easier job. In our eagerness to fill vacancies we may be guilty of hiring or promoting individuals who cannot meet the requirements of the job, even after a reasonable trial period. Such employee might actually be happier on a job for which he is better suited.

Followup Important

In those cases where an employee is out of his job through no fault of his own, it would be wise to save him on some lower job rather than release him outright. A followup should be exercised to make certain he is not overlooked later when a higher position for which he qualifies becomes available.

In any event, demoting an employee is no easy matter. It calls for tact and diplomacy in order to let him save face before co-workers. It is actually easier to dismiss a worker than to demote him, for while the hurt may be greater on impact, at least he doesn't have to hang around to wonder whether his fellow workers look upon him as a failure.

A demotion, in addition to hurting a man's pride, might also hurt his pocketbook. No man should be paid more than he is worth. If he has not been able to "cut the mustard" in his previous job, then possibly he was overpaid. This overpayment should not be carried to the lesser job. However, when the demotion is for company convenience, or if the company granted his raise more on seniority than performance, then he should not be penalized.

Most companies are reluctant to cut a worker's pay when he is downgraded in his job . . . unless this is absolutely necessary, or a union agreement spells out such terms. Usually, if his present earnings do not conflict with the wages of employees in the job category to which he is being demoted, there is neither need nor desire to cut his pay. In a lower job classification, of course, he has a reduced earnings potential.

For a suggested policy, see Wage Administration.

TERMINATIONS

A policy, preferably in written form and published for the guidance of managers, should be used for terminations. When an employee is separated from the payroll, for whatever reason, the specifics should not be left to chance, or worse yet, left to individual whim.

Voluntary. Most terminations are voluntary. The employee takes the initiative and quits. He may be unhappy with his job, or he may be quitting because of personal reasons or for circumstances beyond his control. It is customary to expect the courtesy of a notice, usually two weeks.

Involuntary. An employee may be separated from the payroll with the action initiated by the company. This action usually follows a warning or two to an unsatisfactory performer, possibly even a period of probation. When this release occurs it is considered proper, although legally not required, to give the employee a two-week notice or two weeks' pay in lieu of notice. Most of the time the company elects the latter option, preferring to pay off an undesirable employee rather than have him, unhappy and disgruntled, riding out his time without being very productive anyway.

A typical company policy is to pay two weeks' pay in lieu of notice to an employee with at least one year's service. The same policy might allow one week's pay for employees with less than one year of service; while this consideration may seem generous at times, especially if the employee has been working only a few weeks, it is nonetheless fair since the employee, at time of hire, quit his previous job, or at least surrendered any other job offers, and now needs paid time during which to start looking for a job all over again.

Discharge. Apart from employees who are terminated involuntarily, there are also occasions where an employee must be fired. The reasons are many and are well known to employers. Here the action is generally more sudden, and separation from the payroll is immediate. It is still customary to give such a fired employee two weeks' pay at time of discharge.

Retirement. At time of retirement an employee is paid up to retirement date, plus any unused earned vacation, severance pay if such program is in effect, and there may be special amenities such as official lunch, unofficial party, gifts, etc.

Maternity. Most companies grant some form of leave of absence or furlough to married women who leave because they are pregnant. It is unusual to continue the employment beyond the sixth month of pregnancy; departure may be earlier if medical advice indicates this to be advisable. Considerations include continuation in the company's employee hospital-medical insurance program, and reassurance of rehire, with no loss of previously earned seniority and benefits upon return to work. The return to work is within a prescribed time, generally no more than three months following delivery.

Furloughs. There are other circumstances when it might be in the company's interest to furlough an employee who leaves instead of giving an outright termination. This practice is followed, of course, only when the employee leaves because of personal reasons; it is not used when an employee quits to try another job, only to keep the door open in case the new job doesn't work out and the employee wants to return. A furlough protects previously earned seniority credits and benefits, and carries certain rehire rights. Seniority and benefits do not accrue during the period of the furlough. They are held in abeyance and reinstated upon return to work.

Pay for Unused Vacation. An employee who terminates his employment from a company, for any reason, ordinarily is paid for any vacation accrued under the company's vacation policy which is still unused at time of termination.

Exit Interviews. Whenever possible, it is sound practice to exit interview employees who leave, especially those terminating of their own accord. This gives the employees an opportunity to express privately their real reasons for leaving the company, and it gives the company a last chance to learn from them any thoughts they may have about company practices or about supervision.

SEVERANCE PAY

At time of termination an employee is paid for all time worked since his last pay period until the date of separation. In case he is dismissed he may be given an additional two weeks' pay in lieu of notice. It is also customary to pay a terminating employee for any earned vacation still unused.

But many companies have a severance pay program which pays an employee extra money when he leaves. This severance pay plan may benefit all employees who leave for any reason, or it may be a program which applies only in cases of layoffs. There is a difference between the conditions under which an employee loses his job through no fault of his own (as a relocation of the plant or a cutback in production) and another separation in which a worker quits of his own accord. Many companies feel an obligation to longtime loyal employees who lose their jobs because of a change in circumstances initiated by the company.

Severance pay arrangements are clearly spelled out in many union contracts. One, for example, provides for 3½ days for each year of service, with a maximum amount equal to 70 days' pay. Every employee with five years of service or more is eligible for this consideration.

Another union agreement refers to severance pay as "Dismissal Indemnity." This is paid to any employee discharged, in addition to two weeks' notice of dismissal. A lump sum at the rate of two weeks' pay is paid for the first six months of service plus one week's pay for each subsequent six months of continuous service up to a maximum of 64 weeks' pay for 378 months or more.

Many nonunion companies also have provisions for severance pay. A typical layoff-plan calls for

2 weeks' pay	less than 5 years' service
4 weeks' pay	5 years up to 10 years
6 weeks' pay	10 years up to 15 years
8 weeks' pay	15 or more years of service

Programs such as these are ongoing plans which are applicable in the normal course of business. There are circumstances, of course, which are special for which arrangements peculiar to the situation are made. When a company moves to another state, for instance, those staff members who stay with the company can expect to be paid their moving expense and may even get help in selling their present homes and buying new ones. However, those who cannot make the move   (and this is by far the majority of rank-and-file workers) are usually "paid off" over a period of time in order to cushion the blow. The same is true when a firm goes out of business. Employees are given all the help possible to find new jobs, but for those who are just "thrown out of work" some form of financial assistance is provided.

MOONLIGHTING

The employee handbook of the Fort Worth division of General Dynamics Corporation contains the following statement:

Secondary Employment

Your job at the Fort Worth Division is your primary employment. Any other job is secondary.

If you have an extra job that, in our opinion, affects your work, or causes you to lose time from your job, or is contrary to the best interests of General Dynamics, you must either quit it or you will subject yourself to dismissal from General Dynamics.

HOW GOOD ARE FIRING PRACTICES?

Many companies that have well-established hiring procedures are very stupid when it comes to firing methods.

That's what the man said—this friend of mine who, after 30 years as an electrical engineer, was promoted to chief engineer. He faced the unpleasant task of firing a young man. He couldn't bear to take a job away from a man who had a wife and family to support. He didn't know how to fire the man, and there was no place to go for direction.

To those of us who are making a lifetime career of personnel and industrial relations work, this charge sounded like a severe indictment. So I decided to investigate . . . and by gad, the man is right. There is nothing available on the subject.

I began by reviewing our own statistics for the past year. Approximately 11 percent of our terminations were involuntary. The most common reason was "poor attendance" and "unsatisfactory work" was second. All in all, however, it appeared that we were reasonably tolerant and could have fired more. Some employees were retained who, perhaps for their own good, should have been fired.

Justifying our patience with problem employees, we pointed to the labor market at this time, arguing with ourselves that the replacements, in addition to being untrained, would most likely be no better.

In other situations we were optimistic, eternally hopeful, that with continued understanding and kindness the problem employee might somehow develop into a productive worker. Besides, those who anticipate being fired often make it difficult by being well-liked, exceptionally cooperative, or otherwise acceptable.

The truth is that in most instances the supervisor just disliked the unpleasantness that goes with firing a co-worker. This did not reflect so much his inadequate training or his inability, but rather it revealed a soft heart behind a gruff exterior, which hesitated to inflict a hurt upon another sensitive human being.

This analysis of our own practices disclosed little of value except to show that in this respect we were behaving very much like other companies, as we discovered when we widened our research to other firms, local and national.

From all of our discussions we learned who is being fired, how this is being done, and also how it can be done better.

Who Is Being Fired

Comparing notes with other companies it appears that workers are discharged for five main reasons: (1) for cause, such as dishonesty; (2) continuous disobeyance of necessary orders; (3) personality conflicts; (4) inability to perform (didn't measure up); and (5) what is even worse than lack of skill, that is, lack of will.

Dismissal seems to be the line of least resistance to apply to the employee who:

Lacks initiative or concentration.

Has outside interests which interfere.

Makes too many errors.

Becomes hopelessly confused with unfamiliar terminology.

Is slow.

Develops questionable behavior.

Has a poor memory.

Makes disparaging remarks against management.

Shows no capabilities.

Has inadequate skill for the job.

Is undependable.

Can no longer cope with reasonable volume of work.

Borrows money.

Is a disturbing influence.

Has chronic tardiness.

Becomes involved in a personality conflict.

One mental health expert reported that "from 20 to 25 percent of all employees in every corporation or industrial unit are suffering from mental disorders. They range from psychoses to industrial maladjustment, manifested in absenteeism, accidents, dissatisfaction, alcoholism, turnover, and poor job performance."

He added: "In dealing with these problems the essential factor is the understanding of the individual, rather than labeling his behavior with a diagnostic tag."

When the employees become serious deterrents to production or morale, two courses of action are possible. A supervisor can get rid of them by firing them, or he can attempt to provide or obtain sympathetic guidance which will help to reduce or possibly eliminate the problem.

What should companies do with employees who become problems? To many of them the answer apparently is to fire them. Even when this is the best choice, is their method of firing good?

How Firing Is Being Done

Firing is always distasteful regardless how carefully done and how proper the motive. A professional baseball general manager is fired. The sports world is stunned but nobody questions the owner's right to take such action. A national television personality is fired. His followers are disappointed, but nobody criticizes the network. Both cases were blazoned across the front pages of practically every newspaper in the country.

Both these men continued to receive full pay since their unexpired contracts were honored. But this legal compliance doesn't impress the public, which reacts more to the unexpected suddenness. Continuing their salaries as a legal requirement took some of the onus off the owners. But getting fired hurts people's pride more than their pocketbooks. No matter how the blow is cushioned, it leaves an indelible smear on their work record.

In some instances firing may actually be best for the worker—the old argument that a change of scenery will do him good. But even sympathetic firing leaves a scar; it hurts his ego.

Firing for cause is relatively easy—especially for the self-righteous manager. A variety of techniques, however, are used in the other situations.

Many supervisors use crude measures, believing better methods are not called for. They feel it is better to "get it over as fast as possible." Another trick is the "do it when I'm out of the office" routine.

Sometimes a boss "releases" a certain employee to reassert himself. It's either "him or me" . . . but as long as the boss has the power of life and death over the employee's job, you know who gets the ax! In the process the boss loses face with other employees whose sympathies tend to lie with the underdog.

Oftentimes it is difficult for some supervisors to explain the real reason for firing an employee. Supervisors put up with an employee who has an undesirable habit or characteristic, as, for example, carelessness; then when action is finally called for they hang their hats on some more convenient excuse, such as excessive absenteeism caused by poor health. This eases the employee out of the company, but it does not help him understand his own shortcomings, which were serious enough to cost him his job.

Many supervisors want to retain their right to the decision to fire, but expect to shift the act of firing—"giving him the bad news"—to some removed source such as the personnel office.

A heartless separation reflects a cruel company to the general public. A stupid firing reveals a poorly trained management. A company's reputation in the community is often measured by such acts.

How to Do It Better

Since it was assumed at the outset that hiring procedures are better than firing practices, possibly a review of existing employment practices might contain a lesson or two for us.

Hiring procedures are quite formal in most companies. Even in companies where procedures are not generally considered to be formalized, they are nonetheless well established through practice.

Firms have such practices as personal indoctrination, group orientation, organized tours, first day or first week checklists, bench interviews, big sisters or sponsors, and the like. Actually, the initial interview has a three-fold purpose: to get information, to give information, and to make a friend.

The object, of course, is to have the new employee, as soon as he is hired, become a well-adjusted and productive citizen of the worker community in which he chose to place himself.

If by comparison firing techniques are not as good, perhaps it is because they have not been as well planned. To be more effective these procedures should be clearly spelled out. The supervisor ought not to be left to his own devices, required to stumble through as best he can.

Possibly taking a cue from hiring practices, it might be in order to suggest that, like employment interviewing, it is most important who does the firing, and how it is done. This does not mean that one person should do it all, but it does suggest that all who do it should be properly trained. The termination interview could also have three purposes: (1) to give reasons and in that way try to get understanding; (2) to inquire what the action may do to him, thereby learning how best to be helpful; and (3) to part company as friends.

The fact remains that firing unwanted employees is one of the toughest problems a manager has to face. He should try all sorts of means to avoid excessive firing—by transfer, training, or counseling those worth saving. He should be careful, however, not to evade his responsibility of firing through the use of transfer, thereby merely transplanting a problem case and expecting someone else to eventually do his dirty work for him.

227

Maybe companies should not fire so many. After all, in so doing they merely send their problem to another employer . . . and take the chance of getting one from him in exchange. People earmarked for dismissal should be carefully re-evaluated to determine whether the objection on the surface may conceal hidden worth beneath. A few rough edges worn down can change a stone into a gem.

When the employee is not entirely at fault, as in the case of personality conflicts or misassignments, perhaps a shift to other duties, other supervision, or another work environment might solve the problem and spare him the hurt that always accompanies a firing, particularly one that he does not understand.

Whenever firing seems to be the better choice, supervisors should try to do it without hurting the individual. That way they stand a good chance of not hurting themselves or their companies. Even when a separation is made to appear as a resignation, or by mutual agreement, there is always the suspicion that the action was initiated by management—that the employee was fired.

Generally it is safer all around to be straightforward in each situation. A fair and honest appraisal of the conditions leading up to the firing of an individual leaves less to be disputed. A blunt approach is not necessarily recommended; it may be better to generalize and infer that management shares the fault in that it "might not have used the employee properly."

Wherever possible, offer termination pay and other considerations. The employee who resigns usually gets considerations, such as payment for unused vacation. The fired employee is out of work suddenly, as contrasted with the one who does so by choice, and he needs all the assistance he can get.

Just how to go about this may depend upon circumstances. Consider the effect of firing an employee on the community; in a small town this is far more critical than in a larger impersonal city. Consider its effect on the product or service; will it cause customers to doubt or respect the firm's good intentions? Consider also the nature of the business; obviously a business with face-to-face dealings, as a department store, must treat firing different from a factory where the employee has less opportunity to affect customer relations.

Everybody would gain if we could learn to do this better. Any improvement would have a wholesome effect on the person involved, on company relations with friends and outsiders, and on other employees whose feelings of security in their jobs and trust in their future progress may otherwise be shaken.

What is the most satisfactory or effective way to fire people? There appears to be no authoritative source material to turn to for guidance. It is difficult to learn by example of others, as in other facets of employee relations. There is no pooling of ideas on the subject of firing, no publishing of experiences, as on other management problems. Apparently no one has yet come up with any "one best way" to do this.

Since the act of firing is of major importance to the individual involved, it is absolutely necessary that it be done with tact, discretion, and sincerity of purpose. Because there is always the possibility of untoward ramifications, it is vital that it be thoroughly contemplated and skillfully executed.

EXIT INTERVIEWS

The exit interview is the final step in the employment procedure. It is conducted in the personnel office during the terminating employee's last day on the job. The purpose is to:

1. Try to uncover the real story behind the termination.

2. Locate trouble spots that contribute to turnover.

3. Assure the terminating employee of his rights—insurance, pensions, and other benefits.

4. Distribute the Unemployment Compensation brochure as required by law.

5. Go over final paycheck and other settlement compensation (pay for unused vacation, separation pay, pay in lieu of notice, etc.).

6. Make a necessary record of the circumstances surrounding the termination to satisfy government regulations and union agreements.

7. To part as friends.

PATTERNED EXIT INTERVIEW

Date_____

Employee's
Name_____ Clock No._____ Dept._____ Shift_____ Supervisor_____

Job_____Length of Service_____ Selection Rating: 1 2 3

Final Disposition: ☐ Quit ☐ Discharged ☐ Laid Off ☐ On Leave ☐ Salvaged

Interviewer's evaluation of real reason for termination_____

Rating for rehire: 1 2 3 4 Why?_____

I. INTERVIEW WITH SUPERVISOR

I understand_____ is leaving. Did he work directly for you? ☐ No, ☐ Yes; How long?_____
      (Name)   Does supervisor know him

What was his job?_____ What was his final pay rate?_____
            Does this check with records?   Does this check?

What did you think of the quality of his work?_____
                                        A careful worker? Thoroughly trained?

What about the quantity?_____
                                  Industrious? Properly trained?

Has there been any change in his performance recently? ☐ No, ☐ Yes; What?_____ Why?_____
                                          Correctable? Temporary?

How did he get along with others?_____
                                  Well adjusted socially? Given proper orientation?

What supervisory problems did you have with him?_____
                                Is he a trouble maker? How well has supervisor handled him?

Why is he leaving?_____
                                  Is this the real reason? Can termination be avoided?

Why right now?_____
                                  What is the full story? Can termination be avoided?

Is he worth trying to salvage? ☐ Yes, ☐ No; Why?_____
                                  Does this affect his suitability for all jobs?

(If yes) Would you like him back on his old job? ☐ Yes, ☐ No; Why?_____
                                  Is this consistent?

Do you know of any other jobs he can handle? ☐ Yes, ☐ No; Specify_____
                                  What is the best job for him?

What is his home life like?_____
                                  How has it affected his work? Does supervisor know him as well as he should?

Has there been any change in his home life recently? ☐ No, ☐ Yes; Specify_____
                                  Temporary? Correctable?

What are his strongest points?_____
                                  How does this affect his job suitability?

Where is he weakest?_____
                                How does this affect his job suitability?

Exit Interviewer_____

Exit interviews provide personnel people with meaningful information. This patterned model, developed by Dr. Robert N. McMurry, is distributed by The Dartnell Corporation.

II. INTERVIEW WITH EMPLOYEE

rstand that you're leaving. Before you do, I'd like to find out a little bit about your experience with the company. Let's see now . . . . . .

have another job? ☐ Yes ☐ No (If "Yes") Where?_____ What is new rate?_____

ng have you worked here?_____
_____Reasonable time? Evidence of improper selection?

ind of work have you been doing?_____

ther kinds of work have you ever done?_____
_____Are these related to work here? Helpful in salvage?

ind of work do you like best?_____**Why?**_____
_____Evidence of poor selection?

you first started here who introduced you to the people you worked with?_____
_____Proper orientation?

lly was your job explained to you?_____**By whom?**_____
_____Proper training?

d you like your supervisor?_____
_____Good supervision? Enough supervision?

ll did he seem to know his job?_____
_____Good supervision? Adequate training?

bout his handling of gripes or complaints?_____
_____Good supervision?

have "pets" or play favorites?_____
_____Good supervision?

oubles have you had with him?_____
_____A trouble maker? Good supervision?

as your final pay rate?_____**When was your last increase?**_____
_____In line?_____Understandable?

you feel about your pay?_____
_____Reasonable attitude?

you feel about your progress with the company?_____
_____Reasonable? Has he been overlooked?

ould tell the president of the company exactly how you feel about the way the company is run, what would you tell him?_____

_____

ave you liked best about your job here?_____
_____Are policies made clear? Legitimate gripes?

ave you disliked about it?_____
_____Healthy attitude?

e you leaving?_____
_____Is this real reason? Can termination be avoided?

ht now?_____
_____What is the full story? Can termination be avoided?

ge seems possible) If a more satisfactory arrangement can be worked out, would you be willing to stay? ☐ No, ☐ Yes; Specify changes

_____
_____Reasonable?

_____Exit Interviewer_____

Other side of McMurry's patterned exit interview affords lots of space for obtaining the terminating employee's side of the story.

The exit interview procedure is intended to insure fairness to the worker as well as protection for the company. It applies to both voluntary and involuntary terminations. In those cases where the employee is not in the office on his last day (at another location, absent, or unreported and removed from payroll) the best substitute is to have someone in personnel write a letter and offer to be of service.

One company's policy manual reads, "An exit interview, like any other interview, is a 'conversation with a purpose.' During the exit interview the employee will be permitted to express himself freely about the reason for leaving. Any misunderstanding that might have resulted in his leaving will be corrected. Insofar as it is possible to do so, each employee who leaves will be sent away with the feeling that he has been given a sympathetic, full, and unbiased hearing; that he has an understanding, or at least a knowledge, of the company's position; and that he has satisfactory information about rights and benefits for his personal use."

The report of the exit interviewer should be in writing. Eventually it will be placed in the employee's file to become part of his permanent record. In the meantime it may be discussed with the supervisor. If quits and/or firings are unusually high, it would be well to summarize and analyze the reasons to determine whether any corrective action may be called for. A high turnover rate may indicate that supervisory training is needed, that hiring patterns should be re-examined, or that pay rates may have fallen below the community average.

LAYOFFS

In the American way of doing business, it is inevitable that there will be periodic adjustments when production overtakes demand. From the standpoint of employment, this means layoffs. The alternative is to sacrifice the free enterprise system in favor of a planned economy with the government establishing controls. Both the industrialist and the worker feel this is a price they are unwilling to pay for the guarantee of constant employment.

Adjusting supply to demand would not be so difficult if it were the nature of people to put aside some of their earnings in good years for the possible rainy day. But in an era of credit buying and deficit spending, few people save to provide for their own financial security. As in so many other voids created by the people, government has moved in to help fill the gap. Unemployment insurance, paid for by a tax on employers, provides at least subsistence living for a period of time during which the worker waits to be recalled or looks elsewhere for other employment.

When cutbacks in employment are called for, the employer should think not only of his problem but also that of the employees being laid off. He cannot afford to be impersonal. If he deals only in number of workers and forgets that these workers are human beings, he is entitled to all the grief such a selfish viewpoint will surely bring him.

First Step: Explanation

As a start he should try, as best he can, to explain the need for the retrenchment in the hope that through understanding he may gain the sympathy and support of his workers. If they know the problem they will better accept his action. Nothing is as cruel as abruptly cutting off a man from his job without a satisfactory explanation and some hope for rehire or some help for relocation.

There are many ways to communicate the layoff policy to workers. The house organ, bulletins, announcements, or memos are all available. But these are merely substitutes for the best method, that of a straight and honest face-to-face talk. To the individual employee this is a more sincere approach than that of hiding behind an impersonal piece of paper. "Give 'em the bad news while I am out of the office" is the worst possible way of handling this delicate problem.

Instead of laying off half of the work force, it might be better to work all employees half time. This should, at least, be considered. Maybe a shortened workweek will help spread the work. Every effort should be made to lay off as few workers as possible.

What about the employees who are let go? These are the same workers who until recently were lauded for their loyalty and value to the firm. Are they now simply cut loose? Or is there a serious attempt made to give them assurance, guidance, and hope?

Do they understand the method of recall? How soon may they expect to be contacted? Do they understand their rights to their job? What benefits, such as unemployment insurance, are explained? What provision has been made for continuing their group insurance? Is some program put into action to keep in touch with these temporarily laid-off employees so that their valuable training and experience does not go elsewhere?

What happens if they fail to return to work on the call-back? Do they realize the stake they have in the company and the investment they had accrued through previous service? Are they aware of where they stand in the pension or profit-sharing plans?

Any layoff of employees is critical and even the most sympathetic approach does little to lessen the sting. Layoff and recall are difficult problems. They are further complicated when a union agreement is involved. Usually the terms are clearly spelled out and, to some degree, the union can take some of the pressure off management since it is not involved in the *decision* for the layoff, but in the mechanics of handling it.

Moving Problem Similar

But a curtailment of production or services is not the only cause of layoffs. The same problem, without the prospect of recall, obtains when a company moves to a new location afar off. Except for management, top staff personnel, and some specialists, very few employees will move with the company. They will, by choice or necessity, stay behind when the company leaves.

In such case many things can be done to soften the blow. Among them are:

1. Early announcement of the move so that workers may plan accordingly.

2. Use of temporary workers to reduce the number of permanent employees who are affected.

3. Severance pay arrangement; example: so much for each year of service.

4. Job-seeking assistance and time off to look for jobs with other friendly and cooperative employers.

At best, any layoff is a nasty and unpleasant task. Handling it in the best interest of the workers, their families, the community, and the company calls for management skills of the highest order.

HOW MANY REALLY ARE UNEMPLOYED?

Unemployment figures coming out of Washington can be misleading. Without a doubt this is the most significant single figure given common currency in the country. The White House watches it, both political parties seize upon it, business and labor leaders argue over it, and economists try to interpret it.

But what does it really tell us? Who is included and who is not? The Bureau of Labor Statistics has its own interpretation of what "being unemployed" means. The arbitrary standard is 30 days. Anyone who has not worked within a 30-day period is officially unemployed even if he has signed a contract to go to work.

A teacher on summer vacation waiting to start teaching at a new school is considered unemployed. A teacher on summer vacation who is not changing schools is considered employed.

A Million Boys and Girls

A baby sitter who has not received a call is unemployed. The definition takes in teen-agers down to the age of 14, but only when the 14-year-old has held a job or says he is looking for a job. At any given time, it is likely that at least one million boys and girls, aged 14 and 15, may be included in the official Washington figure on unemployment. This, despite the child labor laws and the minimum wage laws which bar full time work for these same youths.

As many as a million persons—teen-agers, housewives, older persons—switch in and out of the labor market, and the lists of unemployed and employed, at any time. They work as little as one hour a week.

One has to wonder what the unemployment figure might be if there were no war effort or defense activity to absorb so many thousands of men and women who would otherwise be available in the job market. There are those who feel that the Peace Corps, Vista,

Job Corps, and similar programs are convenient government schemes for keeping the number of unemployed at a respectable low level.

The irony is that there are more jobs unfilled than there are people unemployed. The challenge then, for government and industry, is to make the unemployed employable. This is presently the number one domestic problem both from the standpoint of humanitarianism and of economics.

WHY EMPLOYEES QUIT

Much has been written about the reasons employees quit. Many good speeches have been delivered on the same subject. Yet all over the country workers are quitting jobs at an increasing rate. Turnover percentages are going up.

Perhaps very little can actually be done to stem the tide. The restlessness among workers may be a product of the full employment era, especially in offices, in which it is easy for workers to transfer. Part of it may come from living in a mobile economy in which workers and families move about.

If little can be done to control turnover, at least something might be done to control the literature on this subject. Most of the articles and speeches come under the heading of "talking to ourselves."

The same can be said for the assortment of curatives which these articles and talks advocate. Some are discussed in great detail, and in a most convincing manner. But the sad fact is that very few, if any, have any effect on turnover.

The only article which would make sense would be one written by the terminating employees—not by their bosses. Many companies, recognizing that the stated reason is often not the real one, attempt self-correction through exit interview procedures. Some companies use followup questionnaires 30 to 90 days later in an effort to learn whether a study of their former employees' new jobs or later explanations might reveal hidden significant data. While these devices serve a useful purpose they are not entirely factual, nor are they really necessary.

Most supervisors know why their workers leave. The reasons given are usually quite close to the truth. Such statements as "husband transferred," and "illness in family," and "going back to school," are correct. And supervisors generally are close enough to their people to get explanations like these which are understandable and acceptable.

The only way to cut down terminations such as these is not to hire vulnerable employees in the first place. A quick analysis of a company's turnover report will indicate the weak spots in the hiring process. But in today's tight labor market it is imperative that many such applicants be accepted.

But it is the employees who quit to try their luck elsewhere that should concern management. In these cases, supervisors also know the reasons their workers leave. But because they hate to face facts, especially when these facts reflect unfavorably on their own abilities and personalities, they hide behind any available procedure which produces a more plausible excuse.

The typist who reports that she is taking a job closer to home for more money is telling the straight story—but not the whole story. In her job hunt she would not even consider another position where transportation was worse or the take-home pay less . . . would she? But the reason she went out looking in the first place is the one which the supervisor tries to avoid.

The underlying cause of excessive terminations has been, is and always will be salary. A climbing turnover rate is a direct barometer of what workers think about their earnings opportunities. Nothing in any employee relations program should be depended upon to offset inadequate rates of pay.

Impersonality and Pressure

In most companies, however, salary structures are satisfactory, or are quickly adjusted simply as a matter of survival. Yet terminations persist. Why?

There are many reasons, perhaps, but the chief ones are impersonality and pressure.

Both of these factors are behind controllable terminations. Both of these factors are getting worse in the present conduct of business.

Whatever labor unrest exists today can be blamed directly on the boss. American business has neglected its most important asset—its employees—causing more disquietude and restlessness than ever before in the history of the country.

This blunt accusation may sound harsh at first, especially in view of the social development of employee relations programs. "Look what we're all doing for our people," is the stock answer . . . which is usually followed by throwing up the hands in desperation. The reason the problem is more serious than ever before is simply that employees are finally able to react to unfairness and lack of job satisfaction by asserting themselves. They are no longer at the mercy of heartless or blundering managers (one is as bad as the other) and they express their displeasure quietly by taking matters into their own hands—by quitting.

Much of this is caused by poor communications, which often deprives a well-intentioned management of credit for having employees' best interests at heart. Downward communications are bad enough; upward communications just do not exist to any effective degree anywhere.

Some of the best advice which managers receive with open notebooks but closed minds, is the following:

1. *Acquire the confidence of people.* Don't proceed on any program unless and until you can do so in a climate of mutual trust and respect. Otherwise your employees will be apprehensive, suspicious, and defensive against management.

2. *Try to gain understanding of the workers.* This means relating your planning, your program, and your progress with it individually, not collectively, since no two workers are alike. Different people have different fears and require different considerations.

3. *Keep people properly informed.* Misinformation you may not be guilty of; but you will be guilty of something worse—lack of information. Remember, in the absence of information from management, workers will have a tendency to furnish the missing link of information themselves, as they see it. And you may not be happy with the consequences.

Still the problem of terminations continues . . . and worsens. Why? Because managers cannot reverse their habits to coincide with an about-face in the employment situation.

Regain Leadership

There is no easy cure, least of all wages, which have never been so favorable. Impersonal means cannot be used to solve personal problems. Human understanding is necessary.

The president of a national corporation suggested some obvious steps toward a solution:

1. Speed up the flow of ideas from employees.

2. Scrap "company policy or practice" and listen to the workers.

3. Make personnel management a top job.

4. Give more thought to picking supervisors.

He added that "businessmen lost their leadership because they failed to lead."

For the first time in history, ours is no longer an employer market. Today it is an employee market. Procedures and attitudes which were developed out of the pattern of the past won't work in today's changed situation.

We know why employees quit. Changing a method or procedure won't help much. Trying to change our people is futile. Improvement will come only when we are willing to change ourselves which, after all, is the only element over which we have control.

REDUCE TURNOVER—INCREASE PROFITS

Of all the problems in personnel management the one pertaining to labor turnover is one of the most perplexing—and unanswerable. Many companies are concerned with turnover. They are searching for some answer, some guidance, but finding nothing that is really helpful.

Comparisons of turnover rates between companies prove nothing. Apparently there is no standard formula for figuring turnover rates. Hence, percentage comparisons are meaningless.

In an effort to dispense the fog, a search was made through

dozens of management textbooks to see what the academic approach might be. This effort resulted in the remarkable discovery that many of the recognized texts on office management and personnel administration hardly mention the subject at all. Makes one wonder what practical ideas the newly-hatched technicians from the campus are bringing into the business world.

And yet, although few companies agree upon the nature of turnover, they all admit that it is costly and therefore worth worrying about.

One author referred to turnover as "Management's Blind Spot," an area, he said, where management could cut costs sharply but many companies do little about it.

The term labor turnover is an adaptation from the field of merchandising. It is defined as the gross movement of people into and out of active employment status. The index of this movement is the measurement of labor turnover known as the turnover rate.

Turnover is one of the few readily measurable aspects of industrial instability. It is one of the best tests of the relative value of employee relations policies and practices within a company.

The three standard methods of computing turnover are based on accessions, replacements, or separations.

In any computation, the rate is generally defined as the number of accessions, replacements, or terminations per month or year per one hundred of the working force.

The working force is the average number on the payroll during the period for which the computation is made. In the above methods the terms are defined as follows:

Accessions are the hiring of new workers or the rehiring of former employees.

Replacements are persons hired to fill vacancies caused by terminations.

Separations include all quits, layoffs, and discharges.

Besides these three standard methods there are various other computations that are sometimes made. They are mentioned here but not necessarily recommended.

The stable force rate is the proportion of all employees not absent more than two pay periods per year.

The labor flux rate is the ratio of total accessions and separations to the fulltime working force.

The continuance rate is the proportion of employees hired at a specified date who are still on hand at the end of a given and fairly extensive period of time.

The net labor turnover rate is the number of replacements per hundred workers in the average work force.

In most companies there exists what is known as the "refined rate." This merely slants the computation to a figure which is less embarrassing than the bold facts. It is the "true" rate watered down to a more favorable percentage.

The "Quit Rate" Formula

Here again no uniform deviations are used; the modifications vary from one company to another depending up on what each one wants to prove. Eliminated from consideration are such items as unavoidable separations, as caused by illness, death, military service, moving from the area, following husband who transfers, and the like. Many companies do not include part-time or temporary workers. Others deduct pregnancies and retirement.

In these cases a more realistic figure would be the Quit Rate. This ignores the above separations as well as the involuntary terminations. It considers only employees who quit, whom the company lost to competitors or to more fertile fields. Actually this is the only group over which management is usually concerned.

For most purposes a simple arithmetic computation is satisfactory, and tells the truest story. A simple method is subject to limitations, however, since it does not take into account seasonal or cyclical fluctuations.

One simple and straightforward method presents a very practical picture. The average number of employees during the month (or the number at the end of the month if the force is stable) is divided into the total number of separations during that month. This gives the turnover rate for the month.

This formula is expressed as follows:

$$labor\ turnover\ rate = \frac{number\ of\ separations}{average\ number\ on\ payroll}\ X\ 100$$

The same-average or end of month number of employees divided into the total number of separations for the past twelve months gives the annual turnover rate. Each month the current month's figures are used and the 13th-month figures dropped so that a moving average turnover rate results.

Plotted on a graph, the year's high and low figures are easily recognized and trends from one period to another can be charted.

In calculating the turnover rate certain facts need to be known. To arrive at the average work force the number of employees on the payroll at the beginning and end of the period must be established. All terminations, whether voluntary or involuntary, must be accounted for, as well as all accessions, both hires and rehires.

Transfers between departments and divisions should not be included in a company's turnover rate since these shifts do not represent separations from the company.

Some of the factors affecting turnover are changes in wage rates, working hours, working conditions, and inconsistencies in policies. One of the most important factors is supervision.

Wage-Turnover Ratio

Turnover is a direct barometer of wage levels. When turnover is high, wages should be examined for they might have fallen to substandard level. High turnover is also a sign of serious other problems. It signals the need for more careful selection procedures and more extensive training programs.

Some turnover is inevitable. Some turnover is *desirable*, to bring in new blood and new ideas. A certain amount of turnover is not unhealthy—it prevents an organization from stagnating. But excessive turnover is expensive, too expensive to ignore.

The cost of turnover is measurable in dollars. Included are such items as acquisition costs (advertisements, agency fees, interview, tests, etc.), medical examinations, training time (both formal and informal are costly), and perhaps severance pay for the employee who left. Anyone who estimates these expenses soon learns that they add up to sizable amounts.

But turnover costs are more than money. Employees who quit because of dissatisfaction are a permanent source of ill-will that frequently counter-balances expensive public relations programs and prejudices potential employees against the management.

To improve the turnover picture these recommendations are presented:

- Make the initial employment contact pleasant.
- Give honest recruiting information.
- Utilize turnover analysis to improve selection techniques.
- Establish realistic hiring rates.
- Indoctrinate new employees thoroughly.
- Follow through after they are on the jobs.
- Counsel regularly.
- Provide training to permit growth.
- Develop better supervision.
- Always keep improving personnel planning and policies.

A company's turnover experience has considerable immediate significance. It should be computed honestly and studied carefully. But computing the turnover rate, no matter how, is only preliminary to analyzing it.

Analysis of turnover seeks to find out when, where, and why turnover occurs, in terms of any classification that will help in explaining it. Turnover can be analyzed by type of employee, sex, age, marital status, education level, or any other criteria which may be meaningful.

Generally, unskilled workers show higher rates than skilled workers. Older workers have lower turnover rates than younger employees. Long service employees run lower than new hires. The bulk of terminations are among new workers; one company with

13 percent of workers with less than one year of service has over 50 percent of turnover in this less-than-one-year group.

Observations such as these, when properly documented, can be very useful in influencing policy and in effecting cost reduction.

Few supervisors concern themselves with the high cost of labor turnover. They must be made cost conscious and extend their appreciation of cost reduction beyond waste, scrap, and similar apparent extravagant practices to the less obvious labor cost which is a much bigger item.

Unfortunately top management is often as indifferent toward the cost of labor turnover as are the supervisors. This opportunity to cut costs does not receive proper emphasis on top management's priority list of problems. Consultants have discovered and pointed out that annual cost of turnover in some cases was more than the profit for the year.

Anything done to improve the turnover situation automatically enhances the profit picture.

It would be convenient if some standardized approach or formula could be agreed upon so that true comparisons between companies could be made. Until such uniformity is accomplished it is almost impossible to evaluate how serious the problem really is.

Nevertheless, studies of turnover are not without value. Regardless of how they are computed, they do call attention to the problem, they help to pinpoint the causes, and they definitely suggest where and how improvements can be effected.

AUTOMATION

A cow is a completely automated milk manufacturing machine. It is encased in untanned leather and mounted on four vertical movable supports, one on each corner. The front end of the machine, or input, contains the cutting and grinding mechanism, utilizing a unique feedback device. Here also are the headlights, air inlet and exhaust, a bumper, and a foghorn. At the rear, the machine carries the milk-dispensing equipment as well as a built-in flexible fly swatter and insect repeller.

The central portion houses a hydrochemical conversion unit. Briefly, this consists of four fermentation and storage tanks connected in series by an intricate network of flexible plumbing. This part also contains the central heating plant complete with automatic temperature controls, pumping station, and main ventilating system. The waste disposal apparatus is located to the rear of this central section.

Cows are available, fully assembled, in an assortment of sizes and colors. Production output ranges from two to 20 tons of milk per year. In brief, the main externally visible features of the cow are: two lookers, two hookers, four stander-uppers, four hanger-downers, and a swishy-wishy.

There is a similar machine known as the bull. It gives no milk but has other interesting uses.

What is this thing called AUTOMATION?
And why the great concern?

The following is taken from *Automation and Employment*, published by E. I. du Pont de Nemours & Company.

Automation has emerged as one of the magic words of our times.

It has taken on the coloration of glamour—and at times has been wrapped in the austere cloak of fear.

It is a word sometimes used to invoke visions of massive production systems wherein tireless and ingenious machinery takes over man's age-old burden of work, requiring only the most casual attention from a carefree human race given over to full-time leisure.

It is a word sometimes used to raise specters of a frustrated and idle population denied gainful employment, rendered obsolete and perhaps even hungry by robot machinery.

Neither of these extremes is remotely realistic. But the conflicting pictures reflect very real and contrary feelings about automation as both good and evil, as both friend and foe of man. Some of the split vision stems from confusion about what automation is.

When the term was coined early in the 1950's, it had a very limited and specific application to one developing aspect of technology which promised easier and better means to get certain parts of man's work done. Engineers still prefer to use the word "automation" in this rather precise sense: The substitution of control devices (mechanical, hydraulic, pneumatic, or electronic) for human organs of observation, decision, and control. As such, these devices are the most recent and powerful extension of the industrial revolution which increased man's welfare by substituting powerful machines and energy sources for the very limited muscle power of man and animal.

The word is newer than the fact. Automated devices are neither recent nor revolutionary, as is demonstrated throughout industry. Nonetheless, these control devices and techniques have been so greatly improved in the past 10 years, and their use has spread so rapidly, that the glitter attached to the word, "automation," is well deserved.

Du Pont a Pioneer

This glamorous facade, however, has encouraged the loose employment of the term to describe or refer to developing technology in general. Indeed, postwar technological advances on the farm, in the factory, and in the office have been so breathtaking that some new and striking word seemed necessary to define the age. "Automation" has been seized and used for this purpose even though a great part of recent technology makes no use, or very little use, of automation as the engineer thinks of it.

During this period of stunning technological advance society has also experienced some disappointments. In the United States, a principal frustration has been the failure of a booming economy to provide jobs for all members of its work force. Because one of the functions of technology is to get more work done with less human effort, there has been an unfortunate and inaccurate tendency to charge "automation" with the blame for continued pockets of recalcitrant unemployment.

Du Pont, as a member of the chemical industry, was among the first to make use of automated techniques, long before the term itself was conceived. This company's experience suggests that all technology, including the automated segment, has tended to create new products where none existed, and to produce better products where old ones were less than satisfactory. In doing so, technology has contributed to a general expansion of business, and thus of employment opportunities.

AUTOMATION IN THE OFFICE

Automation has become a dynamic force in our changing economy. It is a phase of the technological progress that has made America great. The pace of our technological improvement has gradually quickened, rising in a geometric progression with each new development. Automation is the latest and the most dramatic example of this rising pace of advancement.

Automation may be defined as a means to a new level of productivity and a new era of industrial progress. It is a way of doing things faster, better, and easier than before, and, in many cases, of accomplishing tasks that previously could not be done at all.

Of all the factors that will determine the speed and direction of automation, the most important is its effect upon people. The installation of automation machines or electronic equipment will have a greater impact upon workers than it will upon methods.

The fantastic predictions of push-button factories and offices have in general been psychologically harmful to the attitudinal development of workers. This results in a blind fear of automation, the fear of unemployment, which persists in many circles. The fear is unfounded, of course, and in time the success of automation will dispel this fear.

The Promise Unfolds

The facts are already on our side. Machine-made unemployment as a consequence of labor-saving equipment in the office is a misconception. Surveys show that in 1940 some five million people in this country were employed in clerical work. Today the figure is more than double. All the while the use of office machines became more widespread. The long history of the arithmetic machine, from abacus to adding machine, cash register, calculator, and punched cards, shows very clearly that the faster the machine process, the more jobs were created for the men and women who operate the machines.

Actually, automation should not cause any unemployment. What it may cause is some personnel displacements. There is no natural law which will routinely adjust the employment market to automation changes. This causes confusion in the minds of businessmen and doubt in the minds of workers. In the long run this problem, following the pattern of history, should resolve itself. Society will gradually adjust to it. However, it is difficult to paint the broad picture, depicting a new abundance, to the individual who does not understand automation and who sees it only as a threat to his job security.

Handling this change skillfully and in everybody's best interest will require managerial ability of the highest order.

Increased emphasis on automation in the meticulous advance planning for all company operations will be necessary to solve the two most pressing problems facing office executives today. Automation can slow the increasing pressure for office workers and it can increase per capita productivity.

Freedom from Drudgery

Automation may someday be the only way of getting certain work done. Even now no one is left who "wants" to do the back-breaking labor jobs in factories. In 1850 muscle power performed 65 percent of all work; in 1950 only 1½ percent. It will also become increasingly difficult to hire people to do routine and tedious work in offices. They will be demanding more challenging duties, which are more satisfying.

Machine development will be the emancipation of many workers from drudgery. This has already happened in the factory and is now taking place in the office as routinized jobs are transferred to automatic and electronic machines.

Manufacturing will lean more heavily upon automatic machinery to eliminate dull, monotonous, low-paid jobs. Repetitive office work, when in sufficient quantity as in department stores, insurance companies, and utilities, will rely upon automation principles to get the work done.

Not only will automation not reduce job opportunities, it will be needed to make it possible for the available labor supply to go around. By 1975, when automation is expected to reach its full impact on U.S. industry, it is conservatively estimated that there will be a demand for some 20 million more workers than are in the present-day labor force. This demand for more workers will result from the growth in population, with the increased consumption of goods and services.

Population experts tell us that America in 1975 will be a nation of 220 million people, 40 million more than we have today. These additional Americans will need many things. The number of workers (people in age bracket 24 to 60) will not increase by the same ratio. This means, percentagewise, fewer people will have to produce far more, at a time when pressures will be exerted to reduce the workweek and possibly the work day. Managements, therefore, will be grateful to automation as the one way open to them for increasing productivity.

Compared with the factory, the productivity of office workers is below par. At the present time there is no one phase of industrial activity that has more expendable fat than office systems and procedures.

The increase in the number of office workers in relation to the number of plant workers reflects a steady increase in the efficiency of plants. The development of automation has contributed to the narrowing of plant-office worker ratios.

The thing to do now is apply to the office the industrial engineering techniques and devices that have worked toward improving the efficiency of plants. The modern office can be the nerve center of cost control and operating efficiency it should be only if the office executive is alert to the new dimensions in his field—such as automation and electronics.

Automation in the office should not be greeted with skepticism, fear, apprehension, or misgivings. It should be welcomed. For it is our best hope of providing the answer to many of the problems that are coming up, not the least of which are the labor shortage and the need for increasing productivity.

Jobs Change, Not Workers

Machine development is not eliminating jobs; it is changing jobs. The automobile did not replace the horse and buggy; it replaced staying at home. The new family circle is the steering-wheel and this development opened up an entirely new industry.

As farming moves toward scientific and away from primitive methods, the result is more production per acre and more production per available man. One man today can do the job of a dozen and do it faster and better. We all know that people are migrating away from farm work. Thank goodness technology and machine development are coming to the rescue.

The telephone company moved into the early lead of the automation parade with the introduction of the dial system. This change did not cut employment of telephone operators. It made possible an increase in the value, efficiency, and attractiveness of the service, which in turn brought on the great expansion in installation and use of phones. If we were still using manual telephones there would soon not be enough women, 24 to 60, to be operators.

What's happening, you see, is that jobs are changing as our way of life changes. Domestic help is no longer available, but the housewife doesn't need a maid. In her completely modern kitchen and laundry what she needs is a mechanic.

Our big bakeries are run without bakers: in up-to-date plants bread is baked by machinists. And so it is also in our offices. Much of our accounting, billing, and payroll work is done by technicians, many of whom don't have to know debits from credits.

Yes, the complexion of our work force is changing. And automation is making it possible for industry to adjust to the changing satisfactions demanded by our workers.

In applying automation principles to office operations there are many things to consider. All of the problems of automation are there. All of the benefits of automation are also possible. The application of principles may be the same, but these must be adapted specifically to office procedures and office needs.

In the factory the raw materials are usually the same in each type of operation. In the office the raw material fed into equipment is also of one kind—information. But the information is of a great variety of types and the end product is almost as varied, with as many different end products as there are varieties of incoming information.

The office is like a sorting device in which a mass of incoming material is sorted into various combinations at various stages in different processing lines. The raw information finally emerges from the various processing lines in the form of separate end products.

Since the design of a system to accomplish this is far more difficult than the design of a work flow system in a factory, the achievement of automation in the office must be built from the ground up. Throughout all stages, systems revision must be performed. The manual methods won't adapt themselves to most machine requirements.

In considering automation for the office, the areas to be studied are three:

1. Where production or clerical operation costs are high.

2. Where manual and interrupted operations predominate.

3. Where speed of reporting is inadequate for management needs.

The objectives of such study are three:

1. Lower costs.

2. Faster reporting.

3. Additional information.

Automation should not be thought of primarily as a labor-saving technique. One of the main functions of automation in practice has been to take the guesses out of top-level decisions by giving managers more complete answers soon enough to be of use.

Now should the installation decision be based solely on direct dollar savings. Frequently office automation installations do not reduce total office costs. Progressive companies are content with improvements that are hard to evaluate in dollars and cents. These improvements may be: more information, faster information, and more accurate information.

In the office the various business systems and machines have permitted a limited amount of automation in processing clerical data. The utilization of automatic machinery and electronic computer systems will unquestionably permit a very high degree of automation in the office, but more important still will permit the development of planning and control information of a kind never before possible.

Integrate All Functions

This will be slow and gradual. A large number of individual operations, such as payroll, billing, stock control, etc., have been programmed and are now processed by various computers. However, not one company has yet turned over all of its major clerical functions to an electronic computer system.

When this happens, functional areas such as payroll, accounts payable, etc., will probably cease to exist as such, since a coordinated and consolidated system of processing data in one transaction will take place. It can be realized that piecemeal operations such as customers' orders, invoicing, stock control, production planning, and all other related activities will have to be integrated to make effective use of machines having the capacity to utilize the source document for simultaneous processing of subsequent requirements. Traditional line divisions will have to bend as total office operations become more functional.

The need for unskilled clerical workers will greatly decrease. However, there will be a demand for skilled people who will not be available unless this difficulty is overcome by individual companies through well-planned employee training programs. This is by far the most important undertaking and the greatest challenge to office management today. In fact, a planned program of employee education is a prerequisite to a change of this magnitude.

The problem of introducing automation principles to office operations can be simplified if management will remember three rules:

1. *Acquire the confidence of people.* Don't proceed on any pro-

gram unless and until you can do so in a climate of mutual trust and respect. Otherwise your employees will be apprehensive, suspicious, and defensive against management.

2. *Try to gain understanding of the workers.* This means relating your planning, your program, and your progress with it individually, not collectively, since no two workers are alike. Different people have different fears and require different considerations.

3. *Keep people properly informed.* Misinformation you may not be guilty of; but you will be guilty of something worse—lack of information. Remember, in the absence of information from management workers will have a tendency to furnish the missing link of information themselves, as they see it. And you may not be happy with the consequence.

The new management era will emphasize sympathetic understanding, sincerity, and consideration of the human element in our businesses.

Summary . . .

The forward march of automation will invigorate, not threaten, our economy. It will do for the businessman what the power-driven saw did for the carpenter.

It will take the work out of work. It will relieve workers, not replace them.

Automation will—

- Result in more production at a time when increases in population are demanding more.

- Upgrade workers who no longer are satisfied with menial tasks but are educated and trained for more challenging assignments.

- Contribute to a higher standard of living for a nation which is looked upon as the example for all the rest of the world.

- Lead to a reduction in hours of work for people who are rapidly learning to appreciate and utilize spare time.

Yes, automation is ready. The question is, "Are we?"

EMPLOYMENT POLICIES

Every company should have a clear understanding of its employment policies. The terms should, preferably, be in writing. They pertain to the attitude and conditions related to—

Hiring workers

Full time: Full employee benefits.

Part time: What benefits do they get?

Temporary: Usually get no benefits.

Reemployment of former workers: Do they start over as new employees or are they given credit for past seniority and earned rights?

Employment of relatives: If husband and wife may both be hired, must they be in different departments?

Married women: Any hesitation?

Under age

18 years and older: No limitation.

17-year-olds: Verification of age certificate.

16-year-olds: Work permit; may be employed for any number of hours and during any period of time, except in occupations declared hazardous by the U.S. Secretary of Labor.

14- and 15-year-olds: Limited to certain occupations outside school hours and under specified conditions of work.

Age limit: Usually cannot be hired over 65 years of age as regular employees where a retirement program exists.

Education minimum: Is it general (no one below high school graduate) or specific by job?

Nondiscrimination by:

Race, color, creed, national origin.

Sex.

Age.

EXIT INTERVIEW FOLLOWUPS

Some companies have a practice of sending questionnaires to former employees óne month or so after they have left. Firms which use this procedure feel that the mail questionnaire brings franker comments after the fact of termination than face-to-face exit interviews conducted on the last day of work when employees may be emotional about leaving their jobs if they've been happy, or reluctant to give the real reason if they are unhappy about being separated.

The information, of course, while interesting, isn't worth the effort it costs to get it unless appropriate action, when called for, is taken. Some jobs may need to be redesigned, supervisors better instructed, and training instituted.

SEX DISCRIMINATION

Business was invented by men to get away from women. Now women, aided by government, are asking men to accept them as business equals.

What has transpired during the transitionary period, known as the industrial revolution, tells the story. Let's summarize this progress briefly.

The industrial society as it is known today is hardly more than one century old. But industrial history goes back much further. It is divided into four eras.

The first was "domestic" production. This was production by members of one household, from raw materials furnished largely by the household itself.

This was followed by "handicraft" production in which the worker made a custom-built item which was sold locally by himself or exchanged for a different handicraft of another worker.

With the development of capital and transportation the "cottage" period of production came into existence. Much of the work was done in cottages just outside the town. Handicraft workers still owned the tools of production, but the contact with consumers of their products was made for them by merchants. This practice still continues in many parts of the world and in some sections of the United States.

The "factory" system, wherein factory workers were brought together to perform their duties under one roof, had its start in England about the time of the American Revolution.

The Industrial Revolution had begun.

In all of this two factors stand out. First, work which was initially done in the home was gradually moved out. Second, production work was a man's responsibility.

Ever since they won the battle for suffrage, women have moved steadily forward into territory formerly considered sacred in man's domain. It was inevitable that women should invade the business world, which man had originally designed for himself.

A Shortage of Workers

There were many reasons, not the least of which was the shortage of trainable workers, especially during wartime. In World War II the nation's greatest manpower reserve was women. In the factory Rosie the Riveter did more than fill in for a man in uniform; she proved to be a crusader for her sex. Women's wartime contributions to industry helped push back the limitations and dispelled some of the prejudices. It is sad to reflect, but in any particular taboo it takes a stress to crack it.

In the office the introduction of the typewriter opened wide the door of opportunity. Over the past several decades, women have been successful in all types and levels of office work. In the process, women have also revolutionized the office. The contribution of women to offices has been more than chintz curtains and flowers. Many of the improvements which men take for granted are a direct result of the influence of increasing numbers of women into the workforce. Such things as rest periods, coffee breaks, modern work environment, fancy drapes, pastel wall colors, are the result of the woman's touch . . . which men enjoy as much as women. Men will permit women to outnumber them so long as they don't outsmart them.

Once women workers found their way into business and industry they signified their intention of not wanting to relinquish their gains.

But not content to play a passive role, nor willing to stay within bounds on jobs which were ideally suited for them, they set out to acquire job equality. Instead of remaining satisfied with work as secretaries, nurses, hairdressers, manicurists, waitresses, or teachers, women began spreading their talents all over the industrial map. The fact is that while shortages exist in the areas of work peculiarly adapted to women, any number of women are sacrificing and struggling to gain recognition in occupations heretofore dominated by men. They are attempting, with measurable success, jobs as switchmen, brakemen, dockwallopers, stationary engineers, meat cutters, oilers and greasers, taxicab and bus drivers.

Fundamentally, their basic interests are still centered in the home. Yet business has much to contribute to a woman's life. With its many uncertainties, life cannot always be directed as women would want it to be. In a changing social philosophy, business is also becoming a part of the personal life of many women. Gradually women are being attracted to a business career, either as a primary source of income or as supplementary earnings—in either case for a higher level of living. Besides the monetary incentive, many women, eager to exchange the monotony of domestic and personal service for more interesting pastures, are responding to the change of pace of office or factory employment.

Women workers have proved their point. They are here to stay. But while men welcome their presence in the labor force, they are reluctant to accept them as equals.

This is where the complications come in. Men are not ready to move over and let women share their lofty perch. Women, in the majority of cases, are not asking this. Besides, there is psychological resistance to women getting complete economic equalization. The prejudice against women in positions of authority appears to be even more deeply rooted in our culture than the concept of white supremacy.

The Law and Its Problems

But we have a law—Title VII of the Civil Rights Act—which says everything is equal between the sexes. But passing a law does not establish instant equality, anymore than passing a law against rheumatism would eliminate that scourge.

If women were ever to demand, and receive, full equality, then obviously they should be drafted for military duty and fight side by side with men. It is doubtful that anyone, man or woman, wants to go this far. But how far should government machinery go to guarantee women a fair deal in the business arena?

Some Key Questions

This raises many questions as sincere and law-abiding employers attempt to obey a law. Here are but a few:

- Is legal solicitude for women worth the price?

- Are state laws limiting hours of work for female employees in conflict with the federal act?

- Are arbitrary weight limitations imposed by some state laws enforceable?

- Are male and female help-wanted columns in newspapers discriminatory?

- Can women be required to retire earlier than men?

Maybe women don't need legal protection against exploitation. Women lawyers, physicians, and proprietors needed no law to help them in their ambitions. The tired argument that women's health would suffer if work hours were too long, is a laugh to the average housewife.

The fragility of womanhood, safeguarded by a variety of local, state, and federal laws, is being sacrificed on the altar of equality.

The egalitarian Equal Employment Opportunity Commission has a difficult, almost impossible, assignment. At best, all the EEOC can do is look after the legal rights of women. But in the long run, what is morally right, emotionally satisfying, psychologically proper, financially rewarding, and socially acceptable may be of far greater significance.

As we said at the outset, the truth is that women are really competing in a man's world. Right or wrong, the simple fact is that man was there first.

AGE DISCRIMINATION

Laws which prohibit discrimination in employment because of age are based on the declaration that the practice of discriminating in employment is contrary to American principles of liberty and equality of opportunity. Further, a hiring bias against older workers deprives society of its most important resource of experienced employees, adds to the number of persons receiving public assistance, and denies older people the dignity and status of self-support.

The federal "Age Discrimination in Employment Act of 1967" bans discrimination in employment for workers aged 40 to 65. Its provisions became effective June 12, 1968. It applies to employers, employment agencies, and labor unions engaged in interstate commerce.

Companies cannot refuse to hire or may not discharge any individual because of age. They cannot indicate any age preference in job ads. Some concession is allowable if age is a condition of the job, if age can be shown to be a *bona fide* qualification.

Such laws, federal and state, are careful not to affect the retirement system of any employer nor the varying of insurance coverage according to an employee's age. They do not interfere with compulsory retirement requirements.

COMPLIANCE WITH GOVERNMENT REGULATIONS

Equal Employment Opportunity simply means the hiring or promoting of any person based on the individual's qualifications.

But it is not always as easy as it sounds. Here is a checklist which may help in determining whether a company has established a "positive program" of affirmative action as required under Executive Order 11246 and Title VII of the Civil Rights Act.

1. *Internal Communications:* Is your company policy written and published, and is it well-known to management and employees through meetings, posters, and other instruction?

2. *Community Relations:* Is the policy and attitude known outside your company, particularly to minority group headquarters and agencies interested in helping them?

3. *Recruitment:* Do your advertisements and referral agencies know your policy, and do you go out of your way to reach the minority group applicants?

4. *Selection and Placement:* Is your application blank clear and are the tests you use fair and properly validated?

5. *Promotion:* Are transfers and promotions based on objective data so that every qualified candidate has an equal chance?

6. *Training:* Are learning opportunities open to everyone or only offered to subjectively selected individuals?

7. *Employee Activities:* Do nonwhites participate in recreational programs and other employee activities, serve on committees, hold office, or is the leadership function denied them?

8. *Action:* Are your programs in this area continuous; are follow-ups made to determine that the nondiscrimination policy of management is carried out in practice?

EXECUTIVE ORDER 11246

Executive Order 11246 on equal employment opportunity consists of three parts.

PART I—Nondiscrimination in Government Employment

Section 101 reads, "It is the policy of the Government of the United States to provide equal opportunity in Federal employment for all qualified persons, to prohibit discrimination in employment because of race, creed, color, or national origin, and to promote the full realization of equal employment opportunity through a positive, continuing program in each executive department and agency. The policy of equal opportunity applies to every aspect of Federal employment policy and practice."

PART II—Nondiscrimination in Employment by Government Contractors and Subcontractors

Subpart B—Contractors' Agreements, Section 202 reads in part, "(1) The contractor will not discriminate against any employee or applicant for employment because of race, creed, color, or national origin. The contractor will take affirmative action to ensure that applicants are employed, and that employees are treated during employment, without regard to their race, creed, color, or national origin. Such action shall include, but not be limited to the following: Employment, upgrading, demotion, or transfer; recruitment or recruitment advertising; layoff or termination; rates of pay or other forms of compensation; and selection for training, including apprenticeship. The contractor agrees to post in conspicuous places, available to employees and applicants for employment, notices to be provided by the contracting officer setting forth the provisions of this nondiscrimination clause."

Section 203 reads in part, "(a) Each contractor having a contract containing the provisions prescribed in Section 202 shall file, and shall cause each of his subcontractors to file, Compliance Reports with the contracting agency or the Secretary of Labor as may be directed. Compliance Reports shall be filed within such times and shall contain such information as to the practices, policies, programs, and employment policies, programs, and employment statistics of the contractor and each subcontractor, and shall be in such form, as the Secretary of Labor may prescribe."

PART III—Nondiscrimination Provisions in Federally Assisted Construction Contracts

Section 301 reads, "Each executive department and agency which administers a program involving Federal financial assistance shall require as a condition for the approval of any grant, contract, loan, insurance, or guarantee thereunder, which may involve a construction contract, that the applicant for Federal assistance undertake and agree to incorporate, or cause to be incorporated, into all construction contracts paid for in whole or in part with funds obtained from the Federal Government or borrowed on the credit of the Federal Government pursuant to such grant, contract, loan, insurance, or guarantee, or undertaken pursuant to any Federal program involving such grant, contract, loan, insurance, or guarantee, the provisions prescribed for Government contracts by Section 203 of this Order or such modification thereof, preserving in substance the contractor's obligations thereunder, as may be approved by the Secretary of Labor, together with such additional provisions as the Secretary deems appropriate to establish and protect the interest of the United States in the enforcement of those obligations. Each such applicant shall also undertake and agree (1) to assist and cooperate actively with the administering department or agency and the Secretary of Labor in obtaining the compliance of contractors and subcontractors with those contract provisions and with the rules, regulations, and relevant orders of the Secretary, (2) to obtain and to furnish to the administering department or agency and to the Secretary of Labor such information as they may require for the supervision of such compliance, (3) to carry out sanctions and penalties for violation of such obligations imposed upon contractors and subcontractors by the Secretary of Labor or the administering department or agency pursuant to Part II, Subpart D, of this Order, and (4) to refrain from entering into any contract subject to this Order, or extension or other modification of such a contract with a contractor debarred from Government contracts under Part II, Subpart D, of this Order."

EXECUTIVE ORDER 11375

Executive Order 11375, covers "Equal Opportunity for Women in Federal Employment and Employment by Federal Contractors." It is an amendment to Executive Order 11246 relating to equal employment opportunity which outlaws discrimination on the basis of race, creed, color, or national origin.

Although the new Executive Order does not substantially alter the employer coverage under prohibitions against sex discrimination established by 1962 Civil Service Commission regulations and the 1964 Civil Rights Act, it will strengthen enforcement procedures.

The Civil Service Commission is authorized to hear directly Federal employee complaints of discrimination based on sex. The Labor Department is authorized to investigate complaints of sex discrimination by all Federal contractors or subcontractors.

EMPLOYER INFORMATION REPORT EEO-1

The "Equal Employment Opportunity Employer Information Report EEO-1" is a single report form to be used by employers subject to the jurisdiction of one or more of the following:

- The Equal Employment Opportunity Commission, under Title VII of the Civil Rights Act of 1964.

- The Office of Federal Contract Compliance of the United States Department of Labor, under Executive Order 11246, dated September 24, 1965.

- The Plans for Progress program.

In the interests of consistency, uniformity, and economy, Standard Form 100 has been jointly developed as a single form which meets the statistical needs of all three programs.

Supplying the required information is not to be considered as participating in a voluntary survey. The filing of the report in accordance with instructions is required by Federal law.

In the instructions accompanying the use of Standard Form 100, two sets of definitions should be noted in particular.

Minority Group Identification

Section E provides for reporting American Indians, Orientals, and Spanish Americans where any of these groups is sufficiently large to constitute an identifiable factor in the local labor market. For purposes of this report, the term Spanish Americans means those of Latin American, Mexican or Puerto Rican origin, and it is to be noted that the following states are among those having large concentrations of Spanish Americans: Arizona, California, Colorado, Florida, New Jersey, New Mexico, New York, and Texas. Large concentrations of Spanish Americans are also found in particular localities in other states.

Description of Job Categories

Officials and Managers. Occupations requiring administrative personnel who set broad policies, exercise overall responsibility for execution of these policies, and direct individual departments or special phases of a firm's operations. Includes officials, executives, middle management, plant managers, department managers and superintendents, salaried foremen who are members of management, purchasing agents and buyers, and kindred workers.

Professional. Occupations requiring either college graduation or experience of such kind and amount as to provide a comparable background. Includes accountants and auditors, airplane pilots and navigators, architects, artists, chemists, designers, dietitians, editors, engineers, lawyers, librarians, mathematicians, natural scientists, registered or licensed nurses, personnel and labor relations workers, physical scientists, physicians, social scientists, teachers and kindred workers.

Technicians. Occupations requiring a combination of basic scientific knowledge and manual skill which can be obtained through about two years of post high school education, such as is offered in many technical institutes and junior colleges, or through equivalent on-the-job training. Includes draftsmen, engineering aides, junior engineers, mathematical aides, nurses, photographers, radio operators, scientific assistants, surveyors, technical illustrators, technicians (medical, dental, electronic, physical sciences), and kindred workers.

Sales. Occupations engaging wholly or primarily in direct selling. Includes advertising agents and salesmen, insurance agents and brokers, real estate agents and brokers, stock and bond salesmen, demonstrators, salesmen and sales clerks, grocery clerks and cashier-checkers, and kindred workers.

Office and Clerical. Includes all clerical-type work regardless of level of difficulty, where the activities are predominantly nonmanual though some manual work not directly involved with altering or transporting the products is included. Includes bookkeepers, cashiers, collectors (bills and accounts), messengers and office boys, office machine operators, shipping and receiving clerks, stenographers, typists and secretaries, telegraph and telephone operators, and kindred workers.

Craftsmen (skilled). Manual workers of relatively high skill level having a thorough and comprehensive knowledge of the processes involved in their work. Exercise considerable independent judgment and usually receive an extensive period of training. Includes the building trades, hourly paid foremen and leadmen who are not members of management, mechanics and repairmen, skilled machining occupations, compositors and typesetters, electricians, engravers, job setters (metal), motion picture projectionists, pattern and model makers, stationary engineers, tailors and tailoresses, and kindred workers

Operatives (semiskilled). Workers who operate machine or processing equipment or perform other factory-type duties of intermediate skill level which can be mastered in a few weeks and require only limited training. Includes apprentices (auto mechanics, bricklayers, carpenters, electricians, machinists, mechanics, plumbers, building trades, metalworking trades, printing trades, etc.), operatives, attendants, (auto service and parking), blasters, chauffeurs, deliverymen and routemen, dressmakers and seamstresses (except factory), dyers, furnacemen, heaters (metal), laundry and dry cleaning operatives, milliners, mine operatives and laborers, motormen, oilers and greasers (except auto), painters (except construction and maintenance), photographic process workers, stationary firemen, truck and tractor drivers, weavers (textile), welders, and flame-cutters, and kindred workers.

Laborers (unskilled). Workers in manual occupations which generally require no special training. Perform elementary duties that may be learned in a few days and require the application of little or no independent judgment. Includes garage laborers, car washers and greasers, gardeners (except farm) and groundskeepers, longshoremen and stevedores, lumbermen, raftsmen and wood choppers, laborers performing lifting, digging, mixing, loading and pulling operations, and kindred workers.

Service Workers. Workers in both protective and nonprotective service occupations. Includes attendants (hospital and other institution, professional and personal service), barbers, charwomen and cleaners, cooks (except household), counter and fountain workers, elevator operators, firemen and fire protection guards, watchmen and doorkeepers, stewards, janitors, policemen and detectives, porters, waiters and waitresses, and kindred workers.

Apprentices. Persons employed in a program including work training and related instruction to learn a trade or craft which is traditionally considered an apprenticeship regardless of whether the program is registered with a Federal or State agency.

On-the-job Trainees:

Production (includes persons engaged in formal training for craftsmen—when not trained under apprentice programs—operative, laborer and service occupations).

White Collar (includes persons engaged in formal training, for official, managerial, professional, technical, sales, office and clerical occupations).

McNAMARA—O'HARA SERVICE CONTRACT ACT

General Provisions

The McNamara-O'Hara Service Contract Act of 1965 applies generally to Government contracts, the principal purpose of which is to furnish services in the United States through the use of service employees. It is effective as to contracts entered into pursuant to negotiations concluded or invitations for bids issued on or after January 20, 1966.

Contractors and subcontractors performing work under such contracts are required to observe minimum standards of compensation for employees employed in the contract work. Compensation in accordance with that prevailing in the locality and safe and sanitary working conditions are required for service employees engaged in work under contracts in excess of $2,500.

The act applies to contracts to furnish services in any state, the District of Columbia, Puerto Rico, the Virgin Islands, Outer Continental Shelf Lands, American Samoa, Guam, Wake Island, Eniwetok Atoll, Kwajalein Atoll, and Johnston Island.

Service Employees

As defined in the act, service employees include guards, watchmen, and any person engaged in a recognized trade or craft, or other skilled mechanical craft, or in unskilled, or semiskilled, or skilled manual labor occupations; and any other employee including a foreman or supervisor in a position having trade, craft, or laboring experience as the paramount requirement. All such persons are included regardless of any contractual relationship that may be alleged to exist between a contractor or subcontractor and such persons.

Minimum Wage for All Covered Contracts

Every contractor who enters into any contract with the Federal Government the principal purpose of which is to furnish services through the use of service employees and every subcontractor under such a contract is required to pay employees engaged in performing the contract work not less than the minimum wage specified under section 6 (a) (1) of the Fair Labor Standards Act.

Covered Contracts in Excess of $2,500

Contractors and subcontractors performing work under any contract entered into by the United States or the District of Columbia in excess of $2,500 which is subject to the act must observe the following additional requirements:

MINIMUM WAGE

Service employees engaged in the performance of the contract or any subcontract thereunder shall be paid the applicable minimum monetary wage specified in the contract and in any bid specification therefor, which in no case shall be lower than the Fair Labor Standards Act minimum provided for all covered contracts. The act provides for determination by the Secretary of Labor or his authorized representative of such minimum monetary wages for the various classes of service employees in accordance with prevailing rates for such employees in the locality, and requires that they be specified in the contract and any bid specification therefor.

FRINGE BENEFITS

Service employees engaged in the performance of the contract or any subcontract thereunder shall be furnished such fringe benefits as have been determined by the Secretary of Labor or his authorized representative to be prevailing for such employees in the locality and which are specified in the contract and any bid specification therefor as applicable to such employees.

As required by the act, provisions specifying fringe benefits to be furnished to a class or classes of service employees performing work on the contract will be included in the contract documents whenever the Secretary or his authorized representative determines the furnishing of benefits such as the following to be prevailing for such employees in the locality: Medical or hospital care, pensions on retirement or death, compensation for injuries or illness resulting from occupational activity, or insurance to provide any of the foregoing, unemployment benefits, life insurance, disability and sickness insurance, accident insurance, vacation and holiday pay, costs of apprenticeship or other similar programs and other bona fide fringe benefits not otherwise required by Federal, State, or local law to be provided by the contractor or subcontractor.

The obligation of a contractor or subcontractor to furnish any specified fringe benefits may be discharged by furnishing any equivalent combinations of benefits, or by making equivalent or differential payments in cash, in accordance with regulations of the Administrator of the Wage and Hour and Public Contracts Divisions, Department of Labor.

SAFE AND HEALTHFUL WORKING CONDITIONS

Contractors and subcontractors are obligated to assure that no part of the services covered by the act will be performed in buildings or surroundings or under working conditions, provided by or under the control or supervision of the contractor or any subcontractor, which are unsanitary or hazardous or dangerous to the health or safety of service employees engaged to furnish the services.

NOTICE TO EMPLOYEES

The contractor or subcontractor must provide a service employee, when he commences work on a contract subject to the act, with a notice of the compensation required by the act or shall post such notice in a location where it may be seen by all employees performing on the contract, using such poster as may be provided by the Department of Labor.

RECORDKEEPING REQUIREMENTS

The contractor or subcontractor must make, and maintain for a period of three years from the completion of the work, the following records for each service employee performing work under the contract:

1. Name and address.

2. Work classification or classifications, rate or rates of monetary wages and fringe benefits provided, rate or rates of fringe benefit payments in lieu thereof, and total daily and weekly compensation.

3. Daily and weekly hours so worked.

4. Any deductions, rebates, or refunds from the employee's total daily or weekly compensation.

These records shall be made available for inspection and transcription by authorized representatives of the Wage and Hour and Public Contracts Divisions.

Notice to Subcontracts

Each contractor under a contract subject to the act is required to insert clauses relating to the Service Contract Act in all his subcontracts, as prescribed by regulations of the Administrator.

Exemptions

The McNamara-O'Hara Service Contract Act of 1965 does not apply to the following:

1. Any contract of the United States or District of Columbia for construction, alteration, and/or repair, including painting and decorating of public buildings or public works;

2. Any work required to be done in accordance with the provisions of the Walsh-Healey Public Contracts Act;

3. Any contract for the carriage of freight or personnel by vessel, airplane, bus, truck, express, railway line, or oil or gas pipeline where published tariff rates are in effect;

4. Any contract for the furnishing of services by radio, telephone, telegraph, or cable companies, subject to the Communications Act of 1934;

5. Any contract for public utility services, including electric light and power, water, steam, and gas;

6. Any employment contract providing for direct services to a Federal agency by an individual or individuals;

7. Any contract with the Post Office Department, the principal purpose of which is the operation of postal contract stations;

8. Any services to be furnished outside the United States as defined in the act; and

9. Any contract exempted by the Secretary of Labor under section 4(b) of the act. This section authorizes the Secretary to provide such reasonable limitations, variations, tolerances, and exemptions to and for any or all provisions of the act as he may find necessary and proper in the public interest or to avoid serious impairment to the conduct of Government business.

Violations and Penalties

In the event of violations, the act authorizes the withholding of accrued payments due on the contract to the extent necessary to pay covered workers the difference between the wages and benefits required by the contract and those actually paid. The Government may also bring court action against the contractor, subcontractor, or surety to recover any remaining amount of the underpayment. In addition, the contract may be terminated because of violations and the contractor may be held liable for any resulting cost to the Government. The Government will not award another contract for three years to a person or firm responsible for violations, unless the Secretary of Labor recommends otherwise.

Enforcement

Authorized representatives of the WHPC Divisions investigate for compliance with the Service Contract Act. Anyone can request the Divisions' assistance if he thinks a firm is violating the act. Complaints, records, and other information for employers and employees are treated confidentially.

Other Obligations

Observance of the labor standards of the Service Contract Act does not relieve the employer of any obligation he may have under any other laws or agreements providing for higher labor standards.

Assistance Available

Whether contracts and particular employees are covered by the McNamara-O'Hara Service Contract Act depends on the facts in each case. If you want to know about the application of the law in a particular case, contact the nearest office of the WHPC Divisions. Give information on the name of the contractor, the Government agency that issued the contract, the contract number, the amount of the contract, what service the firm furnishes under the contract, the method and rate of pay, the hours of work, and any other details you think will be needed for an adequate reply.

Inquiries about the Fair Labor Standards Act, Walsh-Healey Public Contracts Act, McNamara-O'Hara Service Contract Act and their application will be answered by mail, telephone, or personal interview at any regional or field office of the Wage and Hour and Public Contracts Divisions of the U.S. Department of Labor. These offices also supply publications free of charge.

ANTI-DISCRIMINATION LAWS

Discrimination in employment is legally obsolete. State and federal laws prohibit discrimination against job applicants or employees because of

- Race
- Color
- Religion
- National origin
- Sex
- Age

Title VII of the Civil Rights Act of 1964 establishes a federal right to equal opportunity in private employment. It is effective July 2 of

- 1965 for employers of 100 persons or more
- 1966   75
- 1967   50
- 1968   25

There are very few exemptions; private clubs, government offices are not covered. But the law applies to employment agencies and labor unions.

With few exceptions, Title VII prohibits discriminatory practices in industries affecting interstate commerce in

1. Hiring
2. Discharging
3. Promotion
4. Layoff
5. Pay

These policies extend to

1. Training
2. Selection
3. Referral
4. Recruitment

An Equal Employment Opportunity Commission of five members is charged with enforcing the law. The EEOC cooperates with state and local antidiscrimination agencies, and defers for up to 60 days investigation of complaints to the applicable state agency. The EEOC also encourages voluntary compliance with the letter and spirit of the law through various educational means.

Title VII requires employers to *refrain* from discriminating. But Executive Orders, issued by the President to employers having contracts for government work, go a step further. They impose *positive* obligations. They require that companies take *affirmative action*. This is defined in many ways, but it means, simply, doing whatever is necessary to provide additional job opportunities to those people who have not been given these opportunities before.

Executive Order 11246 covers race, creed, color, national origin.

Executive Order 11141 covers age.

This nondiscrimination policy, covering government contractors and subcontractors, is administered by the OFCC (Office of Federal Contract Compliance) of the Department of Labor. One of its requirements is the inclusion of the statement, "Equal Opportunity Employer," in all Help Wanted advertisements and other recruiting literature.

Compliance reviews or on-site inspections are results oriented. The inspectors are not interested in words, or devices, or changed programs except as these produce results. There are two routes to trouble for companies:

1. A complaint from an individual.

2. An unsatisfactory report by an inspector.

Title VI of the 1964 Civil Rights Act forbids discrimination in employment in any federally assisted program or activity which has a primary purpose of providing employment. Such programs include accelerated public works projects, out-of-school youth programs, training and apprenticeship programs, area redevelopment programs, and State-operated youth camps providing employment. In addition, Title VI prohibits the racial assignment of staff duties where, as a result, participants receive services on a segregated basis—for example, where Negro children are taught only by Negro teachers.

In public employment, it is the policy of the Federal Government to provide equal opportunity in federal employment for all qualified persons, to prohibit discrimination in employment because of race, creed, color, sex, or national origin, and to promote the full realization of equal employment opportunity through a positive, continuing program in each executive department and agency.

The U.S. Civil Service Commission is required to supervise and provide leadership and guidance in the conduct of these programs covering civilian employment in federal government offices.

Many of the 50 states have passed their own antidiscrimination laws. State laws are aimed at employers, employment agencies, and labor unions. These laws prohibit discrimination because of race, color, religion, national origin, ancestry. Discrimination because of sex is banned in some states, and in some age discrimination is included.

Where state laws exist, these will be considered first where compliance, enforcement, and complaints are involved. The federal EEOC works with the states and will yield where states can do an adequate job. The EEOC will not, however, defer to those states with antidiscrimination laws which call for voluntary compliance only.

It is well for an employer to become familiar with the state laws as well as the federal Civil Rights Law. These laws are likely not to be identical in every respect.

No company can assume that its policies and practices, no matter how effective they have been, will be sufficient to meet demands made upon them in the future. More than mechanics will change. Companies, like other institutions, will have to change many of their attitudes towards people in order to fulfill their role in this era of social revolution. Managements must become sensitive to the strain, stress, and even turmoil which will surely follow as personal prejudices, no matter how subdued, meet head-on with the practical realities of this movement.

PART 3

EDUCATION

Indoctrination

Employee orientation

Interviews

On-the-job instruction

Creative letter writing

Telephone techniques

Training films

The company library

Adult education

Tuition aid plans

INDOCTRINATION

Once the employee is hired he needs to be educated in the business. This is generally known as training. Employee training may be conveniently divided into four broad areas:

1. Indoctrination
2. Orientation
3. On-the-job instruction
4. Education

The entire gamut of training may be defined as "the process of aiding employees to gain effectiveness in their present or future work. This is accomplished through the development of appropriate habits of thought and action, skills, knowledge, and attitudes."

In any company training goes on all the time. Somehow new workers learn their jobs; employees increase their skills; people learn to work together. This learning, however, may be hit or miss, slow or fast, right or wrong. It is better for management to give direction and assistance to this learning.

The first phase of employee education is that of indoctrination or induction. It is intended to get the new worker off to a good start. It occurs on the new worker's first day on the job.

First-Day Review

Much information is exchanged with an applicant during the employment interview. Many things are discussed, some in general terms, depending upon the person and the job for which he is being considered. Other significant details, if they come up at all, may not be remembered since they did not contribute to the decision to accept or reject the job offer.

Therefore, when he reports for work on his first day, the details about the work situation should be reviewed with him, preferably before he begins working. It is best to do this individually, although there could be times or circumstances when this can be done effectively in groups. The indoctrination is usually done in the personnel office or central employment department before the worker is referred to the department in which he will begin his duties. Upon his arrival in the department a local indoctrination also takes place.

Internal Revenue Service

Print full name ....

Social Security
Account Number ....

Print home address .... City .... State ....

EMPLOYEE:
File this form with your employer. Otherwise, he must withhold U.S. income tax from your wages without exemption.

EMPLOYER:
Keep this certificate with your records. If the employee is believed to have claimed too many exemptions, the District Director should be so advised.

HOW TO CLAIM YOUR WITHHOLDING EXEMPTIONS

1. If SINGLE, and you claim your exemption, write "1"; if you do not, write "0" ....

2. If MARRIED, one exemption each is allowable for husband and wife if not claimed on another certificate.

  (a) If you claim both of these exemptions, write "2"
  (b) If you claim one of these exemptions, write "1" }........
  (c) If you claim neither of these exemptions, write "0"

3. Exemptions for age and blindness (applicable only to you and your wife but not to dependents):

  (a) If you or your wife will be 65 years of age or older at the end of the year, and you claim this exemption, write "1"; if both will be 65 or older, and you claim both of these exemptions, write "2"
  (b) If you or your wife are blind, and you claim this exemption, write "1"; if both are blind, and you claim both of these exemptions, write "2" ....

4. If you claim exemptions for one or more dependents, write the number of such exemptions. (Do not claim exemption for a dependent unless you are qualified under instruction 3 on other side) ....

5. Add the number of exemptions which you have claimed above and write the total .... ☐

6. Additional withholding per pay period under agreement with employer. *See Instruction 1* .... $ ....

I CERTIFY that the number of withholding exemptions claimed on this certificate does not exceed the number to which I am entitled.

.... 19...... (Signed) ....
(Date)

1. NUMBER OF EXEMPTIONS.—Do not claim more than the correct number of exemptions. However, if you expect to owe more income tax for the year than will be withheld if you claim every exemption to which you are entitled, you may increase the withholding by claiming a smaller number of exemptions or you may enter into an agreement with your employer to have additional amounts withheld. This is especially important if you have more than one employer, or if both husband and wife are employed.

2. CHANGES IN EXEMPTIONS.—You may file a new certificate at any time if the number of your exemptions INCREASES. You must file a new certificate within 10 days if the number of exemptions previously claimed by you DECREASES for any of the following reasons:

(a) Your wife (or husband) for whom you have been claiming exemption is divorced or legally separated, or claims her (or his) own exemption on a separate certificate.

(b) The support of a dependent for whom you claimed exemption is taken over by someone else, so that you no longer expect to furnish more than half the support for the year.

(c) You find that a dependent for whom you claimed exemption will receive $600 or more of income of his own during the year (except your child who is a student or who is under 19 years of age).

OTHER DECREASES in exemption, such as the death of a wife or a dependent, do not affect your withholding until the next year, but require the filing of a new certificate by December 1 of the year in which they occur.

For further information consult your local District Director of Internal Revenue or your employer.

3. DEPENDENTS.—To qualify as your dependent (line 4 on other side), a person (a) must receive more than one-half of his or her support from you for the year, and (b) must have less than $600 gross income during the year (except your child who is a student or who is under 19 years of age), and (c) must not be claimed as an exemption by such person's husband or wife, and (d) must be a citizen or resident of the United States or a resident of Canada, Mexico, the Republic of Panama or the Canal Zone (this does not apply to an alien child legally adopted by and living with a United States citizen abroad), and (e) must (1) have your home as his principal residence and be a member of your household for the entire year, or

(2) be related to you as follows:

Your son or daughter (including legally adopted children), grandchild, stepson, stepdaughter, son-in-law, or daughter-in-law;
Your father, mother, grandparent, stepfather, stepmother, father-in-law, or mother-in-law;
Your brother, sister, stepbrother, stepsister, half brother, half sister, brother-in-law, or sister-in-law;
Your uncle, aunt, nephew, or niece (but only if related by blood).

4. PENALTIES.—Penalties are imposed for willfully supplying false information or willful failure to supply information which would reduce the withholding exemption.

One of the first pieces of paperwork to confront a new employee—the W-4 withholding exemption certificate.

275

In the personnel office items of general nature are presented. In the department the specifics are covered.

In Personnel	*In Department*
Work week and work day	Work hours for his job
Length of lunch period	Time for his lunch period
Location of cafeteria or outside eating facilities	Usually assigns someone to go to lunch with first time
Rest periods	Time of his rest periods
Pay day and method of payment	How to check in—time clocks or time sheets
Where to cash paychecks	Overtime arrangement
Starting job and starting pay	Job opportunities
Holidays	Absence reporting; tardiness
Vacation policy	How vacations are scheduled
Sick pay allowances	Location of cloakroom or locker, and washrooms
Location of clinic or first-aid	Location of nearest emergency exit
Group insurance with literature	
Employee activities	Introduction to sponsor or other co-worker available for training or questions
Availability of personnel services	

This "first-day-on-the-job" indoctrination in the personnel or employment office is the time to have the new worker sign the necessary papers to process him on the payroll:

- Form W4—Employee's Withholding Exemption Certificate

- Group Insurance Application blank

- Employee gift fund participation.

Recognizing that a new employee is likely to sign anything placed before him, it is inadvisable to sign him up at this time for contributory Life Insurance, Credit Union membership, United Fund payroll deductions, and the like. Items such as these should be thoroughly explained to him at some later time.

Many companies have found the sponsor system effective in welcoming the new worker. The manager has many duties and is often too busy to concern himself with every new employee, especially to the extent that is necessary. He therefore selects a trustworthy employee to serve as sponsor with the responsibility to make the new employee feel at home, introduce him around, answer his questions, and generally "show him the ropes." The sponsor, although he has his own job to do, tries to stay close to the new worker until he feels he "belongs" and can get along on his own.

The purpose of the indoctrination is to welcome the new employee in a friendly manner and accept him as part of the employee group. It also provides the company with the initial opportunity of providing the new worker with useful and accurate information about the company and its products or services. It also advises the worker as to company requirements pertaining to working hours, safety regulations, and other rules and procedures. This is a good time to give the new worker a copy of the Employee Handbook, in which the employee program is covered.

SPONSORS

The following paragraph is taken from the employee handbook of Motorola, Inc.:

"To make you feel at home in the Motorola family as soon as possible, a sponsor is assigned to you when you start work on your first day. This sponsor introduces you to Motorola, answers your questions about us and makes starting on your new job as pleasant as possible. Sponsors are chosen who have been with Motorola for some time and can answer your questions while you are learning your way around. On the first day the sponsor will take you to the cafeteria for free lunch and coffee breaks and help you get acquainted."

BENCH INTERVIEWS

In connection with the indoctrination, some companies perform what is known as bench interviews. A bench interview is a conversation with the new worker at his work station on his first day on the job.

Someone from the employment office visits the new worker late in the day, at the worker's desk or machine. He makes it appear as though this were a casual "drop in" instead of a planned trip. It is amazing to discover how reassuring a familiar face is to the new employee after he has struggled along all day in unfamiliar surroundings with work that overwhelms him.

By the use of the bench interview the company has a chance to learn how the new worker is getting along, to answer questions, to determine that he is off on the right foot. This very personal action reminds him that the company is interested in seeing to it that he makes good.

EMERGENCY ARRANGEMENTS

Business as usual is the normal order of the day. But every once in a while the best organized plans go awry.

Nature can easily upset the status quo. A blizzard can foul up public and private transportation making it virtually impossible for employees to get to work. A flood can call an overnight halt to industries along the river. Any time Mother Nature goes on a rampage she makes a mockery of man's puny efforts to maintain order.

But man himself can cause trouble. Strikes can throw a monkey wrench in the finest industrial machinery. The walk-out doesn't even need to be in the company, or in a related firm. When elevator operators go on strike, for example, all businesses in tall buildings are literally at a standstill. Their daily operations must, of necessity, be rearranged. In some situations firms may shut down completely, operate on a curtailed schedule, or work with only a partial shift.

During the past few years a new danger has entered upon the scene to disturb the industrial calm. This is the threat of civil rights or other riots that take over a community and endanger the lives and property in a large sector of the city. When this flares up to riot proportions, police and military forces set the rules, and business is pushed aside.

In any of these unfortunate situations the results, as far as business is concerned, lead to confusion. Is the plant open? If not, when will it be reopened? What is happening in the meantime? The employee wonders what to do. What is expected of him. As a

EDUCATION

conscientious worker, should he make the effort, at great inconvenience and possibly danger, to get down to work? How does he feel when he shows up, only to find that no one else did?

Since the likelihood of these emergency situations appears to be increasing, companies are willing to consider the advisability of setting up "Operations Emergency" programs and committees.

One plan calls for a telephone communications system whereby every employee would be directly assigned to his immediate supervisor. The chain of communication, both downward and upward, would follow the organization chart. Once a decision is made by topside, the president would report it to his vice-presidents, they in turn to their assistant vice-presidents, who would relay it to their managers . . . down the line to the individual workers. The worker would understand the procedure and know from whom to expect to "get the word." This would also make it clear to him how to reverse the procedure in the event he fails to get a message and wonders whom to call to inquire.

The arrangement, of course, requires that all supervisors be equipped with the telephone numbers of their people. Most importantly, it means that these lists would be kept up to date. As a precaution, alternates should be named (in case a key supervisor is out of reach) and this means duplicate lists. It might be a lot of work to set up and maintain this type of program but, like any other precautionary measure, it is probably better than the alternative of doing no planning in advance.

Get the Decision

The big problem, however, is not so much in the mechanics of delivering the message as it is in getting the decision made. The man at the top is away and lesser executives hesitate to usurp his authority. Or even if he is accessible, he may prefer to consult with some other executives before he declares himself. While all this is going on questions come up, employees do not get answers, hasty makeshift actions are improvised, helpful outside agencies get no cooperation, and confusion runs rampant.

It is imperative that the problems be considered before they happen and a committee, preferably a small one, be empowered to act. This committee might center around the personnel executive, who would take the initiative and move into action, the building superintendent, since building facilities must be considered, and a senior officer, to lend official sanction to any emergency decisions made. These three people should be quickly in touch with each other, arrive at a decision with a minimum of delay, and then trigger the emergency program.

Questions about telling the employee to report or stay home, to ask for police escorts, to shut down air conditioning, heating, motors, etc., to set up plant protection, to notify shippers and suppliers, to cooperate with radio and television media for free or paid announcements, to work with the press—all of these and other problems should get prompt attention. Unless some program is worked out in advance, and certain individuals authorized to proceed on their own, the procrastination, indecision, and illwill created by waiting for top management to get together by remote control, will result in chaos.

Decisions not of an emergency nature may be made later. Whether to pay employees for the day or days the plant was closed could be decided after the plant is reopened and the officials are back on the job.

Programs of this type cannot be effective if they begin after the emergency has struck. The problems must be anticipated and the solutions worked out in advance. Preplanning is the answer.

ORIENTATION

In the training program of workers, that part known as "Orientation" is an organized effort on the part of the company to get the new employee acclimated to his company, his job, and his co-workers. It is an attempt to have the new worker learn quickly and accurately what he would otherwise pick up over a longer period of time, and perhaps somewhat incorrectly, through osmosis.

Its purpose is to inform workers about rules, regulations, and policies so as to enable him to understand them and give willing compliance.

EMPLOYEE INDUCTION — ORIENTATION — PROBATION CHECKLIST

Employee: _____ Job: _____ Date Hired: _____

Department: _____ Supervisor: _____

ORIENTATION — FIRST DAY
Date: _____

	Initial by Supv.		Initial by Supv.
WELCOME: Give your name		**3.** PAY DATA—(Cont'd)	
Determine name employee wishes to be called by		Merit rating. policy	
Discuss: Employee's background—Family, experience, hobbies, etc.		Answer any questions	
		4. PROCEDURES AND REGULATIONS	
Tour department—Explain organization, company history, product & services		Safety rules	
		Safety shoes	
Introduce to fellow workers and give copy of Employee Handbook		Safety glasses	
		Other safety equipment	
DAILY ROUTINE		Fire regulations	
Location and use of time clock		Reporting accidents	
Starting and stopping time		Importance of punctuality	
Lunch period & Break periods		Absenteeism	
Work clothes		Tardiness	
Dressing and rest rooms		Sickness	
Vending machines or cafeteria		Reporting absences	
Parking facilities		Care of equipment	
First aid facilities		Leaving job during working hours	
Where to get information and help		Use of telephone	
PAY DATA		Smoking	
Rate for Job		Housekeeping	
Pay deductions		Personal business	
Pay week		Package passes	
Pay day and pay period		Horseplay	
If job will go on incentive, discuss pay opportunities		Penalties for violation of rules	
Pay for overtime		Handling employees' problems	
Errors in pay—What to do		**5.** Encourage and answer any quesitons.	
Job evaluation		**6.** JOB INSTRUCTIONS	
Job description		(See training)	

ORIENTATION — THIRD DAY
Date:_____

	Initial by Supv.		Initial by Supv.
Briefly review material covered on first day		To effect on other employees	
Answer questions on items covered under—		To total process	
DAILY ROUTINE		**4.** Importance of teamwork	
PAY DATA		**5.** Bulletin Boards	
PROCEDURES AND REGULATIONS		**6.** Tour of Plant	
Discuss importance of his job:		**7.** Answer any questions	
To production		**8.** JOB INSTRUCTIONS	
To quality		(See training)	

ORIENTATION — FIRST PAY DAY
Date:_____

	Initial by Supv.		Initial by Supv.
Rate of pay and how figured		Group Insurance Plans	
Pay deductions—Insurance, Social Security, Income Tax, etc.		Opportunities for advancement.	
		4. Vacations and Holidays	
Discuss employee benefits—Company's Policy on pay increases and fringe benefits—Review Employee Handbook.		**5.** Recreation facilities	
		6. Answer any questions	
		7. JOB INSTRUCTION	
		(See training)	

66 EMPLOYER'S SERVICES CORPORATION
X 314, BRISTOL, TENNESSEE 37620

(OVER)

FORM NO. 29

This induction-orientation checklist keeps tab on the new employee through three stages, including his first payday.

TRAINING ON THE JOB
(Continuous Until Employee Knows Job)

	Initial by Supv.		Initial by Sup
1. GENERAL—Discuss importance of job—Use job description.		b. Stressing key points.	
Production Standards and expectations.		c. Telling him why.	
Tools and Supplies.		d. Being complete and patient.	
Avoiding Waste.		e. Going as fast as the employee can learn.	
Safety.			
2. PREPARATION FOR INSTRUCTION—Analyze job—Break it down into steps and reduce it to writing for employee's guidance. Prepare training time schedule.		f. Designating to whom he should go for help.	
		Evaluate Performance by:	
		a. Having him tell, show and illustrate.	
3. INSTRUCTION PROCESS—Prepare employee for training by: a. Showing interest in him.		b. Praising him when he is right; correcting him if he is wrong.	
b. Determining previous training and experience.		c. Checking progress frequently.	
		d. Encouraging questions.	
Explain job operations and procedures by: a. Telling, showing, and illustrating one important step at a time.		Continue training until employee is thoroughly familiar with job. Follow-up by putting him on his own.	

PROBATIONARY PERIOD RATING REPORT
(by Supervisor)

If for any reason the employee is unsatisfactory after he has been with you three (3) workweeks, the rest of this form should be completed and sent to the Personnel Department. If employee is making SATISFACTORY PROGRESS, the following questions should be answered at the end of probation period. Send this form to the Personnel Department to be placed in Personnel File of employee.

EMPLOYEE'S PROGRESS

	YES	NO
1. Job Knowledge: Does employee know job requirements well?		
2. Quality of Work: Is quality of work good?		
3. Quantity of Work: Is quantity of work meeting standards?		
4. Safety: Does employee try to work safely and follow Safety Rules?		
5. Initiative: Is employee a "Self Starter?"		
6. Dependability: Can you count on this employee to follow instructions and do what you expect?		
7. Conduct: Does employee try to follow company rules?		
8. Punctuality: Is employee at work on time regularly?		
9. Cooperation: Does employee try to work as a team member?		
10. Attitude Toward Job: Does employee seem to like present work?		
11. Attitude Toward Company: Does employee seem to feel "at home" in present job?		
12. Has this employee been fully trained?		
13. Does he make production standards regularly?		
14. If he has not made production standards, is he making satisfactory progress in training and in meeting production standards?		
15. Do you think employee is satisfied with the job?		

16. Attendance: How many days has employee been absent since hired?   **Number**_____

17. How do you rate this employee on his job as compared with other employees with equal experience.

Definitely Unsatisfactory	Substandard but Making Progress	Doing An Average Job	Definitely Above Average	Outstanding
☐	☐	☐	☐	☐

	YES	NO
18. Your Recommendation: Do you recommend this probationary employee be permitted to become a regular employee?		

Date: _____   _____

                  Supervisor's Signature

Back side of checklist has followup for the employee's training, probation periods.

Further than that, Orientation programs instruct employees as to the company history, personality, products, and philosophy. This is important to a worker since it explains a company's reputation, character, and future—all of which are meaningful to him in his personal job ambitions.

An Orientation program gives the company an excellent opportunity to show how much it depends upon the workers. Workers are made to feel that they "belong" and that they are important—otherwise they would not have been hired. It also provides a channel for presenting information to employees and influencing their reaction to it.

Care should be taken in planning such Orientation program that the material is presented for the benefit of the new workers and not simply to glorify the company. Unless it is made meaningful to the employee it is a waste of time.

Program Deserves Good Planning

Don't assume that just because you are impressed that your people will also be impressed, and by the same things. Plan your program carefully because it will represent a big investment in time, money, and talent of both those who participate in its presentation and those who attend.

In larger firms particularly, Orientation programs may be developed and conducted by staff officers, possibly from the personnel office, who arrange classes for groups of workers. It is generally conceded that the best Orientation programs consist basically of two parts and should be handled by two different sets of people. The first part, that of necessary rules, regulations, and policies, should be the responsibility of the line organization. The second part, that of explaining the history and background of the company, can perhaps be best handled by a staff officer in classroom or discussion fashion.

While Orientation programs are generally conducted for new employees, the value of holding refresher courses for older employees should not be overlooked. Sometimes older employees can attend the classes for new workers; often a happy blending of workers results which aids in the discussion. In other situations it might be advisable to design special programs, to avoid unnecessary time-consuming repetition and to keep the discussions on an advanced level.

ON-THE-JOB INSTRUCTION

It may be assumed, if selection techniques are effective, that the new worker possesses the ability to perform the job for which he was hired or to which he was promoted. Now he must learn the job itself. He must be taught how to apply his talent to his new duties. This is known as on-the-job training. Whether this job is in a factory, office, shop, hospital, or store, the worker must learn how to perform it and perform it well.

The methods and techniques of job instruction are simple:

    a. Telling—prepare the worker

    b. Showing—present the operation

    c. Testing—try out performance

    d. Checking—follow up.

Most of this type of on-the-job training can best be handled by the supervisors in the departments where the workers are assigned. Often another worker on a similar job shows the new worker "the ropes." Occasionally, this training function can be centralized in one specific area within the department; someone or some group can be given the responsibility for training all new workers within a department or division. Some aspects of on-the-job training can possibly be transplanted to a central training staff or delegated to other departments which are more specialized in a specific type of work. For example, supplementary training in telephone courtesy could easily be referred to the local telephone company which is glad to provide the assistance.

The responsibility for job instruction must always lie with the line manager or supervisor. Skill training, or the operation of a particular machine, may be learned on the outside, in school or elsewhere; but its application to the company's operations must be done by the line department.

RESPONSIBILITY FOR GOODWILL

In this era of technological change, work is shifting from manufacturing to service. The percentage of manufacturing jobs (blue collar) is going down and the percentage of service jobs (white collar) is going up. A few words to employees in service jobs may therefore be in order.

The major responsibility of each employee is service to the customer, whether this customer is a buyer of the company's products or its services. In your contact with the public you will have the opportunity for creating and maintaining goodwill. How can you do this? By observing the following:

1. Always be courteous. The tone of your voice is as important as the actual words you use.

2. Recognize the fact that questions directed to you are based on understandable lack of knowledge—not on stupidity.

3. Remember that when a customer is irritated, his irritation is not aimed at you. In all likelihood he is perplexed or confused about some problem connected with the company's product or service. A calm and courteous response from you is the best remedy.

4. Answer only questions pertaining to your individual responsibility and on which you are thoroughly informed. Arrange to refer questions which you cannot answer to the proper person.

5. Keep telephone referrals at a minimum to avoid having the customer repeat his story. If you are not sure where the call is to be transferred, ask for the caller's name, telephone and extension number, and follow up as quickly as possible.

6. See that correspondence is answered promptly and that all parts of a letter are covered. Never file a letter until all questions are answered.

7. If checking is necessary on your part, take name, telephone and extension number, and give assurance that you will call back, indicating whenever possible, the time at which your call may be expected.

8. Always call back, if you said you would—even if it is to report that you do not yet have the answer.

9. If your work is with material or forms rather than directly with the public, see to it that information is correctly recorded and filed—to insure prompt handling of requests, bills, or claims.

10. Hold the dealing of the company and its customers in confidence. Whatever information is shared by the customer is reported only to get an answer to his question or problem. No matter how interesting or unusual this may be, it is not intended for general publication and good ethics requires that it be treated as personal and confidential.

CREATIVE BUSINESS LETTER WRITING

A cross-section of management personnel were recently asked how often they used the specific knowledge and skills offered by each of 62 college courses. Results showed that communications and human relations skills were by far the most frequently used.

About 80 percent of the respondents put "skill in letter writing" at the top of their list. Only about 2 percent of the people are natural letter writers. Very few people can write good business letters, but with practice everyone can learn to write better letters.

There are three kinds of business letters:

1. Favorable—completely satisfying.

2. Unfavorable—make the reader mad, disgusted, discouraged.

3. Colorless—leave the reader cold.

The most common complaints against business letters is that they are:

1. Too long.

2. Stilted and stuffy.

3. Tactless or offensive.

4. Vague, involved, repetitious, disjointed.

A study of business letter writing begins with a review of the history of business letters.

Letters originally were prepared by heavy-bearded gentlemen in frock coats, written with a flourish at roll-top desks, with steel pen points dipped in messy ink. The process was conducive to thoughtfulness. The communications, at least those which were preserved for us today, were classics, both of substance and of style.

Today we do much more communicating, squeeze this duty in between many other more pressing assignments, and dread the job so much that we turn out ill-conceived and lifeless letters. The fact that the average businessman signs his dictated letters without looking them over indicates how much he wishes he could dispense with this unpleasant chore with as little fuss as possible.

We Fear to Write

This is a strange paradox. We are educated sufficiently to write good letters. We actually like to communicate; witness our desire to talk at the drop of a hat. But we fear the task, knowing that our efforts will forever be recorded on paper for endless second-guessing by ourselves and others.

The old way letter writing was taught was to copy successful letters. The original textbooks were merely collections of other people's successful letters. They taught the form of a letter . . . nothing else.

Letters were put together by remembering the rules for the format. The finished letter was a patchwork of ready-made phrases which made it impersonal. In today's concept of letter writing these old-time words, phrases, and symbols are hackneyed and inadequate. In their place the modern writer uses natural expressions.

The business letter should not be impersonal. It should be warm and friendly. It should also be sincere. Remember, we don't answer letters; we answer people.

In addition, business letters should be effective to be efficient. A good letter costs over $3 according to the latest Dartnell survey average. An unfriendly, tactless, carelessly composed, ineffective letter costs infinitely more, in further unnecessary correspondence and lost customers.

Before we can learn effective letter writing we must first unlearn many bad habits. Included are the use of—

- Stereotypes
- Overworked phrases
- Negative words
- Stilted formalities

- Superfluous wordage
- Attempted legal lingo
- Ultimatums

Richard H. Morris, correspondence consultant from Ridgefield, Connecticut, suggests the following tips for writing good letters:

1. Organize, before starting to dictate
2. Get off to a fast, gracious start
3. Make letters easy to read
4. Avoid nonstop sentences and paragraphs
5. Create confidence
6. Impart personality and life into the written word
7. Learn what makes your reader "tick"
8. Give your letters sales appeal
9. Let your reader "save face"
10. Adopt a friendly "you" tone
11. You want action—ask for it
12. Build goodwill even when saying "no"
13. End each letter with an appropriate close
14. Remember, you are dealing with situations and people— not just facts and figures.

The most important characteristic of business letters is tone or goodwill. Those who read our letters do not see us; many might not even know us. They judge us, therefore, entirely by the effect produced by our letters. This makes the tone of our letters very important.

The warmth of our letters lies not in the format or style, but in the message. It is necessary that we build goodwill into our letters, and the tone helps us accomplish this.

The tone of a letter is like the flavor of coffee. We know that the flavor makes a cup of coffee good, but we can't really define or describe it. Just as the flavor of coffee must be "brewed in" so also does a good letter contain "a little bit of yourself."

Ask yourself—

- Do your letters have a warm, human spark?
- Do they build goodwill?
- Do they reflect the character of your company?
- Do they fit into the corporate image you try to project?
- Do they get the results that are wanted?
- Are they holding customer friendships?

The normal flow of a letter is from the opening, through the body of the letter, to the close. These are the three essential parts. Too many letters begin with mechanical openings and end with mechanical closes. Don't waste the opening and the close. Use the opening to introduce the subject and to create the mood; use the close to build goodwill or ask for action.

- Energize the opener.
- Neutralize the negatives.
- Chart the right course of action.
- Simplify sentence sense.
- First, last, and always—add a goodwill gesture.

Next to doing something that deserves to be written about, there is nothing more rewarding or satisfying than writing something that deserves to be read.

In the opening, don't emphasize the obvious. Make the opening establish the fact that you are doing the reader a service, a favor, or telling him what he wants to know. Never, but never, begin mechanically.

Don't waste the closing paragraph. Use it to advantage by innovating, if necessary. Always end the letter on a positive note. Put any necessary apology or excuse in the middle of the letter. Make the close friendly and courteous so the reader will do what you ask or expect. Always try to part as friends.

The 11 C's of WRITTEN COMMUNICATIONS

clear	—unambiguous; one reading should be sufficient to get the message
correct	—facts must be right; no excuse for incorrect grammar and spelling
concise	—message conveyed as briefly as consistent with effectiveness
complete	—all necessary data in logical order; no guesswork
courteous	—say "please" and "thanks"; courtesy is genuine; flattery is counterfeit
considerate	—write the kind of message you would like to receive
confident	—be the authority without acting it; assume the reader will do what he is asked
cheerful	—no one likes bad news; whatever the burden, give it graciously
conversational	—write as naturally as you talk; avoid offensive familiarity
clever	—there is little enough wit in the world so share yours
careful	—written words can carry implications never intended by the writer; avoid emotionally charged overtones which can offend the sensibilities of the reader

Some suggestions for letter writers—

1. Don't be afraid to write letters, or to dictate.

2. Get a good reference book as a guide.

3. Practice letter writing. Learn by doing.

4. Write in a natural conversational tone.

5. Learn what to avoid—useless jargon.

6. Review the fundamentals of good English.

7. Organize thought before writing.

8. Analyze your letters for style, clarity, and effectiveness.

9. Rewrite letters occasionally to see how much better they could be worded.

10. Study incoming letters and borrow good ideas.

11. Put your letters on trial periodically.

12. Ask someone far removed from the situation to read your letters to see if he can understand or follow them.

Maybe you don't consider yourself a writer. Does five average-length letters a day sound like a lot? Yet this means the annual output of written words reaches 300,000. When we consider that a professional writer is likely to turn out but 150,000 words a year, we get an idea of the magnitude of the businessman's writing job.

There are many useful business letter writing aids available—form letters, guide paragraphs, suggestions—and there are many good courses offered by schools and by consultants who specialize in this field. None of this is of any value to the executive or manager, however, until he admits that he might be part of the 98 percent who could profit from qualified letter writing assistance.

The Dartnell Corporation has just prepared a new edition of a classic manual for company correspondence, *The Dartnell Business-Letter Deskbook*.

THE SIMPLIFIED LETTER

It took a while, but finally the railroads were streamlined and modernized. Also at long last, house construction became more functional once grandfather's traditional models were discarded. In business office design, too, change has gradually taken over and brought with it much needed improvement.

But most of the letters which these railroads carry between modern business offices and to new homes are still old-fashioned in format and appearance.

There is little concern about waste motion caused by antiquated style. The cost of old-style letters in time, money, and goodwill is appreciable but not appreciated. Yet these letters could be made more practical in design without sacrificing appearance or effectiveness.

Much emphasis is placed upon other phases of office operations today. Work simplification, automatic machines, and other technical advances are accepted as proper in modern operations. Yet letter writing is generally neglected.

This is tragic since letters are the basic means of business communications. They serve as substitutes for personal contact, and as such ought to reflect the up-to-date, intelligent, businesslike company they represent.

Letters are also costly. Conservative estimates run over three dollars each. Any streamlining of letters which does not impair their effectiveness should be welcomed as a practical cost-saving measure. When such improvement can bring, in addition to cost reduction, a more impressive modern form, there would seem to be every reason for considering it.

The conventional letter style is still influenced by outmoded tradition. It should be reviewed merely to keep pace with the concept of change which underlies all management principles in this scientific age.

To assist progressive managements with their letter writing problems, the Administrative Management Society has developed what is known as the Simplified Letter. Introduced some years ago, its popularity is increasing steadily as more and more companies adopt it.

Most present letter styles are modifications of what is called "block." The simplified form is really nothing but "pure" block style. Everything is lined up with the left margin—and the salutation and complimentary close are omitted while a subject is added.

Every line starts at the left margin—where the typewriter starts. This feature alone eliminates the time-consuming and tedious job of "positioning" the typewriter for each part of the letter. The typewriter follows its simplest mechanical course with the minimum use of space bar, tabulator set key, and tabulator bar.

The first item at the top of the letter is the date. At least three spaces down the full name and address is entered in block style. This makes easy use of the window envelope.

The subject to be discussed is shown in capitals about three spaces below the address. Use of such title provides a provocative opening and also suggests a filing clue.

The body of the letter is prepared in block paragraphs. The useless indentation is ignored, which means no tabular delay.

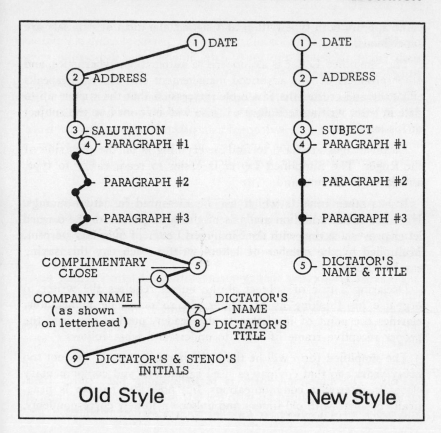

After the closing paragraph the typewritten signature, with title, appears, usually in capitals. The initials of the typist, if used, are placed below the signature also at the left margin. If copies are directed elsewhere this information may be listed on the last line.

In this simplified style several customary items are omitted. The formal salutation, the complimentary close, the company name, and the dictator's initials are not used.

The salutation is actually meaningless, and often poses a problem of correct usage as the dictator fumbles around not knowing how to address the reader. The complimentary close really adds nothing to the letter. The company name is shown at the top of the letterhead; hence, it is not necessary to repeat it. And since the writer's name appears both typewritten and signed, the dictator's initials are superfluous.

The Simplified Letter is as modern as automation, cybernetics, and other products of this advanced management era. Its use bespeaks efficiency and creates the favorable impression that the writer, up to date in letter writing techniques, is also well informed on the subject of his letter.

Disadvantages are hard to find; everything is on the plus side of the ledger. The Simplified Letter is easier to read, easier to type, and easier to file and find.

It has other benefits which can be measured in actual savings. Here are facts: a motion analysis of the typing alone on a 96-word letter proves a saving with the Simplified Letter of over 10.7 percent. Multiplied by the number of letters written each day this saving can be sizable.

Declaring a title or subject at the outset requires the writer to organize his thinking as he begins. In so doing he immediately clarifies the point of his letter to the reader, putting him into the proper receptive frame of mind to understand what follows.

The simplified form will be the style of the future. It was not too many years ago that companies used salutations and complimentary closes in interoffice communications, but now that custom is practically obsolete with old-timers and unknown to new correspondents.

The Message Is the Message

Letter writers must be cautioned, however, that changing the style, or simply adopting the Simplified Letter, will not automatically make them experts in business correspondence. It is not the inclusion or omission of the salutation and complimentary close that makes a letter courteous or effective—it is the message and the manner in which it is written that counts.

Users of this simplified form are urged to consider a few helpful instructions. The dictator must clarify his thinking in order to spell out the subject. Use of the title will immediately tell the reader what to expect.

He should dictate as though he were facing the reader, not his secretary. Really he should not dictate at all, but should speak in a natural manner, avoiding stock phrases as well as oversimplification. This will help to make the letter warm and friendly.

The message should then be presented in a straightforward and coherent manner.

No, adoption of the simplified form will not be a cure-all to a company's letter writing problems. It will not provide the creative thinking that is necessary in good letter writing.

But the philosophy behind the Simplified Letter formula seeks to reduce slow starting and the often stodgy results of conventional letter writing styles. With the Simplified Letter philosophy, a writer can stray the least from a normal, friendly, relaxed type of attitude such as is used in a successful conversation.

Instead of remembering a string of dusty clichés to link thoughts together, the dictator can seek the fresh, orderly flow of a clear mind, informed on the subject.

It may be well to remember the AMS slogan that there is much more to a truly Simplified Letter than simply dropping "Dear Sir" and "Yours truly."

TELEPHONE TECHNIQUES

Everytime the telephone rings, the employee has an excellent opportunity to make a friend for himself and his company. The voice on the phone becomes the company's personality, its image.

At the same time, proper use of the phone makes for efficient operation of any business, no matter how large or how small.

If a company has grown like the proverbial Topsy, it is probable that the telecommunications facilities have sprouted in the same manner, but not as profitably. A personnel administrator might assume the responsibility of coordinating this important phase of the organization; certainly he can—and should—advise that one person be given responsibility for the telecommunications services.

With the variety of telecommunications services and equipment available to modern business and the varying needs of each firm, telephone companies have specially trained Communications Consultants to advise these organizations. The consultants study a company's operations, the goals, bottlenecks and problem areas; the flow of communications in and out, and among departments; they confer with employees; they consider the growth prospects and trends. And from their study they recommend the most efficient services and equipment to do the particular communications job most economically.

This could mean a Dial-Pak service which would free an employee from the switchboard (where she has placed all outside calls) to a clerical position where she answers only incoming calls of a general nature and can assume other responsibilities; extension users save time by dialing their own outside calls and save their caller's time because they dial the extension directly.

Many Alternatives

It may be a recommendation of dial intercom; a tie line between the company's locations across town; or a Wide Area Telephone Service (WATS) line as a savings when many long distance calls are made to many phones within a geographic area. The recommendation may include a Speakerphone set for the personnel administrator so he is able to consult files while continuing his telephone conversation, thus saving both his and his caller's time; he can also include two or more of his staff in on a long distance call when he's making arrangements for a management training program.

Perhaps a system is recommended to automatically distribute incoming phone calls to a group of employees, for instance, order takers. Or, dialed conference calls within a firm would save executive time for department heads who otherwise must leave their offices to attend a meeting to resolve a problem. The Communications Consultant's recommendations might include installing phone booths in a company cafeteria as a convenient location for making personal calls rather than tieing up business phones with personal calls.

The Introductory Pages of the local telephone directory include the number to call to reach a Communications Consultant.

Regardless of who it is who coordinates the communications services for the firm, the personnel administrator must arrange for training in any new service. Often, the Communications Consultant will train the users in the service after it is installed. Or he can arrange for a service adviser to conduct a series of training sessions for all the extension users. It is up to the personnel administrator to schedule people for the sessions and to reserve the room.

Efficient use of the telephone by all extension users is of vital importance to any business. Of course, this is particularly true in those offices where telephone contacts represent a substantial portion of a firm's total business contacts.

Two films which present good telephone usage for business users are available free from the local Bell Telephone Company. They are:

A Manner of Speaking (16 mm, sound motion, color) an entertaining as well as instructive story on the benefits of good telephone manners for business people. 28 min.

If an Elephant Answers (8 mm, 16 mm, sound motion, color) supplements shows of "A Manner of Speaking"; instructs business extension users, under guidance of trained Traffic Department representatives, how to use their telephones more effectively. 20½ min.

Each features situations which show how business customers can receive full benefits from their communications facilities.

A personnel office may get assistance from the service adviser in the telephone company's traffic department, or a company may plan its own telephone program. In any case, the program should include general rules of telephone courtesy, finding numbers, how to answer the phones, and how to place calls—both local and long distance.

Courtesy

Basic to good telephone usage is a pleasant, natural speaking voice. Employees should be encouraged to use a normal conversational tone and to talk directly into the transmitter, with the mouth about an inch away. Enunciate clearly, and no one should be afraid to spell a name or repeat a number. Show interest by inflection and always end the conversation pleasantly: saying "thank you" adds to your image and to the image of a friendly business. And always hang up gently. If, for some reason, a call has been cut off, the calling person places the call again.

How these courtesy pointers are made depends in part on the employee group. For "first jobbers," actual practice conversations may be valuable to help these young people acquire good telephone habits from the beginning of their business careers.

Finding Numbers

Because each telephone has an identifying number, any training program should include appreciation of having the correct number before making any call. This not only saves employee's time but also eliminates time required to answer a wrong number or the time and annoyance of transferring calls.

In most business organizations there is a *house directory* with which all employees should be familiar. It may be a simple list, with name, room number and telephone extension; it may be a small booklet. And in some offices there are both telephone booklets and a list for the office or division.

Familiarity with names and positions is always important and discussion of the house directory can serve as orientation for the corporate structure and organization of the business. Familiarity with this directory also gives numbers for various house services, numbers to call in an emergency, as well as the extension numbers of employees. Knowing what the out-of-hours numbers are can have added benefits for both employees and customers; and employees should know whom to call at home in event of emergencies.

A home telephone number list may be of valuable service to each office and it may be up to the personnel office to develop one and maintain it.

In large organizations the house directory probably lists all office locations as well as the tie lines and other special telephone services. It very likely includes information on how to make long distance as well as local calls.

Sometimes the personnel office issues these directories, but most often it has the responsibility for updating the directories by issuing sheets that show new names and numbers as well as changes of numbers. The frequency of updating depends upon the number of changes. Employees should be encouraged to keep the list handy and to refer to it often. Further, each telephone location should be supplied with such a directory and/or list.

Each telephone should also be "equipped" with the local telephone directory. Any training program might well include appreciation of the Introductory Pages for information about emergency calls as well as calls to the telephone company (repair, business office, Communications Consultant), secretaries often use the postal zone maps. The Introductory Pages also include important information on how to reach "Information" as well as how to place local and long distance calls. The area code map and lists are important for those who make long distance calls. Most persons are familiar with the alphabetical directory, but may not appreciate the use of Yellow Pages for quick reference not only for telephone numbers but also for addresses and full names of firms. A practice session might include looking up the firm's own listings in both the alphabetical and the Yellow Pages directories.

Armed with this knowledge of his own firm, the employee can more intelligently participate in the business of the firm.

Answering the Phone

Every business knows the importance of proper answering of the telephone. The first rule: always answer promptly. And be ready to talk when you pick up the instrument.

Identify yourself! How you do this depends on company policy. If calls are received through a switchboard, the operator should greet the caller with "Good Morning, First National Bank" and then put the call through to the extension. That extension should be answered by "This is the Trust Department, Mr. Jones speaking" or "Trust Department" or "Jack Jones."

When calls are dialed directly to an extension, the person answering identifies himself and his department as "Jack Jones, Trust" or "Trust Department, Mr. Jones." Large firms with direct dialing to extensions frequently urge that only the name of the person be used.

Answering your own phone is not only recommended for speed in transacting your own business, but also to avoid lost calls and irritated callers.

Answering a phone often means taking a message. Always do this cheerfully; you are helping a colleague as well as the caller. And no caller will think you rude if you spell out his name, with a pleasant question-mark inflection, or repeat the telephone number or address he gives. Always offer to take a message. It's possible, of course, that you can answer the question the caller poses and when you do, it is thoughtful if you leave a note to that effect for the person to whom the call was intended. In any case, a correct message makes for friends and efficiency. Always be certain that messages taken at another phone location are placed on the called phones immediately; this avoids needless and embarrassing calls should the called person return to his office and call the person who had previously left a message.

If there are no printed message forms, the personnel office may consider having one printed. Such a form should include blanks for writing the name of the person being called; the person calling; his telephone number with sufficient space to include the area code and a four-digit extension number; four or five lines for message; as well as a check-off list including: "telephoned" "returned your call" "please call" "will call you later" "wants to see you" and "called to see you." There should also be space for the name or initials of the person taking the message, as well as the date and time of the message.

Always Explain Transfer

Transferring a call pleasantly is also important, and the method depends on the type of telephone equipment used in the particular office. But whatever the equipment and the circumstance, apologize for the need to transfer and explain why the transfer is necessary. If possible, "hold" the call while you verify that the person to whom you are transferring the call is in his office. If he is not, then be certain to thank the caller for waiting and tell him Mr. Jones, extension 2345, handles compensation cases, but Mr. Jones is out of the office this morning "but I will have him call you as soon as he returns." Take the message, check the telephone number, and then be certain Mr. Jones gets the message.

Had Mr. Jones been in his office the person would have thanked the caller for waiting and explained that Mr. Jones handles compensation cases and "I'll signal the operator to transfer you . . . just a minute please." The person *slowly* signals the operator, and stays on the line until the operator answers, then "will you please transfer this call to Mr. Jones, extension 2345." With some telephone instruments the call is transferred by a signal to another extension that there's an incoming call; no operator is involved.

Practice in transferring calls lends itself to practice and training in telephone courtesy as well as in knowledge of the company personnel and company operations.

How to "hold" a call while you get information or while you answer another phone is also important. First, it is courtesy: "May I put you on 'hold' while I get the files?" or "Would you mind waiting just a minute while I get the files?" Then depress the "hold" button on the instrument and get the files quickly. If the phone does not have a "hold" button, put the handset on the desk gently. When you get back to the phone-call, press the line button to release the "hold," or pick up the handset, and always thank the person for waiting. If a search for information will take longer than a minute, it is suggested that the person tell the caller it will be necessary to search and perhaps "I could call you back within 10 minutes." Abide by the caller's wishes; he may choose to wait.

Making Calls

Training for making phone calls presupposes familiarity with the telephone directories; it also depends in part on the telephone equipment and the office policies for making calls. But always wait for a dial tone before dialing.

Today most offices have four-digit extension numbers for dialing interoffice calls. Some offices also have one- and two-digit code dialing for extensions within an office organization. But some firms still use a PBX operator to connect them with extensions.

To make a local call outside the company it is usually necessary to dial an access code ("9" for example) then after you get the outside dial tone, dial the telephone number. In some organizations an operator gives the caller an outside line. Always dial the number carefully. A local telephone number has seven digits or that equivalent in two letters and five numbers.

For emergencies it is wise to remember to dial "O" for "Operator" for police or fire.

If a number is not listed in the telephone directory, consult the

Introductory pages of the directory for the local Information operator. When you get the number, hang up; then dial the number.

Long Distance calls are frequent in business operations. They are made when information is needed quickly, when there's need to discuss an issue, when there's need for understanding, confirmation, or obtaining decisions. Long distance calls are easily made and often cheaper than writing a letter.

Some business firms require an extension user to ask the PBX operator for long distance. She gets the extension number and name of the person calling before giving you an outside line or connecting you with a long distance operator. This is for billing purposes, primarily; the company wants to know who calls where.

Types of Calls

Any training program should include the types of calls, their characteristics, and the techniques for making them.

Station calls are those made to a number when the caller will talk with anyone who answers. These calls are as simple to make as local calls; the difference is in dialing an access code where required, then dialing the three-digit area code plus the local telephone number. Not all states have access codes, and some states do not require dialing the area code when it is the same as the calling number—but these instructions are included in the Introductory Pages of the local telephone directory.

If you don't know the number for the telephone you want to call, dial the area code for that number, then 555-1212. This is Long Distance Information.

Since November 1, 1967, there are four schedules of rates for station calls, with rates decreasing from the day rates:

Day Rates—in effect from 7 a.m. to 5 p.m. weekdays

After 5 Rates—in effect from 5 p.m. to 7 p.m. weekdays

After 7 Rates—in effect from 7 p.m. to 7 a.m. weekdays, all day Saturday and Sunday, and 5 holidays

Special Dial Rates—between midnight and 7 a.m. on those calls which do not require an operator.

Using direct dialing of calls saves time and money because of the ease of making the calls and the speed at which they are completed.

Person calls are made when a caller wants to talk to one particular individual or to an extension (when direct inward dialing to extensions is not available). Charges begin when the called person begins to talk.

To place a person call it is usually necessary to dial "O-Operator" and give the operator the calling number, the name of the person being called and that person's telephone number, including the area code if you know it.

Special Business Aids

In some larger cities it is possible to dial person-to-person calls by first dialing "O-Operator," then the area code and the local telephone number. The operator will announce herself after dialing is completed, and after the called person answers the operator goes on to another call. This telephone service is known as Expanded Direct Distance Dialing. The Introductory Pages of the local telephone directory tells whether this service is available.

There are two classes of rates for person-to-person calls:

Day Rates—in effect from 7 a.m. to 5 p.m. weekdays.

Night Rates—in effect from 5 p.m. to 7 a.m. weekdays and all day Saturday and Sunday.

When business firms have offices in different parts of the city or in several communities they may be connected by *tie lines*. Whenever tie lines are established, instruction in their use should be included in any training. In some instances a tie line is dialed, in others it is necessary to ask an operator for the tie line.

Employees should also be trained in receiving *collect calls* if this is a practice encouraged by a business firm. The calls and their costs are often recorded by several departments of the organization.

Businessmen often save time and expense of travel when they make *conference calls* which may bring up to nine locations together. This is a form of person-to-person call which involves an operator to set up the call for a predetermined time convenient to everyone.

Details for making conference calls are given in the Introductory Pages of the telephone directory.

Overseas calls are commonplace for many firms, a rarity for others. Training in making these calls should be provided if they are made frequently. Station and person rates exist for many countries, but in many parts of the world only person calls may be made. Time of calling is important in any overseas call; night rates also prevail for calls to some countries.

Other Calls

Because the business activities vary with each firm's requirements, the telephone services also vary. Instruction should be provided whenever any of the following telecommunications services are available to employees:

WATS lines—who uses them, how they are marked, what areas they cover

Inward WATS—who uses them, what areas they cover, how they are marked, how they are answered, necessary supplies adjacent (such as order blanks, invoices, etc.)

Bellboy Personal Signaling service—what it is, who uses the service and why, how to call the person, importance of judgment and message-taking

Mobile telephone service—what vehicles have the service and why, what it is, how to call the persons in the vehicles, how to list the number in directories, how to call from a vehicle

Telephone Answering service—when such a service is used, need for checking when returning to office, need for reporting when leaving office, hours of coverage, and for some—the billing arrangements

Telephone Answering and Recording sets—where it is, why it is used, how to operate it, how to record messages, how to play back messages, how and when to transcribe messages, service calls

Automatic Dialers (three kinds)—when they are used, who has them, how to record new numbers, how to change numbers, how to make a call using the automatic nature of the instrument.

It is always better to train employees on the actual equipment that is in use in an office. When such equipment and services are installed the telephone company provides instructional material. If such services are in use but the informational material lost, the personnel administrator can obtain additional copies from the telephone company.

Whenever a major change is made in the telephone service for a firm it is advisable to plan for a training program. This is particularly true when a Centrex system is provided, when many extensions will have direct inward and outward dialing. This becomes a "natural" for reviewing telephone courtesy, and for showing the films which make for good business usage.

SALES TRAINING FILMS

For some years, The Dartnell Corporation has been carefully developing a library of outstanding sound-motion pictures and sound-slidefilms on salesmanship. These films deal with tested techniques of proven value and are prepared with an eye for easy adoption into the training curriculum of any company—no matter what type or size.

These films may be used for:

1. *Sales Training*—as part of a sales-training course or sales-refresher course for the existing sales staff or as part of an indoctrination course for new salesmen. The film can be used to supplement other sales or product training a company may have, or a sales-training course can be built from scratch using selected films from this library.

2. *Sales Meetings or Sales Conventions.* Any of the films can be used alone, as each is complete in itself, or a selection can be made to cover different aspects of a meeting. With the meeting guides and supplementary material available, any one of the Dartnell films can be used to build up an entire sales meeting.

3. *Dealer and Distributor Training Meetings.* Where it is desired to run a series of sales or training meetings for dealers, distributors,

or their sales personnel, company representatives equipped with the new lightweight projectors, and with suitable script material, can stage effective sales and training meetings at the local or regional level.

These films and filmstrips may be rented or purchased.

Following is a list of some of the Dartnell Sales Training Films. All are 16-mm. sound films and all run 30 minutes:

The Second Effort, with Vince Lombardi.

How to Take the Butt Out of a Sales Rebuttal.

Solid Gold Hours, starring Monty Woolley and Geraldine Brooks.

Autopsy of a Lost Sale.

The Selling Secrets of Ben Franklin.

How to Make an Effective Sales Presentation.

What it Takes to be a Real Salesman, featuring Dr. Norman Vincent Peale.

Developing Your Sales Personality.

How to Succeed in the People Business, featuring Dr. Joyce Brothers.

How to Prevent Objections in Selling.

How to Sell Quality, by J. C. Aspley, founder of Dartnell.

The Power of Enthusiasm.

The Bettger Story.

Presenting Your Sales Case Convincingly.

Opening the Sale.

Closing the Sale.

How to Sell Creatively.

Overcoming Objections.

How to Up Sales by Better Sales Supervision (executive development).

How to Lead an Effective Sales Conference (executive development).

How to Select Salesmen Who Can and Will Sell (executive development).

With more and more American companies setting up manufacturing facilities and sales organizations abroad, plus increasing impact of the European Common Market, many of the above Dartnell Sales Training Films are now available with lip-sync foreign-language sound tracks.

During the past several decades, salesmanship had become a lost skill in Europe because of shortages. Those days are gone. Production now exceeds demand, and those companies competing in foreign markets would be well advised to consider introducing sales-training films for their foreign sales organizations.

Films are available in these languages: Danish, Dutch, Finnish, Flemish, French, German, Italian, Japanese, Norwegian, Spanish, and Swedish.

Catalog Available

In addition to its library of sales-training motion pictures, Dartnell has films available for executive development, entertainment films for sales meetings, and sound-slidefilms on various subjects.

A catalog of Dartnell films may be obtained from:

The Dartnell Corporation
4660 North Ravenswood Avenue
Chicago, Illinois 60640

Vince Lombardi, a legend in his own time, gives salesmen the philosophy that built the champion Green Bay Packers in The Second Effort, *a sales training film produced by The Dartnell Corporation.*

SALES-TRAINING PROGRAMS

"Selling is Mental" is a sales manpower development program designed by Training Services, Inc., to give salesmen a fresh, more effective approach in selling. It is sparked with positive facts that assure increased sales and profits. It puts new fire into established salesmen, and puts new men into action faster and better equipped to sell successfully. The program consists of a series of six hard-hitting, sales stimulating color filmstrips, 15 minutes in length, with sound on 12-inch 33-rpm records. Each filmstrip sparkles with color photographs. They include field-tested, proven sales strategies and techniques. A detailed leader's manual is provided for conducting sales meetings with minimum preparation and ease of presentation.

The filmstrip topics are:

The Power of Mental Attitude in Selling

Selling the End Result First

Turning a Deaf Ear to Sales Resistance

Developing the Right Attitude Toward Price

Closing the Sale

Developing the Right Attitude on a Call Back

Previews Arranged

Any single film, or the complete set of six, including meeting materials, may be purchased. Previews for a five-day examination can be arranged with the preview cost applied toward the purchase of the complete program.

"Supervisor Training on Human Relations," also presented by Training Services, Inc., is a basic course designed to equip supervisors with the vital knowledge of the principles and techniques of effective management. It consists of eight black and white filmstrips, 15 minutes each, with sound on 12-inch 33-rpm records. A comprehensive guide for leaders to use in conducting the eight one-hour or two-hour sessions on each subject is included. Also included are sample personalized letters to be used as followup mailings to each participant as a concise recap of the ideas, attitudes and practices in good human relations emphasized in each of the eight sessions.

The filmstrip titles are:

> *The Supervisor's Job*
>
> *Interpreting Company Policies*
>
> *The Supervisor as a Representative of Management*
>
> *Induction and Job Instruction*
>
> *Handling Grievances*
>
> *Maintaining Discipline*
>
> *Promotions, Transfers, and Training for Responsibility*
>
> *Promoting Cooperation*

The complete series, or any single filmstrip, may be purchased. Also, additional manuals may be purchased. Previews for a five-day examination can be arranged with Training Services. Inc., 130 Orient Way, Rutherford, New Jersey 07070.

"An Audio-Visual Approach to Management Science," another product of Training Services, Inc., is a series of 12 color sound filmstrips designed to meet the need for an understanding of the latest applications of behavioral sciences as it applies to managerial positions. Each subject in the series provides material for a one-to two-hour program and covers a phase in the development of the professional manager. It includes a 20-minute color sound filmstrip, discussion materials, and comprehensive directions. The material leads to a stimulating and challenging interchange of ideas that reveal the inner core of management needs and ability.

The 12 titles are:

> *Evaluation: A New Integration of Management Theory*
>
> *Self-Analysis for Executive Success*
>
> *Your Inner Dynamics as a Communicator*
>
> *New Frontiers in the Motivation of Others*
>
> *Setting Goals for Self and Others*

The Measurement of Proficiency
Counseling to Produce Results
Predicting Behavior Through Interviewing
How to Achieve Successful Delegation
Installing Your Own Work Simplification Program
Executive Controls That Really Work
New Demands in Executive Leadership

BUSINESS-TRAINING FILMS

A library of several hundred business oriented films and film-strips is offered as a public service by the Audio-Visual Center of The City College of New York.

A counseling service is also available to companies and organizations desiring to establish audio-visual implemented training.

Subjects include:

Accounting	Insurance
Advertising	Labor
Art	Management
Banking and Finance	Marketing
Business Education	Music
Clothing and Fashion	Office Management
Credit	Personnel Management
Economic Geography	Psychology
Economics	Retailing
Education	Safety
Engineering and Industry	Salesmanship
Foreign and International	Speech
Foreign Trade	Statistics
Government and History	Supervision
Graphic Arts	Textiles
Health Education	Time and Motion Study
Home Decoration	Visual Aids
Intercultural Understanding	Vocational Guidance

The motion pictures are 16-mm. sound; some are in color, others are black and white. The filmstrips are 35 mm.

These films and filmstrips may be "booked" on a rental basis for a nominal fee. A catalog (for which a charge of 20 cents is made for handling and mailing) may be obtained from

> Miss Islyn Hurdle
> Film Rental Service
> Audio-Visual Center
> The City College
> Bernard M. Baruch School of Business and Public Administration
> 17 Lexington Avenue
> New York, New York 10010

OTHER TRAINING FILMS

The following training films are available from

> BNA Incorporated
> A Division of the Bureau of National Affairs, Inc.
> 1231 24th Street, N. W.
> Washington, D. C. 20037

Title	Subject
The Marvelous Mousetrap (starring Wally Cox)	Quality consciousness
Cash on the Barrel Head (starring William Bendix)	Fringe benefits
The Real Security	Mental retirement and organizational lethargy
You, Yourself, Incorporated	Self-development, self-fulfillment
The New Truck Dilemma	Role playing in group decisions
The Berlo Effective	Avoiding communication breakdown
Communications Series	Meanings are in people
	Communication feedback
	Changing attitudes through communication
	Communicating management's point of view

Supervisory Training
(series of 7 films)

The Trouble With Archie	Discipline
A Good Beginning	Induction and training
The Winning Combination	Cost control
Listen, Please	Listening
The Case of the Missing Magnets	Boosting productivity
Instructions or Obstructions	Giving instructions
The Challenge of Leadership	Leadership

These are 16-mm. sound color films. Running time is approximately 24 minutes. These films may be purchased, rented, or previewed. Guides for their effective use, and viewer's booklets are available.

ADULT EDUCATION

Adult education is a vital necessity in our fast-moving modern life. Never has there been greater need for knowing more about ourselves and the world in which we live.

Education can no longer be regarded as completed with the preparation for vocations, whether at the close of the secondary-school period or at the completion of a professional course in a higher educational institution. Whether viewed from the standpoint of social need or of individual development, education is a process which continues through adult life.

This is the first generation in which our earlier training is no longer sufficient to carry us through life. A formal education received years ago is no guarantee that we can meet successfully the demands of modern living. New skills, ideas, facts, and attitudes are required to cope with the rapid and continuous changes now going on.

Just as obsolescence occurs sooner in the material world, so also is it noticeably visible in the realm of knowledge. This is certainly understandable when we think of the outstanding advancements in the field of medicine; would we entrust the delicate operation on a loved one to a surgeon who had learned nothing new since he received his diploma years ago?

The need to keep apace of changing conditions is just as important, although not as dramatic, in other occupations.

Today much knowledge is out of date as fast as it is learned. More complete, extensive, and reliable facts supplant earlier conclusions in all fields. More new knowledge has already been accumulated during the lifetime of the present adult population than the total amount that existed at the time of its birth.

Single-Skilled Worker is "Unskilled"

In the vital area of vocational skills, this obsolescence is even more apparent. Automation, electronics, and other technological improvements dictate that adults adapt to new methods and learn new skills. Flexibility is the key word as employers prefer to move workers about instead of releasing them. Many jobs in offices, factories, and shops are in a state of flux, and even if the number of jobs in a company or industry is not reduced, certainly the "mix" of jobs will be different.

The single-skill worker, the one who cannot adjust readily, becomes the victim of technological unemployment at the very time that skilled jobs go begging.

For survival and for progress, America needs all the experience, guidance, and dependability of all available workers. But in an industrial economy these commendable traits are useless without skill development. Adult education, therefore, can no longer be a marginal activity.

This emphasis on adult education should not be considered unusual. Organized education was originally devoted to the development of the mature, not child, mind. Plato and Aristotle taught men and women, not children. Even today, progress is founded on the ability of the adult mind to change by learning new things.

Since our society is controlled by adults, not children, it is foolish to pass over adults and concentrate on children in trying to develop a better world. Education can no longer be considered as the occupation of childhood but of a whole life. The full substance of education can be acquired only in adult life, when grownup men and women, stable in character and serious in purpose, bring varied backgrounds to the process of learning.

Yet in the truly American tradition of freedom, adult learning has always been optional. Beyond the formal education in youth, which is required, any additional learning was left heretofore to informal means, such as occasional books, mass communication media, and voluntary study groups, many of which were poorly planned, poorly executed, run more for social purposes, and with little resemblance to study in the school sense.

The curriculum of adult education originally consisted of an *a la carte* menu of miscellaneous subjects. It was concerned with remedying deficiencies in the education of youth, and in the areas of literacy, citizenship, vocational skills, and better use of leisure time. It filled a limited need despite any ill-defined goal.

In more recent years adult education has been coming in for its share of attention and is getting assistance from government and social forces. During wartime, when Americans displayed an emotional antipathy for all things alien, the emphasis was on Americanization education. Later, the appeal of group dynamics had an impact on classroom discussion. More recently, education for the aged became popular.

The Horizon Broadens

Today the concern is for the common man. This is the era of the disadvantaged, the under-educated, the unemployed, the dropout. Welfare programs reveal there is a causal relationship between poverty of the mind and poverty of the body. A nation dedicated to human dignity is trying to help people who have never known that dignity.

Added together, nowadays the need is greater, more permanent, and more demanding. Fortunately, adult education is no longer a hobby or pastime, a fifth wheel on the cart of learning. It attempts to expose the mind to a new body of knowledge that was unknown years ago, to train in new skills that were unheard of years ago, and to broaden the scope of living in a social world whose horizons are much wider.

Any definition of adult education includes these characteristics:

1. The persons concerned are beyond the compulsory school age.

2. They are engaged in an organized educational activity conducted by a responsible educational agency.

3. They are continuing their education on a partime basis.

4. They are attending classes voluntarily.

5. There usually is a fee.

Most definitions will exclude incidental learning picked up by casual conversation, newspaper or magazine reading, or radio-television listening. This could be labeled "education of adults" as differentiated from adult education, which is better planned and directed.

Adult education is not recreation, nor a program of arts and crafts to provide busy work. Adult education does not have as its goal the primary purpose of providing worthy use of leisure time. Likewise, it is not exclusively a program to teach individuals how to make a living.

Adult education is as broad as life itself. The objective is to enable adults to function more efficiently as citizens, parents, homemakers, workers, and human beings.

The aim of all education is to open the mind, not fill it as we would a bottle. The purpose of adult education is more than merely "to teach"; it is to reopen the mind and create within the individual the desire to learn. Adults need to be taught, yes, but even more so, they need to be stimulated.

But adult education is not an extension of previous formal classroom instruction. It is different. The adult has a few advantages and a few disadvantages as a learner.

The adult learner advantages:

1. Knows what he wants.

2. Recognizes an immediate need.

3. Expresses a definite purpose to learn.

4. Is self-motivated.

5. Feels his responsibility.

6. Brings with him a wide range of experience.

7. Is usually financially able.

Disadvantages:

1. Has limited time for education.

2. May be tired after working all day.

3. Struggles with preset ideas and habit patterns.

4. Must often "unlearn" before he can learn.

5. Could have a critical attitude.

6. May feel inadequate and need his confidence built up.

7. Expects too much and becomes easily discouraged.

There are two main reasons for grownups participating in adult education: (1), to fit themselves for better jobs; and (2), to make their lives more interesting and enjoyable.

The results of a national survey showed that the emphasis of adult education is on the practical rather than the academic subjects. Technical courses, business classes, and other vocational subjects make up the largest segment. The humanities, religious, and public-affairs categories, which are more representative of the realm of ideas and values, run second. Television, a medium capable of attracting the largest audience ever, does not as yet loom up as a very significant force as a form of adult instruction.

The educational agencies in academic circles and in industry have recognized the obligation and the opportunity. The public has accepted the offer and has responded. One of five Americans pursues some kind of voluntary education each year. About three-fourths are high school or college graduates. In some respects the current boom in adult learning is gradually approaching the dimensions of a national craze.

New Concept Emerges

Just as it is normal to expect children to attend school, so it is becoming accepted for adults to keep on studying. Instead of putting a period at the end of school days, we use a comma, as we do not stop but branch out into a more spacious version of life. A new concept of education is emerging. The accelerating pace of social change makes education a lifelong, not a terminal, process. The

ADULT EDUCATION FACTORS

1. Adults must want to learn.

   a. Children may learn in response to compulsion.

   b. Adults must develop their own desire.

2. Adults will learn only what they feel a need to learn.

   a. Children learn many things for which they feel no need.

   b. Adults are more practical in what they study.

3. Adults learn by doing.

   a. Adults will forget within a year at least 50 percent of what they learn in a passive way; within two years they will forget 80 percent.

   b. Adults retain more of what they learn by practice.

4. Adult learning centers on problems, and the problems must be realistic.

   a. Adults expect more than rules, principles, and hypothetical illustrations.

   b. Problems should be based on experience and solutions should be practical in helping resolve these problems.

5. Adults learn best in an informal environment.

   a. Children may need to be regimented and controlled to get their attention and cooperation.

   b. Adults have progressed from school days and rebel against standardization.

6. Adults need a variety of learning methods.

   a. Information should reach the adult learner through more than one sensory channel.

   b. Movies, film strips, flipcharts, other visual aids can heighten the impact of a lecture or other verbal exposition.

7. Adults want guidance, not grades.

   a. They are not interested in competing or excelling.

   b. They resist tests and other devices for comparative evaluation; they fear embarrassment.

social, economic, and cultural climate in which adults live is no longer the same as that for which they trained in early life. Continued learning enables us to understand broadening responsibilities, to detect opportunities, and to build a philosophy in the art of living in a changing world.

But the benefits of adult education are not yet universally accepted. Some people are enmeshed in a mood which worships leisure time as idleness. They know of no pleasure other than the gratification of the senses and the delights of society, leaving their minds unenlightened and their faculties unchallenged. They indulge themselves in the conceit that they are making good use of free time when they are only engaged in the humbler occupation of killing time. Breathing is existing, not living.

Tennyson said, "Come my friends, 'tis not too late to seek a newer world." We can find happiness by understanding and directing the current of progress. This requires continuous study. The human nervous system has great adaptive capacity if we keep it vibrant and working. Each one of us can choose to keep an active open mind or elect to become inactive, forgetful, and depend upon emotional patterns fixed from early experiences. The latter is the sign leading to unhappiness, old age, and discontent.

Adult education offers everybody the chance for self-betterment . . . to keep in step with our jobs and our place in the world.

LIBRARY

Another way to stimulate employees in their ambitions to grow is through company libraries. A central library will serve employees of a large office, or of a company with both office and factory workers housed in the same, or at least nearby, buildings. In multiple-building plants, convenient branch libraries, or "reading centers," may be opened in cafeterias, recreation rooms, or other handy areas.

The purpose is to widen the reading habits of employees. Company libraries contain good books and quality magazines, as well as the weekly news magazines and a file of back issues of newspapers. Homecraft and hobby books are included. Technical textbooks and trade publications are available for specific interests. There are also books and articles on management, supervision, human relations, and on economics, government, and politics. The company library often contains books relating to the business and the industry which are not usually found at public libraries.

The library is under the supervision of a librarian, possibly part time. This person is responsible for loaning books and for their return in good condition. In large cities arrangements may be made with the public library for the lending of books.

How many books should a company library contain? One rule of thumb is one book per employee; at least this is as good a starting point as any. An appropriation may be set up to purchase a certain number of new books each month in order to keep the library up to date. The new books can be reviewed in the employee publication (house organ); such review also reminds employees of the library service.

In this day of popular paperback books, the establishment of a library can be done with a much smaller budget. Not only are these books cheaper to purchase, but employees are likely to donate their personal pocket books instead of throwing them away. Anytime the number of paperbacks becomes too large the surplus can always be shipped to USO clubs or veterans organizations for our men in military service.

THE BASIC 30

A Bibliography of First Purchases for the Business Library

(Budget $800—Prices are approximate)

Ayer's Directory of Newspapers and Periodicals. Philadelphia: N. W. Ayer & Son, Inc., annual. $30.00.

Business Periodicals Index. New York: H. W. Wilson Co., annual with supplements. (Cost prorated $40.00 est.).

County and City Data Book. Washington: U.S. Department of Commerce (Supt. of Docs.) 1962. $5.25.

Dewey Decimal Classification. 8th abridged ed. New York: H. W. Wilson. 1959. $8.00.

A Dictionary of American-English Usage. New York: Oxford University Press. 1957. $6.50.

A Dictionary of Modern English Usage. By H. W. Fowler. New York: Oxford University Press, 1956. $5.00.

Directory of Post Offices—With ZIP Code Numbers. Washington: U.S. Post. Office Department (Supt. of Docs.), annual. $2.50.

Dun & Bradstreet Million-Dollar Directory. New York: Dun & Bradstreet, Inc., annual. $98.50.

Editor & Publisher Market Data Book. New York: Editor & Publisher, annual. $10.00.

Editor & Publisher Yearbook. New York: Editor & Publisher, annual. $8.00.

Encyclopaedia Britannica and Annuals. Chicago: Encyclopaedia Britannica Press. $254.00 (annuals $5.30 each to subscribers).

Encyclopedia of Associations. Detroit, Michigan: Gale Research Co., 5th edition, 1966. $29.50.

Etiquette: The Blue Book of Social Usage, by Emily Post. New York: Funk & Wagnalls, 1960. $5.95.

Familiar Quotations. By John Bartlett. Boston, Mass.: Little, Brown & Co., 13th edition rev. 1955. $10.00.

Famous First Facts. New York: H. W. Wilson Co., 1964. $18.00

GPO Manual. Washington: Government Printing Office (Supt. of Docs.), revised edition, 1959. $1.25.

Hotel and Motel Red Book. New York: American Hotel Association Directory Corp., annual. $7.50.

Poor's Register of Corporations, Directors and Executives. New York: Standard & Poor's Corp., annual. $84.00.

Primer in Parliamentary Procedure. by Marie H. Suthers, Chicago: Dartnell Corporation, 1965. $3.95.

Rand McNally Road Atlas. Chicago: Rand McNally & Co., annual. $1.95.

Readers' Guide to Periodical Literature. New York: H. W. Wilson Co., annual with supplements. Costs prorated. $25.00 (est.)

Roget's International Thesaurus. New York: Thomas Y. Crowell Co., 3rd edition, 1962. $5.95.

Schofield Reference Bible. New York: Oxford University Press. $5.50.

Standard Handbook for Secretaries. by L. I. Hutchinson, New York: McGraw-Hill, 7th Ed. $5.00.

Statistical Abstract of the United States. Washington: U.S. Department of Commerce (Supt. of Docs.) annual. $3.75.

United States Government Organization Manual. Washington: Office of the Federal Register (Supt. of Docs.), annual. $1.75.

Webster's Third New International Dictionary of the English Language. Springfield, Mass.: G. & C. Merriam Co., 1963. $47.50.

Who's Who in America. Chicago: Marquis-Who's Who, biennially. $29.50.

World Almanac and Book of Facts. New York: N. Y. World-Telegram and Sun., annual. $1.50.

World Atlas. Maplewood, N. J.: C. S. Hammond & Co., 1961. $15.00.

EMPLOYEE EDUCATION

Employee education is not to be confused with employee training. General education equips the person for life; training equips the worker for better job performance.

The motivation for employee education lies with the individual, although it is often encouraged by the company. It can be taught by a teacher or be self-taught. It can be in-house or off the premises. It can be on released (company) time or on the employee's own time. It can be in classrooms or by correspondence. It can be degree-related or noncredit courses.

Employee education can be on any work level. Rank-and-file workers may want to broaden their educational backgrounds or executives may want to participate in non-job-related development programs. Studying art or music may not make a man a better accountant, it's true, but this could be useful in rounding out his personality and making him more suitable for an executive position.

Not Easy to See

Every employee is hired initially for a specific job and it is the skill he possesses that makes him employable. The typist in the office and the machinist in the factory are put to work because of a single skill which is well developed. The same is true of upper-echelon positions where an applicant is recruited because of his specialty—engineering, law, math, marketing, etc. But as an individual moves up the ladder he broadens rather than deepens his qualifications.

It is easy for workers to enroll for vocational education programs which enhance their earnings potential. It is not as easy for workers to understand why they should want to participate in adult education which has no direct or noticeable bearing on their hopes of getting better jobs.

Likewise, it is easy for companies to conduct classes, or support workers, in the broad arena of training which enhances the employees' value to themselves and to their companies. It is not as easy for companies to accept the idea that any contribution, financial or otherwise, which they make to nonspecific education may, in the long run, even return a greater payback.

MATHEMATICS VOCATIONALLY

To earn a living, it is better for a girl to know how to read Gregg than Homer. That sober advice has been given to many girls upon entering high school or college.

Too many liberal arts graduates enter the job market without any salable skill to offer in exchange for a paycheck. It must disillusion these otherwise ambitious applicants to yield attractive job opportunities to high school graduates who are commercially trained.

Typing or no typing—for many jobs the choice is obvious. But other less apparent weaknesses in education and training can, nevertheless, be just as costly.

Every high school student's program should include some courses in mathematics. Many students, such as those planning to go into engineering colleges, take math in high school. But what about the others, those who see no immediate need for it, or who shy away from math because it involves too much work?

Naturally, math training equips for many positions such as statistics, accounting, cashiering, inventory control, and the like. It is also necessary in everyday living for budgeting, marketing, taxes, and other purposes. But aside from these specific considerations, let's evaluate math training on general principles.

The knowledge of math is directly helpful since almost all jobs make use of some figure work at some time. But math training is also generally useful in all types of work. It organizes thinking and therefore permits organization of work. It encourages the mind to think further than the problem at hand to see the effects of the solution, to recognize and be prepared for other problems that might arise out of it. Mathematics is like the arts. The ideas, the logic, the patterns of mathematics fit together in an elegant, harmonious way like the sounds of a musical composition, the words of a poet, or the colors of a painting.

Math training is good also as an attitude of mind. "There is an answer to the problem so I will find it." It gives confidence. In general, it is of value for the whole approach to any job.

For the person as a whole, mathematics stimulates the mind and trains it to think. It helps to develop a wondering mind which asks the why and how behind the answer. It causes the mind to think fast and logically, to understand problems first, to find the quickest approach, and then go directly to the solution.

Of course, there can be disadvantages. A mind that is mathematically trained might get into the habit of believing that there is only one solution to a problem and therefore might miss a better one. This could make a person opinionated, by giving the feeling that he is always right—and make him prejudiced. Too much confidence could result in thinking too fast without weighing the reasons properly, thereby coming up with the wrong solution.

When a mind is so trained in math that it forgets the arts, sometimes it becomes narrow and stodgy and loses its creativeness; it goes so directly to the answer that it might miss something that could be more important than the solution itself.

A well-integrated mind is the ideal. This in itself indicates the need of math training. But this also recognizes that the more a mind delves into one subject, such as math, the more it should strive to interest itself in related subjects also. But just as mathematics is not the whole answer, an education for the total life pattern is not complete without its share of mathematics.

TUITION REFUND

It has often been said that the growth of any company is merely the sum total of the growth of its people. In the belief that it is in their best interest to do so, many companies pay part or all of the cost of education for their employees.

Aiding and encouraging employees to improve their educational background is considered good practice in the hope that this will:

1. Upgrade employees in their training, thus enhancing their value to the company.

2. Assure employees that the company is interested in their advancement and future security.

A policy of paying the cost of education is easy to implement when the courses are directly related to the industry. Sending insurance people to a school for underwriters, for example, is common. Many

INTERNATIONAL SALT COMPANY	CORPORATE INDUSTRIAL RELATIONS MANUAL	DATE EFFECTIVE
		APPROVED Administrative Committee

CORPORATE TUITION REFUND POLICY

I. PURPOSE

The company recognizes that educational development is becoming increasingly important and should be encouraged. For that reason, this policy has been established to provide an opportunity for the men and women of our company to obtain additional education or training in order to increase their competence in present jobs and to prepare for advancement in the future.

II. POLICY

Under this policy an employee will be reimbursed for tuition and laboratory fees up to $200 a term or $400 a year if the eligibility and procedural requirements are met. Participation in the plan is voluntary and in no case is to be made a condition of employment.

While it is the company's intention to continue the plan indefinitely, the company retains the right to amend or terminate the offering of reimbursement at any time.

III. ELIGIBILITY

A. Employees

1. The tuition refund is available to any full-time employee who has completed 13 weeks of continuous service prior to the date on which the course begins.

2. Tuition refund will not be given to an employee who qualifies for educational benefits under the G. I. bill. However, a veteran who is no longer eligible for government benefits may participate in the plan.

3. The lay-off or release of an employee after he has been enrolled in an approved course will not alter his eligibility for tuition refund benefits.

4. The resignation or discharge of an employee automatically terminates his eligibility for benefits under this policy.

B. Courses

1. Tuition refund will be given for courses by technical institutes, trade schools, correspondence schools or accredited colleges and universities.

2. The course must be related to the employee's present job.

3. There must be a probability that the course will contribute to the employee's development.

4. Course attendance must be on the employee's own time and should not interfere with his regular job.

International Salt Company's tuition refund policy (continued on page 326).

324

trade associations conduct seminars and specialty schools to which member companies send employees.

The practice of paying for general education, more tailored to the individual than to his company, is a different matter. Companies ought not embark upon such a program without first thinking seriously upon some of the problems which might result. Once the program is underway it is almost impossible to backtrack and revise the rules. It is best that the terms and conditions be clearly spelled out.

Many companies, large and small, have a policy of "tuition refunds" for their employees. This means that under certain standards part or all of the cost of tuition, books, and supplies will be paid back to the employee upon satisfactory completion of the course.

The rules are usually—

1. The course of study must be in line with the employee's work.

    a. Shorthand for a typist—yes.

    b. Sewing for a typist—no.

2. The course must be studied at an approved (not necessarily accredited) institution of learning.

    a. University night school—yes.

    b. Carnegie course—maybe.

    c. Dance studio—no.

3. The employee's enrollment must be approved by the company.

4. The employee must make a passing grade to receive the tuition refund.

Refunds vary from 50 percent to the entire bill. The refund includes tuition, registration, laboratory fees, books and supplies, but not insurance, recreation, or travel.

In some companies the policy is quite restrictive and covers only those courses of study judged to be directly related to the employee's job. Example: Sending a budget assistant to a finance school. Other companies take a liberal position and willingly pay for general education. Example: Postgraduate study toward an LL.B degree for a salesman.

INTERNATIONAL SALT COMPANY	CORPORATE INDUSTRIAL RELATIONS MANUAL	DATE EFFECTIVE
		APPROVED Administrative Committee

C. Approval

1. Approval for courses must be granted in advance of enrollment by the employee's district, plant or headquarters department manager and by the head of the division involved.

2. Each subject must be approved individually.

3. Blanket approval must not be given for all courses to be taken for a degree, unless the major course involved is judged to have a relation to the employee's job or future.

D. Reimbursement

Reimbursement for tuition and laboratory fees up to $200 a term or $400 a year may be obtained when the course is completed if, within 30 days of its completion, the employee submits to his district, plant or headquarters department manager:

1. Evidence of his earning a passing grade for the course.

2. A verified statement of his tuition and laboratory costs or adequate receipts.

IV. PROCEDURE

A. When an employee wants to participate in the tuition refund plan, he should complete a Tuition Refund Application which may be obtained from his personnel manager.

B. The employee should discuss his plans with his immediate superior to determine whether or not he is eligible to participate in the plan.

C. If eligibility is determined, the employee's immediate superior should forward the completed Tuition Refund Application to the district, plant or headquarters department manager for disposition.

D. If approved by the appropriate manager, the application should then be submitted to the head of the division involved for final approval.

E. The approved or rejected application should then be returned to the location personnel manager who will inform the employee of the action taken.

F. A new application must be completed and approved each semester.

G. When an eligible employee applies for reimbursement, a Reimbursement Authorization form is to be completed and sent to his payroll department.

H. Payments made to employees under this policy are considered wages and subject to the provisions of the Federal Income Tax Law. Therefore, the appropriate taxes will be deducted from the gross amount.

I. All records will become part of the employee's personnel file.

Continuation (from page 324) of International Salt Company's tuition refund policy.

There is, of course, the other side of the picture. Many companies, in good conscience, feel that training is the responsibility of the individual. Workers such as typists, accountants, lawyers, nurses, and others are already trained or they would not be hired. Since they have acquired this training at their own expense of time and money, is it fair to "give" others this kind of education? These companies, of course, are prepared to train their employees on the job and teach them the business. But they expect them to be already qualified in the basic skills needed to perform the duties of the job once these are learned.

The fact that the cost of an across-the-board policy of tuition refund can be charged off as a business expense makes the decision easier. Nevertheless, the decision is more generally one of principle, whether the education of its workers is a management or societal responsibility.

TUITION AID—A FRINGE BENEFIT THAT PAYS

Dean Paul H. Sheats of the University of California Extension Division tells of a friend who suggests that universities issue diplomas that disintegrate in 10 years. After the student updates his knowledge with further study, he would then be issued a replacement sheepskin.

Dean Sheats believes that the effective period of the diploma might even be further reduced because "professional people now regard continuing education as a necessary career *process*—not as a step, or something which can be finished."

The California educator has made an equally interesting proposal: That America "move as rapidly as possible to build into the 40-hour week eight hours of paid time for voluntary participation in organized programs of continuing education. The paid time off for continuing education could be either on job-related or liberal arts oriented programs."

This proposal, he says, is based on two results of the explosion of knowledge. One is what Yale Professor Neil Chamberlain calls "the steady downgrading of the occupational competence of all who are employed." A second factor is "the changing requirements of the work force as a result of automation and cybernetics."

No record exists as yet of "disintegrating diplomas." No union contract as yet provides for 20 percent of a worker's paid time being devoted to study.

But right now there are business-sponsored programs that provide part of that "necessary career process" of which Dean Sheats speaks. These are the "tuition aid" plans, devised to encourage employees, first, to do something to avoid their own obsolescence and, second, to assist them in a financial way thus to increase their capabilities and develop their full potential.

INVESTMENTS IN EDUCATION

Hercules Incorporated, Wilmington, Delaware, along with many other corporations, is aware of the very real financial problem faced by our colleges and universities. More and more young men and women are seeking higher education and the fields of knowledge continue to expand. Funds are needed by institutions of higher learning not only for the enlargement of their facilities, but also to provide an adequate and competent faculty.

With a growing and complex technology, Hercules requires more people with advanced education than ever before if it is to remain competitive both at home and abroad. Each year heavier demands for such personnel are placed on the colleges and universities by all branches of industry, including Hercules. If the colleges and universities cannot supply these needs, then it is clear that the entire economy will fall behind.

The philosophy which has guided Hercules in its aid-to-education program is expressed by Henry A. Thouron, company president: "All segments of American life are putting more and more emphasis on higher education, and our colleges and universities are being forced to expand their facilities. To help overcome the problems of trained manpower shortages and maintain scientific and economic advances, Hercules and other corporations must invest in education."

Hercules has been financially supporting education in colleges and universities for more than a quarter century. Within the past eight years this program has been revised and considerably broadened to include aid to individuals as well as to institutions. The present Hercules program consists of four types: Grants-in-aid, matching grants, scholarships for employees' dependents, and 4-H entomology scholarships.

Grants-in-Aid

The Hercules unrestricted grants, first established in 1956, are based on the belief that each department head in the colleges and universities knows best the needs of his department and is able to derive the maximum benefit from these funds. Grants under this program are given to a specific department at the designated college or university to be expended at the discretion of the department head. Colleges and universities receive grants on a cyclic basis so that over a period of years a greater number of institutions will be aided.

Grants are made to departments of colleges, universities, and technical institutions in fields of learning in which Hercules is most vitally interested. These include departments of chemistry, chemical engineering, mechanical engineering, mathematics, forestry, and others.

Selection of the colleges and universities to participate in the program is based on a number of considerations. Among these are the academic standing of the university and of its science or engineering departments, the number of alumni of the university employed by Hercules, and its proximity to Hercules plants, laboratories, and offices.

Occasionally, grants are made which do not conform to any of the above criteria but are given because of the contributions made by the institution to the community at large.

The head of a department receiving a grant is invited to visit the company in Wilmington, Delaware, for a few days at company expense. During these visits there is presented to the academic representative a cross-section of company activities, and he is provided an opportunity to discuss mutual interests and needs with industrially oriented scientists.

The value and usefulness of such unrestricted grants in support of academic research and higher education have been demonstrated by the response of educators charged with administering the funds and by the many worthwhile projects for which the funds have been used.

Matching Grants

To extend the company's assistance to liberal arts and to other colleges not usually included in the grants-in-aid program, the company established a matching grants program in 1960. Under this plan, contributions of employees and pensioners are matched by the company. The plan, which broadens the base of support for higher education, encourages Hercules employees to make annual contributions to the colleges of their choice as well as to participate in fund campaigns such as those for capital purposes.

Any full-time Hercules employee, all retired employees, and employees absent on military or other authorized leave may participate. The employees may select any college or university, including professional and graduate schools, in the United States, its territories and possessions, certified by the appropriate professional or regional accrediting body. In most cases this will include any four-year degree-granting college or university. The company will match, dollar-for-dollar, contributions made by its employees and pensioners to such accredited institutions up to a maximum of $1,000 per employee in any calendar year.

Employee gifts in the form of marketable securities will be matched at the dollar value of the gift on the date of transmittal of the securities to the school.

Donations may be made to one or more colleges or universities at the donor's option. If the employee's gifts total more than $1,000, the company contribution is prorated according to the employee contribution, unless the employee requests otherwise. An employee need not be an alumnus of the institution selected in order for the gift to be matched by the company.

The company's matching grant will be unrestricted, even though the employee's gift may be marked for a specific use. Gifts to provide scholarships or to pay the tuition of specific students will not be matched under the program.

Hercules College Scholarship Program

In 1964 Hercules initiated the Hercules Incorporated College Scholarship Program in cooperation with the College Scholarship Service (CSS), an activity of the College Entrance Examination Board. Each year the company will award to five dependents of Hercules employees four-year scholarships to colleges of the recipients' choice. Scholarships are awarded on the basis of performance in the Scholastic Aptitude Test, total school record both in academic work and extracurricular activities, and other available indications of character, capability, and potential for success in college and later life. Final selection is made by a scholarship committee composed of college and university educators. Each scholarship pays $1,000 per year for a maximum of four years.

Hercules scholarships may be used by recipients at any accredited college or university.

4-H Entomology Awards

In 1952, Hercules began sponsorship of the 4-H Club's National Entomology Awards, to help 4-H Club members understand insect life and its relation to human health and comfort, to recognize insect pests, and to learn the fundamentals of insect-control practices. Through the professional guidance of entomologists, county agents, and 4-H leaders, Hercules helps young men and women to become better equipped technically, and assists in the 4-H Club's objectives of character and citizenship training.

The Entomology Awards program is administered by the National 4-H Service Committee, 59 East Van Buren Street, Chicago, Illinois 60605, and is conducted by the Cooperative Extension Service of the land grant colleges and universities in cooperation with the United States Department of Agriculture. The annual awards consist of a maximum of four gold-filled medals of honor for county winners; an all-expense-paid trip to the National 4-H Club Congress held in Chicago for state winners; and college scholarships of $500 to six of the state winners.

Eligible 4-H boys and girls can obtain complete information from their County Extension Agent. Over 75,000 boys and girls now participate in the 4-H Club entomology program each year.

331

Although Hercules hopes to continue its education program from year to year, the company reserves the right to modify, improve, or discontinue the program at any time.

All inquiries concerning any part of the Hercules education program should be addressed to:

Secretary, Aid-to-Education Committee
Research Department
Hercules Incorporated
910 Market Street
Wilmington, Delaware 19899

TUITION REFUND PLAN

The "Tuition Refund Plan" of International Salt Company, Clarks Summit, Pennsylvania, was introduced in its current form in 1962 for active employees, hourly and salaried.

"It has indeed been successful," says Arnold F. Campo, director of industrial relations. He reports excellent participation in all divisions of the company.

He adds that "one of the key points in our program is that participation is voluntary and in no case may it be made a condition of employment."

TRAINING

TRAINING—TEACHING or LEARNING

Training is big business.

A speaker reports, "Already there are more trainers in business than there are business teachers in the schools."

An editor writes, "American business may soon spend more to train and re-educate its own personnel from the most marginal clerk to the most capable president, than all our school and college systems combined spend to educate youth."

A consultant says, "The training budgets of industry add up to one-half the total budgets for all the colleges and universities."

On-the-job training has been going on since the first worker was hired. Someone shows the new employee what to do. This could be an individual designated to "break in" every new employee, a supervisor or leader who knows what the work entails, the outgoing employee who is vacating the position, or simply the handiest coworker who takes the new employee under his wing. This type of training is generally informal although lately, because of increasing turnover, much on-the-job training is structured.

Skill training has traditionally been delegated to the schools. Ideally, such employees as typists, secretaries, bookkeepers, and teachers are qualified in their skills before they are employed. This is also true of some shop and technical jobs as printers, telegraphers, architects, and the like. The company normally does not teach the skill but does train a new worker in applying his previously-acquired skill to the business. With the shortage of skills in all categories, much of the burden for skill training has been absorbed by industry under the training function known as "upgrading skills."

When it comes to supervisory training or executive development the picture changes. Formal education in college may qualify a graduate in his particular specialty, such as engineering, law, or accounting, but does not ordinarily equip him for a general business career. True, most universities run extension courses, but these are attended by people already employed. This is precisely the point: Once employed, a man's education begins—from experience, from outside formal education, from internal development programs, from seminars, meetings, travel, coaching, and so on.

Training in business is an unending process. The individual who feels he is through learning is through in his job also. Simply stated, jobs today grow faster than the people in them. Keeping up is the obligation of training.

But that isn't the problem. Companies have recognized the situation and have accepted the challenge. Facilities are available, if not in one form then surely in another. The problem lies in the motivation of the trainees. Managers, for example, do not need to be trained as much as they need to be stimulated.

The purpose of any training is to create within the individual the desire to learn. The best training program will be useless unless the trainees attend willingly and participate freely. This they will do more readily if the training program helps them and serves their purpose.

In discussing training it is not enough to consider it from a teaching viewpoint—with capable instructors, well-developed courses, good facilities and equipment, and company support. More important is the learning point of view. In the final analysis, self-development, utilizing whatever aids are available, is the best assurance that training will be successful. Abraham Lincoln proved that years ago.

TRAINING MACHINES

Industry has undergone tremendous change in the past half century. In the process, the unskilled workman and the labor foreman have virtually disappeared. The specialist, the technician, and the manager have taken their place. Worker productivity and effective work management are vital to survival in the competitive business of today and tomorrow.

Change brings progress, but it also brings the requirement for new knowledge and new skills to adjust for new tools and equipment, new processes, and new procedures. The supervisor is therefore constantly confronted with the necessity for training and retraining to meet these changes.

The ability to train workers quickly and effectively is an increasingly important requirement for supervisors. The majority of supervisors, however, lack the know-how to do the job successfully. The need for improving the ability of supervisors to train is so evident and the benefits so certain that special efforts to set up programs for this purpose will be on the increase. The well-planned supervisory development program must put strong emphasis on how to train subordinates.

Perceptual Development Laboratories, St. Louis producers of training programs, provide services which include:

1. A specially designed projector, the *PerceptoScope,* a modern, electronic multifunction projector providing important new concepts and approaches in visual aids to training.

PerceptoScope is one of many good visual aids to training. This unit projects slides, motion pictures, still pictures, art work. Nineteen different speeds allow precision in pacing a training program.

2. Standard training programs: Complete "package" programs including *PerceptoFilms,* manuals, workbooks, tests, and instructor guides in various subjects, to answer a wide and common training need.

3. Custom training programs, similar in composition to the standard programs, but tailored to the specific needs and circumstances of the particular user.

4. Consultation service, surveys, audits, and consultations to evaluate overall programs, develop general or specific programs, and assist in the solution of specific training problems.

The important *PerceptoScope* features are:

1. Multifunction: Still, flash, motion picture projection and film analysis with a single device.

2. Variable speed: Nineteen speeds from 1 to 24 frames per second, which permits high degree of precision in pacing projection for paced training.

3. Indefinite dwell: Single-frame movement at will; indefinite dwell on a single frame without damage, warping, or distortion of focus.

4. Reverse: Instantaneous reverse at all speeds, automatic or manual.

5. Remote control: Activation of all functions and control of film movement and projection speed through a hand-size electronic remote control unit on a 25-foot cord.

6. Easy portability: Weight less than 50 pounds; compact, sturdy, easy to set up and to move from one location to another.

The list of standard programs includes—

Basic and Advanced Typing	10 Key Adding Machine
IBM Cardpunch Operator Training	Reading Improvement
Introduction to Data Automation	Methods Improvement
Fundamentals of Computer Programming	Job Attitudes
	Safety

In addition to this list of standard programs, there is a long list of custom program productions in all fields of training, produced as desired by the individual organization.

PDL also offers a program on "Training Techniques for Supervisors" which is an ideal solution to the problem of qualifying supervisors to organize and conduct job training.

PROGRAMMED LEARNING

By Ralph A. Drekmann
Manpower Development Division
The Equitable Life Assurance Society of the United States

Today's personnel specialist is facing a difficult manpower problem: He has to hire the skills he can get and develop them into what his organization needs. To help him bridge that gap, he will rely on training.

One of the most promising training methods is programmed learning. Here is a discussion that may sound familiar to you:

> "Let's pay more attention to the individual learner and give him a chance to experience achievement."

> "Okay, but let him learn by doing the thing. He may think he knows it, but he can't be sure until he tries."

Programmers discussing training strategy? No, that's quoting Quintilian and Sophocles in free translation.

Then programmed learning isn't really something new? That's right. You can trace its beginning all the way from Plato's Socratic dialogues to Pavlov's study of conditioned reflexes in dogs, from Thorndike's stimulus-response studies to Pressey's multiple-choice testing machine and Skinner's Ping-Pong-playing pigeons.

So why all the excitement about programmed instruction and teaching machines? Because the rediscovery of programmed learning principles may be one of the most significant contributions to human learning in this century. For the first time, behavioral psychologists have taken the results of their scientific experiments out of the laboratory to apply them directly to human learning.

What are some of the psychological principles underlying programmed learning? Most importantly they are: Operant conditioning, reinforcement, discrimination, and behavior shaping.

These principles have to do with habit formation. Here is an oversimplified example: Suppose you want to teach your dog a trick. You want him to retrieve a ball out of the water. By chance you see him run to pick up a stick. He is responding to something, he is showing operant behavior. That is, his behavior operates on the environment.

Right away you give him a piece of Yummy. It's a stimulus. He likes it, feels rewarded, and tries again. You have given him immediate reinforcement. Note that your dog must be active. You cannot reinforce his behavior unless he is busy doing something.

Next you introduce the ball and give him that reinforcing Yummy stimulus only when he picks up the ball. Now you are using selective reinforcement to make him react to the difference between ball and stick. You are trying to bring about conditioned discrimination.

By designing a logical, systematic learning sequence, you can eventually train your dog step-by-step to retrieve the ball from the water. You are shaping his behavior. You are building a new skill. If you help him maintain this behavior, we can observe it, and will conclude that he has learned.

You can see that animal trainers have practiced certain principles of programmed learning for centuries. These principles can also be applied to training the human animal. In fact, Brethower and Rummler of the University of Michigan have pointed out that in your daily work with people, you are probably using operant conditioning right now, unwittingly, as a management technique. If you have shaped employees' behavior by deliberately encouraging only desirable practices, you have used operant conditioning.

How do programmers apply these principles to programmed learning? They have designed instructional sequences, called programs, with special characteristics. These training materials are carefully planned to combine these typical features: (1) Step-by-step build-up, (2) active response, (3) feedback, and (4) self-pacing.

Let's look at each of these features briefly.

Step-by-Step Build-up

A well-constructed program is organized into clearly defined portions called frames. A frame may range in size from several pages of an overview chapter to the smallest step in a multiplication exercise.

Frames are sequenced in what the programmer perceives to be a logical order. If tryouts of his program show that trainees will learn a process more efficiently in an "illogical" order, he will use that tested order as the more effective teaching sequence.

Frames are built one upon the other in steps of increasing complexity. An earlier notion that all material to be learned must be broken down into small steps did not prove very useful. Instead, the programmer must find the optimum step-size by testing his frames, as they are written, among his intended audience.

Active Response

After studying the one specific point presented to him in a frame, the learner must respond. He may have to analyze a diagram, discriminate between typical examples, or form a concept. In this way he is actively engaged in the learning process. He learns by doing.

An earlier "rule" of programming suggested that all active responding should be observable behavior. For example, answering out loud or completing statements in writing. But humans seem to do a great deal of covert responding, hidden but very active. Many learners appear to carry on a silent but incessant dialogue with themselves. They let thoughts race through their minds, manipulate concepts, attempt verbalizations, and keep answering questions to themselves. These, too, are active responses and must be recognized and acknowledged by the programmer.

Feedback

A well-written program will guide the learner through problem-solving exercises which will reveal to him step-by-step that he is answering the questions correctly and finally that he has solved a problem correctly. In addition, the learner will find the correct answer to each frame printed in the program. This will give him a chance to check how he is doing. If he wants to, he can test himself and correct his own work. The printed answer will either confirm that he is right or show that he must correct his response.

At one time programmers thought that such feedback should always follow the frame right away. It would then serve as immediate reinforcement for the learner. But finding out that he made an error was not always a rewarding experience. So, the right answer in the program did not necessarily give reinforcement.

As a result, programmers became preoccupied with the design of programs in which the learner would rarely make a mistake. They wanted programs to be as error-proof as possible. However, many adult learners would check for correct answers only once in a while. They didn't seem to care about immediate confirmation. They became so engrossed in their exercises and action projects that they rejected any interference. All they wanted to do was solve a problem and still another problem. Never mind some of their errors on the way. After completing the program they too demonstrated that they could perform the task just as well. They had achieved mastery; they had learned.

From these observations programmers concluded that immediate feedback is not always necessary or desirable. They have found out that confirmation is not synonymous with reinforcement. Many adult learners do think: "Let me make my own mistakes. And get off my back, so I can try this by myself."

Personnel specialists are usually looking for this positive problem-solving behavior in trainees. And they want them to be able to cope with their own mistakes. To be effective, programmed learning materials must therefore modify some of the features developed in the learning laboratory to adapt to practical needs and conditions.

Self-Pacing

Since the learner can check his answers without waiting for an instructor, a program can be both self-instructional and self-pacing. Of course, there is nothing new about a self-teaching workbook. It was already popular when Thomas Edison wrote his manual, *Telegraphy Self Taught.*

Many learners prefer to work their way through a course at their own speed. The fast learner can go through it in a breeze and the slow learner can take his own good time. Both should be able to perform the training objective after they have completed the program.

Trouble is that some trainees find it difficult to finish a program on their own. Programmed learning may be self-teaching but it is not self-administering. Some time control and selective supervisory monitoring is often helpful. Moreover, if study time varies too much, it may conflict with established training programs. To introduce programmed learning in an organization you must use common sense and suggest reasonable completion schedules.

These four features: Step-by-step build-up, active response, feedback, and self-pacing combine to form a repeating learning cycle. As each segment of knowledge is presented to the learner in frames of increasing complexity, he is required to respond to it in some way, and can then check for feedback to see how he is progressing. On his own, he can speed up this cycle or slow it down, as desired.

How is a program developed? Briefly, here are some of the essential steps used in the process of programming:

1. Examine existing system.
2. Investigate environmental factors.
3. Define trainee's job.
4. Establish need for program.
5. Analyze training task.
6. State training objectives.
7. Write final performance test.
8. Specify course prerequisites.
9. Determine program design.
10. Select suitable media.
11. Write test frames.
12. Write teaching frames.
13. Conduct individual tryouts.
14. Revise program.
15. Validate program through field-test by group.
16. Revise, publish, install, and monitor program for next edition.

Let's review some of these steps. The programmer should question:

1. Under what conditions is the program to be used? Is it a hostile environment where line management gives only lip service to training and thinks it's a nuisance? Does top management fully support the training effort?

2. Does the existing system reward the completer or is there a penalty for the trainee who does the job exactly the way it is taught? Does the training program direct trainees one way while their supervisors direct them in another?

3. What is the trainee now doing? What isn't he doing? What is his present repertory? Is it only a minor deficiency that keeps him from doing what you want him to do? Can he, in fact, do it, but doesn't want to? What are his needs?

4. If it is a case of "can do, but won't do," it's not a training problem. Maybe there is a need to improve communications, working conditions, compensation, or leadership. But there is no need for programmed learning materials.

5. Exactly what is the task the learner must accomplish? What are the typical steps in its performance? How does a master performer do it? What experiences do we observe in the field, on the firing line, at the gut level?

6. How do you define in measurable terms the specific behavior you can observe when the trainee demonstrates mastery? Does management accept these terminal behavior specifications as useful performance objectives?

7. Does the final test simulate real life conditions and the actual job as closely as possible? Is it a valid test? Does it measure what it is supposed to measure?

8. What must the trainee be able to do before he is admitted to the course? What pretest will serve best to screen out those who have not yet met the prerequisites for taking the program?

9. What teaching strategies will be most effective? Should we use a linear format, a straight-line tell-and-test routine? Do we want to accept the learner's constructed response, such as a written answer, as a receipt that our "goods" have been delivered? Or does this particular training problem call for a fast track in the program? Or for branching into extra drill or refresher loops? Should we use a multiple-choice format and accept selective responses? Can we develop enough plausible choices? Will some combination of these techniques give us a more effective program to let the learner reach his objective as quickly and efficiently as possible?

10. What medium shall we use to communicate? Should the learner look at videotapes, movies, film strips or slides? Listen to records, audiotapes, or lectures? Read a text? Are teaching machines suitable for this training job? Is computer-assisted instruction practicable for this particular task? Can a multimedia combination perhaps give us an even better simulation of the real life task? Can we employ other training devices, such as role-play, to get the learner into the act of simulating the job for which he trains?

11. How can we create and develop a series of increasingly difficult task-simulation tests to measure the gradual change in behavior, the behavior shaping we want to engineer? How can we make these tests as close to real life as possible so training will transfer to job?

12. Can we develop task-simulators and real-life examples to prepare a sequence of as few learning steps as necessary? Can we develop exercises which will guide the learner quickly to making critical discriminations and solving problems until he can pass each test frame?

13. How can we set up as realistically as possible tryouts with individual members of our intended trainee population to observe how they work their way through the program? Are the instructions in the program clear for proper use? Did we overteach?

14. Do we feel like revising the whole program because we tend to overlisten to the tryout learner? Does a resequencing of materials really improve the program? Did we provide enough practice? Can we trim verbiage to come up with a lean program?

15. Does the program teach what it is supposed to teach under actual field conditions? What are the problems of administering the program to groups in the field? How does the program fit into the ongoing training effort? Is support equipment and material available when needed? What are the trainer's needs and attitudes?

16. How can we monitor the program's use, after it has been installed, through opinionnaires, routine feedback from reports, or personal observation? What must we do to maintain the skills our trainees have acquired?

This long list of questions is only a sample of the programmer's analytical approach. He is a nosy fellow who wants to find out about things. He is not pleasant to have around, because he can ask a lot of unanswered and uncomfortable questions. Perhaps you would like to ask some of these questions about the task you are now working on.

This review of how a program is developed will now help us in spelling out a definition of programming:

Programming is a systematic process of developing and validating instructional sequences designed to change learner behavior in specific measurable ways.
In programmed learning five key ideas stand out:

1. Systematic analysis	4. Testing and validation
2. Behavioral objectives	5. Focus on the learner
3. Task simulation	

First, programming means a systematic, organized approach to the analysis and effective coordination of all elements and influencing factors of a training problem.

Second, programmed learning is goal-oriented. A program should separate "nice to know" from "must know." One goes out, perhaps to be recommended as enrichment material; the other goes into the program, because it is necessary for goal achievement.

Third, before we send our astronauts into space, we want them to experience as many contingencies as possible in a task simulator. Before you send your trainee into the cold world to face your precious customers, you want him to handle many real life situations under suitable hothouse conditions.

Fourth, testing and validating will give you vital feedback for accomplishing the programming task. It is at the core of the programming process.

Fifth, programming puts renewed emphasis on the learner. You are selling ideas and he is the consumer. He is the final authority on whether you have communicated. And to serve him is the programmer's ultimate goal.

Guidelines Only

Are all programs developed in this systematic way? Far from it. We are only looking at guidelines. And they sound much simpler in theory than they are applied in practice. The problem is that humans are so much more than animals. Programming practitioners have convinced themselves that trainees are not learning like dogs or pigeons. For the behavioral psychologist this means going back to the laboratory for reappraisal. That does not mean his approach is not valid. It means that new questions have come up, but no definite answers. As in all science, there may only be an answer and an answer beyond that. Programmed learning has no special claim to solid scientific foundation, as it is practiced now. It is above all an art.

What are the advantages of programmed learning? In hundreds of published studies there is evidence that programs will reduce training time, will reduce training cost, and will help increase the effectiveness of training. Any disadvantages? Yes. You still cannot make a trainee learn, if he does not want to learn. Some learners do not like to be led by the nose—ever. Some like to have a tutor present at all times to lean on when in doubt. Some miss the outside pressure to complete the program, if left to their own devices. Some training problems do not seem to lend themselves to a programming approach. Other techniques may work better. If so, it does not make sense to program for the sake of programming. Programming is no cure-all.

Who is using programmed learning? Today almost every major organization working with people and concerned about manpower development is making some use of programmed learning. Dr. Gabriel D. Ofiesh, an early proponent of the programming method, has published 35 of the many case histories he collected from all branches of the Armed Forces, from a roster of leading industrial companies, banks, insurers, government agencies, giant retailers, and other organizations. Many of these reports tell of remarkable success through judicious application of programmed learning materials.

The important thing to remember is that a program is NOT a product, is NOT a medium! A program is a process. Programming is not the rewriting of training manuals or textbooks to cover prescribed subject matter in a gimmicky way. Programming is a training method, a pedagogic strategy.

Alert personnel specialists who recognize that all training is basically communication have taken programming concepts and applied them to other communication jobs. For example, management consultants like Dr. George S. Odiorne have used programming principles to propose "management by objectives."

True Scope, Potential Revealed

Progressive educators at the Oakland Community College in Michigan have applied the same systematic development and evaluation used in programming to define, design, produce, and implement all elements necessary for an entire institution of higher learning. All performance specifications were identified and defined in behavioral terms. They spell out the knowledge the student should demonstrate at the end of the course. Course content is sequenced meaningfully and based on a flexible time schedule. The student knows what is expected of him and he is kept informed of his progress. Criteria tests serve to evaluate his achievement of interim goals. An array of media is employed to present materials which allow active responding, give feedback, and permit reasonable self-pacing. The entire complex is learner-oriented, from time schedule to physical design of "learning laboratories" which make up the college plant.

Viewed and applied in this way, programmed learning reveals its true scope and great potential. Programmed learning techniques can be used to develop adjunct training materials to support your present training efforts. Programming can help you develop a year-long training course, redesign your total training program, or even your training center. Properly applied, programmed learning can make a valuable contribution towards more efficient and more effective training for your organization. It will help you solve some of your urgent manpower problems.

DU PONT COURSES

Programmed instruction courses, developed by E. I. Du Pont de Nemours & Company, Wilmington, Delaware, for training its own employees in basic industrial skills have proved so successful that they are being made generally available.

With increased national attention being given to problems of training, retraining, and upgrading of skills, the company feels it can make a real contribution to business and industry by making these proved training courses available to others.

Largest Available Library

The library of training courses, now totaling 106 and the largest available from any one source, was initially developed by Du Pont for its own use. Since these courses were offered to others, many thousands have been used by both large and small companies, vocational schools, governmental agencies, and individuals. Also available are a number of additional courses on safety training.

The courses are made available at nominal cost. Included with each course is an administrator's guide for conducting programmed instruction courses. Inquiries may be directed to Bates McClean, Public Relations Department, Du Pont Company, Wilmington, Delaware 19898.

AUTOMATION COURSE IN 30 HOURS

By Ralph D. Hultgren
Section Head, Engineering Division
The Procter & Gamble Company, Cincinnati, Ohio

This case is a report of work done by Procter & Gamble to solve a problem which is often faced in manufacturing operations—how to teach plant people to operate complex control systems.

Two parts of the case may be of interest—the general approach to satisfying a training need, and the specifics of the particular solution.

The Training Need—Problem Definition Phase

The development of hard-hitting, efficient training material is costly, both in calendar time and in effort. In order to justify such development cost, then, there should be a substantial return. And, when contemplating such a development, it is difficult to predict, with any accuracy, the development cost or the savings results. So, the decision to start the development depends largely upon management judgment.

What were the factors that led our company to the decision to "do something about instrumentation effectiveness in the plants"?

First, the company was faced with the need for more production from existing facilities.

Second, spot studies of the reasons for low efficiencies often showed a lack of understanding of the automatic process control systems. This lack seemed to be more concentrated among the operators, their supervisors, and the area maintenance supervisors, than among the instrument maintenance mechanics.

Finally, the engineers who design new facilities were concerned from several points of view—the need for more sophistication in the controls for new process plants (because of expanding technology and rising labor costs), and the concern over proper use of the existing control systems by plant people.

Having reached a decision to undertake the development of training for plant people, we entered a problem-definition phase. We realized that there are many established approaches to automatic controls training, such as lectures, dummy people, analog simulators, and movies such as "Principles of Automatic Control" and "Automatic Process Control." (These films are available from the Instrument Society of America, 530 William Penn Place, Pittsburgh, Pennsylvania 15219.)

We also realized that, for greatest effect, we needed to define the objectives we wanted to reach through training. Following the principles advocated by R. F. Mager in *Preparing Instructional Objectives* (Fearon Publications, San Francisco), we established the following:

1. The entering student has no special qualifications in the area of automatic controls. He has met normal plant operator selection criteria, and normal employment standards.

2. The graduating student should be able to demonstrate a basic understanding of the operating characteristics of closed loop control, by passing a performance-type qualification examination.

3. The course should be effective with one or two students, placing few demands on the instructor.

Objectives Become Clearer

So, our objectives, as we started the development, were to remove student concerns about the "mysterious little black boxes," and to replace them with self-confidence, based on fundamental understanding, and an ability to learn quickly how to operate the specific controls in the student's department.

It would be less than accurate to infer that our thinking at this point was as sharply focused as the above statements indicate. However, the objectives became clearer as we researched the work done by others.

We then started a program of talking with other companies, the Instrument Society of America, and the U.S. Navy (as being representative of technical training being done by the armed forces). We wanted to make use of any available work by others, and to seek fresh approaches. We found a number of companies who were willing to share their experiences with us. Our problem involved nothing that they considered proprietary, and a few hours' discussion often produced useful information.

One of our early findings was that our *general* problem was a common one—obtaining effective operation of automated manufacturing processes. However, the detailed solutions were always different enough to preclude direct reapplication to our situation. Here are a few examples:

- One company had changed its processes to use numerically-controlled machine tools, and had developed an extensive program for updating the qualifications of its maintenance personnel.

- Another company had developed a short movie that explained how the internals of control instruments work.

- The Navy had developed efficient ways for training large numbers of students in electronics, using many specially-developed training aids.

This does not mean, however, that we found such discussions fruitless. In fact, we found a number of elements of our ultimate solution through this discussion approach. And we obtained confirmation of our suspicion that we must create our own training program—that piecing-together various existing training programs would require too much student time to be justified by the probable results.

Finally, we felt that we were ready to start our training program development. At this point, about eight calendar weeks had elapsed since the start of the project.

The Training Course—Development Phase

As we started this phase, we had several concepts in hand. One was that we need a miniature factory, similar to a "wet process" trainer developed by E. C. Baran of Standard Oil of Ohio. Another was that the student should be required to manipulate the unit as a part of his learning process, following "functional training" principles developed by the U.S. Navy. Finally, the course was to focus on *operation* rather than maintenance (auto driver training rather than an auto mechanic's course).

Development of the Hardware

The first thing we had to do was create a training device which the student would be required to manipulate in order to learn. It might be worthwhile to review some of the features of the unit, which was specially designed as a trainer.

The trainer is a "wet" process—it circulates water through a series of pipes and tanks, which are permanently interconnected. Its dimensions are 30 inches wide by 5 feet high by slightly more than 6 feet long. With shipping container, it weighs about 1,200 pounds. It is designed to be transportable between plant locations by motor truck, ship, and air.

Full-size, operating industrial instruments are used, similar to those the student would encounter in the plant. The control instruments are pneumatic, rather than electronic.

All parts are in the open, arranged in one vertical plane, to resemble a typical process flow-chart. There is no panelboard, as such. Instrument connections are stubbed out directly toward the front of the unit. The level transmitter is partially disassembled, to uncover its basic mechanism. The trainer tank is made of clear plastic.

Most of the gages are calibrated in percent, to ease calculations and aid student learning. The normal "PSI" markings are also provided, to give drill in converting pressure signals into percentages, and vice versa.

The particular types of control loops were selected to illustrate "fast" and "slow" processes. The trainer tank is sized to make the level loop fast enough for instruction purposes, but significantly slower than the flow loop.

Globe and gate valves are installed in a bypass loop around the diaphragm control valve to permit comparative testing of their throttling characteristics.

The flow loop is intentionally designed to discharge into the top of the plastic tank, to provide an adjustable amount of "noise" in the output signal.

Quick-connect plastic tubing is used for the instrument interconnections. This permits the student to focus his attention on *relationships* rather than the manipulation of pneumatic fittings.

While it might sound as though we had "put the cart before the horse" in building the unit first, we had several reasons for doing this. We were fairly confident that the basic processes in the unit would provide almost any instructional situations we could want. (This proved to be correct. In fact, others have used the same unit to teach college-level automatic control theory.) Also, we wanted to teach only those things which the hardware could demonstrate clearly.

Development of the Text

While the unit was being built, we started development of the text material. We settled upon a "training block" format, where each major topic would be treated as a separate unit. A training block does not, therefore, represent a uniform amount of student time. Some can be covered in less than two hours, others might require several two-hour sessions to complete.

Our first training blocks were written to provide terminology and concepts necessary for the students to deal with the hardware. Basically, the student is taught the language of automatic control, in word form, symbolic form, and in physical appearance.

Finally, the trainer prototype and the first draft of the text were completed. The text had to be modified more than once because the trainer experiments could not be reproduced consistently. Similarly, we modified the trainer several times in order that it could prove an important point which we wished to make in the text.

Next, the course was tested at identical processing units at two plant locations. It should be noted that one of the test conditions required that all instruction of the students be handled by a plant instructor. Accordingly, lesson plans in outline form were prepared, and the instructors were taught the material.

In a second round of plant testing, it became necessary to use less qualified instructors. Results were not satisfactory until the text was completely rewritten. The text material was expanded from the previous instructor's outline to a full textbook, addressed directly to the student. Detailed instructor's notes were also provided, giving answers to all of the questions and experiments. This round of training progressed much more smoothly as a result, and the average training time dropped from the original 40 hours to about 30 hours.

Manager Judgment Deferred

Prior to starting the experimental training program, we asked the plant manager of the two plants to take such "before" measurements as they felt might be indicative, and be prepared to comment on the effectiveness of the training at the conclusion of the course. Each plant manager decided to wait for at least six months after completion of the training before he made his judgment. While facts of a cost nature turned out to be difficult to obtain, and even more difficult to interpret, each plant manager concluded that the material was worthwhile, that he would like to commit his funds to extend the training to other people in his plant, and that he would recommend the training to other plant managers.

As a further check on the training material, a retention test was made. Three of the original students were retested some nine months after they had completed the training course. Only one of the students was still involved with automatic process controls—the other two had moved to other assignments. Despite their misgivings about their retention, two of the students completed the qualification exam in less time than they had originally. The third took about 30 minutes (20 percent) longer, and required some instructor coaching on a couple of trouble-shooting difficulties.

It is important to note that all through this development period we continued to refine our statements of objectives, discussed earlier.

Chart 5A—Trouble:
            Correction:

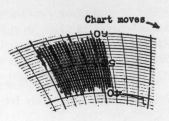

Chart 5B—Trouble:
            Correction:

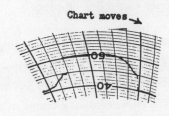

Chart 5C—Trouble:
            Correction:

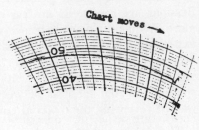

Chart 5D—Trouble:
            Correction:

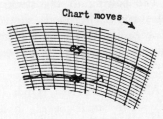

Part of qualification exam on flow-level instruments developed by Howard W. Sams & Co. of Indianapolis.

The qualification examination represents the final statement of our objectives. This exam requires the following:

1. That the student make an acceptable elementary flow diagram of a process and its associated instrumentation, from a word description.

2. That the student be able to associate his diagram with real hardware and make the necessary control loop connections.

3. That the student demonstrate his ability to place all of the control elements in their normal condition, start up the process, transfer to automatic control, and "line out" the controllers. (There are 26 performance checks that the student must make.)

4. That the student demonstrate that he can find three simultaneous malfunctions (taken from a list of 20).

5. That the student be able to identify four cases of grossly improper controller "tuning."

Course Administration

As a final step in our development, we settled on the way we wanted to administer the course.

We chose two-man teams, working at their own pace, as providing optimum results. Each session is nominally two hours in duration. Sessions are conducted no less often than once per week, and no more frequently than once per day. These intervals are based on experience, which indicates that some time between sessions is necessary for the material to "sink in" (and we regularly note vigorous locker room arguments over points covered in the day's studies). If the interval between sessions is long, much time is wasted reviewing the material covered in the previous session.

The pairing of the students is quite important. Their learning rates and backgrounds should be approximately equal. Differences in organizational rank (particularly employee-boss) can have a substantial negative effect on the learning process, unless handled very carefully.

Although the text is not truly "programmed," it does treat the subject in small pieces, in a manner similar to good home-study material. While we have had a number of graduate engineers complete the course using the instructor's notes, without the benefit of an instructor, the text is not intended to be used by an operator, unaided. The text depends on the part-time availability of the instructor to "help the student over the rough spots," and to augment the text by citing examples in the student's own department. The instructor should be available on a full-time basis at the beginning of the course, and toward the end. In the middle portion, only an occasional check by the instructor is required.

Most of our experience has been in training incumbents, and particularly members of the first-level management group (both production and maintenance). Average time for completion for management and experienced operators is 30 hours, with times of 25 to 35 hours considered as normal variations. Time for less experienced operators averages 40 hours, with about the same variability. The best time to date was achieved by a pair of highly experienced operators who completed the course in 12 hours, completing the qualification examination in 40 minutes, without a single error.

This training has been given at several overseas installations, with similar results. In each case, a bilingual local instructor was trained, and he taught the student groups. In some cases, the text was converted to "basic English" and in other cases, the text was translated into the native language.

Our experience shows that no educational prerequisites are necessary for students enrolling in the course. Any man who is judged by the local plant management to be trainable as an operator can satisfactorily complete the course.

It is interesting to note that, although we have a standing offer, "If you pass the final exam, you don't need to take the course," we have had no takers in the more than two years that the course has been offered. We believe this is because most plant people feel quite inadequate about "instruments," and do not wish to give up an opportunity to "really learn how the little black boxes work."

Results

Since it is on-the-job performance that produces the real dollar savings, it is important to look beyond the qualification examination before deciding that the problem is solved. While it is always difficult to associate direct dollars savings with the results of training, we have noted the following results:

- A number of significant incidents, wherein a "graduate" has returned to his department and used his newly-gained insight to detect instruments which have been malfunctioning for long periods. The aggregate of the first-year savings in our best plant is in excess of $30,000.

- A substantial and universal enthusiasm on the part of all students over the new-found understanding of the "little black boxes." While it may sound like an overstatement, we frequently encounter comments such as, "This is the best training I have ever had since I joined the company. I wish I had had this training 15 years ago."

- We found out that some of our instrument mechanics, who presumably had been tuning controllers for years, lacked a basic insight into the principles of closed loop operation. In these instances, the supervisors report a significant improvement in mechanic performance.

- The training helps "green" men learn some of the basics of chemical plant operation—for example, the difference between a globe valve and a gate valve, what a centrifugal pump looks like, etc. This is particularly helpful in a "corn field" startup situation, where operators must be trained locally. One such plant reported an estimated net saving in training time of four days for a crew of eight people, as a result of using the trainer and the training materials.

- Finally, and perhaps most important of all, our cost-conscious plant managers have each committed several thousand dollars of their funds for the hardware, plus a substantial amount of their people's time, to put management and key operators through the course. To date, our company has trained about 500 people in our domestic plants, and about 100 in our international operations. Each plant manager made his own decision to conduct the training, based on the results of tests performed in his plant.

RETRAINING

Training is a big problem that is getting bigger. But there is another aspect of this problem that is, or should be, of even greater concern. That is the immediate need for retraining programs.

Industry, which traditionally relied upon the schools and other outside agencies for much of the training needed by workers to qualify for jobs, has only in the last decade come out of its cocoon and accepted some of this training as its own responsibility. But this move may not have come in time.

The biggest problem today is not training, but retraining. Again industry is slow to face up to the problem it created. Token gestures in this direction have been made but collectively they do not even ripple the waters.

Retraining is necessary for many reasons. Technological progress has eliminated many jobs, rearranged others, and created new opportunities. New products and new processes are affecting jobs. Complex and competitive business is obsolescing jobs faster than ever before. For the first time in our industrial history a man's earlier education and training is no longer sufficient to carry him through life.

So where do we look for a solution? Not to the schools which have proven to be inadequate even for original training so that more and more of that burden has fallen to industry. Not to industry, apparently, which seems to have its hands full at the moment trying to cope with the training needs it reluctantly accepted only lately. What then is left? The answer is easy—government.

The responsibility for retraining is going to government by default! And government, as usual, seems quite willing to move into the void. Already there are a host of programs in operation under the Manpower Development and Training Act. Businessmen who complain about unwelcome government interference should be reminded that leadership forsaken in one place will find expression elsewhere.

FEDERAL ASSISTANCE FOR TRAINING EMPLOYEES

The Federal Government is eager to encourage on-the-job training programs and will help pay for training costs under certain conditions. A company may be eligible if it meets these tests:

1. It needs additional workers and can use unemployed individuals in its area.

2. Employees are working below their capabilities or working less than a full day.

3. Obsolescence of any employee's job skills is likely to reduce or eliminate his work.

4. There is a shortage of workers experienced in the occupations slated for the training program.

Complete Program Available

For a company that is eligible, and whose proposed program meets certain specifications, the Federal Government will:

- Reimburse job instructor fees.
- Pay for materials used in training.
- Pay for instructional supplies.
- Provide consultation and advice on training problems.
- Assist in developing training programs.
- Recruit job applicants.
- Arrange for group training for small shops.
- Arrange for area-wide training programs.

The employer must satisfy local Labor Department officials that a job will be available for everyone who finishes the training, but he isn't bound to hire if unforeseen events change his plans.

For details about the on-the-job training program, write the United States Department of Labor, Bureau of Apprenticeship and Training, Washington, D. C. 20210.

THE MANPOWER DEVELOPMENT AND
TRAINING ACT OF 1962

The Manpower Development and Training Act of 1962 (as amended) provides for a job training program that enables many unemployed and underemployed workers to learn new skills, better skills, skills in demand. This program is intended to help them obtain better jobs and to make workers with needed skills available to employers.

Kinds of Training

The following kinds of training may be included in the Job Training Program:

- Basic Education and/or Pre-Vocational training combined with occupational training.
- Vocational Training in Public or Private Schools.
- On-The-Job-Training.
- A Combination of Vocational and On-The-Job-Training.
- Individualized occupational training when class size training is not available or planned.

Need for training courses is based on the demand for workers in specific occupations as indicated by employing establishments in order to provide "a reasonable expectation of employment."

Length of course varies according to the skill involved.

Unemployed Adults

Those to be trained—

- Unemployed
- Available for a full-time job
- Ability to learn the work

Cost of course to trainee, none.

Those to be granted allowances—

- Training allowances are paid to trainees while in school who are heads of households, or heads of families, and who have had two years of work experience for pay or profit.
- Single persons are paid training allowances who live alone, or who live with parents or other persons without a dependency relationship, and who have had two years of work experience for pay or profit.
- Members of a family may be eligible for training allowances under certain conditions when the head of the household is unemployed, providing they have had two years of gainful employment.

Unemployed Youth

Those to be trained—

- Unemployed
- 16 through 21 years of age
- Available for a full-time job
- Ability to learn the work

Cost of course to trainee, none

Those to be granted allowances—

- Youth training allowances are paid to trainees 17 through 21 years of age who have been out of school one year or more and who are enrolled in a Special Youth Program.

- Regular training allowances are paid to trainees 17 through 21 years of age who have been out of school one year or more, and who are heads of households or heads of families, and who have had two years work experience for pay or profit.

- Regular training allowances may be paid to trainees 17 through 21 years of age who have had two years of work experience, and who live in a dependency relationship in a household while the head of the household is unemployed.

Look Ahead—Upgrade Skills

Train for tomorrow today—

- A worker who has no skill or whose skills have not been kept up to date is usually the first to lose his job. Training is provided to fit this worker with skills needed to work with new ideas, new methods, new products.

Those who may be trained—

A worker selected for training must be:

- Working below his skill capacities, or
- Working substantially less than full time, or
- Will be working less than full time or will be unemployed

because his skills have become obsolete or are becoming obsolete.

Part-time employment while in training—

- Trainees are allowed to work 20 hours per week in outside employment without any reduction in their weekly allowance. Salary or wages for hours worked for more than the 20 hours allowed are deducted from the weekly training allowance on a dollar-for-dollar basis.

Cash Allowances

Amount of allowances—

- Trainees may qualify for weekly cash allowances while in training. Adults, or youths 17 through 21 years of age who are heads of families or households, and who have had two years work experience for pay or profit may be eligible to receive from $40 to $70 per week, based upon the number of dependents.

- All trainees 17 through 21 years of age may qualify for the youth training allowance of $20 per week while enrolled in a Special Youth Program if they have been out of school one year or more.

- Trainees eligible for weekly unemployment compensation benefits exceeding $50 will be paid the higher amount while qualified and in training.

Duration of allowances—

- Allowances are payable for the duration of the vocational training course, or combination of basic literacy, and/or pre-vocational and vocational training up to a maximum of 104 weeks.

Subsistence and allowances—

- Subsistence allowances of $5 per day, but not to exceed $35 per week, are paid to trainees who attend training facilities not within commuting distance of their homes.

Transportation allowances—

- Transportation allowances based on the cost of the cheapest form of public transportation (generally not to exceed 10 cents per mile) are paid to trainees who commute or travel to training facilities within or outside of their residence. However, the first 50 cents of the daily round-trip fare or the accumulated weekly amount of $2.50 is excluded from allowances.

Employers

Advantages—Training will result in adequately trained workers, reduced turnover, increased efficiency, decreased supervision, decreased waste, reduced accidents.

On-the-job training is a most effective method for employers to increase the efficiency of their workers through up-grading, and for workers to learn new skills. The workers are trained on the job while producing, and, when off-the-job instruction is required, it is given at or apart from the work location. Employers are reimbursed for training costs incurred in providing on-the-job training.

The U.S. Department of Labor's Bureau of Apprenticeship and Training is responsible for the on-the-job training phase of the Manpower Development and Training Act of 1962.

The Employment Service promotes the development of training programs which include on-the-job training by employers, trade associations, labor organizations, industrial and community groups, public and private agencies, state and local governments.

SUPERVISION

Every manager, department head, or administrator is a supervisor. He supervises an activity or people—sometimes both.

A supervisor is engaged in supervision. The word "supervisor," if not by definition then at least by connotation, means someone possessed not with ordinary vision but with "super" vision. He must be capable of seeing over and beyond the obvious.

Ideally he ought to wear bifocal glasses: The short vision focused on the job to be done here and now—the distance vision adjusted to the impact this decision has on the future.

Look forward with wisdom and you'll look back with pride.

SUPERVISORY TRAINING

Supervisory training sessions, to be effective, should consider typical everyday problems based upon the experiences of the trainees, and offer solutions which help to meet their expressed needs.

The discussions should·not be built around textbook problems whose answers are in the "back of the book." This type of classroom exercise may be suitable for students. But trainees in a business environment look upon theoretical learning as appropriate for night school bright boys. They welcome any chance to talk over their operating difficulties in the hope of getting useful ideas which they can apply in their work.

Training programs which the trainees attend reluctantly and in which they participate passively are those designed and conducted by outsiders who may know how to construct and lead classes but who are unfamiliar with the trainees' specific problems. On the other hand, training programs which the trainees are eager to attend and in which they become enthusiastically involved are those in which the trainees are encouraged to present and attempt to solve the problem situations in which they have a direct interest and in whose solutions they have a personal stake.

Most of the discussion about supervisory training pertains to the instruction provided by management for its workers. But companies should also become concerned with the training a manager or supervisor provides for himself, for his own self-improvement.

The reasons for this type of training are obvious. They may be stated in these two observations:

1. In today's fast-moving and competitive business operation, jobs grow faster than the people in them. Training attempts to help managers and supervisors grow into their expanded duties, which grow deeper as they grow broader.

2. A man's earlier training is no longer sufficient to carry him through life. This is easily understood when we relate it to medicine; we expect a doctor to keep up with the advances made by medical science. In business and industry the changes might not be as dramatic but they are just as real.

Simply said, a supervisor who rests . . . rusts. Remember, as long as we're green, we're growing; once we're ripe we begin to rot.

The purpose of Supervisory Training is not to teach but to create within the individual the desire to learn. Managers and supervisors don't need to be taught as much as they need to be stimulated.

The subject is a very comprehensive one. A practical approach to this training can be developed from the following thoughts presented in outline form rather than in detail.

The two-fold need for supervisory training

- For effective performance now.
- For assurance of continued effectiveness as business expands or as qualified replacements are called for.

Supervisors need training

- To perform better on their present assignments.
- To keep apace of change.
- To prepare for greater opportunities in the future.
- To attain an attitude and philosophy of the real opportunities inherent in their jobs.

Supervisors must learn

- To manage things.
- To manage situations.
- To manage people.
- To manage themselves.

To accomplish this, management must

- Provide training.
- Give broadening experience.
- Establish the climate for growth.

All training may be accomplished in five training procedures

- Training classes organized and led by training specialists within their own companies.
- Training classes conducted by an expert brought in from the outside.
- Attendance at seminars, lectures, and conventions sponsored by various management associations.
- Training classes run by universities as part of their adult night school or extension service.
- Training activities planned and handled largely by the trainees themselves under the guidance of an experienced training counselor.

365

The four tests for measuring the usefulness of the several training practices

- Training objectives must be founded upon the expressed needs of the trainees.
- Training programs and procedures must be built upon the experiences of the trainees.
- Objectives, training procedures, evaluation methods must have flexibility and open-endedness; learning situations are dynamic.
- Learning is achieved through activity—through the process of seeking truth and insight—and not by the collection of the wise conclusions of others.

Objectives

- To acquaint all levels and types of supervisors with company policies, practices, and procedures which affect them and their people.
- To review with supervisors the accepted practices of modern management, including planning and control.
- To make available increased technical information and encourage the development of technical know-how.
- To emphasize the fundamentals of human behavior in a manner that will help them to improve their skill in communications and in other human relations activities necessary for personal and for company progress.
- To impress upon them the purpose, beliefs, and philosophy of the company as it relates to stockholders, customers, workers, and the community.

Areas

Presupervisory: Designed to prepare a steady stream of potentials by informing likely candidates of the requirements of supervisory jobs to which they aspire. This includes an appreciation of the scope of the supervisor's job, its many obligations, and the management viewpoint and attitudes that differentiate it from the job of production worker or clerk.

Basic supervisory training: Begins with a comprehensive review of necessary technical and human relations skills. Also disseminates additional information as needed for satisfactory performance in a new activity. Included are orientation, methods of organizing work and work groups, motivation, morale, attitudes, grievance procedures, and the like. Leadership is stressed.

Advanced supervisory training: Proceeds from a review of fundamentals to a more comprehensive program of management skills. Included is training in how to lead and participate in conferences and meetings, as well as all other forms of appropriate communication.

Executive development: Preparation for higher positions in management before or after promotion has been made. Advanced skill in management of things, situations, people, and self to meet the changing and ever-increasing demands of executive positions. Includes training in organization structure, labor-management trends, costs and cost reduction, and other facets of this important work. Emphasis is on decision making and policy formation with the understanding that these are not made on authority, as is so often the case, but on logic, impartiality, and judgment since there is seldom the opportunity for a second chance to correct mistakes at this level without a very high price.

CASE STUDIES for SUPERVISORY TRAINING

Just as it is impossible to deliver a gift-wrapped solution in advance, so it is unrealistic to present a set of canned problems which would lend themselves to supervisory training classes. The following 12 case studies are offered only as illustrations of "thought starters," used to stimulate lively discussions. The problems must be those they feel, and the ideas that are developed must be useful to them, in order to make the training program interesting and meaningful.

1. The central employment office uses a system of requisitions to fill job vacancies. Two applicants come in together. They are average girls with average typing abilities. The employment interviewer feels that they should be separated in the company and the girls concur. One girl is hired promptly by an eager and not-too-experienced supervisor. The other girl, about as well qualified and personable, is not hired by a more critical supervisor who is harder to please. *Since they seem to be close friends influenced by each other, what is the next best thing to do?*

2. A job is hard to fill. The girl must operate a billing machine. In this community experienced operators are not available and training inexperienced workers on the machine has so far not worked out too well. Quite unexpectedly a woman walks in one day to inquire about jobs. It turns out that she had been such an operator years ago and could very easily regain her former skill. References check out, salary is no problem, the applicant impresses with her sincerity. In fact, she is so straightforward that she mentions, without any prompting, that she is an epileptic, albeit a controlled case. *Should she be hired?*

3. As a way of controlling costs, should offices insist on hiring 60-word per minute typists, even if it costs more to get them, or settle for less than 60 words per minute if the starting salary is not sufficient to attract better-qualified applicants. *What complications must be considered?*

4. Secretaries are hard to get. A manager has been without one for some time. He interviewed a few prospects but none qualified. Finally a business college sends in a young man, well qualified, who applies for stenographic work. The company has never before em-

ployed male secretaries. *Should the young man be hired, and if so, what adjustments will be required?*

5. A secretary for a section manager is capable, busy, satisfied, and adequately paid. A secretarial job for a higher executive opens up. She is recommended, interviewed, and accepted. Now she has a higher rated job, one with more prestige, but with less work. When she was promoted she received a raise. Is it good to waste a capable secretary on a job that does not challenge her sufficiently, and is a higher salary fair when her contribution to the company is less? *If this is not right, what can be done?*

6. Many men who require secretaries dictate very seldom and possibly not at all. Yet to accept an office girl who cannot take shorthand might lower their own jobs in the eyes of others. But to insist on shorthand is a waste of talent and could easily lead to making a skilled stenographer unhappy with her duties. *What should be done?*

7. Your company hired a correspondent for the customer service department. On her first day the personnel manager told her she would be trained until she became familiar with the work. He also said that she should "think big" and ask questions and offer suggestions for improving the job. Six months have gone by and the new employee feels she has mastered the job. The supervisor, however, will not permit her to use any of her ideas. He simply tells her to do the work his way because it is the right way. When she explains to him that his instructions to her do not coincide with the assurance she received from the personnel office, he tells her, "If you don't like it, go see Personnel!" *What should the employee do?*

8. A typist works for a strict and unimaginative supervisor on a routine job. She is not unhappy, but one day she hears of an opening in another department, where she feels the girls have more fun. She requests a transfer. Because she is a good worker and no problem, the supervisor feels he cannot let her go; in fact, he says he cannot afford to lose her. For that reason he tells her she cannot be transferred because he would never approve her release. *Should she be transferred or retained, and what about the supervisor?*

9. You are a section supervisor over 10 girls in a typing pool. Susie is one of your best typists but is constantly tardy. She is a widow and has three school-age children whom she must care for

each morning before she goes to work. Seven of your girls like Susie and realize her problem, but two others don't like her. They tell you that if Susie is permitted to come late so can they. Susie's tardiness problem seems to have no solution; until now you've decided to live with it. Now under pressure, if you release her you are heartless; however, if you continue to put up with it, you are spineless and can expect to have other challenges placed in your path. *What should you do?*

10. A new training film on "How to Handle People" has just been shown to the assistant managers. They are very much impressed and enthusiastic in their praise for the film and its message. Almost everyone in the group says, "I wish my boss could see this film; he's the one who needs it." *What is the next step?*

11. For years the offices have been clean and painted. The colors were few and standard throughout. In an effort to modernize the premises an outside firm was consulted. They designed a complete program recommending different pastel shades for specific areas, combining several hues to arrive at the desired effect. Gradually areas were repainted in keeping with these recommendations. In a general way, the offices took on an impressive modern look. One weekend a department was painted. When the people came in Monday morning they found a striking new effect. To the artist the walls were nutmeg and sunburst, which blended in with the total decorating scheme. To the people the walls were a hideous brown and orange which clashed with everything, including their mood. When they asked their manager he shrugged his shoulders and said it was none of his doing. When members of the services department were asked they explained that they had shown the color chart to the manager the previous week and that he then had his chance to say something if he thought his people would not like it. Nothing more was done. One day shortly thereafter Personnel received a sealed envelope which contained individually signed notes by approximately half of the people in that department saying that they did not like the color of the new paint job. *Now what?*

12. You are a newly promoted section supervisor. You were promoted because of your ability and because management thinks you are a good potential. Your company has opened a new section in its operations. You have been asked to train the workers in new

methods. The workers are long-time employees some of whom have been with the company for 20 years. They resent your youth and the fact that you were promoted over them. They are obviously reluctant to cooperate with you. *How do you win their necessary cooperation?*

SENSITIVITY TRAINING

Sensitivity training is an educational experience in which the goal is to help individuals work more harmoniously and responsibly together. To work toward such a goal, each person has to learn something about the many factors that interfere with or disrupt communications, decision-making, and active cooperation.

In formal education, the instructor explains how groups are formed and how they interact. This produces theoretical or abstract knowledge. This knowledge is useful but not necessarily put to use by the individuals involved.

In sensitivity training, group members study their own behavior as they go through the process of forming a working group. They learn by doing and in the process of trying to do something, the group members begin to get feedback from other members in the group as to how they see what he is doing. Such feedback is a rich source of information about possible frustrations and conflicts which impede and disrupt the working of a group.

Members are encouraged to communicate with each other in a more open and honest manner than is typically done in the usual social or work situation.

The idea is being used socially in cities as well as within company operations. There are church and civic-sponsored groups which bring together people with diverse interests and ideas into one program. Results are being reported as excellent.

THE IN-BASKET TRAINING METHOD

The In-Basket training method is designed to improve the managerial decision-making process.

It is a special case-study tool which incorporates the best that the traditional case study has to offer, while embodying refinements to allow greater flexibility, realism, and involvement.

A major problem of the traditional case is that it provides either too much or too little information, usually the former. Some cases run to astonishing lengths, the idea being to give the trainee in business or the student in the classroom as much background information as possible to make up for lack of actual experience with the particular situation.

The superabundance of information provided by the traditional case bears little resemblance to actual practice. No company burdens its executives with every minute bit of information that just might be relevant to a situation. After all, what a company requires of its managers is the ability to make sound decisions from the information they have.

The crucial difference is that the In-Basket provides only significant items of information with few extraneous facts. It is designed around typical business situations, which allows the trainees to transfer and relate these study situations to their own experience. Here is where the organization and structure of the In-Basket distinguish it from the lecture, case, or discussion method of training. It is situation oriented.

Using the In-Basket technique, the participant starts out by first working through the case by himself. Moreover, he has to do this within a specified time limit. There is no opportunity to review and discuss details of the case with "the other boys." The participant is thoroughly involved because he takes the role of the man "owning" the in-basket and because he has a limited amount of time in which to arrive at his "answers." Further, he must commit himself on paper. He applies his normal methods of making decisions and solving problems on the job.

Subsequently, all the participants meet to discuss the In-Basket exercise. At this time, each participant gains individual feedback by comparing the discussion results with his earlier record of notes. It is in this phase that true learning (i.e., behavior change) occurs. And because the situation studied is a simulation of real business life—using his own company's background—what is learned is naturally transferable to the job. The participants analyze and discuss the who's, what's, where's, why's, and when's of each decision with an accent on understanding—an opportunity too rarely presented during busy working days. It is done in a permissive learning atmosphere, rather than within the confines of the boss-subordinate relationship.

For this feedback session to be fruitful, the discussion leader must be generally knowledgeable and well prepared. His job is to get the participants to thrash out the reasons for their proposed actions in terms of their own experience with company policies and philosophy. They should be able to justify their reasoning and appreciate the inherent assumptions on which it is based. They should also have some idea what the results of their decisions will be in both the long and short runs.

A manager can learn to come up with good solutions by gaining greater expertise through practicing with the tools at his disposal. The manager's tools are his company's policies and traditions, its channels of authority and communication, plus his skill at separating fact from opinion to identify the real issues involved. The manager who has never learned the systematic use of these tools relies on buck-passing and guesswork.

The strength of the In-Basket is that it is concerned not so much with solutions as with *how* and *why* they arose.

EXECUTIVE DEVELOPMENT

Business management is growing in importance and need. Yet its appeal as a career seems to be waning. This, despite the fact that in collegiate circles business administration is the nation's most popular major. Industry, eager heir to these graduates, is having increasing difficulty recruiting the next generation of managers.

The colleges and universities are careful not to acquire the image of trade schools. They are not guiding enough of their bright young prospects toward the executive suite. The students themselves are not responding to the corporate talent hunt, where jobs appear to be characterized by pressure, conformity, and superficial values. Instead they prefer careers in government, social work, professions, research, and the academic community.

Several large universities are phasing out undergraduate programs. They are opting for business education at the graduate level. They are deemphasizing business courses in favor of social science, humanities, physical science, and mathematics. They argue that teaching specialized business subjects too early deprives the student of a broad background. These schools feel their role is to train men for top management.

But what about the other, *and greater,* need of business for managers and executives below top management? What about men with a good general knowledge of accounting, marketing, finance, and economics? Can business education be developed without becoming vocational in nature? Whatever is offered should equip the student with a background that will stand up under technological and social change.

There are still many excellent opportunities for students interested in preparing for business careers. Fortunately, not all universities have abdicated their responsibility in this area. Some are still maintaining and expanding their curricula with well-qualified and properly oriented professors.

Many good facilities are also available to the worker. Most universities conduct night schools where a worker may take a "how to" course in any subject where he recognizes a deficiency exists in his training or background. Trade associations and industry groups operate schools and seminars for members.

The American Institute of Banking was started by a group of bank clerks who felt there might be a better way to advance in business than waiting for the guy at the next desk to die. Today the AIB has about 105,000 bank employees enrolled in courses in 350 chapters and 200 smaller study groups across the United States.

In Canada the Associated Office Administrators have developed a course of study with the local universities leading to the Certified Office Administrator designation. The program is in effect in most of the Provinces. It consists of night school classes, usually twice a week, over a four-year period.

A typical course includes economics, accounting, human factors of administration, business organization, finance, statistics, and office management. The aim is to educate for the whole business career, not primarily for the first job.

Much can be done by the company creating a work environment which is conducive to the growth of people. The increasing complexity of their jobs will be the stimulation but the climate must be such that permits the self-development of people who respond to the challenge.

A company which wants its executives or managers to develop should offer them:

1. Clearly defined responsibilities.

2. Delegation of assignments.

3. Freedom to make decisions.

4. Arrangements to acquire needed additional knowledge.

In addition it should:

1. Have confidence in these people; give them a chance.

2. Provide coaching instead of criticism; every man who fails is a reflection on his boss.

3. Keep score; progress should be recognized and rewarded.

A baseball rookie going to bat in the big leagues is not left to his own devices. He is told what to do on every pitch—whether to bunt, hit away, take the pitch, etc. He draws upon the extensive backgrounds and varied experiences of seasoned veterans. In business we are inclined to hire an applicant or promote an employee into a management position and then, instead of oversupervising him we actually become guilty of undersupervising him. We have the feeling that once such a job is filled our problems are over and we retreat into our own busy world.

EXECUTIVE TRAINING

The best executive training is a combination of

1. *In-house training sessions* conducted by professional trainers assisted by senior officers: A problem encountered on the operational floor of business calls for results.

2. *Off-the-job training* in universities and in association seminars: A problem discussed or a trend revealed in the relaxed academic atmosphere permits thinking.

3. *Work experience:* This is, in the final analysis, the testing ground that teaches responsibility.

To accomplish executive training use

- Work within the company
- Job rotation
- Lectures and seminars
- Audio-visual equipment
- Meetings (away at hotels and resorts)
- Outside study
- A number of observation points.

To be successful, allow for the expression of

- Ideas
- Imagination
- Enthusiasm
- Judgment
- Ingenuity
- Decisions

Otherwise the executives or potential executives being given this special training will soon determine that it makes sense to play according to the established and accepted ground rules.

The key to success in executive training is guidance. This can be provided in the direction of thought by outside professors and seminar leaders. But probably the best training comes from guidance on the job by seasoned and successful older executives—if they can commit their experience and success to understandable training techniques. What is done is to assign the individual trainee to a "model boss" or trainer-coach.

Work experience means more than simple routines, but does include routines. These teach responsibility for planning, coordinating, and controlling . . . and for getting results. A trainee's knowledge, skills, and abilities are deepened through experience. Ideally, the jobs he is assigned to should be over his head in order to challenge him. Once he masters these he should be moved on to more difficult assignments. In each case the trainer-coach should delegate the specific duty but not spell out how it should be done, and only keep the control to see that it comes to a good conclusion. In other words, he should give the trainee a destination and a green light, but not an old road map.

The trainer-coach must realize that the distinction in performance is not always between right and wrong ways. There may well be several right ways. He must expect that the trainee, unfettered by tradition and past practices, might come up with a different way which could be as good or better than the one which was expected.

When this practical work experience, properly directed, is supplemented by other training, as it should be, the trainee will advance in position, prestige, and compensation as fast as his increasing capabilities will take him and appropriate promotions and job vacancies open up for him.

ASPEN INSTITUTE FOR HUMANISTIC STUDIES

The Aspen Institute for Humanistic Studies, Aspen, Colorado, is a nonprofit educational institution which serves as a conference and study center. It confronts leaders from all vocations with a wide spectrum of ideas and values in order to stretch the minds and lift the horizons of men.

The Executive Program

The purpose of the Aspen Executive Program is to broaden the perspective and excite the imagination of each participant through an informal intensive exchange of ideas.

The program is concerned with self-renewal and further personal development of business and professional leaders. The demands on executives are now so great that there is little time either for reflection on the changing nature of the executive's role or for an exchange of views about fundamental values for the business organization, its employees—or the executive himself.

Aspen provides a special opportunity for self-evaluation through continuing debate and interchange of ideas among intelligent, successful men. Discussions center on such relationships as the individual and the state, freedom and equality, justice and power, and labor and property. Since history shows that there is nothing absolute about such concepts, it becomes the task of the business leader to determine how he is to apply them in a constantly changing society. His success in doing so will ultimately determine the atmosphere in which business operates, the profitability of his enterprise, and even the nature of our future society.

The role of the Aspen program is to encourage the executive to clarify personal values which must form the basis for his working philosophy and his relations to others.

The distinctive feature of the Aspen program is that it gives participants enough time for reading, reflection, discussion, and association with others to make a difference in their lives.

Seminar Sessions and the Aspen Readings

The seminar discussion, based on the Aspen Readings, is a dialectic in which all of the participants become deeply involved. The two-hour daily sessions and the preparatory readings are the core of the Executive Program.

The readings are selected to present ideas concerning the individual and his relationship to society and to the state. The historical perspective is used to deepen the understanding of ideas of great current significance.

Since the readings entail about three hours of preparation for each day of the seminar, a complete set of books is sent to each participant several weeks ahead of time. The following list is representative of the readings in a typical year. The readings are grouped by key ideas that were stressed in the seminar sessions:

Basic Assumptions:
   Pericles: *Funeral Oration*
   Montaigne: *Of Repentance*
   Plato: *The Republic*
   Locke: *Of Civil Government*

Man's Commitment:

Plato: *Apology and Crito*
Thoreau: *On Civil Disobedience*
Camus: *The Stranger*
Martin Luther King: *Letter from Birmingham City Jail*

The Survival of Society:

Machiavelli: *The Prince*
Marx and Engels: *The Communist Manifesto*
Lin Piao: *Long Live the Victory of People's War*
Shulman: *Beyond the Cold War*

Decision Making:

Sophocles: *Antigone*
Melville: *Billy Budd*

Man in 1980

A continuing series of conferences within the theme of "Man in 1980" bring together specialists to study and report on selected critical problems. During one season the "Man in 1980" program included conferences on Liberal Learning; Government and Higher Education; Moral and Ethical Values; and The School Curriculum in 1980. The first publication from this series, *American Higher Education in 1980—Some Basic Issues,* is now available.

Each conference is a continuing one, and annual meetings are based upon interim research and exploration. Significant reports, summaries, and working papers are published and widely circulated as the basis for a plan of action. Conference participants themselves are in a position to develop policies and precedents formulated at Aspen.

The Physics Division

The institute's Physics Division offers theoretical physicists the opportunity to confer with colleagues working in the same fields and to learn firsthand of progress made in other areas.

The program gained its first Nobel laureate in Professor Richard P. Feynman, whose field is quantum electrodynamics. And the National Academy of Sciences sent to Aspen a Russian physicist, Dr. G. Zharkov, thus giving the division international significance.

Participating physicists publish over 20 papers resulting from work in Aspen each summer. Some of the fields represented are: high energy physics, solid state physics, theory of low temperature liquids, and nuclear physics. The work of these physicists is supported by grants obtained through their home universities and by donations from the Alfred P. Sloan Foundation and the Office of Naval Research.

Physicists have the opportunity to meet with participants and resource guests from other institute programs. During the summer a biweekly seminar involved both physicists and executive program participants in discussion of the impact of science on society.

The Lecture Series

Most Aspen seminars are closed to the public, on the grounds that primary communication between participants is of basic concern and that participants too often deliver public lectures to each other when an audience is present.

To make the human resources gathered in Aspen available to a larger audience, the Aspen Lecture series was created. Each summer, Tuesday evening is set aside for a talk or panel discussion open to the public. For one such summer series, Dean Acheson, former Secretary of State, and Mortimer Adler, creator of the Great Books Series, were among the speakers.

In addition to its continuing conference and study programs, the Institute creates special convocations on men and ideas. In May 1966, friends, critics, and admirers of Albert Schweitzer from as far away as Korea, Jerusalem. Lamberéné, Gabon, Holland, France, and the Philippines gathered in Aspen to assess "The Intellectual Contributions of Albert Schweitzer."

MANAGERS DON'T JUST HAPPEN

Reprinted from the Esso Eastern Review

Published by Esso Standard Eastern, Inc. and Esso Eastern Chemicals, Inc.

Some bright young Filipino who joins Esso Standard Eastern in the 1970's may find himself a director of Esso Philippines or Esso Standard Eastern in the late 80's. The same holds for Indian, Thai, Australian, Vietnamese, Pakistani, American, Malaysian, Japanese, or other nationals of the 25 countries in which the company operates.

It is next to impossible for an ambitious, intelligent person to "get lost" in Esso Standard Eastern. Anyone with the capability and will to succeed is noticed. Once his capabilities are demonstrated, his career is guided so he can be ready to take over the highest position he is qualified to attain.

Regularly on the job, and at least once a year in more formal sessions, his accomplishments will be examined. Both successes and failures are noted, and men who are concerned that he succeed try to help him across future hurdles. He is given new assignments to gain experience in his weak areas and to take advantage of his strong points.

Several Programs Available

In every organization affiliated with ESE, there is a management development program to prepare men to be ready to take over important executive roles on both an immediate and long-range basis. There is also a management development committee.

When a young man is hired in Esso Standard Eastern, he will generally spend the first few years putting his college education to work, developing knowledge of and relationships inside the company and carrying out other people's assignments.

If the new employee is able, he will probably move along within his particular area of the company and—while doing so—be given varied exposure both in assignments and to different supervisors. From a variety of assignments and supervisors it will be easier to assess his ability.

It is a goal of management development to have trained men

ready to take over jobs as the men are needed. To insure adequately prepared candidates for the jobs, it is in the company's interest to identify and begin training their future managers as early as possible. Young men, therefore, are not relegated to the end of the line; they are given places in relationship to their demonstrated ability.

The listing of such men with high executive potential and the preparation of plans to develop them into trained managers is basic to the management development program.

Individual career development plans—drawn for four-year periods—are made for each man who is thought to have executive potential. A man's present position along with his next logical jobs to fill out his company knowledge are charted. An attempt is made to give him both functional and geographic experience as part of his development.

To become a manager, the company believes a man must be given the chance to manage. He must learn how to work with people, how to compromise when necessary, how to get his own objectives off the ground, and how to stay within a budget.

Somewhere along the way, the man who is moving toward top executive positions should gain experience in financial management, economics, long-range planning, cost control and profit improvement, budgets and investments; personnel, executive, and organization development, and government, public, or employee relations.

Plans Are Flexible

Plans which are drawn up for each person are not hard and fast things. They are regularly examined and adjusted to meet new situations. A man may, for instance, prove to be more—or less—talented than was earlier thought. Development plans are adjusted accordingly.

If the man has risen to the top of his ability, he is developed in depth at that level. If he can move ahead—on he goes.

A man's professional area of training is not as important as his personal qualifications. Being an engineer or a marketer is not necessarily more valuable in Esso Eastern than being a lawyer or an employee relations specialist, for example. If it was ever true that people with academic backgrounds in certain disciplines were more favored than others for top jobs, it is no longer the case.

There is a theory always extant that "old-fashioned virtues" (being "out-of-date") should be avoided. Such virtues, however, make up a good part of the list of things generally considered to be executive characteristics.

Each man is compared to outstanding employees around him as to his articulateness, commitment, creativeness, decisiveness, and his willingness to help others develop.

Also considered are his flexibility, drive, initiative, intellectual abilities, business and human judgment, leadership, managerial abilities, motivation, health, ability to solve problems, stability, and potential for self-development and discipline.

Satisfying every one of these items is something a Boy Scout could envy. But no one is expected to meet all the requirements. There are men who are outstanding in many areas but lacking in others. Part of the program's goal is to help men to develop areas in which they are lacking and to match them to jobs which maximize their strengths.

A Simple, Workable System

There is nothing mysterious about the activities of Esso management development. It is a responsibility of management which does not end because current affairs are well managed; it demands that an equally good or better successor management be provided. Finally, it boils down to an organized system whereby people who have been seen to be effective are pushed ahead as fast as they can go.

Although machines and tests are used to help in assessing a man's potential, the real tests are human ones—how does he work with and for people and how does he do his job?—and the real assessments are from human beings. Since so many more than one person are involved with assessment, there is little chance that prejudice will keep a really capable man down.

It's a simple system. It's open to everyone. And it works. It is, in short, the reason there are so many people moving ahead.

ORGANIZATION DEVELOPMENT
St. Regis Paper Company, New York, N. Y.

In St. Regis—or any other company—success of a department, a division, or the whole firm depends primarily upon your skills as a manager in getting results.

Organization Development is simply an approach to improving results through getting the best from your people, both as individuals and as members of working groups.

Most of Your Managing Activities Are Directed Toward Improved Results

PLANNING—which involves:

- Forecasting future problems and opportunities.
- Defining objectives.
- Programming the steps to reach objectives.
- Scheduling target dates for completion.
- Selecting procedures and methods to use.
- Budgeting resources to reach objectives.

ORGANIZING—which involves:

- Developing organization structure.
- Delegating authority and responsibility.
- Establishing effective working relationships.

LEADING—which involves:

- Initiating action.
- Making decisions.
- Communicating.
- Motivating others to act.
- Developing and coaching subordinates.

CONTROLLING—which involves:

- Developing measures of results.
- Appraising performance.
- Taking corrective action.

These are the recognized steps of managing any activity.

(Charts tracing the "how" and the "why" of the St. Regis Paper Company organization development plan are on the following two pages. The outline above is concluded on page 386.)

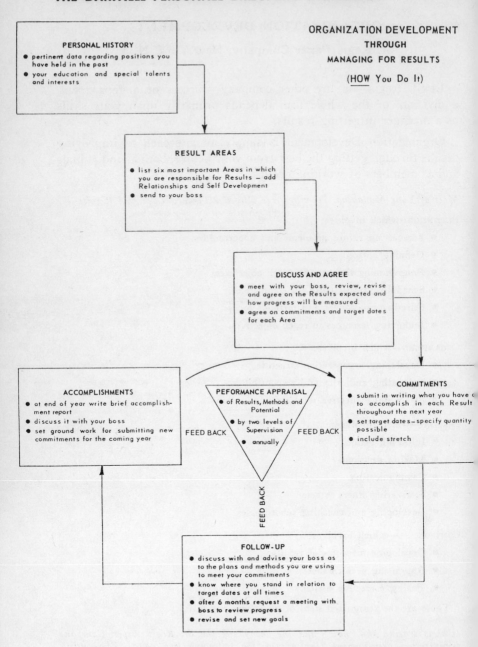

PERSONAL HISTORY
- pertinent data regarding positions you have held in the past
- your education and special talents and interests

ORGANIZATION DEVELOPMENT
THROUGH
MANAGING FOR RESULTS
(HOW You Do It)

RESULT AREAS
- list six most important Areas in which you are responsible for Results — add Relationships and Self Development
- send to your boss

DISCUSS AND AGREE
- meet with your boss, review, revise and agree on the Results expected and how progress will be measured
- agree on commitments and target dates for each Area

ACCOMPLISHMENTS
- at end of year write brief accomplishment report
- discuss it with your boss
- set ground work for submitting new commitments for the coming year

PEFORMANCE APPRAISAL
- of Results, Methods and Potential
- by two levels of Supervision
- annually

FEED BACK   FEED BACK

FEED BACK

COMMITMENTS
- submit in writing what you have [ ] to accomplish in each Result throughout the next year
- set target dates—specify quantity possible
- include stretch

FOLLOW-UP
- discuss with and advise your boss as to the plans and methods you are using to meet your commitments
- know where you stand in relation to target dates at all times
- after 6 months request a meeting with boss to review progress
- revise and set new goals

The mechanics, or the "how" of the St. Regis organization development plan.

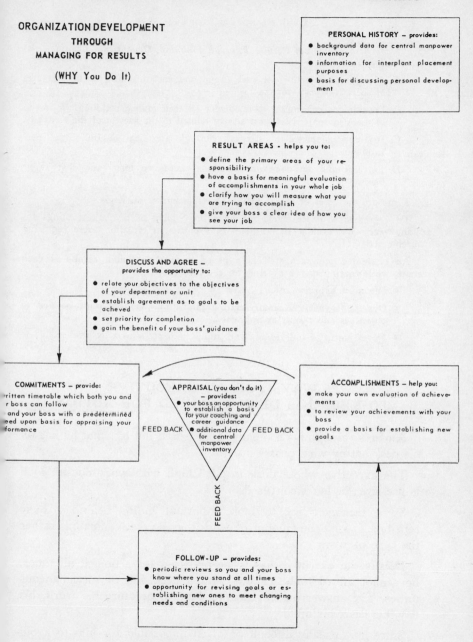

The goals, or the "why" of the St. Regis organization development plan.

(Outline continued from page 383)

To Accomplish Maximum Results Through Planning, Organizing, Leading, and Controlling You Must—

    A. Clarify the objectives of each group and each job, and define measures of successful performance.

    B. Provide for continuing development of each manager through followup of those job objectives most closely related to the success of the company.

    C. Inventory management strength through appraisal of individual performance.

    D. Forecast and act upon organizational needs on long- and short-range bases.

These are the bases of Organization Development at St. Regis.

To a greater or lesser extent we have been doing each of these things for many years—but usually in isolation as a particular situation arose requiring specific action.

An integrated approach will help us to achieve maximum results at each stage, while continuously preparing for the future.

    • We must appraise results based on established objectives.

    • Our management inventory and organization planning must be tied to objectives and results as appraised.

    • Development of individuals and groups will occur as a by-product.

25 WAYS FOR AN EXECUTIVE TO KEEP HIS DESK CLEARED FOR ACTION

A man's value to his company is measured not by what he has *on* his desk but by what passes *over* it.

The executive whose desk is piled high with work doesn't look impressive; he looks confused.

Some managers try to look important hiding behind a busy schedule. It isn't the amount of work they do that counts but rather the type of work.

Because an executive has to be prepared for action at all times, he cannot afford to be caught with a desk full of miscellaneous duties. The answer lies in learning how to organize his work, his day, his desk, his mind.

Since it is usually difficult or often impossible for him to avoid much of his work, it might be well for him to review some of the techniques available to him which can be useful in clearing a desk and keeping it ready for action.

Some of the following 25 suggestions may be considered:

1. Delegate some of your work to subordinates. This not only relieves you of much of the detail but it also helps to develop others who will then be better experienced to take some of the load from you.

2. Allow your secretary or assistant to do some of your work. Oftimes they can actually do a job better because of fewer interruptions and closer acquaintanceship with other workers or departments that may be involved. Ideally, every duty should be performed by the lowest paid individual who is qualified to handle it. Anything else is a waste of company money and your valuable time.

3. Quit trying to keep your fingers in every detail. Don't become a slave of insecurity. It breeds incompetent "yes sir" men who complement the executive rather than challenge and stimulate him. Ultimately it discourages the ingenuity of subordinates by competing with them. Unless the executive can build up his staff so that he can trust them, he will wind up doing all the work whether he wants to or not. And who will get the nervous breakdown?

4. Schedule and evaluate your work. Get out of the woods and take a look at the trees occasionally. The usual executive rushes around doing 40 or 50 different and unrelated things. Too often when he goes home at night it is because he has run out of time, not work.

5. Arrange your work so as to dispose of those things which can be handled promptly. The few projects remaining are then not hard to cope with if the pile of work no longer looks like a hopeless task to tackle.

6. Attack the unpleasant or difficult jobs first and get them out of the way while you're fresh. Don't become attached to them by letting them accumulate.

7. On the other hand, stop wrestling with a problem that, for the moment at least, has you licked. Put it aside temporarily and come back to it when your mood and mind toward it have improved. Be careful, however, not to put it off indefinitely.

8. Develop organizational ability in your own work and that of your area of responsibility. The word "supervisor," if not by definition then at least by connotation, means someone possessed with "super" vision. Look over and beyond the obvious to determine what effect the action of the present may have on the future. Look forward with wisdom and you'll look back with pride.

9. Keep work on top of your desk where it will haunt you and thereby stand a better chance of getting done. Burying it in desk drawers keeps it out of sight and away from completion.

10. Check every single item that is on or in your desk at least once a month. Perhaps if it has had no attention for 30 days it could be filed or even discarded.

11. Put your many miscellaneous duties on trial periodically. By putting them to the test you may discover that some are habit and can no longer be defended as necessary. Habit and routine have an unbelievable power to waste and destroy your time and energy.

12. Develop short cuts wherever possible. For example: Writing your reply to a letter at the bottom of the page, instead of dictating a formal answer, saves both time and money.

13. Don't fall into the pattern of documenting everything. In some cases a telephone call may not only be quicker but actually better than some slower form of communication.

14. Don't file everything either. Much of the material placed carefully into file cabinets is never referred to again until years later when it is tossed out. Make certain there is a justifiable reason for filing something; don't do it routinely.

15. Stop vacillating. This wastes not only your time but also that of others who are depending upon you for sound direction. You should have firmness of conviction, based on sound moral standards. To be head and shoulders above the crowd a man must be willing to stick his neck out. Humpty-Dumpty was a fence-straddling egghead, and when he fell there was no hope of reconstructing him.

16. Learn to make quicker decisions. It takes time to investigate a situation or listen to a problem. "I'll let you know later" only means that the scene must be recreated later when the decision is given. If the answer can be forthcoming when the problem is posed, the job is done.

17. Make decisions that are sound, fair, and logical so that they will be acceptable. Decisions based on authority and unconcern can cause no end of repercussion. Making the decision is important, but making it right is essential. Unless the decision is the right one it will some day return to haunt you.

18. Take time to communicate with others who may be interested or involved with you in a project. A few minutes spent at the start explaining something can save endless hours afterwards should an unintentional mistake need correcting.

19. Discourage visitors and interruptions, however, especially when these do not pertain to your job and you are busy. An open door policy is fine, but remember that every door still has hinges so that it can be closed when necessary.

20. Try to say "no" to some of the requests made of you. Everyone is flattered by being asked to serve on numerous committees and functions where he can share his talents, which he feels are valuable to the cause, and give advice, which is limitless. But these invitations are also cruel demands upon an executive's time and energy, which are certainly not limitless.

21. Concentrate more on your work and less on maintaining the symbols of status, many of them useless anyway. These visible appurtenances are not what gets the work done, you know.

22. Accept authority. Be big but don't act big. The unnecessary acting is what takes up the time.

23. Do not resist authority either. Many people who give orders cannot take orders. They can criticize freely but even well-intentioned suggestions upset them. This puts them in the wrong mood and prevents them from functioning at their best. Anyone given the right to command should first have learned to obey.

24. Accept responsibility. Don't run around looking for a crutch to lean on—either some item of company policy to protect you or a decision by a higher-up to hide behind. This approach not only builds weak managers but it is also time consuming.

25. Finally, don't let the briefcase become a grief case. Develop a balanced way of life. Outside interests and relaxations are needed to round out the whole personality. Work, play, love, worship—this is a good prescription for executive health. Unless the executive enjoys good health and peace of mind, he cannot be on the job and working well to keep his desk cleared for action.

Some years ago my first boss passed along bits of wisdom he had acquired in the school of hard knocks. One of his axioms made it clear that "the more important a man becomes the less work he does." This truism has been restated in an assortment of ways in later business textbooks and management courses. No matter how it is phrased, it suggests that the executive cannot afford to become bogged down in all the details of his job but that at all times he must keep his desk cleared for action.

TOASTMASTERS CLUBS

A Toastmasters Club is an organized group of men, over 18 years of age, who seek to increase their self-confidence through improvement of their speaking ability. Toastmasters is primarily designed for the mature mind.

The organization was founded in Santa Ana, California, by Ralph C. Smedley. Incorporated in 1932 as a nonprofit corporation, the movement has grown until now there are clubs chartered in every state of the United States and in 49 other countries. Since its inception, more than a million men have benefited from membership in Toastmasters clubs.

Insignia of the Toastmasters Club, international organization dedicated to improvement of members' speech-making abilities.

What Can Toastmasters Do For the Members?

- Aid him in mastering the art of effective speaking.

- Help him make a poised, self-assured appearance before any audience.

- Prepare him for chairmanship and for participation in meetings of all kinds.

- Increase his qualifications for business and civic recognition.

- Provide an enjoyable fellowship and a forum for the stimulating exchange of ideas.

The frequent opportunities to speak provide increased effectiveness and self-confidence. Constructive criticism is a vital part of Toastmasters training. Following each program, members evaluate each speaker. A General Critic reviews the entire program. The constructive criticism, or evaluation, is always done by members themselves.

A Toastmasters Club usually meets weekly for dinner. The meetings, including dinner, should not exceed two hours.

Every member, except those scheduled to make speeches, has an opportunity for extemporaneous speaking during the business portion of the meeting and through the regular program feature, "Table Topics," in which he speaks briefly on assigned topics of general interest. A Toastmaster of the evening presides over the formal program, which includes four to six short speeches, all prepared in advance and based on principles set forth in a "Basic Training Manual."

Initiation fees of $5 to $10 and modest monthly dues are set by each club, depending on its needs and activities. From these dues, a small per capita fee is paid by the club to Toastmasters International for maintenance of the World Headquarters, for the general work of supervision, promotion and publication for the good of the clubs, for educational materials and services, and for the conduct of district activities.

Who Belongs to Toastmasters?

There are no occupational, educational, racial, or religious bars to Toastmasters membership. Men in business and professional life are usually the most readily interested in the club. However, any man interested in self-improvement can make good use of the opportunities offered by a Toastmasters Club.

So that members may enjoy frequent opportunities to speak, preside, and evaluate, each Toastmasters Club is limited to a maximum of 40 members.

Toastmasters International is a nonprofit educational organization governed by a Board of Directors. Educational material and other services are provided by the World Headquarters, which is under the administration of the Executive Director. For convenience, the organization is divided into districts, each headed by an elected District Governor. Isolated clubs are under the direct supervision of Toastmasters International.

To *organize* a club, write to Toastmasters International, Santa Ana, California, for detailed information, which will be sent free of charge and without obligation. With this information, a group of men could become interested and form a temporary organization.

To *join* an existing club, an interested prospect should send a postcard to Toastmasters International, Santa Ana, California, asking for information about the club nearest to him. He will be invited to go to a meeting and to form his own opinion.

EXECUTIVE SUCCESS

Contrary to popular opinion, an executive is a specialist. He is a specialist who became a generalist. He used his particular specialty as the ladder upon which to climb to success. Even a chief executive is a specialist; he is a specialist at picking the brains of other specialists.

A discussion of executive success shifts the emphasis away from the specialist to that of the administrator. Let's use a few examples to make the point. To bake a pie and deliver it fresh, delicious, and unbroken to a neighbor calls for technical know-how. To bake thousands of pies each day and deliver them unbroken, on time, and acceptably priced to a series of outlets, calls for management skills. Or . . . in our offices, much of the accounting is no longer done by bookkeepers but by tabulating machine operators, many of whom do not know the difference between debits and credits. Or how about this . . . bread is no longer baked by bakers, but in today's modern automated bakeries, bread is baked by machinists. The question is: How much of the work the executive finds himself doing is not the work for which he had trained himself? What skills does he need beyond the technical knowledge he acquired?

Shortage of Qualified Executives

Speaking within the framework of business and industry generally, let me say first that there is no shortage of people in executive positions. The jobs, for the most part, are filled. But there is a very definite shortage of qualified executives. In fact, the scarcity of management skills is becoming a serious menace to industrial growth and expansion.

We see this disturbing situation all around us in business offices. It exists elsewhere too—in the fields of religion, education, science, government, and so on. It is also true in the professions. There is no problem with the technical skills; the problem is with the skills the technicians or specialists need for the executive or administrative part of their work.

In any program for the development of executives there are two sides to consider. First, what can the employer or the company do, and second, what can the individual do?

In our business offices we find the need for development of present and potential executives is caused by the simple fact that in today's complex competitive operations, jobs grow bigger first, ahead of people. Getting the people to grow to keep pace with their enlarged duties is the responsibility of management. It is a sad commentary that in many well-known companies management is content to fly in a jet age with nothing better than a broomstick.

To develop our people, three things are necessary:

1. Provide training.
2. Give broadening experience.
3. Establish the climate for growth.

Giving a man a title, a rug on the floor, or a secretary won't make him an executive. Somehow we've got to equip him mentally, intellectually, emotionally, psychologically, and spiritually—in addition to giving him physical facilities and visible appurtenances.

Neglecting our need to develop executives can be serious. But the fault may not lie entirely with management. No company can develop individuals who do not reach out for help on their own. Not everybody aspires to become an officer in the industrial army.

The key to executive development lies in self-betterment. Individuals must be awakened to the serious consequences of standing still . . . and to the realization that the world does not remain static. Those who do not keep pace in effect fall behind.

The purpose of any training program is not primarily to teach but to create within the individual the desire to learn. The proper philosophy of training does not believe in spoon-feeding the trainees but encourages self-improvement, motivated from within.

Since in the case of training, the improvement depends more upon the patient than upon the doctor, let's concentrate on what the individual may do for himself in the development of necessary executive skills, especially as they relate to his dealings with others.

Executive Patterns

Executive ability does not come automatically. Many people who are promoted or who suddenly find themselves in positions of management wish it could come to them overnight. A man who is a good technician may have a genuine feeling of inadequacy as an administrator, with duties that call for skills which he has not had the chance to acquire.

Anyone who wants to become proficient in the administrative field should perhaps have some sort of model to pattern after. Let's look at some of the people who earn their living as business executives. No two executives are alike, but all fall into definite patterns. It is possible to group them into four types:

First we have the *originator*. This is the executive who thinks for himself. He can analyze his particular problem and arrive at an independent decision. He is not afraid to explore something new. He may make mistakes but he will contribute many useful ideas to the situation in which he is serving.

Then we have the *improvisor*. This is the executive who must first have the boundaries surveyed for him. Within these limits he operates with vision and imagination, understanding the problems and adapting accepted ideas.

Next we have the *follower*. This executive rarely designs any new programs or any part of a program. He observes what others in the field are doing to meet their problems, accepts what is common practice, then determines the minimum action necessary to keep abreast of competition.

Finally we have the *relaxer*. This is the satisfied executive who grew up with the system, is quite comfortable in it, and has no desire to change anything. He finally got where he is, feels it was hard work getting there, and now wants to sit back and enjoy the luxury of his position. He is willing to work hard but along the lines he understands, accepts, and enjoys.

In any case, the executive function is measured in terms of work goals. Increasing emphasis is on administrative ability, coupled with adroitness in human relations and communications skills.

Executive Qualities

There are certain broad and basic skills which the executive should possess, identified as technical, human, and conceptual. All three skills can be developed by training, but conceptual skill is essentially a matter of raw intelligence and judgment, and is an indispensable element in top-level policymaking.

The executive job differs from the supervisory job in that it does not directly involve the control of people, but rather, the control of ideas. While most executives would make good supervisors, good supervisors do not necessarily make good executives.

The qualities to look for in executives can be grouped into three categories:

Mental	Personal	Physical
verbal ability	self-confidence	vitality
reasoning ability	level of aspiration	endurance
memory, concentration	decisiveness	general health
judgment	work habits	feeling of well-being
flexibility	marital adjustment	balanced life
organization-mindedness	social, ethical standards	peace of mind

The executive should be made to realize that what he is learning or being taught along the lines of scientific management is new. But his trouble with the human element can be traced to conflicts as old as mankind. All human problems are rooted in a few basic weaknesses of man. Theologians have long ago narrowed these failings to seven deadly sins, which the executive should try to avoid in the conduct of his work with others. These are:

Pride —*all wrapped up in oneself.*

Envy —*inability to be objectively honest.*

Laziness —*not being industrious.*

Anger —*this betrays personal shortcomings.*

Unchastity —*lack of integrity and moral uprightness.*

Greed —*hunger for power.*

Gloominess —*fear and pessimism to cloud our thinking.*

Great leaders are known for their great strengths, but what we forget is that they also may have great weaknesses. Executives must be convinced that their success depends upon their ability to build on their strengths and to recognize their weaknesses and keep these as far behind them as possible.

A man was trying to explain to another man why he had not spoken to his wife for six weeks. He said that he had a violent temper and that if he pursued their difference of opinion he might say something in anger that would hurt her. "You probably can't understand this," he added, "because you have no temper." But the other man answered, "Yes, I too have a terrible temper, but knowing this, I've learned never to use it."

When we compare the successful executives with their less successful brethren we come up with the *positive* factors of success. Sometimes it is easier to make our point by turning the record over and emphasizing the *negative* side. Here are a few of the more common reasons for executive failure:

1. Limited viewpoint: cannot see the forest; too preoccupied with the trees.
2. Unwillingness to assume his share of the responsibility: Looking for a crutch to lean on.

3. Using some other status, such as professional, to hide behind and to avoid facing up to executive duties.

4. Impatience in dealing with the slowness of others to grasp those things which may come easy to him: Tolerance is the oil which takes the friction out of life.

5. Inability to participate in a free spirit of cooperation: Insecurity.

6. Indifference to authority: Dislikes discipline. Anyone given the right to command should first have learned to obey.

7. Difficulty in supervising: Cannot see the other person's side.

8. Prejudices which affect independent judgment: Closed mind with cherished notions and fixed ideas. The trouble with some of us is that we want to get to the promised land without leaving our own wilderness.

9. Overwork: Unwilling to delegate.

10. Poor health which interferes with tending to business: Simply cannot do justice to his responsibilities.

Now as to some of those positive skills that are necessary for executive success, a management survey might shed some light. Some 70 large corporations were asked what traits they considered most important to success. Of the answers, 70 percent said, "The ability to get along with people." They listed these requisites for getting along with others:

1. The ability to work cooperatively with others in a group.

2. The ability to communicate—to talk, teach, persuade.

3. Enthusiasm—initiative and drive. The executive who is not fired with enthusiasm should be . . . fired . . . with enthusiasm!

4. Appearance—not fashion plates but neatness and proper dress and manners.

5. Balance—especially emotional balance, personality balance.

6. Leadership—the kind of person others are impelled to follow, not compelled to follow.

The Carnegie Institute, after studying records of 10,000 employees, concluded that 15 percent of success is due to technical competence and 85 percent to personality development. Just as technical skills can be acquired, so also can personality traits be acquired and improved.

What we're saying is that the operation of business today is scientific, but success in business, as elsewhere, is still a personal matter. And while in technological achievements we are supermen, in human relations we are barbarians in dinner jackets.

Can You Communicate?

It must be obvious by now that whatever we bring up as necessary skills somehow gets us right back to this business of dealing with others. And in this part of our jobs that involves dealing with others, one important factor of success is the ability to communicate effectively at all levels.

There are three types of communications: Verbal, written, and nonverbal. It is the nonverbal which are the most effective if properly applied and the most dangerous if not properly applied . . . for they include our attitudes, our expressions, our actions, our beliefs, and our convictions.

Personal contacts in day-to-day procedures provide the most commonly used means of communication between people. In some situations this may involve dealing on the same level. Sometimes downward, as a supervisor giving instructions to a subordinate, which is ordinarily not a consultation between equals but orders to be carried out unequivocally. Oftimes this is from an executive to one of his peers, a person over whom he exercises no direct authority.

But levels should not enter into the consideration lest this complicate the method used. A good executive, no matter where he finds himself in the management hierachy or where he appears on the company organization chart, never should rely upon his position or prestige for the accomplishment of his purpose. He cannot succeed, any more than others can, by imposing his will upon others. It is better to get results without resorting to the prerogatives of authority. The idea that is being promoted should stand on its own merits; it should not ride in on the coattails of executive authority or professional standing.

This is true especially of delegation, the passing of authority and responsibility to others. In dealing with others, and in this art of delegation to others, the usual procedure is to give orders or to command. There are five ways to accomplish this need to command:

1. Command through superior articulation; achieved through skill in persuading others to bring about acceptance of an idea or decision.

2. Command through technical competence: Decisions rest with those who have the technical skills and knowledge which others do not possess.

3. Command through status: Prestige and position in the organization have a bearing upon the right to decide issues.

4. Command through sanctions: A man not in a position to make the decision may exert his influence upon another who, in turn, makes the decision.

5. Command by default: One man is left to make the decision in situations where someone else has taken no action either because of inability or willingness to pass the responsibility.

Rules Not Possible

When it comes to the full area of communicating with others, not just getting acceptance to orders and commands, we run into something else. It is difficult to give out any set of one-two-three rules to help an executive in his efforts to deal properly with people. What works with one man may not work with another because the two people are not alike, therefore do not react in the same way. One rule or principle which works in one situation may not work when transposed because circumstances may not be quite alike.

The point to make is that "just following the book" may not produce the desired result. The principles may be standard but their application must be tailored to the situation.

For example: it is often said, and often proved, that an executive will find the going easier if he consults with others before he makes his decision. This is the theory that says, "Put 'em in the boat with you and they'll not bore holes in it." So he embraces consultative decision-making in the hope that it may be the mysterious key to unlock the door to success. He tries it only to find that while it seemed to make sense, and obviously worked elsewhere, it failed in his situation. Why? The employees were not properly conditioned for this sort of executive approach. They were reluctant to co-operate for any of several reasons:

1. They fear punishment if they are parties to a wrong decision.

2. Some people lose respect for the executive who, to them, should be the sole authority on a particular matter (a doctor, for instance, would not be expected to hold a conference with patients; he tells them and they accept).

3. They don't want to lend a flavor of participation to a decision that they feel has already been made.

What we're trying to emphasize is that any technique that is recommended carries with it the promise of success but may also have some built-in pitfalls or risks that must be recognized.

The issue of whether an executive should operate as a one-man show or, in the interests of better dealings with others, should occasionally bring them into the act, presents interesting observations. The industrial autocrat, the professional dictator, the strong individualist is, oftentimes, quite effective. When right he puts on quite a show of rapid-fire decision-making. This may be very impressive for it does save a good deal of time for everybody.

But what is the percentage for a man being right all the time? One authority says, "It is rare indeed for more than 25 percent of his decisions to be right." You make your own estimate if you don't like his. But it is doubtful if any of us would be foolish enough to claim that such a personality is 100 percent right all the time.

What happens when the decision is wrong? It is just as forceful and just as final as the right one. But others who are affected by it have little recourse. Chances are they know it is wrong and, when it is crammed down their throats, they give it only lip service. That may actually be the better of the two choices. The other is to fall in line with authority, be resigned to the ill-fated decision, go along with it and do things wrong.

We're not advocating that every decision should be referred to the group. What we would like to put across is that any group, through the exercise of teamwork, functions better than the hard-hitting executive who says in effect, "I'll do the thinking around here," as though he had a corner on brains. Whether the executive sits down in committee meeting with his staff, or whether he occasionally consults with them as individuals before he proceeds on his own, doesn't make much difference. In both cases he has the benefits of anything they might contribute to a sounder decision, plus the advantage of having pretested his idea on them before it becomes final. It is better, if an adverse reaction is coming, to be tipped off early enough to make a correction or an adjustment.

This business of dealing with others should not be taken lightly. On this skill rests our entire chance for success. This is true not only in our business but also in life generally. For after all is said and done, the great problems of the age—international, national, and corporate—have to do with the relationships of people. We must be skilled in getting along with others. But this skill must rest upon some such foundation as this: technical competence in our chosen field, broad intellectual outlook, high sense of honor, moral and spiritual values, attention to the public interests, understanding and respect for the other fellow.

Five Keys to Success

In this presentation we've been all over the pea-patch of executive skills. As my personal contribution to you I should like to leave you with five factors which I believe are essential to executive success.

The first is *motivation*. An executive's value is in direct relation to his ability to motivate himself and his workers to more and better production. Since the other elements in business—materials, money, methods, machines, and markets—are fixed, or at least the same among all companies, the opportunity for improvement lies in the only variable element, the available workers.

The second factor is *vision*. Every executive is a supervisor; he supervises people or an activity or both. The word "supervisor," if not by definition then at least by connotation, means someone possessed with "super" vision. Hence, a supervisor must be capable of seeing over and beyond the obvious. Look forward with wisdom and you'll look back with pride.

The third factor is *decision-making* ability. The man who can make decisions gets paid for it; the one who cannot must yield the authority and salary to the higher up who has to make the decisions for him. It's as simple as that! To be head and shoulders above the crowd a man must be willing to stick his neck out. The executive who wants to get somewhere must be able to take a stand; he cannot ride both horses forever. Humpty-Dumpty was a fence-straddling egghead, and when he fell there was no hope of reconstructing him.

The fourth factor is *good health*. To be on the job as needed, and to meet the demands of his increasingly heavy work load, an executive must be in sound physical condition. Much has been said and written about the broad subject of coddling employees, of benefits expanded and working conditions improved. But it is high time that management also take steps necessary to ease the tension, frustration, strain, and effort of executives. Don't let the briefcase become a grief case.

But health is a many splendored thing. It embodies more than physical fitness. It may be likened to the Maltese cross. On each arm of the cross is a word representing a main element by which a normal human being lives. The words are: work, play, love, worship. When a person is short on one of these he should arrange to round out his life. Lopsided living is a common cause of ill health, and the four-sided cross comes close to the prescription for executive health.

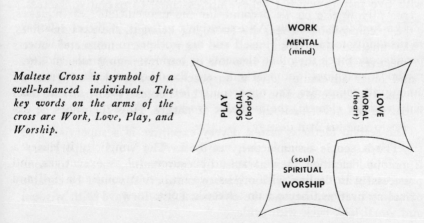

Maltese Cross is symbol of a well-balanced individual. The key words on the arms of the cross are Work, Love, Play, and Worship.

The fifth factor is *humility*. As important as good health is, even more necessary for success is peace of mind. A true spirit of humility provides a source of executive help that is greater than all others. It is a pattern of well being and adjustment to life that has been found effective for centuries.

It is quite obvious that no one of us succeeds alone. We are all interdependent upon one another. It was Tennyson who said, "I am a part of all I have met." But there is more to success than that. Let me remind you that in life all of us have met more than each other.

The Unseen Helper

Throughout our lives there is an invisible means of support, which guides and directs our individual and national destinies. Whether or not we openly profess any religious affiliation, we are nevertheless living and prospering in the afterglow of a great Christian heritage.

That this climate is a factor in our personal success in dealing with others is evidenced by the fact that many problem situations in life, which may not conform to the obvious laws of nature or man, often find easy solution in the spiritual laws, which also exert an impelling force in the universe.

The unseen helper in our lives could well be the influence of a guiding philosophy that recognizes the shortcomings of self-sufficiency. For isn't it true that whenever we are carried away by our materialistic success we are given stern warnings of our misplaced trust? How else do we account for the unpredictable earthquakes, the uncontrollable floods, the damaging drought, the ravaging fires, the unseasonable frosts, and the many other unexpected upsets whenever Ma nature goes into one of her rampaging moods. These and other adversities have a purpose—to teach us the virtues of humility. These are painful lessons but necessary to prove to man that he can never tame the forces of nature. How then does he expect to rule his own destiny!

The lesson is a simple one, but by its very simplicity it leaves a profound message. If we want to be successful as executives, and successful in dealing with others, we must first come to a full and final realization that no man succeeds alone.

PERSONAL TRAITS OF AN EXECUTIVE

Desirable and Undesirable

In describing what makes an executive good or bad, the personal traits must first be divided into two categories—good and bad. By matching his performance against this list it is easy to determine whether an executive is effective or not.

Undesirable personal traits:

1. The inability to see the forest: Bogged down in details.

2. Failure to accept responsibility: Looking for a crutch—a written policy or a higher boss.

3. The inability to lead: People must want to follow.

4. The inability to make room for other people: Insecurity.

5. Unwillingness to communicate: Afraid to share and build.

6. Resistance to authority: Dislikes discipline.

7. Prejudices which interfere with judgment: Closed mind with cherished notions and fixed ideas.

Desirable personal traits:

1. A desire for achievement: The pleasure of accomplishment.

2. An acceptance of authority: Be big but don't act big.

3. A strong driving force: Self-motivation.

4. Organizational ability: Order out of chaos.

5. Decisiveness: Decision-making ability.

6. Firmness of conviction: Believe in something and live it.

7. Activity and aggression: Mentally and emotionally alert and alive.

8. A balanced way of life: Outside interests and relaxations.

SUPERMANAGER—
TOMORROW'S CHIEF EXECUTIVE

The thoughts expressed here are drawn from research of current business literature and observations of the changing patterns of management in the economic environment, and are taken from *Men & Management*, published by Edward N. Hay & Associates, Philadelphia, Pennsylvania, management consultants.

The management pattern of almost every organization has been shaped more by the personality and intelligence of its top managers than by any other factor. The economic climate, the business environment, our culture, our scientific technology, and many other factors influence the "pattern," but successful managers ride atop these factors, harnessing them and using them to the advantage of their companies. These other factors are constantly changing, but our successful manager is flexible; he readily anticipates and adjusts to change.

The successful manager has been compared to a champion bronc-buster. They both are professionals; both are expert in quickly sizing up new situations, making a plan of action, and doing their utmost to stick to it. A semiwild horse is unpredictable and the bronc-buster must be prepared to adjust his seat with the horse's every move. It is unlikely that any move is new to the experienced rider; his problem is determining what moves the horse will make, in what sequence and timing and with what strength he'll make them. If he guesses wrong, he hits the dust—and someone else is champion.

The rider's chances of success depend on a number of things, but primarily:

His experience—how many similar horses has he previously ridden?

His communications—how much he was able to learn about that particular horse from others or from watching him in action?

His thinking experience—how fast can he synthesize what he has learned from his experience and communications with his intuition into an effective reaction?

His motivation—how strong is his need to master that horse?

This analogy is an interesting one if we are thinking of the successful manager of yesteryear. The bronc-rider rides "by the seat of his pants," a way many managers managed years ago. A few still do, but they are almost an anachronism today. The analogy fails because today's manager isn't riding a horse; he's flying a jet and tomorrow he'll be flying a rocket. Neither a jet nor a rocket can be flown by the seat of the pants.

At the outset, we stated that the successful manager is flexible and able to harness the changing forces of his environment to serve his own ends. The manager of tomorrow will need some of the characteristics of a superman if he is to harness his environment. Some managers already are becoming obsolete because today's swiftly changing environment requires a different mental outlook, different aptitudes and interests, and indeed a different management intelligence than they are used to.

Decisions on Too Much Data

This is an era dominated by communications methods so rapid and so enveloping that the problem has changed from making decisions based on insufficient data to making decisions on too much data. Today's manager must sift through masses of information to pick out only the most meaningful. He must do it quickly because while he is making a decision an endless stream of new data is flowing to his desk. He cannot wait for the final chapter because there is no end. This constant flow builds up tensions caused by impending crises, some of which never do quite happen because the next influx of information might resolve one crisis and cause another.

It is most valuable to have complete information and quick communications, but it does take a specially-gifted manager to evaluate the data, to recognize and classify what is important and to discard the extraneous. This information assimilation builds tremendous tensions that must be overcome so that the proper decisions can be made at the proper time.

The manager of tomorrow will not be a specialist in data analysis, but he will be familiar with the techniques of analysis, programming, and communications. He will have expert statisticians and mathematicians on his staff who will analyze data for him, but he will also have economists, psychologists, sociologists—possibly even anthropologists—reporting to him, each of whom will sift through separate information sources and data and submit reports to him. Tomorrow's manager will be intelligently educated in each of these fields so that he can recognize and select, from all the data handed him, what is most pertinent to a problem at hand.

Not only must he be something of a physical scientist and a social scientist, he will have to be a political scientist and an international diplomat.

As automation increases our productive capacities, the top manager must become even more marketing-oriented than he is today—and this orientation must be global. Those who have had dealings with our own government are aware of the differences in attitudes and objectives that you run into in the various agencies and departments. The manager of the future will be dealing with possibly over a hundred governments, over a hundred national bureaucracies, over a hundred different national aspirations. He will not only need a superb grasp of what makes each of these governments operate, he will have to understand the aspirations and needs of the populations wherever he wants to do business.

He'll Follow the Market

Wherever there is a market potential, present or future, that is where the top manager will be going. He will maintain "ambassadors" of his own in each of these markets, but he will have to be familiar enough with each local situation so that he can make judgments and decisions based on the reports he receives from these ambassadors.

The manager of the future will be more than a "Jack of all trades." He will have to be a "Jack of all sciences." If he has the time, he should be equally at home in conferences of economists, space engineers, and psychologists. His education and all his training will be directed to making him an all-around expert. It is doubtful that he will be any 30-year old genius. More likely, he will acquire his seasoning through exposure in his thirties and forties and will be in his fifties and sixties when he takes the helm in a large international operation. The fact that our life-span is increasing is the only reason that we may be optimistic about our chances of raising these "supermen."

As we are already moving into the era of the "super-manager," a look at the characteristics of those men who get to the top and stay there in today's changing world provides us with the best clues to what the manager of the future will be like.

A Thinking Risk-Taker

First is the drive for power. All successful managers have this drive, and it is a genuine, deep, and constructive drive. The image of the executive walking on the corpses of his competition has faded away. Instead, we have the individual who seeks power through his continuous growth and his ability to make adjustments to quick and radical changes. He wants power and in many cases he must emerge with it from status-quo company environments.

His second characteristic is foresight and anticipation of challenges. He is a thinking risk-taker. Self-confidence makes him eager to anticipate the future and to turn to the past only for facts and experience required for handling the problems of the future. Successful managers act in terms of probabilities and make assumptions that cannot be submitted to a quick test of validity before decisions have to be made. This is not managing by hunch; rather it is better and quicker evaluation of information and situations.

He uses professionals to anticipate the future problems in their special areas, but he is their leader; no one of them leads him. He uses them, and he evaluates them. This is no easy job in itself. These are professional technicians of high intellectual caliber, and they usually have different kinds of attitudes and interests than does the average middle management group. Directing this orchestra of prima donnas requires a very special kind of conductor. This kind of professional staff will be extended more and more as we move to the future.

The third characteristic of successful managers is good physical and mental health. This is best seen in the manager who realizes the specific potentialities of his personality and is not ashamed of being what he is. We have found that instead of avoiding tensions, managers who are basically healthy people look for them and in so doing enjoy rich and full lives. The successful manager has an absorbing aim in life which gives unity and coherence to his thinking and to his activities. He is a man with strong emotions who knows where he is going.

The global aspects of his thinking and his work require a strong physical structure that permits him to work without sickness. The manager of the future must be vigorous, strong, mentally alert; able to handle tremendous changes in climate, in people, and in his environment.

Good Emotional Adjustment

His self-confidence also permits him to accept friendly cooperation and friendly competition. He realizes the great importance of society and of well-structured organizations in permitting individuals to achieve more and to function more effectively despite their individual shortcomings.

Another important characteristic is his ability to integrate with spontaneity. He has the ability to grasp relationships of great complexity and to synthesize the numerous parts into an effective whole pattern. The emotional adjustment of successful managers is superior to the general population. Distrust of people is a handicap. Trusting people makes it easier to cooperate with them constructively.

Managers are brighter than the average population but, more important, they have an exceptional speed of mental productivity. The element of timing is important in decision-making. Not all decisions must be made in a rush but there are some that do, and the manager must be able to handle them.

No single set of traits describes all managers. The manager of the future will be as individual as people are, but within this individuality, each will have those psychological characteristics we've mentioned. We will still find different kinds of managers handling different kinds of companies because of the different environments and needs.

The much-publicized "Brain Drain" has drawn attention to exasperated "eggheads" emigrating in droves. They complain that they are undervalued, misunderstood, misused, and generally "messed about." They add that they are at the mercy of bureaucrats who know little—and care less—about their work or the facilities they need to do it. This piece examines the problem in the wider context of industry.

DON'T SCRAMBLE EGGHEADS

By Eric Webster

Creative Director of Pemberton's, London, England

(Mr. Webster is author of *How to Win the Business Battle*, copyright by Putnam's & Coward-McCann, from which book the following is reprinted with permission.)

The difference between creative and executive functions is the difference between sit-down-and-think and get-up-and-go. This pinpoints a growing industrial problem.

Ideas are the octane of progress. As the pace quickens, consumption of ideas in all occupations—particularly in manufacturing, marketing, and selling—increases in geometrical progression. As a result, there is more specialization. Some people become identified as "creative," or "eggheads," or "backroom boys." Others are recognized as "executives," "administrators," or "managers."

As a rule, the administrators—at some point in the organization chart—become responsible for the "eggheads." This is usually where the trouble starts.

Mutual Misunderstanding

All too frequently the executives develop a distrust of the creative section which is exemplified by the very words "eggheads" and "backroom boys" in which they come to describe them. It is implied that to have a mind and to use it for thinking is both weird and in some way reprehensible. Thinkers must be "licensed to think" rather as agent 007 is licensed to kill. They must carry out this dangerous act of imagining in suitable seclusion while restrained and controlled by "normal"—this is noncreative—people.

In its turn the "creative" section of the organization often comes to regard the executives as a bunch of philistines in hob-nailed boots with armour-plated egos who substitute conditioned reflexes for thought and create an unending flow of problems for their more gifted brethren to solve.

How is such an impassé to be resolved—particularly when both viewpoints are so clearly wrong? Your company needs good ideas, new products, new processes, new ways of cutting costs and new marketing methods. It must keep ahead of competitors. Yet how much must you sacrifice in cost, dislocation, and executive frustration to gain an adequate supply of usable ideas? How do you measure their results? What sort of treatment produces maximum output? The entire future of your business may depend on your getting the right answers.

The first step is to understand the problem. We all combine in our makeup varying proportions of "thinker" and "doer," so we are all equipped in some measure to see both points of view. Let us now proceed as if the pure "creative" and "executive" types really existed and examine their characteristics. The province of one is thought and of the other action. This means they live in different worlds, with different feelings, different reactions, different sensitivities.

Executives Tend to Be Extroverts

The executive sets out to be always decisive and sometimes right. He can't hope to be infallible. He's there to play the game and win, so he has no time to question the rules or to have doubts. In order to act, he must behave as if things were certain. Soon they *become* certain in his own mind. His world therefore is solid, substantial, largely unquestioned. His ability to act is based on the premise "things will go on happening in the same way." He is therefore a fairly *secure* person.

The creative man, on the other hand, can only do his thinking in terms of "things will be different." His world is uncertain and imprecise, because he believes it is constantly changing and *can be changed*. He must question everything. He thinks in terms of probabilities rather than certainties. Where executives stand firm on solid ground, he balances precariously on a whirling flux of minute and indeterminate particles. He is almost bound to be a pretty *insecure* person.

The executive tends to be aggressive and extroverted. He knows what an immense amount of drive must be supplied to keep the organization moving. His world is of people rather than problems. People are instruments for achieving his objectives. He admires them, if at all, for their utility. His term of greatest contempt is "so-and-so is useless."

The creative man is usually shy and introverted. To get his work done he must withdraw from the world for lengthy periods and live in his own head. Personality clashes of any kind interfere dreadfully with the process, leaving his nervous structure vibrating like a well-struck tuning fork. Consequently, he may either go to extreme lengths to avoid disagreements, or alternatively, he may enter into them with what the executive feels to be excessive warmth. In this latter case, his indignation is usually due more to the effect the fuss will have on his capacity for tranquil thought than to the actual subject of disagreement.

Executive Is Pragmatic

The executive lives in the present. He is alert, vigorous in debate, sure of his facts—even when they are wrong—utterly pragmatic. The creative man lives much more in the future. He is apt to disappear into a trance at the slightest opportunity. At meetings, therefore, he may appear vague, inconclusive, incompetent and irrelevant. Actually he was thinking of something else at the time, but who was to know?

The executive can occasionally allow himself the luxury of feeling satisfied with a job. The creative person is always bound to feel it could have been done better—otherwise his motive power for further effort would disappear. Hence his relief (and often surprise) when his work is praised.

The executive spends much of his time actively giving orders and seeing that they are carried out. In contrast, the creative man spends long periods giving order to his thoughts. He moves at the speed not of light but of enlightenment, and this can be pretty irritating to the man who is impatiently awaiting the result of this elephantine gestation in order to get something done.

The executive is nothing if not a practical man. The creative man often seems anything but practical. After all, his best ideas are those which disagree with what is currently supposed to be the practical method of procedure.

Take an example from more primitive times; the executive, who was then the courageous hunter, would organize a mass attack on a sabre-toothed tiger. He got action. He might get half the tribe killed, but he got the other half fed and that was life. He wasn't the sort of chap to speculate whether the tiger could be persuaded to come to a prearranged rendezvous and conveniently kill itself. This, he would argue, just didn't make sense in terms of tiger-like behavior. Yet ultimately some craven fellow who preferred to think and stay alive succeeded in digging a pit, putting sharp stakes in the bottom, and camouflaging and baiting the top. And lo, thereafter the wild beasts came and committed suicide for man's benefit!

Would the practical primitive, setting out on a storm-bound journey, have wasted any time wishing his cave could come with him, let alone that it could transport him? No, he wouldn't. "Caves are immovable," says the practical mind. Yet what else but a traveling cave is a caravan, car, jet plane, or railroad compartment?

Action Is More Noticeable Than Thought

This brings us to another point. Biologically speaking, action came first and contemplation later. The world of the executive still approximates in some ways to life in the jungle. It's a rough, tough, challenging existence. Its characteristics are risk-taking, quick decisions, competition, a certain amount of controlled ferocity and a great deal of overt activity. In contrast, the whole essence of the creative man's world is that there should be reasonable security and time to think. Competitive spirit does exist in creative people, but its edge tends to be dulled by the need to cooperate. They are less aggressive and, since at times of their greatest effort they tend to be physically inert, they may easily come to be looked upon as a "lazy lot."

We have now examined enough points of difference to come to the conclusion that creative and executive types don't mix very readily. We can sum up: Where the executive is certain, the creative man is doubtful; where he is active, his thoughtful colleague seems passive; where he is sociable, self-assured, aggressive, extroverted, the creative man tends to be shy, diffident, pacific and introverted.

Recently some experiments were done on the effects of stress on job performance. It was found that whereas increased stress, up to a point, encouraged people to do routine, repetitive activities better, this effect was far more limited on those doing more complex tasks. *Creative work is the most complex of all tasks—and sufficient stress is already built into the job.*

We are now at the crux. *The basic mistake made by most managements in handling their creative people is to use the same methods that proved effective in dealing with their executive staff.*

It may work quite well (although even here there are limits) to haul an executive in, give him a brisk dressing down, point out his defects, and solemnly warn him that he must do better in the future. In this case you are giving a fairly secure individual a mild taste of fear. He may benefit. Do the same thing to a creative person and you give an insecure individual a wild taste of panic. He may not be able to think of anything else for weeks!

The best stimulants for creative people are enthusiasm and excitement. These are achieved by giving encouragement and praise.

How to Keep Creative Workers Working

The best working circumstances are those which combine reasonable job security and freedom from emotional disturbances with the most varied supply of problems and the maximum exemption from administrative chores. If a creative man has to combine administrative and creative functions, the administrative work will always seem the more urgent. He is not likely to do it well and he will seldom find time to be creative.

There is another reason for this. Creative work requires immense effort. Each new act is a perilous step into the unknown. Any noncreative operation will serve as displacement activity to put off the testing time a little longer. Beware of providing such ready-made excuses. The only exceptions to this rule are people with an exactly equal endowment of creative and executive skills, and even here the creative side always suffers.

You will also be wise not to isolate your creative staff. Don't keep them like battery birds laying golden eggs. Pretty soon in such circumstances both eggs and eggheads become addled. It may seem like sacrilege to the cost-conscious executive to keep expensive people in a state of anything less than frenzied activity, but with creative staff it pays, provided you don't go to extremes. There is a rhythm in creative work—a rhythm of effort followed by relaxation in preparation for fresh effort. If the tempo is speeded up too much for too long, the only result is a drop in creative efficiency.

On the other hand, it is a mistake not to expect your creative people to submit to normal office hours and discipline. Being too soft is nearly as bad as being too rough. To a large extent it is a fallacy that creative people get used up. They usually get messed up by unskilled handling. Don't encourage turnover in creative staff in the hope of "getting fresh ideas." This only works if the wrong people were picked in the first place and there is now some reason to hope that the selection procedure has improved.

Give Them Opportunity

The rules for getting the best out of your creative staff are very simple. Give them a chance to replenish their mental capacity from time to time. Give them the opportunity to mix with their own kind. *Give them the constant stimulus of knowing that management is keenly interested in their work and has a warm personal appreciation of them.* And, particularly, work hard to see that mutual understanding and respect develop between them and the executives they serve. *This seldom happens without a lot of managerial effort.* Achieve all this and you will have less and less need to worry about whether they are working efficiently or producing the right results. You will know that they are.

When the administrator of your creative people comes to speak of his charges in terms of pride and understanding, an important battle will have been won. The executive and creative viewpoints are both right—in their own contexts. They are both necessary to the well-being of the company. Without the one there would be little motive power and without the other not much sense of direction. If therefore you wish to create something more useful than disturbance, it is desirable that each group should recognize the other's points of difference so that both become reconciled to working in harmony.

LEADERSHIP

By Herman C. Krannert
Chairman of the Board, Inland Container Corporation

Indianapolis, Indiana

A basic change has taken place in the raw materials for leadership. The men I worked with when I managed a corrugated box plant in Anderson, Indiana, and the men I brought with me to Indianapolis when I started in business for myself 40 years ago, were dedicated loyal employees. They fully expected to serve many years of apprenticeship before they became managers.

Seven of my associates, who later rose to high positions in Inland, had no college education. They educated themselves by paying diligent attention to the lessons that the business taught them and by studying at home after working hours.

I must say that it is mostly men trained in this "school of hard knocks" who have built the paperboard and paper box business to a $2½ billion industry today, one employing about 66,000 people. The packaging industry is a service industry, still growing at the rate of 6 percent a year and providing new opportunities for new designers and managers.

But, in contrast to my day, many young men in industry come from very permissive family backgrounds. Their mothers will have driven them to school, picked them up on every rainy day. They will have served on hundreds of school committees and student governments. Somehow the whole family and school apparatus will have led them to believe that if they are effective, success will come to them quickly. They will expect, when they come into business, to be treated like partners. In fact, some of them even go so far as to tell me that they expect to become president of my company in the near future.

Nothing could better show the complete shift in attitudes from one generation to the next than to have a young man come in and tell me he expects to replace me in a very few years. None of the young men I hired in the early years of my business talked to me that way. They expected to be helpful to me for years and then, if they were lucky, they hoped to be picked for positions of responsibility. From my vantage point, it looks as though the world has been turned upside down.

Loyalty to Profession

Let me deal with another change that has come about—and this is in loyalty. The men I hired expected to stay at Inland Container for their lifetimes. They accepted my orders and knew they would be rewarded. But this is no longer true. Today's young men are primarily loyal to their own aspirations. They will stay with you so long as they feel they have opportunities for development and advancement; and if they don't, they will leave. They are mobile and they don't mind moving from one company or one part of the country to another. Sometimes I think they are a little arrogant. But possibly they are just different.

And this is not all: Business nowadays uses many specialists—accountants, engineers, chemists, economists and so on. Every one of these professional groups has its own society. And these specialists tend to be more loyal to their professions than they are to their companies. When things don't go in the company as they think they should, they use their professional contacts to change employers. In the old days we did a very good job of running a business without these professional groups. Now, as things stand, every business must depend on these specialists.

And so I must conclude that your world is going to be quite different from the one I grew up in and that you must practice a new style of leadership to succeed.

But before I leave this, I want to defend some of the old leaders. When you stop to think of it, they did some really great things. They took over an undeveloped country and created whole new industries, which have in turn brought a standard of living unmatched anywhere else in the world. And I must say, the leaders I knew expressed themselves vigorously in the way they ran their businesses.

I think, for instance, of George W. Swift, Jr., of Bordentown, New Jersey. He had a machine shop and a group of engineers who spent their time developing new machines for the manufacture of paper products.

The first corrugator consisted mainly of two notched drums. Paper was run between these drums, and flutes were formed in the paper. The machine was such a secret that it was enclosed under lock and key in a room with a slot cut in the wall. A man with a hand saw was stationed on the outside to cut off the corrugated paper as it came through the slot at the rate of no more than 10 feet a minute.

As demand increased, George Swift developed a heavy knife that traveled on the machine and cut off the paper automatically. However, as we increased the speed of the machine—and we simply had to increase productivity—the frame of the knife tended to break. At one of my meetings with George Swift, we discussed the feasibility of a rotating cut-off. He took the risk of developing a model. The company I was managing took the risk of placing an order for the first such machine. The rotary cut-off enabled us to increase speed to 100 feet a minute (today, corrugators are running at 650 feet per minute).

Dreamers, Risk-Takers

There are many characteristics of these great innovators which I hope you will have. They were all willing to dream big dreams. They were all willing to take risks. If they believed they could get a new market by introducing a whole new technology, they did it. Every organization constantly faces threats to its very existence and somebody has to deal with these threats. And these risk-takers— whether they were Andrew Carnegie, Henry Ford, or Henry Kaiser —never flinched when it came to doing new things.

In contrast, the specialist never really wants to deal with the big problem. He is content to work out a cost-accounting system, a new scheduling program, or a new manning table. He always wants to work within an established framework which he hopes will never be modified. Unfortunately, as I see it, the same is true for many of our professionally trained managers, who restrict the scope of their interests rather than risk failure. They don't actually want to be concerned with the major problems the company is facing.

It may be, and here I have to speculate, that these men have been over-educated. They want too much evidence before they make a decision. And usually by the time they get all the facts their competitors have captured the market. I don't know why, in this area of strategic decision-making, modern society produces so many "Nervous Nellies." In any case, in my generation of businessmen we seldom flinched if we had to make a risky decision. We rather gloried in it. And as a result, the people around us had few doubts and were willing to move with authority to deal with a new threat.

I think that this capacity to accept the world as nonguaranteed, tricky, full of accidents and unexpected events, is necessary at all levels of management. You will never have all the facts you need. Leadership means risk-taking; and this is particularly true of a world which is changing as rapidly as ours. This great quality which my peers had of being willing to move in the face of uncertainty is something you are going to need in generous amounts if you are going to succeed.

But here is where the parallel ends. The new style of industrial leadership is going to be very different from the style of the past Let me develop this by an analogy: Let's think of the master managers of the past as painting great murals, their employees standing by, mixing the paints, handing them the right brushes, admiring the painter's work and making sure they were well supported.

But now the situation is reversed. The murals of the future will be painted by hundreds of eager young men, each painting his portion as best he can. The new leadership is going to be largely concerned with making sure that each of these young men has the materials, the brushes, the paints and the palettes necessary to do a good job. The efforts of the many will somehow blend together to replace the picture the old master painted by himself.

This is going to be a much more difficult job than we faced. You are going to need great patience to work with these aspiring young artists. Human beings are difficult. They are both wonderful and terrible, courageous and frightened, timid and brash, factual and deceitful, cooperative and destructive, innovative and bureaucratic. You are going to need a genuine understanding of the way your organization works. You must know how communication moves up the organizational ladder, as well as down.

In the future, the company must represent the creative inputs of many prospective leaders. And so I have come to the conclusion that the leader of the future will have to be a very complicated person.

On the one hand, he must be bold—willing to face the world in all its complexities. He must see big designs and have all of the great qualities of business daring. But, on the other hand he must be willing to sense the needs of the aspiring young men coming up in his organization and be primarily concerned with providing a framework in which they can express their own individuality. He must invite their genuine participation in the setting of the company goals, even though his job is always to challenge and to raise their sights. He must be deeply concerned with establishing a reward system which will encourage the "wild duck" and not the slick conformist.

This new type of leader must have what amounts to a split personality. Bold, and yet, in dealings with people, a person of great humility. Courageous, and yet able to listen to the tedious babblings of those who are fearful. Articulate, but able to remain silent while other people awkwardly express their views. This is a tremendous assignment.

Faults of Specialists

When I talk to people in universities I get the feeling that they think trained specialists can replace leadership. Underlying this view is the faith that knowledge by itself will solve all problems. I can understand why college professors, who are devoted to the search for knowledge, would believe this. And I can understand also why public-opinion makers, who are for the most part rebelling against the facts of organizational life, would like to instill this belief. Neither group really knows what it is talking about.

The specialists are just as near-sighted as the loyal servants of the past. They are unwilling to deal with the big problems and they are as human in their failings as any other group the world has ever known. They gossip. They destroy communication channels. They denigrate each other. The whole organization, without active positive leadership, will deteriorate rapidly. If anything, leadership is more necessary in these days of specialists than it was in the past.

There is another prevailing view which I would like to deal with briefly—and that is that brilliance can take the place of leadership—that the man with the so-called great thoughts can supply the specialists with all the stuff they need to build the enterprise. This is

---

WILBERT E. SCHEER

presents his

personal formula for success, which he has recommended to thousands of employed workers, applicants seeking work, and students preparing for work. It applies to any person, on any job, any time, anywhere. It will keep the person from being fired, get him a raise, bring him the satisfaction of being appreciated. It can be stated in two words:

PERFORM

BEHAVE

This is the only advice he can offer workers which carries with it a built-in guarantee for individual success. It simply can not fail.

---

wrong. We need bright people in industry, as in every other walk of life. But being bright is not enough. The person who aspires to leadership must be both imaginative and *patient*. He must deal with human beings. *They* are his raw material.

Not only will tomorrow's leader have to contend with misconceptions, but he must face some special pitfalls which my generation did not encounter. As I said before, you are going to have to gain acceptance for a new idea before your subordinates will move ahead with authority toward a new goal. And there is always a danger you will mistake consensus for truth. I always knew in the 40 years I was building Inland Container that for the most part my colleagues would agree with me. They came out of a generation which tended to agree with the boss; and I always earned their support by taking the full responsibility for the success of the enterprise. But I never made the mistake of believing that just because they supported me I was right. I had to adopt a self-questioning attitude and thus be my own best critic. The cushioning attitude of consensus should in no way make one less exacting of himself.

Another pitfall is that it is better not to make a decision than to make a mistake. This is stultifying. If I hadn't made enough decisions to be wrong some of the time, Inland wouldn't be where it is today. It is best to be right about the big decisions, of course, but it is downright disastrous to let fear of being wrong keep you from ever sticking your neck out.

Still another pitfall is the idea that the leader has to know everything that is done in the organization. The leader doesn't have to know everything his subordinates know, but he should know enough about each specialty that he can test the validity of their knowledge.

As one of tomorrow's leaders, you must know the limitations of your specialists and try not to overuse them. And at the same time you must respect them and never downgrade them. This is a very difficult role to play. This is an easy place to fail; it is truly a pitfall. You must learn to delegate, but you must remember that you never delegate responsibility.

HUMAN FACTORS IN MANAGEMENT

By Colonel John Slezak
Chairman of the Board, Kable Printing Company

Leadership has been defined as the art of being able to get people to express more ability in action than they are aware of having in reserve.

The human being, wherever and whoever he may be, is capable of far greater creative accomplishments than he has had an opportunity to show. Nobody yet has invented a machine to match the miraculous quality of the human mind. Nobody ever will.

Sincere competent management has for its purpose the release of this pent-up productivity and usefulness so that human resources all over the world may adequately and fully be employed toward ever-increasing standard of living. Management practices, when based on sound moral ethical and spiritual principles as well as on professional and scientific knowledge, are the most powerful and creative of social as well as economic forces with which to maintain and advance mankind's interests.

Even from strictly material point of view, in the total cost of the national product and services, the cost of labor amounts to approximately 75 to 80 percent. Where else can you work in a field that has as promising a potential as this!

I am looking forward to the day when corporation balance sheets will include its human as well as its material resources. Some of them do it now, but in a very feeble fashion.

Naturally, my approach to the problems of management is to a degree colored by my personal experiences. On many occasions I have been used as a doctor to "treat" sick corporations. In every case the cure was accomplished not so much by finding more abundant material resources, but by more effective use of the available *human* resources. It is largely developing the quality that enables the management leader to get ordinary people to do the work of superior people.

If I were to select only one basic formula for more effective utilization of human capabilities, I would suggest that you ask them as *individuals* to help you to solve your problems.

You may set it down as a law of human psychology that, in general, human beings taken in groups are incapable of action that is the result of reasoning. When you want men to pursue a desired and well-defined course of action, you should take the time and trouble to convince the individuals one by one instead of addressing them en masse. The individual approach is effective because it essentially tends to satisfy the main psychological needs of the employee.

You recognize him as an individual, you give him a sense of belonging; he is part of the team, not an outsider. You give him a real chance to be heard; to express himself, and you give him a chance to be proud of his work.

Five Basic Principles

I would like to mention here a few principles that I have found workable and effectively useful in my work.

First: Since no two human beings are alike in their capabilities, or in their responses to motivation, the solution to each case should be individually tailored to fit the case.

Second: In the use of men, always create conditions so that the success of the man is inevitably tied up with the success of the job.

Third: Create an organization structure that will make it possible for all of your employees to help solve your problems.

Fourth: Give the individual the broadest possible scope for exercising his ingenuity in accomplishing the predetermined objectives. And reward him promptly for the results accomplished.

Fifth: Make sure that there are free, open, and easy lines of communication from the management to employees and from employees to management.

I am sure most executives realize the fact that as soon as you start supervising other people's efforts, an iron curtain starts to be built around you. The higher you go, the tighter that curtain is. And there is nothing I fear more than acting and making decisions on incomplete facts. Because you see I always get the good news, but not always the bad news. We are all human beings—we prefer good news. A bearer of bad news is not always welcome. And some people, by their attitude toward bad news, almost exclude it. The trouble with most of us is that we would rather be ruined by praise than saved with criticism.

But let us go back to fundamentals. I believe that if every job, every task, is so set up that the individual performing it can not only use his full native capability, but also has a chance to participate in improving it, that will be a sound beginning toward more effective utilization of our tragically wasted human resources.

We cannot standardize human beings and still have them act as human beings. No two of them are alike and, for that reason, standardization, like slavery, tends to kill the very thing that makes human beings human—personal initiative, desire to create, desire to produce, desire to excel.

For that reason, it seems that the recognition of the individual for what he is and creation around him of an atmosphere of great freedom of *individual* opportunity is a foundation for making us not only the most productive but, I also believe, the happiest people in the world.

This problem has been with us ever since one man decided to direct the efforts of another man. Those of you familiar with your Bible will recall that Moses, when leading the Jews out of Egypt, made a tremendous mess of this project until he began to listen to his father-in-law who showed him how to make use of competent individuals (Exodus: Chapter 18). We have learned very little that is new since then. We are just rediscovering more old truths, but we do need more wisdom so that we may apply these obvious and eternal truths more effectively in our everyday living.

In about 600 B.C. the famous Chinese philosopher, Lao-Tse, had this to say about leadership, and it is as true today as it was 2,600 years ago:

A leader is best when people barely know that he exists.

Not so good when people obey and acclaim him.

But of a good leader who talks little, when his work is done,

His aim is fulfilled, they will say, "We did this ourselves."

Or, putting it still another way:

A good *leader inspires men to have confidence in him,*

but

A great *leader inspires them to have confidence in themselves.*

MOTIVATION

Companies no longer have any natural advantage over each other. What then distinguishes one firm from another? The company which enjoys a more profitable position in today's competitive economy is the one which makes the best utilization of its resources.

There are six elements of an enterprise. These are the six M's—

- Material
- Machines
- Methods
- Money
- Markets
- Manpower

Since other elements in business are relatively fixed, the opportunity for improvement lies in the only variable element, the available manpower. All companies have access to the same material, machines, methods, money, and markets. They even have access to the same manpower. It is the utilization of the only variable element, the workforce, that determines whether one firm operates better or poorer than another.

The most promising source of increased productivity is not in machine development or methods improvement; it is locked up in the human will to work. This is also the most neglected area of management since most of the emphasis has traditionally been on the material side of business.

A veritable gold mine awaits managements who succeed in moving workers to greater productive activity and greater efficiency. We know that people do not work at 100 percent efficiency. Nor are they expected to. Andrew Carnegie said that the average person puts only 25 percent of his energy and ability into his work. Psychologists have estimates that run all the way from 17 percent to 50 percent. You may make your own guess. But the fact remains that people do not work up to 100 percent capacity except in a few isolated instances. One such example might be the Czechs who worked around the clock and reached for unknown strength to thwart the Communist despots who threatened their homeland. Another illustration is that of the drowning man who managed to save himself despite the fact that he did not know how to swim. In the ordinary conduct of business, however, we do not get or expect such dedication. Whatever the percentage, one economist estimated that just a 1 percent improvement factor in the United States workforce would result in enough additional manhours of work to run United States Steel, General Electric, and International Harvester for one year.

Explore This Frontier

This then is the frontier that managers are encouraged to explore. The fundamentals and procedures that are used, the necessary scientific techniques that have been developed, and their human application, comprise what is generally termed "motivation."

Motivation efforts must be directed toward improving company operations. To be effective, however, they must also be designed to show benefits to the employee. In fact, motivation can best be accomplished when workers are able to merge their personal ambitions with those of the company.

In initial employment, for example, finding the right person for any job is only half of the task. The applicant must feel that he, too, has found a job opportunity which meets, or exceeds, his expectations. Only when there is a happy job marriage, in which both sides are satisfied, does the placement stand a chance of being successful. In such cases the company will provide the worker with the job satisfaction he needs to be happy; and he, in turn, will have that built-in motivation companies look for in order to make his employment profitable.

Motivation Through Individuality

To utilize the human element in business effectively, it is well to devote adequate attention to the fundamentals of motivation. Unlike machines and other material matters, people have personalities, can think, have beliefs, and exercise some control over their work both in how well it is done and how much is done. Leadership, communications, and good attitude play very important roles. Creating conditions that provide interest, job satisfaction, and personal reward are vital.

Managements do well to emphasize this aspect of the line manager's responsibility. The four functions of a manager or supervisor are

- Planning
- Motivating
- Organizing
- Controlling

Plans and organized efforts are of no value until they are put into action. It is necessary to actuate these efforts by motivating members of the workforce to start and continue to work along the lines determined best by managers.

Since management is accomplishing a predetermined objective through the efforts of other people, it is evident that motivation is extremely important. Stated simply, without manpower the machines would be idle, material would remain unused, and so on. Conversely, a well-staffed, carefully-selected, and well-motivated workforce enhances the value of the machines, methods, and other elements of business.

The degree of success in motivating employees is in direct relation to the manager's ability to help employees realize personal ambitions and aspirations. The basic wants of workers are economic, psychological, and social.

Man does not live by bread alone. While money is necessary, it is not the only form of wealth, nor in the final analysis the most important. In addition to material wealth, employees need to increase their cultural wealth, social wealth, and spiritual wealth.

In trying to understand employees it is well to learn about individual and group behavior. Individuals often react differently when in groups. But always, whether alone or in league with co-workers, employees are individuals. Attempts to motivate workers are more successful when related to individuals and not groups.

It takes some doing on our part to comprehend this. In business we've become so accustomed to using mass techniques—in manufacturing, advertising, marketing, bargaining agreements—that we also try to apply these methods to individuals.

This is what psychologists call the "fetish of symmetrical development." It is not recommended as a motivation technique for the simple reason that no two people are alike. Different people have different fears, different problems, different desires and hopes, and different ways of reacting to similar situations. They require different treatment.

A realistic approach leads to a recognition of individual strengths and weaknesses and then giving consideration accordingly. Only as people are different do they become noticed in a world of conformity. Only as we as managers and supervisors play up to the individuality, rather than the sameness, do we succeed in getting through to people with our message.

We must never forget that the people whom chance has brought our way, who spend a good portion of their waking hours in our trust, are not only trying to make a living . . . they are also trying to make a life!

What People Expect from Work

Sometimes it appears that the reasons people like to work are better known to workers than to managements. A poll to decide what motivates employees brought interesting results.

Bosses gave these reasons, in this order: Good wages, job security, promotion and growth in company, good working conditions, interesting work, boss' loyalty to workers, tactful disciplining, full appreciation of work done, help on personal problems, and feeling of being "in" on things.

Employees, on the other hand, listed much these same reasons, but in a different order of priority. They said: Full appreciation of work done, feeling of being "in" on things, help on personal problems, job security, good wages, interesting work, promotion and growth, loyalty from boss, good working conditions, and tactful disciplining.

It is significant to note that three factors considered least important by management seemed most important to employees. Maybe managements don't know as much about their employees' needs and wants as they imagine they do.

Workers require certain satisfactions from their jobs. Managements which identify these basic needs and attempt to satisfy them are on solid ground. Managements which are preoccupied with other matters will continue to muddle along, wondering, "what's the matter with people today?" The opportunity to minimize problems is there for all. The landscape is the same; the difference is in beholders.

The worker must see that his contribution flows into the common ocean of human effort. The telephone lineman is not merely tying together two strands of wire; he is linking patient to doctor, and so forth. Similarly, the manager or supervisor is more than a skilled technician; he is engaged in a form of human engineering.

The executive who thinks his people are working only for a paycheck is deluded. Only when he tries to understand that his workers are flesh-and-blood human beings with individuality expressed in the way they act and respond, is he on the right track and going in, the right direction—toward success for his workers, his company, and himself.

Basic Job Satisfactions People Need

To get workers to respond, company programs should understand what job satisfactions people require of their jobs. Each worker wants

1. Recognition as an individual, not as a number or robot.

2. A meaningful task: Its purpose and prestige understood by him.

3. An opportunity to do something worthwhile and recognition for his contribution.

4. Job security: For himself and his family.

5. Good wages: Fair in community and fairly administered.

6. Adequate benefits: Protection against the unexpected.

7. Opportunity to advance: Chance to earn a better living.

8. Information about what is going on, especially about what concerns him.

9. Freedom from arbitrary action: A voice in matters affecting him.

10. Satisfactory working conditions: Consideration of his safety, comfort, convenience, and health.

11. Congenial associates: The best part of day, week, and life is spent at work and it should be pleasant.

12. Competent leadership: Bosses whom he can admire and respect as persons, not as bosses.

Motivation in Training Programs

Motivation has always been a likely topic for training, particularly in supervisory development courses. Most of the training lies in the academic approach to motivation. This stresses basic human needs and tries to associate them to employee on-the-job behavior. Consequently the discussions are theoretical and not always useful. They look good on the agenda, and they often sound good to conference leaders and observers. But how much impact do they have on actual office or factory operations?

Too many are designed to provide the supervisor with a magic formula, or convenient push button, which when pressed into use will galvanize every subordinate into action and immediately increase his productivity. In real business life this just does not happen.

A more down-to-earth type of training would suggest less textbook problem solving and more practical discussions in the laboratory of day-to-day business activity. A supervisor brings in an actual problem and places it before the other members of the training group. This focuses attention and invites constructive thinking on a familiar, or easily understood, problem situation. Members of the group discuss the problem in terms of their own experience. In so doing they reveal how they would react to a similar situation and what possible approaches toward meeting it they would consider using.

The discussion is realistic, the problem understandable, and the conclusions meaningful. The practical value is apparent. They are on their way to becoming successful managers and supervisors once they realize that problems of this sort do not lend themselves to any pat back-of-the-book answers.

The History of Motivation

Learning the techniques is not as important as knowing the reasons people react as they do. Perhaps a quick resumé of the history of motivation will be helpful in understanding it.

Motivation in business and industry is identified with three distinct phases.

1. Years ago it was *Fear*. The danger of losing a job, or even worse, the threat of having it taken away, was all the motivation hard-fisted bosses had to use. This type of motivation has long ago been discarded simply because it is not in harmony with managements' new concept of dealing with people.

Any supervisor who still thinks he can motivate workers by threatening them had better "wise up" to the facts of life. Fear actually never was a good motivator. Examples: Fear of lung cancer has not decreased cigarette smoking; fear of imprisonment has not lowered the crime rate; fear of highway deaths has not diminished traffic accidents; fear of the hydrogen bomb has not lessened preparations for war.

2. If not fear, which was used in early days, what do we use for motivation now? Today it seems to be *Fringe Benefits*. "Look what we're doing for our people," we say. But we all know that increasing the company-paid group life insurance, for instance, from $1,000 to $2,000 has no noticeable effect on a worker's daily output. As

important as fringe benefits are, they are no longer effective as motivation forces; they are conditions of employment. Fringe benefits are productivity's contribution to social development.

3. Tomorrow it will be *Leadership*. The manager of tomorrow will be the kind of person others want to follow. He must set a good example. He must be competent, of course, but he must also be considerate, fair, and understanding. His success in motivating others will be dependent not upon what he says, or what he does, but what he believes.

Conclusion

The three basic wants of American citizens which find expression in management's employee relations are economic security, personal freedom, and a rising standard of living.

What then do we suggest companies do to motivate their workers to more and better production to help them reach personal goals and at the same time meet company objectives?

1. Establish the kind of climate wherein people will give of themselves without giving up themselves.

2. Give workers optimum communications, not maximum. Neglecting to keep workers informed is dangerous; in the absence of authoritative information the rumor mill will fill in. But over-communicating is even worse. This is like overclogging the channels with noise. One word of trust and respect will carry more impact than a thousand words of double-talk.

3. Don't imagine you can develop others. No one can develop anyone else except himself. The door to development is locked from the inside. We can keep knocking at the door but the other fellow must respond and open it for himself.

4. Try not to change behavior. This is a head-against-the-wall futility. Make the worker aware of his strong points and capitalize on them. Keep the weaknesses out of sight and under control.

5. Do not try to teach the worker how to behave or what to think. Teach him instead how to learn and think for himself.

INTERNAL vs. EXTERNAL

A manager's involvement with the human side of business leads me to a pet theory.

Most companies, in expanding and improving their personnel programs, dwell on the impersonal aspects of employee relations by building external benefits. In a welfare program, for instance, they concern themselves with putting together a good vacation policy, sick pay allowance, income protection, hospitalization, life insurance, and retirement, plus payment for holidays, jury duty, death, and marriage leave. They spend endless hours in planning and thousands of dollars in administering these items. And yet, what are they doing?

They're worrying about an employee when he is *away* from work.

Look at these items: Sick pay applies only when a worker is absent because of illness; hospitalization protects him when he is flat on his back; retirement income helps him when he is too old to be of value to his employer; and how useful is he to you when life insurance pays off? Firms establish liberal vacation policies for two weeks of the year—when the worker is *off* the job.

How about thinking more in terms of the worker when he is *on* the job?

While these external benefits are necessary increments of a good employee relations program, they only partially meet the needs of workers. The better programs recognize also the internal side of a person's job.

These internal considerations may be divided into four categories:

Physical: To make work comfortable and convenient.

Mental: Provide workers the chance to grow.

Psychological: Build up their prestige.

Spiritual: Help them put love in their hearts to push hate out.

It is gratifying to note that most offices and factories are making progress in improving the physical side of the workers' jobs. Adequate heat and light, air conditioning, and modern equipment and facilities are becoming more common every day.

As for the mental side of a job, it must be remembered that work which challenges the beginner only bores him after he has mastered it. A worker's growth must first be recognized and then rewarded, and a good practice is to promote from within in order to keep him interested.

Psychologically speaking, an employee must be made to feel that the work he is doing is worthwhile and useful so that he can feel good about it. It is not enough to tell a worker how to do something; he must also be told why.

On the spiritual side of a job, we must accept the fact that by nature the heart becomes a museum of ugly traits. By putting a healthy and wholesome construction on our day-to-day dealings with people, by treating co-workers with respect, and by being fair and understanding in our interpersonal relationships, we can keep these natural personality weaknesses from rising to the surface, and do our work in an atmosphere of harmony, trust, and cooperation.

Motivating the employee to more and better productivity becomes easier when we consider the internal as well as the external aspects of his job needs.

EFFICIENCY

Any attempt to help the supervisor increase his personal efficiency logically begins with a definition of efficiency. The dictionary defines efficiency as, "effective operation as measured by a comparison of production with cost in energy, time, money." Yet, a definition, by itself, is useless. It is much like a theory which is different on paper from what it is in practice. It is easy to state, but difficult to apply.

"Each duty should be given to the lowest-paid person qualified to do it. Anything else is a waste of company money."

This statement is a beautiful theory on efficiency. As a theory we defy anyone to challenge it. But it is only a theory. In the practical operation of our offices and plants we are satisfied to settle for less—much less than the perfection implied in this theory.

So it is with efficiency. The truth is that we cannot expect 100 percent efficiency. But we can and should expect to improve our efficiency and that of our people. Efficiency may be defined as the best utilization of whatever we have available to us. This includes our talents, money, methods, people, and so on.

When we look for improvement we think in terms of procedures and machines—and try to make them better. Work simplification and methods improvement are substantial contributions to more efficient operations. But even the application of electronic principles and the introduction of computer equipment, fantastic and revolutionary as these may turn out to be, pale into insignificance compared with the potential that is locked up in the human will to work.

It is generally accepted that people seldom, if ever, work at full capacity. Under ordinary circumstances workers coast along at a much lesser rate which employers have come to accept as satisfactory. Workers are not expected to perform regularly and consistently at capacity. But even a small improvement would produce phenomenal results.

Our present productivity rate, which is good enough to provide the highest standard of living on earth, still reflects a tragic extravagance in the utilization of our human resources. With skilled labor in short supply, a growing emphasis on cost cutting, and competition getting tougher, one must wonder how much longer we can afford the expensive luxury of squandering this greatest of all natural resources. While we can point with pride to the headway we make along technological lines, we cannot make similar claims for our accomplishments in the human area.

The True Nature of "Waste"

Some managers may try to dismiss this part of their responsibilities in the belief that a certain amount of inefficiency in business is not necessarily bad. They argue that our entire standard of living is built upon waste. They may even contend that there is a divine implication in this concept of waste.

In many respects nature is just as wasteful as man. If all the seeds that fall to the ground were to grow, within a year there would be no room for man. So, many persons conclude that if biological waste is acceptable, possibly even good, perhaps our economic waste may also have its useful purpose.

We must remind ourselves, however, that even biological waste is constantly being challenged. For example: We probably consider weeds as worthless. But Emerson described a weed as "a plant whose virtues have not yet been discovered." Each time a botanical specimen is moved from the weed category to that of a useful medicinal plant, we reduce the area of biological waste.

That's what we must do with the economic waste through better utilization of the human element in business. We must recognize that some waste is inevitable, possibly justified. But we must never become resigned to the acceptance of this waste. We must probe continuously for ways to minimize it.

No one can tell the supervisor how to do this. He alone knows his people and the conditions under which they perform. However, we can suggest that the best way to motivate workers to more and better production is through helping them derive greater personal satisfaction from the work they do.

In his efforts to install cost-cutting methods or laborsaving techniques, the supervisor should not overlook the impact these changes may have on people. Scientifically sound procedures will do more harm than good unless there is also understanding. For without understanding there cannot be acceptance, and without acceptance how can there be any benefit?

When we hire workers in our offices and plants we are not buying people. It may be true that what we are buying is a certain amount of their time. Actually, we are buying results. But since these results are realized through people, we must focus our attention on people and not on things.

A good supervisor believes in people. He genuinely likes people, and by his words, actions, and beliefs lets them know this. Finally, he likes his own job, he lives it, and gets excited about it. This enthusiasm rubs off on workers and stimulates them to a similar appreciation of their jobs. Can anyone suggest a more effective motivation device?

Whatever we do, as we strive to increase the productivity of our work force by improving ourselves and our people, we should not try for 100 percent efficiency. This is not possible nor perhaps desirable. Just a percentage of increase in efficiency is all that is needed to show progress. And in the final analysis, progress, not perfection, should be our goal.

Z IS FOR ZERO DEFECTS

By Philip B. Crosby

International Telephone and Telegraph Corporation

New York, N. Y.

(Reprinted with permission from *American Machinist*)

The idea is to prevent errors, not just detect them. It takes real cooperation all down the line, plus some real horse sense, but this program for perfection pays off.

Let us begin by citing three present-day Parables of Human Frailty and Foible:

- The garage attendant wiped his hand on a rag. "There you are, Mr. Thompkins, as good as new. Don't know how they could have gotten the blinker wires switched on your new car, but from now on when you signal for a right turn no one will think you're turning left. By the way, that's a nasty bump on your head, did you have it looked at?"

- A florist received a call from a worried young swain. Seems the corsage he had ordered for his girl hadn't arrived, and they were off to a dance in a few minutes. "Let's see," said the florist, "that order was delivered to 1324 East Sampson Street early this afternoon." "But she lives at 1324 *West* Sampson Street," the young man said. "Hmmm, must remember to speak to the delivery boy," said the florist.

- Seven hundred miles away, the sky burst into a wild display of burning fuel and exploding dynamite. A huge intercontinental ballistic missile had swerved off course and the range safety officer had pressed the destruct button. Millions of manhours sputtered into the sea. Three days later, the operations chief was told the disaster had been caused by failure to remove the caging pin in the autopilot. "Well," shrugged the chief, "guess nothing will ever be perfect as long as people are involved in it."

The common denominator in all three of these parables is human error—and contrary to most opinion it is *not* inevitable.

The tragedy of modern business is that it is plagued with just such mistakes every day. No great incidents in themselves, they can cause an operation to fail, a customer to be disappointed, or costly rework of an end product.

From the football field to the launching pad, these are the little unpredictables that result in big disasters—"tremendous trifles."

The cost of these errors is immeasurable, and the reason they cannot and have not been measured is that we are inclined to accept them as inevitable. Yet each and every mistake made in the world today has two things in common: It is performed by somebody, and it could have been prevented.

We are going to talk about preventing errors. *Preventing,* not detecting. Detecting costs a lot of money and only saves you future grief. It can't do a thing to solve the problems with which you've already been blessed.

And detecting is only as successful as the detector, the inspector, or the checker happens to be at that very moment.

Prevention means getting people and systems to do the job right the first time. There are several techniques involved, but the goal is the same: Do it once and do it right.

Positive Attitude Helps

In order to go wholeheartedly into the study of prevention, it is first necessary to examine the attitude of prevention. The positive attitude is the constant companion of success. What mountain climber ever inspired himself by chanting, "I can't do it. I can't do it"? Prevention is as much a state of mind as it is an understanding of management techniques.

People are carefully conditioned throughout their lives to accept the fact that they are human and humans make mistakes; "To err is human, to forgive, divine."

By the time they enter a business career, this thought is so firmly fixed in their minds that it no longer bothers them to make errors, within reason of course. Acting on the principle that one must not be perfect in order to be human they will permit themselves a defect level. "I am 95 percent accurate, which is about all you can expect."

The Philosophy of 95%

Thus they drill holes correctly 95 percent of the time, deliver packages correctly 95 percent of the time, design a circuit right 95 percent of the time, and so forth. They have established a defect level of 5 percent. The exact figure varies with people, but there is a limit in each one of us at which we begin to become upset over our errors. We do not become upset within our 5 percent level.

So, if this defect level is standard within us, it should become apparent that we will be shortchanged 5 percent of the time when we cash our pay checks. We should go home to the wrong house 5 percent of the time, by mistake. We should go through the back of the garage 5 percent of the time.

However, these things do not happen. It is possible that people have developed one standard for the things they do for themselves and one for their business tasks? Does a dual attitude exist? Yes.

We set a higher requirement on the tasks we perform for ourselves than on the ones we do at work. Why? Because the family will tolerate less error than the company.

Mistakes are caused by two things: lack of knowledge or lack of attention. You can measure lack of knowledge and fix it by tried and true means. But lack of attention is an attitude problem and must be repaired by the person himself. He must develop a constant conscious desire to perform the job right the first time. He does this when cashing his pay check, for he knows that there is one chance and one only to obtain the correct return. Once he steps away from the teller's window, he has had it. He is very conscious of what must occur.

The Dual Standard

So people have accepted a dual standard. In cases involving work, they are not bothered by a few errors, but in personal requirements the standard must be zero defects.

Zero Defects is the name given to a motivation and improvement program developed at Martin-Orlando that has achieved a great deal of success in the weapons industry. Some commercial firms have tried it and feel that it provides real gains for them, too.

The whole program is based on explaining to people that it is not necessary for them to prove their humanity by fulfilling their requirement for error. Rather, they can accept as a challenge the task of making a constant conscious effort to do the job right the first time. You will find that most of them have never been told that.

The usual improvement programs are based on the principle that "Quality is everybody's job. We must do better." No one will disagree, yet if it is everyone's job, then it is nobody's especially.

The challenge of Zero Defects is that it requires the individual to pledge himself to improve. He is given a pin or card in return to seal the bargain. There is one stipulation, however; the worker must sign up for the program as an individual, pledging himself to the cause, "Z-D means prevention, not detection."

There are three phases to Martin's Zero Defects program:

- Show workers why they should join the program.

- Review specifications and requirements to eliminate the unattainable or the overly strict.

- Develop errorproof processes and/or instructions so that anyone who wants to do a good job can do so.

The most dedicated, conscientious "Zero Defect minded" person in the world couldn't be expected to deliver a package from Peoria, Illinois, to Paris, France, in 20 minutes and return. That requirement is unattainable today.

Automobile gasoline tanks made out of paper are going to leak after a while, no matter how dedicated the workers that make them. Cutting a sheet of aluminum to a tolerance of 0.0001 inch with tin snips would tax the patience (and talents) of a saint.

Thus there has to be give and take on the part of management and the worker if perfection is to be attained. Management must not set ridiculous and unattainable goals for its workers, and it must eliminate those that already exist. In instances where the ridiculous and unattainable cannot be eliminated (such things do exist in the precision industries), something must be done to bring them within the range of human skills. You can, for example, order a man to lift 10,000 pounds. He can't do it by himself, but he can do it with the help of a crane.

Down from Cloud Nine

Thus a proper combination of management skill and employee willingness can pull just about any requirement down from Cloud Nine and into the realm of attainment. One by-product of this is drastic cost reduction.

The next step is to develop processes and instructions that will make any task defect proof. First off, it's a matter of attitude. You can't, for example, find a way to drill a perfect hole in just the right spot every time if you don't think it can be done.

Now, assuming that you *do* think it can be done, let's take a look at how a Zero Defects program can be accomplished.

A Z-D program can be carried out by a one-man shop, or it can be carried out in a shop that employs 35,000 people.

Thus Z-D begins with making employees aware of quality. Build them up slowly to make them more conscious of the need for better product quality. This can be done effectively with signs, pamphlets, and little personal talks about how important it is in this day and age to turn out a good product in the face of stiffening competition.

Anyone can make a fly swatter, but the successful fly swatter is the one that will stand up to its job time after time yet be inexpensive and attractive. (Come to think of it, who ever heard of an attractive fly swatter? But be that as it may, that's the principle of a successful product.)

If you take defect level measurements within your operation— that is, if you have an inspection function that examines work in process or at the end, and records defects—hang a defect level chart over each area so monitored. This chart should show the percent of units found to be defective as submitted to inspection. These charts show trends in performance, and people like to be measured.

Here is what you need to launch the program formally:

- A kickoff date for Zero Defects Day—this should be recognized as a big deal. Top management of the company should be available on that day (on the floor and in the office areas) to show by their presence that they take it seriously.

- Posters, pamphlets, and other giveaway material that describes the logic of the program should be ready.

- Pledge cards should be prepared. These should be in two parts. The first should be an IBM-sized card that carries the pledge, "I freely pledge myself to make a constant conscientious effort to do my job right the first time, recognizing that I am an important part of the company's effort to move toward the Zero Defects goal." (Once this card is signed, it should be taken with great formality to the vault and locked up.)

  The second card should be wallet-sized and should restate the pledge, plus some of the program logic. The employee keeps it.

- Zero Defect pins, simple but dignified, should be presented to the employee when he signs up.

  Try some special attention getters. If you have a cafeteria, have a Z-D luncheon bargain. Place tent cards around the building saying, "It means prevention, not detection."

Next, it must be emphasized that no disciplinary action will result from employees making an error. The idea is to help them get better, not become perfect over night. If the wrong impression is given, they start hiding mistakes.

And, *everybody* must participate. Don't make the mistake of concentrating on the assembly line or manual workers. They can do very little to improve the quality of the hardware. All they can do is *not* make it worse than the design and material. Put a lot of effort into the engineering and business side of the house. That is the fruitful area.

The motivation phase of the program must be followed up periodically—some rededication effort every four months helps.

It is fair to ask why such a program should be required. Or, rather, why don't people automatically do their jobs right? Why don't they want to?

Well, people do want to do a good job. They want to have the proper attitude. But they receive their attitude and standards from their supervisors, and the supervisors work on the things that they think the company wants. Thus every time management has a schedule-emphasis period, they may find quality or cost suffers.

It is not enough to depend upon the eyeballs and the skill of the detection personnel, they are at best 85 percent accurate in their trade. The only way to produce defect-free products or services is to not have the error occur in the first place. The only way to have that happen is to convince people that that is the company's standard.

Now let's examine the second phase of Z-D requirements:

The most difficult part about starting a realistic requirements program is getting people to understand that it doesn't mean just getting rid of tough jobs—only the unnecessary.

Let's suppose that you were making parts to 125 mu-in. rms finish—which is pretty good. But if you looked at the assembly you'd find that the part came in contact with nothing on that surface and you could go to 250. Thus the job is easier, cheaper, and just as useful. Well, you say, that's not very exciting. Smacks of common sense.

But each organization is filled with sincere people who are interested in protecting their judgments and prerogatives. They do not want to be found wrong. Thus they issue specifications, requirements, and regulations that contain a margin of safety.

When these people are indoctrinated in the Zero Defects concept, they can have the feeling of confidence that people will then respect the *real* requirement and they won't have to fudge it.

Now how do you go about formalizing this requirements-evaluation business?

Task Force and a Plan

First, a steering task team must be established. This team should represent four functions: manufacturing, quality, engineering, and finance. If the operation is small, all of these might be one man. But he must consider each viewpoint individually to make sure that he is not biasing the program.

Second, a plan of attack must be defined. The order of priority for investigation: (1) The most troublesome area, (2) which areas are the most expensive? (3) which things seem unreasonable or unnecessary?

Once the group investigates and gets into its first problem, the order of execution will have defined itself. The success of the task will be proportional to the enthusiasm of the participants.

It is a good idea to conduct classes for personnel, so that they can see the results of the first few efforts. The understanding they obtain, plus the opportunity to have another crack at the difficult areas, will more than pay for the time spent.

In the final analysis, you are not after the clarification of individual requirements here and there. The goal is to ingrain into every person in the operation the feeling that rules should always be followed, but if the rule is not compatible with common sense, it should be modified. The channel for modification needs to be short, and the judgments sincere. But once people find out that you will listen to them, the ideas will flow and blossom.

Directions and Instructions

The processes for conducting a business are one of any company's most significant possessions. Call them instructions, or directions, or recipes (there are all kinds of names) but essentially they are a detailed documentation of the way to do a job.

In electronics, the processes are quite complex; the chemical industry is very heavy with these directions. And what bleary-eyed father has not tried on Christmas Eve to "place bolt K in hole #4 making sure that Fin V is perpendicular to the red side of the main body?"

Most instructions are written with the thought that the people who are going to do the job already know how and thus need just reminders. When I purchased a swimming pool, I received much literature on the art of placing chemicals in the pool to assure safe swimming water. However, all of it talked about the refinements of the art—nowhere did the basics appear for someone who was not quite clear on what H_2O was. Sort of like reading an instruction booklet for airplane flying that begins "Once up in the air . . ."

Each step of the operation should be examined in detail, each tool or instrument used must stand the test of why it has been selected. And most important of all, the process must be written in language that the worker will understand, so the minimum amount of interpretation will be required.

Review of Difficulties

As the operation progresses, any difficulties encountered should be reviewed with the task team and specific correction obtained. In a brief period, repeatability will set in; then the cycle can start anew with an eye to improvement. If this repeat cycle is not encouraged and demanded, the new process will become as troublesome as the old within the course of time. Problem magnitude will be lower, but your organization will be much more sensitive to potential discrepancies and less easy to satisfy.

What does all of this concentration on attitude bring you? A new way of life—both professionally and personally. A desire to eliminate the error potential becomes part of your thoughts. It is not possible to sit down and say, "Now, for this 45-minute period, I am going to concentrate on preventing defects. Then I shall return to normal operations." The mind does not work like that unless the basic orientation has been accomplished.

Although I have been out of the Navy many years, the words "deck, ladder, bulkhead" still creep into my conversations. They were deeply ingrained there by an organization that was determined that all sailors would talk like sailors. It's the same with the thought of Zero Defects.

How does management set the tone of Z-D in daily operations in order to assure that this occurs? Let's take the example of "breadboard." As everyone knows, a breadboard (and each business has its own word for it) is a device where you build up a potential product strictly for feasibility, just to see if it'll work. The name comes from the practice in electronics of pinning parts to a big board and making a circuit out of them. It is a most useful technique.

However, it is much misused, to the detriment of the eventual product. Research and development has been confused with breadboarding. If management permits the engineering and research (or sales types) people to develop the basic product on strictly a functional basis, then the production of it will be up to its you-know-what in troubles.

It is essential that the processes, controls, documentation, etc., be developed in parallel with the new product. This is not a big effort. But, oh! How many units perform perfectly until they are taken from the laboratory and given to the production line to build. Every error, every misinterpretation, must be learned all over again. You can tell by looking at your rejection rate when your suppliers have made the switch from lab to production.

The manufacturing man is in the position of one who hears a knock on his door and opens it to find a black box nestled in a wicker basket. An accompanying note says, "make a thousand a month." He has had little or no input to the packaging of the unit, or to the material used. Companies that think this way are going to have an interesting problem.

The mind set must be carried into personal dealings with subordinates and associates. "I won't be able to give you that report Friday afternoon as I promised, but you'll get it first thing Monday morning." Now there's a familiar statement. If you accept it, then the Z-D mind is cracking. If you request that the man keep his promise and look like you mean it, you'll never hear the request again. People will do what you put up with.

Is the difference between Friday afternoon and Monday morning that important? Usually not. However, the difference between keeping promise dates and not is life and death to your business. Many companies with good quality and competitive costs have failed because they couldn't deliver on time—consistently.

The attitude of defect prevention—Zero Defects—is all that stands between mediocrity and a great performance.

PROJECT "TOTAL"

A major program to encourage and reward employee efforts to reduce costs, improve efficiency, and assure the quality and reliability of its aerospace products was launched by Textron's Bell Aerosystems Company of Buffalo, New York. The program saved the company about $4 million during its first year of operation. Substantially more is expected in each succeeding year.

Many giants of the aerospace and defense industry have heard about the success of this program and have written or sent representatives to study the reasons for TOTAL and its rapid success for the company and its 5,300 employees.

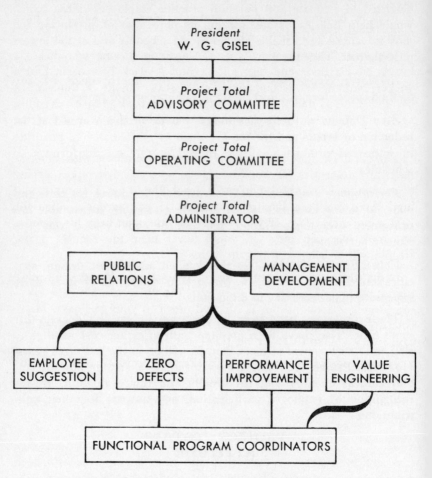

Project TOTAL Organization

President
W. G. GISEL

Project Total
ADVISORY COMMITTEE

Project Total
OPERATING COMMITTEE

Project Total
ADMINISTRATOR

PUBLIC
RELATIONS

MANAGEMENT
DEVELOPMENT

EMPLOYEE
SUGGESTION

ZERO
DEFECTS

PERFORMANCE
IMPROVEMENT

VALUE
ENGINEERING

FUNCTIONAL PROGRAM COORDINATORS

The organizational chart of Project "TOTAL" clearly
shows how every departmental program is integrated.

The new program is called Project TOTAL for *Team Offensive
to Achieve Leadership.* It coordinates the company's existing Employee Suggestion, Zero Defects, Performance Improvement, and
Value Engineering programs and provides the framework for
promoting, evaluating, and implementing employee ideas for the
improvement of Bell Aerosystems' products, plans, and procedures.

The four programs now encompassed by Project TOTAL are designed to evaluate and put into practice employees' ideas which would help Bell Aerosystems fulfill its objectives of producing the most advanced and reliable equipment on schedule and at the lowest possible cost. They are:

Employee Suggestion Program for the improvement of any method, procedure, product, system, facility, or equipment.

Zero Defects, an aerospace industry-wide program aimed at the reduction of errors and the improvement of craftsmanship, resulting in improved product quality, reduced costs, and conformity to schedules.

Performance Improvement Program covering ideas for time and material saving measures which provide a tangible, measurable improvement over the operation, function, or activity as it was previously performed.

Value Engineering involves the detailed analysis of design, specification method, system, or product to determine if it is more expensive than necessary to do its job.

These programs have been in operation in varying degrees for some time. They have been credited with effecting cost savings to Bell and its customers of more than $7 million in the last three years. However, Project TOTAL is now inspiring a greater flow of employee ideas by providing for prompt and fair evaluation, greater recognition of employee participation, and awards for their contributions.

ATTITUDE

We all know that attitude often makes the difference whether a job is performed well or not, or whether a person is successful in it. As managers or supervisors, we're inclined to question the attitude of our workers. Our employees, on the other hand, must often wonder about the attitude of their bosses or of the company they work for. In actual practice there is something to be said on both sides.

Certainly we like the employee who has a good attitude toward his duties, his superior, and the company. As executives we do much toward that end, discussing the value of good attitude with workers generally, counseling with individuals who need correction or improvement, and as in the case of fringe benefits actually trying to buy better attitudes.

Attitude may be defined in different ways. In the dictionaries it reads: "A state of mind that is revealed by our behavior or conduct, which demonstrates our opinion or purpose regarding some matter."

I like to think of it as putting a little of ourselves into our work, over and above the skill to perform it. We are already being compensated for what we do; it is this little extra which attracts attention, which pays off in recognition and inner satisfaction. How many times have we heard the truism that the more we put into our work the more we get out of it.

What distinguishes the professional from the amateur? Is it talent? I doubt it. More likely it is attitude. The professional writer, for instance, is a workman with a good attitude toward his work. Only in the movies does a man suddenly get an inspiration and then proceed to cash in on his brain child. In real life he schedules his work and then attacks it systematically.

The greatest musicians practice many hours every day. The first-rate artists are incessantly sketching or painting. The athlete never stops training. Greatness in any field is ability plus a right attitude to develop and use this ability.

Here Are the Real Rewards

In this one word "attitude" lies the difference between having just another job and in being happy and successful in our life's work. A good attitude toward our duties will bring contentment in our place of employment which, in turn, will be reflected in our pattern of living.

In trying to explain attitude and its importance to workers I have used a very simple illustration quite effectively. I try to draw a parallel between our working life and our happy school days. As school children, for example, we had recess; in the office or factory we call this coffee breaks. We know about the three R's of our earlier school days. There are also three R's of adult life. And by that I don't mean: Romance at 25, Rent at 45, and Rheumatism at 65. The three R's of adult life are: Resources—training and other gifts we offer, Resolution—what we decide to do with these, and Responsibility—the sincerity of purpose we put into life.

Just as there are three R's of both our childhood and adult lives, so are there three A's of business life. These are: Ability, Ambition, and Attitude.

Ability establishes what a worker does.
Ambition determines how much he does.
Attitude guarantees how well he does.

Ability will bring a worker a paycheck.
Ambition will get him a raise.
Attitude will lead to success.

Attitude is defined as the "you" in the job. When ability and ambition in two persons are about equal, how does the supervisor select one over the other for promotion? Here is where attitude becomes the deciding factor. Attitude refects a little plus—that something extra that is given willingly although not required.

But attitude, like arguments, contracts, and many other aspects of everyday life, is no solo affair. One person has an attitude toward something, but others help create it. In fact, it represents a mutual relationship.

Look at the word itself. A-T-T-I-T-U-D-E. Is it a mere coincidence that "I" comes first and "U" later? If this has any significance, then in trying to understand the attitude of people we should first examine ourselves in relation to those people. In cases of disappointment, perhaps we should wonder what we might have done to help bring about this negative attitude, or what we might have failed to do which could have prevented the development of a wrong attitude.

Isn't it easy to criticize the other fellow and comment, "What's wrong with his attitude?" When two of us talk about a third person, all the blame is placed on him. But notice how much different the question sounds when just two are involved and we ask, "What's wrong with his attitude toward me?" About this time we begin to wonder about ourselves and our attitude, don't we?

It is well to understand that when we point an accusing finger at someone else, there are three other fingers of that hand that are turned inward and that point back to us.

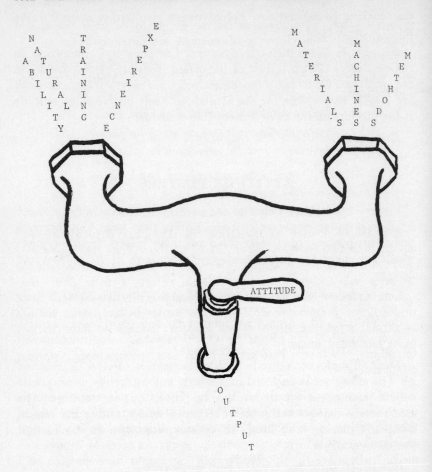

This is what I have tried to point out in the accompanying drawing of a double-intake and single-outlet faucet. The worker brings to the job his natural or acquired ability, previous training and experience, all of which are needed for effective performance. On the other side of the coin, he can expect the employer to provide quality materials, good equipment, and understandable and workable methods. If any of these are lacking then obviously production suffers.

By the same logic it may be assumed that if all these requirements are fully present then production will be high. Here, however, is where attitude must be considered. A poor attitude will affect the output regardless of how qualified the worker may be or how good the working conditions are. For optimum results this attitude valve must be wide open.

Attitude is like a two-edged sword. Certainly it is important in the employees. But it is just as important, possibly even more so, in the employer. Or to put it more succinctly, managers and supervisors are largely responsible for the attitude of their people since attitude is the product of the environment they provide.

Remember, attitudes are caught, not taught!

ATTITUDE POSTERS

Posters, colorful and catchy, are used quite successfully by many firms to improve employee attitude. Rather than print and illustrate their own posters, companies purchase them in sets from suppliers who have, over the years, perfected them both as to content and design.

One excellent source is Careers, Largo, Florida 33541. Their multicolored posters are 22½ by 17½ inches in size, large enough to attract employee attention but compact enough to hang in key office and plant areas.

Their "Employee Attitude-Builder Series" is offered in units of 24. The entire set is enclosed in a sturdy and attractive metal frame with a transparent acetate overlay to protect against spoilage. The user merely changes the poster every two weeks, taking the one in front and placing it in back. When completed, the display can be started over again.

It is hoped these posters will help employees—

- Build interest in better work habits.

- Overcome negative attitudes with positive views.

- Accept change in job content and methods.

- Prepare for new ways of doing things.

- Improve human relations skills.

It is a fact that the average employee will spend less than 5 seconds glancing at a poster message. These are intended to get the point across in that amount of time.

Typical captions and text are—

- "How Far You Go Depends on How Hard You Try"

- "Don't Blow Your Top! It's the Only One You Have"

- "More People Are Run Down by Gossip Than by Automobiles"

WASTE...

You Can't Afford It

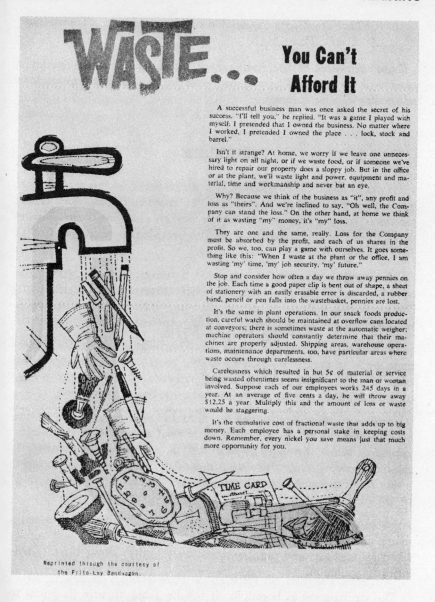

A successful business man was once asked the secret of his success. "I'll tell you," he replied. "It was a game I played with myself. I pretended that I owned the business. No matter where I worked, I pretended I owned the place . . . lock, stock and barrel."

Isn't it strange? At home, we worry if we leave one unnecessary light on all night, or if we waste food, or if someone we've hired to repair our property does a sloppy job. But in the office or at the plant, we'll waste light and power, equipment and material, time and workmanship and never bat an eye.

Why? Because we think of the business as "it", any profit and loss as "theirs". And we're inclined to say, "Oh well, the Company can stand the loss." On the other hand, at home we think of it as wasting "my" money, it's "my" loss.

They are one and the same, really. Loss for the Company must be absorbed by the profit, and each of us shares in the profit. So we, too, can play a game with ourselves. It goes something like this: "When I waste at the plant or the office, I am wasting 'my' time, 'my' job security, 'my' future."

Stop and consider how often a day we throw away pennies on the job. Each time a good paper clip is bent out of shape, a sheet of stationery with an easily erasable error is discarded, a rubber band, pencil or pen falls into the wastebasket, pennies are lost.

It's the same in plant operations. In our snack foods production, careful watch should be maintained at overflow cans located at conveyors; there is sometimes waste at the automatic weigher; machine operators should constantly determine that their machines are properly adjusted. Shipping areas, warehouse operations, maintenance departments, too, have particular areas where waste occurs through carelessness.

Carelessness which resulted in but 5¢ of material or service being wasted oftentimes seems insignificant to the man or woman involved. Suppose each of our employees works 245 days in a year. At an average of five cents a day, he will throw away $12.25 a year. Multiply this and the amount of loss or waste would be staggering.

It's the cumulative cost of fractional waste that adds up to big money. Each employee has a personal stake in keeping costs down. Remember, every nickel you save means just that much more opportunity for you.

Reprinted through the courtesy of the Frito-Lay Bandwagon.

- "If You Can't Do Extraordinary Things—Do Ordinary Things Extremely Well"
- "Thimk! Don't Louse Up Your Job—Work Safely"

- "When You Come to the End of Your Rope . . . Tie a Knot In It and Hang On!"

These are some of the functions of "Employee Attitude-Builder" posters, designed by Careers for better employee communications and on-the-job performance.

BOREDOM

As we make progress along scientific lines we seem to fester problems in human relations. This is true in life as well as in business. In our eagerness to strive for the new we often distort real values. For the answer we need to reevaluate our concept of a well-balanced life.

Relating this to business, we need to reevaluate our concept of a well-balanced job to offset the drift toward job deterioration. There are many situations in the office and factory that cause problems in human relations. One of the big problems is that of boredom.

Work measurement and work simplification are useful management tools, and can be justified on the basis of reducing operating costs, training time, and skill requirements. But if not properly understood and applied either can do more harm than good.

Sacrificing individualism on the altar of efficiency is one of the big causes of boredom. When the personal satisfaction of job performance is lost through standardization, and when the worker is required to work "for" his boss instead of "with" him, his interest in the job wanes and boredom sets in. And this boredom goes beyond the job and back into life—with serious consequences.

Surveys indicate that the average American family watches television six hours a day, seven days a week. Few families will admit this because most everyone feels obscurely guilty about this modern form of addiction.

The explanation is boredom. It results from an unwillingness to learn, to grow in spiritual and emotional dimensions.

Boredom often masquerades in the passive forms of entertainment. This is the reason our religious and national holidays have lost their higher meaning and are now observed by people "who couldn't care less" about their significance as they enjoy a day off with pay away from the routine.

Boredom develops its own escapism—as addiction to drugs, alcohol, gambling, all the way to suicide, as forms of relief. The highest rate of drug addiction, alcoholism, suicide, and death from violence occur in countries which enjoy material wealth and have the most effective social legislation and political stability. The lowest rates exist in countries where life is harder and more uncertain.

Boredom explains better than anything else the growing spread of juvenile delinquency—youngsters with no aims, no horizons, no values, no challenges to their abilities and energies.

Yes, material prosperity poses severe problems. High production is not enough unless with it comes a similar degree of high creative activity.

So when you make changes or improvements in your operating procedures and in your jobs, don't think only of your worker's pocketbook and his stomach; think also whether you may be contributing to the very destruction of his soul.

FATIGUE

The supervisor should recognize that signs of fatigue are not warnings of overwork but symptoms of something else.

There are three kinds of fatigue in the working world:

1. *Physical fatigue:* Years ago men worked long hours at physical labor. They had to rest their bodies to be ready for the next day's work. Once refreshed, they were ready for another strenuous day's work. Where before, after a hard day's work, a man needed rest, today he needs exercise.

2. *Nervous fatigue:* Fatigue in modern industry is nervous rather than physical. The worker may go home tired but still have plenty of energy for gardening, bowling, or dancing. Nervous fatigue comes from strain and fear.

3. *Mental fatigue:* This is not tiredness but mind laziness. A

worker may feel mentally drained from writing, or figuring, or making decisions of some kind. Just let a fire break out at that point and he is instantly as fresh and alert as ever. Better yet, watch a group of "mentally exhausted" men perk up when a pretty woman sweeps into the room. Psychologists claim that mental fatigue is chiefly loss of interest.

Employees who are fatigued are probably on wrong jobs, assigned to work for which they are not best suited, or simply not sufficiently challenged to keep them interested and keyed up. In such cases, don't treat the symptom; look for the cause.

MORALE

Employee morale is the attitude of an individual or group as related to work, co-workers, supervision, management, the company, and the product or service that is provided.

It is generally assumed to be axiomatic that higher morale results in increased productivity. Hence, there are serious efforts made to improve employee morale.

Good human relations builds better morale. This does not mean a scientifically designed personnel program, which may or may not contribute to better morale. It does imply fairness, understanding, and a respect for the dignity of man.

Communications also helps; employees appreciate being kept in the "know." They like to maintain their self-respect. They like also to respect their supervisor, not only as a boss but also as a person. They need to be reassured of their job security. They want, and should have, a voice in decisions which affect them.

Employees, as individuals, have their own hopes and ambitions. Morale is good when employees can use their jobs to fulfill their own personal aspirations. To the extent that these can be dovetailed into company objectives, both the employees and the company gain.

The key to better employee morale lies in good supervision. In supervisory training programs emphasis should be placed on dealing with employees as human beings and not as human machines. Their personal feelings and emotions must be considered as well as their work performance and production schedules.

"Whatever is good for people is good for business" would be an appropriate slogan or credo with which to inculcate the philosophy of supervisors and their attitude toward their responsibility. A department with high morale will get its work done easier and better.

Developing and maintaining good morale among workers is somewhat of an art. But it can be taught. With some supervisors this comes easy; others must work at it.

Good morale is difficult to define and explain. It is not hard to recognize. The evidence is in the payoff.

ATTITUDE SURVEYS

Who knows better than the employees themselves how working conditions are or what they ought to be? So why not ask them?

Done formally, this is known as an Attitude Survey. This is an industrial relations adaptation of opinion polls, used in political campaigns, market research, and television ratings. In the employee relations program this becomes a "Morale Reading."

It is not easy for companies to conduct an Attitude Survey. Not that the procedure is difficult, but the idea of getting employees into the act is, to some managements, deliberately disturbing the calm. Why upset the status quo? Maybe conditions are not perfect, but when employees are given a chance to express their feelings, isn't some form of action called for? What if companies don't want to act? What then?

This is one of the problems of an Attitude Survey. The workers are closest to conditions which affect them and they have opinions of what is good, what is less-than-good, and what should be improved. To ask them and then ignore their well-intentioned advice is worse than not asking them at all.

The other problem of an Attitude Survey is that companies are afraid to face facts. In respect to some questions, they know what is wrong and have learned to live with the situation. In other cases, they don't know and actually don't want to know. Once the undesirable or unpleasant situation has been laid on the table, management loses its right to ignore it. The workers have spoken and this, in itself, demands they be given an answer.

Despite these obstacles, many companies have engaged in employee Attitude Surveys with excellent results. The program, to be successful, must be well planned, publicized to the employees, conducted carefully and openly, and the answers analyzed honestly, thoroughly, and announced to the participants. Most important, corrective action that is called for must be taken promptly and directly.

This is where many Attitude Surveys break down; companies like to know what their employees are thinking, and once they learn this (too often chuckling privately over the answers) they procrastinate, or even worse, fail to take any action. In that case, they have done more harm than good.

Tested Procedures

Properly done, however, it can be helpful to sincere managements. The procedure calls for

1. Announcing the program to the employees.
2. Preparing a questionnaire.
3. Distributing the questionnaire.
4. Collecting the completed questionnaires by an announced deadline.
5. Reviewing the data.
6. Collating the answers.
7. Summarizing the results.
8. Publishing a report.
9. Taking all corrective action that becomes necessary.

The usual method is to employ a multiple-choice questionnaire on which each employee is asked questions and directed to select the answer which seems most appropriate to him.

In designing the question-and-answer sheet

1. Make it easy to complete.

2. Ask general questions.

3. Keep questions simple so they will not be easily misunderstood.

4. Don't slant questions toward desired answers.

5. Don't skirt the important issues.

6. Don't editorialize.

The questions should ask for personal opinions about

1. The company in general.

2. Job satisfaction.

3. Working conditions.

4. Knowledge of company and its products.

5. Compensation.

6. Benefit program.

7. Personnel policies.

8. Co-workers.

9. Supervision and management.

10. Any special problems peculiar to the company, its location, etc.

The only identification seeks information about the employee's

1. Sex.

2. Age (perhaps in 10-year brackets rather than specifically).

3. Job level.

In conducting the survey

1. Get full participation.

2. Don't keep the survey secret—do it out in the open.

3. Keep it anonymous—don't require it be signed, otherwise you'll get a name and little else.

4. Don't try hidden codes or colors; people will become suspicious.

5. Take time to study the answers.

6. Announce and publish results.

7. Tell employees fast, while the project is still fresh in their minds.

8. Do something—this is not just a pet exercise for the amusement of executives. The findings must be translated into action.

Pitfalls to Avoid

As mentioned earlier, conducting an employee Attitude Survey is not easy. There are certain pitfalls to guard against.

1. A clever questionnaire writer can phrase questions to fit preconceived answers.

2. Answers, summarized statistically, can be expressed to create misleading impressions.

3. A little gripe, such as a drinking fountain that is constantly neglected, may cause an employee to fire full blast at management. Trivial complaints, not serious enough for formal grievances, can be blown out of proportion under the protection of anonymity.

It is also important to keep in mind the caution that opinions are expressed from the employees' point of view, which could differ from that of management.

In summary, it should be mentioned that an Attitude Survey will point up *what* is wrong, not *why* it is wrong. Nor will it tell how to correct anything that needs attention, or for that matter, whether the well-intentioned corrective action taken by management is what the employees expect and will accept.

An Attitude Survey, or morale reading, is a useful tool if properly planned and administered; it can become a "loaded" bomb if improperly used.

EMPLOYEE COMMUNICATIONS

If "creativity" is the most overworked word in advertising, then "communication" is just as misused in employee relations.

When a problem arises, the blame is often laid to poor communications. Improve the communication and the situation gets better. That seems to be the theory.

Good communication is vital to good employee relations. But it should not be assumed that communication, any kind of communication, is a cure-all for personnel ills. Do we really understand what is useful communication?

Too much *mere information* is being passed off as communication. The business world, according to one authority, is "suffering from an epidemic of worditis."

He continued, "We are being buried under mountains of memos, letters, carbon copies, duplicated copies, bulletins, directives, house organs, newsletters, copies of speeches that never should have been made in the first place, and press releases that are absolutely of no interest to anyone except the sender."

All of this goes by the mythical name of "communication" and we assume that it is good, necessary, and serving our purpose.

Much Communication Wasted

One of the difficulties is overstimulus of response. Employees hear the sound or read the words but fail to get the message. Much of what we call employee communication is wasted simply because the human sensory apparatus reacts negatively to the sheer volume and constant flow of information.

Much information is designed to fill a vacuum, not a need. Genuine communication creates a bridge between minds; mere information takes up time, energy, and paper—makes the sender seem busy and the receiver seem important.

Overcommunication creates more problems than it solves. But it must be pointed out that many companies are guilty of something worse, that is, undercommunication. Saying something is generally better than saying nothing. In the absence of information from management, employees will arrive at their own conclusions. Rumors and the grapevine, the only tools employees can use under these conditions, can produce strange results and easily destroy goodwill. In such cases, companies should blame only themselves if they don't like what they get.

Occasional but meaningful communication instead of endless messages, planned presentations instead of a hit-and-miss assortment of verbal barrages, employee-centered information instead of pronouncements which impress the company—this is being on the right track and traveling in the right direction.

Employees like to know and be kept informed about things in the company which affect them. Communication, in any form, to be effective, should be simple, direct, straightforward, and sincere.

Employee Communications Media

Bulletin Boards—Company or departmental, prominently located and well maintained.

Employee Magazine (house organs)—For personals, news, social activities.

Company Magazine—For products and services, history, plans.

Newsletter—Digest of news and current events relating to company business.

Employee Handbook—Rules and regulations, working conditions.

Benefit Book (companion handbook)—Welfare programs, insurance.

Policy Manual—Helpful guide on official company position.

Indoctrination—Individual consultations to get new worker off to a good start.

Orientation—Group meetings of both new and old employees to influence attitude of employees toward company objectives.

Individual Counseling—On job-related and personal problems.

Performance Rating Interviews—To tell the employee how he is doing and where he may improve.

Suggestion System—To give formal recognition to good ideas.

Grievance Procedure—To resolve problems in troublesome areas.

Group Meetings—To announce or explain organization changes, new products, financial stability, results, progress, programs.

Public Address System—For quick messages and late news.

Annual Report—To reassure employee of company growth and personal job security.

EMPLOYEE COMMUNICATIONS
AND FREEDOM OF DISCUSSION

A good approach to better employee relations, called "Consultative Supervision," is used by Public Utility District No. 1 of Klickitat County, Goldendale, Washington. This policy, as well as the District's emphasis on communications and freedom of discussion, is outlined below:

Consultative Supervision

Because it emphasizes respect for the individuality and dignity of each employee and encourages his development, the District believes that the most satisfactory and enduring personnel relations will be attained by means of consultation and explanation. This means

1. That employees should be encouraged to express their views on matters affecting their jobs and interests;

2. That consideration should be given to their views before reaching decisions materially affecting their jobs and interests;

3. That any criticism to an employee of his work, activities, or expressions should be made privately, and in no case should an employee be criticized in the presence of employees of equal or subordinate position;

4. All who direct the work of others should see to it that in the daily operation of our business, no one is ignored on those matters about which he thinks he has or ought to have a right to be consulted;

5. That promotions, individual wages or salary changes, and disciplinary actions should be communicated to an employee, after proper approvals, only by his immediate supervisor; and

6. That all matters affecting employee relations should be fully explained.

Employees are assured there will be no discrimination as a result of exercising their rights under this method of administration.

Communications

It is the policy of the District to give the employee prompt and full information on matters affecting his job, either directly or indirectly. This includes background information on social, political, and economic events and problems about which the employee needs adequate information if he is to make good decisions and promote the District.

Freedom of Discussion

One of the principal objectives of the District is to encourage and maintain freedom of contact between the employees and management. Employees should feel free to seek the counsel of their supervisors and to learn about District policies and operational problems, to offer suggestions or to ask advice on any matter which is troubling them. No employee need hesitate to do this.

MEMOS TO ALL PERSONNEL

There are frequent occasions for memos to be sent to all employees. Information must be disseminated, news distributed, announcements made. The easiest and most effective way to reach all employees promptly with the official statement is to send a memo (blanket, not individually addressed) to each employee.

The problem is not writing or sending out the memo. Many people are qualified to prepare, publish, and distribute it. The question is who should do it and under what circumstances.

A good policy is to clear all such memos through the personnel office. In many cases the personnel staff might be required to write the memo, although this is not always necessary. Usually the person closest to the information is in the best position to draft the memo unless, of course, he is not a capable writer in which case he should expect someone, possibly in the personnel office, to polish it up for him.

The personnel people have a right to check and approve every memo that goes to employees just as the public relations staff would expect to see anything sent to the newspapers. In approving each such memo the personnel people do not second-guess the message or the content but they look for conformity to policy, standards of preparation, schedule of distribution, etc. Clearing all memos through the personnel office keeps everybody and his brother from sending messages indiscriminately throughout the house.

Some discretion must be exercised, otherwise if employees are bombarded with a steady flow of ordinary or inconsequential memos from all kinds of people and departments they may not take proper note of a message from top management when it arrives.

Make It "From the Top"

A good rule to follow is to use an executive letterhead, instead of blank paper, to differentiate official memos from routine notices. A message from the president should by its appearance immediately impress the recipient with its importance. It is too bad when a reminder of a bowling league meeting gets more attention than an announcement authorizing extra time off for voting.

Another suggestion might be to limit executives or managers in sending messages only to their own people, with informational copies to their peers or counterparts in other divisions who may then decide whether or not to relay the information to all or some of their own people. Not every memo needs to be sent routinely across the board and some check should be established to stop this practice.

For that matter not all memos should be broadcast to all employees. Some are intended only for limited or specific distribution. The army used a good system in World War II known as the "message center." All outgoing messages were coded and distributed accordingly. In business we tend to address them to the group they're aimed at, such as "All Personnel," "Sales Staff," "Management," "Exempt Employees," and so on.

General memos are addressed to groups and not individually identified. A memo "To All Employees" is given total or company-wide distribution. There are, however, occasions when letters might be individually addressed and mailed to the employees at home, or individually marked by name and hand delivered in the office or plant. The nature of the message should determine the treatment it receives. Certainly a year-end report of progress from the president should get personalized attention whereas a routine announcement of Mother's Day candy for sale at a discount may not merit any special consideration.

A good suggestion would be to limit the number of memos and concentrate on the important ones. Too many notices tend to dilute the significance of all of them. Writing up the story in the company

465

house organ, while not as fast, still gets the message to all employees. Or posting notices on the bulletin boards may suffice. Surely it isn't necessary, or advisable, to send out a memo for every bit of general-interest information.

At any rate, let somebody or some office look over the written messages for content, wording, grammar and composition, importance, and distribution. At least this will keep these "Memos to All Personnel" under better control.

UNDERSTANDING COMMUNICATION

By Lawrence A. Appley

Chairman, American Management Association

Many, many times have people in positions of great influence said that the greatest need in this world is for better communication between people. It is extremely difficult to understand why, in a time when communication is most needed and when the facilities for attaining communication are the greatest in history and developing rapidly, human beings are paying less and less attention to and becoming less and less skilled at accomplishing effective communication.

Please note the care with which I have used the word *communication*. I did not say *communicate* or *communicating*. Despite the dictionary definition, I am taking some liberties for the purpose of clarification.

Possibly, we would understand communication better if we thought of it as a result rather than as a process. When good communication has been attained between human beings, there is enthusiastic support in the search of a common objective. The proof of good communication is the attainment of a desired result by a person, or group of persons, who has the right to desire it.

There is an inclination to think of *communication* as the spoken or written word, or as an instrument such as a telegram, a telephone, a microphone or a letter. It is commonly believed that training in writing and in speech ensures good communication.

Effective communication sometimes exists between people without any mechanism or transmission of the spoken or written word. There is an understanding that exists to the extent that a jointly desired result is attained. Absolute silence sometimes exists at the center of the most effective communication.

The attainment of desired communication requires certain skills and integrity. Underlying all good communication is basic, human, mutual confidence. This does not occur without the exercise of considerable skill. Full cooperation in the attainment of a given result requires fundamental understanding of the desires and viewpoints of other people.

It is obvious that I am rambling a bit in search of an interpretation that may not be commonly accepted. What I am trying to say is that, if a person is in a position that gives him the right to desire a result that requires the help of other people, he will have attained good communication if that result is realized. In order to have this kind of communication, verified by a desired result, he must have the skill to understand people and to have them understand him.

The skill to do this frequently produces mutual confidence even though it may not bring about mutual agreement.

Some skills are bred into people; some are acquired; all are increased with special training and practice. Communication is a way of life rather than a skill, but it takes a lot of skill to attain it.

Reprinted from *Management News,* an AMA publication.

BULLETIN BOARDS

In the area of employee communications, the company bulletin board, conceived and administered internally, is by far the oldest mechanism for conveying information. It was in existence long before the first so-called "house organ" was produced. Its growth has been slowed because of management's failure to view the medium's potentials, but it is moving ahead more recently as a member of the oral and written communication team.

A bulletin board program, to be useful, needs to be meshed officially into a company's total communications effort, not left to drift by itself. Otherwise it could deteriorate into a junkyard for shop-level trivia. Nor should it become a catch basin for syndicated morale stuff that management buys to save itself the trouble of speaking for itself. It is, in reality, a tool of communication and used properly it is a powerhouse of persuasion. At bargaining time it is management's most reliable friend.

Advantages and Pitfalls

According to Newcomb & Sammons, 3200 North Lake Shore Drive, Chicago, Illinois 60657, publishers of *The Score,* a monthly report to management on developments and trends in employer-employee communications, the advantages of a good bulletin board program are—

1. It is generally the fastest and most accurate medium of communication. Even in plants where public address systems are dependable, or where the telephone recording device is used, the bulletin board lets the employees *see* all day what they *heard* earlier possibly only one time.

2. It is gaining fast recognition as a medium of information on labor-management developments. It is a dependable medium for presenting the company's story promptly.

3. In the multiple-plant company, it has an "umbrella" effect. Headquarters can supply solid, interesting, pictorial information on matters of company concern simultaneously to plants in different locations, thus putting a friendly arm around all the people.

4. It is the classic rumor silencer. The one-two-punch effect of a bulletin board program can put a rumor in its place in a few minutes.

5. The board becomes a meeting place. It has its own captive audience. It gets their attention at least once a day, maybe oftener, and this gives the company an opportunity to be as persuasive as the talents of the communicator permit.

What are the roadblocks in the way of effective communication by bulletin board? Here are pitfalls to watch for.

1. Shortage of manpower needed to implement the program. At the plant level the personnel assistant often assigned to this task may have his hands well occupied with other chores. *Remedy:* Straighten this out first with the plant manager, sell him on the

importance of the medium as a tool for his communication, emphasize the fact that bulletin board preparation doesn't take too long.

2. Training the local-level personnel in bulletin board preparation. These people are usually inexperienced. *Remedy:* Set up a briefing session, probably on a regional basis in a company of any size, to coach the people. Also issue a manual in order to keep these plant representatives on the beam.

3. Employee lack of interest. Some communicators complain that employees will not read bulletin boards, no matter how good. The answer obviously is that they're not good enough. *Remedy:* Determine by personal check or simple survey the subjects that interest employees most.

4. No real interest at top management level. This can be serious. If the top man is lukewarm, subordinates will be the same. Therefore it is essential that the sales job be undertaken again. *Remedy:* Link the bulletin board program directly into the total communications program; sell it as an arm of total communications, not as an independent agency. Stress low cost; minimum manpower requirements, value of the medium in talking up productivity, quality, competition.

5. Boards offer little subject variety. To the unimaginative, they don't. *Remedy:* Let the communicator solicit subject themes from employees themselves (see No. 3 above), add to it the topics he knows management would like covered.

In connection with item No. 5 above, one of the biggest headaches involved in bulletin board handling is getting the local level representative to spot "the news." One communicator, cudgeled by this problem, compiled for his field staffers some "typical subjects"—personnel shifts; production, expansion plans; building specifics; product quality; elements of cost; taxes, both corporate and personal; labor negotiations and developments; research projects; business economics; special employee events; retirements; service club news; plant people in community affairs, etc.

News sources are: Top management, this is the key source; public relations, for corporate news; personnel, for news about people; club officers, for social activities, games, scores; community, for news in the area; advertising, for public announcements; and similar places.

Change of Pace

The office bulletin board program calls for an understandable change of pace here and there. Here are some specifications adopted by Rockwell-Standard Corporation, Detroit:

1. Single approval. One department should be responsible for posting notices, and everything cleared through the department head.

2. Irregular change. Avoid the once-a-week routine, or readers will soon notice the pattern and read the boards only once a week.

3. Signed notices. For authority, make certain all notices are signed with the name of the originator or the originating department.

4. Make boards attractive. Avoid the appearance of sameness and don't overuse plain white paper for typing notices; try a felt-tip pen for printing attention-getting headlines; use colored paper and change colors often; use sketches or comic strip cutouts to illustrate notices.

5. Eye-catching titles. Stop the reader with live headlines. For that matter, give the boards themselves live titles. Suggestions: Message Center, Hitching Post, Cracker Barrel, On Target, The Word, Now Hear This, Action Board, Postings, The Notebook.

6. Good location. Across from the elevators is an ideal location, if space and other conditions permit. Consider the cafeteria or coffee lounge. Bulletin boards near time clocks could jam up traffic when good-reading items are posted.

In general, avoid posting notices on other than clean paper and replace if the paper becomes soiled through handling. Don't use notices that "flop over" the board edges. Stay away from too many "don't" notices from management; keep track of the "negatives" that are posted and bring this information to management's attention. In short, accentuate the positive.

The consensus of companies boils down to this: "If you're not using your bulletin boards to the fullest extent—in single-and multiple-plant operations, in small shops as well as large—you're passing up a real opportunity to communicate."

EMPLOYEE HANDBOOK

Many companies, especially the larger ones, have their policies, regulations, and employee benefits written out in an Employee Handbook. A copy is given to each employee.

The purpose is to acquaint new employees and remind old employees of their benefits and opportunities.

Such booklet describing the employee program may become the basis for discussion during the initial indoctrination which takes place on the new worker's first day on the job. It may be distributed at that time or at the orientation program some few days later.

The contents of the book cover company organization, established policies, personnel practices, and operating rules. Specifically, the following types of items are included:

A greeting of welcome to the new employee.

Brief story about the company and its products or services.

Company people.

Location, including branches.

Employment policy, including part-time, rehirees, minority, etc.

Exempt employees defined, and how rules apply to them.

Work day—regular hours and exceptions.

Time records or time clocks.

Overtime.

Rest periods.

Lunch period.

Eating facilities available; cafeteria, if any.

Lounge.

Records and the importance of keeping them up-to-date.

Clinic and health.

Job security.

Promptness (not tardiness).

Income continuation program.

Disability insurance.

Life insurance.

Retirement income.

Sick pay.

Illness absence.

Personal leave of absence.

Furlough.

Pregnancy.

Military leave including National Guard duty.

Extended military service.

Reporting accidents.

Workmen's compensation.

Safety.

Fire drills.

Care of equipment and machines.

Company sponsored employee parties, picnics, dances.

Service recognition dinner.

Service awards.

Employee sponsored activities.

Recreational programs.

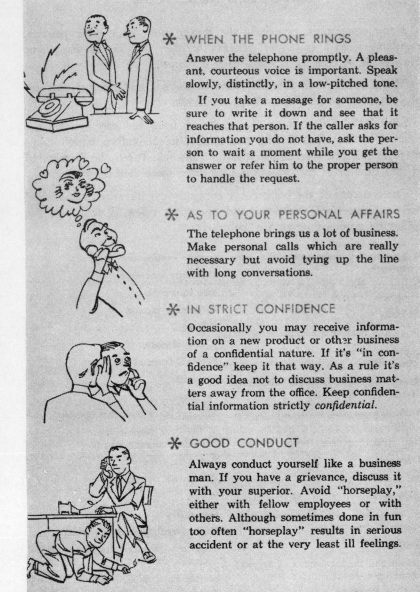

✳ WHEN THE PHONE RINGS

Answer the telephone promptly. A pleasant, courteous voice is important. Speak slowly, distinctly, in a low-pitched tone.

If you take a message for someone, be sure to write it down and see that it reaches that person. If the caller asks for information you do not have, ask the person to wait a moment while you get the answer or refer him to the proper person to handle the request.

✳ AS TO YOUR PERSONAL AFFAIRS

The telephone brings us a lot of business. Make personal calls which are really necessary but avoid tying up the line with long conversations.

✳ IN STRICT CONFIDENCE

Occasionally you may receive information on a new product or other business of a confidential nature. If it's "in confidence" keep it that way. As a rule it's a good idea not to discuss business matters away from the office. Keep confidential information strictly *confidential*.

✳ GOOD CONDUCT

Always conduct yourself like a business man. If you have a grievance, discuss it with your superior. Avoid "horseplay," either with fellow employees or with others. Although sometimes done in fun too often "horseplay" results in serious accident or at the very least ill feelings.

Page from an excellent employee handbook, Welcome to Firestone.

Attendance (not absence).

Dependability.

Personal appearance.

Personal telephone calls and mail.

Smoking—where permitted.

Performance rating.

Job evaluation, a fair system for setting wage ranges.

Payday and where to cash checks.

Social security; company matches employee deduction.

Withholding tax deductions.

Savings bonds—how to buy them through payroll deduction.

Credit union.

Wage assignments—how these are handled.

Employment referrals.

Holidays, national and religious.

Vacations.

Death, time off for funerals.

Marriage leave.

Jury duty and witness summons.

Voting—time off in national elections.

Hospitalization insurance.

Medical-surgical insurance.

Health and accident insurance.

House organ.

Communications.

Orientation program.

Gift or flower fund.

Canvassing and soliciting.

Fund-raising drives endorsed by company.

Bulletin board.

Lost and found.

Notary public.

Counseling on personal problems.

Grievance procedure.

Exit interview.

Unemployment compensation.

Compliance with government laws and regulations.

Plus these where applicable:

Profit sharing.

Incentive pay.

Company discount purchases.

Tuition refunds.

Layoffs.

Probation or suspension.

Policy on gambling.

Attitude toward outside activities.

Moonlighting.

Civic responsibilities.

It is impossible to describe the one best format for an Employee Handbook. It might be advisable to use the assistance of others, such as public relations or advertising people, who will introduce imagination into its creation. The use of color, photographs, drawings, or graphs, will help get the message across. But it must be written, or at least influenced, by the personnel executive who retains the responsibility for its accuracy, compliance with policy, and effectiveness. In addition to detailing the specifics of the employee program, it should reflect the personality of the company.

Companies that plan to prepare or revise their Employee Handbook are cautioned to avoid publishing an obvious *rule book* and should also be careful not to overdo the sickening "you" approach. A straightforward and sincere presentation will be more acceptable, and an interesting style, possibly narrative form, will make it readable.

Dartnell Manual Available

The Dartnell Corporation, 4660 North Ravenswood, Chicago 60640, has published a helpful report, *How to Prepare a Company Policy Manual.*

The following is a unique section of the employee handbook, *Welcome to Firestone,* of the Firestone Tire & Rubber Company of Akron, Ohio. It is unique in the way it is expressed.

Your Part of the Bargain

What We Expect of You

GOOD BUSINESS MANNERS

Courtesy and a pleasant disposition are as necessary in business as they are in your social life. Remember that you represent Firestone in all your contacts with people and everyone is a potential customer.

HOUSEKEEPING

You will want to make it part of your job to help keep your area clean and orderly. Form the habit of putting things in their proper places. When everyone does his part, the entire office becomes a more pleasant place to work. Make it a practice to keep your place of work as clean and orderly as you do your home.

WHEN THE PHONE RINGS

Answer the telephone promptly. A pleasant, courteous voice is important. Speak slowly, distinctly, in a low-pitched tone. If you take a message for someone, be sure to write it down and see that it reaches that person. If the caller asks for information you do not have, ask the person to wait a moment while you get the answer or refer him to the proper person to handle the request.

AS TO YOUR PERSONAL AFFAIRS

The telephone brings us a lot of business. Make personal calls which are really necessary but avoid tying up the line with long conversations.

IN STRICT CONFIDENCE

Occasionally you may receive information on a new product or other business of a confidential nature. If it's "in confidence" keep it that way. As a rule it's a good idea not to discuss business matters away from the office. Keep confidential information strictly *confidential.*

Good Conduct

Always conduct yourself like a business man. If you have a grievance, discuss it with your superior. Avoid "horseplay," either with fellow employees or with others. Although sometimes done in fun too often "horseplay" results in serious accident or at the very least ill feelings.

When You're Absent

Your hours will be explained to you by your superior and you will be expected to report for work on time. If for any reason you are unable to be on the job or must be late, you should immediately get in touch with your superior so that he can arrange to have someone handle your work in the meantime.

Cooperation and Loyalty

Firestone is a great company and a good place to work. And we hope that some of this feeling will rub off on you. The spirit of cooperation between all divisions of the company and all employees is our great strength. By giving your fellow employees and your superiors your full cooperation you will be helping to guarantee future progress. And you can't do your best on the job if you don't have loyalty—to your company, your superiors, your fellow workers.

READING RACKS

Employees think about many things. Interests vary according to the individual, but in general they cover vacations, buying a car or home, hobbies, gardening, crafts, and the like. Women think about recipes, clothes, home furnishings, families, and entertaining friends. Men think about sports, guns, money, and such matters. Both men and women, fathers and mothers, think about taxes and government, war, and voting.

Since what people think about determines what they do off the job, some companies give consideration to activities or projects to guide the thinking of their workers into constructive channels. Distributing useful literature should never be used as an excuse for selfish propaganda, but rather to clear up fuzzy ideas employees may have about things in life that concern them and their well-being. At the same time, companies make available to their workers helpful hints on a variety of subjects.

These companies subscribe to one of the several reputable booklet rack services. This keeps the material neutral as well as easy to obtain. The distributors furnish display racks which are then conveniently located in the office and around the plant.

475

The suppliers often offer a purchaser a choice of material. A new set of pamphlets is sent out periodically, usually monthly. Companies may, in some cases, get a preview and can make a selection. The companies purchase the booklets at a nominal quantity rate and make them available free of charge to employees who are encouraged to take whatever is of interest.

In addition to booklets, some publishers supply newspapers, posters, and other items which contain articles or messages that are in keeping with the booklet theme.

An analysis of subjects breaks down as follows:

- Sports and pastimes.
- Skill development.
- Home crafts.
- Economics and government.
- Leisure hobbies.
- Health.

The objectives, according to the National Research Bureau, Inc., of Burlington, Iowa, distributors of the material, are

1. To aid the development of employee goodwill.

2. To create better employee understanding of our American business system and good government.

3. To give employees self-help information about health, sports, hobbies, money, and a variety of similar topics.

Their program is being used by more than 2,000 companies, large and small, throughout the United States and Canada . . . reaching more than three and one-half million employees.

The employee Information Rack program serves as a medium of communication between management and employees, to create an improved relationship.

The contributing factors making the program successful are

1. *Voluntary use.* Literature is placed in a rack for voluntary pickup by employees.

2. *Diversification of material.* A variety of topics with different titles is available at regular intervals.

3. *Brevity of articles.* Educational messages covering good gov-

ernment, economics, human relations, success stories, health, and employee welfare are condensed into short articles for quick reading.

4. *Source of material.* Articles are obtained from original manuscripts by writers who are recognized authorities in their fields.

LUNCH-HOUR FILM SHOWINGS

Apart from movies or filmstrips used during training sessions or official meetings, some companies, particularly large factories, often show motion pictures to employees as entertainment or recreation.

Such films are usually shown in a large open area on the employees' own time. One popular arrangement is to run short movies once or twice a week in the cafeteria. Employees may sit in that section where the screen is placed and watch while they eat.

Or films may be shown on a scheduled or continuous basis in a room nearby. Employees eat in a hurry, then move to the movie room. There they may occupy chairs or benches or stand as they watch the movies.

Films for lunch-hour showings fall into four categories:

1. *Entertainment* —Comedies or skits by professional actors, or animated cartoons.

2. *Recreational* —Travel, spectator sports, fishing, races. The annual World Series film is a good example.

3. *Educational* —Economic information, health, community relations, investments.

4. *Promotional* —New company products or services, advertising commercials, employee services.

Films may be borrowed or rented. There are regular film lending libraries that are glad to supply films on a rotating basis. Films may also be obtained from other companies and agencies which make them available as a public service.

It is best to schedule films in advance and to post the list. Employees may then plan to watch those films which appeal to them.

OFFICIAL EMPLOYEE GROUP MEETINGS

There are occasions when it is necessary that the employees be brought together for a meeting. "The boss wants to talk with them."

This happens when an official report needs to be delivered or a special announcement is to be made. Telling the workers directly is to be preferred over the rumor mill. There is information the employees are entitled to know and they should get it straight.

There are many times when employees are asked to a meeting. The subject might be a United Fund campaign, U.S. Bond drive, or other program which affects employees and has the endorsement of the company. Of course, new products, next year's models, relocation of plant, organization changes, revision of benefits, business trends, cost-cutting, mergers or acquisition are all subjects for discussions with employees. It is good, also, for the chief executive to simply reassure employees that business is good and their jobs are secure.

Another Task for Personnel

Official meetings of this type are usually presided over, informally or otherwise, by the executive who has the message, but the details are handled by the personnel director. He writes the memo announcing the time and place of the gathering and, hopefully, explains the reason. He arranges for facilities. He makes certain that the employees show up, on time, and that they are adequately accommodated. He may even be expected to write the agenda and possibly even a speech. In short, when employee meetings are held, the personnel director takes the responsibility for them.

There are other meetings of employees which are not officially conducted but still have company support. Examples are credit union elections, bowling league, gift fund, and the like. While the personnel director is not in charge, in fact, may not even be present on the occasion, he should nevertheless be consulted to make certain that these employee get-togethers are run within company policy. Should anything go wrong, the personnel director will surely hear about it. He is the link between the employees and the company.

MANAGEMENT MEETINGS

There are occasions when management has a report or announcement to make to officers, managers, foremen, and supervisors. The news needs to be dramatized to emphasize its significance. This calls for more than a memo or president's letter. The occasion calls for a meeting.

Management meetings may be called as required or scheduled on a regular periodic basis. To add to their importance they may be arranged "after hours" in the evenings. Any gathering during the regular work day is usually referred to as a "staff meeting" whereas a special meeting with extra arrangements is called a "management meeting."

Informality with Dignity

Such a management meeting may be held on the premises, if adequate facilities are available, otherwise in a local hotel or private club. In all these instances the formal meeting is preceded by a dinner with an excellent menu. Since this is a business meeting and not a party, premeeting cocktails may be considered inappropriate.

The atmosphere should be informal but businesslike. Any attempt at corny innovations should be avoided. The dinner should be "class," to set the proper tone for the rest of the evening. A head table is unnecessary unless the business session is held in the same room. If possible, the group should be transplanted to another location more suitable for meeting purposes. The business session should begin on time.

Inasmuch as a management meeting has as its theme some timely and important topic of official concern, the presiding chairman should be the president or other top officer who is in charge of the activity under discussion. The format will depend upon the nature of the subject that is being presented. An annual report meeting will be treated differently from a problem meeting. In all cases it is imperative that all levels of management who have been invited get an opportunity to be heard or ask questions. They should be 100 percent behind the program when the meeting is over.

HOW TO MAKE YOUR MEETINGS MORE EFFECTIVE

A meeting is a means by which information is communicated to or from or among a group of people.

There are two necessary parts to any meeting: (1) those who conduct it and (2) those who participate in it. Often this might be a speaker and the audience. In other meetings this could be the discussion leader and the members of the group.

For a meeting to be effective, both sides must be prepared. Those in charge should provide capable and informed leadership, adequate facilities, and necessary equipment. Those for whom the meeting is conducted should show an interest by their faithful attendance, willing cooperation, and active participation. Neither side can alone effect satisfactory results.

Kinds of Meetings

All meetings are not alike. Before a meeting is conducted a number of questions should be considered:

What is the purpose of the get-together?

What is the meeting intended to accomplish?

What should be discussed and what should be withheld?

Who should attend?

How should the presentation be planned?

What is the best method of conducting the meeting?

Who is best qualified to lead it?

In an informational meeting the leader dominates by presenting facts and other information which are new or unfamiliar to the audience. The group listens. There might be some time allowed toward the close for questions mainly to clarify points.

In a lecture-type meeting the leader dominates during the first part while he presents his subject in his own way. Then he opens the meeting to the group to discuss his topic and to ask questions for further elaboration on items of interest.

In a conference the members of the group confer with each other and the leader merely presides over the meeting making certain that the discussion does not stray or get out of hand. The leader will not dominate the discussion but he will keep control of the meeting, and at the close will summarize the discussion.

There are other kinds of meetings, such as conventions, banquets, after-dinner meetings, seminars, workshops, training sessions, and the like. But essentially all meetings fall into these three categories.

The following graph illustrates these three kinds of meetings and shows how the parts played by the leader and the members of the group differ in each case.

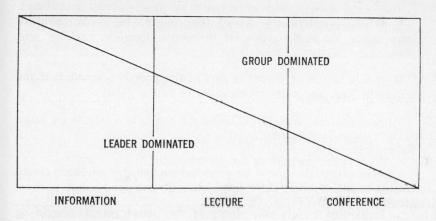

Arrangements

Before a meeting is conducted there are necessary arrangements which the person in charge should make.

1. Arrange for a room that is appropriate for the type and size of meeting. There is a difference between a lecture room, with its theater-style seating, and a conference room with chairs around the table. A room too small is obviously unsuited; but in a room that is too large, the meeting could appear to be poorly attended or the people might spread out too much.

2. Reserve the room for the date and time of the meeting or conference. This is understandable when the meeting is held in an outside hotel, but it is also important when the meeting is planned

on company premises. Get confirmation in writing, if this seems advisable. This will avoid embarrassing confusion.

3. Send out a written notification to all participants, giving the date, time, and place, as well as the purpose of the meeting. Remind them to bring along whatever data or material will be needed.

4. Have the room ready in advance with any necessary equipment. The leader may want a podium or table. If the room is large, have a turned-on microphone ready. Determine if he needs a stand for charts, screen, projector, or other visual-aid props. If a blackboard is requested make certain that chalk and a clean eraser are there too.

5. When outsiders are invited they should be given complete information about the name of the room, location, parking, and other such details.

6. If a luncheon or dinner is part of the program, schedule it for a definite time, and make menu plans to fit the group.

Essentials

Certain essentials should be provided on the day of the meeting so that it will get underway promptly and proceed properly.

1. Individual tablets and plenty of sharpened pencils should be handy.

2. A pitcher of fresh ice-cooled water, with one or more glasses, should be placed at the speaker's or leader's position Water and possibly paper cups should also be available for the members of the group.

3. A sufficient number of ash trays should be conveniently distributed.

4. The location of washrooms should be made known.

5. Cloak rooms or racks should be handy and indicated.

6. Arrival of any outsiders should be mentioned to the receptionist in order to have her ready to receive guests quickly and impressively.

7. An agenda of the meeting should be prepared for the leader and gone over with him.

8. Any and all supporting information, charts, and exhibits should be ready for him.

Chairman

To be effective, the chairman of the meeting, the officer who is presiding, should follow certain rules acceptable to the group. The chair should

1. Keep control of the meeting.

2. Try to maintain a good atmosphere.

3. Be firm, but fair, and stay "in charge."

4. Recognize members before they talk and then insist they stand and address the chair.

5. Give voice to both sides of a debate.

6. Restate the motion before the vote to make certain it is understood.

7. Call for the vote, giving everyone a chance to vote. Even when it appears the "ayes" have an overwhelming majority, he should still call for the "nay" votes.

8. Take a second vote, in case of doubt about the outcome, using a different method.

9. Respect member's wishes to abstain from voting and, upon their request, ask that this be noted in the minutes.

10. Announce the results of the vote.

11. Relinquish the chair when he wishes to speak on a motion or involve himself personally in a discussion.

12. Use good judgment in any conflict between the letter and the spirit of the law.

Agenda

The order of business should be prepared in advance of the meeting. It follows this fairly well standardized order of business:

1. Call to order by the presiding officer.

2. Roll call.

3. Reading of the minutes of the previous meeting.

4. Reports.
   a. Officers.
   b. Standing committees.
   c. Special committees.

5. Unfinished business.

6. New business.

7. Announcements.

8. Adjournment.

Minutes

When meetings are run orderly or businesslike, a record of the proceedings is usually kept. In a formal organization the elected or appointed secretary will do this. For an occasional office meeting, the chairman's secretary may take the minutes.

The secretary will take notes and make a documentary record of the meeting. The important action and decisions, not all the discussion, should be written into the report. The minutes should also include the name of the group, date, time, and place of the meeting, the presiding officer, attendance, the time of adjournment. Any papers or reports that are read become part of the minutes.

Verbatim notes are not necessary, except for special occasions such as stockholders' meetings of large corporations, or board meetings when there is dissension among the directors. In such cases stenotypists or court reporters are brought in.

Ordinarily no attempt should be made to put everything down in full. Verbatim record should be made of important statements, resolutions, or when someone asks that his views be made a part of the record. If in doubt, do not err on the side of brevity.

The minutes are a record of the meeting and a report of the proceedings. They are written for the minute book as the official record. Ordinarily there is only one copy made and it is ready to be read at the next meeting. Sometimes it might be advisable to distribute copies of the minutes of the last meeting to all who attended. This will give them a chance to agree with the report and especially their participation in it. At the next meeting it may then be possible to dispense with the reading of the minutes and merely accept them as submitted or with any necessary changes or corrections.

Parliamentary Procedure

In most cases it is enough to conduct meetings in a businesslike or orderly manner. When the occasion calls for a more formal method, the established rules of parliamentary procedure are applied. Parliamentary rules are as old as democratic legislative bodies. The rules followed by business or social organizations are usually adapted from these congressional and legislative rules. An authoritative source on parliamentary procedure is *Robert's Rules of Order*. Another, just as accurate but easier for laymen to understand is *The Primer of Parliamentary Procedure,* published by The Dartnell Corporation.

By following parliamentary procedure, or a satisfactory adaptation, it is easier to handle official matters in a businesslike manner and also maintain order during the meeting. But the real value lies in guaranteeing the will of the majority and in protecting the rights of the minorities.

Constitution

The purpose of the constitution is to identify the organization, explain its purpose, define the duties of the members, and set up the framework within which they operate. An organization drafts its own constitution which should be compatible with public policy and in conformity with any applicable laws.

A constitution consists of the fundamental provisions, written clearly and concisely. There are at least seven provisions which are usually expressed in separate articles. Each article, in turn, may be divided into sections.

Article I—The name of the organization.

II—The purpose and powers of the organization.

III—The qualifications of the members.

IV—The officers, their duties, and length of term of office.

V—The board of directors, or any governing board or executive committee—and the method of selecting its members.

VI—The time for regular meetings and provisions for special meetings.

VII—The method of amending the constitution and the vote required.

Drafting a constitution is the responsibility of a special committee appointed for this purpose.

Presenting the constitution is done by the committee chairman. He makes his report and moves that the constitution be adopted. He or the secretary then reads the constitution, each article and section separately to make certain the members understand thoroughly the details involved and have a chance to ask questions and discuss anything that may not be clear. Following this procedure the entire constitution is then voted on as originally submitted or as amended.

Adopting the constitution is done by the members. A majority vote is sufficient. The constitution becomes effective immediately upon this vote.

Amending the constitution may be necessary from time to time. There is a provision in the constitution itself which spells out: (1) the type of notice to be given members (usually one or two readings at meetings preceding the one at which the vote is taken), and (2) the vote necessary to adopt amendments.

Bylaws

The bylaws delineate the details necessary to carry out the provisions of the constitution. Those dealing with the same general subject are grouped under one article, which may be divided into sections.

Bylaws ordinarily cover the following:

1. Kinds of membership.

2. Membership qualifications.

3. Procedure for admitting new members.

4. Dues, method of payment, penalty for delinquents.

5. Powers and duties of officers.

6. Authority and responsibilities of committees.

7. Election of officers and the vote needed.

8. Appointment of standing and special committees.

9. Provision for calling and conducting meetings.

10. Parliamentary authority.

11. Number constituting a quorum.

12. Vote required for decisions.

13. Procedure for amending bylaws.

Standing Rules

In addition to the necessary constitution and bylaws, organizations often set up standing rules. These standing rules are ordinarily not as rigid as the bylaws since they cover details of lesser importance.

Commonly included in standing rules are items such as these—

1. Order of business.

2. Hour of meeting.

3. Fines for minor infractions.

4. Limitation on discussions.

5. Regulations concerning guests.

6. Special assessments.

7. Entertainment of guest speaker.

Standing rules are adopted by majority vote. No previous notice is necessary. Any part of these standing rules may be abolished this same way.

Introducing a Speaker

The chairman of the meeting, or the individual who arranged for the program, should introduce the guest speaker. This should be impressive, and it will be, if done properly. When the moment arrives—

1. Address the audience, not the speaker.

2. Be brief!

3. Don't overdo the build-up.

4. Explain, but do not apologize, if the speaker is a substitute.

5. Mention those details only which qualify him for the meeting.

6. Give one or two reasons why listeners would want to hear him.

7. Avoid telling personal stories which might embarrass him.

8. Don't crab his style; let him tell the jokes.

9. Always close your introduction by giving the speaker's name *correctly* and the subject of his talk.

10. Remain standing until the speaker has taken his place on the platform; then sit down in the background.

After-Speech Courtesies

After the talk, lead the applause for the speaker and thank him on behalf of the audience. If a question and answer period follows, let the speaker answer or clarify the questions. Avoid rehashing what the speaker said. If an honorarium or gift is given, present this to him privately.

Conclusion

Meetings are an effective means of communication, if run properly. They serve many useful purposes. They represent quite an investment in time, not only on the part of those who must plan and prepare for them, but also on the part of participants who are required to give up their own time for the meeting and possibly for travel. It doesn't take much to figure that the cost of a meeting can become sizable.

Consequently, it is important that meetings be run right. A poorly run meeting can do more harm than good. A good meeting, on the other hand, can bring untold benefits to everyone who is involved.

WHY MOST SPEECHES FAIL

Our country has been called a public speaker's paradise. People in all sorts of organizations seem to be eager to listen to someone delineate on a popular topic. Subjects range from peaceful applications of atomic energy to the life and love of zebras in Africa.

The reason for so many speeches is difficult to explain. Why do busy men and women sit passively with their hands in their laps while someone else expounds his knowledge? Perhaps some of them are trying to get a night out, husband and wife together, with little cost. Others may be escaping from the monotony of a card-playing routine. Many undoubtedly are seeking satisfaction by participating, or at least supporting, a worthwhile cause.

In our industrial society the occasions for some people to talk and for others to listen are certainly increasing. Associations and organizations of different types conduct regular or periodic business meetings or conventions which feature outside speakers. Ofttimes subjects are technical in nature and pertain to the objectives of the group. In other cases subjects are general and are justified on the theory that members should get away from their daily grind and broaden their intellectual outlook by exploring unfamiliar fields. In a few situations the subject matter makes little difference since the members of the group are merely enjoying a social night out with their companies quite willing to pick up the tab.

In all these situations, what are the audiences getting? Their attendance at the function implies that they want to be told what to do and how to do it. Yet advice from a speaker is usually futile. People in the audience accept those ideas of his which they agree with, and reject other ideas which run counter to their own personal prejudices.

As a result, a speaker tries to be careful not to offend his audience. In an effort to be amiable more than effective, he makes a mild attempt to entertain and then feeds the group, as eloquently as he can, a diet which may be nourishing but is as bland as pap. The members of the audience then applaud the speaker, politely and occasionally enthusiastically, and return to their homes and jobs doing precisely what they did before they heard the words of wisdom which they praised at the meeting.

This is the condition as it exists. Whether it is bad depends upon the views of each individual who is involved. Many people who attend meetings and conferences regularly may be quite content with the present pattern. Those, however, who seek improvement, must ask where the fault lies and where changes should begin.

Three Areas of a Speech

There are three component parts to each meeting, each of which contributes to the success or failure of the event. These are: (1) the audience, (2) the program planners, and (3) the speaker.

Not much needs to be said about the audience . . . except possibly that part which stays away, leaves early, or in other respects is not present at the time of the speech. Usually the audience has little to say about the choice of speaker or his topic. For the most part, the audience remains faithful because of respect, loyalty, or habit. This is certainly true when the speaker and his message fail to inspire. Still there are times when an audience does not do justice to a capable speaker, who has traveled far at great personal inconvenience, and who has labored long to prepare an adequate paper. Certainly he is entitled to a suitable listening group and it is indeed unfortunate when the audience is in a party mood, more concerned about libation than oration.

The audience is, of course, important. But more significant to the success or failure of a meeting or conference is the program planning. Generally the planning is done by a committee and in many cases, because of the pressure of time or the diversity of interests, the program is thrown together.

The things which, in addition to martinis, impress the program committee members are big names in big companies. They will always be attracted to the president of the corporation, if he can be inveigled to appear, in preference to some lesser light, despite the fact that Mr. Big has not established himself as a speaker. They hope to use the magic of a prominent name to swell the advance sale of registrations. The possibility of short-changing those who attend is secondary.

The usual practice for program committees is to hold regularly scheduled gatherings during which all sorts of names, titles, and topics are bandied about—with no tangible results. Then with time running short, the program is "put together" with whatever talent is available and fits the limited budget. When the haze of meaningless conversation is lifted, the bald facts reveal why one speaker was "selected" in preference to others:

1. He has let it be known that he is available.

2. He is willing to participate.

3. He can be obtained because somebody knows someone who will intervene.

4. He comes well recommended by a vague third party.

5. In the interests of good public relations, his company is interested in having him cooperate with groups.

6. Like a salesman, he likes to talk.

7. He is a good story teller.

8. He has a selfish motive in behalf of a particular service or product being promoted.

Whether he has a message of particular interest to the sponsoring group is of minor importance. Often a program chairman suggests to a speaker that he may choose his own topic. This is a dangerous practice because some speakers, having attained prominence on one limited subject, cannot resist becoming self-styled experts on other far-flung topics. Even when the program committee spells out the subject or subjects in accordance with some loosely defined overall theme, the speakers are not necessarily chosen because they are the recognized authorities on the assigned subject. By their availability and willingness they happen to make the committee's thankless job easy and they also coincidentally just manage to fit the budget.

The Touchy Matter of Fee

This matter of budgets causes many program planners to be short-sighted in the fulfillment of their responsibilities to the people they represent. They do not hesitate to charge a registration fee, or add a premium to the cost of the meal to cover "expenses" for the meeting. Yet they express amazement at a speaker's reasonable demand for a modest fee to compensate him, in part at least, for his services.

Chairmen are completely unashamed in their requests for a free speaker. They even feel that a speaker should be grateful for their invitation to let him ventilate his views. The same people who would not give away their products, or render their services free, expect a speaker to give his talents, preparation, travel, and time.

Although they sincerely believe they should not pay for a speech, nevertheless they want not a speech that is worthless, but they expect only the best. It may be that a speaker who works free is either a propagandist for a special interest, in which case he should be avoided, or he is not good enough to command even a modest fee, in which case he doesn't merit the collective time of his unsuspecting audience.

What the program chairman considers a privilege a speaker thinks of as a chore, albeit a pleasant one. Like others who work, he too should be compensated in proportion to the contribution he makes. When he is paid nothing the listeners should not be surprised if they get nothing.

Why Speakers Fail

When it comes to explaining why most speeches fail, most of the fault can be laid right at the doorstep of the speaker himself. Where planning is adequate and audiences receptive, many meetings fail to serve their intended purpose because the speaker or discussion leader does not measure up to expectations. The plain truth is that few people know how to make a good speech.

Good speaking requires far more than an ability to use words, such as is necessary for good writing. A speaker needs a good voice and a certain quality that actors have of projecting the personality into a live audience. Some excellent writers have poor voices and little dramatic flare. Similarly, a speaker is lost who cannot utilize his personality to put his thoughts across.

To be effective, a speaker *must*

- Be able to prepare his material.
- Be able to present it.
- Have something to say.

It is surprising how few men and women who ascend the platform know how to prepare their message. They use warmed-over ideas which proved successful last time and wonder why they did not meet with similar success the second time. This is because the conditions change but the speaker's preparation does not.

The message and manner of presentation must be tailored to each audience. The type of listening audience makes a difference. So does the time of day. The place on the agenda should be considered; an opening keynote address at a conference calls for a different approach from that of a late afternoon bread-and-butter technical session. A luncheon talk may be intended as a "change of pace" whereas an after-dinner speech may be either humorous or serious on a topic of widespread general interest.

Audience Often Sets Style

The makeup of the listening audience also determines the way a talk is prepared. The same material, such as advice on how to succeed in business, must be rearranged depending upon whether the message is directed to businessmen, secretaries, technicians, machine operators, bank women, scientists, students, or others.

The mechanics of "packaging" the material must be understood. Some speakers start too soon. The playwright postpones any crucial line of the dialogue until he establishes the projectory of the "arc of attention" between the voices on the stage and the ears beyond the footlights. A speaker, likewise, should not get into the "meat and potatoes" of his message while his audience is still tuning in.

The style of presentation depends upon the amount of time available. For the usual half-hour address a lecture-type of delivery may be recommended. When the time slot is an hour or more, no speaker should expect his audience to sit still for any straight lecture. He should vary his format by using gimmicks, such as flannel boards or blackboards, hand-out material, demonstrations, and exhibits. He might want to intersperse his lecture with questions from the floor. Where the group is small he may want to engage in a more intimate discussion-type presentation involving members of the group on a voluntary basis.

Upon the ability to organize his material to suit the type and size of his audience depends much of his chance for success. It is important to prejudge as accurately as possible what the people in the audience want. A speaker skilled in appealing to a group's feelings is like an organist playing upon the keys of human nature. If he inadvertently goes contrary to what people expect, his magnetism won't help much. The audience has to accept the speaker as a person before it will accept his message.

Therefore a speaker's ability to present his ideas is also vital. His platform manner should reflect sincerity for if the people cannot believe him they will not believe what he says. He must also display an air of authority but not superiority. He must be looked up to as someone worth hearing. A firm smooth voice denotes confidence and poise. But an apologetic beginning will negate any good that may follow.

He should be able to speak . . . effectively. Here practice and more practice is essential. Critical self-analysis before a mirror or in listening to a tape recording can be very useful. A wife or disinterested observer can tell whether a speaker mumbles, slurs his words, cuts off sentences, stumbles over words, or delivers in a monotone. An unpleasant voice irritates and distracts. A succession of "ahs" causes the listener to focus his attention upon the speaker's inadequacies. Starting every third sentence with "now" tells the audience how unprepared the speaker came. Reading a speech the way a professor reads a scientific paper is an imposition upon listeners who are supposed to be courteous enough to remain attentive. When the audience doesn't listen, it's the speaker's fault. When the audience falls asleep, it is time to wake the speaker.

The Power of a Pause

No humor may be bad, but the misuse of humor is worse. No speaker should pretend to be a comedian until he becomes one in which case he will forsake the podium for Sunday night television performances. A glib tongue and a fast line will tend to make a speaker appear fluent as he overburdens his listeners with his machine gun delivery. A good speaker, however, is one who has learned the drama of the emphatic pause. There are times, as we all know, when more can be said with silence than with any number of words.

While preparation and presentation are necessary, most important is that the speaker have something to say. Isn't it tragic how often a speaker sends his audience home empty-handed because he came empty-headed? A shallow message insults the intelligence of the audience.

The Importance of Something to Say

Some speakers rely upon their familiar name, or the reputation of their companies, to gain acceptance. A name may attract but only a message will impress. The chairman of the board who hopes to satisfy his audience by recalling the days gone by merely succeeds in making them wonder whether his personal success is due to his uncanny memory or his family's inherited wealth. The company president who refers vaguely to "the challenge before us" without ever identifying it or offering any solution, only encourages people to stay away from the meeting next month no matter how attractively the program chairman bills it.

To hold the audience in the palm of his hand, a speaker needs more than an impressive title, personal charm, or a big build-up by the master of ceremonies. He has to have something to say. He has to believe in something which he wants to share. This motivation may, or may not, be related to his regular job. His enthusiasm for it must be genuine, however. Only when he is fired up on something will he take enough interest to research the subject, enough time out of a busy schedule to develop his material, and enough spirit to present it convincingly. Actually, the only speaker worth listening to is the one who is crusading.

It is a tremendous responsibility that a speaker accepts when he agrees to participate in a meeting. Multiplying the number of people in attendance by the amount of time and money each one has expended, the obligation at once comes into proper perspective. The speaker who does not prepare his material, who has not learned how to present it, and who has no message worth listening to in the first place, must expect to be pointed out as the reason "Why Most Speeches Fail."

This can be summarized in the following story. A man accepted the invitation of a friend and his family who were driving his way. First they stopped at a nearby service station to pick up the spare tire which had been left for repair.

HOW TO MAKE A GOOD SPEECH

1. Acknowledge your introduction graciously. Recognize the chairman and other dignitaries at the head table. Greet your audience.

2. Start off smoothly. Never begin apologetically. Try not to be clever lest you be corny. Don't try to "hook" your listeners before they are ready. Take a few sentences to warm up the speaker and the audience.

3. Don't "read" your speech as you follow the script. Be familiar enough with the contents of your paper so you can maintain occasional eye contact with different individuals.

4. Don't memorize your speech. This makes it sound canned and unreal. Rather select some persons in the audience and talk with them as individuals on a personal basis.

5. But don't talk "off the cuff" and expect to get any well-balanced presentation. At least use well-organized notes to avoid rambling and unnecessary wordage.

6. Use illustrations to make a point. It helps if these examples are funny or catchy, but don't tell jokes which are not pertinent to the topic.

7. A degree of nervousness, even for the "pro," can endear a speaker. The listeners respect a speaker who has obviously worked on his material and his presentation over one who appears cocky and lords it over them.

8. It doesn't hurt to jolt the audience occasionally. The speaker is working; the listener is sitting passively and may let his mind wander. Bring him back with a question, anecdote, quotation, poem, or similar device.

9. Stay within the prescribed time limit and quit when you're through. A summarization of what you've discussed may be in order. A fast wind-up can be very effective.

10. Finally, don't follow any standard pattern, such as may be implied in the well-intentioned suggestions offered above. Accept them for what they are, nothing more than suggestions, and adapt them to your own personality, to the situation, and to the audience. Like any formula for success, the rules for making a good speech must be individualized not only for the speaker but also for the occasion.

The guest, trying to make conversation, asked the driver if he knew how much the tire weighed empty. He answered, "fourteen pounds." Then the guest asked, "How much air did the service station put in?" And he was told, "Thirty pounds." So he asked again, "And how much did the tire weigh then?"

The driver said, "As long as our daughter is going to high school and learning such things, let's see what she answers." And immediately she said, "Forty-four pounds." The father commented, "See, their learning today doesn't teach them properly. She hasn't learned the difference between air pressure and air weight." And then the mother interposed, "I don't see what's wrong. If it weighed fourteen pounds empty and had thirty pounds added, why wouldn't it weigh forty-four pounds?"

The guest felt that the father should not make sport of his wife's and his daughter's error. "It's a common fallacy," he explained, "and I don't think they should be criticized."

Then he added, "The same thing is true with speeches. When a speaker tries to fill a specified time period, say a half hour, he often inflates his speech. Like the motorist, he too should realize that there is no weight to wind."

Yes, only when the audience is interested in listening, when the program planners are thorough in their selection, and the featured speaker prepares well, delivers well, and has something solid to say, will speeches no longer fail.

HOW TO HANDLE CHANGE

There is a widespread notion that people resist change. This is not entirely true. Otherwise why do car buyers prefer newer models, why do women's fashions differ from year to year, why are people willing to take unfamiliar jobs in completely new and strange surroundings?

When it comes to daily work procedures, however, people tend to resist change. This is especially true when the new method is rather drastic. Put a long-standing manual operation on the computer, for example, and a good share of the planning is concerned with presenting this conversion to the employees and getting their acceptance.

For some reason workers dislike having a regular routine, one which they have learned and mastered, disturbed. Yet in the name of progress, improvements in equipment and systems must be made. This means upsetting existing methods in favor of better ones. This would appear to be advantageous from a company point of view, but to the individual it means only adjusting his way of doing his job. Since he sees no direct personal gain, he cannot be expected to embrace the idea with the same enthusiasm as the company which stands to profit.

No change, big or small, should be attempted unless and until the employee understands fully why it is necessary and how he fits into the picture. After all, the full cooperation of every involved worker is necessary for the accomplishment of its purpose.

When something big is being considered, such as the introduction of a computer system, the relocation of the plant, or the merger with another firm, a complete communications program should be included in the overall scheme. Employees should be informed about the plans as soon as these can be announced, the program which is finally designed, and progress as the changeover is implemented.

Most modifications of office procedures or factory operations are not this dramatic. Usually they involve only a small part of the total organization, often occur in only one department, possibly are as small as one step in a worker's day. Nonetheless, these innovations are also important—to the company which would otherwise not make them, and to the workers who must adapt their ways to the new method. Therefore, no adjustments should be undertaken without careful thought, not only related to company cost-saving or productivity, but also to the consequences should the workers inadvertently resist. After all, the company can authorize the "go ahead" but it is the workers upon whom the ultimate success depends.

Checklist for Change

When changes are to be made, a manager or foreman should

1. Study his group in order to understand how it operates and what feelings and ways of life make up its attitude; then

2. Introduce change in such a way as to cause the least upset and the shortest period of readjustment.

Thus, he will be able to influence and direct the thinking of the group so that it is in harmony with the objectives of the company.

The work climate has a direct bearing, too. Where the climate is uncooperative, upsetting an established procedure may trigger a whole new set of employee problems. Where employees and supervision work together in a climate of mutual respect and trust, a change is easier to make and could, in fact, be welcomed.

From a manager's or foreman's point of view, good human relations exist when workers are

- Voluntarily giving a little extra to their jobs.

- Getting along with him and with each other.

- Working not only for him but also with him.

The extent to which workers do these three things depends upon the degree to which they are getting satisfaction out of their jobs. It is the company's responsibility to blend the "satisfaction of wants" of the individual with the wants of the company.

These are the sort of satisfactions which people want from their jobs.

1. Job security: What is expected and how they stand.

2. Freedom from arbitrary action: No favoritism or discrimination.

3. Opportunity to advance: New challenges as they grow.

4. A meaningful task: Its purpose and prestige.

5. Congenial associates: Best part of day, week, and life is spent at work: it should be pleasant.

6. Satisfactory working conditions: Comfortable and convenient.

7. Fair wages: Fair in community and fairly administered.

8. Adequate benefits: Protection against the unexpected.

9. Recognition as an individual: Not a number or robot.

10. A voice in matters affecting him: No feeling of being pushed around.

11. Competent leadership: Bosses whom they can admire and respect as persons, not as bosses.

It is the last three factors of personal satisfaction that should be taken into consideration when changes are contemplated and introduced. If the worker can see value to himself in the company change he is more likely to understand, accept, and apply it. In the final analysis, this is the only way to look upon change, for whom are companies trying to benefit with technological improvements except people?

THE INDIVIDUALITY OF PEOPLE

We've become so accustomed to using mass techniques in education, advertising, manufacturing, marketing, and even in bargaining agreements—that we also apply them to individuals. But these techniques do not always work in the same way because no two people are alike.

Let me explain it this way: Take a piece of wax, some meat, some sand, some clay, some wood shavings, and throw them all into a fire. One immediately melts, one starts frying, one dries up, one hardens, one blazes. They are all acted upon by the same force but they all react differently. Just so, under identical influences of circumstances and environment, one person becomes weaker, one becomes stronger, and one withers away.

Different people have different aspirations and different fears. They require different considerations.

Four centuries ago Charles V was emperor of the German empire, which then included most of Europe. Like other monarchs, he found the job of ruling people a troublous occupation. In his old age he retired to a monastery to rest his frazzled nerves. There he amused himself by tinkering with clocks. He had a house full of them. His pet ambition was to regulate them so that they would all strike at precisely the same time. But despite his most persistent painstaking efforts, he could not make them do it. Finally, he gave up. One day he philosophized: "I was a fool, trying to make my subjects think alike on everything. I cannot even make these helpless clocks strike alike."

Only as we are different do we become noticed in a world of conformity. The Tower of Pisa is just another landmark but it is distinguished because of a different slant.

In our social structure there is value to uniqueness. Imagine what a world we'd have if all people were alike. Differences are physical, mental, and emotional. In our business structure it is better to build upon individuality than to try to impose sameness upon people who do not all respond in the same way to the same kind of treatment.

The problems in human relations, brought about by technological improvements, may be said to be the price of bigness in business. Mass production methods, work simplification techniques, and other developments of the machine age have been big gains. But every gain has its price. The curse of bigness, which afflicts every level of our society, not only dehumanizes us in our personal contacts, but also corrupts our sense of values.

Progress along scientific lines is to be encouraged but no such advance should be made unless at the same time it improves the human consideration. After all, whom else are we trying to benefit by these technological changes except people?

INDIVIDUALITY vs. CONFORMITY

There is both individuality and conformity in our makeup. On the one hand we have a tremendous compulsion to conform, and on the other hand we insist on expressing our individuality.

Driving my daughter and her girl friend home from high school, I commented about their habit of carrying textbooks and note paper in their open arms, something they did every day even in the rain. I offered them a choice of handsome, convenient briefcases. I was almost laughed right out of the car for being so antediluvian. All the kids did this and anyone who was sensible enough to use a handy carrying case was simply a "square."

The big thing was to conform, not be the oddball, not to defy the youthful tradition. Yet, in a period of a few short years these girls would have to go through a complete change of attitude and be willing, even eager, to assert their individuality. Would an employer select a new worker at random, eenie-meenie-minee-mo fashion, or would he want one who stood out from the group because of noticeable personal qualities? And how will a girl ever be that "one in a million" for somebody's wife if she insists on going through life as anonymous as "Brand X"?

When Henry Ford introduced his "flivver" he standardized on the model, style, color, and power in order to provide a mass-produced automobile which the average wage earner could afford to buy. Every car was a black one-seater with one door on the right side (the side by the driver did not open). This mode of individual or family transportation, new to the nation and within reach of thousands, was very much appreciated, of course. But just as soon as this new car became commonplace, the individuality of man began to express itself. People wanted the car but now they wanted it to be different from that of their neighbors. This individuality has gone so far that today, if a Ford dealer were to display every different model, size, color, and combination available from the manufacturer, he'd need a showroom large enough to accommodate over a million cars.

Some Unrealistic Formulas

In personnel administration we tend to develop programs and policies for the *masses* and not the *classes*. We think we're being fair by treating all employees alike. In one sense this works; giving them all annual vacations is acceptable. But expecting all employees to go at the same time, or to the same place, or for the same purpose, is unrealistic.

Our regular working hours fit some people better than others. Some of us are early risers and do our best work in the mornings; others don't even think clearly until later in the day. Creative and scientific people are often oblivious to time and do not understand the regimen of fixed hours; they work by the challenge and not by the clock. That is the reason many companies place their research and technical laboratories in out-of-the-way locations so that the idiosyncrasies of these specialized personnel do not come into conflict with the mundane nine-to-five routine of rank-and-file workers.

There are similarities in people and there are differences. All people get hungry, but we don't all like the same food. Millions of people feel the need to worship, but they do not have the same beliefs. Not everyone depends on television for his entertainment; some participate in sports, recreation, movies, nightclubs, reading, card-playing, and the like. The need for diversion is common but hobbies range all the way from gardening to chess.

Many young people go to college but their academic programs vary, they major in different subjects. Workers have a common need for training but their ability to learn is not the same.

We Accept Animal Differences

But this differentiality is also true elsewhere in nature. No two animals are alike. Think what would happen if we tried to handle all animals the same way. If we tried to teach every animal to swim, climb, run, and fly. In the name of democracy and equality, all animals would be developed in the same skills. On that basis, ducks would be forced to waddle instead of swim, pelicans would flap their short wings in an attempt to fly, eagles would be required to run, and so forth. Some abnormal creature which could do all these things would become class valedictorian.

This is what psychologists call the "fetish of symmetrical development." It seemed easy enough to understand when we applied it to animals just now, didn't it? Why is it so hard to comprehend when we apply it to people? But this gets even more involved. Let's take a simple example.

There's a lot more to color than meets the eye. A given color does not look the same to everybody. We are not speaking of people who are color blind, but of average persons. Each sees a color a bit differently—some very differently. This may explain why a certain color combination may seem attractive to you but not to your wife. You may be seeing different colors.

This same illustration can be made with food which is not the same to all people. During World War II the American GI was sent into battle with rations which were nutritionally ideal in proteins, carbohydrates, fats, vitamins, and minerals. They were packaged to meet all climatic conditions. They exceeded all standards of quality control.

But something was missing. Cans of discarded foods filled the gutters along the road to the front line. They piled up in storage dumps. A reappraisal of the facts developed what was wrong, or what was overlooked in the planning. The missing factor centered about taste. The food, so carefully planned, was designed around the similarities of soldiers; but taste is an individual matter.

Few Monuments to Groups

In the military, in government, in business, in life—people are trying to maintain their individuality against growing odds. Society is being collectivized into faceless mass and the big word is "conformity." And we wonder why so many of our industrial and political programs are in trouble.

Excepting identical twins, everybody is biologically, genetically different from everybody else. Diversity should not, however, be confused with inequality. Equality and inequality are sociological; identity and diversity are biological phenomena. Diversity is an observable fact; equality an ethical precept. Society may grant or withhold equality from its members; it could not make them genetically alike even if this were desirable.

In designing our programs it is not enough to understand the desire to conform brought on by the need for acceptance. Building on similarities is fine for groups, but the separate and varied aims and aspirations of the individuals within groups must also be taken into account. It is worth remembering that there are few monuments in parks to groups.

THE ILLUSION OF SECURITY vs.
MAINTENANCE OF OPPORTUNITY

It is not the purpose of personnel administrators to make men happy. Men must make themselves happy in their own way, and at their own risk. The functions of personnel management lie entirely in the conditions or provinces under which the pursuit of happiness is carried on.

Management insight into the basic human needs is the discovery that work is not only an economic but also a psychological necessity. Freud called work man's strongest tie to reality. It is our most effective way of relating ourselves to the world, finding out what we can do and where we belong—of being somebody and meaning something to others and to ourselves.

It is amazing how few personnel executives realize this. Consequently, they build employee relations programs on the wrong foundation, then wonder why they are not effective.

One of the weaknesses of personnel administration is that over the years it has acceded to social demands and has permitted itself to gravitate in the direction of least opposition. It has followed and not led.

In expanding personnel services most of the thought has been given to security measures—paralleling the similar trend in government. Perhaps this is good and possibly it is necessary, on the theory that building for security brings to the individual a steadiness of purpose. But that path in business tends to dull individual enterprise, something which business sorely needs.

Incentive Is the Challenge

Only lately are we coming around to understand that, more important than planning for security, is the need to stimulate personal incentive. Someone once wrote, "A ship in harbor is safe, but that is not what ships are built for." That same truism applies to personnel programs.

After all, there is really no such thing as security—as industry tries to guarantee it. A change in ownership, transfer of location, revised procedures or manufacturing processes, an individual's health, all affect security. But there is no curb on individual initiative.

Man's search for progress should be encouraged by the maintenance of opportunity, not hindered by illusions of security.

The only real security lies in permitting workers to grow, not in inserting clauses in policies or restrictions in procedures which serve only to hamper the free growth of people and companies.

THE VITAL ART OF DELEGATION

A most important consideration in the efficiency of an executive is in knowing how to delegate. He should not try to lead the band and play all the instruments.

We have seen them . . . managers and supervisors who have no time for the concern of others. With others idle, they are hard at work at nights in empty offices. And we have heard them, too, complaining—

> "This job is killing me."
>
> "Route everything through me."
>
> "I don't dare take a day off."
>
> "Check with me before you proceed."

Their trouble lies in failure to appreciate that responsibility in a management position is far greater than the personal capacity to carry out all the details. No one expects the chief accountant to post all the ledger accounts. Certainly no one expects the president to personally service all the customers.

Dispersing authority and responsibility throughout an organization is achieved through delegation. According to the academicians, to delegate is to grant or confer authority and responsibility in equal measure from one executive or organizational unit to another in order to accomplish necessary assignments. By means of delegation one person extends his area of operations, for without delegation his actions are confined to what he, himself, can perform.

From a practical business standpoint, delegation may be defined as unburdening the boss for more profitable tasks. It also offers a basis for sounder and more acceptable decisions, development of subordinates, and all-around better management.

The more delegation, assuming it is done effectively, the more time an executive has to fulfill his top managerial responsibilities. If his abilities, ambitions, or authority keep him close to direct supervision of people or functions, his value to the company diminishes and his personal earnings potential becomes correspondingly less.

Customarily, delegation is considered as being from a higher to a lower level. However, delegation is also from a lower to a higher level, or between levels on the same plane. In other words, delegation can be downward, upward, or sideways.

As examples, downward delegation of authority and responsibility is illustrated by a company president to one of his department managers, or from a doctor to a nurse; upward delegation by stockholders to their board of directors, or by workers to their employer as in the case of group life insurance purchases; sideways delegation by members of a professional or trade association to their committee chairman, as in the case of a conference in which they authorize fellow members to arrange and conduct a meeting in which they then willingly participate.

Delegator Remains Accountable

Actually neither authority nor responsibility can be delegated in the true sense. Authority can be shared and responsibility assigned. Delegation does not imply the permanent release from these obligations but rather the granting of rights and approval for others to operate within a prescribed framework. The delegator always remains accountable for what is or is not accomplished.

There are two types of delegation—general and specific. In both cases, vital to successful delegation are: (1) spelling out the instructions clearly, (2) fixing standards, (3) establishing limits, and (4) keeping control.

General delegation of authority and responsibility is made possible by the establishment of company policies. These statements of acceptable company practices are devices to guide the manager in knowing what is expected of him and within what limits he may make decisions on general matters.

In the assignment of *specific* duties, or one-time jobs, delegation of sufficient authority and full responsibility should accompany the instructions. Some suggestions for specific assignments include:

1. Assign job to the person best suited to it.

2. Don't always use the same person, the handiest one.

3. Make clear the instructions, requirements, and authority.

4. Don't make unreasonable demands.

5. Check up periodically.

6. Set a completion date and follow through on the project.

7. Keep the control.

The occasional job, which does not logically fall to any one employee, but which must be assigned specifically, provides an excellent opportunity to:

- Uncover latent abilities.

- Test the problem employee.

- Train a worker in something unfamiliar.

- Discover leaders.

- Demonstrate confidence in workers.

Once a job is assigned, the manager should not change the signals but let the project run its course as planned. In his eagerness to get things done, he might have formed the habit, when asked a question by the person to whom he has assigned the job, of stepping in and personally doing the work because that is easier than explaining it again. In such case he'll soon find himself doing all the work while his people are standing by, willing to let him do it. And who will end up with the nervous breakdown?

The Point of Action

Although in many cases simple delegation may be all that is required, in practice both general and specific delegation usually involve more than two persons. The chief executive, with unlimited authority and full responsibility, extends these through his senior staff, down the line of command, into the work force. It is recommended that some measure of authority and responsibility be placed as close to the point of action as possible. This creates what is known as the "tapering concept" of delegation. In going downward the amount of authority and responsibility becomes smaller with each successive level.

Now the question naturally comes up, "What can or should the executive delegate and what must he be expected to do himself?" Speaking generally, here are some of his duties divided into three broad categories:

Jobs the executive himself must do:
1. Assuming initiative and responsibility.
2. Planning the work.
3. Scheduling jobs.
4. Building the work force.
5. Establishing and maintaining good morale.
6. Helping employees grow.
7. Communicating at all levels.
8. Settling disputes.
9. Handling grievances.
10. Cooperating with other executives.

Jobs the executive might delegate part of:
1. Interviewing applicants.
2. Inducting, orienting, and training workers.
3. Maintaining attendance and reducing tardiness.
4. Controlling production.
5. Improving methods.
6. Reducing costs.
7. Handling paperwork.
8. Preventing accidents.
9. Keeping equipment in repair.
10. Purchasing equipment, supplies, services.

Jobs normally delegated to others:
1. Opening the mail.
2. Answering telephone calls.
3. Providing proper reception of visitors and guests.
4. Running errands.
5. Making hotel and travel reservations.
6. Filing records.
7. Requisitioning supplies.
8. Caring for equipment.
9. Keeping the premises clean and in order.
10. Insuring company and employees against the unexpected.

It is easy to delegate responsibility. It is harder to delegate authority. There is still another aspect of delegation which is equally important but far more difficult. This is the delegation of decision-making. Some executives find this impossible to do. The executive who operates as a one-man show can't see the wisdom of bringing others into the act.

The industrial autocrat, the professional dictator, the strong individualist is, oftentimes, quite effective. When right he puts on quite a show of rapid-fire decision-making. This may be very impressive for it does save a good deal of time for everybody.

Odds Against Autocrats

But what is the percentage for a man being right all the time? People who have studied this say that "it is rare indeed for more than 25 percent of a man's decisions to be right." You may make your own estimate if you don't like this one. But I doubt that any of us would be foolish enough to claim that such a positive personality is 100 percent right all the time.

What happens when his decision is wrong? It is just as forceful and just as final as the right one. But others who are affected by it have little recourse. Chances are they know it is wrong and, when it is crammed down their throats, they give it only lip service. That might actually be the better of the two choices. The other is to fall in line with authority, be resigned to the ill-fated decision, go along with it, and do things wrong.

Beware of the man who says, "I'll do the thinking around here," as though he had a corner on brains. The executive who consults with others gets the benefit of anything they might contribute to a sounder decision, plus the advantage of having pretested his idea on them before it becomes final. It is better, if an adverse reaction is coming, to be tipped off early enough to make a correction or an adjustment. But even more important, if some of the decision-making can be decentralized, chances are the on-the-spot decisions will better fit the problems and be more understandable to the individuals who are affected.

Perhaps the best reason for delegating authority, responsibility, and decision-making is that the executive who keeps his hand in the details of every job discourages the ingenuity of subordinates by competing with them. His responsibility to share with others, thereby helping to build them, is paramount; his reluctance to do so will cause him to inadvertently develop a group of inadequately trained or inexperienced workers, so that in the end he will have to do all the work whether he wants to or not.

The problem of delegation is a problem of personality. No one else can do it as well, the owner or manager thinks . . . and he could be right. Nevertheless, because of time and pressure he should concern himself with the major factors of planning, directing, and controlling, and let others do much of the work, even that of making some of the decisions. A good rule to follow is this: Every task should be done by the lowest paid employee who is capable of handling it; anything else is a waste of company money and talent.

In many instances it is difficult, often impossible, for an executive to comprehend just where he fits into the management picture insofar as delegation of company authority and responsibility are concerned. On the one hand he is encouraged to deserve and thereby acquire more authority, and to broaden his scope of responsibility; then when he has worked himself into a position of prominence and prestige he is asked to share his well-earned gains with subordinates. Yet this *must be done* in an enlightened industrial society because in building people we are building an organization.

More and more we're relying less and less upon the executive who depends solely upon his own judgment for decisions and his own accomplishments for results. We're moving away from the one-man type of operation to a more democratic form. It follows, therefore, that the more effective an executive, the more his own identity and personality blend into the background of his organization.

Take any well-known department store, manufacturing plant, service organization, or office which enjoys an enviable position in the community. Most likely the individual who built the well-deserved reputation has long been forgotten. His influence is present; his identity is not.

It would be my hope that if I were privileged to visit your company, I should find not a number of good executives but rather a good program—to which all people in the company contribute and from which all benefit. The more we can conscientiously and confidently delegate some of our authority, responsibility, and decision-making to others, the closer we come to realizing this noble ambition.

PART 5

HEALTH AND SAFETY

PREEMPLOYMENT PHYSICAL EXAMINATIONS

One of the many aids used in the selection of employees is the pre-employment physical examination. Where a company is large enough to operate a full-scale clinic, a staff physician may give the examination. In smaller firms a local physician may come in one day a week or applicants may be sent to his office. In all these cases, the interviewer gets additional help in arriving at an appropriate decision.

The medical information provided in confidence to the doctor or nurse, and the results of the tests and examination, are retained in medical files. Details are never divulged to others. Only the medical recommendation is offered, as the doctor classifies each applicant for certain types of work.

A. In good health with no apparent health problem of any kind; fully employable.

B. In good health but with some correctable deficiency (bad teeth, less than 20/20 vision, overweight) which, if given proper attention, makes the applicant employable.

C. In good health but with some definite restriction (no lifting, or very little standing, etc.) which, with the supervisor's understanding, makes the applicant employable but not for all jobs.

D. Not employable, a poor health risk. The decision of who is placed into this category must rest with the physician. The supervisor should never ignore this advice and hire the applicant anyway.

The classification, but not the medical details, should remain in the employee's file so that it will be taken into account when the employee is being considered for a transfer or promotion to a different line of work.

In view of the success companies have experienced in hiring the handicapped, the tendency is to disqualify few applicants. Of greater concern is their proper placement in jobs for which they are suited. After all, very few people are in perfect health all their working lives. Yet almost everybody with a marketable skill is employable if properly placed.

PHYSICAL EXAMINATION RECORD
(Drivers)

Name_____ No._____ M_____ F_____ Height_____ Weight_____

Medical History_____

Surgical History_____

When was a physician last consulted?_____ For what?_____

Ever suffered any injuries?_____ When?_____ Extent_____

Ever have any "fits" or convulsions?_____ Tuberculosis?_____

Eyes: Vision Rt 20/_____ Lt 20 _____ Both_____ Near Rt J/_____ Lt J/_____

Accommodation Lt_____ Distance_____ Binocularity_____

External right eye_____ External left eye_____

Use of glasses_____ Corrected vision Rt 20/_____ Lt 20/_____ Near Rt J/_____ Lt J/_____

Color perception: normal_____; deficient in red_____green_____blue_____yellow_____

Ears: Internal_____ External_____ Hearing: Rt_____ Left_____

Nose_____ Throat_____ Mouth and Gums_____

Teeth Condition_____ Care_____

Neck_____ Goiter_____

Lungs_____

Heart_____

Blood Pressure_____ Pulse Rate_____

Abdomen_____ Scars_____ Hernia_____

Location of_____ Duration_____ Genitalia_____ Ing.-Adenopathy_____

Urinalysis: Color_____ S.G._____ Alb_____ Sugar_____

Sacroiliac_____

Joints: (Describe abnormalities, congenital or acquired)_____

Varicose Veins_____ Flat Feet_____ Deformities_____

Passed_____Rejected_____Reason for Rejection_____

Comments_____

Date_____ Medical Examiner_____

Published by The Dartnell Corporation
4660 Ravenswood Ave., Chicago, Ill. 60640 U.S.A.

Physical examination records make up a vital part of personnel department records. Like other such forms, they should be confidential.

515

The following is taken from the Kimberly-Clark Corporation handbook for general offices salaried employees:

Both you and Kimberly-Clark stand to gain by a check of your physical condition upon reporting for work. The purposes of such an examination are:

1. To determine your physical qualifications for satisfactory performance of the type of work proposed for you.

2. To protect you and your fellow workers by preventing the transfer of communicable diseases.

3. To detect any signs of major or minor conditions of ill health so that we can advise you what steps to take to correct them before they become more serious.

4. To permit a careful comparison of your physical condition at time of employment with your condition as revealed by future examinations. Complete, confidential records are kept in the Health Services office for this purpose.

PERIODIC PHYSICAL EXAMINATIONS

In addition to preemployment physicals, many companies give periodic physical examinations to employees. The practice is more common with executives and managers but by no means limited to this group.

Top-level personnel may be given annual checkups. This is often done on the outside even if an employee clinic is operated. These people are sent to hospitals, sometimes overnight, or to recognized internal medicine specialists. Some corporations have been known to send their senior executives to such places as the Mayo Clinic.

Where a complete employee clinic is operated by the company, these checkups may be done on the premises, especially for middle-and-lesser-management personnel. Some of the work may be done elsewhere, depending upon what is required, and some tests may be sent to laboratories.

As for rank-and-file employees, not as many firms give periodic physical exams and certainly not as frequently. These checkups may be offered, for example, once every three years. Much depends upon the size of the work force, the facilities of the company, and, of course, the attitude toward this type of health program.

A company which offers and pays for such checkups does so on

(Continued on page 521)

PHYSICAL RECORD

COMPLETED
PLICANT OR EMPLOYEE

_____ Soc. Sec. No. _____

_____ City _____

_____ Birth: Date _____   Marital Status: ☐ Single   ☐ Married

] M   ☐ F   ☐ Widowed   ☐ Divorced   ☐ Separated   Children: _____

HISTORY   Check if anyone in your family has or has had:

1. ☐ Tuberculosis   3. ☐ Epilepsy   5. ☐ Diabetes

2. ☐ Nervous or mental condition   4. ☐ Cancer   6. ☐ Heart trouble

---

ATIONAL HISTORY   (Explain further under Remarks if necessary)

particular hazards in previous occupations? _____

compensated for occupational injury or disease? Describe disability, cause, duration, etc. _____

_____

drawing disability benefits from Government or insurance company? If yes, explain _____

_____

ary Service: From _____ To _____   Type of Discharge _____   If rejected, why? _____

_____

HISTORY   Check if you have or have had: (Explain under Remarks)

11. ☐ Diabetes	24. ☐ Rheumatic fever	37. ☐ Ulcer
12. ☐ Tuberculosis	25. ☐ Hay fever	38. ☐ Frequent colds
13. ☐ Epilepsy	26. ☐ Cancer	39. ☐ High blood pressure
14. ☐ Heart trouble	27. ☐ Goiter	40. ☐ Dizziness
15. ☐ Venereal disease	28. ☐ Hemorrhoids	41. ☐ Paralysis
16. ☐ Rheumatism	29. ☐ Kidney trouble	42. ☐ Scarlet fever
17. ☐ Dermatitis	30. ☐ Chronic cough	43. ☐ Tumor
18. ☐ Asthma	31. ☐ Shortness of breath	44. ☐ Bleeding
19. ☐ Hernia	32. ☐ Stomach trouble	45. ☐ Discharges
20. ☐ Nervous breakdown	33. ☐ Backaches—strain	46. ☐ Other (indicate)
21. ☐ Arthritis	34. ☐ Fainting spells	
22. ☐ Pleurisy	35. ☐ Frequent headaches	
23. ☐ Pneumonia	36. ☐ Blood spitting	

X-701

Beginning here is the first page of a four-page folder which provides a complete physical and medical history of employee for personnel files.

517

IF WOMAN: (Explain further under Remarks if necessary)

47. Periods regular?_____Lose time because of monthly cramps?_____

48. Have children?_____How many?_____Pregnant now?_____

49. Pregnancies and confinements free from accidents?_____

50. Any breast or female disorders?_____

SPECIAL HISTORY   (Explain the following in Remarks when necessary)

51. What injuries have you had?_____

52. What operations have you had?_____

53. What accidents have you had?_____

54. Ever in hospital, sanitarium, or institution?_____

55. Taking medicine regularly? Explain_____

56. Ever addicted to drugs or alcohol? Explain_____

57. Smoking habits_____

58. Days off from work because of illness in last 12 months_____

59. What do you consider to be the state of your health?_____

REMARKS   (If referring to specific item, please indicate by number)

(Use additional sheet if necessary)

I certify that the above statements are true and correctly recorded.

Date_____19_____   _____   _____

                                                                        Signature of Applicant or Employee

This second page provides a special space for women employees, plus additional questions concerning all employees (they sign this page).

PHYSICAL EXAMINATION

COMPLETED
YSICIAN:

(Explain under Findings when necessary)

ght_____ft_____in.   Present Weight_____   Usual Weight_____

perature_____   Pulse_____   Blood Pressure_____

eral appearance: Good_____Fair_____Poor_____

elopment: Good_____Fair_____Poor_____

on: Uncorrected: R 20/   L 20/   Near: R   L
        Corrected: R 20/   L 20/   Near: R   L

Color vision_____   Other data:_____

Pupils_____   _____

Eyegrounds_____   _____

ing: R_____   L_____   Hearing aid?_____

(Explain any abnormalities under Findings)

☐ Nor ☐ Abn	78. Abdomen (scars, tenderness, liver edge, etc.) ☐ Nor ☐ Abn	88. Venereal Disease ☐ No ☐ Yes
☐ Nor ☐ Abn	Girth_____inches	89. Reflexes: Patellar ☐ Nor ☐ Abn
☐ Nor ☐ Abn		Romberg ☐ Nor ☐ Abn
t ☐ Nor ☐ Abn	79. Hernia ☐ No ☐ Yes	90. Other:
s ☐ Nor ☐ Abn	80. Inguinal rings ☐ Nor ☐ Abn	
☐ Nor ☐ Abn	81. Genitalia ☐ Nor ☐ Abn	
☐ Nor ☐ Abn	82. Prostate ☐ Nor ☐ Abn	
Glands ☐ Nor ☐ Abn	83. Spine ☐ Nor ☐ Abn	
Thyroid ☐ Nor ☐ Abn	84. Rectum ☐ Nor ☐ Abn	91. Vaccination history:
s ☐ Nor ☐ Abn	85. Extremities (deformities, limitations of motion, etc.)	
Inspiration_____inches	Upper ☐ Nor ☐ Abn	
Expiration_____inches	Lower ☐ Nor ☐ Abn	
☐ Nor ☐ Abn	86. Varicosities ☐ Nor ☐ Abn	
☐ Nor ☐ Abn	87. Lymph nodes ☐ Nor ☐ Abn	

Third page of the four-page folder is for the physician conducting the medical examination. Comparison with employee's version is easy.

LABORATORY DATA

92. Urine: Specific Gravity_____ Albumin_____ Sugar_____

       Color_____ Reaction_____ Microscopic_____

93. Blood_____

94. X-Ray Chest_____

95. Other_____

_____

_____

OTHER FINDINGS AND REMARKS   (If referring to specific item, indicate by number)

(Use additional sheet if necessary)

I have examined_____and would rate

    A. ☐ Physically fit for any job.

    B. ☐ Having remediable defects, which temporarily limit employment to certain types of work.

    C. ☐ Having static defects, which permanently limit employment to certain types of work.

    D. ☐ So handicapped as to be hazard to self and/or others.

In regard to physical fitness for the position of_____

I would classify him/her as ☐ employable, or ☐ not employable.

Date_____ 19_____   Address_____

Final page of report contains space for recording laboratory data, plus generous space for remarks by physician who will sign the record.

(Continued from page 516)

a voluntary basis. No employee, regardless of his job level, is required to participate. Few workers, as a rule, pass up the opportunity to avail themselves of this optional employee benefit.

One exception might be the compulsory periodic checkup in connection with a safety program. Employees in hazardous occupations may be asked to undergo examinations or tests at regular intervals to make certain that their work is not having any adverse effect on their health.

The results are discussed privately with the employee by the medical director or some other qualified professional in the medical division. Any recommendations are made in the interest of the employee. The report and the action are kept confidential.

Kimberly-Clark Corporation, Neenah, Wisconsin, has established a voluntary physical examination program for employees in certain job classifications. Details follow:

POLICY

It is the policy of the corporation to make a comprehensive biennial health examination available to all middle management personnel in specified salary categories. Field salesmen 40 years of age and older and salesmen headquartered at the general offices are also eligible for the biennial examination. Field salesmen under 40 years of age are eligible once every three years.

PROCEDURE

A. *General*

1. The Plan "B" health examination which is made available to employees at corporation expense is limited to diagnosis only and in no case will the corporation pay for subsequent treatment. If, in the opinion of the doctor, certain diagnostic tests in addition to those authorized are indicated, the employee will be expected to pay all costs in excess of those authorized.

2. Examinations shall be done by a private physician of the employee's choice.

3. Employees shall be encouraged to follow through with their personal physician when correction is recommended.

B. *Scheduling and Notification*

1. Notification and authorization will be through the corporation medical director in the form of a letter.

2. This will include instructions to the employee and to his examining physician.

3. The employee will present the examining physician with forms covering a detailed history and examination results. The history will have been completed by the employee prior to the examination.

4. The employee will sign a statement authorizing the examiner to send the results of the examination to the Kimberly-Clark medical director.

C. *Scope of Authorized Examination*

1. History—this shall include a complete medical history covering
   a. Present medical complaints
   b. Past medical history
   c. Family medical history
   d. Occupational history, including nature of job responsibilities which might contribute to emotional strain and tension.

2. Routine clinical physical examination.

3. Single PA chest X-ray.

4. Electrocardiogram.

5. Laboratory examinations:
   a. Routine urinalysis
   b. Complete blood count
   c. Blood sugar
   d. Cholesterol.

D. *Invoices and Medical Reports*

1. The itemized invoice shall be forwarded by the examining physician to the Kimberly-Clark medical director for auditing and processing.

2. The medical report and completed set of forms are also sent to the corporation medical director.

E. *Record Storage*

1. Reports are to be considered confidential with use restricted to doctors and nurses.

2. In units having a nurse in attendance, the medical director shall forward the reports to the respective local health services where they shall be filed under lock and key.

3. All other reports will be filed in the medical director's office.

EXECUTIVE HEALTH CARE

Today's executive is sedentary, with a tendency to be overweight from lack of exercise. His main concern is his job; his concern about his health has a low priority unless, of course, illness has already manifested itself. It is the responsibility of management to safeguard one of its prime resources, the health of its key personnel.

Annual physical examinations should be required of such personnel. Under such program each executive is allowed to select his own doctor or make a choice from a list of recommended physicians, subject to company approval. The cost to the corporation will run from $100 to $150 per examination, depending on the scope of the work done.

For the employee, the examination gives peace of mind and, in the event it turns up a problem, corrective action can be taken in time. For the corporation, there is the assurance that the key employees, or most of them, are in continuing good health. For those not in good health, the report will serve as a warning to take steps to change job responsibilities, ease pressure, or relieve tension. In serious cases plans can be begun for the eventual replacement of any individual whose illness is a progressive one.

Coupled with the executive health policy may be a planned program of physical exercise. Most local physical culture studios will be happy to cooperate. A membership can be purchased for executives at a nearby health club or gymnasium or something like a weekly one-hour workout may be arranged on company premises.

CLINIC

An employee clinic may be established for a number of reasons.

This is where medical interviews or employment physical examinations are given to applicants being considered for jobs. Periodic checkups for workers may also be done.

A clinic is also convenient for first-aid and medical services. An employee who becomes ill can receive medication and care here. The clinic may advise a manager or foreman whether such employee should remain in the clinic to rest a while, return to the job, be sent home, referred to the family physician, or possibly taken to a hospital.

Workers injured on the job get immediate attention. These workmen's compensation cases are ideally handled by the clinic. In addition to emergency treatment and referral to appropriate medical facilities authorized by the insurance carriers, the clinic can process the paperwork involved.

Absences may also be better controlled where a clinic is operated.

Any employee who is absent because of illness may be asked to report back through the clinic where it can be determined whether the employee has recovered sufficiently to return to his job. By having to tell his story to a professional medical specialist instead of his supervisor, it is hoped that abuse of the sick-time-off-with-pay will be minimized.

Services may also be rendered in the form of flu and polio shots. Health education programs may be initiated. One very important aspect of a clinic that should not be overlooked is the counseling that is provided. Employees are encouraged to come in to discuss their problems in an atmosphere of confidence and with some assurance of sincere personal interest.

Every action, from the initial physical examination to later clinic visits, should be made part of the official medical record. Any treatment given, any medications dispensed, any consultations with the family doctor, and any advice given should be documented.

Three cautions must be mentioned. Medical and health information is personal and should be kept confidential. The clinic must not be allowed to take the place of the family physician but should limit itself to emergency or on-the-spot treatment. Finally, the clinic is not to be used as a policeman to determine who is employable, who should be sent home, who should and should not be paid for absence blamed on illness, and the like. Such decisions remain with the line organization which acts on the basis of sound advice and information provided by the clinic.

The following is taken from the Kimberly-Clark Corporation handbook for general office salaried employees.

Health is a personal matter. The basic purpose of the Kimberly-Clark health program is to encourage and assist you to maintain your health at the highest possible level, and to provide adequate medical services on the job for problems of sickness or injury. We cooperate with your own physician to achieve these objectives.

Both you and Kimberly-Clark stand to gain by a check of your physical condition upon reporting for work. Individual health can change. Careful periodic reexaminations are the only way to discover these changes in the beginning. Early detection of serious illnesses such as heart trouble or high blood pressure frequently permits early correction and cure.

The Kimberly-Clark Health Service does not take the place of your family physician. We do cooperate with him, however, by sending him reports of our findings if you request it, or we will ask your consent to do so if we feel it to be advisable. If you are new in this area or do not have a private physician, we will be glad to furnish you with a list of general practitioners or specialists located in your community.

We strongly urge you to not neglect minor ailments. If you feel sick or get hurt on the job or feel an illness coming on, report to Health Services. There are, naturally, certain limitations as to the medical services we can provide for personal illness. We have modern equipment and skilled personnel available for emergency treatment of illness or injury, but we do not consider it our function to undertake extended treatment of illness. We do not give medicines or drugs except those needed for emergency treatment.

EMERGENCY OFF-HOUR PROTECTION

Most offices and plants have some first-aid program for their workers. This service may run all the way from a full-time clinic, staffed with one or more registered nurses with possibly a doctor on the premises or on call, down to a minimal facility in which one person is trained in Red Cross or first-aid work.

But what about people who are working when or where such service is not available? This could include—

1. Workers in smaller locations away from the headquarters building,

2. Workers in any location who are on overtime or irregular-hour schedules when the official first-aid room is closed.

These people are entitled to the same protection as the other employees receive. From a company viewpoint it is dangerous to neglect these people.

To meet any such contingency, arrangements should be made in advance so that every employee is covered at every location and every possible working hour. And every employee, particularly the supervisors, should be adequately instructed what to do in case of emergency.

Usually it is sufficient to have a working agreement with a physician in the locality. He should know what he may expect. The employees should have his name, address, and telephone number for quick reference. His office hours should also be listed.

It may be advisable to make special arrangements for services which are not performed by the general practitioner. For injury to the eye, for example, the emergency patient should not be taken to one doctor only to be referred elsewhere. Delay or unnecessary double transport could be dangerous and costly.

Arrangements should also be made with the nearest hospital. It may be necessary to go there after the doctor's office hours, or in cases when he cannot be reached; on orders from the doctor, or in emergencies or accidents.

In making all these advance preparations, include also ambulance service. It is advisable to have a second, or backstop, ambulance service available . . . just in case. The fire department may also be called for emergency service, so this telephone number, as well as that of the police, should be handy.

All this information should, of course, be posted where every worker may see it.

These off-hour workers, or employees in outlying areas, are generally supervised. The supervisor should not panic but do the best he can under the circumstances. In those cases where the employee may be alone, it is hoped he will be resourceful enough to know what to do, particularly if he has been properly briefed and the needed information is at his fingertips.

In all cases, the incident must be reported at the first opportunity so that care is not neglected. Someone ought to call "the boss" at home or at headquarters as soon as possible to give him a chance to take any further action that may be necessary. Certainly the incident should be reported to the clinic or other appropriate first-aid facility, first thing in the morning. This gives the company a chance to make a proper record for official purposes, such as Workmen's Compensation. But more important, it allows the proper medical authority to investigate and review the case, either by calling in the employee for a checkup, or even visiting him at home or in a hospital, in order to ensure that all possible medical attention is being given.

FLU SHOTS

Most companies are insured against unforeseen losses, but what about the hazards of influenza? The costly effects of the flu virus are often ignored by even the most progressive business organizations until productivity is lowered.

A vaccine is used to produce immunity to influenza. It is especially valuable for (1) persons in whom influenza might represent an added health risk, such as individuals with cardiovascular or pulmonary conditions, (2) persons over the age of 55 with chronic illness of any type, (3) persons responsible for providing essential public services, such as law enforcement officers, and (4) industrial and other commercial organizations.

A transient stinging or aching sensation may occur at the injection site immediately after administration. Redness, induration, and tenderness are common during the first 12 to 24 hours. The vaccine may cause fever, malaise, and backache; the reactions tend to vary in severity with the amount injected.

Allergic reactions due to hypersensitivity to egg protein may occur. Such reactions have been rare, but they may be serious. Although they are uncommon, postvaccinal neurological disorders have been reported following the injection of almost all biological products.

Influenza is caused by different strains of virus in various years. When new, antigenically different strains appear, changes in the strains included in the vaccine are specified by the National Institutes of Health.

Immunization can reduce absenteeism, eliminate the danger of a flu epidemic, avert postinfluenza fatigue, provide evidence of a company's interest in its employees' health, and demonstrate leadership in public health and education.

POLIO SHOTS

Many companies give free polio shots to employees.

Vaccination with Salk vaccine is one weapon available to provide protection against all three types of poliomyelitis. Oral polio vaccine has also been developed.

Of the three types of poliovirus, Type I has been responsible in recent years for between 60 and 70 percent of all paralytic polio in the country. Type III, however, may be increasing in relative importance.

According to authorities, polio vaccination is not complete without four injections. The full series, properly spaced, is 85 to 90 percent effective against paralytic polio. Serious outbreaks can occur until everyone is immunized.

Americans are not adequately vaccinated. Only about 50 percent have had any vaccine at all, and many of these have not had all the shots, even though there is now enough vaccine for everyone.

CHEST X-RAYS

Tuberculosis is a contagious and communicable disease. Tuberculosis or consumption or TB or phthisis—any one of these names may be applied to the disease caused by tubercle bacillus. This germ may infect any organ in the body, but most frequently it is the lungs that are invaded.

For many years tuberculosis of the lungs headed the list of the leading causes of death in the United States, but it has steadily declined until it now stands in seventh place. This is a remarkable retreat for a disease that was once called "The Captain of the Men of Death" and "The Great White Plague."

Yet, tuberculosis still takes the lives of 60,000 people each year. No other disease makes greater inroads upon the health of young people. Between the ages of 15 and 45, tuberculosis kills more persons than any other disease.

Countless millions have had a part in conquering this disease. Included are those who can do no more than buy Christmas seals to show that a contribution has been made toward eradicating the disease.

The much advertised danger signs are not symptoms of early tuberculosis but of active advancing disease. Early TB gives no warning.

Signs of advancing TB are fatigue not relieved by rest, loss of weight, loss of appetite, a cough that hangs on, hoarseness, and possibly spitting blood.

The best time to look for TB is *before* signs or symptoms appear. The instrument that aids the doctor most in his examinations for early evidence of tuberculosis is the X-ray. When an X-ray picture of infected lungs is taken, certain telltale shadows of varying shades of gray are noticeable. To the doctor's trained eye these shadows show what damage has already been done.

Chest X-rays are now considered a routine health check for all persons 15 years of age and over. Modern equipment has made chest X-ray services available in towns and cities across the country. In many cities mobile equipment can be brought to the plant so that chest X-rays can be taken "on the spot." Low cost chest X-rays can be taken with speed and accuracy at a rate of 100 films or more an hour. Each film takes only a few minutes and the picture is developed like a snapshot. Undressing is usually not necessary.

Most persons found with advanced TB have a slim chance of recovery. Most of those who are diagnosed early and receive proper modern treatment without delay have an excellent chance to regain their health. None of the chronic diseases responds more readily to treatment than tuberculosis in the early stages.

HEALTH EDUCATION

Most companies are enough concerned about their employees that they are willing to cooperate in health education. This is true even where no clinic or other medical facility is on the premises.

There is nothing wrong with displaying approved health posters. These may caution employees about coughs and colds, announce diabetes detection week, or stress good eating and sleeping habits. Material of this kind is readily available.

Booklets or pamphlets on artificial respiration, lifesaving, first aid, exercise, and diet can be placed at convenient counters or in reading racks. These tell employees how to look better, feel better, live better.

But companies may go further. When approached by the Cancer Society, for instance, they may agree to show the official film, at employee meetings or in the cafeteria, which points out the common danger signals of cancer.

Where a clinic serves the employees it is not uncommon to have the nurse speak during orientation classes or at other times on personal hygiene, cleanliness, body odor, overweight, and other personal matters.

None of this, of course, should be overdone. After all, personal grooming and health care is the responsibility of each individual. But there is nothing wrong with offering an assist as long as it is done tactfully.

SAFETY PRECAUTIONS FOR NIGHT WORKERS

There is a danger inherent in asking employees, particularly women, to work late into the night. Even though nothing happens in most cases, the women are scared when they are alone in the night waiting for public transportation in a neighborhood that is dark and frightening.

Usually nothing is done by the employer until some tragic incident gets the company and the community alarmed. But why wait until too late? Why not take some precautions?

Guidelines to Safety

Here are safety measures formulated by members of the Commerce and Industry Association and the New York police department:

1. Notifying the local police precinct, which assigns a radio patrol car to accompany employees as they leave the building.

2. Reporting all incidents, no matter how minor.

3. Asking female workers to walk in groups to transportation facilities.

4. Lighting office building lobbies and ground floors adequately to discourage loitering.

5. Reporting any action of a suspicious nature immediately by telephone to the police.

Some companies are using specially hired taxis to pick up employees at prearranged times, to take them either all the way home or to the nearest transportation. Other firms merely allow their women on overtime work or night shifts to take taxicabs home and then reimburse them for the cab fare.

SAFETY

When safety problems arise, the best source of information is the National Safety Council, 425 North Michigan Avenue, Chicago, Illinois 60611. This nonprofit organization, which operates solely on membership fees, is interested and helpful in all areas of safety.

It had its origin in industry, specifically the steel industry. Because of its usefulness, it soon spread to other industry. From there it was only logical to move to offices. Today its services are in all areas of safety—industry, farm, school, and home. A catalog is available listing NSC publications, posters, and training aids.

This Green Cross for Safety symbol is displayed on safety posters and pamphlets used by nearly 10,000 organizations which are members of the National Safety Council.

While safety measures are usually associated with the factory or plant, the need for safety education and precautions is just as great in the office. The biggest office hazard is the belief that there is no hazard. A NSC pamphlet titled "Coffee Breaks" calls attention to the danger of coffee spills on floors, fracture traps such as lower file drawer left open for someone to trip over, or a loose paper clip on a waxed floor for a girl in spike heels to slip on. Open desk drawers, telephone or electric cords, misplaced wastebaskets are all potential danger spots.

The NSC advises holding on to handrails on stairs and using a ladder to reach high shelves. Of course any defective electrical equipment can give an unsuspecting employee the shock treatment. Such electric machines should never be cleaned with flammable fluid.

Razor blades, thumbtacks, and pins can bite if not stored in containers. Paper cuts hurt and can become infected. Keep fingers clear when using paper cutters, and pick up broken glass with a paper towel. Lifting can be harmful and overloaded files, with the top drawer opened, can fall forward.

Over 9,400 business firms, associations, government bodies, and individuals belong to the National Safety Council. The NSC welcomes inquiries from companies and individuals concerned with the problems of safety, both on and off the job.

At General Dynamics

The employee handbook of the Fort Worth division of General Dynamics Corporation contains the following:

SAFETY PROMOTION

We at Fort Worth are proud of our outstanding safety record. The General Dynamics Corporation has a sincere and active interest in providing safe working conditions for the welfare of the people who work here. We have a comprehensive safety promotion program in effect. The best protective equipment and safety devices are furnished to employees. Our safety engineers work constantly to devise safe practices and methods which they pass on to supervisors and employees alike.

Success in preventing accidents depends primarily on people. Experience has shown that most industrial accidents can be prevented.

One of the most important parts of our program is the Employee's Safety Group System. These groups, which include employees from representative departments, meet frequently for specialized training in accident prevention. The employees act as safety representatives and assist their supervisors in the correction of unsafe conditions and practices in their departments. Your cooperation with the members of this group will be appreciated.

Discuss your ideas regarding the correction of unsafe working practices and conditions with your supervisor. He may think your idea is a good one and advise you to submit it through the suggestion plan so it would be considered for a cash award for you.

SAFETY REGULATIONS

The following regulations are for your protection and for the protection of your fellow workers. Observe and comply with them at all times:

1. Do not turn on, use, repair, or operate any machine, tool, vehicle, crane, electricity, gas, steam, air, acid, caustic, solvent, pressure, or other dangerous material or equipment unless your supervisor has authorized you to do so.

2. Horseplay, running, and practical jokes are not permitted on company property.

3. Use compressed air only on work functions requiring its use. It is not to be used for cleaning clothes or hands, benches, floors, or released close to the body of yourself or a fellow worker.

4. If you have trouble with electrical equipment, inform your supervisor. He will call the maintenance electrician if repairs are indicated.

5. Safety glasses or other approved eye protection are furnished by Fort Worth Division and must be worn at all times when grinding, sawing, drilling,

or chipping. Face shields must be worn at all times when pouring hot metal or when handling acids and caustics. Additional or different type eye or face protection will be furnished when you are doing other work where such equipment may keep you safe. You may purchase safety glasses ground to your prescription at the Tool Service Store. They can be purchased by payroll deduction. The Safety Engineering Section maintains surveillance over the program to ensure top-quality merchandise at reasonable prices. Your supervisor will assist you in preparing the necessary paperwork.

6. Loose or torn clothing, ties, open cuffs, etc., shall not be worn around moving machinery. Wrist watches, rings, or other jewelry must not be worn around moving machinery or if your duties involve working with electrical circuits, or if your job requires climbing.

7. Safety guards and devices are provided for your protection. Removal or nonuse is prohibited.

8. Be sure that the power is turned off before leaving a machine. If you are authorized to clean, adjust, or repair a machine, be sure that the switch is locked or tagged in the "OFF" position before you start the work. Do not remove a "DANGER" sign from a machine unless authorized to do so by your supervisor.

9. Be sure that materials are not stored or piled so as to block fire extinguishers, safety valves, sprinkler heads, fire alarm boxes, or emergency exits.

10. Women shall wear approved hair covering when working around revolving machinery or equipment.

11. The wearing of the following type shoes in the factory and yard areas is prohibited unless otherwise authorized by the Safety Engineering Section of the Industrial Relations Department: open toe, open heel, soft tennis shoes (slippers), and all types of high heel footwear. Safety shoes are available to you at cost at the Tool Service Store. They can be purchased on the payroll deduction plan. A complete stock of the most popular styles and sizes is maintained under the supervision of the Safety Engineering Section. We recommend that employees performing production work in the plant, or working on jobs where there are foot hazards, protect their feet by wearing safety shoes.

12. Do not use worn or broken tools or makeshift equipment. Return defective tools or makeshift equipment to the tool crib.

13. Report unsafe conditions, equipment, and practices to your supervisor.

14. Protective equipment, such as respirators, hard hats, and rubber or asbestos gloves, are furnished by the company and must be worn on jobs requiring this type of protection.

15. REPORT ALL PLANT INJURIES, REGARDLESS OF SEVERITY, TO YOUR SUPERVISOR OR TO THE NEAREST FIRST AID STATION IMMEDIATELY. Never attempt self-treatment. A slight injury may become infected if not properly treated. If, after you have returned home, a previously reported plant injury, or one not reported, begins giving you trouble, notify the Medical Section at the plant at once.

16. When using mechanical lifting or hoisting devices, never lift more than the rated capacity of the hoist or crane. Use a proper sling and stand clear of the load.

17. It is a poor practice to pile or leave tools or loose material on ladders, stairs, stands, or scaffolding.

18. Be sure you have proper authorization from your supervisor before you use a high-speed grinder, and then be sure you have the correct wheel and guard for the job.

19. Certain solvents have been purchased to do specific jobs. Contact your supervisor for the correct one to be used and be sure that as much ventilation as possible is provided.

20. Your supervisor is interested in your safety and will inform you of any additional safety procedures or rules specifically applicable to your job. If in doubt about the safe way, ask your supervisor. Practice safety awareness to protect yourself.

21. If your job requires you to lift heavy objects, you should get instructions from your supervisor beforehand. Learn to lift by using the power of your legs instead of your back. Get help if the load is heavy enough to cause strain.

At Aluminum of Canada

The clerk in the safety department of Aluminum Company of Canada, Ltd., in Kitimat, B.C., wrote a letter to be sent to its supervisors, which her employer decided should have broader coverage.

SAFETY

From the Woman's Point of View

by Winnie Gray

It's a well-known fact that a woman is a natural-born worry wart and completely illogical. But perhaps if a few distaff thoughts were correlated, some logic may appear. I'm thinking about safety. For instance:

As a wife, I worry about my husband at work. This was particularly true back in the days when he worked underground. I would hear of men receiving crushing injuries, losing a leg, even dying. In every case, of course, there was a cause. The victim didn't treat his dynamite and blasting caps with respect, or he didn't hose down before commencing work. I would shudder at the thought of trying to raise a family on compensation or, worst of all, watching an otherwise strong, healthy man propelling himself around in a wheel chair. When he left for work each day the worry wart in me would ask, "Will he be next?"

As a mother, I worry about my children and how to prevent them from harming themselves by their immature attitudes and actions. At the moment I'm thinking of my teen-aged son. His chemistry set worries me, and also the fact that he likes to experiment with gadgets. One day I brought home a cabbage shredder, and in less time than it takes to tell, he had scooped a ball of flesh out of his index finger when the gadget's platform suddenly dropped, simply because he was not "expecting the unexpected." Another time I brought home a razor-sharp knife and, because he failed to treat it with proper respect, the back of his hand required four stitches. I can't help worrying, "Will his next injury maim him for life?"

As many of you will know, I'm the clerk in the safety department. It's part of my job to read and record the first aid reports. Noting the careless acts, the disregard for safety rules and regulations, and the late reporting of injuries, I become deeply concerned. A woman finds it difficult to understand a man's love of danger. Is it because he can no longer find a dragon to slay, nor don a suit of armor and tilt a lance at an opponent, that he must find his excitement elsewhere?

I can understand a man's enthusiasm for cars, boats, planes, and hunting, or anything else in which there is an element of danger, but I can't understand why he sometimes appears to deliberately expose himself to known hazards in his normal workaday life. And as I record the injuries for the day, week, month, and year, the worry wart in me says, "It's just about time for the next big one. I wonder who it will be?"

FIRE and EVACUATION DRILLS

In schools we had occasional fire drills. Why not in offices and plants?

A fire or other sudden incident could be disastrous if employees are not prepared to evacuate the premises quickly and orderly.

An evacuation program should not be any one-time practice. It should be covered by a management policy and the policy should be known to all.

The policy, preferably written, should spell out where the authority lies, both during a real emergency and also for the practice sessions: Who sets the evacuation in motion? Who sounds the alarm and who calls the fire department? What responsibility do supervisors have in a mass exodus? Who has final responsibility for the safety of people and the safeguarding of property? Who can and will make on-the-spot decisions? Unless all this is clear, chaos could result.

To get ready for the real thing, periodic drills should be conducted. These need not be surprise drills; they could be announced in advance. For example: "Next Tuesday morning, between 9 and 10:30 o'clock, we will hold a practice evacuation." Employees should learn what the "clear out" signal is, from whom to take orders, where to find the nearest "open" exit (leaving elevators and inside stairwells for firemen and rescue workers), how to "walk, not run," how to fend for themselves in the event leadership is cut off. Even in a practice drill some rules need to be worked out in advance, and explained, about cutting off telephone conversations without panicking the caller, how to shut off machines, power, and automatic equipment; who should pull down the fire doors, whether to lock up or leave unguarded any cash and whether to remove or abandon other valuables, where the emergency first-aid station is located and what services are available. Finally, they should recognize the "all clear" signal and understand how to return to their desks and machines and resume work.

Review Each Drill

After each drill, management would do well to review the procedure. What lessons can be learned? What was the time it took to empty the building? How can this be improved? Did the employees understand what they're expected to do? Were managers and supervisors "on alert" and ready to move into action? What violations were observed?

The evacuation procedure should be discussed with managers and foremen regularly. It should also be included in supervisory training classes. A tour, showing location of fire extinguishers and hoses, and demonstrating their use, would be appropriate.

As for new employees, they should have this evacuation procedure explained to them as part of their original indoctrination. Be careful not to leave the impression that the premises is unsafe, but rather take credit for having established a well-thought-out safety precaution program. Don't just talk about it; walk them over to the nearest exit.

This is something that is easily neglected. One tragic experience will make the point unmistakably clear. Try not to learn that way.

EMPLOYEE SERVICES

COMPANY-SPONSORED EMPLOYEE ACTIVITIES

There are two kinds of employee activities going on in practically all companies. Some are sponsored by the company and others are promoted by employees.

Common among company-sponsored employee activities are service recognition dinners, holiday parties, picnics, and the like. Of course, many companies go much further. Much depends on the location, size of organization, and the nature of the business.

Company-sponsored events are generally organized and promoted by an official committee. This committee is often composed of high-level management personnel and, unfortunately, does not always have employee representation.

Where employees are not included in the planning, it is not surprising if the results are disappointing. The block booking for a musical show or ice carnival may excite the personnel director but few others. The summertime excursion to a place of historic interest may find no takers. Some experiences show employees to be apathetic toward the company junket, preferring to arrange their own social life, apart from work.

Some companies question the time, effort, and money expended. The headaches and problems connected with outings, picnics, and parties may not be worth the trouble.

Should Answer a Need

Companies should not promote events just for the sake of promoting. Employee activities should be sponsored in answer to a need. In a service recognition dinner the company may logically expect most eligible employees, particularly the honored guests, to attend. At other functions, such as the Christmas party, it may be unrealistic to hope to reach everyone. For dances or special attractions that appeal to limited numbers, a break-even attendance should satisfy. Not everybody enjoys going out to a night baseball game, or a concert, or an opera.

The best way to appeal to the greatest possible number is to conduct the affair with dignity, in a first-class location, with a good menu, first-run entertainment, and quality prizes. If an employee activity is worth doing, it is worth doing well.

SERVICE RECOGNITION

Service pins are the most common way to recognize long-service employees. Usually they are issued every five years beginning with the fifth year. For the men these are lapel pins; for the ladies, identical service buttons with a clasp instead of a pin. There are variations. Men may get theirs on a tie clasp or cuff links, and women possibly as a charm for a bracelet or a dress pin.

The same style pin is awarded each time except that the number of years is different. Sometimes a small gem is added to the longer-service pins.

In addition to the pins, gifts are sometimes given. A five-year employee, for example, may get a desk calendar inscribed with his name and the number of years. His 10-year gift could well be a desk pen set. Companies prefer to give a gift which the employee can and will use and display proudly at his desk. The problem is that such gift ideas are almost impossible to apply to factory workers. This leads to giving personal gifts, preferably something the employee and his family can use every day at home.

It is not uncommon to award United States Savings Bonds. The face amount of these bonds increases with the length of service. Gift certificates or some other type of monetary award may be substituted.

The traditional service gift is a good "name" watch for 25-years of service. The only problem here is "how to top this" at 30 years and beyond. It is best to have an established policy in effect.

With or Without Fanfare

Gifts, pins, and other awards may be presented ceremoniously or without fanfare. A five-year employee may get his service pin in the manager's office and be given a ticket for a free lunch in the cafeteria at the same time. A 20-year employee may be escorted to the vice-president's office and possibly even taken out to lunch.

Other companies plan a dinner once a year, in some hotel or country club. This is a gala event to which all honored guests, as well as those previously honored, are invited. The program includes flowers and music and possibly entertainment. It may feature a speaker, usually the president of the firm, who takes this opportunity to thank his loyal long-service hard-core group of employees, and who may also reminisce a bit about "the struggle of the early days." Once a year he is entitled to get sentimental.

Some firms use this annual dinner also to distribute pins and awards. The disadvantage is that an employee could well be months beyond his anniversary date before he receives his recognition. Also, an employee who terminates between his anniversary date and the party will no longer be around to receive the award he earned.

The author prefers to recognize each individual on his anniversary date, the day which is significant to him. This is the day, like his birthday, which is personal to him, when he is unlike co-workers. It is *his* big day! Putting 25 red roses on the desk of an employee the day of his 25th employment anniversary makes much more sense than handing him a watch after he's been with the company 25 years, eight months, and seven days.

Just when to begin a recognition program can be a problem, not at the start but years later when the earlier pattern cannot be undone. Small or young firms may be tempted to invite everyone with five years of service out to dinner. After the firm gets older and the eligible group larger, this arrangement may no longer be practical. But how can it be stopped?

The large banks and utilities, with their record of employee seniority, usually have "25 year clubs." This does not mean that employees with less than 25 years of service are ignored, but it does mean that only the "quarter century group" is feted in grand style. One large utility has 25 percent of its workers in its 25 year club, a record of seniority which in today's fluid employment market is truly amazing.

Do It Well Or Not At All

Seniority and length of service are important to a stable company. Any form of recognition, therefore, deserves to be a quality program. Do it up well, or don't do it at all. Above all, be sincere in your appreciation of loyalty and long service. If a dinner is planned, schedule it in a "big" location (where some employees, at least, may ordinarily never get), have a good dinner, preceded by a reception and possibly a receiving line of corporate officers, and do the party up in style. Don't make it too formal, however, or some-rank-and-file workers may be scared away. Give them an event which they can look forward to and remember afterwards.

The recognition must always be personal, not automatic. Whatever you give, even a pin or a wallet service card, should be delivered and presented personally, properly gift wrapped, and climaxed with a warm hand clasp or other congratulations.

Any anniversary is important to the individual. But it is just as important to the company, isn't it?

ANNIVERSARY OBSERVANCE
(AND OTHER RELATED TRADITIONS)
AT LEO BURNETT COMPANY

Perhaps the most noteworthy element of our company's attention to and preoccupation with anniversary observances and related occasions is a complete lack of premeditated policy in instituting them.

Perhaps some definition of the kind of company we are may help explain why this has been a good place for sentimental business seeds to take root and grow.

We're an advertising agency. Our production machinery is people and our end product is ideas. So our product is only as good as our people. So are progress and profit.

Naturally our management has a healthy respect and affection for good people.

This is why we like to do so many things, little and big, for people that ordinarily a company doesn't bother about even thinking of doing, because it really doesn't have to do them.

Our Company opened its doors in 1935 with eight people. Today we employ about 1,400, with offices in New York, Hollywood, Toronto, and Montreal, as well as our main office in Chicago. We also have a London subsidiary.

When a company is small—when everyone knows everyone else by his first name—internal relations are relatively simple.

When a company grows, many personal elements of working together automatically fall by the wayside.

That's why we feel it's all to the good if a few little friendly and thoughtful traditions can be maintained as the company grows larger.

It is probably needless to point out that this piece does not deal at all with corporate benefits such as insurance, hospital and doctor costs plans, profit-sharing trusts, and the rest. We have them all and more.

Also, our profit-participation bonus is mentioned not as a bonus, *per se,* but to describe the way we handle it.

THE ANNIVERSARY GIFT TRADITION

This dollar per company year per every person on the payroll began in 1950. We presented everyone with 15 silver dollars in a white wool sock with the message, "Something in the Sock," on the company's 15th anniversary.

On August 5, 1950, we didn't know we were starting a tradition, but the money-in-the-sock idea proved so popular that it became almost obligatory in succeeding years to figure out some gag as a carrier for the number of the anniversary we were celebrating.

Over the years gags have included, in addition to the sock, folders and bank bands, some with an apple motif, cigarette lighter, ash tray, wallet, zipper pouch, sugar bowl, Civil War memento, scratch pad, chicken feed, apple extract, pearl-bearing shell, Batman trading cards carrying photos of company executives, utilizing appropriate Burnett currency, medals, simulated Confederate money wrapper, coins, ring, etc.

People enjoyed the gags so much that we're now committed to them—so long as we follow the dollar per-year-of-company-age plan.

The amount forecast as necessary for the anniversary tradition is formally put into the company operating budget at the beginning of each year. (It is now, obviously, quite a substantial item.)

SERVICE AWARDS

The first of these clubs, The Burnett Five-Year-Club, was launched on August 5, 1949—14 years after the Company was born.

Burnett neckties were given all men who had been with the company at least five years. Burnett pins were given to women with the same length of service. (In 1955, the pins for the women were changed to apple bracelets. In 1965, retroactive for all 5-year men, a gold Burnett tie bar was presented.)

On the company's 20th anniversary a luncheon was held for everyone on the staff with five years' or more service.

At this luncheon both the 20-Year Club and the 10-Year Club were founded.

New members of the former received $2,000 checks—$ 100 X numbers of years' service equals $2,000.

The 10-Year Clubbers received Burnett cuff links, if they were men; earrings if they were women.

The 15-Year Club got really out of sequence, not being formed until 1958. We formed it then because we felt it was too long to wait between 10-Year Club and 20-Year Club.

The first service gift for each 15-Year Club initiate was a Polaroid camera outfit. This gift was changed next year to a more popular solid gold men's or women's wristwatch with special Burnett watch band.

Of course, the 25-Year Club couldn't get off the ground till the company was 25 years old. On that occasion, August 5, 1960, first quarter-century members received sterling silver trays, engraved with directors' names and a letter entitling them to 25 bonus days of extra vacation, to be taken any time they wished.

On the company's 30th anniversary, management went all out. The 30-year veteran members each received a gold Burnett apple, a letter entitling him to 30 extra days of bonus vacation *and* a check for $3,000—$100 per year X 30 years of service.

PROFIT PARTICIPATION BONUS

Previous to an official bonus policy, the company had distributed "53rd" and "54th"' weeks' pay as a form of bonus when such distributions were considered practical.

Usually the distribution was "dressed up" as vacation money, Christmas-shopping money, and with some gimmick in the giving out of checks.

However, in 1962 the practice was begun of holding a "Breakfast at Burnett's." These affairs in Chicago have been held in the big Prudential Assembly Hall. Everyone on the staff is invited to come at 8:30 a.m. A light box breakfast is served before the meeting. Promptly at 8:45 the meeting starts.

All employees are told exactly how the company stands for the year; how prospects look for the next year. Material given at the meeting is strictly confidential. Our employees respect this.

At the end of the meeting they are told if there is to be a bonus. After the meeting a more formal breakfast or brunch is held in three Prudential dining rooms, simultaneously.

We feel that the important point of our breakfast is not the money, but that we give all employees the inside facts that we do about the condition of our business—the less pleasant as well as the good.

MISCELLANEOUS COMPANY RELATIONS

Our company has as many employee benefits as most other companies, perhaps more, and more generous, than many.

Here are a few that fall somewhere between our unique anniversary mementoes and service club presentations and the more or less general benefits company managements offer today:

An apple bottle of fine imported perfume, put on each woman employe's desk with a little note, on the occasion of her first anniversary with the company.

A wedding present when an employee is married.

Flowers or a contribution on the death of an employee's close relative.

Generous supper and taxi money policy for late night work.

Extra day's holiday often proclaimed when a regular holiday falls on a Tuesday, Thursday, or Saturday. (For examples: we generally announce a holiday on the Friday after Thanksgiving or give the staff Monday off when Christmas falls on a Tuesday.)

Flowers to Burnett sick people in hospitals.

The company contributes a substantial sum each year to the golf committee to buy prizes for the men's golf tournament.

Employees may purchase travel tickets through our transportation department when the personnel has time enough to take care of personal requests.

Our notary publics handle, at no charge, personal notarization work.

We also get out a fairly elaborate magazine for employees at least six times per year. Two of its basic features are pictures and brief sketches of all new people hired, and pictures and sketches of all people promoted during the time period covered by the individual issue.

Apples have been mentioned in this piece.

Our attitude toward apples warrants some explanation.

When Leo Burnett Company opened its doors for the first time, August 5, 1935, there was a bowl of red apples on the reception desk. (Along with the apples, there was an old-fashioned stereoscope and book of cartoons for the visitors to look at, too.)

We wanted to be hospitable and friendly. If a visitor had to wait, we wanted to help him pass the time. We wanted him to feel welcome and at home.

Since those early days we've always had bowls of apples on *all* our reception desks in all our offices.

We give out currently better than 160,000 apples per year. Burnett employees eat plenty of them, too, but that's just another of our fringe benefits!

Anyway, apples are why we're often known as, "The Apple Agency." The story is explained in a little booklet, "The Apple Story," which is also on reception desks.

_____

The author and the publisher are grateful to Mr. DeWitt O'Kieffe, senior vice-president of Leo Burnett Company, Inc., for the foregoing story of how one company recognizes and rewards long service of employees.

UNITED STATES SAVINGS BONDS

The United States Treasury Department encourages employers to aid employees in the systematic purchase of United States Savings Bonds, usually through payroll deduction. Those employees who participate on a voluntary basis agree to have a specified amount deducted from each paycheck which is then applied toward the purchase of a bond. As soon as the full purchase price has been accumulated the bond is issued.

A representative of the government may call to request the company to conduct a campaign to promote the sale of bonds to employees. Many companies go all out to support such a patriotic program. Even those who do not actively promote the drive, nevertheless do cooperate as a courtesy to employees who may wish to use the convenience of payroll deduction for their purchase of bonds.

A campaign might follow this outline.

1. Appoint campaign chairman.
   a. Select a prominent member of the organization who will act with full support of management.

b. Give him a representative committee of present bond buyers to plan and carry out the program.

c. Pick canvassers at the ratio of one for each 10 employees.

2. Announce the campaign.

a. Issue a strong directive from the chief executive to members of management enlisting their full cooperation.

b. Distribute a letter from the chief executive to each employee telling about the program and the company's interest in it. Enclose a descriptive Treasury leaflet. Sending the letter to employees at home tends to make the decision a family one.

3. Publicize the campaign.

a. Display Treasury posters.

b. Give coverage in company publication.

c. Use official Treasury film.

4. Personalize authorization (sign-up) cards.

a. Put employee's name on card which is meant for his use.

b. Have each card ready so all employee need do is fill in amount and sign his name.

c. Give each canvasser his set of cards.

5. Hold indoctrination meeting. Include

a. Top executives.

b. Other managers.

c. Full campaign committee.

d. Canvassers.

e. Union (if applicable).

f. Treasury representative.

6. Canvass the employees.

a. Contact each employee personally, explain program, and try to have card signed.

b. Return all cards signed or unsigned to campaign committee.

c. Try to interest employees already on the plan to increase their deductions.

7. Prepare report.

a. Tally results, showing participation (number and amount) before and after campaign.

b. Study final figures to determine whether they are satisfactory.

c. Submit report to Treasury representative.

In any type of employee drive—and the campaign for U.S. Savings Bonds is no exception—the employees should not be coerced into signing up. The company sponsorship should not be construed as pressure. Employee participation should be voluntary.

Some employees want to buy these bonds and appreciate the convenience of obtaining them the easy way through the company. Others, and there is nothing wrong with this approach, need encouragement in making up their minds to support a program which is in their own interest as well as that of the nation. Those, however, who are forced or embarrassed into buying bonds against their will, most likely will cash them in as soon as the minimum waiting time has passed. This accomplishes nothing except needless work and employee resentment.

CREDIT UNION

A credit union is a mutual society incorporated for the two-fold purpose of promoting thrift among its members and providing loans for virtually any worthwhile purpose. It is an independent organization, and participation in it is entirely voluntary.

Members must have a common bond of association—be employees of the same company or belong to the same church, fraternal group, labor union, or closely knit community.

Credit unions are chartered by the state, provincial, or federal government, and are incorporated under credit union law. The government that issues the charter supervises the credit union operation.

Under most laws, a credit union charter is granted to seven or more persons, and to a field of membership of 50 or more.

The governing body is a board of directors, whose members serve one-year terms. Expirations and vacancies are filled by the election of members at the annual meeting. The officers are president, vice-president, treasurer, and secretary. They are elected by and from the board.

The directors appoint the credit union clerk. This can be one of its members who puts in the necessary time to do the clerical work. Often this is an employee on the company payroll who puts in some or all of his time doing credit union work. The salary of the clerk may be paid by the company and donated, along with space and equipment, to the credit union. Many credit unions are big enough, and prosperous enough, to pay all or part of the clerk's wages.

The board appoints its own credit committee (which makes loans) and the supervisory committee (which checks all credit union activities). In addition to its own supervision, the credit union has other safeguards. Credit union law requires the maintenance of ample reserve funds to cover any possible bad loans. The government agency which issued the charter sends its examiners to make an audit once a year. All persons who handle funds or records are bonded.

The object of a credit union is a unique financial service for its members—credit, savings, dividends. Only the members can use and profit from its services.

Anyone in the group may join by making application for membership and paying a fee of 25 cents and at least one installment on a $5 share. After a member has one $5 share, he may deposit any amount at any time, in cash or through payroll deduction where this has been arranged. Savings may be withdrawn at any time. Dividends are declared semiannually and credited to each shareholder's account.

Loans Are Protected

Members may also make loans for many, but not all, purposes. The amount of the loan is limited by the charter. All loans are secured by a promissory note signed by the borrower, and for larger loans, cosigners, wage assignments, automobile certificate of title, and collateral are required. The maximum legal rate of interest charged is 1 percent a month on the unpaid balance. This is a $6.50 charge on a $100 loan repaid in 12 monthly payments. Many credit unions charge less than the maximum, and some declare a rebate on interest paid, depending upon the financial status at annual meeting time. Loans are repaid in installments, by cash or through payroll deductions. Most credit unions provide free loan protection insurance which cancels the unpaid portion of the loan if the borrower dies or is permanently disabled.

The reason for credit union popularity and success is easy to understand. The credit union pays good dividends, and at the same time extends credit far more freely and at lower true cost in the long run than most other sources of consumer financing.

The explanation is simple: A credit union requires no heavy capital, no elaborate space, no competitive location. Generally its officers serve without pay. The borrowers are dependable, and losses are few.

In summary, credit union operation is not only safe, but also simple. When a group of people obtain a charter, this is what they do:

1. Put their money (shares) into a common fund.
2. Elect some of their members (as directors) to manage the fund.
3. Lend money to each other from the fund.
4. Charge interest for the use of that money.
5. With the interest (credit union income).
6. Pay the cost of running the credit union, and then
7. Distribute the rest of the earnings to shareholders (as dividends).

Benefits to Management

Whenever the subject of credit unions is brought up, reference is also made to the benefits which come to managements. These are often referred to in general terms and not always spelled out or itemized. But they are real, and they can be justified on the company's profit and loss statement.

Some of these benefits are very apparent. Minimized are those nuisance dealings which relate to employee money problems. The number of wage garnishments, with their unpleasant implications, are reduced. Requests for pay advances are practically eliminated. All this means that loan sharks are kept from preying upon workers. In other words, credit unions stop what may be called payroll sabotage. The time and trouble which this improved condition saves can be measured in dollars; but the effect on morale and better employee relations is substantially bigger.

By eliminating some of the worker's money problems, or helping him at least keep them under control, some terminations can be prevented. Any reduction in turnover naturally cuts turnover cost. In addition, security and contentment resulting from fewer financial worries makes better workers. Worried workers worry the safety director and the nurse; they know that trouble-free employees have less accidents. Yes, the habit of thrift has a stabilizing influence on payroll.

Altogether, an effective credit union builds morale, self-respect, stability, sense of responsibility, and dependability. Fellow employees are better able than management to determine a worker's ability to pay and to judge the soundness of a member's need for a loan. This makes workers more charitable, tolerant, and sympathetic. Understanding of fellow employees' problems helps band them together into a smoother functioning team.

All of this is a new experience for them. Operating under different sets of influence is also good experience for them. Since they are not used to exercising authority, they accomplish their purpose through cooperation. They solve their problems by dealing fairly with others. Through knowledge and practical experience this teaches employees how to understand and deal with other people. All this develops leadership abilities which, once demonstrated, can be used elsewhere.

Credit unions offer a proving ground for the discovery of latent talents among the worker group. Operating a business of their own gets them acquainted in a small way with some of management's problems. All this contributes to self-development, which in turn is beneficial to managements. For the growth of any company is merely the sum total of the growth of its people.

RAYBESTOS SAVINGS CLUB

The following description of the Raybestos Savings Club was supplied by William H. Gay, personnel manager of the Raybestos Division of Raybestos—Manhattan, Inc., Bridgeport, Connecticut 06601. Inquiries about the plan may be referred to him.

The Raybestos Savings Club was organized in 1921. Since then hundreds of employees have received the benefits. It has taught men to form the habit of saving a small amount of their income weekly. This has developed thrift and independence. It has given men a "nest egg" for use in times of necessity.

The company pays 10 percent on the total amount each employee saves weekly. This is in addition to the interest he receives from the bank at its regular savings rate.

HIGHLIGHTS of the Raybestos Savings Club

PLACE OF DEPOSIT

People's Savings Bank of Bridgeport, Connecticut. The account and bank book are carried at the bank in the employee's name.

SAVINGS DEPOSITS

With employee consent, the Payroll Department makes weekly deductions for 50 weeks in accordance with whatever amount the employee designates and credits this to the employee's account at the bank. These deductions must be weekly through the savings club year, except as otherwise stated, and must be started within three weeks of the beginning of the payroll year.

LIMITS OF SAVINGS PER WEEK

Fifty cents to $15. No fractions of half dollars. The company reserves the right to limit the amount of weekly savings, based on the individual's average earnings.

10% PLUS INTEREST

The company will deposit 10 percent of the employee's total yearly savings to his bank account at the end of the year. He will also receive interest from the bank at its current rate, on the net amount of his savings.

REDUCTION OR INCREASE IN WEEKLY DEPOSIT

Because of bookkeeping complications, the employee is limited during the year to one increase and one reduction in the amount of his weekly deposit, provided this change is justified in the opinion of the personnel department.

DRAWING ON ACCOUNT

An employee desiring funds from his account may make one withdrawal, but the 10 percent will only be paid on the balance of the account at the end of the year. He will not be permitted to make any extra deposits to balance this withdrawal.

TERMINATION OF EMPLOYMENT AND ITS EFFECT

If an employee leaves because of a layoff for lack of work, the company will continue to hold the account open and 10 percent will be added to the amount paid in, provided the layoff does not exceed three months.

In the case of enforced unemployment because of ill health, the company will keep the account open for the period of illness and 10 percent will be paid to the amount paid in.

Upon termination of employment, either voluntary or involuntary, the payroll office will process the closing of the account. Under these conditions, the 10 percent will not be added.

NEW AND REHIRED EMPLOYEES

New employees will be given the privilege of opening a savings account within three weeks of the time of employment with full 10 percent benefit.

Rehired employees not previously working during the savings club year will have the same opportunity and receive the same benefits as new employees.

THE PAYOFF

After the end of the savings club year, as early in January as possible, when the amount of each book is counted up and balanced, the company will give each participant 10 percent of what he has saved, *in addition* to the interest paid by the bank. At that time he will be given a People's Savings Bank of Bridgeport check for the total amount credited to his account.

In the words of William S. Simpson, general manager, "It is the desire of Raybestos to have you share the benefits of the savings club plan. We want you to develop self-reliance, foresight, and contentment; we want to aid you financially toward your goal of independence; and we seek your continued loyal and efficient service."

CHRISTMAS CLUB

One innovation of the employee thrift plan is the Christmas club savings program of the Burgess-Norton Manufacturing Company of Geneva, Illinois. This is not a savings account plan but a 50-week deduction program which pays off in time for Christmas shopping.

Arrangements have been made with the First National Bank of Geneva, which maintains a separate account for each participating employee, and pays interest on all accounts paid in full. The bank also issues individual pay-out checks in the employee's name. The checks are distributed through the company and not mailed to the employees' homes.

Each year, around the beginning of November, the company calls this program to the attention of employees and invites them to join. Regular deductions are made from biweekly paychecks in amounts from 50 cents upward. The total deduction is sent to the local bank which makes the separate postings to individual accounts.

An employee who terminates employment with the company may request a refund or he may continue by making payments directly to the bank. In the event of an emergency, the employee may withdraw the amount credited to his account, but then he cannot continue to participate in the plan for the balance of that year.

C. L. Hokonson, manager industrial relations, says, "We have found the Christmas club savings program to be a very worthwhile venture, and each year we have a high percentage of our employees participating in it."

PPG THRIFT PLAN

Pittsburgh Plate Glass Company, Pittsburgh, Pennsylvania, has set up a savings plan for employees. Its object is to encourage eligible employees to systematically save a part of their wages, and through company contributions to acquire a stock interest in the company.

Under the Employee Thrift Plan, an employee may pay in from 2 to 6 percent of his wages through payroll deduction, and he may designate a beneficiary. He may increase or decrease the amount, within those limits, for the next year by giving notice by July 10 of the previous year. He is free to discontinue the plan any time, after giving notice before the 10th of the preceding month.

The company contributes from a minimum of 25 percent to a maximum of 75 percent of the participant's monthly savings to the plan, which is administered by the Employee Welfare Board. Company contributions are invested in PPG stock.

Information about the plan may be obtained from Steve Orosz, employee welfare assistant, Pittsburgh Plate Glass Company, 1 Gateway Center, Pittsburgh, Pennsylvania 15222.

SUGGESTION SYSTEMS

A suggestion system can be either good or bad, depending upon how well it is planned and conducted. Before starting one, it would be well to understand what is involved.

A suggestion system should not be taken lightly. It will require time and effort. To be effective it must have universal endorsement and support from all levels of management.

A clearly spelled out set of rules is a prerequisite. The "rules of the game" should be in writing. The program should be published.

Among the rules should be a statement of who is eligible to participate. Ordinarily, all nonsupervisory personnel may enter suggestions. Supervisors are generally excluded, since improving company operations is considered part of their jobs. Some companies permit a supervisor to enter suggestions which are out of his own area. Some phases of company operations may be "off limits" to everyone. Where to invest corporate funds, for instance, might be "none of their business."

Suggestions are accepted on a "first in" basis, that is, when duplicate suggestions come in, the earlier one is recognized and the others are then returned as having come in "too late."

For ease of submission, suggestion boxes may be conveniently located throughout the office and plant. Also, for ease of administration, suggestions are submitted on entry blanks prepared by the company and distributed at suggestion boxes or other locations, included in house organs, or otherwise made available to workers as gentle reminders.

Most systems let the suggestions come in unsigned. The anonymous entry blank is given a code number and is from that point on referred to by number. Only when the suggestion is accepted and payment is to be made is the suggestor asked to identify himself, possibly by presenting the tear-off coupon from the entry blank which bears the same number. A few systems encourage signatures; this does offer an opportunity for better and more direct communication.

Committee Important

Suggestions should be evaluated promptly. A committee, representing all major areas of operation—production, sales, etc.—as well as neutral functions—systems, personnel, etc.—might meet often and regularly to read, consider, pass on, and decide on all suggestions and the amount of compensation to be paid for those which are accepted. All this takes time. Companies should be prepared to staff such working committee with management personnel who are available, knowledgeable, and interested.

The use of a committee provides a broader base for the consideration of suggestions submitted. It also makes the final decisions more acceptable to the employees. Winners should be recognized and rewarded as promptly as possible. Procrastination, delay, and confusion are insidious enemies that cause suggestion systems to fail.

The committee will acknowledge receipt of suggestions by putting the list, by identification numbers, on bulletin boards, in the employee magazine, or by general memo. As action is taken, the decisions are also announced. A list of rejections, often including the reasons (and these must "hold water") is posted simply because there is no other way of reaching the suggestors who are identified only by number. Suggestions which are being studied, or are in the process of investigation, are also publicized. When suggestions are accepted, the winners are announced, again by identification number, and possibly with the amount of reward to be paid in each case.

A good publicity program helps to maintain interest in the program. Included may be posters, handbills, letters from management, honor rolls of successful suggestions, and human interest stories about winners and winning ideas.

Payment Plans

Payments for suggestions that are accepted can be made in different ways. Most companies feel that cash is the best incentive. The amount is a percentage, usually 10 percent, of the estimated first year's savings to the company. A minimum cash award is made for every accepted suggestion.

Variations of nonmonetary recognition include merchandise awards, paid trips, or a bonus for the best suggestion submitted during a contest period.

This brings up a thought. Many suggestion systems which start out on the right foot bog down into a time-consuming, nonproductive routine program once the initial interest and novelty have worn off. From then on the committee gets more and more useless suggestions from workers who have run out of good ideas but who keep on making suggestions on the "what have I to lose" theory.

To offset this waning of interest, some companies do not run their suggestion systems on a continuing basis. They prefer to conduct a contest. For a 30- or 60-day period they will accept suggestions for possible award payments, with the winning suggestion earning a grand prize, such as a two-week trip to Hawaii, a color television set, or other big item. A number of lesser prizes go to other top winners, and every employee who has a suggestion accepted gets some prize or payment.

Collecting award-winning ideas is but one reason and possibly the least important one. The big benefit that a suggestion system accom-

EMPLOYEE'S SUGGESTION

PROBLEM _____
_____
_____
_____

SUGGESTION _____
_____
_____
_____
_____
_____

EXPECTED RESULT _____
_____
_____
_____

My Name Is _____
Dept. _____
PAYROLL OR
CLOCK NO.   Date _____
ALL SUGGESTIONS BECOME THE PROPERTY OF THE COMPANY TO USE IN ANY WAY.

EMPLOYEE'S
SIGNATURE _____

A simple suggestion form like that shown above will do a satisfactory job in many organizations where the work is not highly complex. The form is available from Staff Builders, Inc., New York City.

plishes is to focus the thinking of the organization on doing things better and developing creativity. The constant stimulation employees get when a suggestion plan is in operation—as long as it is being properly operated—keeps them alert and sparks their interest in their jobs. Knowledge that the "front office" wants their ideas and suggestions, will consider them seriously and sympathetically, and will "share the savings" if their suggestions are adopted, makes them feel they belong, and are important to the success of the business.

Employee suggestion systems are always management oriented. The objective is to increase cash savings and efficiency.

AIR CANADA SUGGESTION SYSTEM

The suggestion plan at Air Canada was established in 1947. H. G. Walker, supervisor, suggestion program, says results were only fair at first, but the plan is gathering momentum.

So far 12,717 constructive ideas have been received from employees. $70,259 has been paid out in cash awards. $586,457 in measurable savings has resulted from the adoption of employees' suggestions (based on savings accruing in the first year following adoption only).

Lead mechanic A. G. Higham of Winnipeg was the recipient of the highest suggestion award in the history of the plan. Mr. Higham received a check for $2,060 for his design of a propeller and cowl de-icer cyclic switch for the Viscount aircraft.

A four-part suggestion form was developed for the easy use of the suggestor. The investigator's comments are written on a suggestion investigation report form. Following are the advantages of these suggestion forms:

1. Suggestor receives an immediate receipt for his suggestion.
2. Investigation can start immediately.
3. Supervisor is not bypassed.
4. Contact is always between suggestor and supervisor.
5. Headquarters have local management's views on the idea before investigating for system use.
6. Local suggestion can be answered verbally; no long written explanation is needed.

7. All replies are countersigned.

8. Suggestion bureau receives a copy of all suggestions and replies.

9. The recording work in the office has been considerably reduced.

Supervisors play a vital role in the program. The areas of supervisory responsibility in the suggestion plan are mainly:

1. *Encourage* employees to submit constructive ideas. Assist them in developing ideas when necessary and within reasonable limits.

2. *Investigate* suggestions completely, promptly, enthusiastically. Try to make something out of them.

3. *Evaluate* suggestions that are submitted. Weigh pros and cons carefully and adopt when the new way is better than the old. Be adequate in measuring benefits.

4. *Discuss* the results. Present awards to employees with complimentary remarks to gain the objective desired in submitting suggestions. Discuss rejected ideas with employees explaining why their ideas cannot be adopted. Commend them for their efforts and encourage them to keep on trying.

Since the supervisor is involved he may logically ask about the advantages to him. The suggestion system program benefits the individual supervisor in the following ways:

Reduces cost of the operation under his supervision through elimination of waste, improved handling, and better utilization of resources for overall effectiveness.

Improves safety through the correction of hazardous conditions.

Improves employee relations through a closer working arrangement with employees in helping them with their ideas and rewarding them for constructive thinking.

IMP—IDEAS MEAN PROGRESS

In the early days of suggestion systems, Nationwide Insurance Companies, Columbus, Ohio, paid $5 for each approved suggestion. From these the best of the week, month, quarter, and year were selected. Small additional payments were made each time for the best suggestion in the period.

In 1959 Nationwide went to the present program, called IMP (Improved Methods Plan). Under the new policy payments range from a minimum $10 and a maximum award of $1,000, based on 10 percent of first-year savings. This has resulted in increased participation companywide, with an average of approximately $100,000 in savings annually for the company.

Present Method or Situation:

Recognize
the
Situation

Get All
The Facts

Print, T
Write

Proposed IMProvement

Analyze
The Facts

Use
Sh
Ne

Develop A
Better Way

San
S

Compute Savings   (Labor, Forms, Supplies, Equipment, Space, Postage, Time, Etc.)
(If Possible)

Sell and
Install The
Better Way

Thor

Other Benefits: (Convenience, good housekeeping, morale, safety, sales, losses.)
Is there an expense involved in starting this suggestion? What is it?....................................
Estimate cost $........................ Approximately how many people are affected?..........................
How frequently or for what period will the benefits result?..

Employee No................................ Agent No.......................

NAME... Disb. Code..

Dept/Div/
Section..Region...............................

Depts. Affected..

Suggestion Subject...

Committee Action: Adopt: Yes...No...............................

For Office Use Only
Date Rec'd........................
Sugg. No...............................
Category No............................
Savings $............................
Award Amt. $........................

The objectives of IMP are —

1. To provide concrete recognition of the importance of broadened participation on the part of employees and agents in developing ideas which will improve service to the policyholder.

2. To provide the means by which the inherent creative ability of employees and agents can be made more effective.

3. To offer stimulation by recognition of individual achievement and by making financial awards commensurate with the value of the individual's contribution.

In order to determine awards for IMP suggestions, the benefits of the suggestion are classified as "tangible" or "intangible."

Tangible suggestions are those that provide a monetary savings. Intangible suggestions, relating to improvements in work quality, schedules, safety, service, public relations, working conditions, provide benefits other than monetary savings.

Suggestions on any of these subjects are generally acceptable:

Eliminate: Operations, equipment, forms, steps.

Reduce: Waste, losses, time, expenses.

Combine: Jobs, forms, procedures, operations.

Improve: Forms, procedures, quality, production, public relations, working conditions.

Devise: New fixtures, new methods, new equipment, new product features.

Increase: Production, sales, cooperation, underwriting gain.

All agents are eligible for IMP awards. Employees up through a specified salary grade are eligible with the exception that supervisors may receive awards only on savings or improvements that fall beyond their scope of authority.

NATIONAL ASSOCIATION OF SUGGESTION SYSTEMS

The National Association of Suggestion Systems is located at 435 North Michigan Avenue, Chicago, Illinois 60611.

NASS is a not-for-profit organization founded in 1942 to encourage the adoption of suggestion systems and to exchange ideas relating to the administration of such programs. It has grown from the original group of 35 members in 1942 to a membership of over a thousand diversified companies and government agencies, and is international in scope. It represents the professional interest of individuals who operate the most successful systems.

The association's broad purpose is to encourage suggestion systems in industry, commerce, finance, and government. Its objectives are to:

1. Gather and exchange useful information on suggestion programs.

2. Study elements involved in promoting good employee thinking.

3. Promote public appreciation of the usefulness of employee suggestion systems.

4. Provide an opportunity for the personal development of those who represent member organizations.

COMPANY CAFETERIAS

Company cafeterias, which received their greatest impetus during World War II, are by no means any war-born frill. Many progressive companies had feeding facilities for years, all the way from free soup and coffee, to lunch wagons, and cafeterias. The basis for any such food service is the contention that there is a correlation between proper diet and production, although this is difficult to prove statistically.

Employee cafeterias or food vending service is referred to in the industry as "in-plant feeding." Installations run all the way from automatic vending machines dispensing packaged ready-prepared meals, to caterers bringing in hot foods cooked in a central kitchen, to elaborate cafeteria and dining facilities with complete kitchens and trained personnel. All together this adds up to big business. In one year 41,000 companies serve 23,000,000 meals each day to their employees.

In many offices and factories of medium and larger size, the employees have available a full-scale cafeteria operation complete with a food service staff with all food purchased, stored, prepared, and merchandised on location. Some attempt is being made to replace manually run cafeterias with partial or fully-automatic food service. This idea is presented more to managements, who hear the arguments for cost reduction, than it is to the employees who still prefer the personal touch.

All Harding—Williams operations: Above, dining area of Guarantee Mutual Life, Omaha; right, serving line at Northwestern Mutual Life, Minneapolis; below, island serving line in cafeteria of Electro Data Division, Burroughs Corporation, in Pasadena, California.

A number of organizations, notably banks, insurance firms, colleges, hospitals, and the military, who formerly preferred to operate their own cafeterias, now seem to be moving toward concessionaires. Other companies have already assigned this responsibility to outside food management firms, content to retain control over scheduling, prices, quality, and cost, but eager to be relieved of the day-to-day work and problems in a field for which they feel less qualified than the professional specialists. Cafeterias in companies are operated on a break-even basis, a cost-plus-fee arrangement, or, as is usually the case, subsidized, with management contributing toward the cost of food and labor in addition to buying the equipment and providing space rent free.

No "Executive Area"

The design is no longer left to chance, utilizing whatever leftover space is convenient, but is well planned, often with the help of restaurant consultants. Kitchens in the newer installations are models of efficiency with stainless equipment. The serving area is moving away from the familiar tray-slide line to the newer "break in" or shopping-center concept of separate stations for different departments. Dining areas are no longer graduated by rank: Insulating executives from the rank and file is a practice good personnel directors usually frown upon. Modern employee cafeterias are air-conditioned, pleasantly decorated, and feature piped-in music. They are intended to make workers feel transplanted into a nonwork environment.

Managements look upon cafeterias as a necessary function of the employee relations program, like work conditions and welfare benefits. Sometimes the provision of a cafeteria is a necessity, especially when firms move to outlying neighborhoods, or where downtown restaurant locations are crowded and expensive.

Other companies shy away from this responsibility, saying to themselves that a worker's eating is his own concern, just as transportation is. Lunch programs, they assert, are paternalistic; they waste space and capital. Besides, they cause headaches and management has enough problems without inviting more. They claim it is better when employees get away during the day for a change.

On the other hand, companies with cafeterias defend their decision by explaining that workers can eat in less time by staying on the premises—usually a relaxed half hour instead of a hurried one hour. This results in better work hours for the entire day. It also cuts down fatigue. In mills and factories, feeding workers in the plant cuts into the nearby saloon trade.

Company cafeterias can serve special needs—menus for people of foreign descent; for others on restricted or low-calorie diets. The company may reward employees with an occasional free meal, or a bargain dinner on a holiday or special occasion. Free coffee can be furnished to call everyone's attention to a new product or a significant anniversary. There are all sorts of possibilities.

Breakfast at Blue Cross

But there are other advantages which are just as real. In the case of Blue Cross-Blue Shield, Chicago, the employee cafeteria, which is operated by Harding-Williams, Division of Saga, opens 45 minutes before the regular office hours begin. Every morning about 175 to 200 customers come in for breakfasts of one sort or another, on their own time, for reasons which are important to them personally. They have a full choice of breakfasts cooked to order—warm food at subsidized prices—and the conviviality at a table of friends certainly beats eating a quickie early morning toast or cereal at home, especially for the person living alone.

The cafeteria is also used for morning and afternoon 15-minute coffee breaks. No food or beverages are allowed elsewhere in the office and this rule helps keep the office clean.

There is still another benefit working in the company's favor . . . and this is considered the most important. Not long after the cafeteria was opened years ago, it was discovered that the smaller tables were seldom used. People gathered at the larger tables seating eight and on many occasions crowded in extra chairs. This circumstance could be peculiar to this office, but the fact is that smaller tables have since been replaced with eights, and several tables can accommodate 12 people.

Here at coffee breaks and during lunch periods friends gather to discuss their common interests. The group often consists of employees who work together; mailroom women might sit with each other, or keypunch operators might be in the same corner day after day. More often than not, the group is made up of people who do not come from any one department, who normally would have no contact with each other, but who somehow enjoy these daily get-togethers with friends in the same circle. Here they visit about all sorts of things in general, telling about vacation plans or reporting on trips completed, discussing last night's television program or the late show, second-guessing yesterday's ball game, commenting on the latest developments in the news, or just talking about personal or family items. Supervisors and managers join in at tables with employees, not necessarily their own, and the conversation which often relates to business crosses divisional lines.

The freedom to meet, talk, listen, and expound, has many benefits. It is good for individual and group morale. It is an excellent communications medium since word of a personal or official nature really gets around. It is an ideal spot for management to plant a well-placed rumor or to listen to a reaction of some official policy or decision. Not to be overlooked is the almost total elimination of the nuisance of employees wasting time while visiting at desks, work stations, or water coolers.

Military campaigns have been told, "an army marches on its stomach," and many a hopeful young lassie in love has been given maternal advice that "the way to a man's heart is through his stomach." So also have the sloganists among the food purveyors advised managements that they can "get to a worker's heart through his stomach." This is naiveté at its worst. Not even the best employee cafeteria can be used as a substitute for a good employee relations program, with recognition, opportunity, and challenges, and above all, adequate wages. But a good in-plant food facility can make the best personnel program even better.

CAFETERIA HONOR SYSTEM

A unique "honor system" is used in the employee cafeteria of Pilot Life Insurance Company, Greensboro, North Carolina.

There is no tray slide serving line. The cafeteria is operated on the shopping center principle. Foods are grouped in stations: there is one location for entrees, another for salads, another for desserts etc.

When an employee enters he takes an IBM card which lists all the food items and prices. The customer goes directly to any food station, helps himself to what he wants, then moves to another station, until he has completed his lunch order.

There are no cashiers or food-checking counters. Since 1929, when the home office cafeteria was opened, it has been operated on an honor system.

Here is the way Joseph W. Gawthrop, second vice-president, tells it:

A number of years ago in order to save manual labor and the time of our dietitian and other clerks in filing and adding totals of menus each day, we devised our IBM card system. Our complete menu, including prices, is printed each day on IBM cards.

As staff members enter the cafeteria, each takes a card, goes through a service area and proceeds to the seating area—all this without any cashier or checker. Upon being seated, he completes the card by indicating each separate item he selected, and enters the total price together with his signature and cafeteria code number.

The cards are placed in a receiving box as each person leaves. They are collected each day by our cafeteria manager, who visually scans them very quickly for any possible errors or omissions (but this does not involve checking any addition).

The cards are then taken to our data processing department where the date is gang-punched and the amount and cafeteria number are handpunched in each card. The cards are then filed. Once each month a list of daily charges and the total is run on data processing equipment for each person. A summary is intro-

day, October 12		*DIXIE SPECIALS*		Tuna Salad	15	Chocolate or Sweet Milk	09
		Hamburger	14	Tossed Julienne	20	Diet or Buttermilk	08
le Soup	10	Cheeseburger	18	Lime Supreme	10	Coffee (Cream Free)	04
		Hot Dog	09	Carrot & Raisin	10	Tea, Juice or Punch	04
STEAMTABLE		Chopped Barbecue	15	Fruit Salad	10		
ork Ham		Wrapped Sandwich	10	Fruit Plate	25	*BREADS*	
TE	31			Cold Meat Plate	25	Sliced Bread—each	01
WICH	27	*SALADS*				Roll or Corn Bread	02
Chicken, Rice	19	Assorted Fruits	05	*DESSERTS*		Muffin—each	03
/Pineapple Ring	19	Cottage Cheese	06	Pumpkin Pie	09	Butter	02
ti & Meat Balls	18	Cole Slaw	06	Ginger Bread	09	Crackers	02
asserole	18	Plain Jello	05	Cherry Pie	09	Mints—each	02
		W/Cream	06	Raisin Pie	09	Jelly—each	02
ABLES		Relish Tray (each)	05	Layer Cake	09		
d Potatoes	07	Tossed Salad		Fresh Fruit	06		
eas	08	WHOPPER	15	Assorted Puddings	05	No.............Amount............	
Beets	08	MIDGET	08	Fudgecicle/Moo Bar	06		
quash	08	Tomato Bits	05	1 Slice of Ice Cream	08	Name............	
Greens	07	Congealed Fruit	09	Ice Cream Sandwich	09		
Fries	08	Potato Salad	10	Cheerio Bar Nutty Buddy	08	*DRINKS*	

duced into our payroll system and each person's monthly charge is deducted automatically from his salary.

The list and the cards themselves are returned to each individual as a receipt and as further evidence that no other employee's meal cost was charged to him erroneously.

VENDING MACHINES

Vending is completely acceptable in thousands of locations, either in place of a company-operated cafeteria or as a supplementary service.

Vending is not new to industry. Candy, gum, and peanut machines began to appear in factories as early as the 1920's, and eventually became as common as the drinking fountain. The cigarette machine soon followed, as did the soft drink vendor. Rather than resulting in wasted time on the job, management soon found that the ready availability of such products helped keep workers on the premises.

World War II gave impetus to the coffee break. The fresh-brew coffee vending machine appeared shortly afterward and met the need for a fast, convenient, economical means of providing coffee on the job.

Strategically located throughout a plant, coffee vending machines required no additions in personnel to serve any or all shifts. Eliminated were time-wasting long walks to and from central cafeterias and the morning and afternoon exodus of people in search of coffee. Not the least of the machine's benefits was the fact that it produced a cup of coffee whose quality was completely satisfying, yet whose price required no subsidy.

With the widespread popularity and continuing rapid growth of food vending, it is difficult to realize that this modern means of in-plant feeding is scarcely more than a few years old. Some pieces of food vending equipment antedate the start of the 60's, such as the hot-canned-food vendor and the "buy on faith" sandwich machine which concealed the product until it had been paid for and delivered. The concealment was not deliberate, to be sure, but reflected an unprepossessing stage in the development of a business which was new to the operator and new to the personnel manager as well. If food at first appeared to have little potential for growth, in common with most pioneering effort, it was also productive of little income. But it did open the way to bring food vending to the relatively sophisticated level it holds today.

Manufacturers of vending machines, taking a lesson from merchandisers in other retail lines, began to provide for display areas where foods behind glass could be plainly seen and exert their appetite appeal.

A Coming of Age

Almost overnight it seems, although designers and engineers would deny it, vending equipment became available in attractively matched units. Gleaming glass and bright metal trims took the place of drably painted surfaces. Machines were illuminated to give showcase display to products. Coin mechanisms became more versatile. They returned proper change and permitted the vending of a far greater variety of products at price levels based on fair values.

No mere mechanical revolution, however, enabled the vending operator to expand his services as a robot restaurateur. Food packers and processors and packaging people saw the future in food vending and prepared to serve it in such a way as to secure their share of its ultimate rewards.

The recent introduction of the electronic oven has done much to speed service as well as to expand menus. Within but eight or nine seconds, the vending machine patron can bring a casserole, sandwich, or entree and vegetable dish from a refrigerated state to table temperature.

There is today scarcely any selection of food for which the customer is willing to pay that cannot be vended. Even gourmet meals offer no problem except that the customer is not yet psychologically adjusted to the vending of "high ticket" items.

Although personnel managers in general turned to vending enthusiastically, some were reluctant to abandon entirely the cafeteria concept of in-plant feeding, even when this change was economically or otherwise advisable. They were concerned that employees, having had things pretty much their own way at the company cafeteria, would tend to find fault with automatic food service. It was suggested that a combination of vending machines and an attended cafeteria counter would bridge the gap between the one and the other, particularly at the noonday meal.

Canteen Corporation saw the wisdom of this thinking and introduced such a combination food service known as CounterVend. In using hot and cold self-service cabinets, a short-order preparation area and an attendant, along with vending machines, the employee patron finds that he can order special items. Perhaps more important to him, he retains the opportunity to exchange a little banter with the lady behind the counter. Interestingly enough, it has been found that, given greater freedom of choice than is provided through vending machines alone, the customer most often tends to select the vended item which is immediately ready and waiting for him.

The aim of the vending industry is to provide the company with facilities which will best meet the particular requirements for in-plant food service, not to replace the manual cafeteria and dining room which will still prevail as the best food service for years to come. The CounterVend concept may be preferred by some. Others find complete vending ideally suited to their needs. Still others may want the full manual cafeteria or dining room, or both.

Vendors and Hospitals

Most hospitals operate their own food service, but many today engage professional food management firms. A caterer, such as Hospital Host, provides the personnel, including back-up staff, plans for regular meals as well as special functions, does the purchasing, sanitation, and accounting, maintains controlled production and quality, and can assist in layout of kitchen, serving. dishwashing, storage, and dining areas. With the advent of Medicare, the rigid accountability and controls which are implicit in the operations of a food service contractor become especially important in accurately reflecting cost information needed by the business office.

Use of an outside food service relieves the dietitian of niggling daily chores and personnel emergencies that arise in the dietary department. It also enables her to concentrate on the therapeutic responsibilities of her position. The hospital administrator can feel he is free of all the day-to-day problems associated with food, while yet continuing to retain complete control of every phase of the operation.

EMPLOYEE LOUNGE

Not all employees go on coffee breaks. Most of them, however, take their scheduled rest periods. For many employees just having a comfortable place to sit and visit is all they ask. It gives them a change in the work routine and a different environment.

An employee lounge need not be fancy, although it should be as pleasant as circumstances permit. The location should be nearby, yet away from the work stations. The atmosphere should be unlike that of the work area so a transplanted feeling results. The chairs and sofas should be comfortable and inviting, similar to living-room furniture. Tables should be available for writing and card playing. Lamps, rugs, and pictures can be used to good advantage. Music helps.

It is customary to equip such a lounge with current popular magazines and other reading material. Some people read to pass the time; others come in to keep abreast of current events. Put the magazines into binders so that no one will be tempted to walk off with a copy.

An employee lounge should be a pleasant place to go so that employees will use it. Someone described a typical office, with its neat rows of identical desks, as looking like "a box of aspirins— filled." Likewise, too many employee lounges resemble bus stations, with a miscellaneous assortment of odd leftover chairs lined up along the walls.

Someone in your organization has a bit of the interior decorator's flair. Let such person or persons rearrange the furniture into groupings to simulate rooms. Display trophies of employee events, safety awards, or United Fund contributions. Add an innovative touch here and there and the lounge will come alive and serve as the hub of employee activity.

RECREATION

One of the fastest-growing fringe benefits is company recreation. These programs range from company-encouraged ball games, parties, or clubs, to company-supported bowling leagues and golf outings, to company-sponsored picnics and choirs, to company-owned swimming pools and country clubs. These leisure-time activities often extend to "family fun."

Small cities may have inadequate facilities for sports, games, and pastime. Companies provide their own in order to attract and hold workers. Some company properties, such as golf links, swimming pools, auditoriums, may also be made available to the townspeople under certain conditions.

The use of outdoor areas, such as wooded groves for family outings, skating ponds, and baseball diamonds, is greater with companies located in small or medium-sized cities where community facilities are often limited. In the large cities, where open spaces are not available or too far out to be practical, the diversionary needs of employees are met with social clubs, indoor play courts, and bowling leagues using public establishments.

Many activities are provided free; others, such as clubs, are covered by dues. Some charge membership fees. Proceeds also may come from vending machines. Typically, company support is indirect and channeled through employee clubs that plan and conduct many of the activities.

Body-building exercises or calisthenics provided in gymnasiums, with the aid of a physical director and a masseur, are for executives and managers—to reduce waistlines, help blood circulation, and "prevent weekend heart attacks." Most programs, however, aim for wide participation and are open to all employees, white-collar salaried personnel as well as the increasingly affluent blue-collar workers.

Companies usually hesitate to reveal how much they spend on recreation since, in the words of one executive, "a lot of stockholders still look on such things as pork barrels." But surveys show that companies and employee groups spend $10 per capita a year to build, maintain, and staff these facilities. Companies claim these programs lead to a reduction in absenteeism and turnover, and aid in recruiting the people they need and want.

Insurance a Precaution

Since companies are involved in some measure in these employee activities, they buy insurance as a backstop against the unexpected. Workmen's compensation covers after-work involvements which are supervised, sponsored, subsidized, or identified with the company, such as by an advertisement on bowling shirts or baseball uniforms. There is, however, a gray area between what is compensable and what is not. No clear line has yet been drawn by state industrial commissions.

Information about company recreation programs may be obtained from:

> National Industrial Recreation Association
> 20 North Wacker Drive
> Chicago, Illinois 60606

The Dominion Foundries and Steel, Limited, Hamilton, Ontario, has an extensive recreation program for its employees. The following is taken from *The Dofasco Way,* the company handbook.

Dofasco has a very large and active recreation club in operation the year 'round. Membership in any of the varied activities is open to all members of Dofasco. There are even some in which members of your family may participate.

All Recreation Club activities are self-governed groups, under the direction of the Recreation Department which may be reached by dialing 3203. The Recreation Director will be glad to give you full details and help you to become established in the activities of your choice.

Activities are carried on at various arenas, gymnasia and bowling lanes throughout the city, while some groups are located in rooms on Company property. Throughout the summer months, softball, blooperball and baseball games, along with tennis matches, are played at our 20-acre Recreation Park located in East Hamilton.

PILOT LIFE COUNTRY CLUB

Pilot Life Insurance Company, Greensboro, North Carolina, offers an extensive recreation facility to its employees. On October 7, 1953, when the home office staff numbered about 300, President O. F. Stafford cut the ribbon that marked the opening of the Pilot Country Club.

Club facilities were designed to provide pleasure and relaxation to all employees and their families. A winding uphill road leads to a parking lot large enough to accommodate 140 cars. A circular drive connects this lot with the carport club entrance.

The beautiful brick building, 143 feet wide, houses the club. The center section rises to a height of over 20 feet. The club is equipped with a manager's office, main lounge with fireplace, cloak rooms, modern kitchen, three dining rooms, ballroom, lower-level snack bar, game rooms, and has a 15- by 75-foot enclosed porch dining area.

The club is located in beautiful natural surroundings. The eight landscaped acres present different moods as the seasons change. There is a picnic grove with barbecue grills.

Above, set in beautifully landscaped surroundings, is the country club for employees of Pilot Life Insurance Company, of Greensboro, North Carolina.

At right, a view of the carport entrance, which boasts its own private road.

Pilot Lake occupies 7½ acres and is stocked for fishing. A 75- by 42-foot swimming pool was built in 1966, together with two additional pools separated by a 3-foot fence. One is shallow and for "toddlers," and the other, deeper, is for younger swimmers and beginners.

The dining rooms allow an employee to enjoy a moderately priced quiet supper on a weekday or to bring the whole family for the special Sunday dinner menu. Numerous dances and parties are held each year for all members and the various facilities can be reserved for such functions as private dinners, showers, receptions, and birthday celebrations.

A club activities advisory committee is elected by the home office staff by popular vote. The committee is charged with the responsibility for arranging seasonal dances, back-to-school parties, bingo games, Easter egg rolls, children's Christmas parties complete with huge tree, and many others. Events also include the Masquerade Ball, New Year's Eve party, and on some occasions fireworks illuminate the sky over the placid Pilot Lake. Sometimes professional entertainment is engaged and at other times home talent provides the shows. The club is also the scene of an annual summer festival.

EMPLOYEE-PROMOTED ACTIVITIES

In addition to company-sponsored employee programs, there are other activities promoted by the employees themselves. These are generally more limited in scope than a program planned by the company for all employees. These employee-promoted activities are offered company-wide but they appeal to special interest groups.

They are often built around and by a certain individual who has a personal interest in some project. He talks it up among his friends, develops enough enthusiasm to bring it to company attention, gets official sanction and possibly some measure of financial support, and the program is underway. Some of these programs fall by the wayside when the spearhead leaves or loses interest.

This is how many bowling leagues start. Someone, usually not from management, gets the idea, sells it all around, and makes it run. Softball teams, basketball teams, volleyball teams get their impetus and development this way. Some of these activities continue year after year, under rotating leadership, while others run their course and die.

Less common than athletic or recreational programs are projects which appeal to only certain individuals. A few employees who share a common hobby might want to meet once a month on convenient company premises. These could be stamp or coin clubs, poetry clubs, foreign travel groups, home movie fans, and the like. Many choral groups are conducted on just this type of informal basis.

The company gets involved by granting official endorsement, some form of financial assistance, publicity, and use of company facilities such as meeting rooms, printing, telephone, and house organ. There is no rule of thumb on how much financial support to give since these activities vary so much. A bowling league involves regulars and substitutes for 35 weeks plus possibly an award banquet, whereas a golf-driving exhibition is a one-time occurrence. Without any guide, most companies are willing to pay entrance fees, league costs, perhaps uniforms, and something toward the group's treasury to be used for prizes or a dinner.

ACCIDENTS AT JOB-RELATED OUTSIDE EVENTS

How much responsibility does a company have when an employee gets hurt outside the regular job but at an employee function which is job-related?

Certainly if a company sends a group of employees out officially, say to a convention, the measure of responsibility is great. These people are, in effect, engaging in company business even though they are away from the office or plant and involved beyond work in pleasure activities. The fact remains that they were directed to go, under company sponsorship, for the good of the firm.

The measure of responsibility is less at a company social event, such as a Christmas party or picnic. The chances are an employee or guest who suffered injury at a company function would be hard-pressed to make a case unless he could prove negligence on the part of the employer.

What it really boils down to is that this is not a legal matter as much as it is a personnel problem. Legally a company may easily be absolved, but it must still live with its employees. Therefore, it may want to do the right thing, whatever is appropriate under the circumstances.

CHARITY DRIVES—ONE or MANY?

Charity drives and fund-raising campaigns run throughout the year. How many should a company participate in? How often can employees be approached? Which of the programs, all worthwhile, should be recognized?

Most communities have a United Fund organization which consolidates most of the major fund-raising activities into one annual drive. By cooperating wholeheartedly with this community-endorsed activity, both the company and its employees feel they fulfill their responsibility to the welfare agencies operating locally and nationally in their behalf.

When a company takes the position that supporting one all-out campaign is the extent to which it can afford to solicit funds from employees, what about the separate programs that come up at other times? One suggestion is that the company may want to cooperate with any additional drive that it feels worthy of supporting, but leave employee participation entirely up to each individual. Contributions might even be made direct.

Posters may be placed on bulletin boards, collection cannisters may be located at strategic stations, literature and mail-in envelopes may be kept handy. In this way, an employee who is moved by the agency's story may donate without any pressure being implied.

It is customary to clear any such appeal for funds through the personnel office. Otherwise a rash of campaigns may spring up for causes which may not be understood and could possibly be questionable. Clearing requests for contributions through personnel would also serve as a control over the sale of raffle tickets, sympathy donations, and similar solicitations.

Companies generally prefer one combined annual fund-raising campaign in which the major agencies share as against a series of many separate smaller donation requests. Obviously, the line must be drawn somewhere, and this arrangement seems to be acceptable to companies and employees.

GIFT or FLOWER FUND

To avoid passing the hat . . .

Companies have established, or allowed their employees to develop, informal gift or flower fund organizations. These are generally simple but effective plans administered by employees for employees.

There is something nice about being remembered on special occasions. But there is something unpleasant about taking up collections, or being asked repeatedly to chip in for some worthy cause. For these reasons a gift or flower fund is formed. It provides an easy and automatic way of giving a nominal amount each payday for remembrances for various occasions, without the necessity of individual solicitations.

It also has another advantage. It equalizes the giving and the receiving. All members get the same benefits and contribute the same amount. Without a plan it is likely that employees in some areas might get more and better gifts, or employees in large departments could be asked to contribute oftener than others.

A typical voluntary plan calls for a contribution of 10 cents per week for the employee, handled through payroll deduction. The company contributes 5 cents per week for every member.

For this the members receive these benefits:

Deaths:	$20 spiritual or floral remembrance for the death of a member, immediate family of a member (husband, wife, children, father, mother, brother, sister, or any other relative residing in the same household as the member).
Illness:	One $10 floral piece, plant, book, or other gift in any calendar year for an illness serious enough to warrant a member being absent from work for 10 or more working days.
Weddings:	A $10 gift or merchandise certificate, if the employee is not terminating at the time of marriage.
Terminations:	The value of the termination gift will be based on $5 for each full year of membership. This could be a check.

The administration of an employee gift or flower fund calls for a president, treasurer, and a few representatives from throughout the work force. These local representatives learn of the need for a remembrance or gift, and they do the gift buying for their coworkers.

OFFICE and PLANT POOLS

Many firms are beginning to clamp down on employee betting. This practice not only disrupts work schedules, but often establishes a plant "bookie" who spends a part of his time collecting and paying off bets.

Sports pools aren't the only problem, although football bowl games and the World Series are common occasions for wagering. One company found its employees paying $1 a week for 13 weeks for a "drawing." Another turned up a lottery based on paycheck digits.

Some supervisors threw up their hands in despair, saying "There isn't much that can be done with so many people involved." What makes the problem difficult is that managers and supervisors, who should control or curb the practice, often participate and are the biggest offenders.

In companies where the custom of conducting an occasional "company pool" is considered little more than employee fun, keep an eye on the goings-on to prevent a harmless practice from developing into a problem situation.

LOST and FOUND

In any medium or large company it is likely that items of intrinsic or sentimental value will be lost or found. Once the employee group grows larger than a close-knit family-type unit, the workers will not know each other too well, which will keep them from readily recognizing each other's personal belongings.

Umbrellas may be left in the lobby, sweaters in cloakrooms, rings or watches in the cafeteria, pens in conference rooms, etc. It is amazing what items are forgotten or misplaced. These are usually found by other employees, supervisors, or the night cleaners.

There should be some convenient central place where lost items may be turned in by those who find them, and reclaimed by those who lost them. This "lost and found" location should be well known to all. Quite often, as in the case of a wallet, it may be important that the loser recover the lost item quickly.

Care should be taken when returning items to people who claim them. Some attempt should be made to have the claimant describe what he is looking for before it is shown. The recovered item should go only to its rightful owner.

Some items will never be claimed. Employees may not realize where they lost things. Once in a while the collection should be cleaned out. Some things, such as soiled or worn-out clothing, may be discarded. Other items may be placed on a table in some public place, such as the cafeteria, urging employees to take anything they recognize as their own.

BLOOD BANKS

Many companies have established blood banks among their employees. Anyone in the work-force who qualifies may volunteer to donate blood, and then employees and possibly their dependents may draw upon the blood supply in the bank as the need arises.

The arrangements are made with the local blood center or with a nearby hospital. The rules for donating blood and for withdrawing blood depend upon the amount of blood available and the wishes of employees who participate in the program.

The qualifications for blood donor usually go something like this. He or she should be between the ages of 21 and 60. Someone 18 to 21 may donate with the written consent or presence of parent or guardian unless married.

A donor may give blood every 10 weeks, or about five times a year.

A donor is rejected permanently if he has ever had jaundice, malaria, diabetes, or syphilis. A donor is rejected temporarily for any of the following reasons:

1. A cold or flu; wait one week after symptoms cease.
2. Childbirth, wait six months.
3. Tooth extraction; wait one week.
4. Appendectomy, tonsillectomy, hernia repair, hemorrhoids; wait two months.
5. Under doctor's care; a note from the doctor will allow donor to be accepted.
6. While taking antibiotics.
7. High or low blood pressure.
8. Certain inoculations (consult blood center).

As for diet, a donor is encouraged to eat during his regular scheduled mealtime; however, he should not eat any fatty foods such as butter, cheese, eggs, meats, milk, soups, etc., within 12 hours. He may have as much coffee or tea (without cream or milk), water, soft drinks, fruit juices, and nonfatty foods as he likes.

Recipients of the benefits of the blood bank may be only those employees who contribute or may include all employees including those who do not or cannot donate. In most such programs employee dependents or close relatives may also share in the benefits.

The arguments for a company blood bank are obvious. The arguments against such program are simply that once a supply of blood is freely available, employees will no longer respond to the individual needs of their families and friends. Once blood becomes a commodity, the opponents feel, it loses its appeal as a health-saving "good Samaritan" act, and they ask, "Has anyone you know ever been denied the blood when he needed it?"

EMPLOYEE COMPLAINTS

Employees, by complaining, are trying to tell their bosses something. Instead of being annoyed, managers should welcome the opportunity to listen.

Complaints should not be taken lightly. Do not let their apparent smallness, from the company point of view, cause you to deal with them in an offhand way. The grievance which may be almost invisible to the supervisor looms large in the complainant's eyes, or he would never have bothered to express it.

Nine times out of 10 the situation is exaggerated. Often it is imaginary. Sometimes it is fabricated. Nevertheless, it deserves to be handled in a spirit of attentive interest.

There are two ways of solving any problem. Management can do something or the employee can do something. Management might not even be expected to resolve the difficulty; it could be enough just to show interest and hear the employee out. When this is not done, the employee might take matters into his own hands. The easiest way for the employee to detach himself from the problem, whatever it may be, is to walk away from it by quitting his job. That way he is free of the annoying situation, but when he departs he leaves the problem behind where it could well continue to plague the company.

More important than saving an employee for the company, or not hurting an employee by letting him quit, there is something else to consider. That is, the *value* of complaints. Every complaint, even the smallest one, is a signpost along the road to trouble.

Why worry about the occasional complaint when the great majority of workers say nothing? Just as nine-tenths of an iceberg lies beneath the surface of the sea, so the complaint may be a signal of something worse that lurks behind the scene.

The ideal way to handle complaints is to prevent things from happening that give rise to grievances, to be careful to give no grounds for a justifiable cause of distress. Thinking of the interest of employees is the best way of safeguarding the interest of the firm.

Even if an employee program were perfect, there would still be complaints. When these complaints are made, they should be turned into opportunities. There is no more satisfying experience than that of turning a discontented employee into a happy and productive worker by the care, attention, and appreciation he was shown.

Finally, if no complaints were ever voiced, how would companies know where improvements are needed? Accept it as a basic law of business life that there is always room for improvement. Complaints are valuable because they direct attention to possible areas of improvement in operating efficiency and employee relations.

Go Looking for Trouble

As an afterthought, companies might go one step further and seek to uncover grievances. When not given expression, irritations will build up to the point of explosion. The principle of stepping out to meet trouble rather than allowing it to fester in secret is a sound one. When an employee sees that his company is making efforts to discover and rectify conditions that displease him, especially when he has not said anything, the action will impress him and make him more appreciative of management's concern for its workers.

In summary, the discreet and skillful handling of an employee complaint is a constructive action in your company's interest. The principal points to practice are to acknowledge the complaint at once, indicate a genuine interest in it, make a speedy investigation, resolve it objectively, and give your decision without delay.

A Sample Procedure

The following description of grievance procedure that has worked well at the New England Medical Center Hospitals was made available through the courtesy of Francis Matthews, personnel director.

Step 1. Discuss the problem with your department head. Most personnel problems can be solved in this manner.

Step 2. If you are not satisfied with the solution offered by your department head, you should present your problem to the personnel director. He will (a) work out a solution to your problem to your satisfaction or (b) act as your representative and advise and assist you in Step 3 of this procedure.

Step 3. If you are not satisfied with the solutions offered by your department head or the personnel director, you should refer your problem to the personnel relations committee. Special efforts have been made to select members of the committee who will be objective and impartial in their consideration of your problem. If the committee includes a representative of the complainant's own department, an alternate may be selected from another department. If you desire, you may select a hospital employee to assist you in presenting your problem to the committee. All information presented to the committee will be considered confidential.

The committee will study your problem and make a recommendation to the administrator of the hospital. After reviewing your problem and the recommendations of the committee, the administrator will make a decision in the matter. This decision will be considered as final.

COUNSELING

Employees have two kinds of problems, personal and job-related. The need to discuss their problems is a real one. Employees should be given an opportunity to resolve their problems.

Employee personal problems relate to money, financing, wage assignments, mortgages, income tax, other tax rulings, court judgments, legal matters, moving, age verification, Social Security or Medicare for self or parent, personal or family health, and a host of other items.

Employee job-related problems relate to supervision, opportunities for advancement, transfer, relocation, wages, lost paycheck, benefits, schools, maternity furloughs, military orders, insurance coverage for self and/or dependents, insurance claims, retirement planning, vested rights, and many other similar items.

The above examples are specific and clearly defined needs. In addition, employees have concerns about their jobs, the company, and their future.

They feel inadequate. They are not clear on just what is expected and how their work is judged. They don't understand other departments and feel sometimes that another department keeps them from doing their best. They want to do quality work but the supervisors keep emphasizing production.

They feel unappreciated. They often suspect favoritism in promotions and salaries. Some employees, frankly, are afraid to open their mouths; complainers, they find, don't last long.

They feel neglected. Their friends in other companies get two more holidays, better vacations or benefits, more privileges. Management never comes around unless there is trouble brewing.

They feel insecure. The company is standing still. Sales are dropping. Deliveries are late. No new products are in evidence. The firm is planning to sell out, merge, or move. The government is taking over.

Not all employees, of course, have all these problems all the time. But there is enough discontent, misunderstanding, confusion, bad feeling, and other problems that their existence should be recognized. No employee can do his best as long as he is plagued with doubt, fear, and similar distracting forces.

Every employee should have an outlet for his problems. In a small place this might well be the boss himself. In larger offices and plants this could be someone in the personnel office. In all cases, the person who is trying to counsel should resist the temptation to say, "I'll tell you what to do." All the person who is doing the counseling can do is help the other employee work out his own solution.

Here are some suggestions for making the counseling discussion effective:

1. Make the employee feel welcome and comfortable. Provide privacy to make the interview confidential.

2. Let him talk. He has a need to express himself and tell about his trouble. Get the conversation going and then hear him out.

3. Hear the problem. Listen, get the full background, find out his attitude toward the problem. Do not assume after a few opening statements that you recognize his situation.

4. Get the pertinent facts. He may be emotionally upset, contradict himself, and confuse you. Keep probing until all relevant facts are clear and fall into place.

5. Don't take sides. Accept what is said but express no judgment of his opinions or actions. Nor be sentimental or sympathetic with his side. Never lecture or moralize.

6. Help him gain insight into his problem. Once he has unburdened himself he may see the situation in a broader perspective. It is not uncommon to find him solving his own problem. Usually he knows what to do but wants first to "go on record" with it and then get some understanding to help him overcome it.

7. Let him suggest the solution. If his plan is satisfactory and you foresee no other involvement which could lead to trouble elsewhere, let him proceed. But you owe it to him to keep him from doing something that might only make the situation worse or lead to more serious consequences.

8. Arrange for followup if necessary. Unless you are involved in the solution, get out of it and let the employee work it out on his own. You might casually check at a later date to see if things worked out as planned.

CHAPLAINS

Chaplains in industry have had enough success during the past decade to dispel the old notion that religion and business do not mix. Both church leaders and businessmen have been impressed.

What does an industrial chaplain do? Very little of his work is directly related to religion. Most of the time he serves as friend and confidant, a man to whom workers—and executives—can go with their troubles. A growing percentage of the ministers entering industry are also trained as psychologists, and their day-to-day work is far more involved with counseling than with preaching.

What do workers discuss? Mostly they bring up personal problems—marital and family troubles, alcoholism, and personality difficulties. Few are concerned with job-related problems.

Regardless of his denomination, the man of the cloth works with men and women of every religion, and also with those of no religion. A bulletin board announces his presence by saying simply he is here "to listen and help if he can."

To be effective, he must be left alone, not directed by the company. Otherwise he may be regarded suspiciously as a new gimmick to improve employee relations, or worse, a company spy. But once the workers discover for themselves that he is "straight," his acceptance is assured and his usefulness begins.

SYMPATHY BOOKLET

At the time an employee experiences a death in the family, a company often does not know how to help.

One practical solution is the "sympathy booklet" developed by the Montag Division of the Westab Corporation.

The booklet contains appropriate poems together with a letter of sympathy. Then follow brief mentions of those company policies and programs which apply, such as final salary payments, life insurance, medical insurance, veteran's benefits, Medicare, income tax. The company offers to help in any of these areas and, what is most important, lists the name of the person who may be contacted.

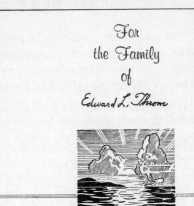

Three pages are shown from a "sympathy booklet" issued by Montag Division, Westab Corporation, to families of employees who have passed away. In addition to expressing sympathy, the booklet contains practical information and advice.

For the Family of Edward L. Throm

In Sympathy

On behalf of our employees, we extend our deepest sympathy to you in your grief.

We know that it is hard for you to think about anything other than your loss at this time. However, we do want to offer our assistance and be sure that you know about the various Company and governmental programs which may concern you.

Please feel free to call on us if we can help you in any way.

COMPANY POLICIES AND PROGRAMS

FINAL SALARY PAYMENTS

The Company will pay to the spouse or designated beneficiary final salary payments.

LIFE INSURANCE

The Company has a Group Life Insurance program. You will be advised if the deceased was a participant.

MEDICAL INSURANCE

There may be a claim for medical expenses. Check with the person named to assist you for this information.

INCOME TAX AID

Employees who seek assistance in filling out their income tax returns may get help from the Internal Revenue Service either by telephone or personal visit to one of the IRS offices.

A special telephone number is designated for telephone inquiries. This service is available each year from January 1 until April 15.

People may also visit their nearest district office where IRS agents are available to assist them in filling out their returns.

FEDERAL BENEFITS FOR VETERANS

Counselors may wish to be alerted to the following benefits, available to veterans and dependents, as they discuss problems with employees who themselves are veterans or veteran's dependents, or who are otherwise related to present or former service personnel:

1. *Allowances* toward the purchase price of an automobile or other conveyance, including special appliances, for disabled veterans.

2. *Social Security Credits,* gratuitous, for period of military duty. In some cases, veterans receiving military retired pay may receive wage credits.

3. *Pensions* for disabled veterans.

4. *Hospitalization* on a priority basis.

5. *Domiciliary Care* for veterans whose disabilities are not so severe as to require hospitalization but who meet certain requirements for a "home."

6. *Outpatient Medical Treatment* for veterans in need of treatment for a disability incurred or aggravated in service.

7. *Outpatient Dental Treatment* similar to above (item 6) conditions.

8. *Prosthetic Appliances* for veterans who qualify for this service.

9. *"Wheelchair" Homes* for certain disabled veterans of wartime and peacetime service.

10. *Medical Examinations* for veterans applying for certain federal benefits.

11. *Aid for the Blind* for any veteran entitled to compensation for a service-connected disability and blind in both eyes.

12. *Vocational Rehabilitation* for disabled veterans.

13. *GI Bill Education and Training* for veterans who served between specified dates.

14. *War Orphans Education Assistance* for children between ages 18 and 23 of veterans who died from disease or injury incurred or aggravated in line of duty in active service during certain specified periods.

15. *Assistance in Obtaining Home Loans* for veterans of wartime and peacetime service.

16. *GI Loans for Homes, Farms, Business* for veterans and eligible widows.

17. *Farm Loan Benefits* for veterans of wartime and certain peacetime service.

18. *Federal Civil Service Preference* (5 or 10 points) for veterans of wartime and certain peacetime service.

19. *Preference in Job-Finding Assistance* for veterans of active wartime service with ability to work.

20. *Reemployment Rights* for veterans under specified conditions.

21. *Unemployment Compensation* for ex-servicemen, as administered by the U.S. Department of Labor.

22. *Naturalization Preference* may be authorized and expedited by eliminating certain requirements.

23. *Dependency and Indemnity Compensation* (DIC) may be selected in lieu of death compensation for service-connected death before January 1, 1957.

24. *Death Compensation* for survivors of veterans who died before January 1, 1957.

25. *Non-Service-Connected Death Pension* for widows and children of deceased veterans.

26. *Reimbursement of Burial Expenses* (not to exceed $250) for veterans of wartime and certain peacetime service.

27. *Burial Flags* for veterans of wartime and certain peacetime service.

28. *Burial in National Cemeteries* for veterans and certain members of their families.

29. *Headstone or Grave Marker* for any deceased veteran.

30. *Memorial Plot in National Cemeteries* for service personnel missing in action or whose remains are unrecoverable.

31. *Six Months' Death Gratuity* for survivors of those who died while on active duty.

For more details in any specific situation the Veterans Administration should be contacted.

A WILL

A good citizen demands the same careful planning for the disposition of property after death as for its use during life. For this he needs a will. A revocable trust may also be used; the same guidelines apply.

What Is a Will?

In simple terms it is a legal document, signed and witnessed, by which a person directs the distribution of his property upon his death.

Who Should Have a Will?

Practically everyone needs a will. A will can be most valuable when the estate is small and assets must be conserved for the benefit of the surviving family.

Both husband and wife should have wills. If a husband and wife own all their property jointly, the will of the first to die will not have to be probated and the property will pass automatically to the survivor. But if both die at the same time—in an accident, for instance—or under circumstances that make it difficult to determine which one died first, then it can be very important that each has a will. In any event, the survivor will eventually die and will need a will to control the disposition of property at that time.

When Should a Will Be Made?

Now—for anyone of legal age who doesn't already have one. The first rule in making a will is: "Don't put it off." No one knows, even young people, when tomorrow may be too late. Besides, when a person waits until he is advanced in age or seriously ill, the chances are greater that the will may be contested on grounds of incompetence or undue influence.

A will can be changed at any time during the lifetime. In fact, it should be reviewed and probably revised whenever a person's family or financial situation change.

What Should Be Included?

A will should provide for dependents—spouse, children, parents, others. You may also wish to name institutions or organizations you would like to remember.

How May a Person Write His Will?

Don't try to write it—get a lawyer. Many wills have failed because they were not properly prepared. A will is a legal document, the preparation of which requires special knowledge. Legal requirements vary depending on where a person lives. The fee for a lawyer's service is small in comparison to the potential benefits to the beneficiaries.

PROBLEM EMPLOYEES

When we think of problem employees here we are thinking of employees with problems. These are not employees who are disloyal, unproductive, or untrained. Their problems are such that the employee usually has little or no control over the situation.

These are the people in our work force who have physical, mental, emotional, or psychological ills. Their handicap may be temporary or permanent. Generally they develop their problem condition after they have been with the company a while. Because their work record is usually good, they have the benefit of job security although they may no longer be able to carry their fair share of the load.

Included in this broad category are all sorts of workers who are no longer performing up to previous standards. And there is no relation between the many types, except that they have become less-than-good workers. The list is long.

The number one addiction problem is the alcoholic. There are five million alcoholics in the United States, cut across all strata of society. They are white-collar workers and blue-collar workers.

There are other problem employees. Many develop mental, nervous, and emotional ills which may not be job-related. Aside from the popular occupational diseases—caused by tension, pressure, worry, and the like—there is an almost endless list of conditions that change an otherwise good worker into a problem employee. A worker's marital or family situation, financial status, health, and such concerns may so disturb him that he can no longer concentrate on his job. Quite often he keeps his troubles locked up inside his heart, ashamed to admit them and fearful of his job.

Understanding Needed

The supervisor, not knowing the real reason, may jump to an erroneous conclusion, and take action that aggravates the situation. But even when the cause of a worker's changed attitude or performance is known, many times the temptation to dispense discipline rather than understanding is too inviting for the self-righteous supervisor to ignore. No supervisor has been endowed with the divine right to pass judgment over a fellow man. Nor is this advisable from a purely selfish viewpoint. A good employee gone wrong becomes a better employee if faith in him is maintained and he is helped over the rough spot in his life.

A big area of problem employees involves those who develop physical limitations. Through no fault of their own they are no longer adequate for their regular work although still useful under new terms. These are the people who recover from heart attacks, who suffer amputations, who develop chronic illnesses, and so on. Is it fair to shelve them when their former value declines? On the other hand, it is fair to other good employees to give all workers equal consideration when it is obvious some of them are unable to compete? Maybe the answer is to transfer these physically limited workers, temporarily or permanently, to jobs that are within their capabilities and to continue to compensate them, as much as is practical, in accordance with their length of service and other previous contribution.

In all these cases, and others like them, it may be well to remember that loyalty works equally well both ways. Companies expect loyalty from their workers. When the shoe is on the other foot, is it asking too much for the company to show its loyalty to the employees? An employee who has given the best years of his life to a company may have no other place to turn for help and understanding.

It might be hard to prove, but it shouldn't be hard to believe, that a company which builds people also builds loyalty, dedication, understanding, appreciation, and character—all of which help to build profits.

THE ALCOHOLIC

Among every 33 people on your office or plant payroll, the national average predicts that there is probably one who has a problem with drinking. If you have 330 employees, you may have 10 problem drinkers. One of these 10 is destined to become an alcoholic, falling victim to the nation's fourth most prevalent health problem.

The national estimate is set at 5 million alcoholics, about 2 million of whom are regularly employed. The annual cost to business and industry is estimated to be over $2 billion.

Progressive managements are coming to recognize alcoholism as a treatable disease. More and more companies are formulating stated policies to govern the problems of the alcoholic employee. It is estimated that nearly 200 major firms have alcoholism programs aimed at helping these people to save their jobs. It is becoming increasingly evident that discharge is not the best answer to this difficult personnel program.

How is that $2-billion cost of alcoholism arrived at? Lost time, absenteeism, accidents, insurance premiums, ruined machines and material—these are some of the costs. The alcoholic loses much more time as a result of job and off-the-job accidents than the average worker. Mistakes caused by the alcohol-fogged mind are costly in this day of complex and expensive machines.

Recent studies indicate that the alcoholic worker loses an average month of working days each year. Time lost by the production worker with a headache or hangover is easily measurable because he either stays home or his production is cut. The problem faced by the white-collar worker is not as quickly calculated because he may be in the office physically.

Larger companies that inaugurated programs to aid their workers are able to report savings running into the millions of dollars. In some cases these companies have full-time staffs working on the program.

For companies that would like to pursue the study of an alcoholism program in office or plant, here are sources of information:

1. Alcoholics Anonymous, P.O. Box 459, Grand Central Station, New York, New York 10017. Practically every community has an AA group, usually listed in the telephone directory. AA works directly with the individual, and assistance is given promptly to anyone with a desire to stop drinking. There are no dues or fees. AA is generally recognized as the single most effective aid to recovery for the alcoholic.

2. The National Council on Alcoholism, Inc., New York Academy of Medicine Building, 2 East 103rd Street, New York, New York 10029. There are 72 affiliated councils of NCA around the country, some of the larger of which have special committees working with business and industrial firms in their areas. Most councils operate Alcoholism Information Centers.

3. North American Association of Alcoholism Programs, 323 DuPont Circle Building, Washington, D.C. 20036. Information available on state alcoholism programs and facilities.

Parke, Davis Policy

Dr. E. M. Rotarius, director of employee medical services, Parke, Davis & Company, describes his company's policy on employee alcoholism as follows:

Our policy on employees with drinking problems has four basic premises:

1. Alcoholism is a serious illness and should be treated as such. All employees with drinking problems receive the same consideration under the company's medical and benefit programs as do employees with other illnesses, if they cooperate wholeheartedly in treatment and attempts at rehabilitation.

2. Our efforts are directed toward rehabilitation of the employee whenever possible. He receives the best advice we are able to provide.

3. Cooperation will be maintained between the individual's department and the industrial medical department. No one-sided action is taken in any

case. Conferences are held about employees who have repeated problems.

4. The employee is given every reasonable opportunity and all possible help to overcome his problem. If he does not cooperate and rehabilitation efforts are unsuccessful, his case is handled as an administrative problem and his future with the company decided jointly by all parties concerned.

SUGGESTED GUIDES FOR DISCIPLINARY ACTION

1. After first relapse, suspend for a short period, say two weeks.

2. After second relapse suspend for one month, with a warning that termination may come after the next relapse.

3. After third relapse, consider desirability of terminating employment. If, in an unusual case, it is decided not to terminate employment, recommend a leave of absence with a firm commitment that the suspension is preliminary to termination—unless the employee demonstrates to the satisfaction of the company that acceptable rehabilitation is accomplished during the three-months' time.

4. If, after that time, there is some evidence of progress, but it is not sufficient to end the suspension, extensions of leave may be recommended up to a maximum of 12 months.

It is important that representatives of management, personnel, and the medical department continue close supervision of the employee during all periods of suspension.

THEFTS

There are figures and statistics available for almost every kind of business loss. But there is no way of knowing how much money is lost each year because of employee thefts, inventory manipulation, juggled books, and other forms of pilferage and "inside" dishonesty. The estimate is that American businesses are losing $1 billion a year because of employee thefts, plus some $3 billion because of embezzlement of company funds.

Company stationery and office supplies which are taken home may seem like a minor item, but if the practice is unchecked or becomes widespread, it can add up to an expensive problem. Stolen equipment is less frequent but because of its greater value adds considerably to the amount of office or plant thievery.

Behind the surge of employee dishonesty are the growing use of part-time workers, the extension of working hours with early or late jobs or overtime workers inadequately supervised, the absence of any specific company policy covering petty thievery, and a reluctance to crack down on dishonest employees suspected or caught in the act.

What should a company do to reduce these losses? If there is no written policy, then draw up one. Make it unmistakably clear how serious the company considers the problem and what the consequences are for any employee caught stealing. Take a position, then stick with it.

If a case is discovered—act promptly and in accordance with the announced policy. Word will get around. Never, however, divulge the details, especially how the deed was perpetrated. This might give someone else ideas.

Look into any suspicious situations such as some items being consumed too rapidly or in unreasonable quantities. Watch for high concentration of certain purchases or other evidence of merchandise transactions that are difficult to follow or explain. There are plenty of signposts along the crooked road and a manager can be alerted to recognize and observe them.

Any form of thievery adds to the cost of goods or services, reduces profits, and ultimately is passed on to the consumer. Most of all, dishonesty on the part of a few employees is an insult to the majority who are honest, not because of any company rule but by virtue of personal integrity.

The Psychology of Bonding

Help prevent thefts from happening with fidelity bonds. It's a fact: When employees *know* they're bonded, the incidence of theft goes down. Tell an employee he's bonded and we create a powerful psychological effect. He's suddenly aware that not only the employer but also the bonding company will hold him to account. And being bonded appeals to his sense of honor and integrity. When men and women *know* they're bonded, the incidence of theft goes down. But they must know . . . and we must tell them.

Leaflets stressing the honor and advantages of being bonded are provided by the insurance company. Many firms distribute them in pay envelopes. To be effective, regular distribution is recommended.

Office-building thefts are on a sharp rise in some cities. Articles from purses to office machines are being removed in large quantities. Some thieves enter buildings on legitimate business and some on the pretext of business.

Sound advice from the police includes these points:

—Never let unauthorized persons wander through an office or even the building.

—Never leave an office unattended without locking the door.

—Never leave a purse on a desktop, and keep the petty cash box out of sight.

—Double check to be sure doors and windows are locked at the end of the day.

—Keep locks on ladies' rest rooms.

—Don't let anyone (including someone in a uniform) remove office machines until he is checked out or is well-known.

—Don't ever assume that a thief does not have the nerve to walk into your office and out with your valuables.

WAGE ASSIGNMENTS

When an employee becomes delinquent in paying a debt it is customary for his creditor to attempt to collect from the compensation due the employee. This places an employer in the unpleasant position of an innocent stakeholder between the employee and the creditor.

The two major creditor remedies are wage assignments and garnishments. Both are regulated by state laws which vary from one state to another.

Collection of a delinquent debt by means of a wage assignment is a convenient procedure available to creditors. Like the wage-deduction process, the source of the collection is compensation payable by an employer to the debtor-employee. Unlike the wage-deduction process, the wage-assignment process may be begun without first obtaining a judgment against the debtor.

There is varied company reaction to this unwelcome intrusion, making the employer a legally constituted collection and remitting agency for an unknown, and often questionable, creditor or finance office. Some employers cooperate willingly in an effort to be helpful to their workers, disregarding the cost in time and effort. Other employers want no part of bad-debt involvement and automatically discharge an employee when he gets into money trouble.

Some companies officially frown upon employees using unsound financing practices. A company may encourage the employee with money problems to visit the personnel office for counsel and advice, or may recommend him to the credit union for a solution. The firm reasons that it is better to seek help before trouble starts.

Many companies simply hold an employee's paycheck as a weapon to move him toward taking action to resolve his problem. They do not give him his paycheck until a written release is obtained from the creditor. Whether this practice is legally permissible is debatable.

In a large number of companies wage garnishments are simply not tolerated, an employee being subject to automatic discharge upon receipt of a wage assignment. As one handbook says, "If you stick your neck out for more installment purchases than you can afford, you may lose your job." These companies take a position that they do not want to assume involvement for their fiscally irresponsible employees. They hope the announcement of a firm stand will serve as a deterrent to indifferent employees.

Generally an employer does not have to put up with garnishments and may fire an employee for having one filed against his salary. However, before doing so it would be wise to check with a lawyer to see whether there might be a state law which forbids discharge. At any rate, a company should not take a hasty dismissal action, because a creditor might have filed wrongfully, or the employee, by taking prompt positive action, might succeed in having the garnishment withdrawn.

Forms of Wage Assignment

A *judgment* served by a court of law must, of course, be honored. This consists of a wage-deduction summons and spells out the terms. It customarily allows for a "living costs" exemption, expressed as a fixed amount or percentage of earnings, and has a limit.

A *notice of levy* is served on an employer by the United States Treasury Department—Internal Revenue Service, when an employee is in arrears in his income tax obligations. The amount due, owing, and unpaid is thereby protected by a lien against the taxpayer.

According to the Internal Revenue Code all property, rights to property, moneys, credits, and bank accounts are levied upon and seized for satisfaction of the unpaid tax. In such cases the demand upon the employer is made on 100 percent of gross earnings of the taxpayer. Deductions are permitted for income tax of current year plus any deductions usually taken out for benefits.

For information only, since this would probably not involve the employer, property exempt from a levy is (1) wearing apparel and schoolbooks, (2) fuel, provisions, furniture, and personal effects not to exceed $500 in value, and (3) books and tools of trade, business, or profession, not to exceed $250 in value.

Wage assignments, garnishments, levies, judgments, assessments, and other forms of attachment should be filed in the employee individual file folder since they do tell something about the person away from his job. It is not recommended, however, that these papers be filed when the assignment is readily resolved by the employee, or if the claim is submitted erroneously. Why retain, for possible future reference, information which might reflect adversely upon an employee if the employee is not at fault and his record is good?

FREE ADVERTISEMENTS

Ever notice the "news tree" on college campuses, used by students to make announcements, inquire about rides home, or offer articles for sale? This convenient clearing house of information is popular because it is an effective means of direct communication.

In business the need for employees to reach fellow workers also exists. Many companies, as an accommodation to their employees, provide for such a medium of exchange. It may take the form of a handy bulletin board, to which workers may attach notices. Where there is a "house organ" magazine, a space is often devoted to this purpose.

Many employee publications offer free advertisements. Here employees may offer cars and other items for sale or exchange, may express a desire to purchase something, and may even seek or offer apartments or homes for rent or sale.

PARKING

The location of the company determines whether a parking lot shall be provided. Firms in outlying neighborhoods have little choice; the convenience is not only necessary but also expensive. In the metropolitan district the expense may be prohibitive and public transportation may suffice.

In most cases the parking lot adjoins the office or factory building, or is next door or across the street. Seldom is it more than one block away.

Quite often such a lot is lighted and surfaced. Blacktop is popular for spacious areas, concrete is sometimes found in downtown congested locations, and occasionally the lot is gravel.

Weather is a factor. Overhead walkways may lead to the building as protection from rain or sun. Use of snow removal equipment is part of maintenance, as is oil and grease cleanup.

One-Way Traffic Advised

For safety, the lot is patroled, walled, or fenced. One-way traffic patterns avoid congestion. Speed limits are posted and attempts made at control. Barricades are set up to prevent speeding. Painted guide marks aid the flow of traffic and identify individual parking spaces.

There are no services, such as car washing. But in below-zero weather some on-the-spot help may be made available for starting stalled vehicles.

Detailed instructions on the use of the company parking lot are given to new employees. Individual employees are assigned to a reserved lot or section but not to a specific space. Drivers use the lot on a first-come, first-served basis, which does not discourage employees from coming to work early. All companies, however, have individual spaces reserved and marked for executives as a convenience, and for others, such as in-and-out salesmen, plant nurse, etc., as a necessity.

Smaller spaces are marked off for foreign and compact cars, and a small corner set aside for motorcycles and bicycles.

One difficulty is spotting trespassers. A parking sticker on a window or bumper is an attempt to meet this problem by identifying those who are authorized to use the lot. Violators of common sense speed regulations, safety precautions, and other rules lose their parking lot rights, usually after a first warning.

There is a problem when the company grows and the parking lot doesn't. In such cases there is usually a waiting list to "get in" and replacements may be selected by seniority or job level. One plan that has been used where the parking facility is inadequate to serve everybody is to give preference to car pools.

Typical Regulations

As one example of the rules governing the use of company parking lots, here are regulations from the manual of the Woodward Governor Company, 5001 North Second Street, Rockford, Illinois 61101:

1. *Parking Lot Regulations.* Only 250 parking spaces will be assigned to the first 250 on the seniority list who drive regularly. We wish to emphasize that members who have assigned parking spaces must drive their car regularly or drive their car as part of a riding pool. Members should not ask for a space when they drive infrequently. Only one member of a riding pool is entitled to a parking space.

2. *Open Parking Spaces.* Members who do not have an assigned parking space will park in the open parking area on the basis of first-come, first-choice, in the area assigned to the exit and entrance used. The dividing line between the assigned area and open parking area will be clearly indicated.

3. *Special Parking Area for Waiting Cars.* The parking area north of the regular parking lot and parallel to the cement drive is for cars and drivers who come to pick up members after they leave work. This area is not to be used for regular parking while the driver is at work.

4. *Numbered Stickers for Cars.* Each member using the parking lot will be given a numbered sticker. This sticker should be placed on the inside of a window of his car, preferably the front window.

5. *Ten-Mile Speed Limit on Company Property.* Drive at a safe speed in the parking lot and on the drive leading out to the highway.

6. *Do Not Pick Up Riders After Leaving Individual Parking Lots.* Riding groups should all get into the car where it is parked. When a car stops to pick up riders in the drive near the gate house, it is hazardous from a safety standpoint and annoying to the occupants of following cars.

7. *Be Careful of Your Neighbor's Car.* Use care in opening your car doors. You probably don't like to have your car dented or scratched, so give the same consideration to the other fellow. Please park in the center of your assigned parking area. The number on the cable indicates the center of your space. Back into your space.

INDUSTRIAL EDITING

There are about 10,000 publications directed to a variety of audiences, with readership totaling tens of millions, sponsored and paid for by organizations still growing in size and number. These publications are serving as the most important link between management and employee, producer and customer, manager and financial backer.

Why are these publications issued? Whenever an organization becomes so big that the people involved are unable to keep up with what's going on by observation or by chatting with their employers, some sort of communication device is needed. A regular publication is one of several effective solutions.

Industrial editing, in general, includes the full range of activities involved in publishing any magazine, newspaper, or newsletter. The most common example is a publication issued to employees of an industrial firm, hence the term "industrial editing." But this profession also embraces those who publish material for other groups: Staffs of hospitals, members of professional or trade associations, sponsors of charities, alumni of schools, civilian employees and servicemen in government units, as well as customers, dealers, retirees or stockholders of commercial concerns.

The Job of the Editor

Although the specific objectives of these publications may vary widely, the one common objective is to convey a better understanding of the organization: its purpose and its function.

Although some publications are concerned largely with entertaining their readers (or lifting their morale), the majority have the job of informing or motivating. This puts a great responsibility upon the publication and, consequently, upon the editor—since it is generally recognized as an official voice of the organization. The material appearing in a company publication is so vital that it can be—and often has been—used as evidence in important legal cases.

It's a big job . . . it's big in the number of subtle nuances needed to relate the organization to its audience. And it's big in the actual performance of a myriad of duties which must be accomplished, or at least supervised, by the editor.

The man or woman engaged in industrial editing is usually called upon to perform a wide range of functions in connection with the publication. These may include selecting subjects, interviewing, writing, photographing, designing and laying out the pages, ordering art and supervising the engraving, printing, and distribution. On some larger publications, these functions may be assigned to specialized staff members or to professionals outside the organization, but it is more common for the editor to do them all. One of the editor's biggest responsibilities is managing the publication's budget —and investigating the various ways of economy without sacrificing effectiveness.

Link Between Management, Workers

Editorial policy is a series of objectives developed and monitored by leaders of the organization. This does not mean, however, that the editor is limited in initiative or in creativity. On the contrary, these are generally the two qualities he needs most to do his job. He has a relatively free hand to select material and treat it in a manner he believes to be effective. Although he is hired to perform as a communications expert, there are times his purely objective news sense must be tempered by what is good for the entire organization.

The editor must understand his role as the link between top management and those who are affected by their policies and decisions. His interpretation of these policies and decisions is crucial in bringing about understanding and acceptance.

The man or woman in editing may be responsible for other techniques in communicating with employees or customers and dealers. These might include bulletin boards, newsletters, letters to employees' homes, a phone information program, tape-recorded messages, closed circuit television, annual reports, movies, plant visits, interim reports to shareholders, paycheck stuffers, suggestion system, direct advertising pieces, sales aids, reprints of speeches, and the like.

Whatever the audience, whatever his initial responsibilities, the editor has an enormous job: he must be helpful. He should give employees information and recognition that enables them to identify their interests with those of the company. He helps stockholders know that their investment is secure and meaningful. He helps customers believe in the quality of products they buy and he helps dealers market the company's products successfully—to everyone's advantage. The editor's readers can be classified into two groups: those who produce and those who buy.

Personal Qualities Required

The successful industrial editor incorporates several personality traits which qualify him for the job he holds:

CREATIVITY: Every issue must be different, interesting, substantive, eye-catching, informative.

EXPRESSION: The ability to express thoughts in logical order is essential to one who tries to motivate others.

INITIATIVE: He cannot wait around for news to come to him.

RESILIENCE: Frustration is an occupational hazard for creative attempts are frequently thwarted.

INTEGRITY: Every publication quickly acquires a reputation, and the kind of image depends largely on the editor.

COURAGE: An editor's opinions and decisions are often challenged by those who hold opposing views.

Information and help may be obtained from—

International Council of Industrial Editors
2108 Braewick Circle
Akron, Ohio 44313

MUSIC

The need for music is so deeply rooted in man that it can arouse strong emotional and physiological reactions even when his attention is not directly focused on it. This is the principle on which the background music of motion pictures and television creates or enhances specific moods.

This subliminal effect of music can also be put to use in industry. But music in offices and factories cannot be just any music. Put another way: Music is sound, and sound can be harmful as well as helpful. As sound is known and understood today, it can be proved that an abundance of it (white sound from rockets) can kill a man, maim him, or cause him to be a deaf mute. On the other hand, the lack of sound, as for example, placing a man in an anechoic chamber, can drive him to insanity.

To serve its purpose, music in industry must therefore be planned. Music by Muzak, a professional supplier, explains that the ordinary music of radio, phonograph records, or juke boxes is designed to entertain and command attention. Entertainment music can create a mood for dreaming, dancing, singing, or marching.

What is wanted in industry is music to create a working mood. The rhythm, tempo, orchestration, and size of the orchestra must be programmed to suit the particular work group. Varying the frequencies of sound and its intensity, and placing these considerations in sequential order, are an important part of programming. Depending on the selections that precede and follow any song, it may sound louder or softer, slower or faster.

Music by Muzak is furnished over leased telephone lines, or through special frequency modulated subcarrier transmissions, whichever is more practical for the subscriber location. When subscribers are beyond the effective reach of either wires or FM, Muzak can supply an automatic, on-site source of music. Special portable units are used on jetcraft, industrial plants, and public areas such as restaurants, supermarkets, hotels, banks, and terminals.

The popularity of this kind of functional music is evident in the statistics. Muzak serves more than 40,000 locations including the "10 best-managed companies," over 80 percent of the nation's 25 largest life insurance companies, commercial banks, and savings and loan associations.

Scientifically planned, properly recorded, and carefully programmed piped-in music may be the answer to the problems of errors, low production, waste, and accidents. At least the professional suppliers can present quite a convincing case. It might be worth looking into.

CHECK CASHING

A check-cashing service can be more than a convenience. Plants which are located away from a handy bank or currency exchange might find it necessary to arrange for cashing paychecks on the premises. But there are also other reasons.

If a company pays its employees by check, and an employee is injured on the way to the bank to cash the paycheck, is the company liable? A New York State court held that the employee was "working for the company" at the time of the injury and that the company was responsible.

The employee was struck by a pushcart while returning from cashing her paycheck during the noon hour, and she sustained injuries. The court concluded that the injuries arose out of, and in the course of employment.

In some plants employees will turn over their paychecks to one of their number to go to the bank to cash them before closing time. There have been numerous instances of these messengers being held up and often injured. Holdup men often frequent public check-cashing establishments where they can select their victims. Not only is this type of messenger service hazardous, but it also allows the earnings of individual employees to become a matter of general knowledge. This can cause personnel problems.

One solution to problems such as these might be to bring in a mobile check cashing service. There are three types of service:

1. Person-to-person. Bonded cashiers wheel money carts directly to each individual at his work station.

2. Central plant location. The cashier sets up a portable service in some central location inside the plant, in the cafeteria, for example, where checks may be cashed during the lunch hour or relief periods, or at some other location easily accessible.

3. Outside plant. Cashiers work directly from armored trucks parked at plant gate or in parking lot, serving employees as they leave at the end of the shift.

Check cashing service has these advantages. It:

1. Discourages tavern check cashing. This eliminates the problems of absenteeism, tardiness, inefficiency, accidents, late home arrivals, and such which are associated with drinking.

2. Cuts unexcused errands. This solves the problem of employees sneaking time, extra at lunch or early at quitting time, to cash checks on the outside.

3. Gives psychological boost. The convenience and consideration of management does, in many cases, result in an increase in production.

As a by-product, the service usually has insurance coverage:

1. For the employer. Each account served is fully covered by liability insurance against any damage, physical or otherwise, for which their trucks or cashiers are responsible.

2. For the employee. The employee who cashes his paycheck is protected against loss of his earnings by force while en route to his home.

A pioneer in this field is Thillens Checashers of Chicago, a service recognized and regulated by the State of Illinois. Established in 1932, its fleet of 20 armored trucks serve more than 125,000 wage earners each week. There are similar check cashing operations in a number of other states around the country.

CHECKLESS PAYROLLS

Service-minded banks are eager to put their new, sophisticated data processing equipment to full-time use—with an eye toward increasing business and adding customers in wholesale lots. The result is that banks have developed and are promoting the "checkless payroll" program. The concept has been around for some years. The earliest systems are mechanical calculators. Today computerization and magnetic ink character recognition devices simplify the job and make it profitable.

A key point is that many banks are capable of tailoring a system to fit the specific needs of a company. The type or amount of service has a broad base. For this reason, the checkless payroll idea is enjoying a steady growth throughout the country. An impressive number of business and industrial operations are already in the fold.

Under this arrangement a company's entire payroll is deposited with the cooperating bank. Each individual employee's "take home" pay is credited to his personal checking account. Instead of a paycheck he receives an "earnings statement" which is, in effect, a receipt for the amount deposited in his name.

The employee gets a checking account with a specified number of free checks each month and there is no service charge. He does not have to take time off to cash his paycheck, nor pay any check-cashing fee, and he does not carry a large sum of cash on payday. He does not have to go out to buy money orders.

Spared Many Details

The employer does not have to allow employees time off to go out to cash their paychecks, nor buy a mobile check-cashing service to come to his premises, nor leave a large amount of money on deposit at a nearby bank where employees may go to cash their paychecks free. More important, by turning over the entire payroll function to the bank, the company is spared all necessary details of check writing, reconciling, filing government reports, and making payments.

The union is agreeable since collection of dues can be arranged by the deduction of union dues from the checks on an individual basis, with the total receipts turned over directly to the union. Each union member signs a statement authorizing this deduction, and the collection of dues becomes a matter between the union, the employees, and the bank.

The bank, of course, is happy to get fuller utilization of its data processing facilities and in the process win new customers and to service them in all of their banking needs.

Marine National Plan

The following is an example of what one bank—in this case the Marine National Exchange Bank of Milwaukee, Wisconsin—offers to a company interested in a checkless payroll plan. The bank's own presentation should answer many questions that might come up if a company is exploring such a program.

Basically, this service entails the preparation and disbursement of the entire payroll (or a portion thereof) by the Marine Bank's Data Processing Center. The procedures used in preparing the payroll are similar to those practiced by companies which are large enough to utilize large-scale tabulating departments, with one major exception: The entire check writing, protecting, distributing, and reconciling functions are eliminated entirely.

A checking account is opened for each employee on the payroll, and each payday the employee's net pay is automatically credited to his account. Instead of receiving a pay check, the employee receives a statement of earnings.

Payroll accounting on tabulating equipment is basically "accounting by exception." All payrolls contain much repetitive information from one pay period to another. After original data is filed with the bank in the form of source documents, the only subsequent information that need be furnished us is that dealing with overtime hours or hours not paid for in the case of nonexempt employees, changes in rate, changes in deductions, additions or deletions from payroll, and similar changes. We then key-punch the information into card form, combine it with the uncharged data, perform the required calculations, check same, and simultaneously print the payroll journal, employee's earnings statements, and account credits. The journal and earnings statements are delivered to you for whatever checking is deemed necessary, and on payday the earnings statements are delivered to employees, their accounts are credited with their net pay by the bank, and a single offsetting debit for payroll is charged against your account.

The bank will automatically prepare and check all quarterly Social Security reports, relieving you of this burden entirely.

The bank will automatically prepare all Federal W-2 statements as well as the required state withholding information forms, and will either transmit them to the employer for distribution or will mail them directly to the concerned employees.

If desired, the bank will automatically prepare the depositary receipt for withheld taxes and deposit same in its Treasury tax and loan account, thus removing this burden from the employer, and eliminating the possibility of penalty for late filing.

The Marine will provide each employee with a Marine checking account. This account may be opened for the individual employee or it may be joint with husband or wife. Each employee will be allowed to write two free checks per month.

Each employee will be furnished with checkbooks, register forms, and with checks imprinted with his name at no charge.

Each employee will receive a regular monthly statement of his account.

If, for some reason, the employee prefers to bank elsewhere, he has only to draw a check for the net amount of his pay as shown on his earnings statement and either cash it or deposit it with his regular bank. Quite frankly, we feel that because of the favorable basis we are offering in this plan, most employees will prefer to maintain their banking with us.

The charge will vary with the complexity of the company's payroll, but in any event the fee will amount to only a small fraction of the company's present cost.

PART 7

WAGE AND SALARY ADMINISTRATION

EMPLOYEE COMPENSATION

Employee compensation is a cost to the company just as rent or purchases. As a cost of production, direct and indirect wages must be accurately planned and intelligently controlled. The cost of manpower services should be kept in line with other operating costs.

Employee compensation, however, is more than just another cost of operation. Properly administered it becomes an incentive for expended efforts, cooperation, and attitude toward the job and the company. It is a potent influence over the nature of the manpower services.

Two factors are inherent in a good wage program: (1) rates should be internally consistent; they should be based on an objective evaluation of each job to all other jobs, and (2) they should also be externally consistent, comparing favorably with community averages.

Three factors make up the individual wage of each employee:

1. The rate for his job in comparison with other jobs. Example: The hourly rate for a carpenter is higher than that of a gardener. A bookkeeper job is paid more than a messenger.

2. Recognition of individual effort. The jobs of two typists may be identical, but since no two individuals are quite alike their output on the job will most likely vary. When the better worker is paid the same salary as the poorer worker, the incentive to give better performance disappears.

3. The wages will reflect labor market conditions. A realistic wage program recognizes the influence of outside competitive conditions.

THE SALARY CASTE SYSTEM

For a country that prides itself on having no social classes, the United States has put up for a long time with a wage structure that epitomizes the caste system.

1. Factory and plant workers, and labor and service personnel, are paid by the hour.

2. Office clerical workers and technicians are paid by the week.

3. Professional, managerial, and executive personnel are paid by the month, often on an annual basis.

Only a few companies have broken the pattern. Some have put production line workers on a salary basis. Others have discontinued the use of time clocks.

WAGE and SALARY RELATIONSHIPS

Salary administrators in the personnel office are inclined to rely upon job evaluation or some similar system to establish the worth of a wage-and-hour job or a salaried position. This is an objective method, and acceptable to many, as long as it is related to the job and not the incumbent.

A chief executive often has his own way of determining how much he wants to pay an individual, particularly someone in a management, professional, or executive position. Whether he recognizes it or not, his decision is based on three determinants: (1) job value, (2) market influence, and (3) personal value to the company.

The personnel executive can advise the president of the value of the job in relation to all other jobs in the organization. This is where his job rating or evaluation system provides objective data. But this is only the starting point for the chief executive. Nevertheless, it is a sound base without which his other considerations would likely be erroneous.

Some jobs are in such scarce supply that the "going rate" reflects market influence more than job value. A physician on the company payroll is paid more for what he knows than for what he does, especially if he is assigned to paperwork or other nonprofessional duties. Computer analysts, fire prevention engineers, actuaries, are scarce in the employment market. A company has to be willing to pay whatever it takes to "buy" a qualified applicant away from another firm, or to keep its present employee from accepting a tempting offer from a competitor.

Finally, there is many an individual with a background, experience, training, or talent that is not required in his job but which the chief executive recognizes is always available to him. Clerical

611

or factory employees who can speak a foreign language, direct an employee chorus, or coach a softball team are examples. A personnel director who can write speeches for the president is a handy man to have around and this convenient talent could well be worth extra money.

This is not to say that a chief executive should ignore the guidance provided by a systematic salary program and go off on unrealistic salary tangents. This is to say that the personnel executive should not look upon his salary system as a straightjacket, but that he must accept that there could well be circumstances for going beyond it. There are reasons for making exceptions which are understood, but often not explained, by the chief executive who, in the last analysis, has the final responsibility.

TIME OFF

There are occasions when employees need time off from work other than vacations and holidays. Companies recognize these needs and provide for them.

Illness

For the infrequent short period of absence due to illness a company usually allows a specified number of "sick days" per year. When an employee is absent for a few days because of illness or accident, he will still be paid his regular salary. When the sick days are used up, he will no longer be paid during illness. These sick days are not a right but a protection; hence, the employee is ordinarily not paid for any sick days left unused at the close of the year.

For the long-term illness or accident, when the time off exceeds a few days, provisions are often made for a definitely spelled-out salary continuation program or a health and accident insurance policy which provides weekly income for a certain period of time. In both cases the allowances are designed to pay less than regular salary as an incentive for the employee to return to work.

Personal

There are circumstances when an employee needs time off for personal reasons. These could be emergencies at home, illness, problems in the family, personal affairs, or any of many similar situations. He tries to work out a solution without disrupting his work, but when this is impossible he will want to be excused from work for a while. Such time off, granted as a favor, is not paid for. Care must be taken to keep people from taking too much time off—the housewife who wants to stay home for a week at a time every few months, or the wife who wants to travel with her husband several times a year. Such on-and-off workers should not be placed on full-time jobs, but should be hired, if at all, under a different set of terms.

Military

Quite a few young men still have military obligations to fulfill after they are employed. Their once-a-week duties are usually in the evenings or on weekends and do not interfere with work. But many are required to go to camp two weeks in summer. Companies do not require them to use their vacations for this purpose, and nowadays companies are paying these employees the difference between their regular salary and their military pay.

Jury Duty

When employees are called for jury duty or to serve as witnesses, they have no choice but to take time off. Companies encourage their employees to fulfill their civic responsibilities and most of them pay either full salary or the difference between regular salary and jury pay.

Religious Observances

The standard 6 to 12 holidays recognized by most companies are considered national holidays, although some, such as Christmas, are religious in origin. There are some employees who observe other religious holidays and who request additional time off. This presents a delicate problem. Denying them the days off is not the answer, and yet giving them more paid holidays than other employees is not the best solution either. Some companies include in their list of holidays a personal day which then can be used by these people. Other firms may have other arrangements such as trading holidays in cases where a few employees may be required to be on the premises or man the switchboard during regular holidays. Otherwise the safest procedure to follow is to grant them the days off without pay. A 1967 ruling of the Equal Employment Opportunities Commission requires an employer must give his workers time off for religious holidays unless he can prove it causes an undue hardship in his business. But it does not say he must pay them for the time off.

Voting

Companies also encourage their workers to vote, and those who need extra time are permitted to arrive late or leave early, generally with no less in pay. Many states have laws which make it mandatory for employers to allow employees time off for voting, say up to two hours, but they do not insist that the employee must be paid.

Taking off all day to work at the polls is another matter. This is considered personal time and the employee is not paid since he is paid by the election board.

Marriage

Some companies have a practice of giving an employee an extra week off with pay at the time he marries. While this policy is appreciated by those who profit from it, it may not be appreciated by employees who were already married at time of hire. To get universal acceptance, a policy should have universal appeal and not benefit only a limited group.

Death

Paid time off at time of death in the immediate family is allowed by most companies. A typical policy provides up to three days off for funerals in the local community and up to five days off if out-of-town travel is involved. The immediate family is defined as parents, spouse, brothers and sisters, children, and any other relatives who had been living in the same household. This policy would seem fair since it covers all employees.

Others

There are, of course, many other occasions for time off. These include furloughs for further education, such as the registered nurse who studies for her academic degree. Short periods of time off for educational purposes include an actuarial employee taking the next exam toward a fellowship, or an accountant sitting for his C.P.A. examination.

There are many requests for extra time to extend vacations. During the height of the summer vacation season it is impossible to have too many employees away at the same time. Granting one or more employees extra time usually means that others have to delay their vacations and it might well be unfair to expect them to do this.

Companies generally are not inclined to dock an employee for an occasional day off, especially if the work record is good and the request is reasonable. Extended time off, however, usually means the employee's income stops, unless an insurance program or definite company policy provides for some degree of salary continuation.

GENERAL INCREASE

While most wage and salary increases are given on an individual basis, many companies give "general" or across-the-board wage increases. In some companies these general (or all-at-one-time) wage increases are given instead of individual consideration. In other cases the general increase is in addition to any program of individual merit raises.

Companies review their wage scales periodically, perhaps annually. When they find their rates are no longer competitive, they take steps to make the necessary upward adjustment. This can be done by either of two approaches.

1. *General wage increase.* All employees (with the possible exception of managers or others who may be on a different program) receive the same raise at the same time. This is either a percentage increase or a flat cents-per-hour increase. A combination of these two ideas may be a specified dollars-per-week up to a certain salary, a slightly higher dollar increase for the next higher earnings group, and a still larger dollar increase for the highest paid workers.

Companies feel such an automatic adjustment is justified when present salaries, especially hiring rates, are no longer adequate; the company has had a good year and wants to share the profit with employees, and the wage scales are geared to the cost-of-living index.

2. *Revised wage structure.* The company raises the entire wage structure but does not make immediate individual adjustments except in those minimum number of cases where this cannot be avoided.

a. Since starting rates are now higher, present employees below the new minimum are reviewed and, if performance warrants, are brought up to at least minimum as soon as practicable (one ground rule might be to space raises 90 days apart).

b. Where this action "bumps" other new employees, at present salaries slightly above minimum, their rates must be reviewed and adjusted where performance warrants this.

c. The idea is to give the least number of "corrective" adjustments in order to eliminate the notion of any widespread general increase.

d. Wage adjustments continue to be given on a merit basis on the employee's regular review date. With a higher wage structure to work with, the increase may be more than the normal increment.

Pros and Cons

Both methods have advantages and disadvantages. Advocates of a general increase point to its ease of administration, the elimination of individual application, and the impact on morale when the announcement is made. They point out that when the wage structure is raised without any significant number of individual adjustments, the company muffs a real opportunity to give employee morale a "shot in the arm." In addition, assimilating the new wage scale into the existing pay pattern puts a prolonged strain on managerial judgment which, at best, could still be fallible.

On the other hand, giving employees a raise that is not related to performance violates a basic concept of wage administration; it is believed that individuals appreciate a raise in pay that is deserved more than one which is granted because of some abstract reason. Also, a general increase rewards all employees alike, the less-than-good workers get the same benefit that the good and the outstanding workers receive. Finally, letting managers decide each case on its own merits at the regular review date, and granting raises based on individual merit, gives them an excellent chance of correcting any inequities that are bound to creep into even the best wage program. Undeserving employees may get no raise, average workers may get a normal increment, and the "big" money is awarded to the better performers.

Ideally, better salaries should be paid to better workers in any wage administration program. When the better workers are not paid proportionately more than the less-than-good employees, there is the danger that they will either lose some of their incentive to do good work (since it is not rewarded anyway) or quit and take their chances elsewhere. Meanwhile, the less-than-good workers, whose wages are increased despite their low production or poor attitude, soon find themselves getting more money than they are worth . . . and they cannot afford to quit.

What is the result? The company loses some of its better workers and finds itself with more than its share of less-than-good workers. Efficiency and production suffer because the work force is no longer up to par. When this happens, companies should not complain about the caliber of workers.

METHODS OF PAY

Originally workers were paid off in cash. At the end of each week, the manager would hand each employee his little brown envelope with the bills and coins carefully counted out. Cartoonists still use the "pay envelope" in their jokes.

But all that has changed. Government demands upon the wage earner and taxes imposed on the employer require accurate record keeping. The use of paychecks serves these purposes.

Hourly employees are customarily paid by the week for the number of hours worked. This is in keeping with the Fair Labor Standards Act which calls for an overtime rate after a certain number of hours in each work week. Since it takes a day or more to complete the computations, there is often "lag time"—a period of a day or more following the close of the work week or work period before the employee gets his money. Firms which prefer to pay "on time" have to anticipate the last day or two as they prepare checks in advance. They make any necessary adjustments in the next check, and this can be confusing.

Exempt employees, those not subject to wage-and-hour regulations, are generally paid on a monthly basis, usually getting paychecks on or about the 15th of the month and again at the end of the month. These checks are distributed "on time," not later, since fewer last minute deductions or adjustments are made. Some firms, in the name of convenience, pay all their employees, exempt and nonexempt, on a common payday. To do this requires the monthly or annual rate of the exempt personnel to be converted into a weekly amount, most likely some odd figure.

To avoid payroll tampering, many auditors recommend that the people who do the calculating and prepare the entire payroll should not be permitted to distribute individual paychecks. Paychecks of terminating employees should be referred to the personnel office where they will be delivered as part of the exit interview.

Deductions from paychecks are of two kinds: those (1) required by law and (2) authorized by the employee. Those required by law are withholding tax and social security tax, and those authorized by the employee cover group insurance premiums, defense bond purchases, United Fund contributions, credit union shares or loan repayments, etc. The check stub should show each specific deduction, properly identified, and possibly in the case of taxes, the amount accumulated to date.

MONTHLY SALARY DEDUCTIONS

Exempt employees (and sometimes other workers) are paid on a monthly basis rather than hourly. The theory is that these people are paid to do a job, not paid for hours put in performing the job. They are theoretically on duty full time, all hours of the day, and weekends.

Ordinarily, an employee on a salaried (monthly) payroll is not docked for time off because of illness absence or for personal reasons. But there are occasions when deductions are necessary. The question is how to figure the salary for less than the full period.

One equitable method is to figure the deductions on an annual basis. To illustrate: Multiply the semimonthly salary by 24 or the monthly salary by 12 to get an annual rate. Divide this annual rate by 52 to get the weekly rate. Divide this weekly rate by 5, if the normal week consists of 5 work days. Then deduct the daily rate for each work day the employee was not on the job.

CHRISTMAS GIFT or BONUS

Are company Christmas gifts a fading practice? Apparently many employees look at a Christmas gift from their employer as an affront. Time and again, companies responding to the Dartnell Survey of Christmas Gift and Bonus Practices stated that the program was dropped because employees thought the gifts were "cheap," or "insufficient," or "unfair."

While a slight majority of responses indicate the practice is still in existence, an undercurrent reveals discontent. Perhaps the "family" concept of the work force is giving way to a colder, more formal employer-employee relationship.

From comments in the survey, it is evident that employees feel they earn everything they get, including a gift or bonus at Christmas. They want it spelled out in advance and they want it guaranteed.

Somehow this takes a little of the shine from a company's attempt to show appreciation. It's also a reflection of today's actual family gift-giving—where the children expect (and receive) many presents which are all but ordered in advance.

A Communication Problem

The problem? It goes back to communication. Does the employee know and understand *why* the company *wants* to give him a gift at Christmas time? If the employees think or feel that the gift is due them, then it would be the better idea to incorporate the gift into annual salary or wages and forget it. On the other hand, does the company make the Christmas gift an actual extra? Is it given in the spirit of the season? Does it have strings attached (or even threads)?

The year-end or Christmas bonus is a different matter. In most cases this is paid on the basis of profits, merit, and perhaps service. Here it is perhaps unfortunate that Christmas falls at the end of the year. Many companies have changed to a fiscal year plan which brings the bonus in February, May, or even July.

An employee today is normally told in his initial interview that the company "has a generous bonus program." This is either explained in detail or vaguely described. At any rate, comes Christmas time, he expects his money. He feels it is ludicrous if the president, the treasurer, or the supervisor comes up on Christmas Eve and slides him a check and a Ho-Ho-Ho.

In some cases, the Christmas bonus is just that, and it should be clearly indicated that it is a Christmas present from the company.

PSYCHIC INCOME

Man does not live by bread alone. While money is necessary, it is not the only form of wealth, nor in the final analysis the most important. In addition to material wealth, employees need to add to their cultural wealth, social wealth, and spiritual wealth.

An awareness of these needs is important in trying to learn how to motivate people. But efforts at understanding what motivates employees should not be limited to rank-and-file workers. The same logic applies to managerial and executive personnel.

Here we are not referring to the trappings of the office, nor to the exemption from rules which the privileged are often apt to accept as rights that go with rank. Any extras which they enjoy are the intangibles that belong to the position.

By psychic income we mean tangibles. These are hard-and-fast, substantial dollar value wages that are not reflected in the paycheck. They are over and beyond the intangibles and are used, frankly, to "buy" executives. They serve as incentives to coax an attractive candidate into joining the firm, and they are also used to keep a good man from being easily lured away.

The list is long and includes such standard provisions as stock options, free life insurance, air-conditioned leased cars, and the like. Country club memberships for prestige are common. Innovations are such items as a toupee for a bald executive.

Many senior executives are today placed under contract. The security such an arrangement offers is often enough to help him make the decision to change. At least he has a guaranteed period of time in which to prove himself, or to effect changes in organization or operations. At least he is protected in the event that, through no fault of his own, he is not successful. Psychic income is used to accentuate his importance on the inside and enhance his value on the outside.

The big attraction, however, is that psychic income cannot be taxed away. Therein lies its practical appeal.

INCENTIVE METHODS OF PAY

How to get equitable wages to better workers is always a problem. On a one-rate job, such as is often the case in a union agreement, all workers on that job get the same wages regardless of their individual differences in production. In many wage programs, both union and nonunion, jobs have a spread or range of pay (minimum to maximum), which allows for variations in wages. The weakness in the administration of too many of these plans is that merit raises, granted periodically, are related more to time (another year went by) than to productivity.

The danger in any poorly designed and routinely administered wage plan is that the good worker, who knows he is out-producing others, will become unhappy if the less-than-good worker, or worse yet the goof-off, gets equal salary consideration.

A policy that pays "a fair day's pay for a fair day's work" is not enough. There must also be a provision for "better pay for better work" or the program won't work.

Some companies, recognizing that pay is a good motivator for more and better production, have gone to incentive methods of pay. Any such arrangement is based upon the concept of results and not upon time put in. A salesman's commission is an excellent example; the more he sells the more he earns.

To make any incentive system effective it is necessary that the company have a continuous supply of work and that equipment always be in running order. Incentives are easier to install in factories where units of work can be measured. Lately, however, incentives have been used with success in offices.

An incentive can be applied best on work which is readily counted or measured. In the factory this would be such tasks as cutting, drilling, stamping, polishing, inspecting, wrapping, etc. In the office, letters typed, keypunch strokes, telephone calls, orders priced or footed, etc. First, standards of performance must be set: How much work is required for base pay and how much extra will be paid to those who exceed the normal or standard output.

One of the oldest pay incentives is piecework. A worker is paid so much for each "piece" he turns out. The usual piece-rate system includes some form of guaranteed pay. Many are combination plans which pay for both results and time.

Where individual incentives are not feasible, some form of group incentive may be developed. There is much indirect labor, work which is necessary to the total result but which cannot be measured or reduced to a standard "so much per hour" output. Supporting jobs in the factory, such as timekeeping, or creative work in the office, are examples. Whenever an activity of this nature meets or exceeds its predetermined quota or goal, it may be rewarded with a group incentive based on overall results. There is logic to the argument that incentives or bonuses should not be segmented, but that all who have a part in the end result, direct and indirect labor, should share.

There are many types of incentives. Bonus or sharing programs are a method of returning to workers some of the benefits they helped accomplish. Supplementary pay plans are a delayed payoff if results are good. Profit sharing is a form of incentive not always appreciated by workers if they do not benefit immediately.

The textbooks are full of incentive plans. Many involve intricate mathematical formulas which could be difficult to explain, hard for workers to understand and therefore embrace, and complicated to administer. To avoid pitfalls a company would be wise to get the assistance of experts in establishing an incentive program.

AUTOMOBILE ALLOWANCE or LEASED CARS

Many companies, because of their sales force activity, have some form of automobile allowance or provide leased cars.

A monthly automobile allowance is usually based upon a percentage of the car's cost or the maximum allowed towards the purchase of a car—such as 80 percent of the retail price of a car up to $4,000. Some companies will advance this amount as an interest-free loan. The monthly allowance is then used to reduce the outstanding amount of the loan.

As to providing a leased car, the Internal Revenue Service will rule that there is additional income unless there is a charge made for personal use of the car. Some organizations charge a flat amount per month for personal use, such as $21 or $28. This charge, being so obvious to the employee, could result in a negative reaction. Another approach might be to furnish a leased car, requiring the employee to keep it washed and garaged, and to provide the gasoline.

Automobiles can be leased under several arrangements. One of these is a maintenance lease where the leasing company assumes all the risks. Another is a finance lease where the lessee takes the risk. With the warrantees in effect today, it would seem financially advantageous for the corporation to take this risk, particularly if the fleet of cars is substantial. Further, with the cost of money at an all-time high, it might be advisable to consider prepaying the leases rather than paying the high interest that the leasing company would have to charge for the use of its money. If this is done, involve legal counsel so that such cars remain unencumbered on the books of the lessor.

DEFERRED COMPENSATION

Companies today look for ways to keep valued key executives. Money is seldom the answer. Taxes dilute the value of salary increases and cash bonuses.

Deferred compensation is one solution. Deferred compensation is an agreement, not insurance in itself. The company arranges to pay a portion of the salary beginning at a specified future date. This guarantees a better income after retirement when the income tax bite is most likely not as severe.

In return a retired employee may offer to make himself available as an advisor or consultant. He usually agrees not to work for any competitor or divulge trade secrets.

Deferred compensation simply means the company maintains a

reserve and pays it either on termination of employment or at retirement, in a lump sum or monthly installments, for a period of time or maybe even for life, to the former employee or his estate.

To provide money for deferred compensation agreements, the employer may become beneficiary of a certain amount of insurance on the life of the employee. The usual policy is a "life paid up at age 65." After the employee retires, the policy remains in force without payment of additional premiums. Proceeds received at the time of death reimburse the company for payments made to the employee. The insurance proceeds the company receives are tax-free. Payments made to the retiree are deductible from current company income, just as though they were normal salary payments. Payments received by the retired employee are taxable as personal income during the year received, but they are usually taxed less because the employee gets an extra deduction for being over 65 and his taxable income is generally less than it was when he was working.

When installing a deferred compensation program, it is necessary to consult an attorney, an accountant, and a qualified life insurance agent.

PEOPLE, PERFORMANCE, AND PRIZES

As an incentive to increase sales, reduce costs, or participate in some other improvement program, cash is certainly a popular award and the easiest for a company to offer. But in many situations it may not necessarily be the best.

Performance Incentives Corporation, headquartered in South Hackensack, New Jersey, one of the three biggest firms in the incentive field, makes a good case for the noncash award. "The winner rarely keeps the cash for himself and the gift loses its identity as it is spent for rent or bills," they explain.

Incentive awards are used to motivate employees to sell more merchandise or services, control absenteeism, reduce accidents, cut waste, encourage recruitment, stimulate suggestions, and the like.

One of the reasons for the success of the incentive programs is that their financing comes from provable increases in sales or improvements in operations. No results—no cost.

The whole notion of incentives is based on the theory that people work hardest for the things they want most. The number one incentive program in terms of popularity provides merchandise. The winner is usually allowed to select his gift from a wide choice. This personal touch in prize selection is a decided advantage over the presentation of a committee's preselected item.

Cash is still used because it is simple to administer. Money earned in an incentive campaign, however, is frequently viewed as deserved income, not as a special award for a special job. All too quickly it becomes accepted salary and resentment is felt when the additional income is withdrawn.

Places also motivate people. One of the fastest growing trends is the travel award. Today it is commonplace for companies to send contest winners on trips, often to faraway places. When this is parlayed with sports, so that the winner of a trip may have the added excitement of attending a major national sports event, it becomes not only a well-accepted award but also a tremendous incentive.

Trading stamps have been used to reward salesmen and employees, but according to one survey, they rank fourth in popularity. The main reason is that a person can stop without attaining his goal, supplement his stamps with those his wife is saving, and get the merchandise he wants.

Points to Consider

From its experience, Performance Incentives Corporation has made several discoveries:

1. An individual can be best motivated by giving him a wide choice of rewards from which he can select the one for which he will work hardest.

2. Salesmen who "shop" a merchandise award catalogue invariably tend to select for themselves harder-to-achieve goals than they would willingly accept from management.

3. Even highly egocentric individuals have a deep need for status and recognition—at home as well as in the office. One way to satisfy this need is to structure the program so that the wife and family may share in the glory of the winner.

4. Men need to compete against themselves as well as against others. This is particularly important for those who are the predictable top producers and for those who have been consistently lowest.

5. The influence the wife and children have in motivating men to make a greater effort is enormous.

It is this last factor which accounts for the big growth of merchandise incentive programs during recent years. PIC President William H. Preis says, "The wife's participation gives her a feeling of pride in her breadwinner, a deeper appreciation of his job, its tensions and rewards, and tends to make her more supportive." Incidentally, of the 100 top merchandise selections, 85 percent are items for the wife or home.

Performance incentives are big business. In one year, U.S. companies will spend some $300 million on merchandise incentives alone. Experts have transformed the incentive business into a highly professional, integrated agency operation. Not to be confused with purveyors of premium merchandise, their agencies are staffed with marketing-oriented account executives, contain creative writers, artists, and production personnel, include client service departments, and in one case, anyway, is backed up by batteries of computers and a string of warehouses stacked with millions of dollars of merchandise.

PATENTS

Employees often come up with new ideas which are patentable. Companies are always in search of new or improved methods or products, and many corporations have large staffs of engineers, scientists, and other technical specialists whose assignment is to find, create, or invent better things to produce and market.

What happens when an employee discovers a new technique, succeeds in fusing a better alloy, creates a new design, or invents a new product? To whom does it belong? Who should hold the patent rights?

Much, of course, depends upon the nature of the business. An isolated discovery in an office or nonmanufacturing plant poses no

INVENTION AND SECRECY AGREEMENT

TO:

I, _____, as part consideration for my employment hereafter by
or by one of its subsidiaries or successors in business (hereinafter called the "Company") and for the wages or salary
now or hereafter to be paid to me during the continuance of such employment, agree as follows:

(1) I will disclose fully to the Company all inventions, discoveries, improvements or developments (hereinafter called "inventions") which during the term of my employment were or were caused to be conceived or developed or reduced to practice by me, either solely or jointly with others, either (a) during my working hours, or (b) at the Company's expense, or (c) using the Company's material or facilities, or (d) otherwise, that relating to the Company's business. All such inventions shall belong to the Company, whether or not patent applications are filed thereon and whether or not the inventions are patentable.

(2) I will assign to the Company the inventions and all patent applications and patents which may issue thereon in any and all countries during and subsequent to my employment, and I will assist the Company during and subsequent to my employment in every proper way in obtaining, at its expense, patent protection covering the inventions, and I will execute any and all documents desired or required by the Company to achieve that end.

(3) I will hold in strictest confidence and will not disclose directly or indirectly [to a]ny unauthorized person and will not myself use for any unauthorized purpose, without the Company's prior writt[en permiss]ion, at any time during or subsequent to my employment, any knowledge not already available to the public. [... ac]quire respecting the inventions or respecting designs, methods, systems, improvements, trade secrets, manufact[...] [tech]niques and processes, sales promotions and ideas, customers lists or other private or confidential matters of the C[ompany].

(4) I have set out below a complete list of invention[s covered] by patents or patent applications, including the numbers thereof, which I had made prior to my employment [by the Co]mpany and which are to be excluded from the scope of this agreement. I agree that any patentable improvem[ent mad]e upon the listed inventions subsequent to my employment by the Company are to be the property of the Company if [...with]in the scope of Paragraph (1) hereof.

(5) At the time of leaving the employment of the Company, I will deliver to the Company and will not keep in my possession or deliver to anyone else any and all drawings, blue prints, notes, memoranda, specifications, devices, documents or any other material containing or disclosing any of the matters referred to herein.

(6) This agreement supersedes all earlier invention and secrecy agreements between us, if any, and may not be modified except by an agreement in writing signed by me and by an officer or other authorized executive of the Company.

(7) The provisions of this agreement shall inure to the benefit of and shall be binding upon the heirs, personal representatives, successors and assigns of the parties.

_____   _____
Witness   Employee

ACCEPTED:

By_____

Dated:_____, 19_____

---

serious problem. If a man were to come up with a better ink pen while working at his desk job, or a better label brush while working in the shipping room, most likely the idea would be his and any benefits would then accrue to him. But what about the man who discovers a new formula while working in the company laboratory, or invents a test model while working in the company shop? Then who has the rights?

To avoid confusion, misunderstanding, and possibly a lawsuit, it would be best to have an established policy and get the employees in agreement with it. There could be situations when the decision may favor the employee and other situations when the employee would willingly consider his innovation as part of his job. A written statement, or even a contract, would be protection for all who are involved.

Ideas processed through a suggestion system become the property of the company. By accepting a suggestion-system award, and signing a receipt and a release, the employee signs away his rights.

Where there is no suggestion system or other established procedure, each invention must be considered individually. One question that must be answered is whether the invention was accomplished during a worker's research for the company. In other words, is it job related? What about postemployment inventions begun while with the company?

Employers may feel the invention belongs more to the worker than to the company. If they can use it in their business they may purchase it outright. Or the inventor may receive royalties when the company sells or licenses his invention.

The following questions and answers published by the United States Department of Commerce may be of interest.

Q. What is a patent?

A. A patent is a grant issued by the United States Government giving an inventor the right to exclude all others from making, using, or selling his invention within the United States, its territories and possessions.

Q. For how long a term of years is a patent granted?

A. Seventeen years from the date on which it is issued; except for patents on ornamental designs, which are granted for terms of 3½, 7, or 14 years.

Q. What do the terms "patent pending" and "patent applied for" mean?

A. They are used by a manufacturer or seller of an article to inform the public that an application for patent on that article is on file in the Patent Office. The law imposes a fine on those who use these terms falsely to deceive the public.

Q. How does one apply for a patent?

A. By making the proper application to the Commissioner of Patents, Washington, D. C., 20231.

Q. How does one obtain information as to patent applications, fees, and other details concerning patents?

A. By ordering the pamphlet, *General Information Concerning Patents,* from the Superintendent of Documents, Washington, D. C., 20402, or through any field office of the United States Department of Commerce.

OVERTIME

Overtime is one of the perennial problems of business. Despite the best efforts to eliminate it, the problem persists. Many companies are unable to control it. Some managers are resigned to it and accept the inconvenience as part of their jobs. Employees generally resist overtime work, but not always. To some it is an easy and lucrative way of enhancing the value of their jobs.

Some overtime work is, of course, to be expected. It results from help shortages when the workers must extend themselves to offset vacancies in the department. Overtime occurs during peak-load periods, such as end-of-month closings in the bookkeeping areas, or inventory counting or pricing done after hours. The reasons are many and easily understood, good solutions are not as easy to come by.

Two Federal Acts Apply

Under the Fair Labor Standards Act of 1938, there is no limit to the number of hours an employee may be required to work, but the employer must pay time and one-half at the employee's regular rate of pay for all hours worked in any one week in excess of 40. There are exceptions. Bona fide executives, administrative, professional, and outside sales personnel do not have to be paid overtime.

Employers operating under government contracts of $10,000 or more must also meet the requirements of the Walsh-Healey Act, which differs in some respects from the Fair Labor Standards Act. The Walsh-Healey Act requires the payment of overtime for all hours over 8 worked in one day.

In plants or offices that are unionized, the overtime terms may yet be different depending upon the provisions of the contract with the union. Quite often the union will bargain for overtime on a daily basis rather than weekly, i.e., for time worked in excess of 8 hours in any one day. It may insist also that workers be paid at overtime rates for all hours worked on Saturdays, regardless of time worked during the rest of the week. In other words, they use the overtime rate as premium pay for Saturday work. Double time for Sunday is not uncommon, and employees who work on a holiday, when fellow workers are off from work and still being paid, often get overtime pay in addition to holiday straight-time pay.

Since overtime becomes expensive, attempts to control it are made. In most companies there is a policy about overtime, or at least a rule of thumb, which sets guidelines within which managers may authorize overtime work. As one example, a company does not question overtime in any department which is less than 2 percent of all hours worked. This says, in effect, that some overtime is expected. But when overtime exceeds the permissible 2 percent, the problem must be explained, analyzed, and special authorization granted.

The Overtime Habit

There are employers who feel that overtime is a disease. Employees get into the overtime habit, find the overtime pay more than offsets the overtime inconvenience, and gradually find themselves enjoying, even seeking, overtime. Then when work slacks off they cleverly manipulate their daily workloads to allow for overtime work. Some employees have actually been accused of deliberately stalling during the regular day, or stretching their work, to make overtime necessary. At any rate, there are managements who believe that workers accustomed to an 8-hour day cannot maintain their level of productivity or efficiency consistently over a prolonged period of 12-hour days, and that they purposely or otherwise taper off during the day, thereby actually making overtime necessary. In these cases the best way to cure the disease is to eliminate, by decree, all overtime and see what happens. Often, the overtime necessity will disappear.

When overtime seems excessive and threatens to develop into a major problem, here are some signs to look for:

1. Is the amount of overtime increasing?
2. Does it go beyond the guidelines established as reasonable?
3. Is overtime general throughout the company or localized?
4. Is it becoming a habit with a certain few?
5. Are people doing overtime work willingly, even eagerly?
6. Are supervisors beginning to schedule overtime as a regular practice?
7. Is top management indifferent to overtime cost?
8. Has the problem been studied lately?

SUPPER MONEY

When employees work overtime, some companies pay meal allowances. This is particularly true for supervisors and managers who are exempt employees and not subject to overtime compensation. This way they are at least reimbursed for their suppers.

But such supper money is not limited to exempt employees. Often it is also paid to wage-and-hour employees who leave the premises to eat evening meals and who do not include the time away in their report of overtime hours.

The conditions are usually clearly spelled out. Employees must work a specified number of hours beyond their regular work day to be entitled to supper money. And they must interrupt their work, i.e., take a supper break, not merely collect the money whether they eat or not.

Similar arrangements may also be in effect for employees who work overtime on a nonworking day, such as Saturday, Sunday, or a holiday. Companies may give them a lunch or supper allowance if they put in a required number of hours. This practice, however, is not as prevalent as that of paying for supper on a regular work day.

During a crisis or emergency all sorts of concessions are made, but these are not considered the same as the supper money policy related to ordinary overtime.

In the majority of instances these meal allowances are fixed amounts. A few firms prefer actual expense account or petty cash reimbursements for the cost of the meals and tips.

SHIFT DIFFERENTIAL

It is customary in most industries to pay somewhat higher wages to employees on a second or third shift. This is known as a "shift differential"—the amount over and above the regular scale.

Premium pay is offered simply because the hours, and possibly other working conditions, are not as attractive as those on the day shift. Transportation during the late evening is not as good as during rush hours, eating facilities not as available, and surely concern for personal safety is a consideration. Besides, the facilities within the company itself may be more limited; the clinic might not be open for just these few workers, the cafeteria closed, personnel counselling unavailable, and so on. To offset these inconveniences companies offer the better wages.

Shift differentials have been common in factories and plants for years. Most union contracts provide for a difference in pay scales for different shifts. The rule is generally 10 percent, although lately the trend seems to be moving to "cents per hour." What this means is that workers on a second or third shift get the same pay which is listed for that same job on the regular shift, *plus* a premium for the night work.

Exceptions to Differential

In office operations there is no universal rule yet, possibly because the problem does not exist in the same measure. Fewer offices than factories operate more than one shift. The night workers in offices operate key punches, tabulating machines, teletypes, or computers. Where this is happening, some extra consideration is given.

A shift differential should be applied to a true second or third shift and not extended to employees who are on odd-hour or short-hour jobs. In offices, for example, most key-punch operators are not on a second shift but are, rather, working a few hours in the evening. These may be housewives who cannot work until the husband comes home to watch the children, or they could be employees from other companies who are moonlighting.

Employees who start earlier, or work later, than the regular workforce are not on a second shift. They are considered to be on the regular shift but with their hours changed. Early morning mail openers, engineers who get the building ready, and those employees who close the office, such as outgoing mail clerks, cashiers who see that the money and books are put away, truck dispatchers, are examples. Nor is any wage differential applied to janitors and maintenance people whose regular duties are performed after the office or factory is closed.

Wage differentials are not only applied to the pay scales of regular workers but are also added to starting rates. The Chicago

Transit Authority, in its recruiting literature, lists a shift differential in its hiring rates for bus drivers. "You receive 3 cents per hour in addition to your basic rate of pay if your work ends after 8:00 p.m.; 5 cents after 2:00 a.m."

A wage differential is intended for workers who do the same work as their counterparts on the regular daytime shift. It is added to the "going rate" to compensate for the less attractive hours and working conditions.

JOB EVALUATION

There are two parts to wage administration. One is the evaluation of the job in relation to all other jobs, and the other is the evaluation of the performance the worker gives on the job. Let's talk about jobs here.

The listing of jobs, that is, the arrangement of jobs by importance, may be accomplished by ranking or classifying jobs through agreement, by collective bargaining, by personal judgment of management (which suffers from all the frailties of human nature), or by the preferred systematic study and comparison of jobs, which is more acceptable to workers because it is objective. This last method, the systematic approach, is widely used because it is fair.

This method is known as *job evaluation*. It is a systematic (not scientific) method for objective determination of the relative worth of jobs within an organization. It is a procedure for measuring the relative contribution of each job and for ranking these jobs in accordance with these measurements.

Preparing for Job Evaluation

The following steps are essential in preparing for a job-evaluation installation. The company must:

1. Recognize the need and decide to install an easily understood system.

2. Assign an individual to administer the program.

3. After he has become knowledgeable on the subject of job evaluation, have him explain in detail to the top executive exactly what is involved.

The top executive should:

1. Call an executive meeting of his management staff to explain the total

program, but only after he has fully understood and accepted what is involved. In this meeting he will:

a. Give his endorsement.

b. Outline the objectives.

c. Announce the appointment of the designated individual who will administer the program.

d. Ask the job evaluation administrator to give a step-by-step explanation of what the program entails to arrive at a clear-cut understanding of the cooperation required of each manager and the assistance provided by the administrator.

e. Discuss details such as the amount of work involved in both the installation and maintenance, the value and benefits to be gained, the limitations to be faced, and the authority to make the program serve its purpose.

2. Repeat the conference if necessary to include everybody who will be *working* on the program.

3. Let employees know what is going on, being careful to stress the significance of an objective procedure which will emphasize fairness in paying wages, and assure all employees that no one will get hurt in the process.

IMPLEMENTING THE PROGRAM

Evaluation of jobs consists of four steps:

1. Preparing job descriptions (following an analysis of each job).

2. Evaluating and grading jobs.

3. Establishing a salary structure.

4. Providing a plan for administering the program.

WRITING JOB DESCRIPTIONS

The job evaluation administrator spearheads the preparation of written job descriptions. He finds out what the jobs are. He writes individual descriptions of all different jobs. These are the essential steps:

1. Distribute sample work sheets to all managers. A typical form calls for a general statement of the overall job, list of specific duties performed daily and at other times, reports or records made, and to whom the job is accountable.

2. Job evaluation administrator and manager go over each work sheet.

3. Administrator writes job description (to standardize write-ups).

4. Submit job description to manager for approval or changes. It is advisable to have the job incumbent review the description and be satisfied with it.

5. When finally approved, have manager sign job description.

6. Administrator merely asks questions; he does not dictate job content.

EVALUATING THE JOBS

Using an informal or formal system (a formal method is preferred), the job evaluation administrator, working through a job evaluation committee, arranges jobs in order of value to company operations. Generally speaking, the factors upon which a job is rated fall into four categories. These are:

1. Skill (job knowledge, experience, education, initiative, ingenuity).

2. Effort (physical, mental).

3. Responsibility (for equipment, money, safety, public relations).

4. Job conditions (working conditions, hazards, annoyances).

Each factor in turn is broken down into degrees, and these separate levels are each defined and point values assigned. The degree to which each of the factors is required by the job is estimated and point value expressed accordingly. The sum of the point values of all factors of the job determines the total point value for the job. After this has been accomplished for all jobs, they are then arranged in point order.

APPLYING THE POINT SYSTEM

The point system may be applied using the following procedure:

1. Using a committee of top management people, decide upon a set of factors. These should be factors that are common to all jobs.

2. Break each factor down into several degrees. It is very important when assigning degrees of factors to various jobs that the levels be identified only by a letter designation. Use of numbers colors the thinking.

3. Against this yardstick, each job individually can be evaluated by administrator and committee. In this evaluation procedure it is advisable to have the manager or foreman whose jobs are being considered sit in to contribute to the discussion.

4. After all jobs are evaluated they should be cross-checked on each factor separately. Reexamine conflicts and make corrections. This purifies the evaluation.

5. Assign point values to each of the factors. Assuming 100 percent for the sum of all factors, establish the relative weight of each factor to the whole.

6. The percentage is then converted to points. A factor which is 15 percent of the total is 150 points if the total of all points is 1,000.

7. The points assigned to each factor represent the *maximum* points for that factor. Assign corresponding lesser numerical values to each degree of each factor.

8. Do not merely adopt the point values which have proved satisfactory in another installation. Establish the relative importance of factors and degrees to fit *your specific situation*.

9. Once point values are agreed upon, it is merely a clerical job to change letter assignments to their corresponding numerical values. Add the

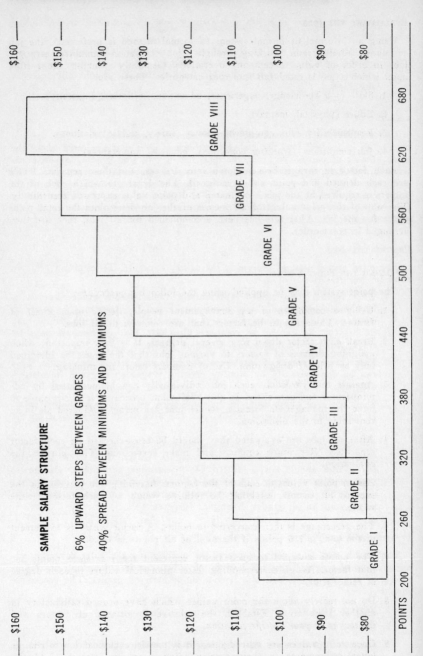

SAMPLE SALARY STRUCTURE

6% UPWARD STEPS BETWEEN GRADES

40% SPREAD BETWEEN MINIMUMS AND MAXIMUMS

point values for each job and arrange jobs in ascending or descending point order.

10. At this time it is well to cross-check all jobs again, considering them not on the basis of separate factors but in total against all other jobs. Jobs which appear out of line in this final evaluation should obviously be restudied.

GRADING OF JOBS

Jobs are divided into grades so that when rates are established they are not applied to individual jobs but rather to groups of jobs that are rated about the same number of points. To break the total list of jobs into grades, use an even-point distribution, recognizing acceptable natural divisions between jobs. The point spread within each class determines the number of grades. Use a constant point spread to establish grades. Example: Beginning with the lowest job or just below, start grades with a 60 or some other constant point interval (60, 120, 180, etc.).

PRICING THE JOBS

The third step is that of designing the salary structure. To establish realistic rates for job grades:

1. Take regularly recognized representative jobs in each grade (known as benchmark jobs) and obtain community rates. Inquiries may be made to companies directly or wage surveys of associations and trade groups may be helpful. Be careful to compare like jobs. Do not compare jobs by titles; this can be misleading. Compare duties.

2. Enter present wages of employees alongside each job in each grade. This can be done visually by plotting existing wages on a graph or scatter-diagram.

3. Show the area comparisons in the same way, using perhaps another color. If wages are shown graphically, plot the area wage comparisons on the same graph.

4. Establish minimum and maximum rates for each grade based on prevailing rates and consistent with company policy. The minimum rates for grades should be separated by a constant percentage. Examples: 6 percent or 8 percent. These should become a pattern of even uphill steps. The percent difference between minimum and maximum should be the same in all grades. Example: 40 percent.

WRITING A WAGE POLICY

The fourth step is to write a procedure spelling out the rules covering administration of wages. These tell how to move between minimum and maximum ranges of any one grade, and also how to move between grades. The procedure should cover:

1. Review dates and their frequency.

2. Method of review.

3. Suggested progression showing increment which should be realistic in consideration of the base rate.

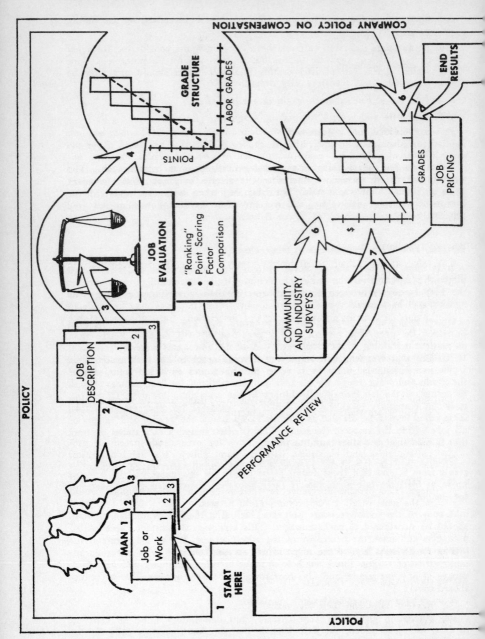

Bureau of Industrial Relations, Graduate School of Business, University of Michigan.

4. Rules for hiring:
   a. Below minimum.
   b. At minimum.
   c. Above minimum.
5. Promotions and transfers, also demotions.
6. Jobs out of line when program is put into effect.
7. Authority and control for making wage rate changes:
   a. On individual adjustments.
   b. For wage program as a whole.

Employees are paid within the ranges depending upon their performance and possibly length of service. Unfortunately, seniority somehow seems to sneak in as an influence on wages paid. The frequency when wages are reviewed, the increment available each time, and the procedure to be followed are covered separately under the subject of Wage Administration.

PUTTING THE WAGE PROGRAM INTO OPERATION

It is important that the top level or levels of management understand and thoroughly approve of the program. Without full understanding and support the very inequities between departments or divisions that the program guards against will be fostered.

Others will want to know about the program, too. There is probably no area in which the grapevine present in any organization will be more active than on matters pertaining to the employee's pocketbook and status with the company. It is likely that everyone will know that a wage program has been undertaken. Upon completion, the program is often published and each individual learns the grade and wage range for his own job. In addition, he is sometimes told of the range of the job immediately higher in the scale than his own. Of course, it is not customary to reveal the actual pay received by other employees. In some cases it may be decided to publish to all hands the grades and ranges of all jobs within the scope of the study. This is often included in a union contract that is published and distributed to members.

Usually it is agreed at the beginning of a program that no wage cuts will result from it and that those found to be below the minimum will be brought up to at least the minimum rate if their appraisal shows them to be adequate for the job.

A copy of the complete wage program, including the job evaluation manual, should be distributed to each manager. This serves as a constant check on all managers and upon the neutrality of the administrator. It also helps extend the manager's horizons beyond the scope of his own activities.

MAINTAINING THE WAGE PROGRAM

A wage program must be dynamic, not static.

Job evaluation should be kept current. Job descriptions must be kept up to date, new jobs added, old jobs deleted. The simplest procedure calls for the administrator as a neutral agency to work out any changes or additions with the manager. Where agreement is reached, the revision is put into the job evaluation manual; where the two cannot conscientiously agree, the dispute can be referred to the standing job evaluation committee.

Likewise, the wage structure must be kept up to date. Community wage surveys must be participated in at regular intervals. Published reports of wage trends and the cost-of-living index should be studied. Adherence to the basic wage policy is assured by promptly making changes in the wage structure when indicated.

OUTSIDE PARTICIPATION

It should not be assumed that the introduction of a job evaluation system and a wage administration policy is always the total responsibility of the company. There could be willing or unwilling outside participation.

The installation of a new job evaluation program, or the revision of an existing one, provide tailor-made opportunities for the use of consultants or professional job-evaluation specialists. As outsiders they bring with them an unbiased viewpoint and can quickly discern abnormalities in jobs and job rates peculiar to the company. Since they are more objective they can serve as arbiters to resolve disagreements which might otherwise be influenced by rank or other unrelated effect.

Their programs are usually well tested in industry, and in a minimum of time they can install a system that will develop few "bugs" afterwards. Caution should be exercised, however, in selecting experts who offer a "gimmick" method in order to emphasize their different or unique approach to job evaluation.

Companies whose employees are organized may be required, or even offer, to include union representation in the planning, development, and operation of any job evaluation program which affects the earnings of union members. This is accomplished by adding one or more union members to the job evaluation committee so that the union will understand the system used, know why jobs rate as they do, and have an opportunity to contribute to decisions which are acceptable. This is the old concept of "put them in the boat with you and they won't bore holes in it later."

JOB DESCRIPTIONS

The following complete job description is from the files of the East Bay Municipal Utility District, Oakland, California.

STATISTICAL TYPIST

DEFINITION

Under general supervision, does varied typing of which statistical typing is the major duty, and performs clerical work requiring the exercise of some independent judgment; performs related work as required.

DISTINGUISHING FEATURES

The duties of this class involve the skillful operation of a typewriter and the use of independent judgment to perform a wide variety of typing tasks,

WAGE AND SALARY ADMINISTRATION

POSITION ANALYSIS

‹ position_____

al Division of the Organization: ☐ Executive ☐ Finance and Accounting ☐ Engineering ☐ Sales ☐ Transportation

‹ Purchasing ☐ Personnel ☐ Other_____

zation nature of the position: ☐ Line ☐ Staff ☐ Combined

port to: Mr._____Title_____Age_____

› located at: Plant_____City_____State_____

sition is: ☐ A new one ☐ An established one ☐ Established but has new factors

at functions in the organization will the person in this position be responsible?_____

_____

_____

_____

› any responsibilities associated with the position such as: Travel, community activities, association activities, public speaking, etc._____

_____

age for this position: $_____ to $_____ Expected hiring rate $_____

› nature of pay incentive_____

positions would next promotion normally lead? 1._____

_____ 3._____

f these should be considered in the appraisal? ☐ 1 ☐ 2 ☐ 3

ed candidate does his job well, how soon could he reasonably expect promotion?_____

_____

ial training, how closely will he be supervised? ☐ Hourly ☐ Daily ☐ Weekly ☐ Monthly Describe_____

_____

ch of the person's work will be checked by others?_____

these qualities should the person have to a high degree? ☐ Flexibility; accepting changes ☐ Resourcefulness ☐ Creativity ☐ Empathy

_____

ds of problems, immediate or long range, are inherent in this position?_____

JA-601   Copyright, 1958, The Dartnell Corporation, Chicago 40, Ill., Printed in U. S. A.
Developed by The McMurry Company

This position analysis form, developed by The McMurry Company and distributed by The Dartnell Corporation, helps gather data for a job description.

SUPERVISORY RESPONSIBILITY

How many employees will report directly to this person?_____,   Indirectly?_____

Titles of all supervisors who will report to this person and number of employees reporting to each:

1._____   7._____

2._____   8._____

3._____   9._____

4._____   10._____

5._____   11._____

6._____   12._____

WHAT AUTHORITY WILL HE HAVE:	TO RECOMMEND		TO DECIDE AND	
1. Allocation of his budget..	☐ Yes	☐ No	☐ Yes	☐
2. Organization of his own section (split or combine sections)...........................	☐ Yes	☐ No	☐ Yes	☐
3. Increase or decrease number of employees under his supervision...................	☐ Yes	☐ No	☐ Yes	☐
4. Release or demote an employee..	☐ Yes	☐ No	☐ Yes	☐
5. Revise standards of quality or quantity of product or service........................	☐ Yes	☐ No	☐ Yes	☐
6. Revise work flow..	☐ Yes	☐ No	☐ Yes	☐
7. Revise operating policies...	☐ Yes	☐ No	☐ Yes	☐
8. Establish his own itinerary...	☐ Yes	☐ No	☐ Yes	☐
9. Establish itinerary of those reporting to him......................................	☐ Yes	☐ No	☐ Yes	☐
10. Expenditures outside of his budget...	☐ $50	☐ $100	☐ $50	☐
	☐ $250	☐ $500	☐ $250	☐
	☐ $1,000	☐ $10,000	☐ $1,000	☐

11. _____

12. _____

13. _____

Analysis developed by_____Date_____

First approval_____Date_____ Approved_____Date_____

Reverse side of the position analysis form pinpoints the employee's supervisory responsibilities and spells out scope of authority he will have.

including the preparation of complicated statistical tables. The class is distinguished from the clerical classes in that the latter use a typewriter only to perform routine letter and report preparation and form completion in addition to their primary clerical tasks. The class differs from the stenographic classes in that the duties of the latter require taking dictation and transcribing from stenographic notes.

TYPICAL EXAMPLES OF WORK PERFORMED

1. Types schedules, columnar data sheets, tables, financial and statistical reports, and similar material from rough drafts and plain or corrected copy.

2. Types letters, memoranda, duplicating master copies, and completes a variety of standard forms with a minimum of instruction.

3. Plans spacing and balanced layout of tabular material to be typed on varied sizes of paper.

4. Proofreads typed work and checks records and reports for clerical accuracy.

5. Performs a variety of incidental clerical duties such as filing, sorting, collating and classifying documents, filling requests for supplies, taking inventory, or operating standard office equipment such as adding, photocopy, and duplicating machines.

MINIMUM QUALIFICATIONS FOR EMPLOYMENT

Education: Completion of the 12th grade or its equivalent.

Experience: One year of full-time clerical employment in which typing was the major duty performed.

Knowledge, Skills and Abilities: Working knowledge of the care and use of a typewriter; of arithmetic; of modern office practices including filing, indexing, and cross-referencing methods; and of correct spelling, punctuation, and grammar. Ability to type accurately at a speed of not less than 40 words a minute from ordinary typewritten or printed copy; to space descriptive and columnar material neatly on a page; to type accurately from copy involving numerical data; to type from corrected rough draft copy with speed and accuracy; to learn the operation of commonly used office machines; and to do clerical work.

The following job titles and descriptions for office positions were developed by the Administrative Management Society for use in the AMS annual office salary survey program:

MAIL CLERK

Circulates office mail, delivers messages and supplies. May process incoming or outgoing mail and operate related machines and perform other routine duties.

FILE CLERK

Keeps correspondence, cards, invoices, receipts or other classified or indexed records filed systematically according to an established system. Locates and removes material upon request and keeps records of its disposition. May perform other clerical duties which are related.

GENERAL CLERK B

Performs clerical duties in accordance with established procedures requiring judgment in the selection and interpretation of data. Job requires a moderate amount of prior experience and considerable supervision.

GENERAL CLERK A

Performs complex and responsible clerical duties requiring independent analysis, exercise of judgment and a detailed knowledge of department or company policies and procedures related to work performed. Minimum supervision required.

ACCOUNTING CLERK B

Checks, verifies, and posts journal vouchers, accounts payable vouchers, or other simple accounting data of a recurring or standardized nature; reconciles bank accounts, etc.

ACCOUNTING CLERK A

Keeps a complete set of accounting records in a small office with or without the use of an accounting machine, or handles one phase of accounting in a larger unit which requires the accounting training needed to determine proper accounting entries, prepare accounting reports, analyze accounting records to determine causes of results shown, etc. May direct work of junior clerks or bookkeepers. (However, excludes supervisors and persons at policy-making levels.)

BOOKKEEPING MACHINE OPERATOR

Operates a bookkeeping machine to record business transactions of a recurring and standardized nature, where proper posting has been indicated or is readily identifiable. May balance to control figures.

OFFSET DUPLICATING MACHINE OPERATOR

Sets up and operates offset-type duplicating machine. Cleans and adjusts equipment but does not make repairs. May prepare own plates and operate auxiliary equipment, and may keep records of kind and amount of work done.

TELEPHONE SWITCHBOARD OPERATOR

Operates a single or multiple position PBX telephone switchboard. May keep records of calls and toll charges, and may operate a paging system and perform duties of receptionist.

TYPIST—CLERK

Types letters, reports, tabulations, and other material in which setups and terms are generally clear and follow a standard pattern. Performs clerical duties of moderate difficulty. May prepare stencils or offset masters.

STENOGRAPHER B

Transcribes from dictating equipment, or records and transcribes shorthand dictation involving a normal range of business vocabulary. May perform a copy typing or clerical work of moderate difficulty incidental to primary stenographic duties. May operate as a member of a centralized stenographic service.

STENOGRAPHER A

Performs advanced stenographic duties which require experience and exercise of judgment. Transcribes from dictating equipment, or records and transcribes dictation of more than average difficulty which regularly includes technical or specialized vocabulary or frequently supplements transcription with the drafting of finished work from indicated sources, records, general instructions, etc.

SECRETARY B

Performs secretarial duties for a member of middle management. General requirements are the same as for Secretary A, but limited to the area of responsibility of the principal.

SECRETARY A

Performs the complete secretarial job for a high-level executive or a person responsible for a major functional or geographic operation. Does work of a confidential nature and relieves principal of designated administrative details. Requires initiative, judgment, knowledge of company practices, policy, and organization.

KEY PUNCH OPERATOR B

Operates an alphabetical or numerical key punch machine to record precoded or readily usable data following generally standardized procedures. May verify the work of others, using a verifying machine.

KEY PUNCH OPERATOR A

Operates an alphabetical or numerical key punch machine or verifier to record or verify complex or uncoded data working from source material which may not be arranged for key punching. Selects appropriate number and kinds of cards. Follows a pattern of operations generally standardized but frequently including rules, exceptions and special instructions which demand operator's close attention. Frequently required to decipher illegible source documents and to assist in preparing new ones.

TABULATING MACHINE OPERATOR—INTERMEDIATE

Sets up, operates, and wires a variety of punched card equipment, including tabulators and multipliers. Wires boards from diagrams prepared by others for routine jobs, uses prewired boards on complex or repetitive jobs. May locate and correct job difficulties and assist in training less experienced operators. This work is performed under specific instructions and may include some wiring from diagrams. The work may involve tabulation of a repetitive accounting exercise, a small tabulating study, or parts of a longer and more complex report.

COMPUTER OPERATOR—INTERMEDIATE

Operates computers utilizing established programs or programs under development. Selects proper tape, loads computer, and manipulates control switches on console in accordance with established instructions. Observes lights on console, storage devices, etc., reporting any deviations from standards. Detects nature of errors or equipment failure and makes normal console adjustments. Maintains operating records such as machine performance and production reports.

PROGRAMMER B

Assists in the review or analysis of the preparation of the program instructions under direct supervision. Fairly competent to work on several phases of programming with only general direction, but still requires some instruction for other phases. May prepare on his own the block diagrams and machine logic flow charts. Codes program instructions and prepares test data, testing, and debugging programs. May also assist in the documentation of all procedures used through the system. Experience of trainee required for entry to this position classification.

PROGRAMMER A

With general supervision, analyzes and defines programs for electronic data-processing equipment. Is generally competent in most phases of programming to work on his own, and only requires general guidance for the balance of the activities. Conducts analyses of sufficient detail of all defined systems specifications and develops all levels of block diagrams and machine-logic flow charts; codes, prepares test data, tests, and debugs programs. Revises and refines programs as required and documents all procedures used throughout the computer program when it is formally established. Evaluates and modifies existing programs to take into account changes in systems requirements. May give technical assistance to lower-level classifications. Normally progresses from this classification to senior or lead programmer.

SYSTEMS ANALYST—INTERMEDIATE

Under close supervision, assists in devising computer system specifications and record layouts. Is qualified to work on several phases of systems analysis, but requires guidance and direction for other phases. Conducts studies and analyses of existing office procedures and prepares systems flow charts for existing and proposed operations. Under instruction prepares computer block diagram and may assist in the preparation of machine logic flow charting.

WAGE ADMINISTRATION

(a typical company policy)

1. *Purpose:* The purpose of the wage administration program is to set the standard for administering wages of employees on jobs covered by the job evaluation system. It is the policy of the company:

1.1 To provide a wage that will attract and hold above-average employees.

1.2 To pay employees equitably for performance.

1.3 To provide financial incentive for sustained meritorious performance of work.

2. *Program:* Minimum and maximum rates are established for all grades. The

progression schedules are attached to this policy, and include the rates and a brief explanation of administration.

3. *Administration:* Wise use of the salary dollar dictates that the emphasis be on the performance of the individual being considered in terms of the specific job to which he is assigned.

3.1 *New Employee:* New employees should, whenever possible, be hired at the minimum rate. An employee may be hired at a rate lower than the minimum if he is hired as a trainee for that particular job. He will be increased to minimum as soon as he obtains those qualifications necessary, but in no case longer than the time specified in the job description.

3.2 An employee may be hired at a rate higher than the minimum, provided he has special training and/or experience in which case he may be paid a starting rate corresponding to his ability, experience, and training. But only in exceptional cases, with the approval of the divisional vice-president and the concurrence of the director of personnel, should an applicant be hired above the minimum. In these cases the time for the first wage review will be on the 9-month anniversary for employees in grades I through V, who are hired below the salary indicated under 9-months merit review. In all other cases the first wage review will be on the 12-month anniversary. The amount of the increase will be the normal next step on the rate progressional table.

4. *Automatic Increases:* An automatic increase will be granted in 90 days or less to full-time employees in grades I through V:

4.1 To new employees hired at minimum.

4.2 To promoted employees whose promotional increase brings them to minimum.

4.3 To trainees when they reach minimum.

5. *Merit Increases:* All increases (including promotional, but not including automatic and longevity) will be based on merit. These merit increases may be granted at intervals and in amounts in accordance with the attached schedules and the terms of this policy. The qualifications necessary for merit increases are spelled out on these same schedules. The decision should not be based on subjective opinion but must be backed up by objective records of performance.

6. *Promotions:* When an employee is promoted he will be given an increase within 30 days effective on the beginning of the next regular payroll period. The normal amount of the increase will be approximately the amount of the next step on the schedule.

7. *Transfers:* No wage action will be taken when an employee is given a lateral transfer between jobs in the same grade. The employee will be considered on his next scheduled review date.

8. *Demotions:* In the event of demotion, the wage rate will be altered to coincide with wages paid for comparable performance on jobs in the same grades, unless—

8.1 The existing wage does not disrupt harmony or cause conflict.

8.2 The demotion is made for the convenience of the company.

9. *Longevity Increases:* The company recognizes that an employee with long

and faithful service may be entitled to special consideration. Accordingly, a seniority raise may be granted to an employee who has completed 10 years of continuous service and who has not had any raise in the past 3 years. A second and final seniority raise may be granted to an employee with 15 years of service who has not had any raise in 3 years. These may be granted even after an employee has reached the maximum for his grade. The increment will be as follows:

Amount of Weekly Raise	When Present Weekly Salary Is
$3	$75 or less
$4	between $75 and $100
$5	$100.50 or above.

10. *Leave of Absence and Furloughs:* An employee who has returned from a leave of absence may be considered for a wage increase on his regular review date.

In the case where a disability absence has been extended beyond 30 days, the wage review date may be properly adjusted accordingly.

An employee who has returned from a furlough may be given consideration for the time worked prior to the furlough, but, of course, will receive no wage consideration for the furlough period.

11. *Less-Than-Full-Time-Employees:* Less-than-full-time employees will be paid on an hourly rate with the first increase consideration 6 months after the start of employment. Subsequent increases will be considered at 12-month or 24-month intervals in conformance with the schedule for hourly employees.

12. *Procedure:* Raise increase recommendations will be handled according to the procedure outlined below:

12.1 The Division will be notified approximately one month in advance, when an employee is due for wage review. It will be the manager's responsibility to recommend the appropriate action to his assistant vice-president.

12.11 When an increase is indicated the appropriate personnel changes reporting form (RB-11) will be submitted.

12.12 When an increase is not indicated the reason for the rejection, and the employee's reaction to the explanation, should be entered on the reminder notice and returned by the vice-president or assistant vice-president to personnel to be filed in the employee's folder for possible reference.

12.13 In either case, whatever action is taken, it is the responsibility of the manager to discuss this action with the employee in private.

12.2 Each increase will be initiated by the manager and referred to the assistant vice-president for action.

12.21 Below review point—if acceptable, the assistant vice-president will approve it and refer it to personnel where it will be audited to avoid any unintentional violation of policy.

12.22 Above review point, recommendation will be referred to the salary review committee through the wage and salary administrator in personnel following endorsement by the assistant vice-president.

12.221 In preparing each case for committee review any additional data, such as salary history, will be provided.

12.222 The committee (see item 13) meeting regularly will review the cases before it and make its recommendations for approval or disapproval.

12.223 Cases below the executive review point will be referred to the vice-president for his consideration to approve or disapprove, and cases beyond this point will be referred to the chief executive officer for his consideration to approve or disapprove.

12.2231 Approvals will be referred to personnel for processing.

12.2232 Disapprovals will be returned to the originator through personnel, with one copy retained in the individual employee's folder.

12.224 In those cases where the vice-president and the salary review committee are not in agreement the vice-president has the right to appeal to the chief executive officer.

12.3 Exceptional merit cases, where the increase is more than one step in the rate progression table and/or less than the prescribed waiting period, will also be referred to the salary review committee.

12.4 Except for automatic increases, the reason for recommending a wage increase should be adequately explained under "Comments."

12.5 No increase will become effective nor should any announcement be made to the employee until all necessary approvals and audits are received.

12.6 All details relating to wage increases should be completed before the effective date as shown on form RB-11. It is especially important that sufficient time be allowed in cases where the recommendations require committee action. Otherwise, when the normal routine processing procedure cannot be completed before payroll is closed, the increase will have to become effective on the first payroll period following approval.

13. *Committee:* The salary review committee shall consist of three members appointed by the chief executive officer: a vice-president, who will act as chairman (and serve for not more than one year when he will be replaced by another vice-president), the systems director, and the director of personnel. The wage and salary administrator will be the nonvoting secretary. In the absence of the vice-president another vice-president will be asked to serve as alternate.

14. *Exceptions:* Any exceptions to this policy require the approval of the chief executive officer.

PERFORMANCE vs. SENIORITY

There are several types of pay raises. These indicate the reason for an upward adjustment in an employee's rate of pay.

Examples are:

Automatic—Given after a beginning period of time, such as probationary or qualifying period, irrespective of performance.

General —A fixed or percentage amount given across-the-board to all employees (or all members of a designated group) as a cost-of-living or similar adjustment with no relationship to individual differences.

Merit —Given periodically to recognize satisfactory, or preferably, meritorious work.

Promotion—Given at the time (or shortly thereafter) that a worker is transferred to a higher rated job with its higher pay scale.

Longevity —Given to old-timers who have reached their production peak but who are nevertheless deserving of consideration because of long experience.

At least these are the labels used in the textbooks to describe wage increases. And this is also the way personnel practitioners refer to salary adjustments when they talk to each other. But . . . what happens in actual practice?

If the truth were ever admitted, most pay raises are granted, pure and simple, on a seniority basis. Another six months or twelve months have passed, salaries are reviewed, and adjustments made, hopefully, to deserving workers. But the reason for the action is "time," not "merit."

Some companies review all salaries at one time, say around the first of the year. The better programs consider wages individually, the review date related to start of employment, transfer or promotion, or most recent wage increase. In all cases a specified period of time has elapsed since the last salary action and another review is called for by the schedule. Again it is the calendar which dictates the action.

It is unfortunate that so many raises in so many companies are granted because of seniority. This kind of wage administration gives the better wages to employees with the longer service. While some consideration should be given to length of service, the most important factor should be job performance. Anything else will discourage the good worker, the very employee that companies can least afford to lose.

PERFORMANCE RATING

Once the jobs are evaluated, the other half of the wage program calls for an evaluation of the employee's performance. This is commonly called merit rating, although performance rating would appear to be more easily understood and applied.

Performance rating is defined as an orderly, systematic method of appraising an employee's performance on the job in terms of the requirements of the job. It is a method of obtaining opinions about an employee; it is not a method of "measuring" productivity or personality traits.

The manager or supervisor (the rater) expresses opinions, usually by asking standard questions that appear on a preprinted form, and checking the most applicable of a series of possible answers. There are any number of forms that can be used: short answer checklists, chart systems, narrative forms, forced distribution systems, linear, etc. The most popular is the graphic form because it is easy to understand and simple to use. On all such forms, the answers are subjective.

The rating is done periodically and regularly. The most popular time seems to be semiannually for wage-and-hour employees and annually for exempt personnel. The time of rating is best related to each individual employee's employment date, or the date of his latest promotion; if done on a calendar basis the manager finds himself burdened with ratings for all his people at one time and possibly cannot be as thorough as when the ratings are spread out and completed one or two at a time.

Performance rating is useful in any personnel action, but should be done independent of the action taken. To be effective it should be done when nothing is at stake, then referred to when some action is called for. To be fair and impartial, and thereby meaningful, it should not be done in connection with a salary increase, promotion, discharge, and the like. Done at a time when the employee is under consideration for some action, the rating merely becomes window dressing to support the recommendation.

The factors upon which a worker is rated fall into three general groupings—what the worker

is   —intelligence, ambition, dependability, initiative

knows—job knowledge, present activity, related procedures

does —cooperation, quality of work, responsibility, quantity of work, diligence, housekeeping.

The factors used should be common to all jobs, otherwise uneven ratings will result. Do not include "attendance" since rating an employee presupposes he is on the job. If he fails to meet minimum attendance requirements he should not even be rated. Dependability is a much better factor than attendance since it embodies arriving on time, not leaving ahead of time, staying within prescribed pass and lunch periods without being policed, and in general being on the job as needed. Avoid personal characteristics such as judgment, personality, and the like.

Point Range Established

For uniform understanding and interpretation, each factor is adequately defined. The factor, in turn, is subdivided into degrees which are clearly spelled out on the scale—usually four to five degrees or levels are set forth. A range of points is thereby assigned to the factors, and a total score or quantitative value arrived at by summing up the points for each separate rating. Where each trait is rated on a numerical scale, there is usually an effort made to weight each trait in proportion to all others; all factors of a job are not of equal value.

Different sets of factors, and therefore different forms, are used for wage-and-hour employees and exempt personnel. A worker is rated only on present performance. Where a worker's potential is considered, a separate system must be used. In the case of rank-and-

WAGE AND SALARY ADMINISTRATION

BLUE CROSS - BLUE SHIELD PLANS
CHICAGO

PERFORMANCE RATING

ᴧE:_____   DATE of RATING:_____

ᴧRTMENT:_____   JOB CLASSIFICATION:_____

JOB WLEDGE	How Well Does This Employee Understand The Requirements Of Job To Which Assigned:				
	Thoroughly understands all aspects of job.	More than adequate knowledge of job.	Has sufficient knowledge to do job.	Insufficient knowledge of some phases.	Continually needs instruction.

ᴧLITY OF ᴧORK	How Accurate, Neat And Complete Is The Work:				
	Consistently neat, accurate and thorough.	Careful worker seldom needs correction.	Work is acceptable.	Occasionally Careless —needs checking.	Inaccurate and careless.

ᴄO-ᴧATION	Does This Employee Work Harmoniously And Effectively With Co-Workers And Supervision:				
	Exceptionally willing and successful as a team worker.	Usually tactful and offers to assist others.	Gets along well enough, no problem.	Cooperation must be solicited, seldom volunteers.	Tends to be a troublemaker.

ᴧPON- ᴧLITY	How Does This Employee Accept All The Responsibilities Of The Job:				
	Accepts all responsibilities fully and meets Emergencies.	Conscientiously tries to fulfill job responsibilities.	Accepts but does not seek responsibility.	Does some assigned tasks reluctantly.	Indifferent—avoids responsibilities.

ᴧTIA- ᴧVE	How Well Does This Employee Begin An Assignment Without Direction And Recognize The Best Way Of Doing It:				
	Self starter: makes practical suggestions.	Proceeds on assigned work voluntarily and readily accepts suggestions.	Does regular work without prompting.	Relies on others: needs help getting started.	Must usually be told exactly what to do.

ᴧNTITY ᴧF ᴧRK	How Much Satisfactory Work Is Consistently Turned Out By This Employee:				
	Maintains unusually high out-put.	Usually does more than expected.	Does sufficient amount of work.	Inclined to be slow.	Inadequate turn-out of work.

ᴧEND- ᴧLITY	How Faithful Is This Employee In Reporting To Work And Staying On The Job:				
	Places company interests ahead of personal conveniences.	Punctual and does not waste company time.	Generally on the job as needed.	Some abuses — occasionally needs to be admonished.	Chronic abuses of working schedules.

ᴧENTS:_____

_____

_____

ᴧy:_____   Discussed With Employee: By_____

ᴧction being taken to help this employee improve his performance?   ☐ No   ☐ Yes—Specify_____

_____

_____   Dept. Manager_____

(See Reverse Side For Instructions in Rating)

653

file workers, the function of the manager as he rates his people is that of a repairman. Where supervisors or potential managers are rated, the rater also serves as a talent scout.

Performance rating systems for administrative, professional, and staff personnel include such factors as:

Planning—Forecasting, setting objectives, determining courses of action.

Technical knowledge and competence.

Organizing—Assembling and arranging resources to meet goals.

Acceptance of responsibility.

Delegating—Assigning responsibility, authority, accountability.

Confrontation Has Value

It should be noted that the significance of performance rating lies not in the form or the way it is filled out, scored, and then recorded. The real value is in the counseling interview, or face-to-face discussion, which follows. Every employee wants to know "How am I doing?" The performance rating then becomes a device to give the manager and the worker the opportunity to sit down together to talk over the worker's progress and find areas for improvement.

In conducting these all-important interviews it is well to remember that:

1. Where workers are rated on the results of their work, and where an attempt is made to orient the discussion to the job, the relationship between superior and subordinate is healthy.

2. Where rating forms focus on personality traits, appraisal interviews are carried out half-heartedly, in an atmosphere of mutual embarrassment, and with little wholesome effect.

There are many advantages to a performance rating program.

For workers, it improves job performance, serves as an aid in promotions, transfers, and layoffs; aids in deciding on wage increases; establishes need for training; improves morale; gets worker closer to supervisor; earmarks candidates for development and other consideration.

For supervisors, it brings them closer to workers, improves their analytical ability, and improves them in the personnel program.

Always keep in mind: Performance rating never fails; the people who use it sometimes do.

SUGGESTED COMPANY PERFORMANCE RATING

Definition: Performance rating is an orderly, systematic method of appraising an employee's performance on the job in terms of the requirements of the job. It is a method of obtaining opinions about an employee's work performance and work habits; it is not a method of measuring productivity or personality traits.

Frequency: The rating of wage-and-hour employees is to be accomplished three months after each salary review; however, in no case should more than six months elapse without a rating. Any employee may be rated at any time that the department manager decides the previous rating is no longer applicable.

Orientation: The department manager will be responsible for rating the employees of his department. He may enlist the cooperation of such assistants who can help him arrive at the most valid rating. Technically, the rating should be made by the immediate supervisor, the person closest to the employee. The department manager, however, will be held accountable and responsible for the ratings of his employees. No one will rate, or assist in the rating of, an employee without adequate preliminary instruction. Semiannually, a meeting will be held during which performance rating and its objectives will be discussed, the procedure explained, and questions answered.

Employee Review: Each employee's performance rating will be discussed privately with the employee by the rater. The rater will discuss both the employee's strong and weak points as revealed by the rating, without reference to point value of factors or total score. This can best be accomplished by conducting a conversation between the rater and the employee in such a way as to give the employee a feeling of individual worth and foster a sense of pride in himself and his work. Anything significant mentioned by the employee during the conversation may be recorded under "Comments," and the form then forwarded to personnel.

Scoring: The factors will be scored as follows:

	Degrees				
	1st	2nd	3rd	4th	5th
1. Job Knowledge	20	16	12	8	4
2. Quality	20	16	12	8	4
3. Cooperation	15	12	9	6	3
4. Responsibility	15	12	9	6	3
5. Initiative	10	8	6	4	2
6. Quantity	10	8	6	4	2
7. Dependability	10	8	6	4	2

Filing: The score of the rating will be recorded on the employee's individual progress card in personnel, and the rating sheet will be placed in the individual employee's file.

SUGGESTED MEMO INTRODUCING PERFORMANCE RATING

To: ALL EMPLOYEES
From: PERSONNEL DEPARTMENT

No matter where you are or what you are doing, your actions are being judged by other people. On the job the manager continually rates the performance of the people working with him so that he knows, for instance, whom to promote or give an increase in salary.

To make this rating procedure in our company orderly and equitable, a formalized system of performance rating has been established which will help the manager in this necessary and continuous task.

Performance rating has been in use in most progressive companies for many years. It is a proved systematic approach to the management of a business which, if used properly, increases the effectiveness of the administration of fair salaries and work opportunities.

The reason for performance rating is to provide those people who are responsible for evaluating the performance of others with a uniform guide. In this way your performance is the sole determining factor in the whole evaluation process.

Since we believe that you would like to know how well you are doing, twice each year your manager or supervisor will visit with you to discuss your performance on the job. This will give both of you an opportunity to discuss your progress on the job, and a chance to do something about the little things which might spoil an otherwise good performance.

With your cooperation and understanding this will be a mutually beneficial program.

APPRAISAL BY RESULTS

Appraisal by results is a performance appraisal at the management level measured against previously-established goals.

It involves these steps:

- An individual manager determines the results he expects to reach during the period ahead, usually one year.

- He and his boss confer about his proposed targets. Adjustments are made to coordinate his goals with those of other managers and blend all of them into unified corporate planning objectives. The manager and his boss reach an agreement on his challenging but attainable goals.

- The manager goes to work doing his job all the while keeping his goals and target dates in mind.

- At the end of the year, the manager's performance is appraised in terms of how well he met the goals he himself set earlier with the guidance and concurrence of his superior. Salary consideration or other action may be taken on the basis of this results-oriented appraisal.

- Based on the previous year's experience, new goals are drafted for the coming year.

SALARY SURVEYS

Companies want to know how they stand in the community salary-wise. Are wages paid still competitive? Are they still able to attract applicants and hold employees? To find out, they participate in salary surveys.

These studies are sponsored by a trade association to which the company belongs, by a prominent corporation against which it competes for applicants, by an industry of which it is a member, by government, or by a group of good neighbor firms who want to share and compare data.

Salary surveys are conducted periodically and regularly, perhaps annually. This gives the program continuity and a note of standardization since after a while the participating firms get to know and understand each other. A better comparison results.

Key jobs are studied. These are benchmark jobs, identical or at least very similar in all companies. They are the common, easily defined jobs, with sizable numbers of employees. Good examples are: key punch operator, typist, computer programmer, janitor, drill press operator, switchboard operator, tool and die maker, etc.

Specialty jobs are avoided. Titles alone are not enough; a comptroller in one company will be different from his counterpart in another firm. It is best to use a few lines to describe the job and then include the job in the study (regardless of title) only if the duties are comparable.

A study of salaries may often include fringe items such as hours worked, vacations, sick pay policies, lunch periods, insurance benefits, etc. It seems easy to gather extra data at the same time.

The method calls for sending out a questionnaire to eligible participating companies. A separate page is used for each job under consideration. It calls for minimum and maximum of the range plus the actual wages paid different incumbents. If time permits, a personal call is preferable to a mailing since it assures better data. All respondents receive copies of the final report.

If medians and quartiles are calculated, the method is explained. The finished report also contains copies of all data used, such as the capsule job descriptions, ranges, number of incumbents, etc.

Individual companies are identified on the index of participating firms so all will know which companies cooperated. But in the details company identification is represented by a code number, known only to the survey team and the company so marked.

SUGGESTED MEMO TO MANAGERS
AND FOREMEN

Our new performance rating program has been thoroughly explained to you. We hope you understand its purpose and also the procedure. After a little experience with it, we know you will find it useful to you in your dealings with your workers.

Performance rating is a continuous process. Although we set aside two dates in a year when performance rating is actually done on paper, the opinions for that evaluation are necessarily formed all during the year. The performance rating will become better as we learn to evaluate each individual objectively all through the year. This does not mean carrying a pencil and pad around writing down all the good and bad things an employee does, but it does mean a conscious appraisal of an employee's work and work habits as they are being formed.

If there is any doubt as to which degree of a particular factor is applicable to a certain employee, the one which is completely true should be chosen, even though in some cases he or she might possess a small amount of the ability or qualifications necessary in the next higher degree.

An important point to consider is that while an employee may conceivably rate very high in a particular job within a very short period of time, this does not mean that he should be given a salary increase to the top of the grade. It means that we are not utilizing this employee to his fullest potential—added responsibility might increase his usefulness; he might be considered for a promotion if there is a higher position or slightly more difficult job he is capable of fulfilling.

Any employee whose rating is below average will be "signaled" out for special consideration to determine if the unsatisfactory record of accomplishment can be traced to some factor which is correctable, such as misassignment, improper supervision or training, or personal problems which we may be able to give guidance on in the interview or subsequent meeting. Department managers are responsible for taking some remedial action which will erase the causes for the poor rating. An employee should not get two consecutive below-average ratings unless the causes are entirely beyond the control of the supervisors, in which case termination should be considered.

The next step, and the most important step in the process, is the interview with the individual. This is the time when confidence and morale can be considerably strengthened and poor behavior and work patterns which may be developing with or without the employee's knowledge can be corrected.

The following are general comments which should be used as a guide in these interviews:

1. An interview means two-way communications. As much, if not more, is to be gained by the employee talking, explaining, and suggesting, rather than our telling.

2. Make an individual feel at ease. Provide an informal attitude and atmosphere—come out from behind the desk. Pass the time of day for a minute or two.

3. Explain to the person what the interview is for and relate the general factors he or she is being rated on, using your own terminology.

4. Start the critique with those items that are praiseworthy. Remember, this person is an individual with an ego, who likes acknowledgment for the things he has done well.

5. Do not read the performance rating form out to the employee, or mention anything about point ratings. Their performance should be explained in your own words—words they will understand.

6. In discussing a person's shortcomings, don't do any preaching. State the facts and then ask the person if there is some reason why—get his side of the story and evolve from it the solution to the problem.

7. The solution to a problem should come from the employee with some guidance on your part. In this way he is much more likely to do something about it.

8. The interviewer should finish the meeting. Don't leave the employee hanging in mid-air; put a conclusion to the meeting with a statement of confidence in the employee.

9. Provide at least 15 minutes for each interview—really get to know the employee.

Surveys on supervision indicate that the most successful and efficient supervisors are those who put over half of their time in the leadership and interpersonal side of their jobs and the rest of the time in the paperwork and technical requirements.

FAIR LABOR STANDARDS ACT

The Fair Labor Standards Act of 1938, as amended, establishes minimum wage, maximum hours, overtime pay, equal pay, and child labor standards for covered employment, unless a specific exemption applies.

Fair Labor Standards Amendments of 1966 extended the act's coverage to more workers and increased the minimum wage for employment already subject to the law. The act applied to employees individually engaged in interstate or foreign commerce or in the production of goods for such commerce, and to employees in certain large enterprises.

The 1966 extension of coverage was achieved through the broadening of the definition of a covered enterprise. Also, some exemptions were revised or eliminated.

Among other changes, more retail and service enterprises were brought under the act. For the first time, the law's standards were extended, in whole or in part, to employees in certain hotels, motels, and restaurants, in hospitals and nursing homes, and in schools. Certain farm workers were made subject to the minimum wage.

The minimum wage and overtime standards for "newly covered" employment differ, for the limited periods prescribed in the law, from the corresponding standards which apply to work subject to the act before February 1, 1967.

BASIC WAGE AND HOUR STANDARDS

Unless specifically exempt, employees engaged in previously covered employment must be paid at least as follows:

Minimum wage.—Current rate, $1.60 an hour.

Overtime.—One and one-half times the employee's regular rate of pay for all hours worked in excess of 40 in a workweek.

WAGE AND HOUR STANDARDS FOR NEWLY COVERED EMPLOYMENT

Unless specifically exempt, employees engaged in work made subject to the act by the 1966 amendments must be paid at least as follows:

Minimum wage for nonfarm work—$1.30 an hour, beginning February 1, 1969; $1.45 an hour, beginning February 1, 1970; $1.60 an hour, beginning February 1, 1971.

Overtime pay for nonfarm work—One and one-half times the employee's regular rate of pay is required for all hours worked over 40 hours in a workweek.

Employees of nursing homes, rest homes, and bowling alleys must receive 1½ times their regular rate for hours over 48 in any workweek.

A special provision permits hospitals to adopt a 14-day period in lieu of the usual 7-day workweek, provided at least time and one-half the employee's regular rate is paid for hours in excess of 8 in any workday and in excess of 80 in the 14-day period.

Minimum wage for farm work—$1.30 an hour. The overtime provisions do NOT apply to farm work.

PREVIOUSLY COVERED EMPLOYMENT

Employees covered prior to the 1966 amendments remain covered under the amended act. They include (a) employees individually engaged in interstate or foreign commerce, (b) employees individually engaged in the production of goods for interstate or foreign commerce, and (c) all employees in certain large enterprises.

a. Employees engaged in interstate or foreign commerce: These include workers in the telephone, telegraph, radio, television, and transportation industries; those who build, maintain and repair highways, railroads, and airfields, or service vehicles or equipment used in interstate commerce; employees in distributing industries, such as wholesaling, who handle goods moving in interstate commerce as well as workers who order, receive, or keep records of such goods; clerical and other workers who regularly use the mails, telephone, or telegraph for interstate communication; employees of businesses such as banks, insurance companies, and advertising agencies that regularly utilize the channels of interstate commerce in the course of operations; and employees who regularly travel across state lines while working.

b. Employees engaged in the production of goods for interstate or foreign commerce: Included are employees who work in manufacturing, processing, and distributing establishments, and in mines, oilfields, and quarries that produce goods for interstate or foreign commerce. This means everyone, including office, management, sales, and shipping personnel, and maintenance, custodial, and protective employees, whether they are employed by the producer or an intermediary. Employees may be covered even if their firm does not ship its goods directly in such commerce. The goods may leave the state through another firm. The workers may produce goods which become a part or ingredient of goods shipped in interstate or foreign commerce by another firm. Also covered are workers who are engaged in a closely related process or occupation directly essential to the production of such goods. Their employers may supply such items as machinery, fuel or utilities to firms for producing goods for, or engaging in, such commerce.

c. Employees employed in the following enterprises, if—
   1. there are, in the activities of the enterprise, employees engaged in interstate or foreign commerce or in the production of goods for interstate or foreign commerce, including employees handling, selling, or

otherwise working on goods that have been moved in or produced for such commerce by any person, and if—

2. such enterprise is one which—

   (i) has one or more retail or service establishments and an annual gross sales volume of $1 million or more, and procures at least $250,000 annually of goods for resale that move across State lines, or

   (ii) is engaged in the business of construction or reconstruction and has an annual gross volume of $350,000 or more from such business, or

   (iii) is a gasoline service establishment which has an annual gross sales volume of $250,000 or more, or

   (iv) is engaged in urban or interurban transit operations and has an annual gross sales volume of $1 million or more, or

   (v) is an establishment of any other such enterprise, where the establishment has some employees engaged in interstate or foreign commerce or in the production of goods for such commerce and the enterprise has an annual gross sales volume of $1 million or more.

The act provides that none of the above enterprises will include any establishment which has as its only employees, the owner, his spouse, parents, or children.

NEWLY COVERED EMPLOYMENT

The 1966 amendments increased the coverage of the act by including employees of additional enterprises and made the act applicable to other employees by repealing or revising specific exemptions. Employment thus made subject to the minimum wage provisions by these amendments is "newly covered." Thus, for purposes of deciding whether an employee is "newly covered," the act as it read before the 1966 amendments must be considered in the light of the changes made by the 1966 amendments.

a. Employees employed in the enterprises indicated below are covered on and after February 1, 1967, under the 1966 amendments, if—

1. there are, in the activities of the enterprise, employees engaged in interstate or foreign commerce or in the production of goods for interstate or foreign commerce, including employees handling, selling, or otherwise working on goods that have been moved in or produced for such commerce by any person, and if—

2. such enterprise is one which—

   (i) has an annual gross volume of sales made or business done, exclusive of certain taxes, of at least $500,000 ($250,000 beginning Feb. 1, 1969), or

   (ii) is engaged in the business of construction or reconstruction (regardless of dollar volume), or

   (iii) is engaged in laundering, cleaning, or repairing clothing or fabrics (regardless of dollar volume), or

   (iv) is engaged in the operation of a hospital (except a Federal Government hospital), nursing home, or school (whether public, private, or nonprofit and regardless of dollar volume).

The act provides that none of the above enterprises will include any establishment which has as its only regular employees, the owner, his spouse, parents or children, or other member of the owner's immediate family.

b. As the result of the elimination or revision of various exemptions, employees of certain hotels, motels, and restaurants and other retail or service establishments have had their exemption status changed. Also, employees of taxicab companies and of additional transit companies have become subject to the minimum wage.

The minimum wage provisions have been extended to certain farm workers, to employees of country elevators in the "area of production," to cotton ginning employees, and to certain fruit and vegetable transportation employees. The minimum wage and overtime pay exemption for employees handling and processing agricultural products in the "area of production" has been repealed. Overtime pay exemptions applicable to certain other agricultural processing employees have been eliminated or revised. More logging-crew employees are now subject to the minimum wage and overtime requirements. The number of hours beyond which overtime pay is required in "seasonal" industries has been reduced.

EXEMPTIONS

Some employees who would otherwise be entitled to the benefits of the act are excluded from the minimum wage or overtime provisions, or both, by specific exemptions. These exemptions apply only in those cases where their terms and conditions are specifically met. Employers should check carefully the terms and conditions of any exemption which they seek to use. The list below merely indicates some types of exemptions contained in the act and does not spell out their conditions. Information on specific exemptions may be obtained from the Division's nearest office.

Exemptions include executive, administrative, and professional employees (including teachers and academic administrative personnel in elementary or secondary schools), and outside salesmen, as defined.

Employees of a retail or service establishment that makes most of its sales within the state and is not in a covered enterprise *or* has less than $250,000 in annual sales (exclusive of specified taxes). Covered hospitals, nursing homes, laundries, drycleaners, and schools do not qualify for this exemption;

Employees of certain seasonal amusement or recreational establishments, of motion picture theaters, of certain small newspapers; switchboard operators of telephone companies which have fewer than 750 telephones; seamen employed on vessels other than American vessels; fish farmers and fishermen;

Certain farm workers employed by an employer who did not use more than 500 man-days of farm labor in any calendar quarter of the preceding calendar year; employees engaged in certain operations relating to specified agricultural or horticultural commodities; and employees in small forestry and logging operations.

Exemptions from overtime requirements only include:

Employees of hotels, motels, restaurants; employees of retail or service establishments who are employed primarily in connection with certain food or beverage services;

663

Certain higher-paid commission employees of retail or service establishments; salesmen, mechanics, and partsmen primarily engaged in selling or servicing automobiles, trucks, trailers, farm implements, or aircraft, employed by non-manufacturing establishments primarily engaged in the business of selling such vehicles to ultimate purchasers;

Employees of railroads, pipelines, and carriers by air covered by specified statutes; operating employees of urban and interurban transit systems; drivers of taxicabs; seamen on American vessels; certain employees of motor carriers; and local delivery drivers *paid on a trip-rate basis* or other payment plan meeting prescribed conditions;

Employees employed in canning, processing, storing, marketing, and distributing aquatic products;

Announcers, news editors, and chief engineers of certain nonmetropolitan broadcasting stations.

PARTIAL EXEMPTIONS

Partial exemptions from the overtime requirements for certain periods are provided for employees in industries determined to be seasonal by the administrator; for certain operations on agricultural commodities; and for employees of certain wholesale or bulk petroleum distributors whose annual gross sales (exclusive of certain taxes) are less than $1 million. Also there is a limited overtime pay exemption for employees of institutions primarily engaged in the care of the sick, aged, and mentally ill residing on the premises; and bowling establishments.

HOW TO COMPUTE OVERTIME PAY

Premium pay for overtime work must be paid for each hour worked in excess of the maximum workweek applicable to the type of employment in which the employee is engaged. Overtime pay must be paid at a rate of not less than 1½ times the employee's regular rate of pay.

The "regular rate" may be more than the minimum wage; it cannot be less. Except for certain types of payments specified in section 7 (e) of the act, an employee's regular rate includes all payments made by the employer to or on behalf of that employee. Assuming that the employee receives no compensation other than that stated, here are some typical cases based, for example only, on a maximum workweek of 40 hours:

1. *Hourly rate.*—The regular rate of pay for an employee paid by the hour is his hourly rate. When he works more than 40 hours in a workweek, he is due at least 1½ times his regular rate for each hour over 40.

Example: An employee gets paid $1.60 an hour; this is his regular rate. If he worked a 44-hour workweek, he would be entitled to at least 1½ times $1.60, or $2.40, for each hour over 40. His pay for the week would be $64 for the first 40 hours plus $9.60 for the 4 hours overtime, or a total of $73.60.

2. *Piece rate.*—The regular rate for an employee paid on a piece rate basis is obtained by dividing the total weekly earnings by the total number of hours worked in the same week. The employee is entitled to payment of one-half this regular rate for each hour over the 40th in addition to the full piecework earnings.

Example: An employee is paid on a piecework basis. When he worked 45 hours in a week, his earnings came to $81. His regular rate of pay for that week was $1.80 ($81 divided by 45). In addition to his regular rate the employee is entitled to 90 cents (one-half his regular rate) for each hour over 40, or 5 times 90 cents for the 5 overtime hours. This $4.50 overtime premium brought his total earnings to $85.50.

Another way to compensate pieceworkers for overtime, where agreed upon in advance of performance of the work, is to pay 1½ times the piece rate for each piece produced during overtime hours. The piece rate must be the one actually paid during nonovertime hours and it must be enough to yield at least the minimum wage per hour.

Example: An employee is paid 8 cents for each piece. In a week in which he worked 43 hours, he earned $68.40 for the first 40 hours at this rate. The employee's pay was piece and one-half, or 12 cents per piece produced in the overtime hours. Assuming he produced 65 pieces during the overtime, he was entitled to be paid $7.80 (65 times 12 cents) as overtime pay. Thus, he earned a total of $76.20 for the week.

3. *Salaries.*—The regular rate for an employee who is paid a salary for a regular or specified number of hours a week is obtained by dividing the weekly salary by the hours.

Example: An employee is paid a salary of $80 for a 40-hour workweek. His regular rate of pay is $80 divided by 40 hours, or $2 an hour. When he works overtime, he will be entitled to get 1½ times the $2, or $3 for each hour over the 40th.

The law provides some alternative methods of computing overtime pay. These methods are given in Interpretative Bulletin, Part 778, entitled "Overtime Compensation," and Regulations, Part 548, on "Authorization of Established Basic Rates for Computing Overtime Pay."

WHAT THE "WORKWEEK" IS

A workweek is a regularly recurring period of 168 hours in the form of seven consecutive 24-hour periods. The workweek need not coincide with the calendar week—it may begin any day of the week and any hour of the day. Each workweek stands alone. Employment for two or more workweeks cannot be averaged out for the sake of figuring overtime or minimum wages except under prescribed conditions in the case of seamen on American vessels and employees of hospitals. The minimum wage must be paid for every hour worked in each workweek and overtime must be paid for all hours worked in excess of the maximum workweek applicable to the type of employment in which the employee is engaged. Coverage and application of most exemptions are also determined on a workweek basis.

WHAT "HOURS WORKED" MEANS

An employee subject to the act in any workweek must be paid in accordance with its provision for all hours worked in that workweek. In general, "hours worked" includes all the time an employee is required to be on duty or on the employer's premises or at a prescribed workplace, and all time during which he is suffered or permitted to work for the employer.

TIPS AND EMPLOYER-FURNISHED FACILITIES

Tips received by a tipped employee may be considered wages for purpose of the act in such amount, not more than 50 percent of the applicable minimum rate, as the employer may determine. A "tipped employee" is a worker engaged in an occupation in which he customarily and regularly receives more than $20 a month in tips.

Wages also include the reasonable cost or fair value, as determined, of board, lodging, and other facilities customarily provided by the employer to his employees. However, such costs are not included in wages to the extent they are excluded under an applicable bona fide collective-bargaining agreement.

SPECIAL PROVISIONS

Unless specifically exempt, all covered employees must be paid at least the applicable minimum wage, regardless of whether the employees are paid on time, piece, job, incentive, or any other basis. However, learners, apprentices, messengers, handicapped workers, and full-time students employed in retail or service establishments or in agriculture under certain circumstances, may be paid special lower minimum wage rates provided that special certificates are first obtained. Also, for employees in Puerto Rico, the Virgin Islands, and American Samoa, industry wage orders may set minimum rates below the statutory minimum.

EQUAL PAY PROVISIONS

The Fair Labor Standards Act, as amended by the Equal Pay Act of 1963, prohibits employers from discriminating on the' basis of sex in the payment of wages for equal work. The equal pay amendment has been generally in effect since June 11, 1964, with deferment in the case of certain collective bargaining agreements. On June 11, 1965, the amendment became effective with respect to all employees subject to its terms.

Under the equal pay provisions, the employer may not discriminate on the basis of sex by paying employees of one sex at rates lower than he pays employees of the opposite sex, in the same establishment, for doing equal work on jobs requiring equal skill, effort, and responsibility which are performed under similar working conditions. The equal pay provisions apply only to employees who are covered by the Fair Labor Standards Act and are subject to a minimum wage under the act; they apply in every establishment where the employer has such employees. They do not apply with respect to any employee who is specifically exempt from the minimum wage requirements.

The act provides an exception from the prohibition against payment of wages at lower rates to one sex than the other for equal work where it can be shown that the wage differential is based on a seniority system, a merit system, a system measuring earnings by quantity or quality of production, or on any other factor other than sex.

An employer who is paying a wage differential in violation of the equal pay provisions of the act may not reduce the wage rate of any employee in order to comply with these provisions. Wages withheld in violation of the equal pay provisions have the status of unpaid minimum wages or unpaid overtime compensation under the act, and back wages due under the equal pay provisions are subject to the same methods of recovery as any other wages due under the act.

The law prohibits any labor organization, or its agents, representing employees of an employer having employees subject to the minimum wage provisions of the act, from causing or attempting to cause the employer to discriminate against an employee in violation of the equal pay provisions.

CHILD LABOR PROVISIONS

Sixteen years is the minimum age for most employment covered by the act. This includes employment in agriculture during school hours or in any occupation in agriculture declared hazardous by the Secretary of Labor.

Eighteen years is the minimum age for employment in a nonagricultural occupation in agriculture declared hazardous by the Secretary of Labor.

Fourteen years is the minimum age for employment specified in the Secretary's regulations, which is permitted outside school hours in a variety of nonmanufacturing and nonmining occupations for a limited number of hours under specified conditions of work.

Employers can protect themselves from unintentional violation of the child labor provisions by keeping on file an employment or age certificate for each young person employed, to show he is at least the minimum age for his job.

RECORDS

Employers are required to keep records on wages, hours, and other items listed in the recordkeeping regulations, 29 CFR Part 516. Most of this required information is the kind employers usually keep in ordinary business practices and in complying with other laws and regulations. No particular form of records is required.

Records required for exempt employees differ from those for nonexempt workers. Special information is required on employees under uncommon pay arrangements or to whom board, lodging, or other facilities are furnished. Employers who have homeworkers must make entries in handbooks supplied by the Divisions. Record of the required information must be preserved for 3 years. Some supplementary items like timecards, piecework tickets, and order and shipping records need be kept only 2 years. Microfilm copies of records are generally acceptable.

SOME REMARKS

The law applies equally to men and women, to homeworkers as well as factory and office workers (certificates issued by the Divisions are necessary for homeworkers in certain industries) and (except with respect to occupations applicable to small logging operations and small country elevators) regardless of the number of employees of an employer, and whether they work full or part time.

The law does *not* require extra pay for Saturday, Sunday, or holiday work, as such, or vacation, holiday, or severance pay or a discharge notice; nor does it set any limit on the number of hours of work for persons 16 years of age or over.

The act does not apply to employees of the United States, or any state or political subdivision of a state, unless employed in a hospital, institution, school, or carrier operations specifically covered by its provisions.

ENFORCEMENT

Authorized representatives of the Wage and Hour and Public Contracts Divisions may investigate and gather data regarding the wages, hours, and other conditions and practices of employment. They may enter establishments and inspect the premises and records, transcribe records, and interview employees. They may investigate whatever facts, conditions, practices, or matters are considered necessary to find out whether any person has violated any provisions of the act. Wage-Hour investigations generally will make suggestions regarding any changes necessary or desirable regarding payroll, recordkeeping, and other practices which will aid in achieving and maintaining compliance with the law. Complaints, records, and other information obtained from employers and employees are treated confidentially.

The act provides methods of recovering unpaid minimum and/or overtime wages: (1) The Divisions Administrator may supervise payment of back wages, and in certain circumstances (2) the Secretary of Labor may bring suit for back pay upon the written request of the employee. (3) An employee may sue for back wages and an additional sum, up to the amount of back pay, as liquidated damages, plus attorney's fees and court costs. (An employee may not bring suit if he has been paid back wages under supervision of the Administrator, or if the Secretary has filed suit to enjoin the employer from retaining the wages due him). (4) The Secretary of Labor may also obtain a court injunction to restrain any person from violating the law, including the unlawful withholding of proper minimum wage and overtime compensation.

It is a violation of the law to discharge an employee for filing a complaint or participating in a proceeding under the law.

Willful violations may be prosecuted criminally and the violator fined up to $10,000. A second conviction for such a violation may result in imprisonment.

A 2-year statute of limitations applies to the recovery of back wages except in the case of willful violations, for which there is a 3-year statute of limitations.

ASSISTANCE IS AVAILABLE

Whether any employee is covered or exempt under the Fair Labor Standards Act depends on the facts in each case. If you want to know about the application of the law to any worker, write to the Divisions' nearest office. Give information on the kind of firm and what it does, with whom it does business, the job involved, the method of pay, the hours of work, and any other details you think will be needed for an adequate reply to your question.

Inquiries about the Fair Labor Standards Act, the Walsh-Healey Public Contracts Act, the McNamara-O'Hara Service Contract Act, and their application, will be answered by mail, telephone, or personal interview at any regional or field office of the Wage and Hour and Public Contracts Division of the U.S. Department of Labor. These offices also supply publications free of charge.

PART 8

BENEFITS

Group insurance
Sick pay allowance
Hospitalization
Major medical expense
Key-man insurance
Retirement income
Preretirement plans
Social security
Profit sharing

GROUP INSURANCE

A company group insurance package includes many or all of the following separate components:

Hospitalization Insurance

Blue Cross.
Commercial insurance.
Self-insurance.

Medical-Surgical Insurance

Blue Shield.
Commercial insurance.
Self-insurance.

Major Medical Insurance

Health and Accident Insurance

(Temporary disability) Some states now have laws requiring disability protection for workers. This is insurance for benefit payments while not working.

Travel Accident Insurance

This may be offered by the company at group rates or paid for in full or in part by the company. It is usually 24-hour coverage, on the job and away.

Life Insurance

The most common is term insurance, only in effect while employed by the company, no paid-up or cash surrender value.

Pension or Retirement Income Plan

This provides a lifetime monthly income after the established retirement age. It may also include provisions for a beneficiary or survivor (spouse). It may be contributory or noncontributory on the part of the employee.

Other Programs

Thrift or savings plan.

Profit-sharing plan.

Stock option ownership plan.

Group insurance programs have been defined as industry's contribution to social development. There are many good reasons for companies to accept this social responsibility.

1. Employees need insurance but do not buy enough protection themselves.

2. No physical examination is required; an insurer accepts all risks in the group. People who cannot pass an insurance physical are still eligible for coverage. In some cases this may be the only insurance they carry.

3. Companies can purchase insurance for employees in group plans at more favorable rates than the individuals would be required to pay.

4. For a low cost, companies try to get increased employee morale and lower turnover.

5. Company cost is further decreased by a tax deduction. The cost can be charged off as a legitimate business expense.

Some characteristics of group insurance are:

1. Premiums are collected or paid for by the employer.

2. One contract is signed but individual certificates are issued.

3. Coverage is the same for all employees, but the amount of coverage may vary with salary, occupation, and/or length of service.

4. There is usually a waiting period which may be to qualify participants or for administrative convenience.

5. An employee who elects not to participate is asked to sign a waiver or rejection card.

6. The company handles the necessary clerical work.

Some considerations are:

1. Should employer pay the full cost or is there something to be paid in favor of having employees share in the cost? Do they appreciate it more? Where employees contribute to the cost, their monthly payments can be arranged through convenient payroll deduction.

2. What about a waiting period? Should this be only to meet administrative requirements (first day of the month following a full month of employment, for example) or should employees wait six months or a year for some of the coverage, just as they wait a prescribed time for some retirement programs to include them?

3. How about including dependents? In a hospitalization and medical-surgical program, spouses and dependent children are usually included.

In other coverage, such as life insurance, they are not normally covered but named as beneficiaries.

The cost of a group insurance program is governed by: (1) kind of insurance included, (2) amount of coverage, (3) number of participants, and (4) their ages. The trend is up and will continue upward. The cost of benefit plans to employers has risen almost twice as fast as wages and salaries in the last decade.

HISTORY OF GROUP INSURANCE

Group health insurance was among the first of the fringe benefits. In both Europe and the United States, associations of individuals "helped" each other during times of personal misfortune. These were often associated with family groups, clubs, or craft guilds. One early example is the Manchester Unity Friendly Society, which was sufficiently organized to publish a book in 1907 with detailed data from their experiences.

As some of the key dates shown below illustrate, early plans developed from the need for them combined with society's need for certain services. For example, if the country wanted merchant seamen or firemen, it had to do something to take care of them during illness or injury.

Typical key dates include:

1798—U.S. Marine Hospital Service established by the United States Congress. Compulsory deductions for hospital service were made from the wages of seamen.

1880—A contract written by the Traveler's Insurance Company for the Board of Fire Commissioners of Baltimore to insure the members of the city's fire-fighting force.

1884—First Compensation Act in Germany.

1910—First group accident and sickness policy issued.

1911—Workmen's Compensation Act. By 1920 all states were covered.

1928—Development of hospital, surgical, and medical coverage for employees and dependents.

1932—First city-wide Blue Cross Plan tried out with a group of hospitals in Sacramento, California. In the early 1930's during the "Great Depression," hospitals had a considerable problem collecting their bills. To prevent the hospitals from becoming insolvent, local societies were formed for the prepayment of hospital-type bills. These groups were the forerunners of the present Blue Cross plans.

1939—First Blue-Shield-type plan formed.

1942—World War II "wage freeze" led employers to offer increased types and amounts of welfare or fringe benefits in lieu of prohibited wage increases. Employees became more dependent upon employers, who assumed responsibilities for workers beyond the payment of wages. Fringe benefits became a competitive necessity. Employers felt that group plans would help attract workers, reduce turnover, and lead to greater productivity.

1949—First major medical-insurance contract issued by Liberty Mutual Insurance Company to the management personnel of General Electric Company.

1949—This year was of major importance to the field of group insurance. In the Inland Steel decision of that year, the U.S. Supreme Court ruled that group insurance was an appropriate subject for collective bargaining. After this decision numerous insurance plans were incorporated into labor contracts.

In the years before unionized labor insisted on being heard, company management decided questions of insurance according to its own criterion, "The best possible coverage for the least amount of money," and it was the company's prerogative to determine what this was. When the situation changed so that managements had to negotiate with unions or keep up with the pattern set by unionized plans, these prerogatives were wiped out.

Since the Inland Steel case, labor unions have taken an increasingly larger share of the decisions away from company managers and placed them on the bargaining table. Even if there is no union present, management has to be aware now of what the competition is granting in fringe benefits as a result of union pressures.

The unions, of course, have kept their demands for group insurance and pensions moving toward ever-increasing coverage. Fringe-benefit bargaining is often balanced against increases in wages or improvements in physical working conditions. Cost data and conclusions on benefits should be in the hands of the employer to enable management to effectively evaluate union demands. It is better to know the strong points of your programs and their inadequacies, if any, from your own estimates than to be told about them in the heat of collective bargaining sessions.

Other agencies besides the unions, including the government, have been drawn into the administration of insured employee benefits. The federal and state governments have conducted numerous studies and investigations of group plans, all of which must be registered with the U.S. Department of Labor. Organizations such as the Foundation on Employee Health, Medical Care, and Welfare offer advice to companies and unions on good practices in buying group insurance.

EMPLOYEE HEALTH INSURANCE PROGRAM

Five major forms of health insurance are common in a company's health program for its employees. These include—hospital insurance, surgical insurance, regular medical insurance, major medical insurance, and loss-of-income protection.

Hospital insurance covers the usual hospital expenses, room and board, nursing care, drugs, operating room and equipment, laboratory, and x-ray. About 82 percent of Americans have some form of hospital insurance. There are many policies available. A low-premium policy naturally pays low benefits. How much of the hospital bill does your coverage pay? Does your program pay a specific daily amount or does it pay all reasonable hospital costs up to a high maximum? Make a study. Your program may have fallen behind the tremendous progress made by medical science and may no longer provide the protection your employees are lead to believe they carry.

Surgical insurance covers surgeon's fees, usually with dollar limits, including some preoperative and postoperative services. This kind of insurance also covers anesthesiologists' fees. About 76 percent have this type of coverage at present. But does your plan pay the physician's customary charge or is it limited by a fixed-fee schedule. Check some time to see how much of the bill your employees are still required to pay out of pocket.

Regular medical insurance pays for nonsurgical care and, in some cases, includes procedures in the doctor's office. There is a tendency to expand this kind of insurance to pay for diagnostic services. About 72 percent of employee health plans include regular medical insurance.

Major Medical, as a rule, pays over and above medical and surgical costs. It supplements basic insurance and comes into effect after other benefits are exhausted. It also includes benefits beyond the scope of basic insurance, such as private-duty nursing, prescription drugs at home, office and house calls, psychiatric care. The typical major medical policy has a deductible (Example: the employee pays the first $100 each year), a co-insurance arrangement (Example: the employee pays 20 percent of the amount over $100, the carrier pays 80 percent), and an outside limit on expenses for a single illness or injury (Example: $10,000). About 33⅓ percent of employee programs now include major medical protection.

Loss-of-income protection provides regular weekly income for a specified period of time to partially replace the income an employee loses during a period of illness or disability. How good is your program? Are payments related to earnings? Are they limited to a period of time, say, 26 weeks? What then? Have you a disability-insurance program for those employees whose illness or injury leaves them permanently disabled?

Check Your Company Program

How long since you've taken inventory of your employee welfare program? What does it include? How good is the coverage? How well does it meet employee needs?

Are you aware of the trends in this field? The tendency is for the company to pay more or all of the premium costs. Unions are asking for annual physical checkups, eye care, prenatal and postnatal care, and psychiatric care is high on their priority list. Many companies are investigating dental care, and nursing home care is coming in for its share of attention. Finally, employees look for paid-in-full benefits.

The big industrial firms—like automobiles and steel—are the pattern setters. Medicare is now a benchmark for other coverages, and labor and management will feel pressure to eliminate differences between what employees get and what oldsters are legally entitled to.

Through Medicare and Social Security all five of the major forms of health insurance are available, to a degree, to retired or disabled workers and their families. Unless companies move to provide at least comparable benefits to workers, the government may take the initiative.

Medicare, while causing problems in one area, is also a blessing in disguise in another respect. Companies no longer have to provide and pay for the full benefit cost for workers and retirees after age 65. These savings can be diverted into better programs for regular employees and their dependents.

COMPENSATING THROUGH FRINGE BENEFITS

Fringe benefits are sometimes referred to as the "salary with the fringe on top." This is an apt label. While not paid in cash to the workers, the fringes nonetheless represent a substantial cost-expense to the employer and a sizable cost-saving to the employee.

In many respects the fringe benefits may be the only difference between earnings in one company compared with those of another. Many factors, such as the tendency toward local and national wage increases, industry-wide policies, the proliferation of compensation surveys, and the practice of tandem adjustments, have contributed to near-equalization of job rates. Fringes, therefore, often make the difference.

Applicants and employees realize full well that there exist only slight variations in wages during days of full employment. Hence, they shop about for the best compensation package which consists of direct and indirect pay plus the intangibles.

Fringe benefits is a relatively new term. The earlier usage referred to "welfare work." But because this was, and still is, an unpopular phrase in the industrial vocabulary, the textbooks tried to promote such substitutes as "service activities" or "employee services." This service work, according to one definition, included "all those activities which are not directly concerned with production, but which make the plant personnel a healthier, sounder-thinking, more forward-looking group." The notion prevailed that those services would better the "condition" of the working men.

Today such features as individual lockers and clean washrooms are considered facilities of employment by companies and as a right of employment by workers. The fact that they are not under the supervision of the personnel executive indicates that they have passed from being employee benefits to being operating necessities.

The personnel office maintains an interest in their adequacy for safety and sanitation but exercises no direct control over their function.

On the other hand, industrial health and in-plant feeding have not only remained under the direction of the personnel officer but have also grown in importance. The medical services in many firms have gone from a small first-aid station to a complete clinic offering free polio and flu shots and annual physical checkups. Cafeterias provide more than convenient, well-planned, low-cost meals; just as important is the change-of-pace atmosphere available during rest periods and lunch hours which permits employees to relax, meet their friends, and engage in personal conversations which are discouraged at their work places.

One-Fourth of Wage Bill

Fringe benefits have increased during postwar years to the point where they commonly add approximately 25 percent to the wage bill. The development over the years is considered by some economists as a handicap of American manufacturers in competing with cheaper foreign products. But in many European countries there is an even greater diversity of nonwage benefits than in the United States. In other countries these are "social charges" which is nothing more than the cost of social legislation passed on to employers.

In analyzing fringe benefits, emphasis must be placed on the cash wages to which the fringes are added. If the base pay is not right the fringes will not be effective. Fringes are "plus" and cannot be expected to offset inadequate wage scales. Fringe benefits will not accomplish their purpose where starting salaries are below "going" rates and therefore do not attract workers in the first place. Where fringes are used to replace rather than to supplement salary, they are a misrepresentation of an employee benefit program as well as an unsound compensation practice.

The reasons for the establishment and expansion of benefit programs are many: tax consideration, legal requirements, increase in leisure time through shorter hours, growing concern with security, questions of public and employer responsibility, and so on. Because the cost can be charged off as operating expense, salary in the form of fringe benefits has the advantage of being tax free, whereas salary in cash is subject to taxes.

Generally, the purpose of fringe benefits is to help attract applicants and to hold workers. Specifically, each type of benefit has its own objective. If, for example, the aim is to increase skills, then a form of tuition refund or off-the-job training is recommended. If the labor market is to be widened, then flexible working hours or company-operated transportation should be considered. Attendance rewards may be tried in an attempt to reduce absenteeism. To maintain workers on the job and keep production going is the reason that convenient health facilities are available. In a cost-conscious climate the reason is selfish, no longer paternalistic.

The "cradle to grave" school of thought has had its day and today fringes are expected to pay their way in order to justify their existence. A true fringe benefit should show a value to both the employee and the employer. Social and humane considerations might appear to be unprofitable to companies, but they are of tremendous worth if they help to prevent strikes, reduce turnover, and the like.

In expanding the company benefit package the question arises as to whether to liberalize present benefits or to enlarge the scope by adding new ones or even possibly experimenting with innovations. Before the program is altered it might be advisable to consider how to justify the change or addition, not only to the comptroller but mostly to the employees.

Don't Copy Other Companies

It is not good practice to copy fringe benefits from other companies. Some fringes are suitable to one company and not applicable to others, such as selling "own goods" at wholesale. Many are peculiar to one locality, such as the wide variance in number of holidays across the country.

Some fringes, although available to all employees, are geared to special groups. When this is obvious the workers who see no gain feel they've been discriminated against and the fringe might actually do more harm than good. A retirement program has little appeal to the young married woman whose immediate ambition is the establishment of her home. Other examples here are: Company-paid memberships for management or professional people, personal time off for women, income tax help for hourly paid plant workers, wedding gifts for newlyweds, remembrances when babies are born, and wedding anniversary gifts for old-timers.

The kind of benefits made available to retired employees are usually in the health and service categories. A number of employers pay the Medicare medical premium for retirees (and sometimes spouses) or offer free or low-cost complementary health insurance. Some permit discount purchases of company products, free telephone use, secretarial assistance, cafeteria privileges, income tax guidance, and the like.

The "Nonwage" Benefits

Nonwage benefits are here to stay. While some of our more pedantic colleagues prefer to speak of "payments other than wages and salaries" or "indirect compensation," the terms "fringe benefits" or "employee benefits" have obtained a fairly clear identity and ready acceptance in management circles. But like many other such terms, while they are convenient to employers, they are not necessarily clear to employees.

"Employee benefits" is perhaps a better description than "fringe benefits." The miscellaneous benefits could possibly be classified as "fringes," but other major or even minor items in the total package are anything but fringes. Such things as free parking, libraries, purchase discounts, notary public services, and the like are the fringe items. They are not universal and depend upon the type of company and its location.

But practically all firms all over the country offer certain standard benefits which certainly cannot be classified as fringes. These substantial items are the wage replacement plans, such as sick pay allowances, income continuation policies, disability insurance. They also include the other insurance programs such as hospitalization, life insurance, and pension plans, which employers know employees need and which can be purchased more conveniently and advantageously in group arrangements than individually.

Anyway, these nonwage extras can hardly be called fringe anymore. But by whatever term these benefits are known, it is well to recognize their existence in the total scheme of managerial operations. Any discussion on this subject takes into account not only the effect of a benefit program but also its cost, which today is larger than most companies realize. Managements should itemize their fringe-benefit bill, just as they make other cost analyses; the results will open their eyes.

Before any meaningful study of costs can be made, however, a definition must be established in order to know what should be included and what should be excluded. Employee benefits are defined by one company as: "Anything which benefits the employee directly or indirectly in the form of extra income or services in excess of the established straight-time earnings, whether required by law or not." Employee benefits have these characteristics:

1. Increase the cost to the employer of a productive work-hour.

2. Add to employees' take-home pay in the form of benefits they would otherwise have had to pay for.

3. Are available to all employees, or most of them.

4. Vary in total cost as the workforce changes in size.

Some Exclusions

Under this definition benefits which generally contribute more to the well-being of the company than to the welfare of its employees, and are designed and developed for that purpose, should not be considered fringe benefits. Such things as safety clothing, first-aid rooms, personnel counseling, physical examinations for applicants, music at work, house-organs, and training material are excluded. The salary of the plant nurse and the cost of medications should not be included under this rule; but the cost of polio shots or other personal accommodation services are employee fringe benefits.

Any study of cost should include a complete inventory of the many separate fringe benefit items and a realistic analysis of the cost to the employer. Everything besides direct wages which is intended to benefit the worker and which costs money to provide should be counted. However, the cost of overtime, shift differentials, and premium pay for Sunday and holiday work should not be included;

such items compensate employees for working at certain times and under certain conditions.

One of the best studies of fringe benefit costs is made periodically by the Economic Research Department of the Chamber of Commerce of the United States.

SICK PAY

The practice of the United States Government in allowing civil service employees "sick" pay has spread to business. It has long been the practice of most companies to take care of salaried employees when they are away from work because of illness. Now policies are in effect which cover all employees, office and factory, on the same or similar terms.

At first there was a reluctance to pay people when they were not at work lest this practice encourage some to stay home every time they had runny noses. But that viewpoint is changing. Now companies prefer to have ill employees stay home to avoid spreading sickness to co-workers and at the same time endangering their own health.

For the occasional one-day or two-day absences firms are willing to write a policy which is fair to all. Many companies simply pay up to a certain number of days, say 10, for each employment or calendar year. Other firms allow so many paid days for each separate illness. Once the allowance is used up, the employee is no longer paid, unless he is covered by some other program.

Abuses of a Privilege

It is not uncommon for companies to have a waiting period, especially during a worker's early years of employment. This might be a waiting period of two days during the first year, one day during the second year, and no waiting period thereafter. The reasoning (which many managers feel is fallacious) is that a longer service employee can more likely be trusted not to abuse the sick pay privilege.

And abuses there are. For an absence of several days an employer could rightfully ask an employee to bring in some report from the doctor who attended him. But most employees do not see a doctor when they are unable to come to work for a day or two because of a cold, fever, upset stomach, headache, and the like. They merely call in sick and return a day or two later, mentioning the reason for the absence. Even with a clinic checking them back in, some of their stories can easily be doubted.

The best control is to check the pattern of absences. An employee who is absent six times a year, all on Mondays or Fridays, might well be suspected of taking long weekends. Supervisors who know their people can usually spot the phony stories and may want to remember these absences when an employee comes up afterward for salary review or other consideration.

The theory of sick pay protection is like insurance—it is intended for the employee who has need of it. This is an assurance that his wages will not suffer if, through no fault of his own, his work is interrupted. This is not a right. Some employees feel that if they do not use their sick leave they should be paid extra for this.

Since the ill employee (and especially the one who stays away for personal reasons but calls in sick) gets paid, the loyal and dedicated worker who never or seldom lets his employer down may feel, with some justification, that the policy of sick pay favors the less-than-honest worker. Therefore some companies do pay for unused sick time but as a principle, good personnel administration must frown upon this attitude.

The amount of sick pay is usually related to seniority. A typical program might provide 10 days per year and then increase this to 15 days after 5 or 10 years. Some plans which do not "pay off" at the end of the year allow unused sick days to accrue and be used later in case of a long term or catastrophic illness absence.

TYPICAL COMPANY SICK-PAY POLICY

The company shall provide regular payment to employees during absences due to illness or nonoccupational accidents in accordance with the following schedule:

Qualifying Period	Sick-Pay Allowance		Waiting Time (each illness)	
	Wage-Hour	Exempt	Wage-Hour	Exempt
First 3 months of employment	none			
Next 9 months	7 work days		3 full days	
First 12 months of employment		10 work days		none
Second year of employment	10 work days	10 work days	2 full days	none
Third, fourth, and fifth years of employment	10 work days each year	10 work days each year	none	none
After five years of employment	15 work days each year	15 work days each year	none	none

After six months of employment, an employee on a wage-and-hour job shall not be charged with the three or two days' waiting time for any absence of 10 or more work days . . . providing the employee presents a doctor's statement upon return to work and the clinic concurs.

An employee who, on recommendation of the clinic, is excused from work, shall be paid in full for the day . . . and this absence shall not be charged against sick-pay allowance.

An exempt employee, who is absent because of illness, will in accordance with federal law be paid for a full week, even after sick allowance has expired, for any week in which he is eligible to be paid for time worked and/or paid under some provision of company policy.

An employee who has been absent because of illness or accident will not be considered "back on the job" until the clinic has given written approval to return. It is necessary to furnish a certificate from the attending physician, which must be presented to our clinic for concurrence. Such certificates may be waived in short stays upon the recommendation of the clinic.

Unused sick-pay allowance may not be accumulated from one year to another.

SALARY CONTINUATION

In addition to sick-pay allowances, to cover the occasional short-term-illness absence, many companies also have a policy to cover long-term illness by continuing salary, on a full or partial pay basis, for a specified period of time.

Where no formal policy spells out the terms, it is not unusual that an employee, particularly a salaried worker, be kept on the payroll under some informal or undeclared arrangement. This is especially true for executives and managers, or for long-service employees.

A typical formal program might be—

Term of Employment	Full Pay	Half Pay
6 months to 1 year	none	6 weeks
1 to 5 years	none	9 weeks
2 to 5 years	4 weeks	9 weeks
5 to 10 years	13 weeks	13 weeks
10 to 15 years	13 weeks	39 weeks
15 to 20 years	26 weeks	26 weeks
20 to 25 years	39 weeks	13 weeks
25 years or more	52 weeks	none

Any such special consideration would begin after sick-pay allowances are gone. If, for example, an employee is entitled to 10 paid sick days per year and had seven left, the special program would be applied starting from the eighth day. Some companies permit unused sick leave from one year to be accumulated and applied later. Under such plan an employee with 20 or 30 unused sick days to his credit would, of course, be paid in full until all this accrued sick time had been used.

As an alternative, companies may purchase health and accident insurance which would pay an employee benefits for a certain number of weeks while he is absent from work because of illness or nonoccupational accident.

HEALTH AND ACCIDENT INSURANCE

Employees wonder what would happen to their paychecks if they were injured at home or at work and unable to perform their jobs. Or what if they were to become suddenly ill and in bed or confined to the house for days or weeks at a time?

Most companies have a sick-pay allowance program which is intended to cover short-term illness. Generally companies allow a specified number of "sick days" per calendar or employment year. But what protection is there for the long-term illness? The rent and other expenses continue even after the paycheck stops.

One way to meet this problem is to purchase health and accident insurance for the employees. All employees are automatically covered in a group policy after a short waiting period—30 days to six months, depending upon the policy purchased. Benefit payments begin from the first day of an accident and usually a little after the first day of an illness. The terms, of course, depend upon the contract with the insurance carrier.

The amount of the benefit is related to salary. It is less than full salary, otherwise it would wipe out any incentive to return to work. A typical benefit schedule might be the following:

Annual Salary	Weekly Benefits
Under $3,000	$ 30
$3,000 to $3,999	40
$4,000 to $4,999	50
$5,000 to $5,999	60
$6,000 to $6,999	70
$7,000 to $7,999	80
$8,000 and over	100

There could be administrative problems relating to "overlap." An employee with 10 or 15 days of sick-pay allowance could still have sick days left when H & A insurance benefit payments begin. The sick pay is full salary; the H & A weekly benefit is less. Which should he get? If the company continues full salary should the insurance company be excused from paying until sick days run out? Or should the insurance company pay according to the contract (and premium charged) and these payments be signed over to the company? Will the employee understand? Or should he be allowed to get both—which means, in effect, he profits financially from being sick.

An H & A policy usually pays benefits for 13, 26, or 52 weeks, again depending on which policy is purchased. This coverage should be adequate for practically all long illness or accident absences. Any case extending beyond these limits would be handled under a disability insurance program, if available, or may get other special consideration.

Any health and accident or disability insurance program should not be confused with workmen's compensation, which covers on-the-job accidents.

GROUP H & A INSURANCE PLAN

This plan, in which participation is entirely voluntary and optional, provides through insurance underwritten by The Travelers Insurance Company, weekly payments for employees of Hercules Incorporated, Wilmington, Delaware, who become disabled due to a nonoccupational accident or sickness.

ELIGIBILITY

All regular employees at Hercules locations where this plan is available are eligible to participate upon the completion of six (6) months of service.

ENROLLMENT

Each eligible employee who desires this insurance should complete his enrollment card and return it to his supervisor before the end of the six (6) months' qualifying period if he wishes to be insured as soon as he is eligible.

If an eligible employee does not apply for this insurance within one month after he completes six (6) months of service, evidence of insurability satisfactory to The Travelers Insurance Company will be required before his application for insurance will be approved.

Each regular employee who has completed six (6) months of service and is transferred from a location where this insurance is not available to one where it is, may enroll within one month after his transfer without supplying evidence of insurability, provided he has not previously waived or canceled membership. If he has previously waived or canceled his membership or does not apply within one month of his eligibility date, evidence of insurability satisfactory to The Travelers Insurance Company will be required before his application for insurance will be approved.

The insurance of any employee who is absent from work shall not become effective until the date on which he actually returns to work.

PLAN PROVISIONS

WAITING PERIOD

Benefits begin after a waiting period of seven (7) consecutive days of total disability.

WEEKLY BENEFIT AMOUNT

The weekly benefit payable to an employee beginning the eighth consecutive day of his disability is $25.

DURATION OF BENEFITS

Benefits are paid beginning the eighth consecutive day for the duration of disability but not longer than thirteen (13) weeks for each disability except that:

1. Benefits for a disability resulting from nonoccupational accident or sickness which occurred after an employee becomes sixty (60) years of age will be limited to a maximum of thirteen (13) weeks during any twelve (12) consecutive month period.

2. Benefits for disability caused by pregnancy will be limited to a total of six (6) weeks for any one pregnancy.

SUCCESSIVE PERIODS OF DISABILITY

Successive periods of disability separated by less than one week of active work shall be considered one period of disability unless the subsequent disability is due to an injury or sickness entirely unrelated to the cause of the previous disability and commences after return to active work.

EXCLUDED DISABILITIES

Benefits will not be paid for any disability:

1. For which an employee is not treated by a duly qualified physician.

2. Resulting from an injury or sickness sustained while doing any act or thing pertaining to any occupation or employment for remuneration or profit, or for which benefits are payable in accordance with the provisions of any workmen's compensation or similar law.

NOTICE OF DISABILITY

Each insured employee, or someone in his behalf, must promptly report his disability to the designated Hercules representative at the location where he works so that the necessary claim forms may be issued. The prompt submission of claim forms completed by the insured employee and his attending physician should assure the timely resolution of the claim.

PAYMENT OF CLAIMS

Upon receipt of due proof of loss, benefits are payable weekly.

EMPLOYEE CONTRIBUTION

The present cost to an employee is $1.35 per month which will be deducted by the company from the employee's wages or salary.

TERMINATION OF INSURANCE

The insurance terminates when an employee (a) is pensioned or retired, (b) becomes seventy (70) years of age, (c) leaves the service of the company, (d) ceases to pay the required amount toward the premium for this insurance, or (e) is transferred to a Hercules plant or sales office at which this insurance is not available.

LEAVE OF ABSENCE

The insurance shall not remain in force for more than thirty-one (31) days after the last day an employee works if: (a) he is laid off, (b) he ceases to have earnings, or (c) he is granted a leave of absence other than for disability.

Insured employees absent from active work because of disability may continue their insurance throughout disability periods by continuing regular contributions.

REINSTATEMENT OF INSURANCE

1. The insurance of an employee who is absent from active work for reasons other than disability shall be automatically reinstated on the basis of his service at the time he returns to work, without evidence of insurability, provided he has not canceled such insurance.

2. The insurance of an employee who is absent from active work because of disability will lapse if he does not continue his contributions. In case of such termination of insurance, the employee, upon return to work and upon application for insurance, may become insured provided he supplies evidence of insurability satisfactory to the insurance company.

3. An employee who returns to work without the restoration of prior credited continuous service, may apply for insurance as a new employee upon completion of six (6) months of credited continuous service.

MODIFICATION AND TERMINATION

Hercules reserves the right to change, modify, or discontinue all or any part of the plan on any renewal date of the group policy issued to it.

PERSONAL ACCIDENT INSURANCE

The personal accident insurance plan of the Boy Scouts of America offers employees coverage for accidental death, dismemberment, or total and permanent disability resulting from any accident anytime. Coverage is available to employees, spouses, and dependent children.

1. Eligibility. Professional employees are eligible to enroll as soon as they are employed; nonprofessional employees wait 90 days before becoming eligible.

2. Amount of coverage. Professional employees may enroll for $50,000, $75,000, $100,000 or more; nonprofessional employees for $10,000, $15,000, $20,000, or $25,000. Spouses are eligible for one-half the amount of insurance which the employees carry, and dependent children under age 23 are eligible for $5,000 coverage. Retired professionals can continue 25 percent of the personal coverage carried immediately prior to retirement.

3. The cost is paid by the employee, or the employer, or shared by both as determined locally. Premiums are payable quarterly and depend upon the rate in effect at the time.

4. Benefits. The full principal sum is paid to the designated beneficiary in case of accidental death or to the insured in case of loss of two hands, feet, or eyes; one-half the principal sum is payable to the insured in case of loss of one hand, foot, or eye.

An insured person, under age 60, who becomes totally and permanently disabled as the result of an accident, will begin receiving 1/200th of his principal sum per month, beginning one year after he becomes totally and permanently disabled. Should the insured die before the total principal sum has been paid to him, the commuted value of the remaining payments will be paid to the beneficiary.

HOSPITALIZATION INSURANCE

Hospitalization insurance is protection in the form of financial assistance limited to a specified number of days and certain definite contract provisions. It pays for (or toward) the cost of room and board in recognized hospitals plus related miscellaneous services performed there by the hospital staff. The coverage ordinarily does not include the services of doctors and special nurses.

Most frequently these miscellaneous or necessary charges cover drugs, use of operating rooms, preparation for surgery, and similar expenses. The following explanation is representative of the term "other hospital charges"—"Whenever the term charges for 'other hospital services and supplies' is used, it means the actual charges made by the hospital, on its own behalf, for services and supplies rendered to the individual, and required for treatment of such person, other than charges for room and board, the professional services of any physician, and any private-duty or special-nursing services (including intensive nursing care by whatever name called), regardless of whether such services are rendered under the direction of the hospital or otherwise."

Value Rises With Costs

It is a well-known fact that the cost of hospital services has increased steadily over the years, and seems to be continually increasing. This means that the cost of hospitalization insurance has a corresponding increase. It also means that people today cannot afford to be without such form of group or individual protection.

The cost in a group plan may be borne entirely by the individual employee, or paid for by the company, or a combination of the two. The trend in both union and nonunion firms is to move toward increasing the employer's share. Some companies even pay the full amount, not only for the employee but also for his family.

Most plans, regardless how they are financed, cover the employee after a brief (one or two months) waiting period, which is nothing more than administrative convenience. For a higher premium rate the employee may also include the spouse plus dependent unmarried children under a certain age, say 19. The worker's share of the cost is usually handled through monthly payroll deduction.

Nonprofit vs. Commercial Plans

The main difference between the voluntary nonprofit plans, such as Blue Cross, and the programs of the commercial insurance carriers is that the former, as a rule, pay "service in full" benefits while the insurance companies allow fixed benefits—so much per day plus so much for extras. Example: the nonprofit plan may pay the entire cost of a semiprivate two-bed room (or the common semiprivate rate toward a private room), whereas the insurance company often pays dollars-per-day toward the cost of the room. The same is true of hospital services. The former may pay in full for all ancillary services that are required, whereas the latter may have a lump sum allowance to be applied toward these extra services.

Not only are hospital costs increasing, as medical science advances and new techniques are introduced, but the average working man or woman is also becoming more sophisticated in the use of hospital care. Now that insurance coverage is so readily provided, and much of the financial sting removed, it is human nature for people to want to take advantage of the benefits for which they have been paying. Consequently, utilization is also increasing. More people are willing to go into the hospital where personal care is available, especially when this costs them very little in the way of out-of-pocket expense. Controls are being applied in hospitals and by the medical staffs, and educational programs are, or should be, initiated by companies to avoid abuses.

One recent development in the control of costs is the "coordination of benefits" provision which keeps two insurance companies from paying for the same basic benefits. The prime carrier, i.e., the one covering the employee, will not pay for his spouse who is covered under another program, except that it will make differential payment if it is better and pays greater benefits or covers more services.

Hospitalization coverage is so widespread today that practically every permanent employee who wants to be covered can arrange for hospitalization benefits under one type or another. Exceptions would be the people in business for themselves, seasonal or temporary employees, the over 65 who have Medicare, some union workers who have access to union welfare clinics, and employees in companies which prefer informal self-insurance.

MEDICAL-SURGICAL INSURANCE

The medical-surgical insurance plans available for groups of workers cover the doctor bills that come with a stay in a bona fide hospital. Some plans cover medical care and surgery no matter where performed within the limits of the schedule of fees attached to the plan.

Companies which provide hospitalization insurance for employees usually have a companion medical-surgical program also. These two coverages are generally administered together, with the same waiting period, dependency coverage, cost-sharing, and payroll deduction applicable to both. A waiting period might be required for certain coverages, as for example, maternity.

Some plans, such as Blue Shield in certain areas, pay "service" benefits, which means the total charge for participating physicians. The charge is based on the employee's income level. Most plans, and this includes practically all those offered by the commercial insurance companies, are indemnity programs which pay flat acounts according to an established fee schedule.

What started out as surgical insurance has gradually been expanded to embrace medical coverage also. These medical services usually mean payments to the insured for doctors' services, in and/or out of the hospital.

Some of the more liberal plans lately have provided benefits for diagnostic services, dental care, office and home calls, home health care, visiting nurses, and nursing homes. There apparently is no limit. Insurance companies are prepared and willing to write almost any kind of contract that employers and employees consider necessary and can pay for.

BLUE CROSS and BLUE SHIELD

Blue Cross and Blue Shield are the pioneer prepaid health care organizations in this country and every year provide protection to increasing millions of Americans. The names are household words. Blue Cross and Blue Shield stand today, as they always have, for

the nonprofit community-oriented voluntary health care prepayment plans and the services they offer in the health care field. Their benefit programs range from local to national in scope.

There are 75 Blue Cross Plans in continental United States and one in Puerto Rico. There are four Blue Cross Plans in Canada. In the United States, enrollment exceeded 65.7 million in 1968 and public service programs, including Medicare, extended Blue Cross functions to an additional 18.2 million people, bringing the total served by the Blue Cross system to more than 83.9 million people, over 42 percent of the population. In the United States, Blue Cross pays out more than half of all the benefits paid for hospital care. Canadian enrollment is nearly five million persons.

There were, in 1969, 72 Blue Shield Plans in the United States, nine in Canada, one in Puerto Rico. These Plans provided medical-surgical coverage to almost 64 million persons under regular underwritten contracts. The United States Plans serve an additional 13.6 million persons under various government programs, the main one being the supplementary medical insurance portion of the Medicare law—Part B. With underwritten and government programs, Blue Shield Plans serve over 77 million persons.

The work of the Plans is coordinated through national association offices located in Chicago, Illinois—the Blue Cross Association and the National Association of Blue Shield Plans. Among other things, these national associations assist member Plans in maintaining quality operations in order to meet approval standards that relate to high benefit performance and associated levels of responsibility.

Plans qualify under state nonprofit or not-for-profit enabling legislation. They must have sponsorship of the local hospital association in the case of Blue Cross and local medical association in the case of Blue Shield. The Plans are governed by Boards of Trustees elected from the community served by the Plan.

Blue Cross and Blue Shield Plans specialize in health care benefits and are the most experienced in the field. They write basic hospital, surgical and medical benefits, extended benefits, and major medical programs. Included in the extended or major medical categories are such benefits as skilled nursing home care, outpatient psychiatric care, home care, prescription drugs, intensive medical care, medical consultations, outpatient x-ray and laboratory services, and home and office calls.

The basic benefits—hospital, surgical and medical—generally are covered on the "service basis" meaning that payments for health services such as care received in a hospital or surgery are fully covered. Many Blue Shield Plans apply income limits to their service programs with a schedule of indemnities applying to over-income subscribers. The Plans also offer indemnity programs and many of them have developed reasonable, customary, and prevailing fee programs for doctors' services to subscribers of all incomes.

Individuals and Groups

All Plans enroll both individuals and groups. All subscribers receive identification cards. Because of the agreements made directly with the providers of care, Blue Cross subscribers may enter any of the 7,000 participating hospitals in the United States without advance deposit for covered benefits, and the billing will be sent directly to the Blue Cross Plan, thus eliminating the necessity of the patient paying his bill and recovering his benefits. Blue Shield offers similar arrangements through their participating doctors. These direct billing arrangements overcome the red tape of handling claims forms by the subscriber or his group.

Subscribers have free choice of doctor or hospital, with special nonparticipating benefits applying when the provider of service is not participating. Blue Cross patients entering hospitals outside their Plan area have their cases processed via direct wire to their "home" Plan through the Blue Cross Association wire system.

Small Groups to Interstate Plans

Blue Cross and Blue Shield cover groups of almost every description, ranging from groups of five to the Federal Employee group of four million members. Seven of the 10 largest corporations in the United States have Blue Cross and Blue Shield for their employees. Upon termination from any group, persons are offered individual coverage which they may continue on their own.

Blue Cross and Blue Shield write both local and national benefit programs. Interstate groups may secure uniform programs in all of the states, such as the aforementioned Federal Employee Program, or the local program of each of the Plans but with consolidated billing. The Plans offer both community rating and, to the larger groups, various forms of experience rating or merit rating, but with consolidated or separate billing.

On the average, including group and individual business, Blue Cross Plans in the United States are currently paying out 96 cents of the income dollar for benefits, and Blue Shield pays approximately 91 cents. Individual Plans, however, may reflect slight operating differentials in their own communities under the influence of varying patterns of hospital and medical practice.

Blue Cross and Blue Shield feature utilization and cost controls "at the source." By working directly with doctors and hospitals through utilization committees and agreements, controls are applied with minimal burden on the patient. The Plans undertake extensive audit systems to assure subscribers that benefits paid in their behalf are based on proper costs.

The Blue Cross system has been designated as intermediary to handle approximately 90 percent of Part A benefits of Medicare. Blue Shield Plans have been designated for approximately 68 percent of the Part B cases.

The National headquarters for Blue Cross and Blue Shield are:

Blue Cross Association
840 North Lake Shore Drive
Chicago, Illinois 60611

National Association of Blue Shield Plans
211 East Chicago Avenue
Chicago, Illinois 60611

For any employer interested in forming a Blue Cross and Blue Shield group, a good place to start would be to call or write the local Blue Cross and Blue Shield Plan in the area.

MAJOR MEDICAL INSURANCE

Major medical insurance pays the big medical bills. It pays where other programs leave off. In addition, it covers services which are not included in the basic programs.

The usual major medical plan has a ceiling, say $10,000 per person for a lifetime. Within this limit, it will pay toward the excess portion of hospital, surgical, and medical expenses which are not paid in full by the basic coverage. If, for example, a surgeon charges $350 for an operation, against which the surgical insurance pays $250, a claim for the difference of $100 may be filed with the major medical program. Or if a hospitalization plan pays 30, 60, or 120 days, the major medical plan will pick up any excess days of the long stay case.

But there are other services which may be collectible only from the major medical plan. These include nursing services, prescription drugs, laboratory fees, home and office calls, and the like.

The design of a major medical plan usually calls for a deductible and a co-insurance feature. A typical plan will not pay for the first $100, and then pay 80 percent of all eligible costs above this first $100. The theory is that the insured should share a reasonable amount of his medical bills but that the insurance will protect him against any medical catastrophy.

People who have been through the tragedy of a complicated illness or accident, or a dread disease, appreciate and approve the security provided by major medical coverage. As an employee fringe benefit, it is gaining in popularity.

GROUP INSURANCE TRENDS

A Dartnell Management Research Survey reporting on "How 325 Companies Control Their Group-Insurance and Pension Costs" reveals definite and significant trends. If one word could be used to summarize current trends in this complex area of employee group-insurance plans, it would be "More!"

What is happening now, and what is indicated for the future, for *employers* is:

1. Higher costs.
2. More record-keeping.
3. More work to stay well informed and in control of how much more of everything is involved.

As a result of these factors, *employees* will gain:

1. More personal coverage in terms of dollar benefits.
2. More coverage for dependents and widows.
3. More mobility (under certain job conditions).
4. More of a certain kind of "protection" through government regulation or participation in more phases of various plans.

Employees must also anticipate certain negative possibilities, such as:

1. More dollar contributions to be required of them in company, union-sponsored, or "association" plans.
2. Inevitable increases in taxes because of increased government activity in this area.
3. Erosion of purchasing power because of added inflationary pressures.
4. Some loss of freedom and related intangibles in return for probable increases in material comforts and improved services to be gained by accelerated institutionalism (private and governmental) of medical care, nursing homes, mental-health facilities, large-scale retirement housing centers, and other geriatric projects.

As everybody moves in these directions together, employers who adapt themselves to the best possible combination of "give and take" may expect to improve and reinforce their practical framework of good industrial relations policies and practices.

The Dartnell survey detected three new types of group insurance coverage entering the picture. These are dental services, eye care, and psychiatric care.

Dental services and eye care plans are still few and far between. There are some indications of their increasing use by large employers.

Most regular group insurance plans do not cover eyeglasses, examinations, and prescriptions. Nor do they include any kind of dental work except limited oral surgery.

Dental plans are gaining momentum but must be carefully written because most everyone could use some dental service. Eye care also could be prohibitive in cost because studies conducted by various government and industrial groups show that half of the employees in office and factory work have visual deficiencies needing attention.

Managements, however, are becoming interested in eye care and dental service programs for their employees.

Poor or bad eyesight has been known to cause abnormal fatigue, headache, vague feelings of illness, increasing errors and lowered efficiency. Indirectly it also has some effect on absenteeism and turnover.

Students of the problem remind us that for thousands of years man used his eyes as nature intended—for distance seeing, out-of-doors. Then, as he became an indoor creature and began using his eyes for prolonged close work, the change in his seeing habits put a heavy burden upon his eyes.

Until the development of artificial lighting, practically everybody worked only during daylight hours and slept during the darkness. Today most men and women live and work indoors much of the time, with their eyes performing difficult tasks far different from the simpler ones before. Reading, writing, drawing, sewing, and operating intricate machinery are only a few of the eye-fatiguing jobs now being performed.

Gone are the days when applicants were required to have 20/20 vision. Job applicants with substandard vision are hired today because they possess skills or other qualifications needed by the company.

Needed dental repair work is neglected by many workers simply because they have to bear the full cost themselves, without aid of an insurance plan. Yet poor teeth, like poor eyesight, can affect an employee's work.

To compensate for poor teeth, a man may change his diet and avoid foods which he cannot handle or which give him trouble. An improper diet can have an adverse effect upon a man's work efficiency.

A sore tooth, a toothache, or an abscess is no different from other health problems which cause unnecessary absenteeism and a lot of other problems. Repair, work, extractions, fittings, and treatment of gums should be taken care of promptly if a worker wants to perform at top efficiency.

While dental services and eye care plans are still relatively unknown, the story is quite different for psychiatric care.

Over half of the companies with group benefit programs have some sort of coverage for conditions related to nervous or mental health.

Perhaps the high incidence of peptic ulcers, which have been called "the leading psychosomatic illness of our culture," and the persistent pressure of alcoholism have something to do with this. Both conditions, although carefully screened on employment, seem to develop in individuals at a significant rate.

It serves no purpose to rationalize by claiming (1) the conditions are caused by modern life, or (2) work pressures cause them. The fact remains they are here, they seem to strike indiscriminately, and something must be done about them.

Treatment is usually so costly that it is beyond the reach of the average hourly paid or salaried employee. The costs include hospitalization, outpatient treatments, psychological testing, counseling, social worker visits to the family, and fees for specialists. If the average employee is not covered by some type of insurance, he is apt to end up at a county or state institution.

The trends toward new programs will be worth watching. As the well-trained, competent employee becomes more and more valuable to his employer, it seems to be good sense to take constructive steps to keep him in good health, aid him in poor health, and thus keep him on the job—in production—as much as possible.

WORKMEN'S COMPENSATION

States have workmen's compensation laws whose purpose is to promote the general welfare of the people by providing compensation for accidental injuries or death suffered in the course of employment.

These laws are designed to provide protection to workers suffering occupational disabilities through accidents arising out of and in the course of employment, and occupational diseases for illnesses resulting from exposure to hazards peculiar to particular employment.

The acts in most states are now a half century old. Prior to the enactment of workmen's compensation laws, injured workers could sue under "common law" but it was necessary for them to prove negligence on the part of the employer. Today, the concepts of blame and negligence have been eliminated and compensation is paid regardless of fault.

The amount of compensation differs in the states, but this is clearly spelled out in each law. Benefits cover payments for medical expenses, time loss, disfigurement or dismemberment, and death.

Generally, lump sum payments are made in case of death, the amount varying by number and type of dependent survivors. Burial expense allowance may be added.

In nonfatal cases the compensation usually includes a fixed schedule of reimbursement for medical services and specified weekly payments during the period of incapacity. The amount again is related to the number of departments.

In cases of long-term permanent disability, settlements are often worked out.

Schedules of benefits are established by law. Circumstances concerning accidents and extent of disability are often disputed.

Employers may elect to self-insure or may prefer to transfer their entire liability to pay such compensation to an authorized insurance company.

UNEMPLOYMENT COMPENSATION

Unemployment compensation is a part of the social security philosophy. It had its origin in countries other than the United States.

Germany set up social security programs to cover old age and sickness in the 1880's, but unemployment insurance was not introduced until 1927. In 1961, social security programs covering work injuries existed in 77 countries, and 59 included old age and sickness. Twenty-six programs provided unemployment coverage, but only 20 pay such benefits without a means test. Russia "suspended" its unemployment insurance in 1930 and eliminated the program in East Germany after World War II.

In 1935, when Congress passed Social Security legislation, it required each state to establish basic unemployment compensation laws. These benefits were designed as a cushion against a cessation of spending when factories cut back work forces. On the whole, the net effect of labor and security laws has been beneficial to the national welfare.

To qualify for compensation, the unemployed had to be "ready, willing, and able to work." Benefits were intended for legitimate wage earners who had lost jobs through no fault of theirs, to tide them over until they could find work.

The unemployment insurance laws provided for Federal tax on employers of 3 percent of wages up to $3,000 paid to a worker in a calendar year. For 1962, the tax was increased to 3.5 percent to finance the Federal Extended Benefits program. For 1964 and after, the tax will revert to 3.1 percent. Timely payment of the state unemployment compensation tax permits employers to deduct 2.7 percent from the Federal tax rate.

This Federal revenue goes to the United States Bureau of Employment Security (BES) in the Department of Labor. BES gives the states money for their unemployment insurance administrative costs and keeps an average of $6 million for its own expenses. The 2 million covered employees are taxed by the states according to the size of their payrolls.

Each state was made responsible for its own program and to meet its cost. The states could set any level of benefits, but could vary the tax, after the first three years, only according to the experience of each employer—the experience rating system.

Largely Successful

Since 1938, when the first benefits were paid, all the state unemployment funds have remained solvent, except Alaska. Though Federal assistance was proposed during emergencies caused by war or recession in 1942, 1944, 1945, 1952, and 1958, the states got along without it.

The average state in normal times pays unemployment benefits equal to at least half of its total state payroll. In 1958, Michigan and Pennsylvania unemployment benefits were larger than their state payrolls. However, such payments usually average less than 10 percent of a state's total budget.

Seven major industrial states have half of all covered workers. Federal equalization grants to the hardest hit states have been proposed periodically. Opponents feel that Federal aid would bring Federal standards. They point out that some states with the highest unemployment have programs that are more liberal than average— such as California, New York, Pennsylvania, and Rhode Island.

The trend has been to liberalize unemployment benefits. Claimants now receive payments sooner and for a longer time. The real protection to the unemployed has increased 100 percent in general, 200 percent in California, and 400 percent in New York.

As a rule, covered workers without dependents receive enough money to pay for food, shelter, clothing, and medical care. Eleven states give larger benefits to those with dependents; Illinois, Iowa, and Michigan use sliding scales.

Benefit Eligibility

How much can an ex-employee collect? The amount and the conditions vary by state. In Illinois, for example, here are the conditions:

An individual is entitled to unemployment compensation for each week if:

1. He is unemployed. (A person is unemployed if in a calendar week, Sunday through Saturday, he performs no services and receives no wages, or if he works less than full time because of lack of work and earns less than his weekly benefit amount, or, if he has seven consecutive days of total unemployment overlapping two calendar weeks during each of which he is ineligible for benefits on a calendar week basis because of earnings.)

2. He registers for work at a state employment office and files a claim for unemployment compensation.

3. He is able to work.

4. He is available for work.

5. He is actively seeking work.

6. He is not subject to a disqualification for any of the following reasons:
   a. Voluntarily leaving work without good cause.
   b. Discharge for misconduct connected with his work.
   c. Refusal to accept or apply for suitable work without good cause.

7. His unemployment was not caused by a stoppage of work due to a labor dispute in which he is involved (see labor dispute).

8. He is not collecting unemployment compensation from another state or from the United States.

9. He is not receiving workmen's compensation for temporary disability (if workmen's compensation is less than his weekly benefit amount, then his benefits are reduced by the amount of such compensation).

10. He has sufficient earnings in his base period.

11. He has not already received his maximum benefits in his current benefit year.

12. He has not received benefits for 26 weeks unless he has had intervening employment of at least three weeks (may requalify by earning three times his weekly benefit amount).

13. He never collected benefits fraudulently until he has repaid such benefits, plus a penalty of an equal amount.

14. He is not receiving a company retirement pension. The following items are deductible from the weekly unemployment compensation benefit:
   a. All of the retirement payment paid for entirely by an individual's former employer.
   b. Half of the retirement payment paid for in part by an employer.

By statute a person is considered unavailable for work if:

1. He moves to a locality with less favorable work opportunities.

2. He leaves work because of marital, filial, or other domestic circumstances until such circumstances cease to exist.

3. He leaves work to accompany or join a member of his family in another community (may requalify under certain conditions).

4. He leaves work voluntarily to marry (does not apply if he becomes sole support of family).

5. His principal occupation is that of a student in attendance at, or on vacation from, a public or private school.

6. A woman who leaves work because of pregnancy (until she is able and willing to accept work but under no circumstances for 13 weeks before and four weeks after childbirth).

Illinois employers are advised to protest a claim promptly if they have information that not all of the above requirements have been met.

Since state programs vary considerably, every employer should become knowledgeable with the provisions of the state law under which he operates, in order to familiarize himself with the tax rate, the base earnings period upon which benefits are based, the benefit schedule, the conditions of claimant eligibility, and the administrative procedures to follow.

CLAIMS PROCEDURE

The usual procedure is for an unemployed person to make application for benefits at the unemployment compensation office nearest to him. The last employer is notified. He has seven days in which to protest, by reporting on the appropriate form the circumstances surrounding the claimant's unemployment.

A deputy considers both sides of the story, that of the claimant and that of the company. On the basis of the information supplied by both he makes a determination. Both parties are notified and have seven days in which to appeal the deputy's decision. If nothing is heard, the decision becomes final.

The next step, in the event of a protest from either side, is for a referee to take over the case. Most likely, both parties will be asked to appear before him to answer his direct questions as he studies the case. The referee interprets the personal appearance of both parties as sincere interest in the case, and he is impressed when an employer takes time to personally state his arguments. This procedure seems unnecessary since the case is that of a citizen of the state vs. the state, and the employer merely supplies answers to questions but does not enter into the decision. Unfortunately, in the administration of these state laws, the employer, or his representative, run the risk of an unfavorable decision by not appearing. After several days the referee makes his decision and again both parties are notified and given seven days to appeal.

When the referee's decision is not acceptable, and either party wishes to pursue the case, the next step is for the case to be referred to a board of review. This board will, in due course, review the entire file, study the facts as they were originally presented, read the testimony given at the hearing, and then make its findings known, most likely without calling in either side for further testimony.

In all these situations, if the decision is in favor of the claimant it becomes retroactive to the date of filing. Quite often the decision does not disqualify a claimant entirely but only for a short period of time until some provision in the law is met.

The recourse both sides have beyond the claim procedure outlined above is in the courts of the land. Very few cases go this far.

KEEPING COSTS DOWN

The following suggestions may help a company reduce its unemployment insurance tax rate:

1. Keep good personnel records. It is better to rely upon facts than to trust memory.
2. Hold exit interviews and record the reason for leaving.
3. Keep improving hiring and indoctrination procedures. Try to reduce the number of misfits who have to be fired.
4. Stabilize employment. Avoid seasonal work as much as possible.
5. Check figures supplied by the state. Make certain the base earnings period is stated correctly and the amount agrees with payroll records. Make sure the tax rate is right.
6. Charge each operation with its own payments. In multiplant operations, recalculate the rate each establishment should have.
7. Get the tax man and the personnel man to cooperate. The two can make a good team.
8. Rehire ex-employees whenever possible. If the former employee's work record is clear, and suitable work is available, it is better to put him back to work than to permit him to receive compensation for not working.
9. Make direct testimony at hearings. This takes time but it is worth it, since it shows the company is sincerely interested in good administration of the law.
10. Watch legislation. Be familiar with the statute and keep an eye on developments. Support the legislators who give evidence of keeping the law within reason.

DISABILITY INSURANCE

There are two types of retirement programs. The one commonly thought of is age retirement; workers reach a designated age, say 65, and are retired from the company.

But there are other workers who are retired from the company, who leave the workforce, even before age 65. These are the people who become totally disabled and are unable to continue working.

It is fortunate for them if they have been associated with a company that provides an income when they are not working. The safest way to handle this is through disability insurance.

Disability insurance, or a disability retirement program, provides a worker with a reduced weekly or monthly income when he becomes totally and permanently disabled.

Benefits are based on salary and length of continuous service. One example might be 50 percent of the first $650 of monthly salary plus 33⅓ percent of that portion in excess of $650. Usually there is a maximum benefit, say $1,000 per month.

This amount is payable monthly for a prescribed period of time. This might be five years of benefit payments for five years of employment, increasing gradually to 15 years of benefit payments for 10 years of employment, with benefits payable for life for all employees with more than 10 years of service.

If the disabled employee is also eligible, or later becomes eligible, for payments under the Federal Social Security system, the amount of these payments will be deducted from the benefits paid by the disability insurance.

Usually there is a considerable waiting period before an employee is covered. This insurance is intended to benefit the longtime faithful employee who would have built his career with the company were he not incapacitated.

Other exclusions might be service in the armed forces, intentionally self-inflicted injury, chronic alcoholism, wrongful use of narcotics, or participation in a felonious or criminal act.

Payments do not begin immediately, but usually start six months after the disability has existed. A medical committee will rule on each case to determine whether the employee is entitled to receive benefits. Further, the disabled employee will likely be asked to submit to medical examination or to furnish continued proof of his disability periodically.

An employee could be declared disabled when he is forever prevented from engaging in any occupation comparable to that which he had held.

GROUP AUTOMOBILE INSURANCE

There's a new wrinkle in automobile insurance. Casualty insurance companies have introduced automobile insurance on a group basis, much the same as hospitalization coverage has been offered over the years.

The procedure calls for an agent or broker to approach a company with the idea of selling individual insurance policies to interested employees and collecting the premiums through regular payroll deduction. They claim the rates are lower if the insurance is handled this way.

Unlike other group insurance, there is no percentage of employees who must participate. The insurance company takes whatever business it can get. Nor are there any uniform rate benefits for all. Instead there is individual underwriting and separate insurance policies. Claims are handled individually. Changes and cancellations are between the insured employee and the insurance carrier; the employer is not involved, nor has he any voice in the dealings between the two parties.

To begin a program of group automobile insurance in a company, a letter announcing the availability of this insurance is sent to all employees. For those who are interested, individual interviews are arranged with the insurance company salesmen. Any employee who buys the insurance signs a payroll card authorizing the regular deductions to be made by the employer to cover his premiums.

Then as an ongoing activity, an insurance company salesman visits the employer's office periodically to talk with new employees, to answer questions, to change the coverage, and to discuss problems.

The selling point is that this is an employee benefit with the company's involvement kept at a minimum. This is fine as long as everybody is satisfied. But it is doubtful that an employer can stand by idly if one of his employees becomes unhappy with the rate, the service, or the treatment. In such a case, the employee is likely to blame his company for letting this happen to him.

GROUP LIFE INSURANCE

One of the big items in the employee benefit package is group life insurance. In most companies this low-cost protection is a combination employee-employer purchase.

The company often provides some basic life insurance. This may be only a nominal amount, say $1,000, equivalent to burial insurance. This coverage is geared to time; it is given after a period of service, say six months or a year.

In addition, the employee may purchase additional insurance at group rates. There is one rate for everyone in the employee group, regardless of age. The amount available is geared to annual salary. As salary increases the employee becomes eligible for more insurance. The company pays the difference in cost; the company also keeps any rebate or credit.

The employee names his beneficiary. Claims are payable on death from any cause. This type of insurance usually includes double indemnity if death results from accidental means. Payments may also be made for accidental loss of limb or eyesight.

Group life is generally term insurance, good from month to month while the employee is on the payroll. But arrangements can be made to have some paid-up feature at time of retirement. The employee share of the cost is handled through payroll deduction. The premiums are usually paid up for life in case of total disability.

A good feature of group life insurance is that no medical examination is required if the employee enrolls when he is eligible for the initial amount or later increases. This may be all the life insurance some people can get. If an employee who originally turned down all or part of this insurance decides during a subsequent reenrollment to make application he will be called upon to produce proof of insurability. This life insurance is convertible at time of termination.

Dartnell Survey

A Dartnell management research survey, covering 308 companies (15 of them in Canada), shows that 263 firms limit life insurance to employees only, and 45 also provide coverage for dependents.

Of the 308 companies studied, 144 firms, mostly the larger ones, require or permit employees to contribute to the cost.

The minimum and maximum amounts of coverage vary considerably. The higher amounts are usually offered to management personnel, but nonexempt workers are protected by substantially more than "burial insurance."

Term insurance is the most popular, with less than 5 percent of the companies offering "paid up" or a combination of term and paid up insurance.

Waiting period is 30 days for 40 percent of the respondents, 60 days for 10 percent, 90 days for 38 percent with a few waiting six months or one year.

ACCIDENTAL DEATH and DISMEMBERMENT

Accidental death and dismemberment insurance is customarily associated with a group life insurance program.

As one company explains, "The prudent person finds that accidental death and dismemberment insurance is of prime importance in a well-rounded insurance program. It gives one's family a financial bridge over the gap that occurs when the breadwinner meets unexpected death. Or, for the tragedy of accidents resulting in loss of sight or dismemberment, it provides a sum that may be needed to train one for a new career in keeping with the handicap."

Most group life insurance plans include some type of A D & D coverage, either as part of the plan or an optional added coverage.

A D & D insurance pays extra for accidental death, usually double indemnity, or twice the amount of the schedule of ordinary life insurance carried. There is also a fixed set of benefits payable in case of accidental loss of one or both eyes or limbs.

The benefits are usually geared to the earnings of the employee. As a rule dependents of employees are not covered.

KEY-MAN INSURANCE PLANS

Key-man insurance is often called "profit protection" insurance, a term that describes its basic function. While most other insurance protects employees, this type of coverage is designed to protect the employer on the following points:

1. The cost of hiring and training a new man, usually an executive.

2. The value of sales, production, or profits which might be lost because of the "key man's" absence.

This type of insurance is highest among the smaller companies, those employing fewer than 100 people. This reflects the serious need for such protection on the part of smaller companies, where the "first team" of executives often includes executives without understudies or immediate replacements.

As would be expected, larger companies are usually in a better position to replace a key executive. They are also apparently less vulnerable to suffering a loss when one man dies or becomes disabled.

In carrying this type of coverage, the "key man" must be identified and a dollar value given to him. Just as manpower programs and replacement plans should be updated annually, so should "key man" insurance. An executive whose replacement was correctly stated at $100,000 two years ago could easily be worth $200,000 or more today.

It is also important never to cut this insurance even when the person covered is no longer indispensable. The insurance value built up over the years represents a considerable investment. It is also possible that the former "key man" may again become important to the company or one of its projects sometime in the future.

One element of this type of insurance has a vital bearing on the welfare of all employees. This is the case—usually in smaller companies—when the death of the principal owner could mean the forced sale or liquidation of the enterprise to settle the estate.

The benefits work both ways—for the employees and those sharing the estate—when insurance is set up to provide funds for one or more of the persons experienced in the business, but lacking capital, to buy the controlling interest from the heirs of the principal owner. This is often arranged with the understanding that such a purchase is for the purpose of continuing the enterprise in a form closely resembling the aims and policies of the original management.

With a combination of insurance and replacement planning, it is possible for most companies to arrive at the desirable goal of reasonable security in this area.

A TYPICAL COMPANY POLICY

To help assure the security of those you leave behind, in the event of your death, a Group Life Insurance Policy and Accidental Death and Dismemberment Policy have been taken out by the company through the XYZ Insurance Company.

The amount of your coverage, free to you and without any physical examination, depends on your length of service. This is the amount of insurance you will receive on the first of the month following:

	Life	Accidental Death and Dismemberment
1 year of service . . . a total of	$1,000	$1,000
2 years of service . . . a total of	$3,000	$3,000
3 years of service . . . a total of	$5,000	$5,000

In addition you may buy at group rates more insurance based on your salary. After you have been employed for one year and your annual salary is $4,200 or more, you may purchase additional coverage according to the following table:

Salary Bracket	Life	Accidental Death and Dismemberment	Your Cost per Month
$ 4,200 - $ 4,999	$ 4,000	$4,000	$ 2.80
5,000 - 5,999	6,000	5,000	4.10
6,000 - 6,999	8,000	5,000	5.30
7,000 - 7,999	10,000	5,000	6.50
8,000 - 8,999	12,000	5,000	7.70
9,000 - 9,999	14,000	5,000	8.90
10,000 - 11,999	16,000	5,000	10.10
12,000 - 14,999	18,000	5,000	11.30
15,000 - 17,499	20,000	5,000	12.50
17,500 - 19,999	23,000	5,000	14.30
20,000 - 24,999	28,000	5,000	17.30
25,000 - 27,499	33,000	5,000	20.30
27,500 - or more	38,000	5,000	23.30

No physical examination is required for this additional insurance. However, if you do not take advantage of the offer when it becomes available, you may not reenroll without a health statement and possibly a physical examination.

HIGHLIGHTS

Your beneficiary will receive the full amount of your life insurance in the case of your death due to any cause. There are no exceptions or exclusions.

When death results from an accident, your beneficiary will receive payment from both life insurance and accidental death and dismemberment. This is double indemnity for an accidental death.

The accidental death and dismemberment insurance also pays when a dismemberment results from a nonfatal accident judged to be involuntary. For instance: The full amount of insurance would be paid for the loss of both hands or for the loss of one hand and one foot. One half the amount of the insurance would be paid for the loss of one limb or the loss of the sight of one eye. The complete schedule is in the certificate.

Your beneficiary may be any person or persons you name. You may change your beneficiary at any time by signing the appropriate change form in the personnel office.

If your employment is terminated because of total disability before you reach the age of 60, your group life insurance will be continued without cost to you during such disability. You will, of course, be required to submit evidence of your continued disability from time to time.

Should you leave the company, your life insurance coverage remains in force for the next 31 days. During this 31-day period you have an opportunity to buy from the XYZ Insurance Company an individual policy at the prevailing rates without a physical examination or health statement.

RETIREMENT INCOME and PENSION

There is to some people in management a fine line of distinction between retirement income and pension.

A retirement income is a form of monthly income after a person's working days are over. A company retires a worker in accordance with the terms of an established program. The customary age is 65, although earlier retirement, say at age 62, is becoming more attractive; in some instances retirement may be postponed beyond age 65.

Workers who have no company affiliation usually do not arbitrarily stop working at a prescribed age. Examples are farmers, shopkeepers, professional men, congressmen, judges, and other elected and appointed officials in public service.

A company asks an otherwise capable worker to vacate his job and accept, in return, a retirement income. This regular monthly income, mailed from a trust, is less than his regular salary. It is less for three reasons:

1. His living expenses are reduced in leisure years.

2. He is usually in a settled financial situation.

3. He is now subject to a third-party income (social security).

The amount of the retirement income is related to (1) earnings during all or part of his working years and (2) the length of employment. Such retirement income is guaranteed for life. Many programs offer options to cover joint pensioner (spouse) or other beneficiary.

A pension, on the other hand, is related to earnings and length of service but not to age. Usually after an employee has worked a certain number of years he is eligible to leave the job and still continue to receive part or possibly all of his salary, regardless of what his age may be at the time.

The best example is the military pension program. A man or woman may choose the armed forces for a career. After 20 years, if he leaves the service, he will receive 50 percent of his "base" pay for the remainder of his life. This amount increases by 2½ percent for every year thereafter, up to a maximum of 75 percent. A serviceman who retired after 30 years would, therefore, receive 75 percent pay for life. This pension pay schedule is uniform in all branches of service.

There are all sorts of variations, of course. The Civil Service Commission, for instance, generally follows the retirement philosophy of industry. Its mandatory retirement age is 70 for employees with at least 15 years of service. Those with less employment may be kept on until they have completed 15 years, and retired employees may be retained on a temporary renewable basis and at salaries reduced by the amount of their pensions.

There are exceptions for government employees in foreign service, law enforcement agencies, and certain hazardous jobs, who may leave at 20 years of service and after age 50 and receive an immediate annuity.

Retirement or pension programs need the approval of the Treasury Department, since their cost is chargeable as a company operating expense. It is well, therefore, to deal with an established insurance company or a reputable consultant when setting up a program. There is too much at stake, considering the amount of money and the number of people involved.

VOLUNTARY EMPLOYEE CONTRIBUTIONS

There are advantages and disadvantages to voluntary employee contributions to a pension plan, according to Arthur Stedry Hansen Consulting Actuaries.

711

Advantages: Generally an employee gains three advantages from voluntarily contributing his own savings to a pension plan:

1. Experts invest his money in a balanced fund of stocks and bonds at no cost to him.

2. The employee does not pay taxes on the earnings of the fund until he actually receives them. Thus the entire amount of dividends and interest earned by his savings are reinvested for further income, instead of being partly used to pay taxes. Consequently, savings grow faster. Eventually, when paid to him, the income must be entered on his tax return, but since that will be after retirement, he will probably pay taxes at a lower rate—or perhaps not at all. If the balance is paid as a lump sum, it may receive favorable tax treatment as a capital gain.

3. The money accumulated can be used to purchase an annuity from the pension trust fund without payment of the commission charges or other expenses incurred in buying an annuity from an insurance company.

Disadvantages: The chief disadvantage lies in the fact that the employee cannot withdraw the entire amount credited to his voluntary contribution account until his employment is terminated. In order to get the tax advantages mentioned above, the government requires the plan to provide that, prior to termination of employment, an employee may withdraw the amount he has contributed, but if he does so, the investment income and gain which has been credited to his account will be considered as forfeited. So savings are not available without penalty for routine purposes or for emergencies, as they would be in a bank account. (In order to avoid the loss which would occur upon a withdrawal, a loan provision could be added to the plan. However, if an employee borrows money from the trust fund, he must, of course, pay back his loan with interest at the going rate.)

In addition, there is always the possibility that retirement fund investments may lose value instead of gaining it. Return of the amount of money contributed is not assured, as it is when invested in United States Bonds, or in an insured savings account.

Another disadvantage, insofar as the company is considered, is that voluntary contributions would cause a considerable increase in administrative details and recordkeeping.

FOCUS ON THE RETIRED EMPLOYEE

The company press pays more attention to the retired employee now. The trend is a sound one. For many years, in too many companies, the retiree has been shunted into his industrial oblivion with only a watch to consult and a few handshakes to remember.

The mounting national concern about the aged has helped shape this newer viewpoint. However, there are other considerations; entirely apart from the fact that it is simply good, old-fashioned human decency to remember the retired employee, it is good business to do so. More and more companies are finding this out.

The retired employee is one of the best ambassadors in the community, provided he is a satisfied and not a disgruntled retiree; provided he terminated his employment with good feeling about the company and did not come away from the plant soured on it and its management. The retired employee can influence favorably local labor recruitment. The retired employee can contribute to the firmness and the soundness of the company's image within the community. As a participant in his company's retirement plan, he is a figure in a growing and important aspect of our national economy.

Surveys of employee attitude constantly expose employee ignorance of retirement benefits. It may be argued—and it generally is—that information is as close as the personnel office, that a handbook on retirement "explains everything." The fact remains that many employees, even on the brink of retirement, have hazy notions about what their retirement holds.

Into this breach the company press appears to be stepping, somewhat hesitantly to be sure, but with some good early effects. *The Score,* published by Newcomb & Sammons, consultants in the field of employer-employee communicators, find the range of coverage wide and impressive.

Enterprising communications people look upon their retiree "coverage" not simply as an opportunity to extol the virtues of long and faithful service, not only to publish the names and address of retired employees. They view coverage as a much-needed investment in corporate goodwill; they view retirement itself as something all employees might reflect upon from time to time.

PRERETIREMENT PROGRAM

This is a description of retirement preparation for employees of the City of Chicago. It was prepared by Mrs. Myrna Casebolt of the training department of the Chicago Civil Service Commission, and was issued by the Mayor's Commission for Senior Citizens.

"Retirement? Look It Over Carefully!" is a program designed to inspire planning well in advance of retirement. Speakers, films, and printed material are used to inform participants and stimulate provocative discussion on the following subjects included in the one-day conference:

Eligibility for Social Security upon retirement with a thorough explanation of how to compute and calculate benefits.

Complete explanation of pension benefits including taxation.

The pro's and con's of investments and explanation of investment "jargon" and opportunities.

The physical aspects of aging, including basic nutritional needs and an explanation of common symptoms to check regularly.

Mental health in later life, noting changes in attitudes which occur during retirement and explaining senility.

Leisure time activities turned into profit-making ventures, and free services available to retired persons.

Housing: Retirement hotels, apartment buildings, and communities; the pro's and con's of relocating.

The conference is offered on a one-time participation basis and is held weekly, accommodating 15 employees per meeting. As part of the project, a member of the training division's professional staff is always available for private meetings with a participant. These personal contacts can precede and/or follow the one-day conference and can be arranged in order to answer any questions an individual would not be willing to discuss in a group situation.

Background

There is no mandatory retirement age for City of Chicago employees with the exception of policemen and firemen. Although in the early 1960's many private employers had already engaged in serious preparation of their employees for retirement, the City of Chicago had no plan. The Mayor's Commission for Senior Citizens was the one city agency actively encouraging and sponsoring retirement programming. In 1961, the Chicago Civil Service Commission became acutely aware of the fact that the city, with its 45,000-plus employees, had made no provisions for helping to prepare its employees for retirement.

During a series of meetings in 1961, it was decided that the Civil Service Commission in general, the training division in particular, would assume responsibility for the establishment of a formal retirement preparation program.

In October of 1961 a retirement preparation program was offered to City of Chicago employees for the first time. The program was a slight modification of the "Making the Most of Maturity" series developed by the Industrial Relations Center of the University of Chicago. Each of the 11 weekly sessions was designed for city employees approximately 55 years of age and over. According to available information, Chicago's Retirement Preparation Program is believed to be one of the first programs of its kind instituted by a municipal government. This program was repeated six times with further modification to eight 90-minute sessions. From October, 1961, to September, 1963, a total of 73 people attended the programs.

Development of Current Program

The program underwent several modifications. A one-day conference was developed to overcome the objections of departmental supervisors that the 90-minute multiple-sessions plus travel time took city employees away from their responsibilities for almost a half day.

The concept of a one-day program had immediate favorable response. During a recent year, 24 one-day conferences were offered to municipal employees. A total of 285 people attended.

"Retirement? Look It Over Carefully!" is offered to all municipal employees regardless of age or level of responsibility. Participation is on a voluntary basis; however, the employees are encouraged to attend. There is no cost to the participant except for coffee and rolls which are available during the conference.

Speakers and Films

Speakers are secured, generally, by referral from the Adult Education Council of Greater Chicago. Certain research contacts, such as doctors, lawyers, stockbrokers, etc., were asked if they would talk with groups in their respective areas of expertise. Topics include social security, pension benefits, wills and estate planning, physical health, and mental health.

Two 16mm black and white sound films are used in rotation; only one is shown at each conference. "Retire to Life" and "Preparation for the Later Years," both under 30 minutes long, are borrowed from the Chicago Public Library's Visual Materials Center.

Followup

A questionnaire is sent to each participant after attendance at the conference which asks them to send the training division their comments about the value of the program. The comments have been helpful in keeping the conference geared to the employee's need for information. In response to their suggestions, plans are under consideration to hold a series of lecture-discussion seminars in order to present detailed information on several topics, including financial planning, wills and estates, and mental health.

Ninety-four percent of the participants replying reported the conferences interesting. Thirty percent of them said they had given little or no previous thought to planning for retirement. More than 70 percent said they had begun planning *after* the sessions.

Financial planning was given as the subject of greatest interest covered in the sessions; health was second, housing, third, and leisure activities, fourth.

The Mayor's Commission for Senior Citizens seeks to help start or improve preretirement programs among other employers. The address: Mayor's Commission for Senior Citizens, 185 North Wabash Avenue, Chicago, Illinois 60601.

RETIREMENT

Several companies issue "lifetime membership" identification cards to retired employees. These companies recognize that—

1. A credit card may be a rarity with some employees, and that often this company card can serve the purpose.

2. An identification card is an important symbol of employee status; it testifies to long service with a respected firm.

3. It is a link of continuing significance between the retired employee and his company.

As one example, the Sunbeam Corporation, 5400 West Roosevelt Road, Chicago, Illinois 60650, introduced what is often called a *gold retirement card*. The card bears the retiree's name and his photograph. It is handed to him in dignified ceremonies. It grants the retiree the right to visit the plant when he chooses (admission past the plant guards), to attend employee functions, and—probably as important as most—to take advantage of all employee discounts on company-manufactured products.

SOCIAL SECURITY

The Social Security Administration administers the Federal programs of retirement, survivors, and disability insurance benefits and health insurance for people 65 and over (medicare).

The basic idea of social security is simple. During working years, employees, their employers, and self-employed people pay social security contributions, which go into special funds. When earnings stop or are reduced because the worker retires, dies, or becomes disabled, monthly cash benefits are paid from the funds to replace part of the earnings the family has lost.

Part of the contributions go into a separate hospital insurance trust fund so that when workers and their dependents reach 65 they will have help in paying their hospital bills. Voluntary medical insurance, also available to people 65 and over, helps pay doctor bills and other medical expenses. This program is financed out of premiums shared half-and-half by the older people who sign up and the Federal Government. Highlights of the program follow:

MONTHLY CASH BENEFITS

Before monthly cash payments can be made to a worker and his family or survivors, he must have credit for a certain amount of work under social security. This credit may have been earned any time after 1936.

Most employees get credit for one-quarter year of work if they are paid $50 or more in covered wages in a 3-month calendar quarter. Four quarters are counted for any full year in which a person has $400 or more in self-employment income or wages from farm work.

For monthly benefits to be payable to a worker when he retires, his dependents, or survivors, he must have worked long enough under social security to be fully insured.

A worker is fully insured if he has credit for one quarter for each year after 1950 and up to the year he reaches 65 (62 if a woman) or up to the year he dies or is disabled, if earlier. In counting years after 1950, omit years before age 22.

No one needs more than 10 years of work to be fully insured and no one is fully insured with credit for less than 1½ years of work. Having a fully insured status means only that certain kinds of benefits may be payable—it does not determine the amount. The amount of monthly cash benefits that may be payable depends on a person's average earnings covered by social security.

If a worker dies before becoming fully insured, some benefits may be paid his survivors if he is currently insured. He would be currently insured if he had credit for at least 1½ years of work within the three years before his death.

RETIREMENT PAYMENTS

The amount of a worker's retirement payment is figured from his average earnings under social security. A worker can start receiving benefits as early as age 62. But, if he starts benefits before he reaches 65, the amount of his benefit will be permanently reduced. A worker's benefit is reduced by 5/9 of 1 percent for each month he received it before he reaches age 65.

If a person works after he starts getting benefits, and his added income will result in higher benefits, his benefit will be automatically refigured after the end of each year.

DISABILITY PAYMENTS

A worker who becomes disabled before 65 may be eligible for benefits. A person is considered disabled only if he has a mental or physical condition which prevents him from doing any substantial gainful work and is expected to last or has lasted for at least 12 months or is expected to result in death.

Disability payments may begin with the 7th month of disability. To get disability benefits, a person must be fully insured and have credit for five years of work in the 10 years just before he becomes disabled.

FAMILY PAYMENTS

Monthly payments can be made to certain of the worker's dependents when the worker gets retirement or disability benefits, or when the worker dies. These dependents are:

1. Unmarried children under 18, or between 18 and 22 if they are full-time students. Unmarried children 18 or over who were severely disabled before they reached 18 and continue to be disabled.

2. A wife or widow regardless of her age if she is caring for a child under 18 or disabled and the child gets payments based on the worker's record.

3. A wife 62 or older, or widow 60 or older, even if there are no children receiving payments.

4. A dependent husband or widower 62 or over.

Payments may also be made under certain conditions to a divorced wife. After a worker dies, monthly payments may be made to his dependent parents at 62.

A wife who chooses to receive benefits before she is 65 and a widow who chooses to receive benefits before she is 60 will receive permanently reduced benefits.

When a person applies for benefits, the people at the social security office will explain how any future earnings he may have will affect his benefit payments.

HEALTH INSURANCE (MEDICARE)

Nearly everyone 65 and over is eligible for the two kinds of health insurance protection often called medicare: hospital insurance and for those who choose, voluntary medical insurance.

Hospital insurance helps pay the cost of inpatient hospital care and certain kinds of posthospital care. Medical insurance helps pay the cost of physicians' services and other medical services and supplies not covered by hospital insurance.

FINANCING SOCIAL SECURITY

Federal retirement, survivors, and disability benefits, and hospital insurance are paid for by contributions based on covered earnings. Employed persons and their employers share the responsibility of paying contributions. Self-employed people pay contributions for retirement, survivors, and disability insurance at a slightly lower rate than the combined rate for an employee and his employer. The hospital insurance contribution rate is the same for the employer, employee, and self-employed person.

Contributions are deducted from an employee's wages each payday. His employer sends them, with an equal contribution as his own share, to the District Director of Internal Revenue.

A self-employed person reports his earnings and pays his contributions when he files his individual Federal income tax return each year.

A person's earnings are entered on his own record by the Social Security Administration. This record of earnings is used to determine a person's eligibility for benefits and the amount of cash benefits he will receive.

SOCIAL SECURITY CARDS

Every person must have a social security number if his work is covered by the social security law or if he receives certain kinds of taxable income. A social security card can be obtained at any social security office.

CHECKING SOCIAL SECURITY RECORDS

Each employer is required to give his workers receipts for the social security contributions he deducts from wages. He does this at the end of each year and when an employee stops working for him.

These receipts, such as Form W-2, will be useful to a person in checking his social security record.

A person should check his social security record from time to time to make sure his earnings have been reported correctly. This is especially important if a person changes job frequently. A person can ask at any social security office for a postcard form to use in requesting a copy of his record. He should complete, sign, and mail the card. Information about any person's record cannot be released without his signed request.

SOCIAL SECURITY OFFICES

There are over 700 social security offices located conveniently throughout the country. These offices have representatives who go regularly to other communities.

The people in these offices will be glad to answer questions about social security. The address of the nearest social security office can be found by looking in a telephone directory under Social Security Administration or asking at the nearest post office.

For more information about social security, ask for a free copy of Booklet No. 35, *Your Social Security.*

QUEST FOR STATEMENT OF EARNINGS

ACCOUNT NUMBER			
DATE OF BIRTH	MONTH	DAY	YEAR

se send me a statement of the amount of earnings recorded in my social security account.

MISS		Print
MRS. _____		Name
MR.		and
		Address
ET & NUMBER _____		In Ink
		Or Use
P.O.,		Type-
E & STATE _____		writer

YOUR NAME AS
USUALLY WRITE IT _____

your own name only. Under the law, information in your social security record is
idential and anyone who signs someone else's name can be prosecuted.

our name has been changed from that shown on your social security account number
, please copy your name below exactly as it appears on that card.

SOCIAL SECURITY AMENDMENTS OF 1967

Calendar Year	Maximum Taxable Base	Tax Rate (percent) Employee Share	Employer Share	Maximum Tax (dollars) Employee Share	Employer Share
1969 - 1970	$7,800	4.8	4.8	$374.40	$374.40
1971 - 1972	7,800	5.2	5.2	405.60	405.60
1973 - 1975	7,800	5.65	5.65	440.70	440.70
1976 - 1979	7,800	5.7	5.7	444.60	444.60
1980 - 1986	7,800	5.8	5.8	452.40	452.40
1987 and after	7,800	5.9	5.9	460.20	460.20

The hospital insurance tax is 1.2 percent in 1969 (divided equally between employee and
employer) and is scheduled to increase in steps to a combined 1.8 percent maximum
in 1987.

RAILROAD RETIREMENT

The Railroad Retirement Board administers the Federal social
insurance system for railroad workers and their families. Under
this system, they are protected against loss of income because of
old age, disability, unemployment, sickness, and death. The retirement and survivor programs are similar to those under the social
security system, but are generally more liberal. The unemployment

and sickness benefits can be compared with some of the more liberal state programs. Coverage is confined to employees in, or closely affiliated with, the railroad industry.

Retirement and Survivor Benefits

REGULAR RETIREMENT ANNUITIES

The minimum work requirement for regular retirement annuities is 10 years (120 months) of service. An employee receives credit for a month of service for every calendar month in which he worked for a covered employer. All railroad service after 1936 is creditable. Railroad service before 1937 and time spent in military service are creditable under certain conditions.

With 10 years of service, an employee may begin to draw a full annuity at age 65 or a reduced annuity at ages 62-64. With 30 years of service, the employee can retire at 60; however, this annuity is reduced if the employee is a male.

An employee with 10 years' service who is permanently disabled for all regular employment can receive a disability annuity at any age. If an employee is permanently disabled for work in his regular railroad job, he may start drawing a disability annuity at any age after 20 years of service or at 60 after 10 years of service. To be eligible for this occupational disability annuity, the employee must have had a prescribed pattern of recent employment in the railroad industry (called a "current connection").

If a retired railroader is at least 65, his wife may also qualify for a monthly benefit. A wife may start receiving a full annuity at 65, or earlier if she has a child under 18 or a disabled child in her care. Otherwise, she may choose to receive a reduced annuity as early as 62.

SUPPLEMENTAL RETIREMENT ANNUITIES

In addition to a regular retirement annuity, the employee may receive a supplemental annuity. To qualify, the employee must be 65 or older and have 25 years of railroad service and a "current connection." Supplemental annuities are payable only to employees who were awarded regular annuities after June 1966.

SURVIVOR INSURANCE BENEFITS

Survivors of railroad workers may receive monthly and lump-sum benefits. The eligibility of an employee's family for these benefits depends on whether the employee was "insured" at the time of his death. The insured requirements are generally the same as under social security, except that an employee must also have at least 10 years of railroad service and a "current connection." Otherwise the social security system has jurisdiction over the case.

If the employee leaves a widow, she is eligible for an annuity at age 60 if she does not remarry. The widow's annuity may begin before she is 60 if she is caring for a child who is under 18 or disabled.

Each of the employee's unmarried children under 18 can receive an annuity. An older child can also receive an annuity if he became permanently disabled before 18 or if he is a full-time student under 22.

If the employee leaves no widow or child eligible for an annuity, his dependent unremarried parents can receive annuities at 60.

An insurance lump-sum benefit is payable when a survivor annuity is not immediately payable. The payment is made to the widow if there is one; otherwise it can be used to reimburse the person who pays the employee's funeral expenses.

Residual Payments

There is one type of death benefit for which an insured status is not required. This benefit, called the residual payment, is made if the regular retirement and survivor benefits paid to the employee and his family amount to less than the total retirement taxes taken from the employee's salary, with an allowance for interest.

Amounts of Benefits

The amounts of the retirement benefits paid to an employee and his wife are generally related to the employee's railroad earnings and the length of his railroad service. Survivor insurance benefits are based on the employee's combined railroad and social security earnings. Under both the retirement and survivors programs, railroad employees and their families are guaranteed that their monthly benefits will be at least 10 percent higher than under social security.

Transfer of Credits

The railroad credits of employees who have less than 10 years of service when they retire or die are transferred by the RRB to the Social Security Administration. Railroad credits are also transferred if the employee is not insured at the time of his death. In any event, survivor insurance benefits are based on combined railroad and social security earnings and are paid by only one agency.

Filing for Benefits

The best way to apply for retirement or survivor benefits is to visit an RRB field office. When a benefit is awarded, the board will explain how working affects benefits and other conditions governing the payment of benefits.

Financing

The regular retirement and survivor programs are supported by taxes paid on employee earnings by the worker and his employer. Railroad employers deduct the employee's share of the taxes from his paychecks and match this amount on all his creditable earnings except tips.

The supplemental annuity program is financed separately by a special tax on railroad employers. Employees do not contribute to the plan.

Health Insurance Benefits

Railroad workers and family members 65 or older have the same medicare protection as workers covered by social security. The medicare hospital insurance plan pays most of the costs of hospital and related care. It is supported by payroll taxes paid by employees and their employers. The medicare supplemental medical insurance plan, which is voluntary, helps to pay doctor bills and charges for other medical expenses. Persons who enroll in the medical insurance plan pay a small monthly premium for the additional coverage. A matching contribution is made by the Federal Government.

Unemployment and Sickness Benefits

Railroad employees may receive unemployment benefits when they are out of work, provided they are able to work and available for work. They can also receive sickness benefits when they are unable to work because of sickness or injury. In addition, maternity benefits are available for women employees.

A new benefit year for unemployment and sickness benefits begins every July 1st. To be qualified in a benefit year, the employee must have earned at least $750 in railroad work in the preceding calendar year (base year), counting no more than $400 in any month. Also, if the employee had newly entered the railroad industry in the base year, he must have worked for a railroad in at least seven months of that year.

The amount an employee receives depends on how long he is unemployed or sick and on his railroad earnings in the base year. Unemployment and sickness benefits can each be paid for up to 26 weeks in a benefit year. Extended unemployment benefits are available for long-service employees who exhaust their normal benefits.

To claim unemployment benefits, a railroad worker should call in person at a railroad unemployment claims agent's office. Sickness benefits can be claimed by mail. The necessary application forms for sickness benefits can be obtained at any RRB office.

The funds to pay unemployment and sickness benefits are provided by a payroll tax paid only by railroad employers.

SERVICE AND EARNINGS RECORDS

The Railroad Retirement Board maintains records of the service and earnings of railroad employees after 1936. This information is recorded under employee social security account numbers.

Each year, the board prepares statements of service months and compensation (form BA-6) for employees working in the railroad industry. These forms are distributed through covered employers. The form gives each employee a record of his cumulative service and earnings since 1936 and of his service and earnings in the most recent calendar year.

RAILROAD RETIREMENT BOARD OFFICES

The headquarters office of the Railroad Retirement Board is in Chicago, Illinois, at 844 Rush Street 60611. There are about 100 field offices in localities easily accessible to large numbers of railroad workers. In addition, the board maintains part-time service in outlying areas. The address of the nearest Board office can be obtained at any post office.

For more detailed information on the board's programs, ask for booklet IB-2, *Benefits for Railroad Workers and Their Families.*

PROFIT SHARING

In Profit Sharing Research Foundation literature, profit sharing is defined as "any method of raising output and lowering costs through human cooperation which is brought about through the direct participation of the employees (in addition to their regular wage) in the total results of the enterprise as measured by profits."

Some people feel that a definition such as the one above tends to beg the question. That is, raising output and lowering costs is a hoped-for result of profit sharing, not really a part of its definition.

In the constitution and by-laws of the Council of Profit Sharing Industries, it is defined as "any procedure under which an employer pays or makes available to regular employees subject to reasonable eligibility rules, in addition to prevailing rates of pay, special current or deferred sums based on the profits of the business."

The essential distinguishing mark of a profit sharing plan is that company contributions to the plan fluctuate with current profit levels. Profit sharing programs are thereby differentiated from individual incentive plans, group production plans, Christmas bonuses (not tied to profits), thrift plans, pensions, and stock purchase plans.

Plans

There are two fundamental approaches to profit sharing:

1. *Current Distribution Plans,* often called *Cash Plans,* where cash is paid to an employee as soon as profits are determined—monthly, quarterly, semiannually, but most often yearly.

2. *Deferred Distribution Plans,* where the employee's share is put into a fund to be distributed to him at some later time, such as retirement, or other dates or stated circumstances, such as disability, death, severance, or under withdrawal provisions during employment.

The cash plans are not increasing in number as much as the deferred plans. The popularity of deferred plans is due partly to tax advantages. Deferred plans seem to be preferred by many medium-sized and large companies, while smaller firms frequently set up cash plans.

All profit sharing plans stem from these two basic types, but can branch into almost endless variations. For instance, plans may have combination cash and deferred elements side by side, be contributory or noncontributory on the part of employees, have broad coverage with all or almost all employees included, or have limited coverage with only specified groups participating.

Further, the percentage of profits distributed, rules of eligibility and participation, methods of payment, and other considerations differ from company to company. Plans may have many features in common and other elements that are as unlike as fingerprints. Profit sharing is an incentive system and productivity booster whose design, application, and approach vary from one company to another, according to the needs and problems of the individual firm.

OBJECTIVES

Among the objectives of profit sharing plans are inspiring a sense of partnership, incentive, security, attract and retain capable people, reward employees, economic education, and flexibility of compensation.

Many executives feel that profit sharing satisfies a deficiency in modern corporations by restoring to individual employees the traditional, vital element of personal involvement in the fortunes of the enterprise. They claim profit sharing both demonstrates and encourages partnership in industry. In that sense profit sharing is not donating a part of the profits to workers but rather sharing with them the earnings resulting from greater efficiency.

The final test of profit sharing must always be, "Can a company get greater profits by giving some profit away?"

TAX TREATMENT

There are many benefits derived from favorable tax treatment accorded deferred profit sharing plans. Once a deferred plan has been qualified by the Internal Revenue Service, company and participants enjoy these major advantages:

1. The amounts contributed by an employer are tax deductible up to 15 percent of the compensation paid to participants. What's more, the 15 percent limit has credit and contribution "carryover" features for flexibility during good and poor profit years. The fund member does not pay a tax on his share of the company's contribution when it is allocated to his account.

2. Profit sharing trust funds enjoy compound growth year after year without taxation. No taxes are paid until distributions are made.

3. Participants may enjoy lower taxes. If they receive their share in installments, it is taxed at ordinary rates, but often this is at retirement when they are in lower tax brackets. If they receive their share as a lump distribution, the long-term capital gains tax, a maximum of 25 percent, applies rather than the ordinary tax rate.

4. The amount in a participant's account contributed by the employer can pass to a named beneficiary free of estate tax.

5. There is also a $5,000 death benefit exclusion from the deceased member's estate.

ADVANTAGES

In addition to tax advantages, deferred plans have these benefits:

1. Profits go into a flexible fund capable of meeting contingencies of retirement, severance, disability or death, and even financial emergencies of employees.

2. Workers are quick to see how their accounts benefit both from earnings and appreciation on investments.

3. As the individual account grows, it builds an increasing long-term incentive on the part of the employee.

Deferred profit sharing plans, however, are not the only types that have advantages. Cash plans have these advantages:

1. Immediate incentive to better productivity and reduced costs.

2. A tangible reward on a regular basis.

3. Acceptable to all employees—money talks.

4. Female and younger members of the firm tend to prefer it.

5. Direct relationship between profits and distribution is easy for employees to see.

6. Simple to explain to everyone.

7. Easy to administer.

DISADVANTAGES

But cash plans have their weaknesses, too:

1. There are no tax advantages. The distribution is taxable as ordinary income.

2. No security funds are built up for layoff times, for retirement, separation, disability, financial emergencies, or death.

3. Cash plans fail at a greater rate than deferred.

4. Employees rarely gain company stock ownership through cash programs.

5. Employees are more apt to consider sharing as their due, with possible adverse effects during years of no or little sharing.

ADVICE

So complex is profit sharing that those who have entered into it temper their advice with almost as many "Don'ts" as "Do's." Some of their recommendations are:

1. Don't expect profit sharing to substitute for competent management; profit sharing is no panacea. It cannot produce profits, even in normal times, if management can't.

2. Don't go into profit sharing unless you are willing to accept the worker as your "partner in business"—with whom you will share appropriate responsibility and information as well as profits.

3. Don't expect profit sharing to work unless you contribute enough to motivate your employees.

4. Don't just copy another firm's plan, even in your own industry. Your objectives, your size, your potential differ from other companies.

5. Don't go into profit sharing unless you are willing to expend time and energy communicating the philosophy of profit sharing to employees, stockholders, and management at all levels.

Information on profit sharing plans, how they are designed, installed, promoted, and administered, may be obtained from—

Council of Profit Sharing Industries
29 North Wacker Drive
Chicago, Illinois 60606

Profit Sharing Research Foundation
1718 Sherman Avenue
Evanston, Illinois

A quick look at profit sharing's two major plans:

	Current Distribution	Deferred Distribution
Distribution of profits	Monthly, quarterly, semi-annually, but most often yearly	On retirement, disability, death, or severance or some financial emergency
Chief advantages	Strong incentive—employee sees "immediate" results, in cash	Earned security—employee sees comfortable, dignified retirement ahead
Service required for eligibility	3 months to a year	Longer periods, usually 1-2 years
Permit employee savings or contributions	None	⅓ to ½ of plans do
Allocation most influenced by	Pay scale and individual performance	Compensation and years of employment
Employee ability to borrow against share	Rare	1 in 5 plans
Vesting rights	Prorated over profit sharing period—up to 1 year	Minimum—1 to 5 years service; maximum—10 to 20 years service
Administration	Relatively simple	More complicated—usually with some employee representatives
Trustees	None	Corporate trustees (banks) or individual trustees
Investments	None	Common stock, bonds, or combination
Average annual distribution per participant	$350 - $450	$450 - $550
Tax-free limits	No tax-free provision for employees	Up to 15% of total compensation of participants, with carryover features

VOLUNTARY EMPLOYEE CONTRIBUTIONS

Provisions permitting voluntary employee contributions to a profit sharing plan constitute a desirable addition to an employee benefit program.

There are several advantages, according to Arthur Stedry Hansen Consulting Actuaries, to the employee who utilizes the contributory feature as a method of savings. If properly designed, the administration of voluntary contributions will not be burdensome, and the expense to the employer will be nominal. The highlights:

Objectives: Voluntary employee contributions are provided under a qualified plan primarily to enable the employee to enjoy the advantages of accumulating savings in a tax-free, professionally managed trust. Because the employee is not required to report the income earned by his savings until he actually withdraws his accumulation from the trust, he is likely to pay a much smaller tax than would have been levied under his effective tax rate during the period of savings.

Benefits: The benefits to the employee and his family in addition to the tax savings are significant. For example—

1. Employee contributions may be invested with the general assets of the fund, giving the employee the opportunity to participate in a carefully selected, properly diversified portfolio.

2. The investment objectives of the fund coincide with the employee's objective of accumulating amounts at the highest yield and appreciation obtainable consistent with safety until the time his savings are needed to provide for him or his family.

3. By proper accounting procedures the employee's savings and earnings are allocated to his own account.

4. No investment expenses are incurred by the employee.

A provision for voluntary employee contributions is appreciated by the employees who participate, or intend to participate, in this method of savings.

A PROFIT SHARING EXAMPLE

Dominion Foundries and Steel, Limited, Hamilton, Ontario, Canada is a basic steel producer, employing 6,500 people. The company has one stated policy—The Golden Rule—and every attempt is made to sincerely apply it.

The following information on Profit Sharing, taken from *The Dofasco Way,* the company employee handbook, is illustrative:

There are many advantages to working at Dofasco. One of these is membership in the Employees' Savings and Profit Sharing Fund and the Employees' Deferred Profit Sharing Plan. Profit sharing enables Dofasco people to share directly in the profits which they have helped to produce.

Profit sharing is designed to stimulate your interest in the successful operation of the company, to build security for you and your family when you retire, and to assist you when necessary in meeting current financial needs. You will become eligible for membership after three years continuous employment.

THE SAVINGS AND PROFIT SHARING FUND

Your Fund credit is built up in two ways. You will save in the fund by regular payroll deductions, 5 percent of your wages to a maximum of $200 annually. Then, at the end of each year, the company will pay into the fund on your behalf, an additional sum based on the profit for that year, to a maximum of three times the amount that you saved during the year. These combined credits are then invested to further increase your savings in the fund.

Under the terms of the fund contract, the full amount of your fund credit will become payable to you when you retire at the normal retirement age, or earlier in the event of mental or physical incapacity. Should you leave the company's service before reaching retirement age, you will receive all the money which you saved in the fund and the accumulated earnings thereon. You will also receive from a minimum of 50 percent to the full 100 percent of the company's contribution on your behalf plus the accumulated earnings. This percentage is based directly upon the number of years you have held membership in the fund. If you should die prior to retirement, your beneficiary or your estate will be paid the full amount of your fund credit. These terms are described in detail in your fund contract book.

THE DEFERRED PROFIT SHARING PLAN

Your New Plan credit is built up by company payments only. To the extent that profits permit, the company will pay into the new plan on your behalf, a further sum, to a maximum of three times the amount that you saved in the fund during the year.

At the end of each year, you have the option of leaving your new plan credits on deposit or taking payment in cash, in whole or in part. If you leave your credits on deposit, they will be invested and the income will be credited to your account in the same manner as in the fund. Under certain circumstances and upon reasonable notice, you may withdraw all or part of these invested deposits at a later date. Of course, if they are not withdrawn they have the effect of increasing your retirement security substantially.

Your credits in the new plan, with accumulated interest, will be payable to you upon retirement or upon leaving the company's service, or to your beneficiary or your estate if you should die prior to retirement.

The profit sharing plans are administered by an advisory committee, which is made up of representatives elected by the employees and members appointed from management. If you have problems or questions in relation to these plans, your area representative will be glad to help you.

THE COMPANY POSITION

THE COMPANY POSITION

"In setting up any profit sharing fund," explains T. J. Hawes, assistant director of personnel, "we are quite convinced that three principles must be followed." These, he says, are—

1. That the company be sincere in wanting its employees to share in company earnings; in other words, the profit sharing fund must be an outward manifestation of an attitude of mind.

2. Profit sharing must be substantial; in other words, there is not much point in asking employees to work harder and try to do a better job and then tell them at the end of a good year that their share of the profit is $15 or $20.

3. Profit sharing must not be used in lieu of wages; it is important that the going wage be paid and profit sharing be something over and above this.

WELFARE AND PENSION PLANS DISCLOSURE ACT

The Welfare and Pension Plans Disclosure Act, as amended by Public Law 87-420, became effective June 18, 1962. The act defines two types of plans for which a description and annual reports must be published. These are "employee welfare benefits" plans and "employee pension benefit" plans.

An "employee welfare benefit" plan is one that provides medical, surgical, or hospital care or benefits, or benefits in event of sickness, accident, disability, death, or unemployment, through the purchase of insurance or otherwise. An "employee pension benefit" plan is one that provides retirement benefits by the purchase of insurance, annuity contracts, or otherwise, and includes any profit-sharing plan that provides benefits at or after retirement.

The two types of plans have certain common characteristics. A plan, fund, or program to be included in either category must be one which is communicated or the benefits of which are described in writing to employees. It must be established by an employer or by an employees' organization, or by both, for the purpose of providing certain specified benefits to the participants or their beneficiaries. The term employer means "any person acting directly as an employer or indirectly in the interest of an employer in relation to an employee welfare or pension benefit plan, and includes a group or association of employers acting for an employee in such capacity." An employees' organization includes a labor union or any other association or group of employees in which employees participate and which exists for the purpose, in whole or in part, of dealing with employers concerning an employee welfare or pension benefit plan, or other matters incidental to employment relationships. It also includes an employees' beneficiary association.

Every employee welfare and pension benefit plan except those listed below is subject to the publication requirements of the act if the plan is established or maintained by any employer or employers engaged in commerce or in any industry or activity affecting commerce, or by an employee organization or organizations representing employees engaged in commerce or in any industry or activity affecting commerce, or by both.

The act does not apply to:

1. Plans which cover not more than 25 participants.

2. Plans administered by the Federal Government or by state governments, by political subdivisions of a state, or by an agency or instrumentality of any of the foregoing.

3. Plans established or maintained solely for the purpose of complying with applicable workmen's compensation laws or unemployment compensation disability insurance laws.

4. Plans that are exempt from taxation under Section 501 (2) of the Internal Revenue Code of 1954 and are administered as a corollary to membership in a fraternal benefit society described in Section 501 (c) (8) or by organizations described in Sections 501 (c) (3) and 501 (c) (4) of such code.

Plans administered by a fraternal benefit society or organization representing its members for purposes of collective bargaining do not qualify for this exemption.

Disclosure Requirements

The Welfare and Pension Plans Disclosure Act places on administrators of covered employee welfare and pension benefit plans responsibilities to disclose certain information. In brief, it requires an administrator to publish, as provided in Section 8 of the act, a description of the plan and annual reports containing the information (including copies of documents relating to the plan) specified in the act. The administrator, in order to comply with requirements for publishing their information, shall:

1. Make available for examination in the principal office of the plan by a participant or beneficiary, copies of (a) the description of the plan (including all amendments or modifications thereto upon their effective dates) and (b) the latest annual report;

2. Upon written request, deliver to a participant or beneficiary a copy of the description (including all amendments or modifications thereto upon their effective dates) and an adequate summary of the latest annual report, by mailing such documents to the last known address of the participant or beneficiary making the request;

3. File two copies each of the plan description (including all amendments or modifications thereto) and the annual reports with the Secretary of Labor.

The Secretary is required to make available for public examination in the Public Document Room of the U.S. Department of Labor the plan description and the annual reports, including copies of documents relating to the plan, filed with the Department.

Title 18, Section 1027, United States Code, provides penalties up to $10,000 fine or five years imprisonment, or both, for any person who, in any document required by the act to be published, or kept as part of the records of any covered plan, or certified to the administrator of any such plan, makes any false statement of fact, knowing it to be false, or knowingly conceals, covers up, or fails to disclose any fact required by the act to be disclosed.

The Secretary of Labor has authority under the act to make such investigations as he deems necessary when he has reasonable cause to believe that the act has been violated. Before investigating possible violations involving annual reports which have been filed, the Secretary must first require certification of those reports (if not initially certified) by an independent certified or licensed public accountant.

The Secretary may, whenever he believes that any person is engaged in any violation of the act, bring an action in the proper district court of the United States to enjoin such acts or practices, and upon proper showing a permanent or temporary injunction or restraining order shall be granted.

A complete description of the Welfare and Pension Plans Disclosure Act, and the information about the necessary reporting forms, is available in the official *Labor-Management & Welfare-Pension Reports,* published by the United States Department of Labor.

LABOR RELATIONS

ORIGIN OF LABOR UNIONS IN THE U.S.

By Paul C. Shedd, Jr.
Assistant Engineer, Central Engineering Division
Unarco Industries, Inc., Chicago, Illinois

Although labor disputes and movements can be traced as far back as the Middle Ages, this section deals only with their origins in the United States. The establishment of labor unions in this country was solely the result of a growing "new country" and the rise of merchant capitalists prior, during, and after the Industrial Revolution. The labor movement in Europe has no visible effect on the birth of unions in this country.

One of the first recorded labor disputes occurred in colonial America around the year 1636. It was over the withholding of wages from a group of fishermen employed by a Robert Trelawney on Richmond Island off the coast of Maine.

The labor movement began in this country after it was sufficiently populated enough to produce settlers with surplus income. When these wealthier settlers needed a home built, furniture made, etc., they would gain the services of what may be called a "master builder." This man soon evolved into a strong employer who gathered together various types of journeymen to accomplish whatever task he had been commissioned to complete. After this master received his pay from the wealthy settler, he would in turn pay the journeymen (withholding, of course, a handsome profit for himself.) In these colonial days it may be said then there existed no employer-employee formal relationship. All prices were set and agreed to verbally, a strong contrast from labor today which must have everything in writing.

As America began to grow, it began to push westward. With this push the number of masters grew and the labor movement began. The movement began to cause labor disputes. The second American labor dispute was recorded in 1676. It appears the city of New York ordered its licensed cartmen to remove dirt from the streets for threepence a load. The cartmen felt this wage was too low and they banded together in protest and refused to comply. This then was the origin of workers getting together in various trades to protest an alleged injustice by a master craftsman. Many incidents of early labor disputes have been recorded between 1676 and 1792. It should be noted, however, these disputes were not organized protests. They were gatherings of groups of workers to protest verbally an injustice.

The Trade Societies

During the latter half of the 18th century many trade societies were established. These societies later became the original unions. They were at that time, however, only social organizations formed by various trades for philanthropic purposes such as death benefits, sickness, insurance, and social activity. Economics fell out of their scope. By the 1790's almost every trade had established a society. In the year 1794 the Federal Society of Journeymen Cordwainers came into existence in Philadelphia. It is considered to be the first real trade union in America. This society was formed for shoemakers. They conducted their first strike in 1799 and picketed a master's shop for the first time in American history. A few months later in New York a group of journeymen printers established another society, and thus began a long line of societies for all the trades. With the beginning of the 19th century there came into existence societies for artisans and mechanics. Prior to the turn of the century the only societies formed were for printers and shoemakers.

The push of society and civilization toward the West opened up new horizons for the employer. The demand for goods increased and large factories to accommodate these demands began to develop. With the expansion of factories came the competitive markets of employers. In order to meet costs under highly competitive conditions in the 1880's and 90's, employers sought to hold down wages. They lengthened the working day to meet production requirements and they looked for cheap labor markets. The search for cheap labor led to the employment of children and foreign immigrants looking for a promised land with no money in their pockets. The employer began to exploit the worker.

With the development of production lines and hiring of unskilled labor there arose a new problem, the discontent of the skilled artisan. He saw this move by the employer as a move to lower the living standard and as a loss of his status. He began to look to the new West for employment. New towns springing up in the West were offering higher wages to the worker. Skilled and unskilled laborers began to move out of the factories in the East, but the employer still ruled the roost. The skilled artisans began to militize, and trade societies began to gain new prominence and take a more active part in economics.

Employer Resistance

The employer in the face of stiff competition and the militization of the artisans started to fight back. Employers grouped together to help prevent closed shops caused by strikers belonging to these new trade societies. In most cases they were unsuccessful, and they turned to the courts when they could not cope. They attacked the workers as being conspirators to the restraint of trade. The first such court action occurred in 1806 and the second in 1815. In both cases the employer won. He won because the workers could not defend themselves in court. The judges ruled not against the workers' rights but their methods.

In 1819 a severe depression swept the country and because of the scarcity of jobs most of the trade societies which were taking a more active interest in economics ceased to exist. During most of the 19th century these societies thrived during prosperous periods and died away during depressions. The only trade society which has been recorded as even partially existing during a depression in the 19th century existed during the 1890's. Some of the early leaders of trade societies during those days were Thomas Skidmore, George Henry Evans, Robert Dale Owen, and Francis Wright.

Union organization and strong leadership gained a foothold in 1870. There was a depression during this year and as a result a great deal of worker exploitation. Workers began to strike and there was intervention by the police which eventually led to bloodshed and killing for the first time in the history of the American labor movement. Trade societies began to unite and increase. In the year prior to the 1870 strike a new society titled the Knights of Labor was formed. After the strike and bloodshed the society began to grow and amalgamate with other societies and so arose the first "one big union."

Interunion Struggles

With the forming of the big union there came a power struggle within the union. Opposition rose in its ranks. There were many voices of opposition to what the big union interpreted as the "workers interest." One of the loudest voices heard was that of a man named Samuel Gompers. He banded together a strong group of workers and opposed the Knights of Labor. Out of this opposition came the American Federation of Labor (AFL) under the direction of Mr. Gompers. Out of this opposition also came the death of the Knights of Labor. The day of the American unions had arrived and the day of the small trade society was part of history.

Although Mr. Gompers gained fame after 1886, he had already been an active participator in the moves of various trade societies which had by this time become small individual trade unions. He was born in England but came to America when just a boy. He was a journeyman cigarmaker and joined the cigarmakers union in 1863. He became such an active member that he participated in its reorganization in 1877 and later became president. He became chairman of a committee of a newly created Federation of Organized Trades and Labor Unions in 1881. It was this organization that grew into the American Federation of Labor and opposed the Knights of Labor. He was president of the AFL from 1886 to 1924 with the exception of the year 1895. He was chiefly responsible for its nurturing and developing. Although unions did not start with Mr. Gompers, it can be said he was the father of the American unions as we know them today. Under his leadership trade societies became local unions, and local unions later became the AFL.

Volume upon volume can be found on labor unions during and after Samuel Gompers. Our discussion concludes with his emergence on the American labor scene since we are concerned here only with its origin. To summarize the history of unions it can be said its history falls into six categories:

1. 1792 to 1827—This was the period of the formation of local trade societies or craft unions.

2. 1827 to 1850—A period of political and social agitation for the craft unions.

3. 1850 to 1866—A period in which the local craft unions began to emerge into a national organization.

4. 1866 to 1886—A period of amalgamation of national craft unions.

5. 1886 to 1935—A period of federation. It was during this period the AFL was formed.

6. 1935 to — —A period of industrial unionism. This period has seen the forming of the CIO and the merging of the AFL-CIO into a giant voice in the American labor movement.

GROWING WHITE COLLAR UNIONIZATION

By Lewis E. Lachter, Managing Editor

Administrative Management Magazine

Over 2.7 million white collar workers out of a total of 31 million belong to unions today. Eventually, such union membership is expected to reach 4 million of a projected total figure of 37 million. What should you know about this important trend, and how can you best deal with it?

Some of the information you should have includes the kinds of firms now unionized, where they are located, present and projected statistics, some data on the unions actively engaged in white-collar recruitment, the immediate and long-range plans of these unions, and finally, how the unionization process works.

The single largest group of firms that have unionized white-collar workers are involved in some phase of manufacturing. This is only natural: Both industrial unions and exclusively white-collar organizations like the Office and Professional Employees International Union have long been engaged in recruitment in this area.

About 65 percent of the OPEIU's 70,000 membership is employed by manufacturing firms. Hotel employees account for about 5 percent; shipping firms, 4 percent; banks and insurance companies, 3 to 4 percent; office personnel at missile and testing sites, 4 percent, and other service-type businesses such as stock exchanges make up the rest.

According to OPEIU president Howard Coughlin, the union's major efforts are now being directed at the shipping industry and banking and insurance firms. In the banking area, Mr. Coughlin believes the recent AFL-CIO resolution instructing unions to place pension and welfare fund money in organized institutions will substantially help in efforts to unionize white collar employees in banks around the country. The resolution also noted that union funds should be invested through brokerage houses that are organized.

In reference to a geographical breakdown of white-collar unionization, the eastern portion of the United States is most heavily organized, as is the eastern section of Canada. Similarly, the western area of the U.S. and Canada are the second most heavily organized. San Francisco and Los Angeles, portions of Oregon and Washington, and cities in British Columbia have proven fruitful ground for white-collar unionization.

The Midwest states have given union organizers the most difficulty, and the South, where unions have met with some success, is going to be the scene of a more concerted organizing effort in the months to come.

"Many firms are moving their offices or a branch into the South," Mr. Coughlin told AM. "We at the OPEIU feel this is fertile ground for us, and we believe we can organize a great many white-collar people in this area."

In terms of percentages, the OPEIU president estimated that 60 percent of the union's members was in the East, 15 percent on the West Coast, 15 percent in the South, and 10 percent in the Midwest.

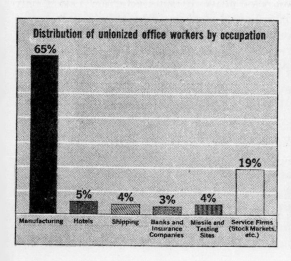

Distribution of unionized office workers by occupation

65% — Manufacturing
5% — Hotels
4% — Shipping
3% — Banks and Insurance Companies
4% — Missile and Testing Sites
19% — Service Firms (Stock Markets, etc.)

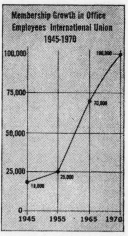

Membership Growth in Office Employees International Union 1945-1970

1945 — 18,000
1955 — 25,000
1965 — 70,000
1970 — 100,000

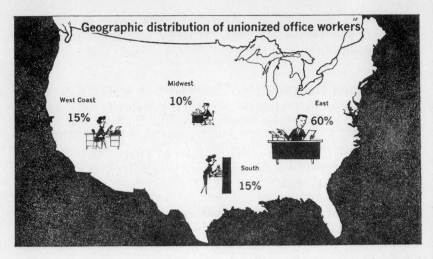

In the general area of statistics, latest U.S. Labor Department figures show that there are over 31 million white collar workers today. The data break down this way: Professional and technical, 8.8 million; sales, 4.5 million; managers, officials and proprietors, 7.3 million, and clerical workers, 10.5 million.

It is interesting to note that in 1950, white-collar workers made up 42.8 percent of the total U.S. labor force. The figure was 46.6 percent for 1960, and the projected total for 1970 is 48 percent of nonagricultural workers. By 1965 there were 72 million registered employed workers in the United States. The projected figure for 1980 is 101 million.

White-Collar Drives On

Out of this tremendous work force, unions feel their greatest organizing potential is with white-collar workers. Some of the largest industrial unions such as the United Steelworkers, Teamsters, United Auto Workers, and Electrical Workers have made concerted, relatively successful efforts to organize the white-collar people working in predominantly blue-collar operations.

There are many unions that deal exclusively with white-collar workers. The OPEIU is the largest under the banner of the AFL-CIO, but there are also many independent unions. Some cover only one company, and some cover one relatively small industry, but they all have one goal in common: Make dues-paying members out of white-collar workers who have historically identified themselves with management.

Independents

There is strong competition between the unions for white-collar membership. Some authorities believe the independent groups have the best chances of long-range growth. These smaller unions are generally more informal and office-oriented than the larger organizations, especially the industrial unions. The independents are highly specialized and understand the workers and their problems more intimately. One expert in labor relations sees the possibility of a new federation evolving which will be made of the independents working cooperatively to organize the growing white-collar "market."

Another factor for the future is a plan for a four-day week. This has been discussed for some time, but Howard Coughlin of the OPEIU has a detailed plan based on an eight-hour day and 32 hour week that includes Saturday.

Let's now cover in general terms the procedure used by unions to organize workers.

Organizing efforts begin when a union seeks out and approaches a dissatisfied worker—or vice-versa—and they discuss what action might be taken. Briefly, the union evaluates the situation, and, where it sees an opportunity, asks management for a voluntary acceptance of union jurisdiction.

According to Mr. Coughlin, 90 to 95 percent of the firms do not voluntarily accept the union, and the National Labor Relations Board is petitioned to call for an election. If 30 percent of the workers in a firm sign the petition, the election is mandatory within 30 days.

When the election is held, a simple majority of the workers voting decide for or against unionization. If management wins, the election procedure can be reinstituted at a later date. If the union wins, workers are classified by salary and job status, and a list of proposals is drawn up. The proposals are approved by the workers, and the suggested changes are presented to management. At this point, a bargaining committee made up of employee representatives and a business agent from the union meet with management people and draw up a contract.

When the contract is approved, shop stewards are appointed in the various office departments, a grievance procedure is established, and hopefully, union and management work together in what several management people call "peaceful coexistence."

The important question for management in the face of union activity is: How does one deal with it best?

A three-point plan would include familiarizing yourself with possible courses of action, deciding on a clearly determined policy, and finally, following through in a positive, decisive manner.

There are three basic courses of action possible: Voluntary acceptance of the union, an all-out election fight, and a carefully evolved program designed to prevent the possibility of unionization.

Let's examine each course of action open to management separately.

1. *Voluntary acceptance.* As noted above, this procedure is followed by some companies when first approached by a union. One manager worked for a firm that had opened the door to the union. "Management was deathly afraid of these people," he said. "They let the union in without a fight and the final contract almost put us out of business. The least a company can do is force an election. Otherwise the union people lose all respect for you, and take as much advantage as they can. And they can lay it on thick."

Of course, election procedures are time-consuming and costly, but it is generally agreed by managers that they are vital to management's best interests.

2. *Election procedure.* If you do decide to force an election, here are some suggestions based on experiences of other businesses.

First of all, don't panic. Many firms do, and the results are disastrous. Plan your course of action carefully, and you might win the election, or if not, you will gain the respect of the union people and a better contract. After all, a union contract is a result of bargaining. There has to be give and take on both sides, but you should set your goals high.

Learn the National Labor Relations Board regulations. There are many and they change, but you should be familiar with the rules so that you don't get involved in "unfair-practice" situations. Some firms have adopted a policy of accepting a "slap on the wrist" by the NLRB in order to win an election, but this should be given careful consideration beforehand.

Get good legal advice. There are special labor relations lawyers, and they can be valuable. They know unions and the NLRB. However, all they can give you is advice. Some of it will be too cautious, and some too radical. You know your company's needs and potential best. The final decisions must come from you.

Consult other management people and management associations. They have experiences you can benefit from, and libraries containing useful information.

When involved in the pre-election battle, tell your story to your employees in direct, factual terms. Explain in some detail the benefits they are now enjoying. Don't get involved in answering the union in a pamphlet-for-pamphlet war. The union usually wins in this situation. Save your ammunition and fire it in strong bursts. Point out that union campaign promises do not have to be kept. Explain that unions can't order changes, they must negotiate them. Of course there are dues and fines to be paid when a union takes over, and negotiated contracts cover all workers, not just some.

If you win the election, you are home free. If you lose, it is to your advantage to bargain in good faith. Peaceful coexistence was the phrase used by many management people we spoke to who are involved with unions. It is a meaningful phrase, and one that best serves management's needs in most cases.

3. *Preventive measures.* The best course of action for a management that does not want its workers unionized is a clearly defined program based on preventive measures. If working conditions and personnel policies are kept at a high level, employees will not seek out unions, and if unions seek them out, organizing efforts will most probably be in vain.

DECISION

Professor A. A. Blum, of the School of Labor, Michigan State University, in his book *Management and the White-Collar Union,* lists five points that may keep white-collar employees in management's camp. They are: (1) give employees the feeling that they have a share in decision-making; (2) make them feel important in relation to blue-collar workers; (3) reassure them in reference to automation changes; (4) give them evidence management is not taking them for granted, and (5) convince them that management institutes improvements voluntarily.

Dr. Blum also discusses proper grievance procedures in his book. He makes the point that employees should be made to feel free to discuss complaints without fear of being fired. The grievance procedure should be available in written form, and if a complaint is found to be warranted, the change should be instituted within 24 hours, if possible.

Other preventive measures include a suitable fringe benefit program (the question today is not *if* there are fringe benefits, but which ones and how much), a salary policy based on merit increases as well as seniority, and a feeling of job security based on good performance. All of these worker benefits, of course, have to be consistent with good management practices. Your efforts to prevent unionization should not put you out of business. However, it is possible to maintain high-level employee programs and operate a profitable company.

ACTION

Historically, the white-collar worker has always been on management's side. The current trend, however, is changing this situation. If you believe unionization is not for your firm, chart a clear course of action based on preventive measures.

In addition to the preventive measures mentioned above (salary, fringe benefits, job security), a vital one is that of identification with management. Status is very important to white-collar workers, and if they think of themselves as close to management, they will be poor prospects for unionization.

The point to keep in mind is that if you don't make efforts to make your white-collar workers happy while productive, the unions will be there to try.

THE UNION POINT OF VIEW
From OPEIU Spokesmen

Caught between low salaries and spiraling prices, more and more office and clerical workers today seek collective bargaining to better their lot. The best-known union in the white-collar field is the Office

& Professional Employees International Union, AFL-CIO/CLC. Although this union has been in existence since 1904, it began its real expansion toward the end of World War II when it received its international charter from the American Federation of Labor. Office workers employed under OPEIU contracts generally earn $1,000 a year more than nonunion employees. They are an elite group.

Since establishment of the International Union in 1945, its membership has grown from 22,500 to more than 80,000 in some 220 locals in the United States, Canada, and Puerto Rico. In giving due consideration to the unusual problems inherent in organizing white-collar workers, the OPEIU has rendered exceptional performance in its field of unionism.

In Many Industries

OPEIU members today include office, clerical, technical, and professional workers in every conceivable type of private industry. These number, among others, the pulp and paper industry in the United States and Canada, Blue Cross workers in Puerto Rico; stock exchanges on Wall Street; the petroleum industry in Texas; motion picture, television, and the radio broadcasting industries in Hollywood; steamship, shipbuilding and repair yards; the Tennessee Valley Authority; public utilities of all types—including atomic power and aerospace projects—the retail, wholesale, and distributing trades, with strong representation in industrial establishments.

This white-collar union's most recent organizing breakthrough has been the unionization of some 2,000 clerical workers and tellers in several large commercial and savings banks in the United States and Canada. Throwing off traditional attitudes, young bank workers today are showing an increasing interest in white-collar unionism, according to OPEIU President Howard Coughlin. He attributes this to low pay of bank staffs, compared with high bank profits, resulting in a loss of social status and economic prestige that bank workers formerly enjoyed in their communities.

From the beginning, organized labor in the United States and Canada has been concerned, above all, with improvement in wages and working conditions. In collective bargaining relationships with employers, labor unions still concentrate on these fundamentals.

Their primary service to members is to improve their economic position.

But labor unions also serve their members in another important way. They give to the individual worker a feeling of belonging, of strength in united action, of membership in a group with a common objective. Where the individual is weak, the union gives him a sense of security. In a world of atomic change, it gives him some assurance of permanence and continuity.

Through the OPEIU an office worker asserts his freedom and expresses his wishes as a member of our economic society, growing ever more complex and perplexing for the individual in this technological age. Finally, through his elected union representative he has a voice in the determination of his wages and conditions of employment—something the nonunion worker does not enjoy.

The Glamor Unions

Most young people today don't realize that every actor and actress they see on television or in a movie belongs to a union. It is also true that every Broadway performer, every musician in the orchestra, those familiar radio voices, the screen writers—even cameramen and directors—all belong to some union.

The famous Radio City Rockettes, so familiar to tens of millions of Americans, and many popular professional sports stars who do commercials—they all belong to unions like the OPEIU—unions affiliated with the AFL-CIO and the Canadian Labour Congress (CLC).

Why do all these prominent individuals belong to a union? Why will a performing artist never set foot on a stage or a movie set without a written contract? Why do airline pilots, who earn as high as $40,000 a year, teachers, and civilian aerospace technicians belong to unions? For the same reason that every American or Canadian or Puerto Rican should belong to a union. It makes *good business sense*. Besides, citizens of the United States, Canada, and Puerto Rico have legal rights to belong to a union—guaranteed by law and court decisions.

Asked why a typical OPEIU member belongs to the union, will get you a reply something like this: "Because I'm *proud* of my job;

it makes me a *better* employee in a *better* job. Our white-collar union puts things on a business-like basis. I like that. We put everything down in a written contract which we, ourselves, negotiate. My employer, who is a businessman, wouldn't think of doing business without a signed contract. It's just as good business for an employee to have a signed union contract. We've found that our union contract benefits all of us, and makes our office a better office to work in."

Of course, unions are changing with the times to keep abreast of modern developments but they haven't changed as much as business has. And the rapid changes in business provide some very strong reasons why a union like the OPEIU is *necessary for the office worker.* Here are a few:

1. Business has grown larger, more *impersonal.* The bigger the company, the more likely you are to be just a number, a work station, or simply part of the "bunch downstairs." People are hired and fired in groups. Where do you stand in that setup?

2. Companies are changing, managements are merging and consolidating; they're transferring people, whole departments, and entire plants. What kind of person-to-person relationship can you have with an employer when that happens?

3. Jobs are growing more specialized with training and skills that often leave an employee with only two choices: Do it *their* way or quit. Even general skills have become so specialized that all you know is how they want the job done where you work. Where does that leave you if that particular job is eliminated?

4. Modern management techniques often result in more and more rules, regulations, and restrictions. When that happens where you work, do you have a *voice* in the changes?

5. Perhaps most alarming, technology and automation are being applied to more and more jobs. Science brings some great advances to help our lives in many ways. The computer and electronic data processing may have helped to create your job. But what happens the day somebody brings in a machine to replace you completely?

WHY EMPLOYEES DO OR DO NOT JOIN

Office employees do not join a union for any number of many reasons, including these:

1. *Satisfactory work conditions.* Office work is considered better than factory work. It is quieter, cleaner, safer, and less tiring. The need to improve work conditions in the office is usually not critical.

2. *Loss of status.* Office employees, more than shop workers, are identified with management. To them it is generally more important to be associated with those "in the know" than with union co-workers.

3. *Loss of individuality.* The office offers the worker the last vestige of individuality, the opportunity to be himself. In the factory the rate and conditions fit the job; in the office these are more likely to fit the person.

4. *Automatic union benefits.* Office employees often get the advantages of unionism without becoming members. As benefits are negotiated for the factory workers in the company, the office employees usually get a "free ride" as the new terms are also made applicable to office employees.

5. *Characteristics of office workers.* People who are cut out for office work tend to be conservative. They are less eager to change the status quo and less likely to be moved by the appeals of union organizers. Many are women or secondary wage earners whose main interest in life is not centered in a lifetime career with long term benefits.

What are some of the reasons that office employees join a union? Here are a few:

1. *Need to improve conditions.* When the work condition, or some part of it, is unsatisfactory, and going through channels fails to bring any results, employees cannot be blamed if they listen to the voice of an outsider who promises to intercede in their behalf.

2. *Discontent with wages.* If wages are below the community average (and workers know) and the problem is not recognized or its solution is not communicated, employees may actually seek someone to champion their cause. This is especially true where factory workers earn more than office employees, which is so often the case.

3. *Inadequate benefits.* Fringe benefits are expected to be comprehensive. They should be known and understood by workers. When a situation arises in their personal or family lives for which the benefits seemed inadequate, workers may feel that management has shortchanged them.

4. *No feeling of justice.* To whom do they go with their grievances, when there is no formal grievance procedure established? They will look for someone to listen to their gripes.

5. *Insecurity.* The fear of automation, procedural changes, management reorganization, and similar changes, if left unanswered, will send employees scurrying for job security measures, such as the protective umbrella of seniority.

6. *Poor supervision.* Employees want supervisors whom they can look up to and respect. If management leadership is missing, don't be surprised if employees go elsewhere for the guidance they need.

7. *Lack of communication.* Companies talk about an "open door" policy. But who walks in? In a union representation there is always a steward handy and eager to listen to employees. What's more, he can get a quick answer from management to the employee's question or problem.

More likely than not, employees join a union or do not join a union because of little things. The big problem situations are either well known or soon become evident, and management generally responds with dramatic and prompt action. It's the little things, ordinarily unrecognized and therefore left unattended, which cause the problem. It doesn't take any talent to spot the obvious, but it does call for real managerial acumen to locate the potential trouble spots that are not apparent on the surface.

ORGANIZING ATTEMPTS

The following is taken from the revised edition of *When Labor Problems Confront You,* published by the Illinois State Chamber of Commerce.

THE RECOGNITION CAMPAIGN

Orinarily you will receive very little warning of the union effort to organize your employees.

Union organizers are expert in their field. Not only do they have the benefit of years of experience, but enlightened unions train their personnel through various workshops and seminars in the practical application of labor laws, contracts, negotiations, strikes, unemployment compensation, safety regulations, fair employment practices and other similar laws applicable to labor relations. They are ready to exploit any weakness that may exist.

They are prepared, as employers should be, for any situation which might arise!

Your warning of union activity may come from the plant grapevine. Or, you may hear of picnics, open meetings, visits to home of employees, or beer busts sponsored by the union. You may see leaflets or handbills distributed at the entrance to your business.

On the other hand, you may have no warning. Instead, you may receive a telephone call, a personal visit or a registered letter in which recognition is demanded by the union organizer claiming that his union represents a majority of your employees. In fact, a picket line may be posted without any advance warning.

What should you do? Remember these two primary reactions: *Do Not Panic! Obtain Competent Advice!*

Here are some further suggestions for detailed planning in particular situations:

In the rumor stage:

Separate the wheat from the chaff. Keep your ears and the ears of your supervisors open, but do not interrogate employees directly. Evaluate what you hear carefully.

Go over your personnel checklist carefully to see what practices and procedures have been ignored or not followed up. Is there some source of discontent which you have overlooked?

Correct any bad situations promptly, but check with your legal adviser first to be sure you are not overstepping the proper bounds of conduct.

Consult other employers in the area to determine if the activity is general or localized. If general, it may be desirable to provide a means of keeping each other abreast of all of the facts.

Solicit the active cooperation of your supervisors. Be certain their attitudes and actions are consistant with company policy. Have them keep careful records of any unusual situations. Keep your supervisors carefully instructed and fully informed.

Foremen should watch out for slowdowns.

Improve communications among personnel, particularly from top to bottom, and encourage contact from bottom to top.

Improve and step up personal contacts.

Note presence of strangers. Keep copies of leaflets you find.

During a telephone call or personal visit from a union organizer:

Be courteous.

Be a good listener.

Be calm! Do not jump to conclusions or be pressed into ill-considered actions! Take enough time both during and after your talk to consider carefully the next step to take.

Be as brief as you can. Obtain but do not give information until you have had a chance to talk to your adviser. The organizer is a "pro" in his field. Most of them have had 15-25 years of experience in just this sort of thing. Think about how much, or rather how little, you have had and act accordingly.

When the demand for recognition is based on a claim of authorization cards signed by a majority of your employees:

Be wary because a request that you check the cards is loaded with legal implications which may result in your being required to recognize the union without benefit of an electioon.

Authorization cards are oftentimes unreliable indicators, as even the Chairman of the NLRB has had occasion to observe. Social pressures, fear, uncertainty, or misrepresentations might have played a part in the signing—you aren't really in a position to know—and the employees' actual views might be diametrically opposed.

If you do not wish to consider union recognition on a card check basis:

You should not discuss, look at, review, or accept the cards.

You should not interview your people to ascertain whether or not they signed (although interrogation is legally permissible in some circumstances, the limitations are many and technical).

You should not agree to a "quickie" election by an impartial third party. It may be just as poor a test of real employee sentiment as the cards.

You should not engage in objectionable conduct, stalling, and the like.

You should not give the impression you are against unions categorically.

You should raise any question you may have concerning the appropriateness of the unit requested.

You should suggest the proper forum for deciding any question of representation has been statutorily determined to be the NLRB.

You should state the need for consulting with your labor relations adviser before you can take any position.

On receipt of a letter from the union:

Be certain to seek guidance as to appropriate response.

Be mindful of the cautions on card check reference.

Be certain that the letter is answered in a reasonable period of time.

During an organizational strike or recognition picketing:

Alert the chief of the law enforcement body in the jurisdiction in which your place of business is situated. Maintain close liaison.

Ask your labor attorney to advise you and to consult with the law enforcement officers concerning the rights of those who wish to work.

Consult with your attorney as to whether the strike or picketing is illegal recognition picketing. Ask what information he will need if he is to take legal action.

Alert your supervisors, office personnel, and other people who are not affected by the strike. Advise them of the facts and your policy regarding the strike.

Instruct all personnel to avoid loitering near the picket line. In general, avoid exchange of conversation with pickets to minimize the danger of unwanted incidents.

Consult the section on strikes included later in this discussion.

Remember that the organizer has certain legal rights, too. He can distribute handbills on public property. He can call on your employees at their homes. He can call meetings of your employees in public places or in such places as he may obtain.

You need not let an outside organizer talk to your employees on company property under most circumstances. The problem arises only if you have made "captive audience" speeches and (1) are covered by the "lack of access to employees rule" which originated with department stores, and (2) are enforcing an unlawful broad no-solicitation rule. These are complex areas but generally can be outlined as follows:

Department store rule—Applies to a business operation in which access to the employees through channels of communication other than on company property is considered by the NLRB to be impossible or impractical.

Unlawful broad no-solicitation rule—A company rule against employee solicitation and literature distribution applicable only to unions (and not to other organizations) or prohibiting such activity during nonworking time and in nonworking areas. Conversely, limitations against such activity in working areas during working hours are permissible. There are exceptions here too, but your guideline should be: "Working time is for work."

This is a changing and developing field and care is warranted. For example: Indications are the NLRB is heading (or would like to head) in the direction of an "equal time" rule whenever an employer makes a speech on company premises.

You need not let an outside organizer distribute handbills in your plant (subject to the above limitations), but your own employees have somewhat wider latitude in this connection.

The governing rule remains: Working time is for work. Conversely, during nonworking time (lunch breaks, etc.) your employees are free to solicit memberships and discuss unions and, in nonworking areas, distribute union literature.

Perhaps you have already concluded—as you should have—just what your response to the organizer will be. Remember:

It is imperative that you act affirmatively and at once if you intend to contest the union claim!

Some employers are willing to accept union demands for recognition without an election. There can be many reasons for such a decision, particularly among employers associated with the building trades and construction industries, where 80 percent of the employees are organized—compared to 5 percent in the retail trade. They may believe sincerely that the benefits, such as a ready source of employees, the union label and an anticipated attitude of cooperation, outweigh disadvantages of organization. These have been persuasive considerations under proper circumstances.

This is your decision. We suggest only that you consider carefully the long-term nature of any relationship; your future financial position and the effect on it and your employees of quick recognition and agreement with the union. Temporary expediency, such as the hope—or promise—of an "easy" first contract, should not be allowed to blind you to the long-term effects of your decision.

And remember, although you may be willing to recognize the union as the representative of your employees, it is nearly impossible to tell how your employees really feel without an election.

The Labor Management Relations Act says, in Section 7:

"Employees shall have the right to self-organization, to form, join, or assist labor organizations, to bargain collectively through representatives OF THEIR OWN CHOOSING, and to engage in other concerted activities, for the purpose of collective bargaining or other mutual aid or protection, AND SHALL ALSO HAVE THE RIGHT TO REFRAIN FROM ANY OR ALL OF SUCH ACTIVITIES except to the extent that such right may be affected by an agreement requiring membership in a labor organization as a condition of employment as authorized in Section 8 (a) (3)." (Emphasis supplied.)

You must be adequately sure that the union does represent a majority of your employees before you may recognize the union. Consult your attorney on the legality of recognizing a union without an election!

If you do recognize the union, nothing in the law gives the union the right to dictate the terms of your collective bargaining agreement. This is a matter for bargaining which is discussed later.

CAN AN EMPLOYER CAMPAIGN, TOO?

Yes! First of all, we suggest again that you refer regularly to the check list under "Preparedness." These are always items of concern. In addition, the law allows you considerable leeway in taking an active part in a campaign, if you desire to do so.

Such campaigns have many times proven successful. Even though a substantial majority of your employees may have signed union authorization cards initially, this does not mean that the union will win a secret election. Employees sometimes sign membership cards much in the same fashion that many of us sign petitions, without reading carefully or fully understanding exactly what we have signed.

But the election conducted by the NLRB will be by secret ballot. Both you and the union will have full opportunity to carry your messages to the employees, who then exercise their choice in the privacy and secrecy of the voting booth.

The result of the election will be determined in many cases, by whether the company or the union has done the most effective selling job during the campaign.

SOME GENERAL SUGGESTIONS AND A CAUTION

Do not overestimate the loyalty of your employees: Your employees may be bored, broke, aggrieved, hurt, or bitter. The union organizer knows the score. He can exploit the weak spots, the points in the fence you failed to mend.

It is a good idea to have your supervisors prepare a private and conservative analysis of probable election sympathies on an individual employee basis. If the analyses are critical in fact and not colored by wishful thinking, and if you count all doubtfuls in the union column, you will have a reasonably accurate indicator. Repeat the process during the election campaign, of course. Another rule of thumb, if you insist on predictions—the union polling maximum will approximate $2\frac{1}{2}$ times the number of people who attended their last preelection meeting. (Not as reliable as well-informed supervisory opinion, but a guideline.)

Your employees have their own image of you, based on what they observe, not necessarily on what you say.

Keep in mind that the union will have inside help. The alert organizer will look for those employees who have a feel for leadership, a need for prestige, or an ax to grind.

Take a positive and realistic approach: There is no time to wallow in self-pity, resentment, or anger either at the union or the employees you thought would never do such a thing to you.

Recognize your weak points, but capitalize on your strengths!

You must win votes in the same way a candidate for office wins them—do not assume that your employees will vote for you just because they may have known you longer than the union organizer.

Your supervisors are on the front line and will carry a heavy portion of your campaign burden. But don't forget they need indoctrinating, too. All too many will hesitate or feel uncomfortable in talking to their people about unions. There are also those who will feel on the defensive, who will consider it slightly sinful to acknowledge that the company is making money, and intends to continue to make it. In other words, you have to sell your supervisors before you can sell your other employees.

Sincere (not phony) identification with your employees through your common background may cause them to identify with you on election day. (Particularly in smaller communities, your common interests are often many—your children may play in the same Little League, you may belong to the same church, the same PTA, the same lodges.)

Remember, this will not be an easy campaign, but unions don't always win, either! True, on the surface at least, it would appear the union has a strong head start since there must be a "showing of interest" in the unit (signed authorization cards) from a minimum of 30 percent of the employees. But, according to an NLRB survey, unions which had signed up from 30 percent to 50 percent in advance won only 19 percent of the time, while companies, on the other hand, won 26 percent of the elections involving units in which more than 70 percent of the employees had originally signed union cards.

Do not stray from the limits of the law in your words and actions: Avoid any statements or actions by members of management which could be construed either as a threat or a promise.

Plan your campaign carefully; review your plans and the text of your letters or speeches with your labor relations attorney.

Be alert to your rights as well as your limitations!

You Can Talk to Your Employees

The Constitution and law itself provide you with freedom of speech, limited only to the extent that you cannot directly or indirectly threaten, promise or intimidate your employees by the words that you speak or by the manner or background in which you say the words. Your professional adviser will caution you about the practical and legal effect of talking to your employees, as well as where and when such talks may be made.

There is, however, a wide choice of things you may say freely, including the following:

You may emphasize your belief and your opinion that the people do not need a union; you may talk about the loss of their independence. You may emphasize that an outsider will come between the employee and you. You may state that without a union your door is always open.

You may refer to the cost of union initiation fees, dues, and assessments.

You may state your personal opinion concerning the union organizers, providing you do not exceed the legal bounds of libel and slander.

You may express openly the hope that your employees vote against this or any union.

You may remind the employees that they have a right either to join or refrain from joining the union.

You may remind your employees that they do not have to vote for the union because they have signed a membership card.

You may describe the good features of working for you—job opportunities, longevity, job security, steady work—your strong points.

You may state the union cannot guarantee additional pay. Only the employer meets the payroll.

You may state that the union cannot guarantee the security and success of the business, only customers can do that.

You may discuss the possibility of strikes and serving in picket lines, and you may review the history of the particular union as to such matters.

You may describe the experiences which other employers have had with this or other unions, including those in your own community.

You may urge all employees to vote.

You may call attention to any union falsehoods.

You may explain the meaning of checkoff and union shop and the effect they may have on all employees.

This is not a catalogue of what you should say. It is a list of statements that are accepted as a proper exercise of free speech. You will have to decide from your own situation, whether it is appropriate to say any or all of those things to your employees.

In addition, if you have never talked to your employees before the union appeared, remember to weigh carefully the impact of a new and dramatic gesture of this kind against possible criticism that you are insincere or "buying goodwill."

LETTERS TO EMPLOYEES

Letters to employees should be short, plainly worded, factual, dignified. They are most effective when limited to one topic. Other suggestions which employers have found useful are:

Plan your campaign so that your letters will be well spaced. Consider the use of letters as followups to talks to employees.

Have a series of envelopes prepared in advance of mailing, personally addressed. Have at least an outline of letters prepared in advance.

Mailing letters to employees' homes may give them more time and privacy to review them, and will give their families an opportunity to hear your side of the argument.

Remember that the same prohibitions apply to the written word as to the spoken word—you must not promise, threaten, coerce, or intimidate, or in any way interfere with the employees' freedom of choice. Your written or spoken word is usually considered in light of your actions to determine if there is any violation of employees' rights. Review your letters with your labor relations attorney!

Do not misrepresent. Be truthful.

Use the NLRB—It's Your Agency Too!

Do not be afraid to avail yourself of the services of the NLRB in a proper case. Union coercion of employees is prohibited by law, and certain types of strikes, picketing, and boycotts are also prohibited.

Be alert to union activity such as excessive spending, threats, following your employees, or other evidence of interference which may be grounds for setting aside an election.

Use your supervisors to keep a record of all that transpires in this connection.

If the union has demanded recognition, but has not asked the NLRB to hold an election, consider filing an employer petition for an election.

Participation by Local Business Groups

Local chambers of commerce and other business groups are often faced with the question of whether and how they can help one of their member companies which may be facing an organizing campaign, or other labor problems.

The Illinois State Chamber of Commerce believes that the most important functions to be served by local chambers or other interested business or civic groups are:

To provide basic information to employers who have had little or no experience with unions.

To assist such employers, upon request, in finding competent, experienced professional help.

If a local group desires, for any reason, to participate more directly in the labor matters of one of its members, it should:

Review with the member-employer the extent to which any such participation can be helpful and is desired.

Review with experienced labor relations counsel any steps it may intend to take.

Hasty action by well-meaning local groups can boomerang in both legal and practical ways, and may hurt the situation more than it will help. On the other hand, action carefully guided by expert advisers and fully integrated with the member company's own plans and objectives may be valuable in some cases.

Avoid the Following Pitfalls

Do not offer wage increases or other inducements during this particular period unless the increases are a part of an established pattern.

You may continue to operate your plant in its established pattern. This is not only proper but vital to you.

Do not threaten to fire, suspend, or otherwise discriminate against anyone because he joined the union, or because he is prounion. By discriminate, we mean a failure to treat both union and nonunion employees alike in making assignments of preferred work, overtime, and the like. Be certain to enforce plant rules impartially.

Do nothing which can be construed as an effort to undermine the union.

Do not threaten to shut down or move the plant if the union gets in.

Do not lay off or discharge an employee for union activity.

Do not prohibit solicitation of union membership during nonworking hours.

Do not ask your employees to name other employees who have attended meetings.

Do not engage in any conversation with employees about meetings that the union has held, or the number, or identity of persons who have signed cards or attended meetings.

Do not promise employees promotions, raises, or other benefits if they get out of the union.

Do not interrogate employees about union activities.

Do not have straw votes.

Do not violate the NLRB limitations on campaigning during the 24-hour period immediately preceding the election. It's a hard, fast rule. For example, answering questions following a last minute speech will void a result favorable to the company if the answers run into the proscribed period, even though the speech itself was concluded in time.

Consult your attorney about any problems you have in this area!

BARGAINING

If you have lost the election, your job is cut out for you—both by law and by economic necessity.

Perhaps your preelection campaign was an emotional one. Perhaps hard feelings were engendered on both sides. These are not uncommon by-products of the election procedure. Nevertheless, you cannot allow yourself the luxury of permitting emotions to govern your thinking. You are faced with contract negotiations which will determine the impact which the union will have on the future operations of your business.

Your first negotiations may be your most important.

Certification of the union as representative of your employees will follow shortly after the election (unless you file objections), and a union request to meet and talk contract will appear on the heels of the certification. Prompt courteous response is recommended.

Duty to Bargain

You are obligated by law to bargain with the union in good faith.

There are standards which determine whether you have complied with this requirement, if the question is raised by a charge filed with the board.

We wish to emphasize the existence of these standards or rules of conduct because employers often overlook the fact that the issue of good faith bargaining is resolved not only by examining the employers' attitude toward negotiations but by an investigation of their entire course of conduct toward the union.

The law does not require you to make concessions or even to reach an agreement, in order to satisfy this statutory obligation. However, the board examiners will look at many factors if you do not reach an agreement. Some of these are: Your general attitude in reacting to each of the events leading up to the election, the manner in which you have accepted the results of the election, your response to the union request to meet, the frequency of your meetings with the union, your bargaining positions, whether changing or unchanging; the general atmosphere or climate you have created by your statements and actions.

In other words, the employer will be judged in the context of all of his activities.

Check Your Every Move

Undue delay in arranging for meetings, unreasonable demands, refusal to discuss or to give your position on issues and antagonistic attitudes or responses to union requests are but a few of the factors which may go into the formulations of an "antiunion motivation" and ultimately undermine an otherwise legitimate strategy.

A word of caution: You are not required to agree to a union "form" contract. Strange as it may seem, some employers have done so under the mistaken belief that all other employers had the same contract with the particular union, or that the union had the legal right to insist on the specific language.

A detailed checklist covering the most important bargaining points is presented on following pages.

BARGAINING CHECKLIST

GENERAL

Your first contract not only establishes the dollar cost of a union but probably will set the tone and pattern for your future negotiations and relations with the union. Even if a second election is held after a year and the union loses that election, your labor agreement has established your economic base.

Another point—anything which goes into a labor agreement giving the union an opportunity to speak and be heard on your business procedures and operations constitutes a relinquishment of a management right. Once you have given up any management right, you will have a hard time getting it back. Consequently, the watchword is deliberation and forethought in negotiations.

ISSUES

You probably will be asked by the union to bargain on the following subjects:

Economic—wages, overtime, premium pay for Saturday and Sunday work, shift premiums, paid holidays, vacations, insurance, and other fringe benefits.

Union Security—union shop, checkoff of membership dues and initiation fees, inplant union representation (the number of stewards, their rights, privileges, super-seniority), grievance procedure culminating in arbitration, seniority during layoffs and recalls and in promotions and transfers.

Job Security—job bidding, job classifications and jurisdictional work limitations, and prohibition on foremen working.

The above represent typical union demands. You may be asked to negotiate on other subjects, of course, such as provision for leaves of absence, sick leave, bulletin boards, military service rights, safety programs, pensions, supplemental unemployment benefit plans, termination pay, and a variety of special fringe benefits.

You will want to look at each one of these demands from the standpoint of how it affects your operation. Any concession will be with you for a long time.

In addition, you will want to present to the union a management rights clause which will preserve for you the right to run your business efficiently and productively. For example, if subcontracting is an essential aspect, you will want to protect it. If the size and nature of your business dictates that foremen be permitted to work in the shop, be certain you do not limit that right. If flexibility in assignment is an essential, cover it. If additional facilities are ever contemplated, limit your recognition clause to the specific location involved in the negotiations and provide for the management prerogative of determining the number and location of your plants.

Seek advice. Remember, your opponent on the other side of the bargaining table will be a skilled and experienced negotiator.

CHECKLIST

Here is a checklist of some of the items on which decisions will have to be made before negotiations start:

Meeting Place

Select a comfortable location. Consider the effect of meeting at your place of business. Will it encourage union showboating for its new members? Will it interfere with customer relations? Will it cause a space problem during recesses? Consider also a neutral location. Will it be available when you want it? Will it be costly? Will the union share in the costs?

Time and Length of Meetings

Decide whether to meet during or after working hours. Can the management group afford the time during the day? Will the loss of production of absent union committee employees be significant? Will you pay the employees if you meet during working hours? (You have no legal obligation to do so.)

Decide how long your meetings will be before they start. Marathon sessions make good headlines but bad contracts.

The Management Team

Determine the number. Select your chief spokesman and stick to it throughout the entire negotiations. Post your spokesman on his exact authority. Assign one of your team to the job of taking notes—particularly of the union position on subjects discussed.

Economic Limitations

Determine what you can and cannot do economically. Decide just how important the rights included in your proposed management clause will be in relation to subcontracting, foremen working, assignment flexibility. All have dollar value.

Ground Rules

Management must present a united front. Any disagreements within the management group must be resolved in recess—not before the union. Profanity and personal abuse are out. Should they appear the meeting should recess automatically. (If you are to make this rule stick, company demeanor must be above reproach.) Sometimes letting off steam is necessary, but orderly negotiations usually are the most productive. Make it clear whether your agreement on a specific provision is subject to agreement on the entire contract, or whether it is final on a piecemeal basis. Strategy will vary depending on circumstances, but it must be made clear whichever way it goes.

If possible, settle all noneconomic issues first. Save your money to buy final agreement on disputed issues.

Union Demands

Obtain as many other contracts as you can to which your union is a party. Particularly, try to find some contracts with newly organized employers. Check with your local Chamber of Commerce and the Illinois State Chamber of Commerce. They can help. Make a survey of wage rates paid in your area for comparable work. Expand it to your industry and to your competition so you can tell what kind of costs you may need to consider. Check with your trade association.

Know your Opposition

The international union will have its problems, too. You can spot them and adjust your approach accordingly. Does the international representative rule with an iron hand or is he still trying to win the committee's confidence—by acting tough with the company—by reciting long experience—by threatening strike? Is he catering to any particular committee members or views?

At some point in negotiations you will have to evaluate the international representative's positions, demands and final goals, and the only way to do it with any degree of accuracy is to assess them without being influenced by meeting room theatrics.

Discussion of Proposals

Review the union demands first with the union and explore, without argumentation, the exact extent and nature of each proposal.

Prepare counter-proposals which will balance union demands. You are not limited to issues raised by the union. Avoid a contract termination date during your busiest season. Note that you are not obligated to grant any benefits retroactively. Consider communications with your employees if you reach a stalemate.

Warnings

Avoid "inability to pay" as an argument, or the next thing to it—according to the NLRB—"refusal of an increase in order to stay competitive." You might be obligated to open your books to the union. Avoid flat rejections. Deliberate consideration of proposals is a requirement of good faith bargaining.

Avoid misunderstandings as to what has been agreed upon. Have union and company officials initial copies of provisions agreed to.

Ascertain union authority to negotiate. If the membership must ratify the committee's agreement, obtain firm commitment from the committee that it will recommend your agreement.

Arbitration Clauses

The union may ask you to agree to an arbitration clause should you request a no-strike clause. Such a clause, of course, gives a third party the right to decide what the contract means in case of a dispute that cannot be resolved between the employer and the union.

Therefore, you must decide at the outset whether the security of a "no-strike" clause outweighs the hazard of having a third party stranger interpret your labor-management agreement.

Should you decide to include an arbitration clause in your contract be sure that you define or provide for the exact method of selecting the arbitrator, the time limits for this selection, the powers he shall have when selected, and the limitations on his authority (that is, subject matters, which cannot be considered, such as wages, rates of pay, the right of subcontracting, etc.)

Of course, it is essential that you know as much as possible about prospective arbitrators before you are called upon to make a choice. An arbitrator skilled in wage rate cases, for example, may have little or no experience in disputes involving discharge or discipline.

THE ELECTION

In this section we address ourselves to a subject of interest only to employers who are within the jurisdiction of the NLRB. Those who are not under the Labor Management Relations Act are considerably less inhibited in what they can do during a fight to keep a union out—but the same holds true for union efforts to get in.

Early in the game—sometimes even simultaneously with receipt of the demand for recognition—you will be served with a copy of a representation petition, filed with the NLRB by the union. The petition seeks an election in a designated employee unit. The exact timing of the filing of the petition will depend upon union appraisal of its own vote-getting position.

Occasionally, of course, the union may not file at all. All you will see is a picket line while the union is working to obtain support. However, the Landrum-Griffin Act amendments fix a time limit of 30 days on organizational as well as recognition picketing and give you some relief in this area. You are entitled to seek an election if the union does not, providing there is a demand for recognition.

The Possibilities Ahead

There is almost an infinite variety of strategic and tactical approaches which can be pursued at this stage. Choice will vary as the facts change. But since eventually all petitions are processed by the Board, you should have a general idea of what is likely to occur when you refuse to recognize the union.

Once a petition has been filed with the NLRB by the union, by the employees, or by the employer, there is an investigation by the board to determine:

If the employer is "in commerce" and if a question of representation exists.

If there is a sufficient showing of interest (in the case of petitions filed by the union or the employees, 30 percent of your employees must have indicated union support before the Board will proceed further).

If there is another contract which might bar an election.

If there has been an election or certification within the previous year.

If there is any objective basis for assertion by the employer of a "good faith doubt of majority status" (in the case of an employer petition).

If the petition has not been disposed of following the investigation by dismissal by the regional director, by withdrawal of petitioner, by the parties in a consent adjustment, either a consent proceeding or a formal proceeding ensues.

CONSENT PROCEEDINGS

There are two types:

Type One—Agreement for consent election.

1. You agree that you are engaged in commerce, the unit requested (as may be modified by the mutual agreement of the company and the union) is appropriate, an election should be held at a set time and place, and a specific payroll date will be used as a cutoff date for determining voter eligibility.

WARNING—Careful attention to the unit is essential. Exclude office, clerical, professional, technical, supervisory, plant protection, and any other employees not clearly part of the requested group if you can. Once in the unit, they will be there a long time. Any decision to include borderline employees in the unit with the hope of thereby affecting the result of the election should be adopted only after a careful evaluation.

2. You waive a hearing at any stage, an opportunity to take exception to the regional director's rulings (unless they are arbitrary or capricious), and the right to have the board instead of the regional director issue certification or amendments of certification or to rule on objections.

Type Two—Stipulation for certification on consent election. Your agreements are generally the same as in a consent election agreement except:

1. The board in Washington, D. C. finally determines all questions relating to elections, and

2. You waive only the preelection hearing.

Unless one of the two types of consent proceedings is adopted, you will have:

FORMAL PROCEEDINGS

A hearing is set before an NLRB representative. You may examine and cross-examine witnesses, present testimony on any relevant point including jurisdiction, existence of a labor organization, and appropriate unit. You may file briefs and/or argue orally. The hearing officer summarizes the evidence, analyzes the issues, and submits his report to the regional director for decision.

Election can be held before hearing under Landrum-Griffin amendments where the union has engaged in organizational or recognition picketing. Board review on appeal from the regional director's decisions is available under certain limited situations.

Unless the petition is dismissed in this proceeding there is a direction of election unless the board accepts a petition for review (in which event indefinite postponement will result).

1. Within seven days of the direction of election you will have to provide the board (and union) with a list of addresses of employees in the election unit. The election will be scheduled within 30 days after the direction.

2. You may campaign during the interim. (The rules regulating campaigns have been discussed earlier.)

3. A preelection conference will be scheduled to determine eligible voters (the employer is required to furnish the payroll list for the period immediately preceding the board's direction of election), the time and place of election, the number of observers for each party, and the places for posting notices of election.

   Questions of eligibility may include the right of temporary, part-time, laid-off, absent, vacationing and striking employees to vote.

4. Your observers must be instructed to challenge all voters you do not consider eligible. A challenged ballot is separately sealed and not opened unless it can affect the result of the election. Challenges must be timely.

This is a highly technical area. Provide your attorney with all the applicable facts so he can properly advise you and your observers.

After the election an opportunity exists to file objections to the conduct of the election or the conduct of the other party which allegedly constituted interference with the election process.

If either the company or the union violates the applicable law and regulations in their election campaigns, the election may be set aside.

Be a graceful as well as a grateful winner. Holding grudges against employees who disagreed with you does nothing but encourage resentment against you.

Mend your fences! Do not give your employees further reason to seek out a spokesman!

COLLECTIVE BARGAINING

Collective bargaining is an American institution of long standing. Employers and employees sit down together to work out their differences and agree upon mutually acceptable terms for the period of the next contract.

They're in this thing *together*. That is the key word. One cannot exist without the other. Workers need a company to hire them, and the company needs workers to provide the service or manufacture the product. But what is happening in too many cases is that Labor *and* Management has become Labor *vs.* Management.

This situation is detrimental to both. Negotiations are not between friendly enemies. They're more like a grudge match.

The two sides have conflicting goals, and the outcome of bargaining is influenced by the skill of the bargainers. But the common interests are far weightier and far more important to both sides than their differences. They have a common interest in protecting and enhancing the competitive position of the company and industry. And they have a common interest in a healthy, growing economy.

A company, in order to fulfill its part of the bargain, should provide realistic wages, adequate benefits, and proper working conditions to meet the reasonable demands and complaints of its employees, in order to build and maintain a capable, industrious, and cooperative work force. Management, despite noticeable advances in the field of human relations, still leaves much to be desired in too many cases.

Workers, in return for their demands, should give loyal, dependable, and dedicated service. In most large industries and many small companies, too, they are now well-paid, even coddled, yet indifferent and indolent.

Management, employees, and labor leaders agree on their common interests but they view them from different vantage points. This is where the disagreements come in. When they meet in a bargaining session these disagreements are placed on the table and an attempt made to work out adjustments that are acceptable to both sides.

This process of reconciling conflicting views in order to serve common interests is not a unique feature of labor negotiations. Almost all business relationships and most personal relationships involve some differences in viewpoint between parties who nevertheless share mutual aims.

Reason, Respect Lacking

Generally speaking, such relationships are conducted reasonably, with goodwill on both sides. The one thing that is unique about bargaining for a new labor-management contract is that reason, composure, and mutual respect are often put aside for the duration of the negotiations. Over the years little progress has been made toward reducing the atmosphere of militancy and crisis that surrounds all too many negotiations.

This unpleasant atmosphere is a dangerous anachronism, an obsolete carry-over from the bitter labor-management conflicts of a generation or more back. It survives primarily because the image of management, portrayed as the exploiter of the worker, has become deeply imbedded in union folklore.

Actual bargaining sessions are usually preceded by announced demands. Much of what is demanded in the prenegotiating period may be discounted, although a lot can be learned from the volume, the tone, and the content of the union's preliminary barrage.

Present trends are making the problem worse instead of better. In too many situations, particularly those which attract national attention, labor and management work *against* each other instead of *with* each other. When they are at loggerheads with each other, and the national interest is endangered, public sympathy is alienated, and third-party intervention results. The United States Secretary of Labor has warned that public pressure will bring about compulsory arbitration of labor disputes unless new private procedures are devised to assure the settlement of crippling strikes in critical industries.

Change Is Essential

To curb this unwelcome development both workers and management must accept that their progress can come only from willing cooperation with each other. To get full cooperation there must be a radical departure from the present relationship between labor and management. Such a change will be difficult to get because of past habits.

Management must regain and retain its logical position as the leader of cooperating workers. The wage-payer still can boss the wage-earner, although in the interests of both, some aspects of this authority can be shared with labor unions.

This is not what is happening now. Labor and management too often are at opposite poles, fighting each other instead of fighting together against the common problems that accompany progress. The worker has had to go to the union to get his due. Management's benighted attitude toward the worker has been largely responsible for the situation that exists.

The need is for understanding. The worker is not interested in increasing efficiency of operation when such increased efficiency will result in his losing his job. But neither must the rights of the workers be forced on management by the union. Cooperation is essential to bring a unified effort to the "division of labor" that we call modern industry.

To create this mutually beneficial and constructive climate the habits and conceptions of labor-management relations must be reexamined.

THIRD-PARTY BARGAINING

Something new has been added to collective bargaining in the last decade. This is the entrance of a third party to the negotiations.

The government has become the uninvited guest, the unwelcome third party. Federal intervention has ranged from the dock workers' strike to the settlement of the musicians' strike at the New York Metropolitan Opera.

A third party is unwelcome unless it is

1. Requested by both interested parties in the bargaining process, or

2. Required by contract as in the case of arbitrable matters, or

3. Called for by law as in the case of the NLRB and the courts.

Third-party intervention is somehow justified by government under the guise of "the national interest"—"the public welfare"—"a national emergency"—"the interest of national defense."

Outside help in negotiations is of three kinds:

1. Volunteer, requested to participate in bargaining or to set the bargaining policy.

2. Paternal, for guidelines but not participation.

3. Intruding, when the President, the Secretary of Labor, or an appointed committee, moves in to avoid a stalemate.

Finally, in order to give a flavor of legality and sanctity to all types of intervention, there is now the possibility of Congressional action through the so-called "arsenal of weapons" approach. In this arsenal there are:

Fact finding without recommendations.

Fact finding with recommendations.

Compulsory arbitration.

Labor courts.

These weapons might well be used for the actual settlement of labor disputes. Another group, which would include court injunction and various forms of seizure, might be proposed to deal with crippling strikes without actually effecting a settlement.

The rising incidence of third-party intervention and the "arsenal of weapons" indicates an increasing vote of no confidence in free collective bargaining. To preserve a sound American institution, both labor and management must rededicate themselves to making two-party free collective bargaining work. Otherwise they will face legislation which really comes to grips with the basic problem, namely, monopoly power.

GRIEVANCE PROCEDURES

By Walter E. Baer
Corporate Labor Relations Representative
Brunswick Corporation, Chicago, Illinois

In many companies, the first-line supervisor is given responsibility and authority to deal with the problems and grievances of his employees—and to resolve them by application of the proper remedy. In these companies, the job of administering the labor contract falls squarely on the supervisor's shoulders.

In most cases, the supervisor had no hand in negotiating the contract, nor did he share in drafting its provisions. Nevertheless, he is the one who deals most frequently with employees and with the union—and he must be equipped to represent management's interests and preserve management's rights, or they will quickly go down the drain.

The following checklist pinpoints the principal practices and pitfalls that the supervisor should be familiar with in handling the grievance machinery. Naturally, all these points are not applicable to every case, but if the supervisor is familiar with all of them—and observes them in his handling of grievances—he will be prepared for almost any kind of case that may arise.

DO

Investigate and handle every case as though it will eventually result in an arbitration hearing.

Talk with the employee about this grievance. Give him a good and full hearing.

Require the union to identify the specific contractual provision allegedly violated. Determine whether the matter can properly be constituted a grievance—as defined by the agreement.

Determine whether the grievance was filed, appealed, and processed from step to step within the contractual time limits and whether the grievance meets all other procedural requirements dictated by the agreement.

Examine the agreement carefully. Is it silent on the matter in dispute? If so, is there a past practice? Is the practice fixed and established? Is it known to both parties? Was it instituted unilaterally or bilaterally? Has it been relied upon before? How long has the practice existed?

Examine the relevant contract provision. Is it either ambiguous or unclear? If so, how has that provision generally been interpreted by the parties? Has the company been consistent in its administration?

Determine whether you have treated employees differently under similar circumstances. If so, why? What has been the prior relationship with the grievant—good or poor? If poor, why? Has the grievant been disciplined on a prior occasion? Why, and what was the outcome?

Examine the grievant's personnel record—if not familiar to you—for length of service, jobs held (qualifications), absenteeism, tardiness, work effort (quantity), discipline record, union offices held (current or prior).

Consult grievance records for similar or identical issues that have been resolved in prior cases, for repeated grievances on the same issue, and for arbitration awards on the same issue.

Examine the contract negotiation record for new or changed contract provisions on the grieved matter. If there is a new provision, which party proposed the language, and for what reason? Which party's language was eventually adopted? If there is a changed provision, who proposed the change, and for what reason? Whose proposal was eventually adopted? What do the negotiation minutes reveal regarding discussions on the provision in dispute—whether it is new, changed, or unchanged? Who was present during discussions on the relevant provision?

Visit the work area of the grievant; be familiar with his working conditions, fellow employees, group leaders, earnings (incentive and straight-time), hours, etc.

Record all results of your investigation.

Determine whether there is a political connotation to the grievance. Is the grievant a deposed union official, or is he now aspiring to a union office? What is his relationship with current union officials? If unfriendly, why?

Establish whether the grievant filed his grievance voluntarily or at the urging of union officials. If through urging, what is the union's motive?

Present any records that are germane to the case—such as time cards, production records, absenteeism reports, payroll records, and prior grievance or arbitration settlements.

Remember, the union is the moving party on all but discipline cases. Require the union to present its arguments, its positions, its case.

Identify the relief the union is seeking. What is the extent of company liability?

Permit a full hearing of the issues. Be sure the union has presented its whole case; be sure you have everything on the record that is pertinent.

Permit reasonable latitude to the union in manner of its presentation of the case, but don't permit the union to take an excessive amount of time or to demean management personnel.

Make a full record of both the union's and company's position, arguments, witnesses, evidence, and participants in discussions.

Treat the union representative with the respect due his office, and demand the respect due your office from the union representative.

Advise the employee of the corrective action you plan to take. Assure him of prompt action. Follow up to ensure it.

Control your emotions—control your remarks—control your behavior.

Pass along to your management labor relations representative your experience with any troublesome contract clauses.

Remember your case may result in an arbitration hearing. Fully inform your supervisor of all discussions about the grievance.

DON'T

Discuss the case with the union steward alone if the (grievant) employee is at work and can be present during the discussion.

Argue with the union representative in the presence of employees. Hold your discussion privately.

Admit to the binding effect of a past practice—for settlement of the grievance—until you have first discussed it with your management labor relations representative.

Forget that the union is a political institution—it must sometimes attempt to justify itself. Some grievances are irreconcilable.

Assume a judicial role. Hear the union's case, then be a company advocate. Represent management's interests.

Argue the merits of the grievance first, if grievance was untimely raised or filed. If untimely, present your arguments on that issue first—give reasons for considering it untimely. Be very clear that you are denying it first on that basis. Do not excuse or waive the timeliness issue on untimely filed grievances (unless you have caused employee or union delay).

Withhold any relevant facts—if they reveal weaknesses in your case, prepare logical and persuasive defenses.

Make settlements that obligate the company to prior approval, mutual consent, or joint consultation with the union before management can act.

Ask favors of the union. They won't forget—they will some day expect a reciprocal concession.

Give lengthy written answers on grievance forms when denying a grievance. If the grievance should be legitimately denied—after exhausting all persuasive efforts to resolve it—give the simple written answer, "No contract violation. Grievance denied."

Make any settlements "outside" the terms of the agreement—unless you have first discussed it with your management labor relations representative.

Hold back a remedy if the company is wrong. Make correction in the amount you calculate to be proper—even if it is less than the relief sought by the union.

Settle grievances on basis of what is "fair"—the contract determines what is fair.

Pay the grievant if the grievant was the improper employee to file the grievance—even if an actual contract violation has occurred. Instead, determine the employee who was wronged by the contract violation and apply the remedy to that employee, even if such action does not resolve the original grievance.

Count on the union to assume authority for resolving your problems; exercise authority and dispose of issues.

Interrupt or stop production to convenience a union representative demanding instant handling of a grievance—but *don't postpone* or delay grievance handling beyond the time when such procedure will no longer interfere with production operations.

Settle the grievance—if in doubt. Discuss the case with your management labor relations representative.

By action or inaction, cause the employee or union to default on their compliance with any time limits. If you do, don't later deny the grievance for reason of their noncompliance with such time limits.

NATIONAL LABOR RELATIONS ACT

It is in the national interest of the United States to maintain full production in its economy. Industrial strife among employees, employers, and labor organizations interferes with full production and is contrary to our national interest. Experience has shown that labor disputes can be lessened if the parties involved recognize the legitimate rights of each in their relations with one another. To establish these rights under law, Congress enacted the National Labor Relations Act. Its purpose is to define and protect the rights of employees and employers, to encourage collective bargaining, and to eliminate certain practices on the part of labor and management that are harmful to the general welfare.

The National Labor Relations Act states and defines the rights of employees to organize and to bargain collectively with their employers through representatives of their own choosing. To ensure that employees can freely choose their own representatives for the purpose of collective bargaining, the act establishes a procedure by which they can exercise their choice at a secret ballot election conducted by the National Labor Relations Board. Further, to protect the rights of employees and employers, and to prevent labor disputes that would adversely affect the rights of the public, Congress has defined certain practices of employers and unions as unfair labor practices.

Regional Office Power

The law is administered and enforced principally by the National Labor Relations Board and the General Counsel acting through 30 regional and other field offices located in major cities in various sections of the country. The general counsel and his staff in the regional offices investigate and prosecute unfair labor practice cases and conduct elections to determine employee representatives. The five-member board decides cases involving charges of unfair labor practices and determines representation election questions that come to it from the regional offices.

THE RIGHTS OF EMPLOYEES

The rights of employees are set forth principally in Section 7 of the Act which provides as follows:

Sec. 7. Employees shall have the right to self organization, to form, join, or assist labor organizations, to bargain collectively through representatives of their own choosing, and to engage in other concerted activities for the purpose of collective bargaining or other mutual aid or protection, and shall also have the right to refrain from any or all of such activities except to the extent that such right may be affected by an agreement requiring membership in a labor organization as a condition of employment as authorized in section 8(a)(3).

THE UNION SHOP

The act permits, under certain conditions, a union and an employer to make an agreement (called a union-security agreement) requiring all employees to join the union in order to retain their jobs (Section 8(a)(3). However, the act does not authorize such agreements in states where they are forbidden by state law (Section 14(b).

A union-security agreement cannot require that applicants for employment be members of the union in order to be hired. The most that can be required is that all employees in the group covered by the agreement become members of the union within a certain period of time after the contract takes effect. This "grace period" cannot be less than 30 days except in the building and construction industry. New employees may be required to join the union at the end of a 30-day grace period after they are hired. The act allows a shorter grace period of seven days in the building and construction industry (Section 8(f)).

THE RIGHT TO STRIKE

Section 7 of the act states in part, "Employees shall have the right . . . to engage in other concerted activities for the purpose of collective bargaining or other mutual aid or protection." Strikes are included among the concerted activities protected for employees by this section. Section 13 also concerns the right to strike. It reads as follows:

Nothing in this act, except as specifically provided for herein, shall be construed so as either to interfere with or impede or diminish in any way the right to strike, or to affect the limitations or qualifications on that right.

It is clear from a reading of these two provisions that the law not only guarantees the right of employees to strike, but also places limitations and qualifications on the exercise of that right.

The lawfulness of a strike may depend on the object, or purpose, of the strike, on its timing, or on the conduct of the strikers. The object, or objects, of a strike and whether the objects are lawful are matters that are not always easy to determine. Such issues often have to be decided by the National Labor Relations Board. The consequences can be severe to striking employees and struck employers, involving as they do questions of reinstatement and backpay.

THE RIGHT TO PICKET

The right to picket likewise is subject to limitations and qualifications. As with the right to strike, picketing can be prohibited because of its object or its timing, or misconduct on the picket line. In addition, Section 8(b)(7) declares it to be an unfair labor practice for a union to picket for certain objects whether the picketing accompanies a strike or not.

COLLECTIVE BARGAINING AND REPRESENTATION OF EMPLOYEES

Collective bargaining is one of the keystones of the act. Section 1 declares that the policy of the United States is to be carried out "by encouraging the practice and procedure of collective bargaining and by protecting the exercise by workers of full freedom of association, self-organization, and designation of representatives of their own choosing, for the purpose of negotiating the terms and conditions of their employment or other mutual aid or protection."

774

Collective bargaining is defined. Section 8 (d) requires an employer and the representative of his employees to meet at reasonable times, to confer in good faith about certain matters, and to put into writing any agreement reached if requested by either party. The parties must confer in good faith with respect to wages, hours, and other terms or conditions of employment, the negotiation of an agreement, or any question arising under an agreement.

These obligations are imposed equally on the employer and the representative of his employees. It is an unfair labor practice for either party to refuse to bargain collectively with the other. The obligation does not, however, compel either party to agree to a proposal by the other, nor does it require either party to make a concession to the other.

THE EMPLOYEE REPRESENTATIVE

Section 9(a) provides that the employee representatives that have been "designated or selected for the purposes of collective bargaining by the majority of the employees in a unit appropriate for such purposes, shall be the exclusive representatives of all the employees in such unit for the purposes of collective bargaining."

A unit of employees for collective bargaining is a group of two or more employees who act together for purposes of dealing with their employer on matters concerning wages, hours, and working conditions. The determination of what is an apropriate unit for purposes of collective bargaining is left to the discretion of the NLRB.

Generally, the appropriateness of a bargaining unit is determined on the basis of the common employment interests of the employees involved. Those who have the same or substantially similar interests concerning wages, hours, and working conditions are grouped together in a bargaining unit.

HOW A BARGAINING REPRESENTATIVE IS SELECTED

Although the act requires that an employer bargain with the representative selected by his employees, it does not require that the representative be selected by any particular procedure so long as the representative is clearly the choice of a majority of the employees. One of the methods by which employees can select a bargaining representative provides for the NLRB to conduct representation elections by secret ballot.

The NLRB can conduct such an election only when a petition has been filed requesting one. A petition for certification of representatives can be filed by an employee or a group of employees or any individual or labor organization acting on their behalf, or it can be filed by an employer. If filed by or on behalf of employees, the petition must be supported by a substantial number of employees who wish to be represented for collective bargaining and must state that their employer declines to recognize their representative. If filed by an employer, the petition must allege that one or more individuals or organizations have made a claim for recognition as the exclusive representative of the same group of employees.

The act also contains a provision whereby employees or someone acting on their behalf can file a petition seeking to determine whether or not the employees wish to withdraw the authority of the individual or labor organization currently acting as their bargaining representative, whether the representative has been certified or voluntarily recognized by the employer. This is called a "decertification" election and a petition seeking such an election can be filed by an employee or group of employees or any individual or labor organization acting on their behalf.

Provision is also made to determine by secret ballot whether the employees covered by a union-shop agreement desire to withdraw the authority of their representative to continue the agreement. This is called a union-shop deauthorization election and can be brought about by the filing of a petition signed by 30 percent or more of the employees covered by the agreement.

Section 9(c)(1) provides that if a question of representation exists, the NLRB must make its determination by means of a secret-ballot election. In a representation election employees are given a choice of one or more bargaining representatives or no representative at all. To be certified as the bargaining representative, an individual or a labor organization must receive a majority of the valid votes cast.

Unfair Labor Practices of Employers

The unfair labor practices of employers are listed in Section 8 (a) of the act; those of labor organizations in Section 8 (b). Section 8(e) lists an unfair labor practice that can be committed only by an employer and a labor organization acting together.

Section 8(a)(1) forbids an employer "to interfere with, restrain, or coerce employees in the exercise of the rights guaranteed in section 7." Any prohibited interference by an employer with the rights of employees to organize, to form, join, or assist a labor organization, to bargain collectively, or to refrain from any of these activities, constitutes a violation of this section. This is a broad prohibition on employer interference, and an employer violates this section whenever he commits any of the other employer unfair labor practices. In consequence, whenever a violation of Section 8(a)(2), (3), (4), or (5) is committed, a violation of Section 8(a)(1) is also found. This is called a "derivative violation" of Section 8(a)(1).

Section 8(a)(2) makes it unlawful for an employer "to dominate or interfere with the formation or administration of any labor organization or contribute financial or other support to it." This section not only outlaws "company unions" that are dominated by the employer, it also forbids an employer to contribute money to a union he favors or to give it advantages that are denied to rival unions.

Section 8(a)(3) makes it an unfair labor practice for an employer to discriminate against employees "in regard to hire or tenure of employment or any term or condition of employment" for the purpose of encouraging or discouraging membership in a labor organization.

Section 8(a)(4) makes it an unfair labor practice for an employer "to discharge or otherwise discriminate against an employee because he has filed charges or given testimony under this act."

Section 8(a)(5) makes it illegal for an employer to refuse to bargain in good faith about wages, hours, and other conditions of employment with the representative selected by a majority of the employees in a unit appropriate for collective bargaining.

UNFAIR LABOR PRACTICES OF LABOR ORGANIZATIONS

Section 8(b)(1)(A) forbids a labor organization or its agents "to restrain or coerce employees in the exercise of the rights guaranteed in section 7." The section also provides that it is not intended to "impair the right of a labor organization to prescribe its own rules" concerning membership in the labor organization.

Section 8(b)(1)(B) prohibits a labor organization from restraining or coercing an employer in the selection of a bargaining representative. The prohibition applies regardless of whether the labor organization is the majority representative of the employees in the bargaining unit.

Section 8(b)(2) makes it an unfair labor practice for a labor organization to cause an employer to discriminate against an employee in violation of Section 8(a)(3).

Section 8(b)(3) makes it illegal for a labor organization to refuse to bargain in good faith with an employer about wages, hours, and other conditions of employment if it is the representative of his employees.

Section 8(b)(4) prohibits a labor organization from engaging in strikes or boycotts or taking other specified actions to accomplish certain purposes or "objects" as they are called in the act.

Section 8(b)(5) makes it illegal for a union to charge employees who are covered by an authorized union-security agreement a membership fee "in an amount which the board finds excessive or discriminatory under all the circumstances."

Section 8(b)(6) forbids a labor organization "to cause or attempt to cause an employer to pay or deliver or agree to pay or deliver any money or other thing of value, in the nature of an exaction, for services which are not performed or not to be performed." This section forbids practices commonly known as featherbedding.

Section 8(b)(7), added by congressional amendment in 1959, prohibits a labor organization that is not certified as the employees' representative from picketing or threatening to picket for the purpose of obtaining recognition by the employer (recognitional picketing) or acceptance by his employees as their representative (organizational picketing).

CONCLUSION

The objective of the National Labor Relations Act, to avoid or reduce industrial strife and protect the public health, safety, and interest, can best be achieved by the parties or those who may become parties to an industrial dispute. Voluntary adjustment of differences at the community and local level is almost invariably the speediest, most satisfactory, and longest lasting way of carrying out the objective of the Act.

Long experience has taught that when the parties fully understand their rights and obligations, they are more ready and able to adjust their differences voluntarily.

NATIONAL LABOR RELATIONS BOARD

The rights of employees declared by Congress in the National Labor Relations Act are not self-enforcing. To ensure that employees may exercise these rights, and to protect them and the public from unfair labor practices, Congress established the National Labor Relations Board to administer and enforce the Act.

ORGANIZATION OF THE NLRB

The NLRB includes the board itself, which is composed of five members with their respective staffs, the general counsel of the NLRB and his staff, and the NLRB regional offices. The general counsel has final authority on behalf of the board, in respect to the investigation of charges and issuance of complaints. Members of the board are appointed by the President, with consent of the Senate, for 5-year terms. The general counsel is also appointed by the President, with consent of the Senate, for a 4-year term. Offices of the board and the general counsel are in Washington, D.C. To assist in administering and enforcing the law, the NLRB has established 30 regional and a number of other field offices. These offices, located in major cities in various states, are under the general supervision of the general counsel.

FUNCTIONS OF THE NLRB

The agency has two main functions: To conduct representation elections and certify the results, and to prevent employers and unions from engaging in unfair labor practices. In both kinds of cases the processes of the NLRB are begun only when requested. Requests for such action must be made in writing on forms provided by the NLRB and filed with the proper regional office. The form used to request an election is called a "petition," and the form for unfair labor practices is called a "charge." The filing of a petition or a charge sets in motion the machinery of the NLRB.

AUTHORITY OF THE NLRB

The NLRB gets its authority from Congress by way of the National Labor Relations Act. The power of Congress to regulate labor-management relations is limited by the commerce clause of the United States Constitution. Although it can declare generally what the rights of employees are or should be, Congress can make its declaration of rights effective only in respect to enterprises whose operations "affect commerce" and labor disputes that "affect commerce." The NLRB, therefore, can direct elections and certify the results only in the case of an employer whose operations affect commerce. Similarly, it can act to prevent unfair labor practices only in cases involving labor disputes that affect, or would affect, commerce.

"Commerce" includes trade, traffic, transportation, or communication within the District of Columbia or any territory of the United States; or between any state or territory and any other state, territory, or the District of Columbia; or between two points in the same state, but through any other state, territory, the District of Columbia, or a foreign country.

Although a company may not have any direct dealings with enterprises in any other state, its operations may nevertheless affect commerce. Using this test, it can be seen that the operations of almost any employer can be said to affect commerce. As a result, the authority of the NLRB could extend to all but purely local enterprises.

Although the National Labor Relations Board could exercise its powers to enforce the act in all cases involving enterprises whose operations affect commerce, the board does not act in all such cases. In its discretion it limits the exercise of its power to cases involving enterprises whose effect on commerce is substantial. The board's requirements for exercising its power or jurisdiction are called "jurisdictional standards." These standards are based on the yearly amount of business done by the enterprise, or on the yearly amount of its sales or of its purchases. They are stated in terms of total dollar volume of business and are different for different kinds of enterprises.

In addition, the board exercises jurisdiction over all enterprises that affect commerce when their operations have a substantial impact on national defense. Also, all businesses in the District of Columbia come under the jurisdiction of the board.

Finally, Section 14(c)(1) authorizes the board, in its discretion, to decline to exercise jurisdiction over any class or category of employers where a labor dispute involving such employees is not sufficiently substantial to warrant the exercise of jurisdiction, provided that it cannot refuse to exercise jurisdiction over any labor dispute over which it would have asserted jurisdiction under the standards it had in effect on August 1, 1959. In accordance with this provision the board has determined that it will not exercise jurisdiction over hospitals that are operated for profit, racetrack enterprises, owners, breeders, and trainers of racehorses, and real estate brokers.

In addition to the foregoing limitations the act itself states that the term "employee" shall include any employee *except* the following: agricultural laborers; domestic servants; any individual employed by his parent or spouse; independent contractors; supervisors; individuals employed by an employer subject to the Railway Labor Act; government employees, including those employed by the U.S. Government, any government corporation or Federal Reserve Bank, or any state or political subdivision such as a city, town, or school district; individuals employed by hospitals operated entirely on a nonprofit basis.

The term "employer" includes any person who acts as an agent of an employer, but it does *not* include the following: the United States or any state government, or any political subdivision of either, or any government corporation or Federal Reserve Bank; hospitals operated entirely on a nonprofit basis; any employer subject to the Railway Labor Act.

NLRB Procedure

The authority of the NLRB can be brought to bear in a representation proceeding only by the filing of a petition. Forms for petitions must be signed, sworn to or affirmed under oath, and filed with the regional office in the area where the unit of employees is located. If employees in the unit regularly work in more than one regional area, the petition may be filed with the regional office of any of such regions. Section 9(c)(1) provides that when a petition is filed, "the board shall investigate such petition and if it has reasonable cause to believe that a question of representation affecting commerce exists shall provide for an appropriate hearing upon due notice." If the board finds from the evidence presented at the hearing that "such a question of representation exists, it shall direct an election by secret ballot and shall certify the results thereof." Where none of the choices on the ballot receives a majority, Section 9(c)(3) provides for a runoff between the choice that received the largest and the choice that received the second largest number of valid votes in the election. After the election, if a union receives a majority of the votes cast, it is certified; if no union gets a majority, that result is certified. A union that has been certified is entitled to be recognized by the employer as the exclusive bargaining agent for the employees in the unit. If the employer fails to bargain with the union, he commits an unfair labor practice.

The procedure in an unfair labor practice case is begun by the filing of a charge. A charge may be filed by an employee, an employer, a labor organization, or any other person. Like petitions, charge forms, which are also available at regional offices, must be signed, sworn to, or affirmed under oath, and filed with the appropriate regional office—that is, the regional office in the area where the alleged unfair labor practice was committed. Section 10 provides for the issuance of a complaint stating the charges and notifying the charged party of a hearing to be held concerning the charges. Such a complaint will issue only after investigation of the charges through the regional office indicates that an unfair labor practice has in fact occurred.

The hearing is before an NLRB trial examiner and is conducted in accordance with the rules of evidence and procedure that apply in the U.S. District Courts. Based on the hearing record, the trial examiner makes findings and recommendations to the board. If the board considers that the person named in the complaint has engaged in or is engaging in the unfair labor practices charged, the board is authorized to issue an order requiring such person to cease and desist from such practices and to take appropriate affirmative action.

If the regional director refuses to issue a complaint in any case, the person who filed the charge may appeal the decision to the general counsel in Washington. Section 3(d) places in the general counsel "final authority, on behalf of the board, in respect of the investigation of charges and issuance of complaints." If the general counsel reverses the regional director's decision, he will direct that complaint be issued. If he approves the decision not to issue a complaint, there is no further appeal.

POWERS OF THE NLRB

To enable the NLRB to perform its duties, Congress delegated to the agency certain powers that can be used in all cases. These are principally powers having to do with investigations and hearings.

The National Labor Relations Act is not a criminal statute. It is entirely remedial. It is intended to prevent and remedy unfair labor practices, not to punish the person responsible for them. The board is authorized Section 10(c) not only to issue a cease-and-desist order, but "to take such affirmative action including reinstatement of employees with or without back pay, as will effectuate the policies of this act."

The object of the board's order in any case is two-fold: To eliminate the unfair labor practice and to undo the effects of the violation as much as possible. In determining what the remedy will be in any given case, the board has considerable discretion. Ordinarily its order in regard to any particular unfair labor practice will follow a standard form that is designed to remedy that unfair labor practice, but the board can, and often does, change the standard order to meet the needs of the case.

COURT ENFORCEMENT OF BOARD ORDERS

If an employer or a union fails to comply with a board order, Section 10(e) empowers the board to petition the U.S. Court of Appeals for a court decree enforcing the order of the board. Section 10(f) provides that any person aggrieved by a final order of the board granting or denying in whole or in part the relief sought may obtain a review of such order in any appropriate circuit court of appeals.

When the court of appeals hears a petition concerning a board order, it may enforce the order, change it, or set it aside entirely. If the court of appeals issues a decree enforcing the board order, failure to comply may be punishable by fine or imprisonment for contempt of court.

In some cases the U.S. Supreme Court may be asked to review the decision of a circuit court of appeals, particularly where there is a conflict in the views of different courts on the same important problem.

THE RAILWAY LABOR ACT

The Railway Labor Act was passed to provide for the prompt disposition of disputes between carriers and their employees.

The term "carrier" includes any express company, sleeping-car company, carrier by railroad, subject to the Interstate Commerce Act, and any company which is directly or indirectly owner or controlled by or under common control with any carrier by railroad and which operates any equipment or facilities or performs any service (other than trucking service) in connection with the transportation, receipt, delivery, elevation, transfer in transit, refrigeration or icing, storage, and handling of property transported by railroad, and any receiver, trustee, or other individual or body judicial or otherwise, when in the possession of the business of any such "carrier."

Highlights of the Railway Labor Act follow:

The purposes of the act are: (1) To avoid any interruption to commerce or to the operation of any carrier engaged therein; (2) to forbid any limitation upon freedom of association among employees or any denial, as a condition of

781

employment or otherwise, of the right of employees to join a labor organization; (3) to provide for the complete independence of carriers and of employees in the matter of self-organization; (4) to provide for the prompt and orderly settlement of all disputes concerning rates of pay, rules, or working conditions; (5) to provide for the prompt and orderly settlement of all disputes growing out of grievances or out of the interpretation or application of agreements covering rates of pay, rules, or working conditions.

The National Railroad Adjustment Board was organized in accordance with the provisions of the Railway Labor Act. By law the headquarters are maintained in Chicago, Illinois.

The disputes between an employee or group of employees and a carrier or carriers growing out of grievances or out of the interpretation or application of agreements concerning rates of pay, rules, or working conditions, shall be handled in the usual manner up to and including the chief operating officer of the carrier designated to handle such disputes; but, failing to reach an adjustment in this manner, the disputes may be referred by petition of the parties or by either party to the appropriate division of the adjustment board with a full statement of the facts and all supporting data bearing upon the disputes.

Parties to a dispute are required to state in all submissions whether or not an oral hearing is desired. Oral hearings will be granted if requested by the parties or either of them, and due notice will be given the parties of the time and date of the hearing. Parties may be heard either in person, by counsel, or by other representatives, as they may respectively elect.

The awards of the several divisions of the adjustment board shall be stated in writing. A copy of the awards shall be furnished to the respective parties to the controversy, and the awards shall be final and binding upon both parties to the dispute. Appeal is through the courts.

It is worth noting that the act was amended to provide that all of the provisions of the Railway Labor Act, except those of Section 3, "are extended to and shall cover every common carrier by air engaged in interstate or foreign commerce, and every carrier by air transporting mail for or under contract with the United States Government, and every air pilot or other person who performs any work as an employee or subordinate official of such carrier or carriers, subject to its or their continuing authority to supervise and direct the manner of rendition of his service."

Section 3, which is excluded above, covers the National Railroad Adjustment Board. In the case of disputes involving carriers by air, a board of adjustment, of temporary duration and of limited jurisdiction, shall be established by agreement of the parties concerned. When it is judged necessary to have a permanent national board of adjustment, the act provides for the selection and designation of four representatives to constitute a board known as the National Air Transport Adjustment Board. Two members shall be selected by the carriers by air and two members by the labor organizations. Their findings shall be stated, served, and enforced.

THE TAFT-HARTLEY ACT

"Nothing in this act shall be construed as authorizing the execution or application of agreements requiring membership in a labor organization as a condition of employment in any State or Territory in which such execution or application is prohibited by State or Territorial Law."

Those 44 words constitute section 14(b) of the Taft-Hartley Act.

Right-to-work laws have long been a thorn in labor's side. Many states now have statutes prohibiting compulsory union membership ("union shop" agreements), and labor finds their existence (as well as the threat of their expansion into other states) a distinct drag on its activities.

This excerpt from the South Dakota Constitution is considered typical of the right-to-work laws: "No person shall be deprived of life, liberty, or property without due process of law. The right of persons to work shall not be denied or abridged on account of membership or nonmembership in any labor union or labor organization."

Such laws were upheld by the United States Supreme Court in decisions in 1949 and 1963.

It was in the early 1940's that the right-to-work concept began to reflect public disapproval of the compulsory membership power exercised by the labor unions, with the sanction of federal law.

The country had come full-circle from the "yellow dog" contracts of the turn of the century. In those, employers required workers to agree, before they were hired, that they would not join unions. These pacts were outlawed in 1932 by the Norris-LaGuardia Act as infringing on the liberties of working men and women. At the same time, Norris-LaGuardia set out the rights of workers not to join unions.

With another complete swing of the pendulum, the Wagner Act in 1935 authorized closed shop contracts between unions and employers and required anyone seeking employment to join the union before he could be hired. So the working man, having escaped from the power of the company to tell him to stay out of a union, was now under the power of the union to force him to join as a prerequisite of working.

THE DARTNELL PERSONNEL DIRECTOR'S HANDBOOK

Public opinion then began to reflect the feeling that such compulsion was contrary to the basic prinicple of freedom of choice. The right-to-work term was first used to describe the movement of voluntarism in unions by the Dallas *Morning News* in 1941. With other papers picking up the phrase, it came to be the accepted term for the voluntary union membership concept.

The National Right-to-Work Committee was organized in 1935 to provide assistance in the right-to-work movements in states, to conduct a campaign designed to promote understanding of the principle, and to protect 14(b). The board consists of clergymen of all faiths, educators, business and professional people, and farmers, as well as union members.

Public opinion polls have shown increased support for the right-to-work principle. Opinion Research Corporation, Gallup, and Harris polls reveal widespread support.

Despite public opinion, opposition to right-to-work continues. Union officials, frustrated in their efforts to kill the movement in the states and through the courts, now concentrate their efforts on eliminating section 14 (b) of Taft-Hartley. They portray the section as "union busting" and predict dire consequences to working men and women.

Union people complain that the laws create an antiunion atmosphere that hampers their recruiting of new members. Proposed union shop bans alone, it is said, channel labor's energies into defensive battles when union men would rather be pressing state legislatures for far-reaching changes in such programs as unemployment benefits, workmen's compensation, and state minimum wage laws. Not least, these battles tend to sap union treasuries.

In the argument for compulsory unionism there are several contentions abroad in the land which, advocates of 14(b) say, approach the proportion of myth. Among these, according to John W. Angle (to whom we are indebted for much of the information in this piece) are:

Union Security. It is contended that right-to-work laws destroy unions. Federal law requires employers to recognize and bargain with unions. Other statutes provide special legal immunities and privileges for labor organizations. No employer, no state could destroy a union today.

784

Free Riders. Union leaders hold that it is unjust for nonunion workers to share in the benefits gained by a union, without supporting the union. They say those who do are "free riders."

No one, apparently, is willing to carry this argument to its logical conclusion: Compulsory membership in all organizations from which we derive any benefit. Many organizations perform worthwhile work—churches, civic clubs, chambers of commerce, boys' clubs—yet they do so without a law compelling membership.

Majority Rule. Another claim is that "a majority vote is the democratic way to determine a union shop."

That is only half true. Granted that majority vote is a basic rule of our democratic system, but going along with it is an equally basic rule—the protection of minority rights. That's why we have a Bill of Rights. Only a sovereign government may compel submission to its rule.

The Chamber of Commerce of the United States believes that right-to-work is important:

For the public, because it helps control union monopoly power, by requiring a labor organization, like other private groups, to sell itself on merit rather than by force.

For the employee, because it protects his freedom of choice—to join a union if he wishes, or to decline membership if he feels the union is unnecessary—or if he disagrees with its aims or leadership.

For the employer, because it protects his right to manage and right to hold the loyalty of his employees.

Debate Goes On

And so the debate goes. In favor of leaving section 14(b) alone, as it was intended in the Taft-Hartley Act, are the employers, or at least most of them. They have a loud voice, individually, and through their trade groups and the National Right-to-Work Committee, Washington, D.C. On the other side of the argument, in favor of the repeal of section 14(b), are the unions with their spokesmen, organizations, and funds.

It can only be hoped that whatever action may be taken—repeal, nonrepeal, modification, on local or national levels—will be in the best interest of the working man and women, and not designed for the benefit of power-hungry union organizations, selfish employers, or opportunist politicians.

United States Department of Labor statistics indicate that states with right-to-work laws have been making more economic progress than the states without them. In the creation of new jobs, the states with right-to-work laws show an increase of 14.6 percent compared with 3.8 percent for states that have no such laws; wage improvement 37.5 percent against 33.3 percent; per capita income improvement 30.2 percent against 25.3 percent. Right-to-work states were ahead in percentage of expenditures for industrial expansion, in bank deposits, in the increase in retail sales, and in several other indices of prosperity.

UNION TRENDS

Union growth depends upon its ability to come to grips with at least three main issues: internal union administration, union responsibility, and union organizing.

1. *Internal union administration.* A popular criticism is that labor has lost the crusading spirit of a social movement. Apathy of union members "who never had it so good" has replaced the zeal of the 1930's. The rank-and-file union member is content that his membership provides protection against the absolute rule of management over wages, hours, and working conditions. He does not participate in the activities of the union except in a crisis when he comes to the aid of the union cause.

The direction is left to professionals who can comprehend the legal and political aspects of unionism. Policy decisions, industry economics, and internal union administration are alien to the average members who, it seems, couldn't care less. Their personal interest, so necessary for growth, can best be stimulated through involvement and opportunities for up-from-the-ranks leadership.

2. *Union responsibility.* Union responsibility means more than living up to agreements and concern with the employment effects of union policies. The common characteristic of the union responsibility theme in all periods is self-denial on the part of union leadership. The labor organizations, in formulating their wage and price policies and other demands, must look beyond the counsel of their tradition and out into the broad field of modern economic realities. A union exists for the benefit of its members, but its concern over their immediate welfare should not endanger their jobs over the long range.

The issues of labor management are far too complex, far too

potent, and far too influential on the rest of society to be resolved in the small arena of one group and on the old testing ground of force and power.

3. *Union organizing.* The "no union" vote measured by NLRB representative elections or by valid votes cast has been higher within the past few years than it has ever been; or conversely, the union vote is lower than it has ever been. Therefore the union batting average is lower. The union attitude toward organizing often is one of pessimism, defeatism, and complacency.

There are three reasons for this: (1) The difficulty in organizing small companies, (2) the indifference of the white-collar worker, and (3) interunion rivalry.

Recognizing these difficulties, attributed to a change in the industrial community, the unions are revising their tactics. The traditional appeals which worked in the evangelical days of unionism are not effective in reaching potential members working in a much more affluent society. The classic blitz campaign must be replaced by a long-run educational program.

Is the day of the "outside" organizer over? Have employees learned to trust their company leadership more than some stranger with exaggerated promises? Is the antibusiness propaganda of unions actually alienating recruits who work for modern, progressive companies that have come a long way from the early days of worker oppression?

In the past union leadership could function from a sense of outrage against injustice and be supported by a sympathetic federal administration and by a sympathetic intellectual middle class. The temper of the times has now changed. The union is no longer regarded as the underdog. Its excesses are not forgiven as readily. The economic atmosphere is uneven. The net effect is that outrage as the dominant mood of the union thrust must be modified to include analysis and reflection.

The public generally accepts the function of the union, but it is a grudging, complaining acceptance. Someday, perhaps, we will talk not only of the union's responsibility to the public but also about the public's responsibility to the union, as an indispensable adjunct to our free society.

ADMINISTRATION

TIME RECORDS and TIME CLOCKS

A fundamental, inescapable factor of payroll accounting is the need, under federal and state laws, to keep adequate records of attendance time and hours worked for all nonexempt employees. They must be paid according to the time worked, and at an overtime rate for all time over scheduled hours.

Time records can be accomplished either manually or mechanically. Individual or group (department) time reports may be done by hand or recorded on individual cards by mechanical time clocks.

Manually, this basic information can be obtained in three ways:

1. Each employee writes in or reports his own time.

2. A supervisor reports the time of his subordinates.

3. A timekeeper checks employees "in" and "out."

Regardless of the efficiency or cost of these methods, they are all dependent upon human nature with its vagaries. When a man enters his own time, his record cannot be questioned without questioning his honesty and integrity. When a supervisor or timekeeper writes in the time, the problems are those of one person checking another. Disagreements relating to favoritism, friendship, partiality, and personal differences could arise.

There is a difference of opinion among personnel experts as to the electric time clock. Many say they are the only certain method of achieving efficiency—but some companies have removed them even on production lines

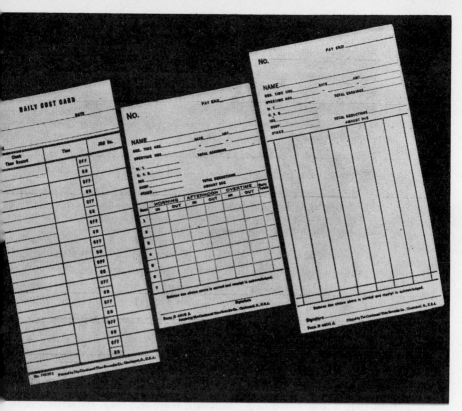

At left, a daily job-cost time chart. In the center, a weekly payroll card registering horizontally. On the right, another weekly card used vertically.

On the other side are the mechanical time recorders. They are completely impersonal and accurate. They can operate only when operated and will show only the exact time. They cannot discriminate nor show favoritism. Each employee has the same opportunity to make his own record fairly, accurately, and impartially.

Since it was first invented in 1884 by a young engineer in a southern furniture factory, the time clock has increased in usefulness until today some 600,000 recorders are providing indisputable time data.

The advantages of mechanical time recording are summarized by the Cincinnati Time Recorder Company:

1. An impartially made record is furnished.
2. Disputes are precluded because of the impersonal record.

791

3. Neither the employee nor the employer can question the completely accurate record showing the exact day or date, hour, and minute of arrival and departure.

4. Automatically printed cards are proof to employees they are being credited with precisely the hours they have worked.

5. Employees have the opportunity to audit and verify their time records without consulting supervision.

6. Employees can record their time faster, easier, and more accurately.

7. Employees have a greater time consciousness of the scheduled work hours.

8. A "partnership in time" is established between employee and employer. The employee is responsible for arrival in the morning and return from lunch. The employer is responsible for the time between arrival and lunch and after lunch until departure.

Some managers believe a mechanical device for attendance time-keeping should not be introduced since this could become a symbol identifying a low strata of employees. In the United States we maintain "all men are created equal" and a time clock, it is felt, is detrimental to this belief. Some firms have ceased using time clocks for production workers and report high productivity.

Either way, working time must be documented. Records must be legible, acceptable for audit, and conform to laws. Exempt as well as wage-and-hour employees should be accounted for. All employees benefit when the method is efficient, simple, fair, impartial, and accurate.

One caution: Time clocks should never be installed as a substitute for poor supervision. If the supervisors cannot get the workers to report on time, no clocks or other system will work either. Even the best device cannot be expected to accomplish what direct supervision cannot do.

TIME AND PAY RECORDS
UNDER THE FAIR LABOR STANDARDS ACT

Employers must keep certain records about each worker who is entitled to minimum wage and overtime pay under the Fair Labor Standards Act. The law requires no particular form for the records. All it requires is that the records include certain *identifying information* about the employee and data about the *hours* he works and the *wages* he earns. And, the law says, the information must be *accurate*.

Here is a breakdown of the basic information that must be recorded:

IDENTIFYING INFORMATION:

1. Employee's full name.
2. Address.
3. Birth date, if under 19 years of age.
4. Sex and occupation in which employed.

HOURS:

1. Time of day and day of week when employee's workweek begins.
2. Hours worked each day.
3. Total hours worked each workweek.

WAGES:

1. Basis on which wages are paid (such as $1.75 an hour," "$70 a week," "piecework").
2. Regular hourly pay rate for any week when overtime is worked.
3. Amount and nature of each payment excluded from the "regular rate."
4. Total daily or weekly straighttime earnings.
5. Total overtime earnings for the workweek.
6. All additions to or deductions from the employee's wages for each pay period.
7. Total wages paid each pay period.
8. Dates of payment and of the pay period covered by the payment.

At first glance, this may seem like a lot of information to keep track of. But most of the information required by law would be kept anyway by any company that observes good business practices.

Records with somewhat different information are required for workers with uncommon pay arrangements, homeworkers, employees who are paid with board, lodging, or other facilities, and those who are exempt from the minimum wage and overtime requirements of the Fair Labor Standards Act.

WHAT ABOUT TIMEKEEPING?

The employer must keep track of the hours worked each day and workweek by every employee entitled to the minimum wage. This is true whether or not the worker also is subject to the law's overtime requirements. It is also true regardless of whether the worker is paid by the piece, the hour, week, month, or on any other basis.

But, because of the law's pay provisions, the employer must keep track of the total hours worked each workweek. That's why it's important that the employer *decide the time and day of the week when the worker's workweek starts.*

Remember, employers must keep track of work hours on a *weekly* basis, even when the workweek and the pay period don't coincide. It's easier to keep track of the total hours worked each week if records clearly separate the number of hours worked each workweek. Work hours must be totaled by the week because overtime pay is figured on the basis of the number of hours worked each week.

A daily and weekly time record must be kept whether the worker is paid by the hour, by the piece, on a salary, or by some other arrangement.

OFFICE EMPLOYEES

Many office employees are on a fixed working schedule from which they seldom vary. In these cases, the employer may keep a record showing the exact schedule of daily and weekly work hours that the worker is expected to follow and merely indicate that he did follow the schedule. When the worker is on the job for a longer or shorter time than the schedule shows, the employer should record the exact number of hours the worker actually worked.

HOW LONG SHOULD RECORDS BE RETAINED?

Keep all records containing the information required for THREE YEARS.

Keep all records on which wage and hour computations are based for TWO YEARS. Records that must be kept for two years are employment and earnings records such as time cards and piecework tickets, wage-rate tables, work-time schedules, and record of additions to and deductions from wages. Other records which must be kept for two years are order, shipping, and billing records; also records which the employer makes which explain the basis for payment of any wage difference to employees of the opposite sex in the same establishment.

All of these records always should be open for inspection by the divisions' representatives, who may request the employer to make extensions, recomputations, or transcriptions. Microfilm copies of records may be kept if the employer is willing to provide facilities for viewing them. The records may be kept at the place of employment or in a central records office.

Complete information about the Fair Labor Standards Act is available at the nearest office of the United States Labor Department's Wage and Hour and Public Contracts Divisions.

UPDATING PERSONAL DATA

At time of employment, personal data about each employee are recorded. Much of this comes from the application blank, resumé, interview results, tests, insurance application cards, and the like. Once the new employee is "processed on the payroll," the information is recorded and filed.

A file may be reviewed at a later date when an employee is up for consideration or possibly in trouble. It is surprising how many employee file folders or record cards are never looked at, except

PERSONNEL RECORD CARD

Name _____ Address _____ Phone _____

Date/hire: _____ SS# _____

D.O.B. _____ Sex: _____

Emergency Notification: _____

_____

Family

Marital status _____

Tax exemptions _____

Spouse _____ DOB _____

Spouse _____ DOB _____

Child _____ DOB _____

Child _____ DOB _____

Child _____ DOB _____

Child _____ DOB _____

Child _____ DOB _____

Termination

Date: _____ Elig. for rehire? ( ) yes ( ) no

Reason: _____

Record of Commendations & Discipline: _____

First side of a personnel record card designed by the Administrative Management Society.

Insurance Coverage

	BC/S—Hosp./Med.	Maj. Med.	Life	Disability
Effective date				
Policy number				
Amount or plan				

Life insurance beneficiary: _____

Personnel Actions

Effective Date	Position/Title	Rate	Reason for Rate Change	Schedule Rate Changes Date	New Rate

AVAILABLE FROM ADMINISTRATIVE MANAGEMENT SOCIETY, WILLOW GROVE, PA. (Minimum quantity 50) Prepared by the Management Employee Relations Committee of the Personnel Division.

Obverse side of Administration Management Society's personnel record card.

possibly to add salary or status changes to the progress card or a paper of some kind to the file folder.

The personal information is seldom, if ever, changed. It makes one wonder what value personal data may have that was obtained say 10 years ago. Surely an employee at age 30 is noticeably different from what he was when he first came out of school.

To meet the problem, some companies make an effort to keep personal data current. Probably the most common approach is to verify addresses and telephone numbers annually, or to get a statement, once a year, about whom to notify in case of emergency. But there are other things personnel offices may do to keep their employee records current and, hence, of more worth.

Changes in marital or family status may be asked for. Additional education acquired or new skills should be noted. Outside activities, particularly offices held or honors received, would certainly enhance an employee's data in the file. Depending upon the nature of the business, or the type of work force, other personal data may be updated.

This is really not too difficult when employee records are processed mechanically. Each employee may be given a print-out of his own record of personal data, with the request that if any of the recorded information is not current, he may wish to have changes or corrections made. When records are handled manually, the updating is done by contacting each employee by written memo or in person, with the same invitation to keep his record up-to-date in order to reflect him at his best.

If people change, then the records and reports about them should also be changed. Otherwise they lose some of their value as time goes on.

LIVING RECORDS

Just as in life we have too much government by law, and not enough government by men, so do we in business have too much automation, not in the machines and procedures, but in the minds of men.

The real danger is not in machines thinking like men but in men thinking like machines.

This sad state of affairs is all the more deplorable when it affects the employee program. In a materialistic age we substitute impersonal procedures for personal considerations. We worry about automation, then try to apply automation principles to human values.

In too many personnel offices the staff is concerned more with paperwork than with people. The clerks, particularly, busy themselves with records, reports, and statistics, keeping track of all sorts of information, which of itself does nothing to contribute to a better organization.

The papers and the figures on these papers are lifeless. But behind each piece of paper is a human being. Viewed in this light, each record, each posting, each statistic takes on real significance.

Any clerk who cannot recognize this distinction does not belong in the personnel office.

VERIFICATION OF AGE

Records are becoming increasingly important. But records are of value only if they are correct.

Employee records should be right. This is especially necessary when it comes to age. A certain percentage of employees will falsify their age for any of many reasons. At some later date, perhaps when retirement vested rights or income payment are at stake, one of these employees will try to have his personnel records changed to reflect a more favorable situation.

What happens when the traditional records are unavailable or unobtainable—birth certificate, baptismal record, earlier school record, etc. When attempting to establish a valid birth record, great care must be exercised in examining the supporting evidence. On a certificate of naturalization, for example, if the birth date recorded on the papers was self-serving, it cannot be accepted; if it was obtained by the court through proper legal channels, then it may be submitted as evidence.

Other evidence than an actual (not delayed) birth certificate, or a baptismal certificate, which is considered sound, is a

1. Notarized statement, by two witnesses who are older than the person involved, and who have known the person since childhood.

2. Permanent grammar school or high school records.

As a last resort, the records of the Bureau of the Census, United States Department of Commerce, may provide an answer. While it is true that the census taker is merely "told" a person's age, and asks for no proof, doesn't it seem likely that an age of 17, during a given year when there apparently was no occasion to "doctor" the birth date, could be used as reliable data for an employee now nearing retirement age?

One Billion Names!

Since its beginning in 1790 the U.S. Census has recorded identifying data for close to one billion names, including, of course, those duplicated from census to census. It has handed copies of these records back to several million of the counted, as legal proof of age, place of birth, citizenship, or kinship.

When the Founding Fathers made constitutional provision for a decennial count of the population to determine allocation of representatives in Congress, they could not have foreseen how the census would yield a by-product of such direct benefit to many of the people it would count. Requests for personal census records range from the routine—persons who realize they are without legal proof of birth or age and want to be prepared "if anything comes up," to those of desperation—citizens with plans made for a trip abroad who are suddenly faced with a no-birth-certificate, no-passport situation; old people unable to obtain needed assistance without proof of age; persons unable to claim their rightful shares of estates because of inability to prove relationship.

Regular birth certificates are not issued by the Bureau of the Census, but by the health department or similar agency in the state in which the birth occurred. However, since it was 1920 before the last state adopted compulsory birth registration, many persons born before that time did not have their births recorded. Even persons who keep orderly records—with or without governmental urging—sometimes find themselves without necessary credentials of existence. Fire and flood and fate in various other forms have a destructive way with even the best-kept records.

Assuming the birth was not registered, and that acceptable proofs, such as affidavits from the doctor or midwife who attended the birth, family Bible records, or baptismal certificate, cannot be offered for a delayed certificate, census records may be the only recourse.

Procedure Outlined

Here is the procedure:

1. Ask the Personal Census Service Branch, Bureau of the Census, Pittsburg, Kansas 66762, for an Age Search Application Form.

2. Read the instructions printed on the form, then fill it out and sign.

3. Send the completed form with remittance—$4 for a search in turn, $5 for an expedited search ahead of turn—to the Personal Census Service Branch, Bureau of the Census, Pittsburg, Kansas 66762.

The personal information in the records of the 1900 and later censuses is confidential and may be furnished only upon the written request of the person to whom it relates or, for a proper purpose, a legal representative such as guardian or administrator of estate. Employers who want this information must therefore get written permission from the employee.

FORMS

Dealing with the human element in business should be personal. Yet the administration of the personnel program involves paperwork. Despite the personal application, which is paramount, the amount of paperwork is increasing steadily.

In the area of personnel forms, here is a list of some of the more common ones already in use:

Application Blank

Employment Requisition

Induction Papers (W4, Bonding, Flower Fund, etc.)

Add-to-payroll Authorization

Termination Notice

Exit Interview

Salary Change

Promotion or Transfer

Status Changes

Job Classification Change

Change of Address and/or Telephone Number

Age Correction

Notification and Instruction pertaining to Leave of Absence or Furlough

Payroll Deduction Authorization

Telephone Reference Check

Mail Reference Inquiry

Reference Reply

Progress Record Card

Medical History

Medical Record

Performance (Merit) Rating

Performance and/or Potential Appraisal

Grievance Statement and Settlement

Warning Report

Probation Notice

Overtime Slip

Suggestion System Entry

Accident Report

Questionnaires

Meeting Announcements

Employment and Promotion Tests

Test Profile

Agreement (patent, conflict of interest, etc.)

Tuition Refund Application

Job Rating Specifications

Job Evaluation Factor Breakdown

Job Description

Insurance Application

Insurance Waiver

Insurance Claim Form

Retirement Application

Retirement Option Request

In addition there are many different report forms to be completed periodically.

Turnover

Compliance Data

Illness Absence

Fringe Benefit Costs

Manpower Inventory

Acquisition Results Study

Layoffs

Seniority Lists

Surveys and Analyses

Not all of these forms are in use in every company. On the other hand, some companies may have other forms necessary for their particular purposes. The use of forms simplifies the procedures. Imagine, for example, what might happen if employment data were not standardized on a handy application blank. At the same time, care should be taken not to become "form happy," since too much paperwork can shift the emphasis in personnel from a personal program to an impersonal system. In any personnel program the important ingredient is people, not paper.

ONE FORM FOR ALL

A personnel changes reporting form, developed for use by Blue Cross-Blue Shield, Chicago, allows reporting on one form all changes which affect an employee from the time he is added to the payroll until he is removed. It replaces sundry individual notices and memos which were previously used.

A separate form is used for each action. It is prepared in triplicate : the original is for the payroll section with instructions to change the record; the second copy is retained in the personnel office which audits and records the change; and the third copy is returned to the originator as his notification that the action has been completed.

The top third is the identification section, with space for personal items such as name, address, social security number, employee number, seniority date, job classification and grade, date the form is prepared, date action is to become effective. The middle third reports the action, such as add (or reinstate) to payroll and on what basis, change in salary, transfer or promotion within or between departments, leave of absence or furlough, and termination. Necessary supporting data and reasons are asked for. This portion is also used for reporting, under Comments, changes in address and telephone number, as well as any exceptions to policy which should be documented. The lower third is for the authentication, providing for the signatures or initials of the manager making the recommendation, the official authorized to approve it, the personnel director who checks it against policy to spare the line organization from inadvertently doing something that might not be in its best interest. The concurrence or approval of the salary review committee and/or the president, when required, are also provided for.

There are many advantages. With one form no one has to wonder about the proper form to use, or invent an acceptable one for the occasion. Those to whom the change is directed recognize only one form. The management and clerical personnel who must see it for consideration, approval, checking, and recording get it in turn since all forms follow a processing procedure which, once learned, becomes the normally accepted pattern. Distribution of copies is clearly indicated, which means information is not easily sidetracked into the wrong office. It makes filing neater and easier since all reports are

PERSONNEL CHANGE
(Fill In applicable section only)

To: **Payroll Section**

Date:_____

Effective Date:_____

NAME:_____

Soc. Sec. No.:_____

ADDRESS:_____

Emp. No.:_____

TELEPHONE:_____DEPARTMENT:_____

SENIORITY DATE:_____JOB CLASSIFICATION & GRADE:_____

_____ ADD TO PAYROLL   Salary: $_____per week $_____per hour $_____per month _____ temporary / regular

_____ TRANSFER
OR
PROMOTION   from Department_____Job Classification & Grade_____
to Department_____Job Classification & Grade_____

_____ SALARY CHANGE   from $_____to $_____ _____Automatic _____Merit _____Promotion _____Longevity
LAST INCREASE $_____ DATE OF LAST INCREASE_____

_____ LEAVE OF ABSENCE
OR
FURLOUGH   from_____to_____
Reason:_____

_____ DROP FROM PAYROLL   _____VOLUNTARY   _____INVOLUNTARY   Would you rehire _____Yes / No
Reason:_____

COMMENTS:_____

_____

_____

_____

SALARY REVIEW COMMITTEE

_____Recommended   _____Not Recommended

_____ | _____   RECOMMENDED

_____ | _____   APPROVED

_____ | _____   PRESIDENT

_____ | _____   AUDITED

_____ | DISTRIBUTION:
White — Payroll
Green — Personnel
Yellow — Division File

DATE   CHAIRMAN

a uniform 8½ by 11 inches. Since reasons and comments are required as supporting data, the frequent use of this form builds up a rather entensive file of recorded objective opinions about an employee and his performance which is available for future reference.

The form, with one-time-carbon, has received immediate acceptance and is serving its purpose well. The idea of using one composite form for all personnel changes is apparently unique. Quite a number of other companies have reviewed it and adopted it to their needs. The form is not copyrighted and there are no restrictions on its use.

REFERENCE REPLIES

Just as the personnel office sends out reference inquiries to former employers, on applicants being considered or already hired, so also does the personnel office receive reference inquiries from other companies to whom former employees may be applying for work.

These inquiries take on many forms. Some are telephone calls and an exchange of information takes place immediately. The majority are mail requests, usually form letters, in which the prospective employers ask about dates of employment, work record, outstanding good and bad traits, and the like.

Most of the time a personnel clerk tries to provide answers to questions asked, abstracting such data from the terminated employee's file. It is easy to verify or provide dates of hire and termination, nature of the work, a general comment about the work performance, last salary earned (if willing to divulge this), reasons for leaving, and whether the record is clear to permit rehire.

Some of the incoming questionnaires are anything but simple. A few are idiotic. Asking about a former employee's personal integrity, honesty, loyalty, or dependability, when the person worked as a summer temporary during a school vacation 10 years ago, for a supervisor who left long ago, is not only meaningless but downright dangerous. Such form may be beautifully designed, expensively produced, and carry the seal of approval of a superior, but it is practically worthless as a tool in the placement process. The best suggestion is to answer those questions which are routine and to ignore those which are impossible and unreasonable. It is better to give no information than to guess.

Some inquiry forms ask for information which may be interesting but of doubtful value. Certainly it is not worth the effort clerks must exert to obtain answers. A school system in a large city established a committee of school guidance counsellors and businessmen to discuss the variety of such questionnaires received by the school and to endeavor to standardize on a form which would provide useful information to companies and still be easy for schools to complete, using recorded data readily available in the administration offices. It turned out that certain questions asked previously. which conscientious school clerical personnel tried to answer, made it necessary for clerks to spend endless hours searching through the archives in the basement, only to have the businessmen who were asking the questions admit that the information didn't help them after they received it. On the other hand, there was information readily available in the offices which the companies were not asking for which would have been far more helpful.

Therefore, personnel offices have fulfilled their obligation when they reply to reference inquiries by giving only such information which is convenient, factual, and current. No inquirer has the right to ask thoughtless questions which put the company to a lot of unnecessary trouble. In those few exceptional cases, when the inquirer is checking on certain details for a specific reason (example, lawyer or FBI agent), he will find companies more than willing to cooperate.

As a protection to employees, it is advisable never to give out any confidential information without the consent of the employee. Information on salaries, for example, should not be released to mortgage houses without the employees knowing about it and authorizing it. Extreme care must be exercised in giving out any information over the telephone, unless the caller is known. When in doubt or suspicious, ask the caller for his telephone number and offer to call back. Employees of a company have the right to expect the personnel office to guard carefully the information to which they have access which is, after all, given in confidence.

CREDIT VERIFICATION

With the proliferation of charge cards, and for the purpose of establishing identity for check cashing services, or to develop a good credit rating in the community, employees are required to give their place of employment as a reference. The credit bureau where the application is made then checks with the named employer to verify certain information.

The information requested depends upon the credit agency and the extent of the risk. For check cashing purposes "verification of employment" (does the person work there?) may suffice. For a first mortgage on a new house considerably more questions are asked about length of employment, prospects of permanency, and income.

Since data is given by an applicant or worker voluntarily as part of his employment record, the information should be considered personal and treated confidentially. Discretion must be exercised as to the amount of data that can safely be divulged and to whom such information may be given.

Addresses should not be given lest this confidential information get into the wrong hands—peddlers, collection agencies, lawyers, or such people as jealous suitors, former husbands, or possibly even the crime syndicate. Keep in mind that this type of information belongs to the person and not to the company, and that the employer has no right to betray an employee and give away his information.

Sometimes the inquiry comes from a representative of the Internal Revenue Service or the FBI. Upon presentation of credentials, it is appropriate to cooperate with any reasonable request.

Offer to Call Back

Over the telephone it is easy to be trapped into revealing confidential or useful details to an unauthorized caller. If in doubt, or if this becomes a problem, make it a point not to reply directly. Ask for the caller's name, his company, and telephone number, and let him tell his reason for wanting the information. Then offer to call back. This cautious approach will cull out the nuisance requests and the unscrupulous inquirers.

Never, but never, give out confidential or personal data without first getting the approval of the employee involved. Whose business is it how much salary or bonus a man receives? If he needs to supply this information to a mortgage house, for instance, he will permit his employer to release this. But when a lawyer asks how much money a man makes, he may be trying to settle an accident claim against him. This is between the lawyer and his client, and the company has no part in the transaction. Similarly, an insurance salesman checking salary data as a procedure for underwriting a policy has no right to expect the employer to give out salary information. Collection agencies, particularly, look for any kind of assistance in forcing settlement of bad debts. But there is no reason for the employer to get mixed up in delinquent accounts which are an employee's personal problem and not related to his job.

A safe rule to follow is that the employer should work in the interests of his employees and should protect personal data which they furnished routinely and in confidence. A company expects loyalty from its employees; it should also expect to be loyal to them. The employer, however, does not owe the same consideration to strangers, many of whom undoubtedly have legitimate and reasonable requests; others, and it is difficult to distinguish the difference, may actually be conniving cleverly to use the information for their own selfish aims and against the employees.

REPORTS

What can be said about personnel reports? All personnel offices issue reports, possibly more than they realize. But there is no standard pattern that applies to all companies. Some firms are report happy, others are quite the opposite. As they used to say in the army, "It all depends on the situation and the terrain."

If the boss wants a weekly report of job openings, or involuntary terminations, or new workers hired above minimum, or whatever—he gets it. Some personnel executives send out reports as evidence that they are working. "Look how busy we've been," they say as they list all the things they did last week while they were not writing reports.

Mechanizing personnel records is conducive to the production of all sorts of reports. These might not be the most useful reports; they are often the most automatic to grind out. People to whom they are distributed find them interesting perhaps, but what do they do with them?

Some reports, of course, are very necessary. The report of an accident is part of the workman's compensation claim. Reports should be made of committee actions and decisions. Reports for control purposes, such as acquisition cost or turnover, can certainly be justified. Reports cost time and money and an attempt should be made to determine whether they serve enough of a purpose to offset their cost.

There are reports which are simply protective, which in itself is a good enough reason for their preparation. Unions make it necessary to record and publish certain activities in the employee program. Government demands reports to assure that companies comply with laws and executive orders. This area of government compliance is growing rapidly and causing increasing work.

Personnel reports are of two classifications: (1) those which are for own use, i.e., documentation, and (2) those which are sent to others for information.

Many actions in personnel administration should be recorded. These include disciplinary cases, warnings, grievances, complaints, requests, and the like.

Reports for the dissemination of information tell about training programs, wage developments, policy changes, employment trends, safety progress, and so on.

Put Them on Trial

Personnel reports, like all other reports in a company, should be put on trial occasionally. It is safe to say that many reports have outlived their usefulness and many others could well be simplified. Let me cite an example from personal experience.

For years we published a monthly turnover report in my personnel office. It showed turnover for the month and for the year by various breakdowns. Originally intended for officers, its distribution was widened steadily as more and more people asked for copies.

What began as a simple report became over the years a much more involved and complicated one as the breakdowns were refined, smaller work units identified, male and female indicated, work groups compared with one year ago, interdivisional transfers listed, temporary help first included and later excluded. Many of the other

EEKLY EXPENSE REPORT

ne_____	Week ending_____ 19____
ed_____	Territory number_____
Mail check to my regular address	
Mail check to me in care of_____	Mail check to arrive by_____

Address_____
City_____ Zone_____ State_____

	SUNDAY		MONDAY		TUESDAY		WEDNESDAY		THURSDAY		FRIDAY		SATURDAY			
KFAST																
H																
ER																
ING																
AND OIL																
ONE - TELEGRAPH																
RY																
NG																
FARE																
OAD FARE																
ARE																
LIMOUSINE																
ENTAL																
@ ¢																
AINMENT††																
ITEMIZE)																
																TOTAL WEEKLY EXPENSES ↓
TOTALS →																
S OF TRAVEL																$
OM																
																TOTAL MILEAGE ↓
MILEAGE Enter Above																

S OF ENTERTAINMENT

DICATE DAY							
MPANY							
IVIDUALS							
E							
CE							
POSE							
OD							
NKS							
ETS							
(Enter Above) →							

WORKING FUND

hand last report	$_____
from office	$_____
ance funds to date	$_____
paid this week	$_____
hand end of week	$_____

OFFICE USE ONLY

Approved by_____ 19____
                Sales Dept.   Date

Approved for
Payment_____ 19____

(See over for instructions)

809

divisions in the company were relying on the "people data" which we in personnel were providing—or so at least it appeared. The budget administrator in particular seemed to be making good use of our report and came in each month to balance the figures.

When I woke up one day to the realization that my senior personnel clerk was devoting two full days each month to the preparation of this report, I felt an evaluation was in order. Others in management apparently liked to receive the report; it made interesting reading and occasionally they could spot a discrepancy and bring it gleefully to our attention. But we discovered that the miscellaneous data that had crept into the report actually served no useful purpose, or was available from their own sources. I made up my mind that our responsibility was not to supply others with data but to observe turnover trends and locate trouble spots. So we streamlined the report to bare essential details. On one page we now show the monthly and yearly turnover percentages of the seven divisions as well as the company in total. That's all. And know what? To this day there has been nary a squawk.

When I was hired I asked my new employer what reports he wanted. I was coming from a company where everything I did in personnel had to be reported. We had reports of number of applicants per week, number of placements, turndowns, terminations, clinic visits, etc.—all broken down into detail and reasons spelled out. "Document everything—and send me a copy," was the standing order from my superior. So I was pleasantly surprised with the answer I received during that final employment interview. "Reports," said my new boss, " I don't want any reports. All I want is a favorable reaction about personnel from the other division heads."

TIME OFF REPORTS

Some personnel offices find it necessary or desirable to issue regular time off reports. Following the completion of a time interval, possibly a payroll period or calendar week or month, a report is prepared showing the extent of time off.

Depending upon its use, this report might indicate the names of the employees who were absent and the days each one was away, or it may simply be a comparison of the total amount of time off in each department.

Information of this sort is helpful since it pinpoints where the absentee problem exists. However, it is useful only if someone does something about it.

If this type of information can be published automatically by machine, it is difficult to criticize the idea. But where the data are gathered, summarized, and typed manually, it doesn't take much to question whether the value is worth the cost. Unfortunately, there are personnel offices full of clerks who spend time on such unproductive duties.

Actually it shouldn't be necessary for the personnel office to report this information to departments. The managers or supervisors ought to know which of their employees are abusing privileges. The personnel office should work with managers, not in reporting the problem, but in solving it.

AUTOMATIC DATA PROCESSING

By Philip L. Morgan
Vice-President, Personnel Data Systems
Information Science, Inc., White Plains, New York

Long gone are the days when a personnel manager could concern himself merely with the hiring and placing of employees and remain isolated from the larger problems of the organization. He then had little reason for interaction with other departments. But the personnel manager today is faced with a wide variety of situations that often cross functional lines, and he must now relate his activities to their actual or potential effect on the organization as a whole. He must make decisions involving great numbers of employees, often in different geographical locations. These decisions necessitate his having a mass of facts available—consistent, up-to-date facts that a conventional filing system simply cannot handle.

Many companies have met this demand by turning to automatic data processing of personnel data. This may sound like a simple solution, but the person assigned responsibility for the functioning of the system soon finds that he is tackling a job that involves broad concepts as well as precise technical details.

It is difficult to generalize about this subject, because each organization has its own set of problems. However, there are principles that have applied, almost without exception, to all organizations—principles which are aimed at solving problems at the operational level, and are not just one more superstructure to be installed at the top of already existing systems.

These general principles are:

1. Establish a data base that incorporates each piece of personnel information you should know about your employees.

2. Establish a single, responsible source of personnel information and eliminate any redundancy of multiple handling and storage of data.

3. Integrate all personnel data into a useful composite record and provide a simplified method of updating.

4. Establish methods of data retrieval that will allow complete accessibility to the information stored.

5. Adopt a systematic approach to personnel data handling that will convince employees that the organization's personnel policies are being applied consistently, day in and day out. Let them *see* what you are doing.

Now let's examine the basic intent of these principles.

1. *Employee Data Base.* This involves the identification of all personnel data meaningful to an organization. In a study of the records and reports of a relatively small personnel department, it was found that over 2,100 items of data were used in the everyday personnel job, but when the analysis was completed and duplicated data discarded, only 160 items or "elements" proved to be different or distinct. And of these 160 elements of data, only 110 were actually relevant to the organization. The rest were discarded and the 110 then became the data for this organization. The economics of eliminating needless duplication are often dramatic. For example, it has been found that the cost of maintaining and transacting personnel information can be reduced by $6 to $15 per employee per year—a substantial saving in a large organization.

How do you isolate the data that should be considered for your employee data base? A matrix analysis is the best technique for this kind of system or information analysis. A computerized matrix analysis especially for personnel information has been developed which considers each report and record and identifies the individual items used in that report or record. Each item is keypunched, with its item number, so that subsequent manipulation on the computer will allow all data to be considered. The result is the identification of those key items essential to the personnel-data needs of the organization, items capable of being handled on data processing equipment.

2. *Single, Responsible Source.* When you attempt to develop an answer to a particular problem or question, it is often necessary to consult many sources.

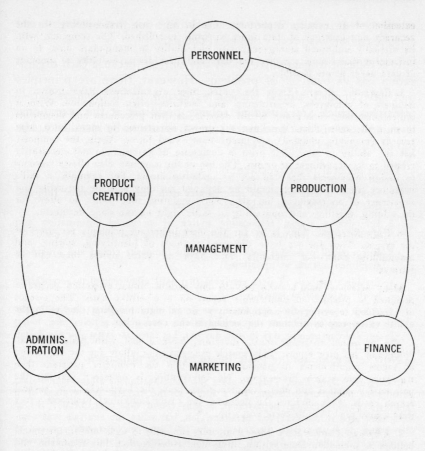

BASIC COMPANY FUNCTION CHART

For example, you may want to study the relationship between salary and age with the education level held constant. To do so, you might have to get part of the information from salary administration, part from personnel, and part from education records. You would then have to combine the data from these different areas into analyzable form. This integrating of component parts is a common problem. A similar one arises when you attempt to develop information across organizational lines, especially when various levels of staff get into the act. The difficulties lie in overlapping information and records that have not been kept up to date. And the moment you have more than one source to consult, you have, in addition, problems of communication, and even varying interpretations of the request for information. Hence the need for a single, responsible source of information.

This single source may entail the information of a new department, or the extension of an existing department, but in any case, responsibility for the accuracy and currency of data must be firmly established. The computer, with its virtually unlimited storage capacity and ability to manipulate data, is an instrument that brings together the data and provides accessibility to amounts of data never before possible.

3. *Composite Record.* Over the years, most organizations have grown in numbers of employees, departments, and facilities—often nationwide. Without central direction, each group would develop its own procedures and documents to store the same data. We have all grown accustomed to many hard copy records (manually updated) and many punch card forms. Again, the computer has the ability to store and print a composite of information not necessarily related to its department of origin. The use of the computer also allows freedom to design documents that can act as updating media. For example, a skills inventory profile document should be designed not only to show the skills and experience of an employee, but also, when updating time comes, to allow for the adding, deleting, and upgrading of skills right on the same document.

4. *Data Retrieval.* This is by far the most important principle for users of the system. Thus far we have discussed methods of identifying, storing, and maintaining data, but obviously data have no value unless they can be retrieved.

Many personnel data systems contain only specific output programs, programs designed to produce an unalterable report on a repetitive basis. The essence of personnel reporting does not, however, lie in regular reports; it lies in the ability to respond to different requestions as the need arises.

The personnel specialist must, therefore, have a tool with which he can "program" his own report. This search program must allow for the expression of report requirements in personnel terms that the computer program then translates into search instructions. No intervention is necessary between the personnel requestor and the computer other than the keypunching of several search cards. This obviates the necessity for costly individual programs every time a new report requirement crops up.

5. *Employee Participation.* Most companies subscribe to such familiar personnel policies as promotion from within, individual consideration, fair treatment, and so on. But employees know that no placement man can, by himself, keep his finger on the organization's total requirements or resources. The use of a computer, however, gives the employee the satisfaction of knowing that his skills are recorded. When he receives a copy of the record itself, he knows that his organization has a systematic approach to recording and using that data. He knows that the company has the ability to put the right man in the right job at the right time. This confirms to him that "the company cares."

Now that we have examined the general principles of the application of automatic data processing in the personnel function, we might see how these concepts can be put to work.

THE INTEGRATED PERSONNEL DATA SYSTEM

Many large companies have turned to or are interested in an integrated personnel data system. This means the integration of all information from current records into one set of computer-produced documents. Key in this system is a *Profile and Chronological Work History Record.* This is the main statistical and report-generator record which automatically adds and deletes employees on other records in the system. The computer now replaces the costly clerical updating of history cards, Cardex files, etc., with automatically updated documents in multiple copies for distribution to line managers, division heads, and personnel departments.

A Skills Inventory, which records the work experiences, work preferences, and such things as test scores, geographical preferences, and foreign languages, is a popular part of the personnel data system. This record can retrieve the minutest facts about manpower resources without overlooking the consideration of any employee, regardless of physical or geographical location.

The Resume-Education Record adds personal achievement, historical, and comprehensive education and training information to the system. Such data as family information, military data, organization memberships, precompany employment, formal and in-company education and training courses can be printed on output documents and are annually reviewed and updated by employees.

Employee Benefit Statement informs each employee of the personal value he receives from various company benefit programs.

Seniority Roster Determination provides the mechanics to automatically record and adjust seniority lists as changes of jobs and work schedules take place.

The Employment Requisition Control completes the full manpower planning cycle of the personnel data system. Using the same format of the profile record, open requisition data can be stored. The total result is head count and projection reports by company, division, location, and function which can relate to budgets and organization planning charts.

Commercial information products have been developed also. PICS (Personnel Information Communications System) allows individuals to describe their skills, experiences, and preferences in computerized form, and the data then stored on a nationwide computer network. Search parameters are established to allow companies to specify job requirements. When these parameters are entered into the computer, a high speed data reduction process quickly matches at their highest levels the skills of people to jobs. The individual receives the company job description and the company receives the individual's resume. Each, then, may use the information provided according to his interest and need. In other words, PICS creates a computerized communication link on a nationwide basis— never before possible—between individuals and employers.

All there are, of course, very sophisticated systems, and may sound far too complex and expensive for the needs of many organizations. Small companies, particularly, are inclined to shy away from the very word "computer," because to them it implies an organization large enough to support an "in-house" computer. However, the question of expense and equipment for the smaller company can be adequately answered.

PS-5000 (a personnel system for companies *with less than 5,000 employees*) is a standard personnel package of records and programs which incorporates many of the concepts discussed earlier. To overcome the expense of programming, fixed record formats are utilized, with free selection of elements or data fields, the design of the output document and the organization of the information center. The same report retrieval program exists which allows the personnel specialist to freely structure and request any combination of information he desires. The concept of PS-5000 will allow the small company essentially the same level of sophistication as the large company at a very low cost.

As for computer equipment, there are many companies—commonly called service bureaus—in the business of selling computer time to smaller organizations. Full key punch and supporting unit record equipment are usually available in these bureaus. There are banks, too, that have full-fledged computer facilities and have found the service bureau business highly profitable as a sideline.

Computer manufacturers and organizations like Western Union are also recognizing the problem of the smaller organization, and have developed the concept of time sharing. This means that a large computer with many input and output channels, rather than the conventional one input and output channel, is available in a data center. Thus, many organizations can use the same computer by processing over telephone or telegraph wires directly into and out of the data center computer.

The smaller organization, therefore, need not fear the computer as an answer to its data handling needs. When it has located the proper data processing equipment, the smaller organization can gain the advantages of a personnel data system as effectively as the larger organization.

Perhaps a brief review of "What not to do" will dispose of other doubts and spot some common pitfalls in undertaking a personnel data system. Plain common sense will avoid most of them; nonetheless, here are a few points to keep in mind:

1. Don't consider the personnel data system a part-time project, to get attention only when nothing else is pressing. Its effectiveness will depend on its priority. Inadequate staffing and direction from the top will almost inevitably bring failure.

2. Don't think the personnel data system can operate in a vacuum; it affects the entire personnel organization. Each personnel department head must recognize that his data requirements are part of a larger whole, and that he must contribute to and cooperate with the other components of that larger whole.

3. Don't expect your systems or programming departments to lead the way. Personnel must provide the leadership for the project; this is the only reasonable way to insure a personnel-oriented system.

4. Avoid piecemeal approaches, each by a different department. Such an approach produces the situation described earlier—many different records containing redundant and unreliable information. Overall direction aiming at the accomplishment of the objectives must be established; all activity undertaken must be contained within that predetermined framework.

The computer, carefully controlled, can be an excellent tool, one that truly frees personnel people from the necessity of performing many dreary clerical tasks. Do not, however, lose sight of the fact that the sophisticated computer system is not an end in itself. It is only the means to an end: accomplishment of the personnel function more efficiently and productively, and extending its service to the rest of the organization.

COMPUTER-BASED PERSONNEL MANAGEMENT

By Robert E. Anderson

Director of Administrative Services

Honeywell EDP, Wellesley, Massachusetts

In discussing the design and implementation of personnel management systems we should first look at our company goals and objectives, since the principal purpose of the personnel function is to support the company's line management in their efforts to achieve the company objectives. Computer-based systems are one of several tools which can be used by personnel in carrying out their mission of supporting company objectives. Any serious effort in information system development should answer the question of how well it will support company goals before a major commitment to proceed is made.

Freedom and imagination must guide the decision process of selecting an area for computerization. The "old way" of doing things is not necessarily a healthy or acceptable way under today's changing conditions. We are not interested in just doing the old things faster, but are interested in achieving higher levels of more effective support to the company. A successful computer system is one that contributes to improved performance of the area which it services. While the voluminous daily flow of data should be handled more effectively and efficiently, profitability will stem from thoughtful analysis of summarized information which is produced as a by-product of the daily flow.

Education and Understanding

The computer, as a tool, should be a catalyst to stimulate improved methods and approaches to daily problems. Since the computer is a tool that has unique characteristics, and consequently potential, it is essential that the people utilizing this tool experience an education process to equip them to effectively harness the tremendous capability. This education and understanding process takes time and effort. A critically important consideration is that personnel management and supervisory staffs actively participate in the design of the overall business information system of which the computer represents one portion. Only through this participation and experience will come adequate understanding of the following principles:

The term *business information system* includes all of the processing and data handling activity concerned with a given flow of information. The business information system *always includes manual systems* and procedures and *sometimes computerized systems* to handle the information flow. The computer system is always bracketed on the incoming and outgoing side by some type of manual system and procedures. The computer system itself manipulates data and converts it into information through various types of processing. The computer system, however, never makes a profit. The profit comes from supervisory and management people analyzing and acting on computer output. This analyzing and action occurs in the area covered by manual systems. The computer system is a very talented middleman, but is limited to its effectiveness by what happens in the information flow before and after. A brilliantly conceived computer system placed abruptly into an environment which has not been modified to work with this system and whose personnel are not trained to utilize the output will not produce anything of real value and will generally have negative consequences.

INGREDIENTS FOR A SUCCESSFUL SYSTEM

The business system then is what is important. The computer system is one of the components. It is significant but not more important than the overall business system as a whole. A balance must be achieved wherein the manual portions and the computer portions are in reasonable balance, where there is participation by the using group in the design of the business system, where there is adequate training and documentation, new procedures are developed, and where a close cooperation and joint effort exists between the computer people and the operating department personnel.

Successful use of computer data processing systems then go back to these principal ingredients:

1. Management support from personnel and other line areas.
2. A good *business systems* approach.
3. An effective manual system design and followup.
4. Effective computer system design and implementation.
5. Followup on *validity* of files and output by personnel.
6. Effective training of all individuals concerned.

INFORMATION SYSTEM PHILOSOPHY

Because the effectiveness of any information system is limited primarily by the skill, training, and knowledge of the people involved, we must recognize that progress and profitability is limited primarily by the level of understanding of supervisory and management staffs. This people limitation fact must be recognized and acknowledged and considerable effect devoted into converting the principal limiting factor into one of considerable strength. Our philosophy for information systems must be evolutionary and be consistent with the needs and capabilities of our own organization. Our information system philosophy should also focus attention on the goals to be accomplished rather than on the specific tools to be used. We should adopt a comprehensive and natural information system philosophy which includes:

1. Sophisticated computer-based management information systems.
2. Computer-based data processing systems.
3. Manual systems and procedures.
4. Continuous people-oriented education.

The results of our efforts should be improved profit and more effective information processing. Improved profit will come from a stronger management capability. This capability will come from improved decisions based on more factual and quantitative information as well as a broader understanding from each manager of how his activities relate to the overall accomplishment of company objectives.

Company profit is directly related to the quality of management decisions at all levels. More effective information processing means getting the proper information to the people concerned on time. It also means reducing operating costs and information processing costs. Significant improvements come from reducing the time required to find desired information and to verify that it is current and valid.

IMPLEMENTATION GUIDELINES

In implementing advanced personnel information systems we are really attempting to achieve coordinated communications. This means speeding up the information flow by streamlining the processing and by making information available to those who have a need to know. The following guidelines will be helpful in undertaking the implementation stages. They are:

1. *Functionally Oriented System Design*

The design of each major segment of the total personnel system should be developed along the natural functional information flows. The normal tendency is to develop systems along organizational lines. This is very shortsighted in that the organizational structure is dependent upon the relative strengths of personalities at a given point in time. The organizational structure in most companies changes quite regularly. By orienting the system along the natural information flows there will be greater efficiency and effectiveness. Any system after being designed along functional lines may be implemented in segments. The size of each segment may be dictated by organizational lines of authority. Again a balance is called for.

2. *Balance Between Man and Machine*

There should be an effective and practical balance between the human side of a system and the automated side. To optimize a computer system at the expense of the human activity in events preceding and following the computer system is a mistake to be avoided. The best capabilities of man and machine should be utilized in balance. A highly sophisticated machine system is a waste of time unless the people using the system have a similar level of understanding and sophistication. In the same sense a simple system for sophisticated people is also inappropriate; therefore, each piece must be in balance with other elements in order to be effective.

3. *Phased Growth*

Each of the principal elements (management capability, system design, and hardware techniques) must all evolve progressively and in stages. These stages may be small or large depending upon the situation. The particular characteristics of each situation will dictate the rate of progress through each level of sophistication.

4. *Flexibility*

In the age in which we live, flexibility is a vital consideration. Mergers, acquisitions, etc. can change the situation quickly. A personnel system is doomed to a short life unless it has the built-in capability to be changed and modified. This flexibility may initially appear to be more costly. In reality, however, the inability to change or adapt to a new situation is far more costly than a small increase in daily operating costs.

5. *Early Data Capture*

We must progress in recording and capturing data as close to the time it is originally created as is practical. This should improve accuracy and integrity and allow faster processing cycles. Maximum automation should be striven for in this area. This includes eliminating the keypunch bottleneck.

6. *Higher Data Integrity and Lower Costs*

By looking at the full information-processing cycle and by balancing machine elements with human elements and by following natural functional flows, a net reduction in information costs will result. By achieving a lower net cost, the utilization of information should increase, thereby achieving a greater benefit to the company. The information will be used to a greater extent as the integrity is improved. The integrity of information will be improved by earlier, more accurate, and automatic recording of data. Thus the real benefits come from information being utilized. This utilization will be achieved when personnel managers have the confidence in the integrity of information and the understanding of how to use the information.

7. *Advanced Personnel Management Information*

This implies producing fewer reports containing less information but increasing the significance of the information and correlating significant information from several areas so that an accurate, broad picture is presented. This applies to all levels including various line supervisors and the senior personnel executive.

How to Get from Here to There

We obviously cannot get from where we are to the ultimate in advanced systems with one fell swoop. We have neither the capability, resources or the precise definition of our needs to make the magic move by putting on seven-league boots. Since the principal limiting factor is the ability of the managers and supervisors concerned to define their specific needs and to understand how to use more advanced and more sophisticated information systems, we must proceed in such a manner as to allow them time to gradually acquire a comprehension and increased capability. We must proceed then in stages. There is a definite pattern to these stages which has been proven by experience several times over. This pattern, however, must be tailored and adapted to the specific needs of your own individual situation. The best precise course of action for one company is not in keeping with the best interest of another company unless their situations are exactly identical.

The stages start off with establishing a clear understanding of what you are trying to accomplish in general terms and then progressing from fairly simple and easy to manage steps into progressively more complex and difficult areas of activity. Once you accept the premise that there is a learning activity which must precede any serious, long-term gain, then you can accept taking a relatively simple, unsophisticated, and easy series of steps initially. You will need to make some early gains at a fairly low cost in order to prove the validity of your concepts and to enlist support for the expenditures of both money and effort which must be made to accomplish the long term goal.

Stage 1. First draw up fairly quickly and briefly an overall functional chart which depicts the entire organization and its major functional components. A highly simplified and general diagram representing this would show the management of the company in the middle, surrounded by the three principal functions of *creating* or designing a product, *producing* it, and *selling* it. These three primary functions all exist to accomplish the goals of the company management. Each of these areas communicate with one another and also with the management of the company. Supporting these three principal line functions we find the personnel function, administration function, and finance function.

At this point we can take the personnel function, after we understand how it relates to the rest of the organization, and go into a more detailed functional study of the personnel area. Another simplified diagram would show the three principal personnel-function elements being the employment function, the wage and salary administration function, and the recordkeeping and benefit function. These all communicate with one another and also into the central or management area, which will include the policy-making area and research and compensation development activities. On an outer circle the areas being serviced are the hourly employees, the nonexempt salaried employees, and the exempt (executive, administrative, and professional) employees.

At this point, with specific details being spelled out in your own situation, it would be fairly easy to spot significant areas and establish a priority list. It may be that the employment of hourly personnel is a major activity with one company whereas in another the salary administration or professional personnel might be much more critical. Each personnel executive must decide, on the merits of his own situation, what his order of priority is. He now has the necessary framework established from which to start making decisions on new personnel-management-system implementation efforts, and he and his people also have a guide or a frame of reference to constantly go back to in the design of a specific subsystem.

Stage 2. In this stage you actually get into the implementation area. A key here is to take something fairly simple for the first attempt. This would be considered more or less a pilot project. One fairly obvious pilot project, and one that is overlooked by many companies, is the area of compensation analysis and research. If there is an existing automated payroll system you may find to your surprise that by merely expanding the current payroll system with the addition of a few codes for each person that a significant amount of analysis

THE DARTNELL PERSONNEL DIRECTOR'S HANDBOOK

may be performed in the compensation research areas. This quite often has the potential of producing significant results for a fairly small investment. From the experience gained in utilizing an existing system as a starting point, you then build up the confidence and the capability of proceeding into original areas. This initial stage should be considered one of basic training and education.

Stage 3. You are now ready to proceed in earnest. A more detailed functionally oriented design will be created, and then you will start in on a completely new approach to some area which has been selected as being of high importance to you. The detailed design of this area will be influenced by the broad functional approach originally taken. The current project may still represent a somewhat restricted activity in that only a portion of an important function may be worth computerizing at a given point in time. It is important to point out here that not all systems should be computerized, and even if they were, we will find out that every business information system has both manual system components and computer system components. The area selected at this time should be worth the effort required and be something within the resource capability of your group. As one major area is completed, other basic data processing activities can be undertaken in related functions. Each one of these basic systems is adding to a data base for later use by more analytical and research oriented activities.

Stage 4. Now with some systems in operation, with confidence built up, and with better overall understanding, work can begin on improving the output of the existing systems. Here we would institute exception reports instead of the voluminous reports currently employed. We would begin finding ways to manipulate the data base established by the Stage 3 systems to produce analytical reports. Here we really start getting into management-oriented information.

The payoff from this activity comes, of course, from the *analysis* by *management* of the reports which are produced by the new system. We are at this point raising the level of sophistication and the complexity of our projects and are beginning to influence management decisions. Another activity at this stage probably would include better and more automatic means of data collection and data gathering. This will help speed up the overall system flow and reduce errors.

Stage 5. By this time we would begin linking across the various systems which have been developed and integrating information from these various systems. This could mean interconnecting information from several companies into a corporate headquarters or it could mean, on a local level, the integration of information from the several data bases established into more comprehensive overall higher level management reports for the particular company concerned. At this point also, there can be much more done in the way of simulation and operations research.

In summary, at this point, I am saying that you should think big but start small. You should have your eyes on the stars but your feet on the ground. You should act with confidence and independence on a knowledge of your own situation. You should recognize that your company's priorities are not necessarily the same as your neighbors' or competitors'. If you think first and use a realistic and systematic approach, I am sure the benefits will be well worthwhile.

In planning and implementing a broad approach to personnel, management information system, I believe that asking the following questions will help you arrive at a sound course of action for your individual situation. These questions are:

1. What system areas are economical to computerize, provide a payoff, and *when* is the proper time?
2. In considering advancing the level of sophistication in a functional area, can related areas match the new pace of sophistication?
3. Where are you starting from? What is your present stage of development?
4. Which areas require improved and advanced management and analytical information first?
5. In which area are your people and the management whom you're serving flexible and adaptable at all levels?
6. What are your resources?

In short, balance your desires with your capabilities.

HONEYWELL EDP APPROACH

A brief review here of the steps taken at the EDP Division of Honeywell may help clarify the preceding points.

Stage 1. At first there were no automated systems supporting the personnel activities. A very rough generalized plan was drawn up initially. This plan was modified several times over in the course of the ensuing years. This is typical since your method of implementation will change from the original plan as the circumstances and relative priorities change within your business.

Stage 2. An early critical area was the recruiting of professional employees as the EDP Division started to grow. The first computerized application was a very simple and inexpensive system designed to keep track of various applicants at the professional level. This inexpensive system was an excellent learning vehicle and provided the stimulant to develop further plans. It provided immediate assistance in keeping track of professional applicants and materially aided the recruiting efforts.

Stage 3. The prospect system was expanded to handle weekly employees and additional features were added to it. As the labor market tightened up, another system in the employment area was added. This was the CASTOR system, developed to help improve and control the college recruiting activities. Another effort undertaken at this time was the beginning phase of an employee information system where basic information on each employee was recorded on tape and manipulated by a simple processing system. Compensation research started to use this information as soon as it was available and provided valuable information in revamping the compensation structure within Honeywell EDP.

Stage 4. During this stage further sophistications were added. A major step forward was the combining of the payroll processing runs and adding it on to the existing employee information data base. This produced one complete file containing all significant information about employees including up-to-date payroll information. This was a major increase in the breadth and level of sophistication of the EIS System. This also allowed the wage and salary administration people to start using the output of this system, and in addition, improve the analytical capability of compensation research. Further reports were added for compensation research due to the improved information base now available.

Stage 5. This phase is still underway. Accomplishments so far have been to further improve the reports emanating from the employee information system. This represents a third level of sophistication. In addition, this data base is being manipulated to provide, on short notice, specialized reports directly into a corporate level employee information system. The basic design criteria for both the corporate system and the EDP Division system are essentially the same. The individual systems vary in their implementation to a great degree; however, the basic compatability of key data elements allow the transmission of up-to-date and complete employee information for a variety of purposes to corporate with relative ease and with much greater speed.

COMMUNITY RELATIONS

In many companies, especially the small or medium sized ones, community relations comes under the personnel director. Since he deals with the community in surveys and information exchanges, he is a logical company representative for other community relations activities.

He keeps in close contact with the schools for the referral of graduates. This relationship can easily overflow to the extent that he may be expected to cooperate with the schools on committees, dedications, honor assemblies, and other programs. He may serve on boards or be a speaker before classes.

By participating in surveys he becomes familiar with other firms and acquainted with their key personnel. He should join a trade association or service club to gain access to other companies. This could well lead him to an active membership involving work for the association which, of course, broadens his connections.

More than likely he is the company chairman in community money raising campaigns such as the United Fund. He may also be the executive selected to receive awards that are granted to the company for outstanding service. The nature of his work makes him a logical choice to work beyond the company on behalf of the company.

This does not mean that others in the company should not participate in community work. They should, in fact, be encouraged to do so. Members of the sales force should join the local service group to expand their contacts. The specialists, such as the EDP staff, accountants, statisticians, and professional people, should be the proper individuals to represent the firm by memberships in trade associations in their particular field. But here again, the personnel officer may be the likely choice for coordinating all these outside activities.

With the personnel director playing a leading role in community relations, both as a participant and a coordinator, it may be that the job of public relations may also fall to him. He knows what is going on in the company, and he is known in the community. If he is good with words, as he ought to be, the job of public relations could well be his.

The size of the company, its relation to community life, the nature of the business, all have a bearing on the extent and depth of the community relations program. The ability and willingness of the personnel director determine whether or not he directs the activity. In many situations he is the logical choice.

INDUSTRIAL SECURITY

The employee handbook of the Fort Worth division of General Dynamics Corporation contains the following guide to plant security:

ESPIONAGE AND SUBVERSION

Today we face a powerful enemy whose avowed purpose is world domination. Espionage and subversion are among his primary weapons. Much of his technological advancement has been accomplished through information obtained by his espionage and intelligence apparatus.

General Dynamics is a primary target of the enemy because of the weapons we produce and the information we possess.

Your security responsibilities are real. In each of us has been placed a trust which is vital to the defense of our nation, our people, our way of life. We must not, through ignorance, negligence, or carelessness betray that trust.

The Fort Worth Division of General Dynamics, as a contractor to the Department of Defense, is contractually, legally, and morally obligated to comply with those government regulations and laws which protect our nation's defense secrets. We, the company, have entered into a security agreement with the government. This security agreement is a basic and legal part of each of our contracts with the government and constitutes a vital contractual obligation.

The Industrial Security Department is responsible for guarding and protecting the premises, personnel, equipment and products, and for ensuring the observance of government and our security rules and regulations.

Industrial Security is responsible for the overall jurisdiction and coordination of security matters.

Your supervisor is responsible for assuring adherence to, and maintaining compliance with, all security rules and regulations applicable to employees and areas under his jurisdiction.

Your cooperation in all matters pertaining to security is essential to an effective security program which will protect General Dynamics, you, your job, and the security interests of our country.

You are responsible as an individual for protecting and safeguarding classified information at all times, both on and off the job. This responsibility continues in the event your employment with General Dynamics is terminated. Unauthorized disclosure or failure to properly safeguard classified information is punishable under federal law.

Violation of security regulations is cause for disciplinary action and discharge and under government clearance criteria is cause for denial or revocation of security clearance.

Remember—each individual is responsible for safeguarding at all times the classified information in his possession.

Knowledge of the following incidents must be immediately reported to your supervisor or the Industrial Security Department:

1. Any act of sabotage or possible sabotage (do not tamper with the evidence).
2. Any act of espionage or attempted espionage.
3. Any subversive or suspicious activity.
4. Any violation or infraction of government or company security regulations.
5. Any unauthorized or suspicious activity.
6. Any loss or subjection to compromise of classified information.
7. Any disclosure of classified information to an unauthorized person.
8. Embezzlement of government property.

GENERAL DYNAMICS PRIVATE AND PROPRIETARY INFORMATION

Private Information is defined as General Dynamics records, data, information, documents, etc., not involving classified military information, which requires controlled distribution and access. This category includes, but is not limited to, wage and salary lists, inter- and intradivision records of major contractual negotiations and commitments, cost figures, etc.

Proprietary Information is defined as General Dynamics trade secrets, "know how" data, or designs developed and/or valued by the company, but not covered by a patent. Since such information does not have the legal protection afforded by a patent, it must be withheld from public knowledge in order to remain valid proprietary information.

Industrial Espionage, which is sometimes called competitive intelligence, is usually motivated by competition or individual personal gain.

The loss of private or proprietary information can be very costly, can result in the loss of important contracts, earnings, and employee jobs, and has in some cases put a company out of business.

You are responsible as an individual for protecting and safeguarding General Dynamics private or proprietary information at all times, both on and off the job.

Examine your own habits and:

> Observe all regulations for protecting and safeguarding information designated as General Dynamics private or proprietary information.
>
> Don't, without prior authorization, reveal General Dynamics private or proprietary information to fellow employees, vendors, suppliers, subcontractors, or other business associates.
>
> Don't discuss company business with family or friends.
>
> Don't discuss company business in public places.
>
> Don't brag or be a "blabbermouth."
>
> Knowledge of the unauthorized disclosure of General Dynamics private or proprietary information must be immediately reported to your supervisor or the Industrial Security Department.

THEFT OF GOVERNMENT, COMPANY, OR PERSONAL PROPERTY

At Fort Worth Division, theft of government, company, or personal property is cause for immediate termination and for prosecution under the law.

Vigilance on your part in reporting acts of theft, pilferage, or embezzlement and your assistance in bringing thieves to the attention of the Industrial Security Department is a sure way of reducing personal losses and losses to your company. Neither you nor your company can afford such losses.

BADGES AND IDENTIFICATION CARDS

Badges and identification cards are issued to all employees at the time of employment. Badges must be worn on the upper left quarter of the body in plain view when entering the plant and at all times while in the plant. Identification cards must be exhibited to guards on duty upon entering the plant. An employee is required to submit his identification for inspection at any time when requested to do so by any member of the Industrial Security Department or by any supervisor.

If you report to work without your badge, you can obtain a temporary badge by asking the industrial security officer at the gate to issue you one before entering the plant. If you report to work without your identification card, you may obtain a temporary pass from the identification office.

A temporary badge or temporary identification card may be issued for three consecutive days, after which you must secure a new regular badge or a new regular card from the identification office. A charge will be made for the replacement of either one.

Badges and identification cards are to be used only by the employee to whom they were issued. If either is lost or mutilated, report it to industrial security immediately. A charge will be made for the replacement of either. If you later find your old badge or identification card, return it to the identification office, and you will be refunded the amount of money you paid for replacement.

All badges and identification cards issued to you must be returned upon request and upon termination of employment.

SEARCH

Industrial Security Department personnel will at such times as are deemed appropriate, and on a reasonable basis, conduct checks of employees' personal property while they or their property are on company premises. The primary purpose of such checks is to protect government material, data, equipment, and property, entrusted to the company. Such checks also provide internal and external protection of the facility against sabotage, espionage, and natural hazards.

PASSES

Employee Gate Pass. The employee attendance cards serve as "gate passes' for hourly employees. If you must leave the plant during your working hours (for reasons other than illness or injury), obtain permission from your supervisor, "punch" your attendance card, and present it to the security guard stationed at the gate through which you leave. If you return during the same shift, pick up your card from the guard and "punch in" in your department.

If you are sent out of the plant on company business you will follow the above procedure, except that your supervisor will sign your attendance card before you leave your department.

Salaried employees are required to sign in and out only on certain days in accord with audit requirements.

Medical Pass-Badge. If you become ill while at work, report to your supervisor or to the nearest first aid station. You will be treated by the nurse on duty or sent to the plant hospital. If it appears advisable for you to leave the plant you will be issued a medical pass-badge. Show the pass-badge to the guard at the gate. This procedure applies both to hourly and salaried employes.

Material Pass. When you want to remove any of your personal property from the premises, your supervisor will issue you a material pass. A material pass is also needed when you remove certain items from the plant in connection with company business.

You do not need a material pass to remove personal clothing, lunch boxes, thermos bottles, magazines, purses, and books which are your personal property. Security regulations require that you offer the above materials for inspection by the guard at the gate when you leave.

Educational Pass. An educational pass is used by employees who carry unclassified educational materials in and out of the plant for a specified period of time. Stationery, notebooks, folders, reference books, textbooks, manuals, etc., may be covered by the pass in general, but such items as slide rules, compasses, and other training aids must be itemized.

The Educational Services Section issues educational passes, as required, to employees attending in-plant classes. Present the pass to the security guard at the gate when you leave and permit him to see the material if he requests you to do so.

Books stamped "FOR TRAINING PURPOSES ONLY—O.K. TO TAKE OUT OF PLANT" and public library publications can be removed without an educational pass.

Books that have been issued by one of the division libraries on a tool slip may be removed by presenting the signed slip to the guard.

Keys

All keys and locks for securing General Dynamics property and equipment are issued and controlled by the Industrial Security Department. You are responsible for any keys or locks issued to you. DO NOT LEND OR DUPLICATE ANY KEY ISSUED TO YOU. Personal locks are not permitted on company equipment. If you lose a key, notify your supervisor immediately.

Fire Prevention and Regulations

Fire regulations are enforced to protect life and property. These regulations will be explained to you by your supervisor.

Knowing what to do in an emergency may help save lives and jobs. If you discover fire, detect smoke or an unusual odor, call the fire department immediately.

Always notify the fire department first before attempting to extinguish the fire yourself.

Learn the location and operation of the nearest fire alarm box and fire extinguisher in your work area. When you use an alarm box, remain at the box until the arrival of the firemen in order to direct them to the fire.

If you use the telephone, be sure you give the proper location of the fire or emergency by stating building number and the column or room number.

For the safety of yourself and others, learn the fire hazards common to your work area. Also, you should learn the best way to prevent fires and the best way to extinguish them.

Be sure your matches, cigarettes, and cigar stubs are out before throwing them away. Put them in ash trays or butt containers only.

Do not smoke in restricted areas marked "NO SMOKING." Strictly observe all smoking regulations.

Wooden "kitchen" type matches, or "strike anywhere" matches of any type and some types of mechanical lighters are dangerous and must not be brought into the plant.

Use only safety type containers for flammable solvents.

Oily or solvent soaked rags must be placed in provided approved safety containers. Do not leave waste materials on floor, benches, etc.

Keep areas in front of fire extinguishers, fire hoses, and fire doors clear at all times. Do not block or congest fire exits or lanes.

Report any fire hazards to your supervisor immediately.

EMPLOYEES IN POLITICS

Believing that everyone has a stake in politics, Humble Oil & Refining Company, Houston, Texas, encourages employees to be active in public affairs. The emphasis has been placed largely upon registering, voting, and local party participation, according to George A. Lloyd of Humble's public relations department, who administers the program.

During the years the program has been in effect, more than 500 employees have held appointive and elective public offices. These offices ranged from precinct committeeman to membership in the state legislature. Most of these activities have been conducted on the employee's own time; only two leaves of absence have been necessary for employees who were elected to serve in their state legislatures.

The company publicizes its policy, and examples of it in action are written up in house organs, *Humble News* and *The Humble Way*. The official company policy, "Employee Participation in Public Affairs" is as follows:

Our company believes in the participation by all citizens in local, state and national political affairs. In order to encourage such participation by Humble employees, the following company policy relative thereto has been adopted:

1. An employee engaging in political activity does so as a private citizen and not as a representative of the company. The company will not discriminate against an employee because of his identification with any lawful political party or activity.

2. The company considers that qualifying oneself to vote (by registration or payment of poll tax), voting, serving in civic bodies and keeping informed on political matters are all highly important rights and responsibilities of the citizens of a democracy and therefore are to be encouraged. The right of an individual to contribute financially to the party or candidate of his choice is an important element of our political system. Campaigning for public office and the holding of such office by employees are also recognized as being a part of their rights as citizens, although they may be instances when the position of the company and the individual employee with relation to a particular office is such that the exercise of these rights might not be advisable.

3. An employee should consult with his supervisor before making himself available for public office, the holding of which might detract from his ability to perform his work assignments.

4. In many cases an employee seeking public office or participating in political party activities will be able to carry out such activity without interfering with his job responsibilities. If, however, this is not possible, he must request the appropriate regular leave of absence.

5. If an employee is elected or appointed to a public office which will demand all or a substantial part of his productive time over an extended period, or which will otherwise substantially detract from his ability to perform his company assignments, or which may create a conflict of interest which

could be eliminated by a special leave of absence, the company may grant the employee a special leave of absence without pay. Such a special leave of absence will not normally exceed two years. This leave may be extended at the company's discretion on request by the employee.

6. The policy set forth is applicable to all employees of the company in the United States, whether they are covered or exempt under the Fair Labor Standards Act.

The company is also interested in Public Affairs Council, the Effective Citizens Organization, of which it is a corporate member along with some 300 leading U.S. companies. The Public Affairs Council initiated the national movement encouraging business people to take a personal interest and participate actively in a political party and serves as a national clearinghouse.

A statement about "ECO and the Public Affairs Movement" follows:

The Effective Citizens Organization was founded in 1954, initiating the national movement to encourage business people to become active participants in the party of their choice. Realizing that our kind of government cannot survive if many of our most able leaders sit on the sidelines, the business community accepted this public affairs concept—in the establishment of over 500 corporate public affairs programs.

The typical corporate public affairs program has these essential elements: (1) A statement of corporate policy encouraging the employees to participate in politics; (2) political and/or economic education courses for the employees; (3) communication with the employees on issues which directly or indirectly affect either the company's or the employee's well-being; and (4) a designated public affairs officer, who is charged with the responsibility for the conduct of the program.

ECO—and the public affairs movement—have grown up. Public Affairs Council will continue the missionary work which created this great awakening to citizenship responsibility; as well as constantly expanding research and counseling service to the men who conduct established public affairs programs.

GOOD CITIZENSHIP

The following is taken from the employee handbook of Motorola, Inc.:

"Good citizenship is important to your country, to you and to Motorola. Among Motorolans you will find mayors, town and county board members and many others holding important offices in their communities.

"Motorola encourages its people to get into community and political activities. Through the Political Science Club, Motorola people receive guidance and are stimulated to undertake greater civic responsibilities."

OPEN HOUSE

There are many benefits to be derived from an open house. But to get any good out of one, it must be carefully planned and executed.

A booklet on open house programs, put out by Northern Trust Company, covers some points which might be considered:

In order to have a successful open house, you must plan every step in detail. Set up committees to work on various phases and appoint a coordinator to keep a close watch on the overall picture. And start early—time slips by quickly.

First block out the broad theme of your celebration, then refine your outline. Remember, close attention to details can make the difference between a smoothly run open house and utter confusion.

If there are outside suppliers to be engaged, such as florists, photographers, caterers, display designers, etc., make arrangements early.

And if you plan to give mementos to those who attend, order the gifts early and make sure they arrive on time.

Printing of tickets, invitations and souvenir brochures should be arranged far in advance.

Reasons for conducting an open house include opening a new building, observing an anniversary, and cooperating in a civic endeavor.

The purposes can be many: to introduce new facilities, recruiting aid, employee morale, get-acquainted between families and company officers, pride in company and jobs, product announcement, demonstrations, community relations.

The best time seems to be late spring or early summer when weather is good and people are in a visiting mood. The most popular hours seem to be nonworking time, such as Sunday afternoon; otherwise after hours—late afternoon or evening.

The question of whom to invite depends upon the occasion:

Employees' families and friends.   Customers.

Retirees.   Suppliers.

Board members.   Students and teachers.

Shareholders.   Neighborhood people.

Service organizations and trade associations.

The guests may be invited through the employee house organ, bulletin board announcements, public address system, paid advertisements in local newspapers, radio and television spot announcements, newspaper stories, mailing inserts with invoices and checks.

Guest tickets can be used to get an even flow of traffic by specifying different hours. They can also be used to get messages across, such as "Smoking in cafeteria only," or "Sorry, no cameras." Return coupons will indicate the amount of activity to plan for.

Many things are "musts" in the planning of such an ambitious undertaking:

Greeters or reception committee.

Commemorative program, with floor plan and directions.

Tour guides or hostesses wearing name badges.

Route markers on floors and walls.

Identification signs.

Ribbon-rope for "off limits" areas.

Handout circulars with appropriate "welcome" message.

Equipment demonstrators.

Parking (mechanic to help with flat tires or motor trouble).

Buses for transportation from parking lot if distance is great.

Guards or police protection.

First-aid room with registered nurse in attendance.

Rest rooms clearly marked, and lounges.

Souvenirs (playing cards w/ building picture, sample of product).

Refreshments—coffee, milk, tea, cokes, finger sandwiches, ice cream, cookies, hot dogs, etc. (if served outdoors, make provision in case of rain).

Other items that might be included in the planning:

Flowers for decoration.

Corsages for hostesses.

Music (organ, strollers, or piped-in Muzak).

Guest book.

Pictures (by company or press photographer).

Press coverage (prepare a press kit).

Entertainment (clown for kids).

Movies, especially about company product or service.

Door prize drawings.

In-receiving line at entrance.

Out-receiving line at exits.

A few final reminders. Give the entire plant and office a thorough house-cleaning. Have the parking lot swept down. The premises should get the "white glove" inspection (a la Army).

Arrange to have a dry run. Experiment a time or two in advance.

Plan to pay people overtime for all hours beyond their regular work schedule.

Keep the United States flag flying all day.

HOW TO SELECT AND USE CONSULTANTS

By John Elliott,
Vice-President—Behavioral Sciences,
Fry Consultants, Inc.
Chicago, Illinois

Written especially as an objective treatise for this handbook.

Management consulting is a necessary and logical service that is only limited by the lack of understanding of today's managers about the functions that a consultant can perform, when and how to select a consultant, how to make best use of the consultant once he is called in, and how to properly implement and evaluate the work of the consultant. It is the purpose of this article to help clear the air on these points, and to help bridge the gap between the needs of management and the services of the consultant.

Practically everybody in industry has an opinion as to the relative worth or lack of it of management consultants. Stories abound as to how a particular consultant lifted a company off the ground when it was on the verge of failure. Other stories are not quite so complimentary. However, when these same storytellers are asked what they mean by "management consulting," the words do not flow quite so easily.

What actually is meant by the term management consulting? According to the Association of Consulting Management Engineers, management consulting is a "professional service performed by specially trained and experienced persons in helping managers of various kinds of enterprises solve managerial problems and maximize economic opportunities by systematic analysis of facts and the application of objective judgment based on specialized knowledge, skills, and techniques."

The principal task of management consultants is to assemble specialized skills for once-in-a-while problems. Management consultants help managers diagnose problems concerning goals, objectives, strategy, organization, operation, etc. Consultants also make recommendations that provide optimum solution to the aforementioned problems and help implement their recommendations when necessary. Management consulting consists of combining managerial, functional, and specialist knowledge into an economic package of expertise and quality, to provide modern management with a competent and objective service.

Profession and Industry

Management consulting is a profession, but it is also an industry. As a matter of fact, management consulting is a 750 million dollar industry comprising about 2,600 firms with some 25,000 employees. Those employed by large consulting firms include industrial psychologists, business school graduates, engineers, economists, mathematicians, public administration experts, lawyers, physical scientists, and accountants. Consultants stress a team approach to management problems. Consulting services include general management, finance and accounting, marketing, engineering, manufacturing, personnel, management of research and development, scientific and technical research, and office and clerical work.

The types of problems faced by management consultants are quite varied. In the area of general management, the problems include those of long-range planning and organization planning and structure. Also included in this area are all types of feasibility studies as well as acquisition or merger feasibility analyses.

Consultants also face problems of a research and development nature. Included here are all types of human factors engineering research; for example, product and process engineering, analysis of product design, evaluation of new products as to consumer use, safety, and acceptance. Also included in this general area are engineering and research administration, as well as organization and evaluation of technical research capabilities.

A third general problem area faced by consultants is that of production. Included here are all services relating to the functions of production; for example, plant and industrial engineering, materials management, production and control, quality control, manufacturing and technological advances, and plant location studies.

In the marketing area, problems may include the planning and evaluation of marketing strategy and product line, marketing controls, procedures and organization, and all types of market research. Financial problems dealt with by consultants include accounting, budgeting, corporate financing programs, cost control. financial planning, and the establishment of an appropriate financial control. An area of vital importance to consultants is personnel. Personnel consultants help managers with such problems as manpower analysis and planning, performance appraisal, candidate and employee evaluation, management development and training programs, executive search, attitude and morale surveys, etc.

Basically, They're Problem-Solvers

Most consultants deal largely with healthy, well-managed companies that want to stay that way. Client companies are usually progressive, and are intent on remaining in the forefront of their industry. "Sick" companies, or companies that have immediate short-term problems whose solutions are necessary for the continuance of successful operation, comprise a very small portion of a consultant's clientele.

Management consultants are basically problem-solvers. In the main their use is indicated whenever problems arise which management is not fully equipped to solve. Personnel problems are often a major concern, since people comprise the most complex factor affecting the operation of any organization. Personnel problems can be extremely difficult for management to detect, yet they are the most important of all, since they are basic to the company and bear directly on its survival.

Consultants are continually asked by prospective clients to justify their cost, and rightfully so. It is not enough for the consultant to prove he can do a better job than the client's own employees. He must do a better job at a lower cost to the company. After all, why should a company pay high fees to a stranger? Would it not be more profitable for a company to employ its own staff? Or if the company's current staff is not capable of handling the assignment, why not hire a few men who are? If a management consultant has something extra to offer, what is it and how is it going to benefit the client?

These questions, and the answers to them, are especially critical for the personnel consultant. It is he who must find his way through the twilight zone of organizational effectiveness; never being truly able to pinpoint his success in a specific cost-benefit fashion, while at the same time dealing with the heart of any organization—its human resources.

The decision to call in a consultant may sometimes be the result of management's inability to solve a particular problem. Sometimes the company does not have the qualified personnel necessary to solve a particular problem. A company may also call in a consultant when a fresh, objective viewpoint is desired. At other times, management may call in a consultant to approve their actions, right previous wrongs, assist them in making decisions.

The decision to call in a consultant may at times be a quick and arbitrary one. For example, the director of personnel may decide that there have been too many complaints from the union local, and that the problems have to be cleared up. He may then call in a consultant to conduct an attitude survey to get to the root of the complaints.

There are, however, certain objective indices that can be used when considering whether or not to call in a personnel consultant. These indices fall into the categories commonly referred to as Direct Performance Factors and Indirect Subjective Factors.

Direct Performance Factors include turnover, absenteeism, accident frequency, union grievances, etc. When these job performance factors rise, company productivity will fall.

No-Man's-Land

The second major criterion to use when considering whether or not to call in a personnel specialist is more subjective. How well are the company supervisors supervising? Are they able to properly motivate the people working under them? What is the attitude of the employees toward the company? Would they go to work for the firm across the street if they were offered a few dollars more? How does management respond to the workers' suggestions? Are these suggestions encouraged and acted upon, or are they thought of as just more rabble-rousing nonsense? What kind of work climate does the company have? What sorts of pressures are put on the employees? Do employees tell their friends and relatives that the company would be a good place to work for, or do they send their acquaintances elsewhere?

As can be readily seen, these problem areas all fit into sort of a no-man's-land. They cannot be readily identified, nor can they be easily measured. But the great effect that these intangibles have on job performance and productivity should not be underestimated. The importance of variables which impinge on the human resources or an organization should not be taken for granted. After all, the quality of an organization is nothing more than the sum of the qualities of the people who work for it.

Check With Other Clients

Successful client-consultant relationships usually begin prior to any specific demands that a business firm might place upon the consultant. A sound investment for any company to make would be to survey the talent available in the areas of expertness it is likely to need. A good idea would be to keep a file of the consulting talent that is available. A company can evaluate the technical skill and business acumen of a particular consultant by asking his previous clients the results of their experiences with him. A reputable consultant will not hesitate to provide a prospective client with a list of the companies he has dealt with in the past. Following this procedure will aid a company in making the right choice of a consultant for both small and large problems.

A management consulting firm is usually selected on the basis of a formally submitted proposal. This proposal consists of a statement of the problem as it is seen by the consultant, the methods by which the consultant plans to attack the problem, the expected results of the study, and the time and cost of the entire operation. But what should a company do when they have had no previous experience with management consultants? Just what are the guidelines to use when choosing a management consultant?

Perhaps the first thing to look for in a management consultant is his integrity. A company should make every effort to determine the consultant's general reputation with banks, business and trade associations, as well as former clients with whom he has worked.

The next thing to ascertain is the consultant's professional competence. An attempt should be made to determine the services offered in light of the consultant's qualifications for performing them. A company should look into the education, business, and consulting experience of the principals of the management consulting firm. It is always a good idea to deal with a well-established practice. How long has a consultant been in business? What type, size, and caliber clients has he served? The answers to these points should give some indication as to whether or not a particular consultant can serve your needs. Don't forget to check the financial stability of the consultant. Check his Dun and Bradstreet rating. A final guideline might be to find out if the consultant belongs to professional organizations, trade associations, and civic groups. If the consulting organization that you are considering is able to meet these criteria, you can be fairly sure that you have chosen the right firm.

Spell Out Your Problem

Now that you have your consultant, how do you best utilize his skill? The first thing to do is to carefully define your problem. There should be specific reasons for considering the use of outside assistance. Try to formulate as best as possible what you think the problem is, the conditions for its solution, and the end results which should be achieved by the solution. Of course, you will not be able to do this in all situations. The consultant can help you to define your problem, but the more you can accomplish in this area the better. You and the consultant should agree with each other on mutual obligations. You must remember that to ensure the successful completion of a project, you must devote the required time and effort. The consultant and management share responsibility for the definition of the purpose and scope of the problem, as well as the study's general time and cost.

Also part of management's responsibility is to determine with the consultant whether the company's personnel are capable of implementing the consultant's recommendations or whether they will need his help in this phase. Proper support of the consultant's work must be insured. The client company should assign a staff member to serve as liaison between the consultant and its own personnel, so that the consultant can obtain necessary assistance as required. Thoroughly prepare all company personnel as to the nature and aims of the consultant's job. A thorough briefing can do much to prevent the development of morale problems in some employees. And, of course, the consultant should be provided with the complete physical facilities necessary for efficient functioning— office space, telephone, needed clerical help.

To fully utilize the skill of the consultant you must make sure to implement his recommendations. To achieve the full value of his services, the normal inertia existing within a company must be overcome. A consultant's report that collects dust in an office file is not going to do anybody any good. The useful way of management to circumvent this occurrence is to require a report from its personnel every 30 days stating the progress being made in installing or implementing the recommendations. In many cases, it will prove useful to retain the consultant for a specified period to help implement the recommendations.

The client company will find that it pays to make a thorough evaluation of the work performed by the management consultant. About six months to a year after the consultant has left, a systematic evaluation should be made in items of the following criteria:

1. Did the consultant perform the work he had originally set out to do?

2. Were progress reports periodically submitted to appropriate members of the company?

3. Did the consultant perform a professional job of fact-finding and analyzing?

4. Did he work constructively with the personnel of your company?

5. Did the consultant leave behind him an accretion in management skills for your own employees?

6. Did his recommendations achieve your original objectives? Were you satisfied with the results?

7. Did the consultant remain in close contact with your organization to help in the implementation stage?

8. Did the consultant perform his tasks in a reasonable period of time and with minimum disruptions?

In the final analysis, the best measure of the success of a consulting engagement is whether or not you are willing to use the consultant again on future assignments.

PERSONNEL BUDGETS

Personnel, like all segments of the business, should have its budget. This gives the personnel staff the amount of money allocated for its operations. It also permits personnel expenses to be charged properly for adequate cost accounting.

A good budget is a guide, not a control. Personnel activities must never be put in a straitjacket. Provisions should be made for "shifting gears" as the year unfolds, for a personnel program, to be effective, must be dynamic.

Some budgets simply set aside sums of money which are earmarked for use during the year for specified programs. In a personnel budget the total amount may likely be broken down by functions, such as acquisition costs, operating expenses, salaries, and the like.

Other budgets may be on an "object of expenditures" basis with itemized charges provided for at specific times when they are expected to occur. Thus, the amount budgeted for help-wanted advertising may be more in winter months than in June when applicants may be easier to get as schools let out.

Items in the budget include acquisition costs—advertising, agency fees, employee referral bonds, applicant travel, relocation reimbursements; expenses—differentiating between expenses of individual personnel staff members and those of employee groups; memberships —annual dues and participation in activities; equipment, stationery, supplies, tests, etc.; payroll and overtime of personnel staff; operating costs—postage, telephone, telegrams.

The above budget covers the activities and expenses of the people in the personnel office. There may be similar budgets for the entire employee group: *company official functions*—parties, dinners, picnics; *employee relations*—handbooks, music, recreation, sports programs; *training*—materials, equipment, reprints; *benefits*—insurance, payroll taxes, etc.; *cafeteria*.

All these can be periodic budgets (annual), progressive (revised as they go along), or moving (12 months with new month added and same month a year ago dropped).

Cover More Than Money

The customary budgets, and the ones described above, are money budgets. But budgets do not necessarily have to be expressed in dollars. There are other types of budgets and some lend themselves to good personnel use. Here are two examples:

Manpower budget—The present number of employees, listed by number, grade, and location, are a starting point. For the period of the budget, say one year, manpower needs are anticipated. The total number may go up or down, and fluctuate from month to month. The expected changes are entered for the month in which they should be made. The accountant will, of course, relate this to labor cost, but the personnel staff uses it as a guide to know when to expect to hire, or transfer (or layoff), workers by grade and department.

Performance budget—The goals of a department or an individual manager are agreed upon a year in advance. Adjustments may be made during the year if changing conditions warrant and management concurs. At the end of the year the department's or the manager's results are measured against the stated objective. Group bonus or individual salary increases may be based on how well the objectives were met.

In any event, the personnel activity is too big to be run by "the seat of the pants" anymore. The use of budgets makes the administration of the personnel program more orderly.

PART 11

POLICY

POLICY

Policy is merely the outgrowth of practice. We have policies whether we realize this or not. Our job is to make policies understandable, fair, and acceptable. Reducing them to writing usually helps accomplish this.

Policies are formulated at the worker level; they are formalized by the executive group.

In any operation there is a customary way of doing things. This is the practice. When the performance of a single task is standardized, a method is established. A series of cumulative and integrated steps becomes a procedure. A system is a network of related procedures. All of these activities are accomplished within the framework of company policy, whether written or unwritten.

A written policy is a commonly accepted statement of understanding or formula. It facilitates delegation of decision making. It assures fairness and consistency in decision-making criteria. It saves time in reaching the decisions since the answer is determined in advance.

Companies which boast that they have no established policies are actually admitting that they have a confusing variety of policies. Whether this plethora of policies is a problem depends upon other factors, such as size of the company, complexity of its operation, and the like.

Resistance to written policies suggests an unwillingness to conform. The argument that "we're different" is usually more in the mind than in reality.

Yet, no set of written policies should become a straitjacket on management thinking. Two of the most elastic terms in the vocabulary of industry are "company policy" and "corporate objectives." The first is often a cloak to hide behind; the second is a managerial haven for generalities.

A policy manual should help a manager solve a problem, not limit him. A book on grammar is useful, not for people who know how to express themselves, but precisely for those who don't. The artist Da Vinci certainly did not need a numbered paint set. Queen Marie of Romania once remarked, "Etiquette is for people without breeding, just as fashion is for people without taste." Any set of rules is at best a substitute for natural talent.

The purpose of any set of standards is to see that everybody is playing the game by the same rules. Following the established practices makes for fewer arguments and less confusion. But men of overwhelming talent make their own rules, guided by some inner ear, by some pulse of the heart, that makes their decisions instinctively right and acceptable. To this type of manager a policy manual is useful as his guide, not as his Bible.

RULES and REGULATIONS

A fundamental of military leadership is that no order should be given which cannot be enforced. A good rule, like a good law, should be in the general interest, and not merely in the company's interest.

Rules and regulations should be known. This is often done in the form of an employee handbook. What is not as well published are the consequences for disregarding or violating these necessary rules.

Company regulations pertain to safety (personal and property)

845

and to conduct on the job. Wearing a "hard hat" in the foundry is a typical rule. Safety rules govern machines, apparel, and behavior. It is obvious that such regulations must be observed.

In the factory and office it is important that employees demonstrate "business sense" toward their job responsibilities. Much of this is self-understood and little more than common sense or good social graces. But because employees forget, become indifferent, or deliberately try to see how far they can go without being reprimanded, they must often be told. In such cases, employees need to be reminded of the customs, spelled out as house rules.

While companies like to be lenient and make things pleasant for their employees, they cannot let people go off in different directions. So they make rules. Employees are expected to comply willingly.

What happens when rules are not followed? An employee who is habitually tardy is counselled in hopes of helping him overcome the bad practice. An employee who starts a fight may be fired. An employee who steals may be apprehended.

If discipline is to be meted out to offenders, the procedure should be clearly spelled out, publicized, and enforced. Rules and regulations should be reasonable so they can be accepted, and they should be respected so that infractions and penalties will be minimized.

SAMPLE EMPLOYMENT POLICY

In the employment of workers, the aim is to hire, from among available applicants, the person best qualified for each job, who also shows potential for development. At the same time it is hoped to give each worker the type of job he wants which he is able to perform.

The continuing policy of the company shall be to use employment and promotion practices based on factors other than age, sex, race, creed, color, or national origin. In the interview procedure as well as in later promotions, appropriate tests are utilized in order to give every candidate an equal chance.

Men and women get equal pay for equal work—which means equal skill, equal effort, equal responsibility, performed under similar working conditions. Any wage differentials are based on seniority, merit, performance, and other criteria of the wage administration program, but not on sex.

COFFEE BREAKS

Coffee breaks, or rest periods, are the single biggest cost item in the fringe benefit package. A company that works a 7½-hour day and gives 15-minute rest periods in the forenoon and afternoon knows that 1/15th of the payroll cost goes for time not worked. The cost is even higher, considerably higher, when rest periods are not carefully policed and employees are permitted to abuse the privilege.

This typically American custom has become more of a habit than a period of rest. The worker of today, using labor-saving equipment and performing his duties in ideal surroundings, is hardly in need of rest after an hour or two of work. Diversion, possibly; rest, hardly.

There is little doubt that the coffee break results more in work loss than in work pickup.

Can the coffee break be abolished? Should it be? Firms which tried met considerable opposition. Others agree they are helpless, and the reason is real: It was popular ever since its introduction, back in the 1950's when less than half of all offices had coffee breaks. In a short 10 years, 94 percent of office and factory workers enjoyed at least one break a day. Now it's a rare company which doesn't have to deal with the problem. Most employees get morning and afternoon breaks and thousands of others simply "break" when they choose.

In favor of coffee breaks are arguments such as these:

"Higher production and accuracy make up for any loss of time."

"People seem to work better when they get their second wind after a cup of coffee."

"The boost to morale makes the cost insignificant."

It is hard to detail the advantages or disadvantages of coffee breaks. Companies don't even try. They are resigned to the practice as a condition of employment. They say, "Employees take the time off anyway. If there were no coffee breaks, they'd duck into the washrooms to exchange the latest gossip or visit more at desks or work benches."

What can be done? Here are a few suggestions—

1. Don't allow all employees to take their coffee breaks at the same time. In a large office this means wasted time waiting in long lines; in small offices there is a complete work shutdown.

2. Time-limit all coffee breaks. Each employee should know what the duration is. If it's 15 minutes, don't let it drag into 20 minutes. When a group breaks at once, a timing bell might be sounded.

3. Schedule coffee break times sensibly. According to the National Safety Council, disabling injuries occur most frequently between 10 to 11 a.m. and 3 to 4 p.m. This is just before weariness reaches its peak, and weariness results in errors in mental work also. Breaks should not be scheduled close to starting time, lunch, or closing time.

4. Keep the coffee convenient. It isn't handy when a restaurant across the street is patronized and an hour of one worker's time is wasted taking orders, making the purchase, and distributing the coffee, or worse yet, when each employee fetches for himself. When a restaurant won't deliver telephoned orders, experiment with other means. Some firms keep community hot water pots boiling so that workers can utilize their own concentrated coffee, tea, and cream. Many have installed commercial vending machines in convenient locations. A company cafeteria is perhaps the best unless the service is slow or the atmosphere lends itself too easily to leisured and lengthy drinking.

5. Consider the "unlimited" and untimed coffee break. This means the worker can take as many breaks as she likes whenever she chooses, but is expected to take these at her own desk. This works out well with office employees who are under pressure to complete specific jobs at a stated time. Now they find themselves working while they are "breaking," and they take refreshment when they really need it.

6. Discourage coffee-breaking cliques. These are the workers who pal around together and who can't wait for the coffee break so that they may enjoy long visits with each other. One good way to dissolve such groups is to assign different break times to each member.

7. Don't hesitate to reprimand the flagrant offender. Returning late from breaks is no different from being late to work or extending the lunch period.

8. Don't be afraid to take charge of the coffee break. Employees are excused from work 30 minutes each day but still being paid. The time belongs to the company, not the employees, and they should understand this.

9. Consider giving a little to get more. Some companies actually serve coffee free to workers. Now many workers feel morally obligated to get right back to the job at the allotted time.

10. Let management set a good example. If executives and supervisors parade their rights by taking their coffee breaks at privileged times, or by going oftener than their workers, or by ignoring the time limit—then employees will soon pick up these bad habits and the situation will get out of control.

PERSONAL TELEPHONE CALLS

Personal telephone calls can be costly in more ways than one. Every company has only a limited number of trunk lines. When a personal call is made during business hours, it ties up the line, interferes with the firm's business, interrupts the employee's work, and creates extra work for the switchboard operator and sometimes for management employees.

Personal phone calls can also be annoying and could cause a conflict between the supervisor and the employee. Few supervisors relish the idea of acting as "personal secretary" to the workers by being required to relay personal messages or to seek an employee who is absent from the desk when a personal call comes in.

It isn't easy to attempt to control personal phone calls and, at the same time, try to maintain a democratic working atmosphere. It is impractical to set rules governing personal phone calls which would be acceptable or enforceable among the company's many different types of employees. Even the conscientious worker resents "restrictions."

If personal calls, incoming and outgoing, can be controlled in schools, why not in business? The answer is simply that companies do not want to be that restrictive. They prefer to treat their employees as adults and hope they will be sensible and conscientious about the privilege.

The problem comes about because some employees cannot resist the convenience of a free telephone. They not only get messages, but they often engage in lengthy conversations. They know full well they are taking unfair advantage of an easy-going supervisor.

In spite of all efforts at control, personal telephone calls continue to be a major source of irritation, loss of work hours, and added costs to large and small businesses. The best approach seems to be sincere efforts to gain employee understanding of the company's side of the problem, followed by sympathetic and effective supervision.

PERSONAL MAIL

Because of the large volume of official or business mail, many companies request that employees arrange not to receive personal mail at work. They don't want to be responsible for letters, bills, or other mail addressed to individuals in care of the company. Where an employee is not identified with his department or location, it means mailroom clerks must take time to learn where such employee works so his mail can be brought to him. Most mail sent to a company is opened in the mailroom to catch cash, checks, and other payments, or to determine where the mail should be routed. Routinely opening personal mail would violate its privacy.

Nor should personal mail be placed in the "out" box, handled by the mailroom, and dispatched with company metered mail.

The same rules apply to personal packages, delivered by mail, express, or parcel service. They should not be sent to an employee at work. This is certainly true of C.O.D. packages. It follows that company time, materials, facilities, and delivery services should not be used to send out personal parcels.

As much as possible, personal business should not be mixed in with company business.

FASHION NOTES

Suitable dress is extremely important in the business office or in the industrial plant.

The well-dressed office woman chooses suits and dresses of neat and conservative design. Too casual and ultraextreme costumes should be saved for other occasions. A man should customarily wear a coat to the office, although he may not be required to wear it all day. If his jacket and trousers do not have an identical match, as in a suit, they should at least be in good taste and complement each other. He should wear a clean shirt, not necessarily white, and

POLICY

also a matching tie. Sport shirts, particularly the gaudy type, are
taboo in most offices. For both women and men, propriety and con-
ventionality are perhaps of foremost importance.

In the plant, personal safety is of as much consideration as is
comfort. Female employees performing production type jobs are
usually required to wear slacks or jeans, blouses or shirts, and
sturdy oxford type shoes. Shorts are not acceptable attire. Men
may wear work clothes or uniforms, depending upon their duties,
and open-collar shirts are appropriate. Safety shoes, of course, are
vitally important for some jobs.

In both the office and the factory, clothing should be appropriate
to the jobs. These are places where work is performed, not opportunities for competitive style shows. Off-beat casual wear, extreme-
style street clothes, and cocktail and party outfits have no place on
the industrial scene.

PERSONAL APPEARANCE

The following is taken from the member's manual of the Woodward Governor Company, 5001 North Second Street, Rockford,
Illinois 61101.

The company believes that there is a high correlation between cleanliness and
efficiency. One who is clean and neat physically and in his dress, and who works
in clean, well-lighted surroundings, will not only do a better job, but will have
more respect for himself and the work he turns out. There is dignity in any
worthwhile work, and certainly the man who can use his hands and head, as a
craftsman, is doing dignified work. Too often in the past, the so-called "white
collar" worker has been put into a different bracket than the shop worker. Some
young people have the delusion that to be a success they have to become "white
collar" workers, when in reality the shop workers may be much more valuable
to society. In asking each individual to report for work clean shaven and neatly
dressed, the company is merely trying to help him to develop respect for the
job and himself.

COMPANY UNIFORMS

Fidelity Bankers Life Insurance Company, Richmond, Virginia,
serving 40 states, supplies complete summer and winter wardrobes
to all home office people. All the personnel, from the board of directors down, get the same uniforms.

For the girls, the outfit includes two lightweight navy blue blazers, with brass buttons and a distinctive gold crest consisting of a wreath surrounding a decorative gothic "F," the company's corporate symbol; three Evan Picone gray summer-weight skirts (slim or A-line style); three white pique blouses with a bow at the throat; two pairs of Hanes seamless stockings in a neutral shade; one pair of blue Naturalizer pumps; and a large blue leather handbag.

The men receive two summer-weight navy blue blazers with crests; two pairs of summer-weight gray slacks; two blue and gold regimental striped ties; three white button-down oxford Gant shirts; two pairs of dark blue Gold Toe socks; and a pair of Florsheim or Bass shoes.

Winter-weight outfits are similar.

The wardrobes retail for $207.50 for the men and $220.80 for the women. The company has arranged for the purchase of replacement clothes at a 45 percent discount. The clothing is deductible from income taxes, as are laundry and dry-cleaning bills.

The outfits were created by Betty Bauder, fashion director at Thalhimers, Richmond's largest department store, which also handles all the custom fitting.

"We decided to create the FBL Look," said Harold J. Richards, president, "to enable our employees to identify themselves with the organization. We believe it will further our esprit de corps, and, of course, will be a welcome fringe benefit. It will keep the company growing by attracting attention and inviting interest in Fidelity

Bankers Life. We don't recognize competition, but we're putting our competitors in a position to recognize us."

Executives have worn their blazers on business trips all over the country and Europe, and the reaction has been favorable. Salesmen think the outfits are "effective for calling on customers."

CLEAN-UP TIME

Employees are expected to perform their assigned tasks from the official starting time until the official closing time. In factories and plants this means working from the starting bell until the signal ending the shift.

There are, however, some jobs on which it is the policy to allow a reasonable amount of time for the employee to clean up, and for cleaning machines, workbenches, etc., or for returning tools and equipment to the tool cribs.

The supervisor is usually more familiar than anyone else with the requirements of each job for which clean-up time may be necessary, and he is relied upon to apply the policy in a fair and equitable manner in his area of operation.

TOOLS and EQUIPMENT

Employees working in certain jobs are required to maintain an adequate supply of personal hand tools necessary for their own use in performing their assigned work. In the interest of safety and good workmanship, these tools should be kept in good condition. They should also be kept locked in the employee's personal tool box when not in use.

Tools and equipment furnished by the company and dispensed from various tool cribs are not to be considered personal. Nor should tools of this nature be brought from home lest they be confused with company items. These tools should not be abused and must be returned in good order. Any tool found to be damaged, defective, or worn out, should be returned to the crib and the attendant told about it. No employee should attempt to alter, repair, or correct any company-issued tool. A tool that is no longer needed should be returned promptly so it will be available for someone else.

An employee will be charged at cost for any company tool assigned out to him which is not returned.

WORK CLOTHES

Certain jobs require, or make good use of, special work clothes. These can be uniforms, to identify the profession, or protective clothing, to safeguard the worker.

The first illustration that comes to mind are professional athletes. Their attire is described as functional. Imagine a lifeguard working in street clothes.

Hospital personnel, except those in the business office, have uniforms which are suitable for the performance of their work and which readily identify their jobs. Besides surgical and floor nurses, there are nurses' aids, dietitians, technicians, housekeepers, service people, and volunteers.

A nurse in a company clinic will wear a uniform, but a nurse doing clerical work in a claims department will don regular clothing. Cafeteria employees will put on laundry-supplied uniforms or large white aprons, possibly chef's hats. Waitresses wear a variety of styles and colors. Mailroom girls and file clerks may wear smocks over, or instead of, regular dresses.

In the factory or plant there are many jobs which require special clothing. Specialists, such as electricians, plumbers, painters, and carpenters are easily recognizable because of their outfits. Maintenance men and engineers usually change to coveralls.

Plant guards wear uniforms resembling the garb of policemen. Doormen are equipped with special uniforms, often gaudy, depending upon the nature of the business. Chauffeurs can be spotted in their black caps and dark suits. Railroad conductors have their own uniforms and we've all become accustomed to airline personnel in their specially designed outfits.

There are a host of jobs which require protective clothing or equipment, all the way from bulletproof vests to lead shields in x-ray rooms. Examples are the welder with goggles and the acid worker with gloves. Safety shoes are needed for many types of work.

In many cases, but not in all, these uniforms or special clothes are furnished free by the company. In other instances, such as safety shoes, the necessary protective equipment may be purchased conveniently, and for a nominal charge, through the company. Many firms feel that if the special work clothes are required on the job they should be provided as are desks, machines, and company cars.

TOOLS, CLOTHES, LOCKERS

The following is taken from *The Dofasco Way,* the employee handbook of Dominion Foundries and Steel, Limited, Hamilton, Ontario, Canada :

Tradesmen (machinists, electricians, patternmakers, etc.) are expected to have their own kit of light tools. Good quality tools may be purchased at cost from our stores department and paid for through pay deductions. Tools required by production workers and special craft tools are provided by the company.

The company will provide you with a hard hat, eye protection, and other special safety equipment which may be required by your job. You may have to pay for a replacement if you lose or misuse this equipment. You are required to provide your own ordinary work clothing. Safety shoes (which all employees must wear in the plant) and gloves may be purchased on a pay-deduction arrangement.

We recommend that you have your work clothes cleaned regularly. The safety department has arranged a low-cost supply and laundry service for work clothes and a safety shoe repair service for the convenience of employees. If you take advantage of these services, the charges are deducted from your pay.

An employee is provided with a locker for the safe storage of clothing and personal effects. A combination lock is also provided and you are cautioned to always keep your locker closed and locked. Since you will "live" out of this locker while you work at Dofasco, do your best to keep it clean.

PENALTIES

Every company has its regulations, sometimes referred to as "house rules," which employees are expected to observe. When infractions occur, disciplinary action may be called for. The schedule of penalties is clearly spelled out in one company's employee hand-book, that of Dominion Foundries and Steel, Limited, Hamilton, Ontario, Canada. This is what they tell their people:

We feel that you will find little difficulty in adapting to our rules. Yet, we must warn you that you may be reprimanded or penalized by suspension or dismissal, depending upon the frequency or seriousness of your offenses. In general, disciplinary action will be applied as follows:

INFRACTIONS OF A MINOR NATURE

1. Absence without notification or reason.
2. Habitual tardiness.
3. Loafing, sleeping on the job, neglect or failure to perform assigned duties.
4. Improper use of company property.
5. Failing to report to main medical office upon returning after sickness or accident.
6. Violation of safety rules of a minor nature.
7. Failure to punch or improper punching of time cards.
8. Leaving the job before quitting time.

An employee committing any of the above offences is open to:
1st offence—warning
2nd offence—maximum 3 days suspension
3rd offence—dismissal

INFRACTIONS OF A MAJOR NATURE

1. Habitual absenteeism.
2. Insubordination (willful disobedience of authority).
3. Theft.
4. Fighting.
5. Being on the company's premises while under the influence of alcohol.
6. Bringing, having, or consuming intoxicating beverages in the plant.
7. Smoking in prohibited areas.
8. Willful damage to company property or property of others.
9. Walking off the job.
10. Gambling.
11. Punching another employee's time card.
12. Violation of safety rules of a major nature.

An employee committing any of the above offences is open to immediate dismissal.

PERSONAL CONDUCT

The employee handbook of the Fort Worth division of General Dynamics Corporation contains the following:

The orderly direction of personnel includes the administration of discipline by supervision. To help us continue operating the business in a safe, orderly, and effective manner, certain rules and regulations are necessary. They are to guide us in our conduct and responsibilities while working for General Dynamics.

Employees who fail to abide by these established rules and regulations will be subject to corrective discipline or discharge. "Corrective discipline" (which precludes or falls short of discharge) may range from a simple or timely warning for minor offenses or omissions to, and including, disciplinary layoffs without pay for more serious or repeated infractions.

Immediate discharge without previous warning may result in cases of major infractions. Also, repeated infractions or uncorrected conduct may result in discharge. Prior to final action, an employee may be suspended by his supervisor while the proper action in his case is determined. Suspension in itself is not disciplinary action; it is the pause in active employment during which an investigation of an incident takes place.

The following are representative causes which may justify disciplinary action, including discharge. No attempt has been made to list these causes in order of severity or seriousness.

Any willful damage to or unauthorized removal or appropriation of property belonging to the company or to another employee.

Committing any act of violence, fighting, brawling, or improper or immoral conduct on company premises.

Disobedience to or insubordination to persons with authority to direct.

Gambling, lottery, or any other game of chance on company property at any time.

Doing personal work on company time or property.

Repeated failure to punch attendance card or deliberately altering card.

Deliberately punching another employee's attendance card, or permitting another employee to punch your card.

The possession or use of intoxicating liquors or narcotics on company property, or reporting to work under the influence of intoxicants or narcotics.

Willful or repeated violations, disregard of security regulations or carelessness in the handling and/or safeguarding of classified information.

Willful violation or disregard of safety, fire, traffic, or parking lot regulations.

Loaning or permitting the duplication of General Dynamics' keys.

Smoking at a time or place not authorized.

Possession of firearms, weapons, cameras, or sound recording devices on company property, unless specifically authorized.

Loafing, wasting working time, being out of your work area without permission, or sleeping on the job.

Taking company property, records, employee lists, GD/FW Private Data, or classified information from the plant without permission.

Falsification of personnel, medical or other records, the omission of pertinent facts, or giving false testimony.

Solicitation of employees for donations or membership in organizations, circulation of petitions or other literature, sale of tickets, merchandise, or magazines, etc., on General Dynamics' property during working time without specific approval of the director of industrial relations or his designated alternate.

Circulating petitions or distributing literature or articles of any kind in working areas on General Dynamics' property without specific approval of the director of industrial relations or his designated alternate.

Posting of notices or signs, or writing in any form, on official bulletin boards, or removing approved notices, without the specific approval of the director of industrial relations or his designated alternate.

Garnishments or wage assignments.

Absence without reasonable cause. Failure to properly notify GD/FW of absence immediately or in no event later than five (5) working days.

Repeated tardiness or absenteeism.

Leaving the plant without your supervisor's permission.

Refusal to perform work as directed, or willful neglect of duty.

Inefficient performance of assigned duties or careless use of General Dynamics' property.

Deliberately permitting another person to use your badge or identification card, or using another person's badge, identification card or special pass to enter or leave General Dynamics' property or restricted areas, or in any way entering General Dynamics' property without proper authorization.

Covering up mistakes or faulty work.

Refusal to identify yourself to any supervisor or guard upon request.

Conduct outside of work of a criminal, dishonest or immoral nature; habitual use of intoxicants to excess; drug addiction; or conduct which would reflect unfavorably toward the company.

Climbing fences enclosing company property or entering or leaving the plant by other than authorized methods.

WORKING CONDITIONS

In the early days, working conditions and other human considerations were secondary to production and profit. The employees were there to serve the interests of the business, not vice versa.

During the past two decades, however, the picture has changed. In a tightening labor market, workers were expecting and getting a better work environment. No longer were they content to spend the better part of each day in dismal surroundings.

The influx of women into factories and offices has also had a marked effect. Their contribution has been more than chintz curtains and periodic rest periods. They brightened up the place in more ways than one; they introduced new concepts of cleanliness, they required quieter and safer equipment. Oddly enough, as women caused improvements, men did not object.

Adequate heat is now taken for granted. Air-conditioning is becoming commonplace in older buildings as well as in new construction. Acousticon ceiling treatment abates machine noise. Tile floors, which are waxed regularly, have replaced the old wood floor which was scrubbed infrequently. Fluorescent light is used in place of the former inadequate incandescent fixtures. Liberal use of glass in walls lets in an abundance of natural night. Bright pastel colors have made even old-timers forget the dingy tan walls of the office and the unpainted brick surfaces of the factory.

Sanitation and health facilities are better and maintenance is done on a daily basis. Good housekeeping is part of everybody's job. Noise, odors, dirt, fumes, and hazards are well controlled and minimized as much as possible through modern methods. Piped-in music is designed to make the day pleasant.

All the while these changes were taking place, managements went along willingly to provide the better working conditions. They liked the improvements themselves and began taking pride in the physical facilities and work environment. More important, they found the new approach was better for business since it contributed to increased production from employees who felt appreciated because their employers demonstrated "we care."

The old notion of "whatever is good for business is good for people" has, over the years, been turned about. Managements today understand and accept that "whatever is good for people is good for business."

SMOKING in the OFFICE or PLANT

Smoking in the office is commonplace these days. Smoking in the factory is generally restricted to authorized areas.

In offices, men and women are allowed to smoke at their desks, except where they meet the public. This means that receptionists, information clerks, ticket sellers, tellers, and interviewers are asked not to smoke on the job. Other office clerical and supervisory personnel may smoke at their desks or in their offices.

Smoking is permitted in washrooms, locker rooms, lounges, and cafeterias, but not at time clocks, in elevators or stairways. The "traveling cigarettes"—carried by people smoking as they walk about from one location to another, or in aisles or corridors—is frowned upon in many places. Pipe smoking or cigar smoking is usually limited to private offices or at least semiprivate areas.

In factories, plants, or shops the regulations must, of necessity, be most stringent. Smoking is forbidden in manufacturing areas as a safeguard to people and property. If the fire hazard is great, the insurance companies will insist on the ban being enforced. Production workers have areas of the plant designated for smoking, with safety ashtrays and other precautions in effect.

Arguments in favor of letting employees smoke on the job include the feeling that it improves production, lessens the time wasted on smoke breaks, builds better morale, and eases complaints against restrictions.

Arguments against include the thought that the practice offends customers, annoys nonsmokers, creates an unbusinesslike atmosphere, gives conference room a pool-hall air, and increases the fire and safety hazard.

There should be no distinction in the rules for men and women anymore. Smoking has become such a habit with many people that companies accept the practice in their offices and plants. Nonsmokers do not get equal rights and have no recourse where their privacy is invaded. About the only control companies may exercise is concerned with safety.

HOUSEKEEPING

The following is taken from the administrative services handbook, *This Is for You, Fair Lady,* distributed to employees of Montgomery Ward:

YOU CAN HELP by keeping your own immediate work area clean and tidy.

The housekeeping staff uses the most modern equipment and technique. But, good cleaning becomes impossible when boxes, records, and other items are left on floors and cabinets after working hours.

If you purge files and organize desk drawers, there will be no need to clutter cabinets and desk tops with stacks of paper and other things that create a disorderly appearance.

Housekeeping personnel do the extensive, overall cleaning of the building at night; however, the main aisles, lobbies, washrooms, refreshment centers and other areas are serviced during the day.

Please call whenever you notice that these areas need special attention. The building service section depends upon your keeping them informed.

Carpeted offices can be thoroughly cleaned during vacation periods. Call two weeks in advance for this special housekeeping service.

WASHROOM PROBLEMS

Washrooms in office and factory buildings often present a problem. It isn't enough to have them on a regular maintenance schedule, such as night cleanup and occasional daytime inspection. Nor is it feasible to keep an attendant on duty in each washroom full time.

For some reason men and women using public washroom facilities are often not so considerate as they would expect to be at home. Sinks and mirrors are left untidy, floor cluttered with thrown paper, drains clogged, and other careless or unintentional indiscretions.

What happens when employees complain about the condition of the washrooms they are assigned to use? The clinic nurse says that while sanitation may be within her domain, the inconsiderate sloppiness of employees is not. The janitor says he cannot stand guard to prevent the careless or deliberate plugging of plumbing. The personnel office says its responsibility is to see that adequate facilities are provided but not to police them.

So where does this leave us? Managers and foremen have little control over their people after they leave their work area. Employees should not be asked to spy or report on each other. The matron, when she happens to be present, has no authority to reprimand offenders.

The best solution calls for clean and comfortable restrooms to begin with, in the hopes that most people will cooperate with management that shows concern. Some regular during-the-day service might be provided as a normal part of maintenance. Should the problem grow beyond reasonable limits, signs or notices might call attention to the need for cleanliness and neatness. If the problem gets out of hand, group meetings, addressed by a "health or sanitation specialist" rather than authoritative management, would not be improper. In such gathering, the educational approach should be stressed.

Montgomery Ward's Approach

The following is taken from the administrative services handbook, distributed to employees of Montgomery Ward:

All washrooms are serviced several times a day; however, each matron is responsible for several washrooms and cannot be on continuous duty in any one washroom. So women employees can do their part in keeping their washrooms clean by:

Using the ash trays provided rather than throwing cigarettes on the floor.

Taking a few extra seconds to clean the washbowls after washing.

Not taking food or beverages into the washrooms.

Using receptacles provided for disposing of sanitary napkins.

Making sure that towels are put into containers.

Being tidy with cosmetics so that lipstick smears and powder smudges are not left on ledges and mirrors.

The building services section welcomes all suggestions for keeping the rooms immaculate and appreciate the prompt reporting of all washrooms not being kept clean, and in a sanitary condition.

NOISE

Factories and offices are getting noisier, jeopardizing the hearing of millions of employees who work in them.

This point is made in a training manual, *Industrial Noise—A Guide to Its Evaluation and Control,* published by the United States Public Health Service national center for urban and industrial health.

"An estimated seven to eight million workers may be exposed to noise conditions hazardous to hearing in our increasingly technological society," it says.

The manual lists two kinds of hearing loss among workers: Temporary loss, caused by initial brief exposure to intense industrial-type noise, or permanent loss, caused by prolonged exposure to the same noise. Besides this auditory damage, other adverse effects cited include interference with speech, loss of efficiency in performance because of the distraction, and the psychological factor of annoyance.

NAMEPLATES

Desk nameplates have a practical value in identifying workers in a company. There is also the psychological importance of making the identified individual feel that he or she is a recognized part of the organization. In addition, there is a matter of being able to exert more competent supervision in an office situation when employees seated at desks are more readily identifiable by name.

JACK FORESTER
PURCHASING AGENT

The Seton Name Plate Corporation, New Haven, Connecticut, manufacturers nameplates and other identifications typical of the many used in industry.

The Vanderbilt model is a typical engraved nameplate with white core letters neatly incised into a choice of any one of nine handsome background colors. It is furnished on a clear lucite base. This is an inexpensive type popular with large offices where turnover and name changes may run high.

The Forester type is used more for people with "titled" positions. This executive desk marker has black-filled lettering in satin-finished solid aluminum or brass on an oil-finished gunstock walnut base.

There are a variety of other plastic and metal identification signs, tags, plates, markers, labels, and badges available for multiple purposes.

HOLIDAY DECORATIONS

What should be done at Christmas time about holiday decorations and trees? This poses an annual problem in many offices and factories.

In stores, banks, restaurants, and similar places of business which serve the public directly, this is no problem. It just seems appropriate to establish a festive atmosphere and charge off the expense as a cost of normal operations.

But what about those areas in offices and plants which are occupied only by employees? From a strictly business standpoint, something as personal as a Christmas mood may not belong. Yet, employees do not leave their personal beliefs and Christmas excitement at home; much of the spirit of the holidays pervades their place of work. Many employees, in fact, get carried away in their efforts to share their Christmas joy with fellow workers.

How many trees should a place allow? Should every department have its own? Should these trees be supplied by the company or does this make Christmas impersonal and hence detract from the enthusiasm?

What about decorations? Aside from regular restrictions about what may be attached to painted walls or suspended from ceiling fixtures, how much latitude should employees be permitted as they attempt to "deck the halls" to spread cheer?

What's more, should this be done on company time or after hours?

There is no hard-and-fast rule, of course. Much depends upon the size of the company, its many separate locations, the nature of the business, the company attitude, and many other factors. Some firms encourage the practice of letting employees enjoy some measure of the holiday spirit at work; others take a firm position against this, arguing that it causes too much interference with work.

In any case, it might be wise to establish certain ground rules. Trees may be permitted for every specified number of workers. They should not be so tall that they cannot be trimmed by employees while standing safely on the floor. Decorations should not be so elaborate as to appear gaudy. While Christmas is a Christian holy day, it is observed by many as a national holiday and therefore the motif of the decorations might have to be somewhat restrained so as not to appear "preachy" to some people.

Much can be gained in the way of employee morale if the spirit of Christmas is allowed to permeate the work climate. But if no common sense restrictions or cautions are exercised, departmental competition for attention could run rampant and hurt feelings might result. This whole subject need not be a delicate one so long as it does not get out of hand.

PRIVATE OFFICES vs. OPEN OFFICES

No one has ever explained why generals sit in private offices and privates sit in the general office.

Officers in the industrial army also set themselves apart from rank-and-file workers by sitting in separate enclosures. There is no pattern, of course. In some business firms, such as advertising agencies, there are many private work areas to accommodate the amount of creative effort. In banks, most all the officers sit out in the open to facilitate easy direct dealings with customers.

Private offices are decided on rank in some firms, and on functions in others. Executives, department heads, managers, as well as professional, research, and personnel people usually have private offices. The three factors to consider are: (1) prestige, (2) concentration, and (3) confidential work. Alternatives to private offices are enclosed or semienclosed work areas made of movable partitions.

Should there be uniformity in private offices or should there be variations? The trend is toward flexibility. Companies try to standardize private offices in such matters as size and location, and allow them to be personalized in the choice of pictures, lamps, and colors. A private office should express the executive's personality.

It is accepted that a private office adds weight, influence, and respect to jobs in the eyes of employees and visitors.

QUIET HOUR

There is an old proverb that reads, "As the first hour of the day goes, so goes the day."

The Michigan Millers Mutual Insurance Company of Lansing, Michigan, has introduced the "Quiet Hour" to promote good work habits.

All employees, including department managers and top management, were asked to adopt this resolution:

THE FIRST HOUR OF EACH DAY (8 to 9 a.m.) IS THE "QUIET HOUR." DURING THIS PERIOD WE REQUEST THAT NONESSENTIAL CONVERSATIONS BE AVOIDED.

They were instructed to please

Hold outgoing calls and the gathering of materials necessary to complete these calls until after 9 a.m.

Avoid contacting other departments on routine matters until after 9 a.m.

Exceptions to the rules are, of course, recognized. These are:

1. When it is necessary for new employees under training to talk with their supervisors, this should be done as quietly as possible.

2. Field personnel, who need assistance before leaving on assignments, may obtain this help.

3. Incoming business calls may, of course, be taken.

4. Matters pertaining to other departments of an urgent nature are excepted from the "quiet hour" rule.

When discussion is necessary during the "quiet hour," employees are asked to be considerate of others.

The idea for the "quiet hour" came from Newell Kiebler, manager of the mill and elevator department, who initiated it in his department. Because of its success from a profit and morale standpoint, the operation of the department became more efficient with fewer personnel.

Upon his transfer, he installed the "quiet hour" in his new department. Efficiency picked up, the number of employees went down, and morale improved. Later the new program was tried on a company-wide basis.

According to Duane Bower, personnel director, the "quiet hour" has been "a good thing" for the company. "Now we can be quite certain," he adds, "that unless an emergency arises the first hour is a productive one."

TARDINESS

There are two basic approaches that are used in dealing with the problem of tardiness: (1) attempts at control through punishment or reward, and (2) through acceptance.

Occasional tardiness is easier to tolerate than habitual latecoming. Both are easier to justify when the employment market is unfavorable and when the employees involved are key workers or good performers.

The chronic latecomer presents a problem few companies can

handle or want to become involved in. The usual method is to warn the offender a few times that if he doesn't, or can't, mend his ways, he will be terminated. Some companies make a more intensive effort to help employees correct the problem and thereby retain their jobs.

A reward and punishment method simply means that offenders are punished by being docked, or the nonoffenders are rewarded in some way over and above their usual pay.

A typical punishment plan consists of perhaps three steps:

1. Face the employee with the facts. Go over time sheets. Point out the extent or frequency of tardiness. Ask about causes. Some employees, when they see that the company is genuinely interested in helping them, will try to do better.

2. If the situation does not improve, it is time for a second interview. This might well be a performance review in which all aspects of the job are discussed. If work performance is good, this is mentioned, and it is also pointed out that the work record would otherwise qualify the employee for a raise, say a normal increment of $25, but because of the uncorrected tardiness, the raise will be only $15. Now the employee understands that he, and not only the company, is being penalized by tardiness.

3. If this doesn't work, and other attempts at reasoning fail, most companies feel they have no choice. They terminate the offender because they cannot ignore the problem any longer and disturb team morale, nor can they permit the bad habit to spread and upset production.

"Preaching" Is Avoided

In these meetings with tardy employees the companies are satisfied to point up the problem. They don't preach to the employees or advise them how to overcome some of the basic reasons for their inability to conform to the standard starting time of the entire work group. To do so would be practicing "amateur psychology" for which they and their supervisors are not equipped.

The exception to this approach is the creative person who feels he must be a nonconformist in order to retain his individuality. Good

WHO NEEDS A TIME CLOCK?

OT JOE!

START TIME
JOE OVERSLEPT AND ARRIVES
8:10 AM (Writes 8:00 on Card)
LOST-10 MINUTES

COFFEE BREAK
JOE MISSED BREAKFAST SO
HE NEEDS AN EXTRA CUP
(10:00 To 10:10 AM)
LOST-10 MINUTES

LUNCH TIME
JOE KNOCKS OFF 15 MINUTES
EARLY TO WASH UP (11:45 AM
To 12:30 PM)
LOST-15 MINUTES

COFFEE BREAK
(AFTERNOON)
JOE'S FEET HURT SO HE TAKES
10 MINUTES (2:30 To 2:40 PM)
LOST-10 MINUTES

QUITTING TIME
JOE'S TIRED AND QUITS 15
MINUTES EARLY TO CLEAN UP
(Writes 4:30 PM on Card)
LOST-15 MINUTES

E WORKED 7 HOURS TODAY BUT
S BOSS WILL PAY HIM FOR 8!

Who needs a time clock? This poster provides the answer.

engineers, scientists, physicists, and others are in high demand and short supply. To keep these people working at full efficiency is the big opportunity, and companies are reluctant to annoy these people with restrictive rules and regulations which actually do not contribute to the creative or inventive process. If their tardiness causes embarrassment, it may be advisable to isolate them from the rest of the work force, so their irregular work habits go unnoticed.

What can be done about tardiness? First of all, the supervisor has to set a good example by being on time himself. His employees expect to see him there when they arrive.

Every employee has to be handled on an individual basis. The problem of tardiness is common, but the reasons for it are many and varied. The employee who is late knows what he is doing. He might not know why. Criticism won't help, and the supervisor who picks on the tardy employee, because he has him at a disadvantage, makes the employee defensive instead of cooperative.

The best way to work toward a solution is with understanding, not of the problem but of the individual. The company responsibility is to help employees develop to their finest potential and the key is leadership.

HOW TO REDUCE ABSENTEEISM

The problem of absenteeism from work goes back a long way. In early Egypt absenteeism was attributed to one of three reasons: The missing person was sick, out appeasing the gods, or just plain lazy.

In modern business the problem is not much different. Half of the reasons are legitimate, but in the other half of the cases, the employee decides he would rather be somewhere else.

Some employees who don't feel "up to it" in the morning when they arise, stay home and call in sick, while others, similarly disposed, drive themselves to work. Why? Some people are more conscientious than others, possibly more honest than others. Some employees like their jobs and prefer going to work instead of staying home even for an excuse that would be quite acceptable.

An analysis of absenteeism reported that:

- 54.8 percent of one and two-day absences follow or precede legitimate time off for holidays or weekends.

- Absenteeism rises as jobs become more plentiful.

- An "incredible" correlation exists between employee "illness" and major sports events.

- Companies without "sick-pay" plans frequently have a record of fewer absences than those who have such plans.

In a full employment market, offices and factories are hiring more secondary wage earners, such as wives who are not the sole breadwinners for their families. A missing day's pay is not enough to offset the urge to stay home to look after the house, go shopping, wait for the drapery man, or to prepare for a party dinner (Example: Wednesday before Thanksgiving). Even married men whose wives are working, or for that matter any worker who has another income as a cushion against being docked, is more likely to take a day off occasionally than the worker who lives from one paycheck to another.

Don't overlook the very distinct possibility of an employee taking a day off to look for another job. Most jobs are filled during regular working hours.

All Reasons Not Bad

There are, of course, many reasons. Everybody probably has his own list. And the reasons are not all bad.

Just as there are many reasons for absenteeism, so also are there many attempts to solve or at least reduce the problem. Most of them do not have much effect.

Docking an employee for taking a day off works against the conscientious employee; it actually gives the secondary wage earner a clean conscience to say, "Why complain when I take a day off.

You're not paying me for it." Rewarding the employees who do not have absenteeism by giving them extra money or time, seems to be one way of circumventing the problem but not solving it.

The consensus of most companies is that the supervisor is the main line of defense in combating absenteeism. This is just another way top management absolves itself of responsibility by shifting the burden to the supervisor who has neither the time nor the authority to do anything about it. This also explains why the problem is not being solved: today's breed of "instant supervisors" just isn't that good. They are work pushers, not problem solvers.

Most companies keep records of the "causes" of absences. Few keep records of the periods of time off. There is a difference between an employee who is absent 10 days in a row and one who is absent 10 separate days in a year.

Also worth watching is the type of day. Some employees have a pattern of time off which can easily be pinpointed. Some are off most on Mondays or Fridays (to give them long weekends). Some stay away before or after holidays or on heavy workload days. One married woman got an extra week vacation (unpaid) three years in a row simply by telephoning in long distance on the last Friday to report she was under doctor's care in her relative's home town.

Control Measures

In order to control absenteeism, or to eliminate the abuses—

1. Gather the facts. The frequency, the length, the pattern, the status of the employee, the job—all these are easily documented.

2. Set up standards of what would normally be acceptable.

3. Determine the accountability for absenteeism. Hold the supervisor accountable, for that is where the problem and the inconvenience are. If it is conveniently "dumped" into the personnel office, far removed from the immediate problem, it merely becomes a recordkeeping function.

4. Set up controls and give the supervisor the authority and backing needed to act.

One thing is certain. Rules and regulations won't solve the problem of absenteeism. Good supervisors may cure it.

ATTENDANCE BONUS

Many companies with nagging tardiness or uncontrollable absence problems try to reduce these problems by offering bonuses to employees. Payoffs are made only to employees with perfect attendance, but it is hoped others will be moved by the incentive to try to improve their records.

Payoffs are sometimes made in the form of cash, but more generally with additional time off. In my first place of employment, a small wholesale drug jobber, it was important to telephone the retail drug stores before the larger wholesalers did. Therefore, anyone who was present and on time every day of the week found an extra dollar in his pay envelope.

Some programs add points or credits for perfect attendance to the employee scorecard which gives credit toward merchandise for many other aspects as well, such as employee referrals, suggestions, etc. There are bonus plans which pay off in trading stamps.

The most common reward comes in additional time off. Each employee who has a perfect record for 30 or 90 days, for example, might get an extra one-half or one day off from work, or added to his vacation. Immediately one has to wonder about the logic of such approach since the company could easily give away more time than it gains.

A typical time-off program might be:

Beginning immediately, something new has been added to our employee program which will make this an even better place to work.

Many employees have through the years of their employment maintained a perfect record of attendance. We have adopted a plan to recognize this perfect attendance by granting free time off from work, in addition to the regular vacation time already provided.

All programs need rules to operate by, and the rules for our Bonus Time Off Plan are as easy as we can make them. It is our hope that before long, all eligible employees will have free time to their credit.

The "rules"

1. One half day will be given to each eligible employee for each 30 consecutive work days of perfect attendance.

2. The 30-day period may begin on any work day of the month.

3. Bonus time may be accumulated to a total of one full day. The bonus time off must be taken within 30 days after it is earned. Holidays, vacation or bonus time off, falling within a work period, do not count against perfect attendance.

4. Perfect attendance is understood to mean:

   a. Being on time in the morning and when returning from lunch.

   b. Remaining on the job until the beginning of the lunch hour and until quitting time.

   c. Observing the time of the 15-minute pass period.

   d. Employees will be considered late if not in their department and ready for work at the established time each day.

   e. An employee sick, tardy, or on leave without pay, begins a new 30 day work period the work day following the break in his or her record.

Any program, such as the one above, saddles the manager or foreman with additional administrative detail. It is almost necessary for the supervisor, or someone he designates, to make separate entries on individual employee record cards several times each day.

Management Misgivings

The whole notion of an attendance bonus is not well accepted by many managements, however, because of two very basic reasons:

1. These firms have serious misgivings about paying any employee *twice* for part of his job. He is already being adequately compensated for being there and doing his work. Why pay him extra for only doing what is rightfully expected of him?

2. This is just another instance of a management using a "device" to do what supervision obviously is incapable of doing. To them the introduction of such a plan is an admission of weak supervision.

HOLIDAYS

Paid holidays are granted nowadays to all regular employees—plant or hourly as well as salaried or office. The minimum number of such paid holidays is six, and when one of these six holidays falls on a nonworking day, such as Saturday, or Sunday, the day before or following is often recognized as the day on which the factory and office shall be closed and employees paid. Apparently few firms want to be accused of giving less than six holidays a year.

The trend is toward more holidays. Many companies have eight or more paid holidays. Generally, in eastern and northeastern states more holidays are observed, and it is not uncommon for a business to be closed 11 or 12 times a year. In southern states and possibly elsewhere there are local holidays which are observed.

Quite often extra holidays slip into a firm's work calendar. When Christmas falls on a Thursday some firms close on Friday too. Or if Independence Day falls on a Tuesday, some firms close on Monday also.

A not uncommon practice is to recognize the regular six standard holidays *plus* two "floating days," the selection depending upon the calendar each year. Thus a Friday after Thanksgiving may be a holiday one year but not the next.

A Personal Holiday

The author likes adding one personal holiday to the list. This would give each employee "one day in the bank" to use as he chooses— possibly for a special religious observance, an extra day of travel, shopping, birthday, or whatever is useful to him.

It is easier to close on a "national" holiday than on a "church" holy day. In this context, Christmas is considered a national holiday, since Christians and non-Christians alike celebrate it.

Full-time employees are paid for holidays; part-time workers are not paid as a rule. When an employee works on a holiday he gets time-and-a-half (overtime) or possibly double-time, in addition to regular pay for the holiday.

The annual survey of the Administrative Management Society shows that in the United States there is a definite trend to a more liberal holiday policy.

27.2% of the firms grant 6 holidays per year
21 %   7
24.2%   8
27 %   9 or more

Eastern United States is the most liberal area with 75.4 percent of the firms granting eight or more paid holidays.

There is also a trend in Canada to a more liberal holiday policy. Among the Canadian firms 97.8 percent give eight or more paid holidays. Of these companies, 31.2 percent give nine days, 29.3 percent give 10 days, and 7 percent give 11 or more.

THREEKENDS

The movement to celebrate most holidays on specified days rather than calendar dates keeps on gathering momentum. And in altering the dates, the trend moves toward weekend holidays.

One noteworthy example is the bill passed by Congress and signed into law by President Johnson which assures five three-day holiday weekends each year. The measure makes Columbus Day a federal holiday and provides that it, Washington's Birthday, Memorial Day, and Veterans Day be observed on Monday each year. Labor Day already falls on a Monday.

Washington's Birthday will be observed on the third Monday in February, rather than on February 22; Memorial Day on the last Monday in May instead of May 30; Columbus Day on the second Monday in October instead of October 12, and Veterans Day the fourth Monday in October instead of November 11.

The bill is limited to observance of holidays by employees of the federal government and the District of Columbia. But most states tend to follow the lead of Congress in providing for holidays. To give the states a chance to act, the legislation does not take effect until January 1, 1971.

Proponents of the idea of weekend holidays maintain that observing holidays on long weekends will result in fewer requests for extra days off. A series of three-day weekends which employees can count on every year will eliminate the four-day holidays that somehow seem to be popping up.

One company magazine has already coined a word for this new holiday plan. It suggests the name "Threekends." Who knows, maybe the name will catch on.

One of the main objections against more three-day holidays is the greater risk of holiday accidents during long holiday weekends. This, explains Columnist Sidney Harris, of the Chicago *Daily News,* is an interesting example of the power of abstract statistics over reason. A case can be made that there is less chance of being killed on the highways during a holiday than at other times. True, there are more accidents on three-day weekends, but not compared to the greater number of cars on the road.

VACATIONS

The policy of granting vacations in business stems from the long-standing practice of giving vacations to school children. But the motivation and reward are changed.

School vacations are a product of a rural economy. The children were excused from classes during the summer months in order to help their parents with the crops. Had ours been an urban society it is questionable whether youngsters would have been given this free time, or at least as much free time, during the hot summer. Whereas farm children had work to do, their city cousins often do not know how to keep occupied. They become bored and in too many cases their idleness leads to trouble.

Workers in business get vacations, not because they are needed elsewhere at certain times, but rather as a change of pace from their regular work routines. For years office employees were given the same vacation privileges as the management people they served, but factory workers, who were paid only for the hours they worked, were not given paid time off for vacation purposes. Since World War II the practice became universal and the same vacation policies are applied to all workers in a company.

A declining number of companies still do as the schools do, close down for a period of time when everyone, or almost everyone, goes on vacation. The reasons, however, are such concerns as plant clean-up, equipment repair, inventories, etc. Practically all firms now remain open the year round and let their employees spread their vacations over a period of time. Even this vacation period, which originally was synonymous with summertime, say May through

September, has, in many companies, been extended so that employees may take their vacations any time during the calendar time.

Permissiveness Growing

Other practices are changing too. Few companies require that an employee take his entire vacation, say two weeks, at one time. Split vacations are popular, especially since policies have been liberalized and many workers today qualify for three or four weeks. It is not uncommon for employees to take both winter and summer vacations. Jet travel has made this possible; it is no longer necessary for a vacationer to spend a good share of his time traveling to and from his destination.

There are, naturally, many variations. The practice of taking a vacation a day at a time is frowned upon. This defeats the purpose of the vacation which is intended to get a worker away from his work long enough so he will come back refreshed and renewed.

Vacations in the United States fall short in a comparison with European ones. By law, in France, a three week annual vacation is required; in practice, through collective bargaining, four weeks is standard. In West Germany, workers receive an average of three and a half weeks of vacation. In Belgium it's only three weeks, but employees receive double pay during their vacations.

VACATIONS

(A Typical Company Policy)

Employees (except temporary) shall be granted vacation with pay depending upon length of continuous employment as of January 1 of each year.

QUALIFICATIONS

Employment for 12 months or more but less than 10 years ....2 calendar weeks

Employment for 10 years but less than 25 years ....3 calendar weeks

Employment for 25 years or more..4 calendar weeks

President and vice-presidents ....1 month

Others on confidential payroll ....3 calendar weeks

New Employees

Employees hired during the first six months of the year, one week vacation after six months of employment, provided it can be taken in the same calendar year. Two weeks vacation in the following calendar year after 12 months of employment.

Other New Employees

Two weeks vacation in the following calendar year, after 12 months of employment, with option of taking one of these weeks after six months of employment.

Carry-Over

Employees shall not be authorized to carry over any unused vacation time from one calendar year to another. Any unused vacation will be forfeited unless such vacation remains unused at the company's request, in which case disposition will be made by the president.

Vacation Pay

Wage-and-Hour: Unless otherwise directed by the employee, and approved by the manager, a payroll check will be issued on the last workday preceding start of vacation, for time worked plus vacation allowance.

Exempt: Prior to leaving on vacation an employee will receive any check or checks which normally would have been distributed during the period of his vacation.

Payment in Lieu of Vacation

Since vacations are intended to provide rest and diversion from the regular work routine, payment in lieu of time off will not be granted.

Holidays During Vacation

When a recognized holiday falls during a scheduled vacation period, an additional day off, mutually agreed upon by the employee and the manager will be granted. This additional day may be taken in advance, if it is contiguous to the vacation. It need not be contiguous if taken afterwards.

Scheduling

Vacations shall be taken at a time mutually agreed upon by the employee and the manager. All other factors being equal, schedules will be arranged on the basis of the work load and employee (companywide) seniority.

Vacation time will be taken in units of not less than one full calendar week, and shall begin on the first day of the week. Vacations will not be scheduled to begin on the last Monday of December when it becomes impossible to complete a 5-day vacation period within the same calendar year.

Reporting

Immediately after January 1 of each year Personnel will furnish each Division with a list of employees and their seniority dates. A supplementary list will be submitted on July 1, covering employees hired after January 1.

Vacation schedules will be reported in writing to Payroll not later than

May 1 of each year. Earlier vacations, cancellations, or other last minute changes will be reported in writing as soon as they are authorized.

ADDITIONAL TIME OFF

Because of the heavy vacation schedules during the summer, no extra time for extended vacations may be granted between June 1 and September 15. The approval of the president is required for any exceptions (exceptions most likely to receive approval are for marriage or overseas travel). Extended vacation time at the employee's own expense may be granted during the rest of the year, when in the judgment of the manager, such time off does not cause undue hardship to the department operations and so long as it does not result in any unfairness or inconvenience to other employees.

TERMINATIONS

Any employee who has been employed for 12 months or more shall be paid at time of termination for any unused vacation. In such cases, the effective date of termination will still be the last day worked.

EMPLOYEES ON LESS-THAN-FULL-TIME OR TEMPORARY JOBS

Employees on regular less-than-full time jobs shall receive vacation time proportionate to the average number of hours worked.

Employees working on temporary jobs, either full time or less-than-full-time, shall not be entitled to any vacation rights.

EXCEPTIONS

Any exceptions to this vacation policy, or to any of its provisions, shall be reported in writing to personnel and must carry the approval of the president.

PAYMENT FOR TIME NOT WORKED

There is more truth than poetry to the saying that when we hire a worker we are actually buying a share of his time. In return for the production he turns out during this time he is paid his wages. This would seem to be a fair exchange were it not for the fact that for some of the time we pay for we get no production.

This is the whole gamut of "payment for time not worked."

Here we must differentiate between direct and indirect wages. Indirect wages cover: (1) taxes—social security, railroad retirement, workmen's compensation, unemployment compensation, state sickness programs, etc., and (2) insurance—hospitalization, medical-surgical, health and accident, disability, life insurance, death benefits, pension and retirement plans, These are among the fringe benefits which add substantially to the cost of labor.

But we're thinking only of direct labor costs. Something like "a fair day's pay for a fair day's work." No extras. Included are the base rate plus any overtime, premium pay, shift differential, earned incentive, and production bonus.

More Items Unaccountable

But it's not that simple or clear cut. Whereas we assume we pay for time worked, in reality we pay for other time too.

Take rest periods, for instance. Wherever these are granted no one expects the worker to punch "in" and "out" and not be paid for this time. This cost is sizable. A company which works a 37½-hour week and grants 15-minute morning and afternoon passes, has 1/15 of its payroll going for time not worked.

Another big item is vacations. Here an employee is paid yet not expected to work. How big is this item? If an average of two weeks vacation is given per employee, then another 1/26 of the payroll is for time not worked. This increases when vacation allowances are liberalized, as is the trend these days. And it increases further when double wages are paid to employees who "sell back" all or part of their vacation.

The cost of holidays also adds up. The minimum number of national and religious holidays is six, and this number is double or more in certain sections of the country. Holidays are not just days off from work; in our culture it is taken for granted that these are paid holidays.

Personal Time Off

These are the big items. These are the obvious costs. But these are not the only ones. There are all sorts of other company policies which provide for pay for time not worked.

It is customary for most firms to "not dock" workers who stay home ill for a day or so. The argument is that the employee's living expenses continue so his income should not be interrupted. Quite a few companies have salary continuation programs, on a full or partial basis, for the long-term illness.

It is not uncommon for employers to pay for an occasional personal day off. Companies generally pay a worker who is serving on a jury or as a court witness, or while he is voting. Lately more firms are making up any difference in pay for employees on temporary military leave or national guard duty.

There are other items. In cases of involuntary terminations or discharges, companies pay two weeks' salary in lieu of notice. It is also the policy of most firms to pay employees who are absent because of death in the family. Some companies have a marriage leave policy which allows an employee an extra week off with pay.

Then there are the special arrangements peculiar to certain companies, types of work, or union agreements. These include paid lunch periods, get-ready time, clothes-changing time, wash-up time, and even travel time. And there are some payments that are required under guaranteed work week or work year.

Wages and salaries are charged against the cost of production. But a growing percentage of the annual payroll never finds its way into finished goods or services. It ought rightfully be considered as a contribution to social customs that have crept into the industrial fabric of our everyday lives.

JURY DUTY
(A Typical Company Policy)

The company has adopted a liberal attitude toward duty as a member of a jury or as a witness, as a way of encouraging employees to be good citizens.

Any employee called to jury service or subpoenaed as a witness will, upon presentation of call, be considered "on-the-job" and will be paid at the regular rate of salary for the period required to serve. In addition, he will be permitted to retain whatever jury pay he receives.

While on jury duty an employee will be expected to return to work during those hours when he is not required to be in court. Exception to this provision can be made when an entire jury is under protection of the court.

Absences for jury or witness duty will be recorded on the time sheets with the letter "J" in black.

VOTING TIME OFF

There is no federal law which requires employers to give their workers time off for voting. But 30 states have laws which set the rules. The terms vary. Companies must give time off, under certain conditions, usually upon request. In some cases companies are required to pay for the time but need not count the hours as time worked.

Most companies encourage their employees to take their civic responsibilities seriously. They urge their employees to vote. Many gladly give them time off, either by allowing them to arrive later in the morning or leave earlier in the afternoon, whichever is more convenient to both the worker's personal voting arrangements and the company's work schedules. In cases such as these, companies usually are more than willing to "not dock" the workers for the time away from work. This is not the problem. The problem is that workers are *entitled* to time off in some states and employers should acquaint themselves with the law in their state.

Some firms have been known to open up an hour or two later than usual, particularly on national election days. This not only takes the pressure off workers, who then have more time to fulfill their voting obligations, but it also allows the younger employees, those below the voting age, to stay home a while with their younger brothers and sisters, while their parents vote.

Occasionally a worker asks for the entire day off. He may have volunteered to serve at the polls either as an unpaid watcher or a paid election clerk. Granting this time off is up to the company. The usual practice is to permit the employee to take the day off but not to pay him since he very likely may be paid by the election commission for working at the polls.

LEAVES OF ABSENCE and FURLOUGHS

Companies try to avoid the "on again, off again" employees—those who do not work steady. But even regular employees sometimes need to take time off for various reasons, such as illness or accident, pregnancy, personal or family affairs, military duty, or travel.

A leave of absence is granted for a short period away from work. In the case of prolonged illness, this leave may be extended upon medical advice.

A leave of absence implies that employee benefits are uninterrupted, seniority continues, vacation rights accrue, and his job is saved for him. Wages stop, although some form of insurance coverage or welfare policy may provide a type of compensation.

When an employee wants to be away for a longer period of time, a furlough may be considered. A furlough is like a termination except it carries with it certain rehire rights. Employee benefits are discontinued, seniority does not accrue during the absence, and the job is not guaranteed to be saved. Wages, of course, stop.

Benefits and seniority are, however, held in abeyance. Upon return to work, to a position of like status and pay (if available), full employee benefits are immediately reinstated where they left off at time furlough began, and seniority (like a rewound clock) is accumulated to the previous record.

LEAVES, ABSENCES, and FURLOUGHS

(A Typical Company Policy)

It is the purpose of this policy to assure employees of certain job rights or considerations pertaining to their employment status in accordance with the conditions and privileges stated herein. Upon the written recommendation of the manager, the division director in charge may grant an employee time off without pay under one of the following arrangements:

PERSONAL LEAVE OF ABSENCE

Conditions: Should be requested by employee. Must be for employee's personal convenience, unrelated to the job. Cannot exceed 30 days or one month. Cannot be extended beyond 30 days or one month. When an employee is absent for personal reasons for one week or more, even when the period includes a holiday, a personal leave of absence should be initiated.

Rights: Seniority continues to accrue. Employee benefits are uninterrupted. Employee maintains the right to his particular job.

DISABILITY ABSENCE

Conditions: Should be requested by employee or initiated by the manager on behalf of the employee who is absent because of illness or accident. (Separate policy for workmen's compensation cases.) Must be supported by written advice of the employee's physician to our clinic. Must have concurrence of the clinic. Begins when sick pay expires. Cannot exceed 30 days or one month. With the approval of the chief executive officer, extensions may be granted for not more than 30 days or one month at any time. In no case should the disability absence plus extensions run more than six months.

Rights: Seniority continues to accrue. Employee benefits are uninterrupted. Employee maintains the right to his job (even when it has been filled temporarily by another person).

DISABILITY FURLOUGH

Conditions: At the expiration of a disability absence, and/or its extensions, an employee who, in the opinion of our clinic, is still medically unable to return to work, will automatically be placed on a disability furlough. The length of the disability furlough will be for any known or at least reasonable period of time, subject to periodic verification that the employee is medically unable to return to work as determined by our clinic. In no case will the disability furlough, including any disability absence immediately prior thereto, extend more than one year from the date sick pay expired. At the end of this one year, employee will be terminated subject to reemployment rights as outlined below.

Rights: While absent from work, group life insurance (both basic and supplementary) (1) waiver of premium (retroactive to date of disability) becomes effective subject to approval of carrier, and (2) if later returns to work, life insurance coverage and payments can be resumed in company group. Health and accident insurance claim, once established will run its normal course, but employee will be dropped from our group. Disability insurance, where applicable, will pay regular benefits according to the contract. Group hospitalization and medical-surgical insurance, single or family coverage may be (1) continued in group with employee making arrangements to pay the total cost while on disability furlough or (2) when disability furlough ends before employee returns to work, employee transferred to direct membership, with employee making payments direct to carrier.

In the event of return to work during period of disability furlough, (1) full credit toward seniority for previous service, with seniority date amended to reflect time off; (2) prompt reinstatement of all employee benefits, with the next scheduled vacation allowance prorated; (3) Every possible consideration for a job of like status and pay provided one is open.

In the event of return to work after employee has been terminated, (1) seniority rights and benefits will be decided at time of reinstatement on payroll and will be based on length of previous service, prior position, etc., and job and salary to be offered will depend upon qualifications of the returning worker and availability of suitable job opening.

PREGNANCY FURLOUGH

Conditions: Upon request of the employee. Must have concurrence of our clinic. For female married employees who have been employed for one year or more. Not to start later than the beginning of the seventh month of pregnancy. Not to extend beyond three months following the termination of pregnancy. Pregnancy furlough cannot be extended. When an employee is available and requests return to work, but because of company convenience is required to wait, the extension of time will be treated as a personal furlough.

Rights: Group hospitalization and medical-surgical insurance—pregnancy furlough is considered a termination with the exception that the employee may elect to continue for all or part of the pregnancy furlough period her coverage as part of our group. An amount will be deducted from the final paycheck sufficient to cover the full cost to the 1st of the month, following the end date of pregnancy furlough.

Upon return to work: Full credit toward seniority for previous service, with seniority date amended to reflect time off, prompt reinstatement of all employee benefits, with the next scheduled vacation allowance prorated, and consideration for a job of like status and pay provided one is open.

MILITARY LEAVE OF ABSENCE

Conditions: Should be requested by employee as a result of his military duty orders. For temporary service in the National Guard or Reserve. For a period not to exceed 15 calendar days.

Rights: Seniority continues to accrue. Employee benefits are uninterrupted. Employee maintains the right to his particular job.

EXTENDED MILITARY SERVICE FURLOUGH

Conditions: For any employee who is drafted, enlists, or is recalled to extended military duty. Furlough to coincide with his military orders.

Rights: Upon evidence of his acceptance into military service the employee will receive pay for one extra week, if he has at least one year of continuous service, pay for two extra weeks, if he has at least two years of continuous service.

Following his military service, he must, under the Selective Service Act of 1948, be reemployed to a position of like status and pay unless the employer's circumstances have so changed as to make it impossible or unreasonable to re-employ him if:

He has an honorable discharge, he applies within 90 days after discharge (or within 90 days from hospitalization following discharge for a period of not more than one year), and he is still qualified to perform the duties of the position he left.

To qualify for full reinstatement the employee will be asked to present his discharge certificate (a photostat copy may be made for personnel records) and to provide such information about his military record as may be considered advisable to bring his personal history up to date.

PERSONAL FURLOUGH

Conditions: When it is necessary for an employee to take time off from work for a longer period than provided under personal leave of absence, or for a reason not covered in any of the preceding arrangements. May be used by the manager in preference to an outright release in the case of an employee who leaves (except to try another job) for whom we want to keep the "return to the company" door open. Cannot be extended and in no case can it be granted for more than 12 months.

Rights: Full credit toward seniority for previous service, with seniority date amended to reflect time off. Prompt reinstatement of all employee benefits, with the next scheduled vacation allowance prorated. Consideration for a job of like status and pay provided one is open.

Furloughs: An employee on furlough will be considered as having terminated, as far as records and payroll listing are concerned. Benefits will also end except that an employee on a disability furlough, pregnancy furlough, or disability claim may continue in the group hospitalization and medical-surgical insurance portion of the benefit program as described earlier. Like any other termination he will be paid for unused vacation, reported as a termination to the employee gift fund committee, replaced on the job (unless the job is abolished), etc. Upon return to work he will be subject to "rights" as explained under each specific furlough.

Benefits Continuation: An employee on a personal leave of absence or a disability absence has the right as explained earlier to continue under the company's benefit program. If he is paying part of the cost as in the case of group hospitalization and medical-surgical insurance family coverage and/or contributory life insurance, he can cooperate to continue these additional benefits. He may authorize a deduction from his final paycheck to cover his share of the cost of the benefits during his leave period or he may make arrangements for payment monthly, in advance, by sending his check to personnel. If payments should lapse, his benefits will revert to employee only protection.

Reports: Notification of leave of absence or furlough must be reported individually to personnel and should be sent whenever possible prior to the effective date. When a furloughed employee is rehired, an "add notice" will be completed to reinstate him on payroll.

POLICY MANUAL

A policy manual is a very useful tool for managers and supervisors. It tells them what the official position is on most of the policy questions they may expect to encounter in dealing with workers.

Employee handbooks cover the more common practices for the convenience of employees. But these handy books are written in general terms, the policies stated briefly, and the information aimed at *selling* the policies rather than *administering* them. The managers need more specific instructions on how to handle a particular situation when it comes up.

Policy information is disseminated to supervisory personnel in many different ways. Often this may be in memo form from a superior officer to a supervisor telling him how to meet a problem. Unless other supervisors get copies, there is little likelihood that the next situation arising elsewhere will be similarly handled. And unless policy instructions are numbered, or issued under some pattern, it may well be that the instructions, issued earlier, may not be found when needed.

One good solution is to issue a policy manual to each executive, manager, and supervisor—those who have authority over other workers. Such a manual should be looseleaf so it can be kept current simply by adding or replacing pages.

Each policy item in a policy manual is on a separate page or pages. Thus, the vacation policy will be separate from the antidiscrimination policy. These policy items, mimeographed or printed on 8½ by 11 punched paper, are filed in alphabetical order in a ring binder, separated by dividers for easy lookup. Jury Duty is under "J," Blood Banks under "B," and so on.

Leave Some Leeway

Each policy should be clearly spelled out in enough detail to enable the supervisor with the question to proceed toward a satisfactory solution. It should not be so detailed, however, that it becomes a straitjacket, but should allow the supervisor some leeway. By staying within the framework of established policy, the supervisor knows that any decision he makes will not conflict with similar decisions made by other supervisors. Everybody, this way, is playing by the same rules.

Policies should not be copied from a book nor borrowed from other companies. They should be written and included in the policy manual only as they are needed to resolve problems. There should be no hesitancy to revise any policy when it is no longer adequate to meet a new or changed situation.

The preparation and maintenance of the policy manual should rest in one location, and the personnel office is the most likely first choice. The personnel staff is charged with the implementation, accountability, and continuing conformance to policies by supervisors throughout the company. Who then is more logical to originate and update policies as they relate to the employee program? This does not mean that the personnel officer has sole authority for initiating or changing company policies; but he has the responsibility for getting the policy-making group, such as senior staff, to listen to and act upon his recommendations and for getting the president to give each policy the approval it needs to be put into effect.

A policy manual is a confidential reference guide to aid supervisors and should be issued to all who need it, but not indiscrimately to others. A good control over the use of these policy manuals is to include in the binder the list of management personnel to whom the original binders, and later changes or added pages, are distributed.

PART 12

PERSONNEL STATESMANSHIP

Personnel administration:
A way of life
History of "personnel"
What is your philosophy?
Some corporate examples
The human element
A management function
A peek at the future

PERSONNEL SHOULD NOT BE A DEPARTMENT

In many organizations the central headquarters for the employee program is referred to as the personnel department. This is done whether or not the chief personnel executive is considered to be the equivalent of a department manager in authority, responsibility, and influence.

This unintentional classification is unfortunate from two viewpoints. First, the personnel officer conducts himself much the same as a department head, even while his opportunity is greater. Second, others in management look upon the personnel activity as a service function about on a par with other departments.

Use of the word "department" unwittingly introduces the unnecessary concept of levels, which adds nothing to the status of the activity, or to the acceptance of an idea, or to the administration of the program. It can only confound the issue since in this case "level" has nothing whatever to do with effectiveness. Each separate aspect of the employee program should stand on its own merits and not be accepted or rejected on the basis of any superficial consideration such as the prestige or position of the individual who is proposing it.

Higher ups who have a natural tendency to look down upon their own subordinate departments cannot be blamed if they then look down upon personnel, if it is tagged as another of many departments. Conversely, assistants who look up to department managers for leadership may be predisposed to accept carte blanche any guidance and direction which the personnel director proffers.

Not Who Is Right, But What Is Right

In any situation involving the establishment or application of policy, the introduction of a new procedure, the evaluation of an applicant's qualifications, the interpretation of placement tests, the granting or rejection of a wage increase or promotion, or any other aspect of personnel administration, any discussion between parties should be objective or neutral, not affected by personalities or organization rank. When an idea is good, it doesn't become better because a vice-president, instead of an assistant manager, proposes or supports it.

Personnel decisions should not be made on the basis of majority vote but only on what is right or wrong in the particular circumstance under consideration. An employee program, to be effective, must reflect the attitudes of the workforce, not the peculiar whims of unprofessional personnel advisers no matter how well-intentioned they are or how high they rank in the organization.

A personnel executive who is content to be a department manager will soon find himself administering other people's ideas, some sound and some unsound. Then when the stew, because of too many cooks, is unpalatable, who will be blamed? He will. And he should be—for letting it happen. Too many corporate officers want to be relieved of the dirty work while still maintaining control.

No man, when he is promoted to an executive or management position, acquires overnight the skill and insight which the trained personnel executive has acquired over the years and which he is continually testing and challenging. Topside should lend support and authority to personnel programs considered to be sound, practical, and in the company's interest, but should be careful not to use its authority to dictate in a field which is potent and volatile and not responsive to the logic of managerial rationale.

The personnel officer should also be careful not to degrade or upgrade himself and his program in relation to other facets of management. What does it matter whether he is, or thinks he is, more or less important than the purchasing agent, or the comptroller, or the production superintendent? His value lies not in prestige nor in the place he occupies on the company organization chart. Just as he should not be expected to let others dictate his program, simply because they outrank him, so also should he not be permitted to impose his ideas and his program upon others.

Needs No Authority

Ideally, the personnel administrator should have no authority. If he needs position or rank to put his program across, then there is something wrong with it. A comprehensive personnel program, well designed and properly communicated to all concerned, will be accepted by employees, by managers, and by the company for the reason that it works.

The easiest way to foul up an otherwise good program is for the personnel officer and the line executives he serves to get all tangled up in needless controversy about rank. Instead of lining up against each other they would be better advised to line up alongside each other to face their common problem and try to arrive at a mutually beneficial solution.

I will never forget a discussion I had some years ago with a vice-president of the company for which I was personnel director. I had been there one year when he called me in.

"Something bothers me," he began, "and I would like to get it off my mind. We had a personnel program before you joined us, and I'll be the first to admit we now have a better one.

"But as you build your program, and expand your influence, all with our approval and acceptance, I have to wonder where you get your additional authority.

"As I picture it, there is only 100 percent in the management pie. I have my share, and for purposes of this discussion it doesn't matter whether it is larger or smaller than that of the other fellow. What does matter is that I worked hard for my share and I don't relish the idea of relinquishing even a small part of it to anyone, including you, regardless how effective you are."

So he concluded with the question, "Where do you fit in?"

The Line-Staff Concept

I explained, by way of oversimplification, that his was a line function and mine was staff. The management pie, as he described it, was the operations end of the business. In effect, I was not part of that pie at all. The responsibility for running the company belonged to him and the other line operators. My sole purpose for being there was simply to make their jobs easier.

"Think of yourself, and the other line executives, as the operating pie," I suggested. "Then think of me as the whipped cream over the entire pie, not as part of the pie itself. The pie, with its several unevenly cut slices, was probably good to begin with. If I am successful, as you admitted earlier, then the entire pie should be better because of the addition of my effectiveness."

This explanation seemed to satisfy him. There never again was any conflict between us. We understood our respective roles in the company and he knew my program was intended to complement his activity, not compete with him.

PERSONNEL ADMINISTRATION IS A WAY OF LIFE

Personnel management is many things to many people. The confusion results from misunderstanding.

If top management is confused, this is to be expected. No two personnel practitioners, it seems, can agree on the scope of their responsibilities or the challenge of their opportunities. They might have identical titles, but that's where the similarity ends. Their programs vary all over the map from centralized employment to service functions to management development to organization planning.

The reason is that most personnel managers have jobs, albeit good jobs. The truly dedicated personnel executive does not have a job; he has a vocation. Expressed another way, only one man in a thousand plays the drum; the others beat it.

Thousands of personnel administrators strive for lifetime careers in this relatively new but rapidly growing facet of management. Depending upon external influences over which they have little control, such as the economic climate and the stability of company operations, many of these personnel executives enjoy a fair measure of personal prosperity. How many, however, are making any notable contribution to better management?

Personnel managers can bring service to their companies, benefit to the employees who depend upon them, and credit to themselves, if they could just be made to realize that personnel administration is much more than day-to-day performance of necessary administrative duties.

Personnel administration is a science that can be learned, an art that can be acquired, and a profession wherein stature can be attained.

Science is knowing how and what to do; it is the accumulated knowledge systemized and formulated. Art is the way the job is done: the application of natural talents. Profession is the manner of performance: conforming to ethical and moral standards of conduct.

Know-Why Important

Many personnel practitioners have the know-how, but not the know-why—scientists but not artists. Some possess a superficial knowledge of many procedures without the depth of understanding. Others work hard at the methods, and become quite adept too. They are the recognized technicians, the master mechanics, learned in all the "tools of the trade" but not the purpose behind them.

All of these people miss the whole point of their opportunity: Where they leave off is where personnel administration first *begins!*

Personnel administration is an area of management that is changing faster than most others. It is no longer safe to learn the techniques, either from books or experience, and then expect to go out and practice them. Personnel administration cannot be run by the book. Neither is it a trade that can be performed with cold efficiency the way a mechanic uses his hands as he follows a blueprint. Nor can it be governed by the head, with emotion or sentiment or tradition dictating the actions.

To be effective, personnel administration must be personal, not in its procedures necessarily, but in its effect or meaning to the individual whom it is intended to benefit. It should deal in human values. What the soul is to the body is what human relations is to personnel administration. Employee programs which are made up of techniques but not understanding have a shell for a body and an ache for a soul.

The field is gradually coming of age. Personnel management is maturing because the growth of companies carries with it a complexity of new duties involving people. And in the total management picture personnel is no longer in the periphery, but closer to the center of activity where the hard decisions are made. In the process the breed of successful personnel practitioners has changed from professional do-gooders to technical specialists, and finally to practical philosophers as the emphasis shifted from making employees happy to making them productive.

CAPSULE HISTORY OF PERSONNEL ADMINISTRATION

Phase	Dates back to	Its service is	Development	Status
Past	1917	Practical	Started with centralized employment	None
Present	1939	Technical	Began to introduce techniques	Departmental
Future	1960	Philosophical	Something to believe in	Executive

Forms Are Not the Job

Fortunately there are personnel executives who are growing as their reservoir of functions is being deepened as well as widened. There are the leaders who are making progress in their profession and in their companies. No company can give recognition to people it feels unworthy of the award; on the other hand, no company can deny recognition earned by the consistent day-to-day performance of the dedicated personnel executive who works from the heart.

The personnel directors who are making a contribution to the field are those who are developing a philosophy of what the work is all about. The forms, procedures, and devices used are not the job; these are merely the paraphernalia of the personnel administrator. In short, personnel management is not something they do, but something they believe in.

To them personnel administration is not a job; it is a calling. It is not a way of making a living. Personnel administration is a Way of Life.

897

WHAT IS THE PERSONALITY
OF YOUR PERSONNEL PROGRAM?

In many companies there is a tendency to discount the significance of personnel management. Where this attitude prevails one or both of two factors may be involved: (1) the company has not yet felt the need for putting all elements of management into proper focus, or (2) the personnel executive has not learned to appreciate fully his responsibility and opportunity.

In either case the impression exists that to be effective in employee relations requires little more than common sense and good intentions. Of course, common sense is necessary if for no other reason than that the employee program be logical and orderly. And good intentions can certainly be helpful in the administration of any program. There is, however, much more to a personnel program— much more.

Take a careful look at some of the personnel programs in your particular locality or industry. What does such a study reveal? It is disheartening to note that many companies still have no clear idea of the nature of personnel work. Often they confuse it with welfare activities and various paternalistic practices.

Many Born of Emergency

Then ask yourself how many personnel programs were established because some far-sighted executive recognized the wisdom of treating employees with the same consideration generally accorded customers. Most personnel programs were emergency-created, and their present status is merely the gradual outgrowth of some earlier problem situations. Some are still considered a luxury or expense, not expected to contribute much to the firm's cost-cutting or operating efficiency.

Consequently the field is cluttered with many personnel managers who have not taken the trouble or time to become acquainted with the fundamental challenges inherent in their jobs. These include former supervisors, foremen, and others who came up through the ranks, some rewarded with promotions because of loyal performance elsewhere in the organization, others actually "demoted uphill" in order to get them out of the way.

Is that what is meant by personnel leadership and personnel administration? What about scientific principles? A few actually become adept and turn into master mechanics in the field of personnel. But operating professionally in the techniques of personnel administration is not sufficient if they remain amateurs in the area of humanistics.

Especially where scientific procedures have been developed to a high degree, the thought of humanizing the personnel activity is considered secondary if it is considered at all. These people fear that such an approach would vitiate what they believe is essentially an impersonal piece of scientific management.

It would be a mistake not to pay attention to the engineering aspects of the personnel program. But it would be an even bigger mistake to imagine that an engineering plan would be the solution to the employee program. Undue reliance upon scientific methods would create more problems than it would solve.

The best plans are no more than frameworks into which living people must be fitted. These scientific programs cannot become straitjackets, precluding all flexibility, initiative, and spontaneity; they can not be iron case regulations covering every action, telling exactly what must be done, and how, on every occasion.

That "Extra Something"

However personnel administration is defined, it is not only techniques and procedures. These are merely the paraphernalia of the personnel administrator. The significance of employee relations goes much deeper to embody the motives and methods of dealing with and organizing people of all levels at their places of work in order to get them to give and accomplish the best that is in them while at the same time getting the maximum degree of personnel satisfaction.

The best way to bridge the wide gap between intent and accomplishment is by developing, in addition to common sense practices and scientific procedures, that extra something that gives substance to the program, namely, the personnel personality. In a sense, every personnel program already has some sort of personality, just as every dog, even a mongrel, has some sort of pedigree. The opportunity facing every personnel administrator is to shape the personality of his program so that it will be a favorable one.

Generally the personality of the employee program is not created— it just happens. Like hash, it accumulates. Usually it mirrors the personality of the chief executive, or the person or persons who influence its operations. It is well, therefore, to analyze some impacts of personality on the employee program. There are a number of characteristics about the leaders which may have a vital influence on the company. They include the basic beliefs of the chief executive and his advisory staff of senior assistants. Their administrative practices, their particular specialty and management experience, their history with the company, and their effect on organizational pressures are all factors to consider.

When Management Overpowers

In these types of situations personnel programs are often a hodge-podge of centralized activity, reflecting the fancies of top management executives who complain about the ineffectiveness of personnel functions yet unwittingly dominate the personnel personality.

Personnel program developers should recognize that their responsibility goes beyond trying to impress officials in whose hands their personal job destiny is centered. To fulfill their obligations they cannot be just the administrators of everybody else's ideas, some sound, some untried. They would be wiser to develop a program which reflects the character and personality of the work force.

Nor should a personnel personality be built by using some other company's blueprint. Too often a business, in its personnel program, will try to duplicate or adapt the successful features of another company's program. Just as men yield to some terrible compulsion to conform in dress and appearance, even in their thinking, they likewise like to copy personnel ideas from other firms. This does not build a company personality. When a personnel program adopts a little item from this company, another from a second company, and so on, it is more nearly to develop a program which is characteristic of chop suey.

Difference Is Important

Why copy another company's program? In that case, why should people want to work for one employer in preference to another? Stepping out of character to imitate others in forfeiture of individual personality.

In referring to the personalities of individuals or business the attention is not on their similarities, but rather on the subtle differences that distinguish one from the other. Actually there is very little difference between one man and another. But that little difference is tremendously important. This also applies to personnel programs. In many respects they are all alike—in their functions and in their responsibilities. So it is not in their similarities that they are distinctive but in their distinguishable differences. These are very significant.

The difference may not be very obvious, but that degree of difference is what determines the personality.

Every personnel program is composed of various elements in varying proportions. What makes one product different from another are not only the elements that go into it but also the proportions of every element used. Take a cake recipe, for example. Different ingredients will result in different kinds of cakes. But even the same ingredients will turn out cakes that are not alike if the amount of the ingredients varies.

With the same 88 notes on the keyboard, why does one man's music sound better or worse than that of another? It is the skill used in arranging the notes, the tempo with which they are played, and especially the touch or feeling that is put into the playing that accounts for the difference. When a musician goes flat on one note he spoils the entire effect.

A personnel program of 88 component parts will likewise not be the same in one company as in another even if the identical 88 components are used. Expressed another way, just putting notes together won't make music; it is more likely to produce noise. Putting separate personnel procedures together will not, of itself, result in an effective program.

The elements that go into creating a personnel personality must all be present in sufficient quantity to assure having a personality at all. But the degree of emphasis placed on each of the component elements will make the difference between one personality and another.

Look for Meaning

The combinations and permutations of these component elements is what makes one personnel personality distinctive from another. What these elements are and what degree of emphasis each element should receive is the decision of the personnel executive as he strives to fashion the type of personnel personality that best suits the needs of his company and his work force.

Conscientious personnel administrators who seek guidance in this matter are reminded that the basic functions of all personnel programs can generally be divided into several broad areas. Academically speaking, the logical subdivisions of a total personnel program (as listed earlier under "The Functions of Personnel) are these: (1) Research and standards, (2) employment, (3) education and training, (4) safety and health, (5) employee activities, (6) wages and salaries, and (7) benefit administration, with the possible addition of labor relations as an extra category. The day-to-day personnel activities, and the scientific or systematic methods used to perform them that fall into these categories tend to make all employee programs alike.

But personnel administrators must be concerned not only with the functions but also with their meaning. The extent to which these functions are humanized determines the meaningful difference between programs.

A good personnel executive knows at all times how closely the program matches the personality of the work force. He studies not only the efficiency but also the behavior and cultural pattern of people available for employment. He builds his program by building people.

Business, you see, does not exist merely to produce more goods or better services, though that is no small part of its task. Business also, especially in today's enlightened era, affords the principal means whereby individuals may gain the satisfaction of accomplishing something more than merely sustaining their own lives.

A personnel program built around procedures, even though each separate instrument is a technical masterpiece, is lifeless. A program built around people is warmly effective because it has a personality. The administrator of a coldly efficient program is an ordinary personnel manager. The administrator of a personality plus program is an extraordinary personnel executive.

What is the personality of your personnel program?

WHAT IS THE PHILOSOPHY
OF YOUR PERSONNEL PROGRAM?

Before we can begin any kind of employee program, we should have a philosophy of what we are trying to accomplish. What is such a philosophy as it applies to the personnel program? Maybe it can be explained with an illustration.

Many young pine trees were planted in their particular forest. A few have already disappeared but most are struggling valiantly. Here is one almost covered over with dead weeds. We must let in the sun to give it a new chance. Here is another that is being choked by large vines. Again we must come to the rescue. Some are lifting their tiny arms into the sunlight free from hindrance. All are trying. This is the glory of creation—all are trying. Man's function here is to help bring order and overall progress out of aimless growth and blind competition.

Individuals Too Must Grow

The human garden is in very much the same condition. Most employees either want to grow and don't quite know how, or they are struggling with a handicap, real or imagined, which they themselves don't know how to eliminate or live with. This is where we come in.

Employee development is a living thing, and like any living thing needs constant attention. Workers need more than working space, materials, and methods. In order to grow, they need the sound cultivation of good work environs, the sunshine of warm-hearted interest, the nourishment of other people's knowledge and experience, the fresh air of inspiring and patient guidance, the good climate of mutual respect, and the deep roots of security and permanence.

Managements must be loyal to the fundamental faith in the very personal quality of the individuals who want to grow with the company. It takes unselfish executive leadership to build others. Yet, unless workers profit, management cannot profit.

At its workers grow, so a company prospers. For the growth of any organization is merely the sum total of the growth of the individuals constituting it.

THE HUMAN ELEMENT IN BUSINESS

Let me philosophize a bit about the human element in business. This is not the type of technical discussion that is intended to put ideas into your notebook. In this kind of presentation we're not trying to move the pen; we are trying to move the spirit.

The really dedicated personnel practitioner, whether he be a staff specialist in the personnel office or a manager or supervisor in the line organization, believes there is a right place in this world for everyone. The difficulty is that we may not always know where to find it. It's just that some folks are easier to help than others; usually these people need our help the least. But all people, including those who pose more of a problem, are entitled to our interest and fairness in our consideration.

Look at this selfishly if you want to. It's a case of "employ 'em or support 'em." Our job is to place people where they are best suited. But in that regard we must never for one moment lose sight of the plain fact that there is good in everyone. If we don't believe that then we're debasing the glory of creation. Because people are not biological accidents; they are created. And things and people are created for a purpose.

Emerson described a weed as "a plant whose virtues have not yet been discovered." Not long ago medical science found in the venom of the deadly cobra a possible cure for polio. The center of your football team is just as valuable as the quarterback . . . even though he does see half of the game upside down and backwards.

Whose Standards?

Yes, there is good in everyone, although we may not always understand it. That's because we insist upon measuring everybody by the same standards—our standards. I heard an award-winning news commentator say that "the only reason some of us are down here while other folks are in the stone institution atop the hill is that for the moment we outnumber them." That's quite a profound statement —worth pondering.

Talents vary, but they are all God-given. Don't we believe that people are created in the image of God? Who is there among us who will suggest that possibly in a few instances the Divine Planner may have made a mistake?

Perhaps it is just that we have not yet learned the proper place for some people . . . the spot for which they are intended. They don't fit as well into the standard pattern of life which the rest of us have established as socially and industrially acceptable.

For example: There are many jobs that outstandingly mature and well-educated individuals would be appalled by, at which individuals with certain exaggerated personality traits fare better. Some neurotics are submissive persons who are glad to do extra hours of work that others reject; some are extreme perfectionists who turn out accurate and reliable work because anything less makes them uncomfortable. These people have a built-in quality control that others acquire only under heavy discipline. But don't confuse these useful neurotics with the troublesome types.

Every personality has a hidden switch. It is up to us to keep trying until we find it . . . even if we blow a few fuses occasionally.

So we may conclude that when people are misfits in our work situation the fault may be more ours than theirs. Those who don't learn as well as others may be learning wrong things. I go back to my grammar school days to remember a chap who probably never earned the diploma he got eventually. But he could drive a steam locomotive on a spur railroad. Those of us who look down upon him, and others like him, can we match his particular skill?

In World War II, I saw conditions eight thousand miles away where natives, God's creatures, lived and existed in primitive surroundings where no one of us would have remained sane very long. Even under army conditions, which meant that a part of the familiar and comfortable U.S. had been transplanted temporarily to a tropical isle, I watched well-educated men gradually go berserk. One of my former tentmates, who was sent back to the states with a boatload of carefully guarded mental degenerates, was later quite normal and again working as an industrial sociologist.

Fits and Misfits

Take him, and some of us perhaps, out of our environment, and we become the misfits. Likewise, take the individual who seems out of place in our office or shop, find a more suitable niche for him in society, and he becomes better adjusted. What I'm saying is that there are three kinds of workers in the labor force: the Fits, the Misfits, and the Counterfeits. The Fits are no problem, and these are the ones we usually brag about as our success stories. But we have little or no right to boast because they are naturally Grade A material and we can't claim much of the credit. The Misfits obviously need help and there is a conscientious effort in most companies to shift them around and to work with them to fit them better into the organization. But it is the Counterfeits who test our talents, patience, and ingenuity as we strive to increase the efficiency of our work force.

Getting all people placed where they do the best for themselves, for their companies, and for society is the obligation that awaits all of us who are privileged to serve humanity.

IS PERSONNEL MANAGEMENT A PROFESSION?

Personnel management is here to stay. Very few people will disagree on that point. But as to the purpose of personnel, and the place of personnel in different organizations, there apparently is considerable misunderstanding.

Some years back this newest member moved in on the management family. At that time, and since then, it received varying degrees of welcome from other members of the family. For the most part this new addition, which gradually became known by the name of personnel, was tolerated and accepted because it was too small to get into anybody's way.

But now it is growing up—and beginning to command attention. Some members of the family are accepting it as an equal, others still seem to look down upon it as a stepchild. What complicates matters further is that this youngster personnel has a tendency to confound the others by its behavior. Sometimes it gets into trouble; at other times it actually shows signs of having outgrown the pecadilles of its mixed-up youth.

A factual appraisal of the situation reveals that personnel has not yet attained the position it deserves. Personnel practitioners can dream about equal status with other segments of management. Planners can place personnel high on the charts on drawing boards. Professors can theorize in the classroom. But the fact remains that in most companies personnel has not yet been recognized as it could or should be.

And this is for only one reason: Personnel generally is not yet making the kind of contribution to general management which merits a place for it topside.

There is an opportunity for personnel to grow up and eventually approach the bigness that the other fellow has already attained. There is also a need for this.

One way might be to grow up professionally.

The Pattern of Professions

Before accepting the thesis that professionalization of the personnel activity is the solution to personnel growing up, it might be well to consider whether the pattern of the established professions is adaptable to the cause of personnel administration.

In the professions are individuals who by their choice of lifetime work and their specialized training have set themselves apart from other workers in the community. Because of their practice they are different from others, better in their particular respect, and therefore to be looked up to. This is the attraction which appeals to the advocates of professionalization of the personnel activity. There is a serious danger for personnel people who follow this path of professionalization, for it tends to isolate the personnel practitioner from the people he serves. While all the evidence points to the fact that top executives come from the ranks of line managers, personnel people move away from the role of manager toward the staff titles which imply consultative work. Instead of joining the ranks of management people they are inclined to set themselves apart. They have even developed a lingo of their own designed to mystify and impress others with their singular importance.

Be the Invisible Man

To be effective the personnel administrator must move more in the direction of generalization, toward a well-balanced personnel service which is integrated into every other aspect of management. Ideally, he should strive for relative anonymity, with his own identity blended into the background of his company. He cannot serve the purpose of personnel by setting himself up as a professional specialist. Only by involving himself in everybody else's business can he hope to earn a place in the everyday councils of management where the hard decisions are made.

The one approach builds the individual who grows in stature by being different from those he serves. The other approach minimizes self as a separate entity and gets its strength from general integration. While these are opposite approaches, they both can lead to professional stature.

On this basis, what can be learned by looking at the established professions such as medicine, law, and the ministry? What distinguishes them from other respected vocations? A quick analysis points up these distinct characteristics: (1) their qualifications, usually an isolated body of knowledge, (2) their progress or relentless drive for improvement, and (3) their standard of ethics, which motivates and guides them toward desired goals.

To qualify in other professions members must first meet definite academic requirements. No one is entitled to use "M.D." until he has completed prescribed courses of study and passed necessary examinations. A lawyer must first pass the bar before he can practice. This is certainly not the case in Personnel. Although there are many courses of study available to personnel administrators, it is not necessary to complete even one of these in order to hold down a personnel job. Personnel management has been considered more a process of osmosis and rote than specialized preparation for a profession; education and practice have been highly fragmentized.

No Promotions From Ranks

When the company doctor leaves the firm who would think of promoting his successor from the ranks? Yet this is often the way personnel vacancies are filled. The same companies that hire a trained accountant to do cost analyses, or a certified actuary to figure insurance rates, seem to feel that any pleasant, understanding sort of fellow can do personnel work. Getting along well with people seems to be the main requisite. While these are fine traits, they do not compensate for knowledge of systematic personnel procedures nor for professional expertness in personnel administration.

Too often the personnel manager is a former supervisor or manager who came up through the ranks, whose loyal performance was rewarded by promotion because he knows the customs, traditions, policies, and personalities of the company. And, of course, he is a friendly and pleasant person.

One danger of such a practice is that these personnel practitioners, while they are capable of following orders from higher up, and are capable of keeping the employee relations program from running into the ground, they do not have the depth of understanding to distinguish right from wrong in various personnel techniques. They are suckers for all sorts of personnel gimmicks which they embrace in an attempt to look good but which they really don't comprehend. They will buy a "pig in a poke" because they cannot appraise its potential value or possible harm. They will adopt another's successful procedure or device, then wonder why they do not get comparable results. They are like the church organist who knows music but cannot get the congregation to sing; he plays with his hands, not his heart.

Being relatively unskilled in their jobs it is not surprising to find these personnel people using outdated or discredited programs. They rely upon their special ability to "size up people." They work on hunches because they don't know how to be objective with facts. They tune in on official thinking before they stick their own necks out, and when they do make a decision they rely upon authority more than judgment. Usually they limp along concerned mostly with keeping their own noses clean.

Possibly some may argue that it is preferable to advance in the personnel field by building upon work experience rather than "book learning"—and in view of the many so-called successful people operating in the field of Personnel this is a strong argument. Yet even in these situations there is nothing to prevent sincere personnel managers, who have come up through the ranks, from determining their understanding of this field by measuring their capabilities against prevailing standards.

Many people in management, including many personnel people themselves, somehow feel that personnel work does not call for any specialized training other than that which can be acquired as they go along. Yet, can anyone practice medicine, or law, or teach?

The Job of Keeping Up

Perhaps another notable feature of the established professions is their eternal struggle to keep abreast of the times. Truth does not change but the ways of propagating it certainly do. Outmoded teaching methods must be abandoned. In medical science the vast accumulation of knowledge is as nothing compared with what it will be 10 years from now. Unfortunately, in personnel work research is by no means as important as practice.

Personnel administrators are still depending upon the old standbys of recruiting, methods which are rapidly reaching the point of no return. In hiring they still pretend to go through a process of selection when actually the selection procedure has become a series of rejections. The tests they use, developed decades ago and validated under conditions existing then, could be losing their usefulness and leading to erroneous conclusions. Their concern over the shortage of skills usually does not go beyond that of typists and secretaries in the office, or tool and die makers in the shop, when the real serious shortage of available skills is higher up, among executives. Companies still devote time and money to training, when the big problem, brought about by technological change, is retraining, which they ignore and thereby let the door of opportunity wide open for unwanted government intervention. Not enough personnel practitioners recognize their responsibility to the field which has provided them with a livelihood.

Pride of Workmanship

But a still more significant distinction between professional people and personnel administrators is something more vital than either of these other two factors. This is the standard of performance. In the conduct of their work true professional people are moved by a belief or a creed which goes beyond their day-to-day work, one which gives meaning to their actions. The clergy is the best example; theirs is a guiding philosophy which does not permit compromise. The medics have their Hippocratic oath which leads them to unbelievable heights of accomplishments. A good lawyer would much prefer to utilize his powers of persuasion to bring a broken family together than make an extra dollar handling a divorce case.

Before personnel administrators can even think of becoming professional they must develop a philosophy to guide them in all their actions. Too many personnel administrators are still concentrating on techniques, their goal being that of becoming master mechanics. On the road to professionalization a technique cannot be a destination in itself but merely a way of travel. A doctor does not practice medicine; he treats patients. A teacher does not teach a particular subject; he teaches students. A dedicated personnel administrator does not perform personnel duties; he deals with factors which affect not only a worker's living but also his life.

The personnel administrator is on his way to executive status who concerns himself not only with the function of things but also with their meaning. He attains bigness when he goes beyond personnel administration and begins to practice personnel statesmanship. As

---

A Profession ...

1. Develops a code of ethics, not only in writing but branded into the conscience and conduct of its practitioners.

2. Possesses a vast body of organized knowledge, developed by predecessors over the years, and available to newcomers, who in turn perpetuate, refine, and add to it for the next generation.

3. Calls for specific skills unlike those of other professions.

4. Requires that its members receive a certain defined formal instruction, preferably leading to a degree from a recognized institution of higher learning.

5. Provides for certification of proficiency before a member can achieve professional status.

6. Follows an orderly process in the fulfillment of responsibilities.

7. Offers opportunity for the promulgation and interchange of ideas among its members.

8. Demands an acceptance of the disciplines of the profession, realizing that the price of failure or malpractice is "out" of the profession.

---

soon as he learns to conduct himself in a professional manner the desire to professionalize his activity ceases to be important.

The desire for professional status is manifest in the many attempts to upgrade the position of the personnel administrator, not by performance but merely by changing the title to a more impressive one.

Personnel management calls for the use of scientific techniques and to some people this makes it a profession. It will be a long time, however, before any educational institution or professional society will accept the responsibility of certification of personnel executives as professional people. Meanwhile some trade groups, such as personnel associations, are toying with the idea, but it seems inadvisable to certify personnel administrators by decree.

Yet there are similarities between personnel management and the professions, especially in their formative years. The early professions surrounded themselves with mystery and paraphernalia. They used a special jargon—some still do. They claimed uniqueness and expected special privileges. They created bizarre titles for themselves. These descriptions fit many personnel executives.

The Fakes and Phonies

Not all professional people, of course, are worthy of the cloak of respectability that shields them from criticism or suspicion. Some are mountebanks and others are out-and-out fakes. Many personnel practitioners are phonies, too, impressing no one but themselves, as they surround themselves with specialized terms and incomprehensible language, involved procedures, trappings of the office and other outward appurtenances to confuse the laity. They forget that it is not through position or prestige that the personnel executive accomplishes his mission.

Socrates remarked that the only man who deserves to be given power is the man who doesn't want it—for he is the man most likely to treat his office as a trust and not as a trough.

A certificate on the wall does not make a man a professional. It merely gives him a label in a particular field. There could be, and sometimes is, a marked difference between professional identification and professional conduct.

The central theme of any profession is unselfish service to mankind, not service to self. The motivation should never be money. The legal definition of a professional worker is different from the one in common usage. In everyday language, being professional merely means accepting money for service. A professional baseball player is paid. The difference between professional golfers and amateur golfers is that the first get paid, not that they are any better or even different. This merely adds dignity to the job but not much else.

Dedication to duty should be ahead of every other consideration. This service, humbly rendered, is associated with guidance, extended

THE JOHNSON'S WAX CREED

We Believe

in fostering the creative power of people to perpetuate the general good and to that end we dedicate our company to serve:

OUR CUSTOMERS...

By developing and marketing broadening lines of superior products that meet the ever changing needs of consumers throughout the world.

OUR EMPLOYEES...

By recognizing their individual rights and dignity and quest for happiness.

By challenging their capacity for creative teamwork and individual excellence and by sharing with them the profits of the business resulting from such industry and teamwork.

By providing fair and liberal compensation, progressive personnel policies, and pleasant working conditions.

OUR FREE ENTERPRISE SYSTEM...

By keeping our company growing and dynamic.

By pursuing sound, forward-looking management policies and organizational practices, governed by the highest standards of conduct and ethics.

By safeguarding our stockholders' investment and providing reasonable and regular return thereon.

OUR SOCIETY...

By embracing our responsibilities as a corporate citizen, providing leadership as a company and as individuals, in the affairs of our community, state, nation, and the world.

S. C. JOHNSON & SON, INC.
RACINE, WISCONSIN, U.S.A.

with pride and authority. But in performing this service there is no turning away from the ways of the world. The profession is a part of the society in which it acts.

Professional people strive to get respect in their field, to be recognized by their peers, to accomplish their purpose, often against struggle and misunderstanding, and always because they are dedicated individuals and believe in what they are doing. But always they try to serve mankind rather than run mankind.

Instead of talking up professionalization, personnel executives would do better to raise the level of their performance. If they would work toward developing a philosophy of what personnel administration is all about, they will increase their effectiveness and thereby enhance their stature. Then the struggle for professional status will no longer exist . . . for they will have arrived there.

A MAJOR MANAGEMENT FUNCTION

Personnel—the "people" function in most companies—has emerged as a major plank in the corporate organization structure, according to a study released by the National Industrial Conference Board.

H. Bruce Palmer, NICB president, noted that "American managements are giving increased attention to their people problems out of recognition that in a world of rapidly changing products and markets, the capabilities and commitment of people may become the most solid, long-term competitive advantage upon which to build the company."

The study, covering 249 large companies, most of them manufacturers, found that:

The personnel unit is now nearly as prevalent on company organization charts as the financial and secretarial functions and is more prevalent than units devoted to research and development, marketing, and public relations.

There has been a steady escalation in the level of personnel titles and reporting relationships. In a majority of surveyed firms, the top personnel man is now a vice-president whose jurisdiction covers virtually all the company's employees. He generally reports to the president or chairman.

In about half the personnel units, staff has grown faster over the last decade than the company's overall work force.

Central factors in changing the concept and structure of personnel are the need for greater productivity in the face of rising labor costs and stiffer competition; the need for more broadly skilled managers and for stable executive succession; and the growing urgency of planning and providing greater flexibility in the status, work and relationships of employees.

Labor relations, the study revealed, is no longer the preoccupation of personnel that it was some 15 years ago. With the emphasis on people and planning, personnel has broadened its scope and is focusing on such newer activities as:

Management Development—assuring that a steady supply of topgrade people is available to staff all levels of management.

Organization Planning—structuring the company's organizational framework (authority, responsibility, accountability, etc.).

Manpower Planning—determining future needs resulting from varied business changes (expansion, mergers, diversification, etc.). Some firms have developed manpower plans which look two to five years into the future.

Employee Benefits—planning and controlling the wide array of benefits outside of wages and salaries (such as vacations, sick leave and other time off with pay).

Personnel Research—studying new personnel techniques and procedures. An especially fast-growing area is behavioral research (analyzing why individuals and groups behave as they do).

Labor relations has not been downgraded, the NICB study pointed out. Rather, the more critical and complex nature of this activity has called for a more systematic approach from management.

Authored by Allen R. Janger, director of NICB's Information Service Division, *Personnel Administration: Changing Scope and Organization* is available to associates of the board as well as to nonassociates. Anyone interested in purchasing a copy may write the NICB, 845 Third Avenue, New York, New York 10022.

The above summary of the study was prepared by Arthur C. Croft, editor of *Personnel Journal*.

A LOOK INTO THE FUTURE

During the Industrial Revolution the emphasis was on technological progress. Human resources did not get into the consideration; it was not in the thinking of the day. There were dire consequences to this neglect, which managements realized too late. One example was the widespread unionization of defenseless workers who responded to the leadership from outside when their own companies failed them.

The past two decades have produced unprecedented progress in the fields of automation and electronics. But again the advances have been all one way; no corresponding improvement has been made in human relations. People, as usual, have been taken for granted and are once again beginning to assert themselves. The pendulum is swinging back to people. Only this time they're getting their encouragement and assistance from government.

Government intervention in the affairs of business is, of course, not new. We've long had government regulating hours, working conditions, overtime rates, minimum pay, and the like, and we've learned how to build our personnel programs around these requirements. Business has come to accept these controls against exploitation of employees by employers. In addition, pensions, insurance, and welfare payments are established and administered by government, and industry has no choice but to fall in step. Business, largely, is in sympathy with the motives.

The new intrusion on the part of government, which we are discussing here, is, however, something entirely different. The socialistic trend so evident in government planning during the last 30 years has produced a geometric patchwork of social programs designed to extirpate all social evils from poverty to rheumatism. These schemes have been so varied and so all-encompassing that government is finding it necessary to form "government-industry partnerships" to carry them out.

A New Burden

In short, business is expected to implement government social legislation. And government is no longer subtle in its efforts to saddle business with this responsibility. The forced cooperation that results does nothing to help business operate more effectively; in fact, it impedes operating efficiency much as a millstone around the neck hampers the swimmer.

Government has all sorts of ways to "influence" business to come around to its way of thinking. It holds all the trumps. There is hardly a business enterprise, no matter how small, that is not involved in some way with government business, if not as a prime contractor then at least as a subcontractor. The contract says in effect that the contractor agrees to do business with government on government terms. This can mean anything from corporate subservience to the laws to willing compliance with executive orders. As the nation's largest direct and indirect employer, government is now setting the standards.

Industry has already been directed to revalidate employment tests, even discontinue the use of some tests, since they work a hardship upon applicants who have little or no chance of passing them. Compliance investigators have "suggested" that nothing detrimental should be included in an employee's file, that negative responses to reference inquiries, prison records, unemployment claims, wage assignments, and the like serve only to prejudice a manager against an individual who may be under consideration for employment or promotion.

Already new words are coming into the industrial vocabulary. First we heard of the *disadvantaged,* then the *unemployed* and *underemployed,* and now we're getting pressure to help the *unprepared.* Industry is told to put them on the payroll, with some measure of reimbursement toward the costs of recruiting, counseling, on-the-job training, remedial education, and supportive services such as minor medical care and possible transportation. The idea seems to be "employ 'em or support 'em" with employment the preferred choice since this supposedly will reduce the skyrocketing tax burden. Whether industry gets its fair share of productivity from these substandard workers, and all the red tape that is necessary, seems to be of little concern to the social planners.

Nothing Is Routine

And red tape there will be. It is not sufficient to submit obediently to the laws and carry out the provisions of the contract, but a company is always suspect to the burgeoning faceless army of government auditors and investigators. Charges against a firm are easily made, and even a routine inspection can call for endless and detailed records and reports just to prove a company is innocent of any alleged or implied wrongdoing.

The penalties for passivity in meeting the government's terms, instead of enthusiasm for embracing a positive program of "affirmative action," are in such devices as prolonged investigations of complaints, public hearings, and always the threat of contract cancellation. Lately there has come the hint of "negative" penalties in the form of assurances that firms which meet the government's terms willingly with an announced program of cooperation may be rewarded with extra consideration in the awarding of government contracts and more definite profit guarantees.

How serious is all this? A representative of the Secretary of Commerce addressed 300 top executives of companies which are prime contractors. He outlined the specifics of the "President's Test Program for Hiring the Hard Core Unemployed." Since by existing standards these people would never be eligible for employment, he told the assembly that in their hiring and employment practices they should "throw away the book and start over."

In summary, personnel administration as we learned and practiced it is a thing of the past. The gradual encroachment of government upon the industrial scene has bent the established and proven concepts out of shape. As a result, we will revise forms, records, reports, tests and test norms, recruiting sources, hiring standards, promotion sequences, training qualifications, grievance procedures, dismissal practices, and other personnel techniques which have served business so well. From now on their primary purpose will be to promote the government's social legislation aims.

CORPORATE PARTNERSHIP

The business philosophy of the Woodward Governor Company, 5001 North Second Street, Rockford, Illinois 61101, is unique. It is based upon implied constitutional concepts in our free enterprise system: That each human being has the right to develop a living standard for himself and his family commensurate with the relative value of his capability and output; that the purpose of an industrial organization is to provide a medium through which he may, in cooperation with others, promote his legitimate aims; that he has the right to individual freedom, dignity, justice and opportunity; and that the sanctity of these rights is contingent upon his individual and our collective determination to defend them.

Although the company is legally a corporation, internally it operates as if it were a partnership subject, of course, to the legal restrictions applicable to corporations. The system is best described by Mr. Irl C. Martin, chairman of the board, in *The Woodward Way—Evolution of a Business Philosophy,* from which the following was excerpted.

The Woodward Governor Company was founded in the year 1870. It has been through a number of booms and depressions. It has had time to age and temper its processes. It was founded by a conscientious unassuming Maine Yankee of the old school, who was more interested in the development of a satisfactory formula of living than in the accumulation of power via the control of wealth. He preferred to enjoy himself each day at a vocation he liked, among people he liked, and in an atmosphere of mutual regard and respect. His son who succeeded him inherited the same fundamental characteristics. Theirs was the gospel of the industrial family. It is to be hoped that those who are now the industrial parents will discharge their inherited obligations as ably and conscientiously as their predecessors.

EVOLUTION OF THE BUSINESS PHILOSOPHY

Prior to the depression of the late twenties and early thirties, the Woodward Governor Company operated pretty much in the orthodox manner of that era. In 1930, business came completely to a standstill for us, as well as for most others. The slow return to normal business began in 1932.

We decided to try the principles of partnership after a careful analysis of the many facets involved. It required a number of years of mutual cooperation, trial and error, acceptance and rejection before we were all convinced that the partnership philosophy was the most fair, harmonious, effective, and efficient. In 1946, a meeting of all stockholders and workers was called and the partnership plan was voted into effect. For want of a better name, we call it the "Corporate Partnership Plan of Industrial Association."

The management members were entrusted with the authority and obligation of making the necessary decisions except in very unusual instances. These instances require full-scale discussion in open assembly and balloting if necessary. The welfare of the company as a whole must, of course, be the basis of all decisions.

THE PARTNERS

There are three general forms of legal organization: sole proprietorship, partnership, and corporation. The Woodward Governor Company is chartered under the laws of the State of Illinois as a corporation and carries on its external operations under that charter. Internally, however, the organization, started operating as a partnership in 1946, with each partner contributing his assets and, in return, receiving his share of the fruits of the organizational endeavor.

The stockholder partners contribute the required facilities, working capital and funds for expansion. The capital is based on 190,000 shares of one dollar par value stock outstanding. In addition, funds for expansion have been provided from income. The stockholder is expected to honor his status as a partner with loyalty, understanding, and complete collaboration. The stockholder members voice their thinking through the board of directors. Presently there are approximately 1200 stockholders.

The worker partners contribute time, talent, and energy. The worker is expected to maintain and improve his capabilities, apply himself honestly and diligently, and exercise due care in the use and maintenance of the necessary facilities. He is kept completely and accurately informed of the company's status and prospective status via monthly plant meetings, bulletins, intraplant broadcasts and through our monthly publication, *Prime Mover Control*. A complete statement of company finances, orders on hand, daily, monthly and yearly shipments is posted in the recreation area and kept up to date.

When long-range decisions of vital company importance are to be made, the worker member registers his approval or disapproval by the orthodox method of a hand showing or by voice or, in exceptional circumstances, by secret ballot. Presently the worker membership consists of approximately 1250, divided about as follows: Research, Development, Design, and Sales Engineering—200; Manufacturing—825; and Nonmanufacturing—225. The management members are promoted from the worker half of the partnership whenever possible. Management is expected to provide effective leadership, assure fairness and utilize the contribution of both partners with honesty, logic, and prudence.

DIVISION OF INCOME

A partnership worthy of the name must be founded upon mutual honesty, fairness, confidence, and capability. The purpose of an industrial partnership is to provide the most effective vehicle for the mutually satisfactory and harmonious self-advancement of both the worker and stockholder partners. The fruits of the partnership activities may be distributed in a number of ways.

The most fair and logical way is to make distribution on the basis of the relative value of each partner's contribution. Over a long period of trial and error, we have evolved a system of distribution which, although not strictly scientific, has proven quite satisfactory. Because our internal partnership method is simulated, we are subject to the legal restrictions and penalties applicable to corporations. However, the "corporate partnership" method has operated so satisfactorily to all concerned for the past two decades that no objections have developed.

Theoretically, such income as is available after all business costs have been deducted is divided between the stockholder and the worker on a mutually approved master formula. Business costs are considered to include, as highest priority items, provisions for the perpetuation of the working force and facilities (the bases of income). In the event of deficits or meager profits, the application of this theoretically logical concept would be restricted by minimum wage laws which apply to employer-employee relationships under the corporate structure, but would not apply to a pure partnership.

The partners receive, when available for distribution, what might be classed as periodic interim payments (wages, salaries, and dividends), with final settlement at the end of the fiscal year. The interim or base remuneration to the currently registered stockholder partner is calculated on the relative value of his investment. The interim or base remuneration of the regular worker partner is calculated upon his relative value as compared to that of his worker colleagues.

A minimum limit for the least valuable regular worker member is established. It is the amount of income required to prudently but decently support, protect, and educate a family consisting of husband, wife, and two children. A maximum limit for the most valuable regular member (officials included) is established at 10 times the minimum. Individual incomes are interpolated between the two limits by a yearly rating and ranking system that is participated in by the entire organization.

It is philosophically intended that the worker will base his living standard on his interim or base income. It is expected he will use any additional income for the purpose of creating an estate. Final distribution, if any, is made to both partners at the end of each current fiscal year. Income accruing to the stock-holders may be retained in whole or in part at the discretion of the board of directors. Retained income is used to increase working capital and for expansion. The workers' share of available surplus income is distributed as a bonus. The bonus may be paid to the worker in cash, or up to 15 percent of the payroll may be paid into the Deferred Profit Sharing (savings) Fund.

MEMBER EVALUATION

The company attempts to evaluate the contribution of each worker member fairly and impartially and base any wage adjustments upon the results of this evaluation.

Evaluation of New Members: The new member's performance on the job is reviewed and his rate considered at periodic intervals during the first two years of his employment. If his work merits an increase, the supervisor recommends a rate change. Rate changes are approved by the next in line of authority over the supervisor at the first and second periods, and by the Member Evaluation Committee at the third and fourth rating periods. These evaluation periods are as follows:

1. Between 60 and 90 days after starting date.

2. Nine months after starting date.

3. Fifteen months after starting date.

4. Twenty-four months after starting date.

First Evaluation: Approximately 60 days after the starting date of a new member, the Personnel Department furnishes the supervisor with a progress report form for the new member. The supervisor reviews the performance of the new member and makes any recommendation for a change of rate. Any rate changes are approved by the next in line of authority over the supervisor.

Second Evaluation (9 months after starting date): The same as first rating.

Third Evaluation (15 months after starting date): Same procedure as in the first and second ratings with respect to progress report. However, after the supervisor has made out the progress report, he places the member on his current department ranking list. This rating is reviewed by the Member Evaluation Committee. The hourly rate is set according to the rates of the adjacent members on the list; usually the same as the next member below, or if there is no member lower in the list, the rate will be equivalent to or less than that of the next member above.

Fourth Evaluation (24 months after starting date): Same procedure is followed as in the third evaluation. In addition, the Evaluation Committee places the member on the master ranking list. This is accomplished by placing the member somewhere on the master list between the names of the two members on the department list above and below the member being ranked. Regular meetings of the Evaluation Committee are held monthly for the purpose of considering the members who have received the third or fourth evaluations.

Rate changes approved at these meetings become effective at the start of the pay period immediately following the evaluation.

Annual Evaluation of Regular Members: After successful completion of the two year probationary period, every regular member of the organization is included in the annual member evaluation program. This program takes place during the months just prior to January 1st as any wage changes developing from the evaluation program become effective the first pay period following January 1st. The evaluation program concludes with a list of the entire regular membership of the company in numerical order according to the overall value of the individual to the company. This listing of members, in order of value, is accomplished through a series of coworker evaluations in which each member of the organization participates, and through supervisor and Member Evaluation Committee review. This Member Evaluation Committee is composed of company officials, executives, and supervisors with extensive backgrounds.

The worker is also obligated to evaluate the relative value of the supervisors. This evaluation is of only indicative value because all workers, particularly the younger ones, are not well enough acquainted with all of the supervisors to apply mature judgment to their evaluation. The final evaluation of the supervisors is provided by the supervisors themselves and by the Member Evaluation Committee whose job it is to know intimately the qualifications of each. The supervisors rate the executives and vice versa. This rating procedure, including a final review of executive ratings by the head of the company, progresses in a final and confirmed listing of every worker in the company—including company officials.

The final step is dividing the master list into pay blocks. Each worker is allotted a base wage commensurate with the relative value of his contribution to the total team effort and, therefore, his position on the list. Changes in his individual position on the list, either up or down, can result only from a change in the relative value of his contribution to the company.

FACILITIES

People are the most important ingredient in any enterprise. Adequate facilities are necessary, however, to provide the means with which the people can do their work most efficiently and effectively. The company facilities include the home plant at Rockford, Illinois, and a manufacturing plant at Fort Collins, Colorado. There are assembly plants in Slough, England; Schiphol, The Netherlands; and Tokyo, Japan. There is also an international sales office at Lucerne, Switzerland.

The home plant is located on 26 acres of ground about five miles northeast of downtown Rockford. The main building is of buff-colored brick, with a Lannon stone front and Bedford stone trim. The office and manufacturing areas are on one floor and the building is windowless. It is completely air-conditioned and all incoming and recirculated air is electrically cleaned of all smoke, dust, pollen, etc.

Year around temperature is held in the 70-degree range and the relative humidity at approximately 50 percent. The ceilings of the manufacturing and office areas are made of soundproofing metal squares. The fluorescent lighting fixtures are flush and the dimensions are such that the lighting and sound-proofing units are interchangeable. The lighting intensity may be increased to a maximum of 150 foot-candles if desired.

The machine and service connections are all introduced from below the floor. The manufacturing area has ceramic tile walls and a terrazo floor. The office has painted walls and cork-tiled floors. A paging system of broadcast quality covers the entire building. In addition to paging and time signals, music and news are broadcast at stated intervals.

The basement area contains many nonmanufacturing service departments; a cafeteria, which is the source of plain but excellent food; a complete medical department, including x-ray rooms; a dental clinic; a library; tiled locker room with air-conditioned lockers; a barber shop; and a rest area containing reading tables and game tables. Above and at the front of the building is an auditorium with a seating capacity of 500.

Also included at the home plant are research and development facilities, an environmental test building, a product test building, storage facilities, a building for storage and maintenance of grounds—care machinery, and a large green-house. The greenhouse provides seedlings for the plantings which surround the building. It also provides cut flowers and plants during the winter months throughout all buildings.

Our tools and machinery, with the exception of some special equipment used in research and development and certain specialized production machines, are general purpose machine tools. Due to the extreme accuracy and cleanliness essential in our specialized business, however, our depreciation and obsolescence rate is quite high. The maintenance cost to minimize machine downtime is well above average.

The branch plants consist, at present, of some purchased and some rented properties. It is expected, however, that each branch will eventually reach a status comparable to the Rockford facilities as each plant's assets expand.

SUMMARY

In conclusion, let us note that the "corporate partnership" plan has operated efficiently and fairly. It provides the flexibility necessary to properly accommodate the fluctuation in production resulting from varying customer requirements. The plan also results in more stable employment. It permits the worker members, for instance, to work long hours in the winter and short hours in the summer without penalizing the stockholder members. It assures maximum quality, the best delivery, and the lowest justifiable prices to our customers. Our volume of business, like that of most others, is determined by quality, delivery and, finally, by price. Our total net income and our individual incomes are dependent upon our individual and collective performance. The "corporate partnership" plan is the only plan of which we have any knowledge that tends to preclude suspicion and misunderstanding and, at the same time, provides an honest incentive for economy, efficiency, and teamwork.

Our formula for determining base incomes and the sharing of additional income has proved quite satisfactory. It has provided a foundation on which the worker members and stockholder members can move up and down the income scale together in harmony and understanding, if not at all times in complete enjoyment. No one likes to have his income reduced but, if it is necessary, there will be far less discord if everyone concerned receives proportional treatment. Such mutual accord encourages liberality on the part of the stockholder in the purchase and maintenance of facilities that will permit the worker to use his aptitudes and energy most effectively. It encourages the worker to strive for the ultimate in efficiency since his income is directly affected. The whole plan pays both partners proportionately a premium for harmony and efficiency and a penalty for discord and indolence.

The worker has sufficient personal power and prestige within the organization to get immediate redress if his personal prerogatives are infringed. He can also get immediate action if he feels that conditions exist or are imminent that will adversely affect the welfare of the company. The full power and prestige of the company are solidly back of him as long as his motivation and conduct are a credit to the organization.

Probably the principal reason our company has had reasonable success and no personnel difficulties in over 90 years of existence is because it is operated *as a means to a satisfactory life* rather than just as a means to money making. Its philosophy takes into consideration that all people have basic economic aspirations; that in a corporate or corporate partnership endeavor both the stockholders and the workers are necessary; that each group has a definite contribution to make; that the relative value of the contribution of each can be determined with reasonable accuracy by people anxious to be fair; that each is entitled to his fair share.

YESTERDAY, TODAY, TOMORROW

What is personnel administration? How do people in the field of personnel view their management responsibility? What do line managers and foremen consider is their involvement insofar as personnel administration is concerned?

At the outset, let's understand that personnel administration is not some responsibility "up front," or the job of one man or one staff, but is the obligation of all who work with people. Whether hiring, training, promoting, disciplining, rating, or whatever, these are all part and parcel of the same activity, commonly lumped together under the catch-all name of personnel administration.

Neither is personnel administration an accumulation of various clerical functions. Many personnel offices consist of clerks who spend unproductive hours keeping all sorts of records and reports which nobody does much about and which do not change the picture anyhow. Keeping track of tardiness and absences, for example, may be better handled in payroll where the time sheets are available. What is done with the information such records reveal is, of course, a responsibility of personnel.

Nor is personnel a central service organization. This concept started with centralized employment and then began to embrace all sorts of odd jobs in an effort to build a staff and to justify its existence.

Let's get something else straight, too. Personnel administration is not to be thought of as a job. It is not an occupation that young people are encouraged to enter for a good livelihood. This is not a series of scientific or systematic procedures that can be learned in the university or on the job. It is rather something that people believe in. Then it becomes a business of arts and crafts instead of science and technology.

To make my point, let me take you back to your military experience. If you're crawling up on a pillbox you'd much prefer to be covered by a guy who thrilled to joining a fighting outfit than some kid who signed up looking for "benefits." Similarly, I'd hate to entrust the ideals and attitudes of our workers to people who went into personnel work because this was better than driving a truck.

In an attempt to understand what personnel administration is, or should be, it is necessary to erase from our minds the picture we see today and go back to its start, see how it came about, how it developed, and where it is heading.

In the Beginning

Before World War II, company management was concerned mostly with only five of the six M's of management—Money, Markets, Material, Methods, and Machines. No money or time was appropriated for the other M—Manpower. It was not in the thinking of that day.

Until the early 1930's, the personnel activity was pretty much restricted to employment, to see that every position in the organization was kept filled with men and women. Then as the employment market gradually tightened, managers found that the chore of finding suitable new workers was becoming more time consuming and that it interfered with their many other duties, which were also becoming more complex and involved. That made them willing, in fact eager, to let some other person worry about the problems of locating applicants, sorting out the undesirables, and referring the acceptable ones for their consideration.

In its modest and unobstrusive beginning certain unwanted tasks related to employment were relegated to this central office. In addition to the actual recruiting and screening, the details associated with keeping adequate records and conforming to company policy and government regulations were permitted to drift into this central office. It is significant to note, however, that while management was willing to share some of the work, there was no thought of relinquishing any of the control.

Where They Came From

Since this new office was given no authority of its own, it attracted the type of person who expected to be bossed by higher-ups. From the outside came school teachers who were lured away from the classrooms by the prospect of better earnings. Welfare workers came to do good in business where certainly much good needed to be done. A wave of idealism attracted do-gooders of high principles and great naiveté. Often when the jobs were filled from within the organization they were given to former supervisors, foremen, and others who came up through the ranks, some rewarded with promotions because of loyal performance in unrelated work elsewhere in the company, many actually demoted uphill to get them out of the way. The personnel people came to their new and undefined jobs from sales, from production, from accounting, depending on who could be spared. In the history of personnel development it is sad to reflect that many men arrived by accident.

There was no precedent to go by and this indecisiveness as it concerned qualifications resulted in personnel making only halting progress. The many different practitioners, using various job titles, had no guidance, either. Literature was sparse and few schools had courses which offered proper training in this new field. The bosses didn't know what they wanted either; they knew only what they didn't want—trouble from unions and government, and release from the nuisance of hiring.

The First Progress

The first personnel administrators were hired as a defensive measure. Management had an attitude that the job was a necessary but unwelcome bother.

From this meager start the personnel activity began to grow. But its growth was uneven and unsteady. In some companies it grew very little; in some places it died out as an activity of its own and its several duties were again absorbed by others. Wherever it failed to make progress, the fault lay with lack of encouragement on the part of management or lack of leadership on the part of the personnel people. But there were some companies that were ready to recognize the contribution a sound employee relations program was prepared to make toward more efficient operation. And fortunately there were some personnel executives who were able to grow with their programs.

The big growth came after World War II. There were three contributing factors. First, employment was no longer hit or miss. With the rapid industrial development that followed war's end, personnel programs began to become necessary to cope with the hiring and placing of men and women. Adequate help was getting harder to find and the entire complexion of the nation's work force was changing. New forces, such as housewives, came into the employment picture. Conditions and circumstances surrounding work were considerably affected.

Second, management no longer had the unqualified upper hand. Somewhere along the line new forces had come into play. For instance, new motivations had to be established when such things as fear no longer proved effective. Workers, including those not organized, were being heard and had to be reckoned with.

Third, something new entered the picture in the development of third party influences. First the arrival of New Deal legislation involved companies in legal responsibilities which logically centered in the personnel office. At about the same time labor unions had grown in size and strength, and this focused management's attention on the practical necessity of getting its house in order. The personnel administrator was destined to become the person to deal with these increasingly important and militant forces.

As business operations, especially in the areas of dealing with employees, became more involved, companies began to attach new significance to their personnel programs. The reservoir of functions was being deepened as well as widened. Personnel, which originally only added more services to its sphere of activities, now began to add influence also. Jobs like training, wage administration, and benefit counseling, which began as minor functions because they received little attention, were, in the process of development, expanded with the expansion of industry, the growth of labor unions, and the increasing complexity of legislation.

Better qualified administrators, most of them technically minded, began to be attracted to the field. They introduced and developed techniques and procedures which, after years of painful trial and error, have become refined and formalized. In the present picture, personnel is attracting a higher level of academically trained "successor prospects" which give the entire activity a fresh and vigorous balance of experience, training, and ability.

All this indicates that there are signs that personnel management, which was originally marked by mediocrity, is now emerging from stepchild status in the corporate community. It has gone so far that some large organizations, having experienced the contribution personnel can and does make, have created vice presidental positions for their top personnel executives. While it is true that not every program has succeeded this well, it is just as true that throughout all companies the personnel activity has been upgraded in the eyes of management and the workers. For the qualified and dedicated personnel executive the door of opportunity is open wider.

A Coming of Age

No longer is personnel staffed with do-gooders or industrial misfits, but with practitioners who approach their responsibilities and their opportunities from both a technical and a philosophical standpoint. The old myth that every management man had, namely that he knows all about how a company personnel program should be set up and run, has long ago been exploded. Many company presidents have said that they go out to hire the best personnel executive available because they realize that in our enlightened era "business is people," and the conditions of employment and development of manpower lie within the province and purview of the personnel executive. The company president is no longer the sum total of all management functions, and he and his senior staff know that they are not expected to understand and direct the employee program effectively with all its ramifications. This is the job for the personnel executive who has the necessary skill, training, background, and outlook to understand not only the personnel functions but also their purpose.

New Responsibilities Evolve

The field is slowly coming of age. Personnel management is maturing because the growth of companies carries with it a complexity of new duties involving people. And in the total management activity personnel is no longer in the periphery but closer to the center where the hard decisions are made. We've gone a long way from making people happy to making them productive. The stardust has been shaken out, and in the process personnel executives have learned for themselves, and demonstrated to others, that personnel administration is much more than day-to-day performance of necessary administrative techniques.

Personnel management is still beset with handicaps, real and imagined. How fast it grows and what kind of progress it makes depends upon the personnel practitioners more than upon the management of the company. No company can give recognition to people it feels unworthy of the award; but on the other hand, no company can deny recognition that is earned by the good consistent performance being done every day by personnel people.

What I've said so far is that the field of personnel management is growing up. Naturally I cannot speak for you as an individual and whether you too are growing up. We'll come back to that later.

Personnel programs have come a long way from the early days when garbage-can tasks were dumped into their convenient central office. No longer is personnel a storage place for unwanted duties. No longer do personnel staffs lose more men and women to other divisions than they obtain from those divisions.

Where once the personnel man symbolized weaknesses in company operations, he now symbolizes strength, for the strength of any company lies not in its products but in its people who design, make, sell, and distribute those products.

Top management may still be disillusioned by visions of holding control and direction, but the personnel man is beginning to make his mark, namely that it is in the best interest of the company to design its employee relations program to fit the workers' needs, not the personal whims of management, and to conduct its personnel programs accordingly.

After experiencing the peccadillos of adolescent youth, there is now some hope that personnel management is growing up. In many places it is taking its rightful place as a full-fledged member of the management team.

Three Examples of Growth

To prove that this is not wishful thinking, let me give you three unrelated illustrations from everyday business life to show how personnel management is growing up.

In the first place, personnel practices are being improved. For example, in the employment of workers there is less discrimination than before. The problem has not been completely solved, nor will it be despite recent legislation, for bias is buried in the heart of man where no law reaches. But simply as a matter of economics, qualified members of minority groups are having less difficulty finding suitable jobs. Companies are realizing that ability knows no restrictions and that unfounded prejudices create artificial barriers to success which are too costly to tolerate.

There is still discrimination in the hiring of older workers, although this situation is coming in for its share of attention. By ignoring this problem managements have left the door open for still more unwanted government intervention. Management should realize that as far as older workers are concerned it is simply a case of "employ 'em or support 'em." Besides, companies need all the available workers; skills cannot be arbitrarily cast aside because of an unrealistic age barrier.

Women, too, are gaining in acceptance. Long ago established as a vital part of the nation's workforce, they are now moving into positions of responsibility and authority. Here again, no one sex has a corner on brains.

In a democratic society these moves spell progress. In our industrial society they indicate that personnel management is growing up.

Better People on Way

Secondly, the field of personnel management is attracting better caliber men and women to be the practitioners. It is true that the field is cluttered with all sorts of personnel administrators operating under various titles and with varying degrees of effectiveness. But as the demands for a really professional-type service increase, the misfit with the title is being replaced by the more competent technician, better trained in the skills and better equipped in the understanding of human relations.

The colleges are turning out hundreds of graduates who are well schooled in personnel precepts. These technicians, trained in the laboratories of the campus, are bound to have a wholesome impact on personnel work as they acquire practical experience in the laboratory of life. More and more their influence will be felt. This also is a sign of personnel management growing up.

In the third place, some of the personnel executives, those who are making a contribution to the field, are beginning to develop a philosophy of what the work is all about.

For the first century and a half of this nation of ours the emphasis was on the development of physical resources—technological progress. Without any slackening in attention to technical improvement, during the last two or three decades there has been far greater attention paid to human values than ever before—from physical resources to human resources. This is no shift from things to people; it is just bringing both into proper perspective and balance.

There are indications that managements are becoming aware of the importance of emphasizing the human side of progress. Technologically we have found the key to plenty. Yet the world that technology can build is only a half-world. For a complete world we must look beyond the sliderule and be concerned with the meaning of things, not merely their function. In the final analysis, people, not science or technology, will determine the kind of world we live in.

When the history of the industrial revolution is written in its entirety, the closing chapters will record three stages in the evolution of personnel management.

In 1917 personnel administration was in its infancy, usually emergency-created. It took on many forms, but amounted to little more than centralized employment.

Approximately in 1937 it emerged as an adolescent with the establishment of scientific or at least systematic procedures which emphasized necessary technical training. At this point it generally acquired departmental standing.

The New Philosophy

For its future, it is expected to move into the grown-up stage, with the development of a philosophy. Once this is accomplished it will have attained executive status.

Before we conclude this recital, it might be well to ask ourselves what our personal future in this field will be. We've heard where the field of personnel management is destined to go. How about you?

Perhaps many personnel administrators might be satisfied with the progress they have made. After all, it is a good way of making a living. As jobs go, there are many, many other jobs that are less attractive.

To me this sounds like the attitude of people who are going nowhere. When they leave to go elsewhere or into retirement the field of personnel will not miss them. People who are content to stand still in effect fall behind, for the world around us is not static. I firmly believe that those of us who make our living in personnel work have a responsibility to the field which provides us our good fortune. But in order to progress beyond our present position we must do more than build a greater central service activity, or introduce more techniques.

The forms, procedures, and devices we use are not the job; they are merely the paraphernalia of the personnel administrator. On the way to personnel success such techniques are not a destination in themselves but only a means of travel. They are the scaffold used to erect a sound employee relations program.

As long as you're content to be a department manager then concentrate on your personnel procedures, all the while administering in your central office other people's ideas and policies, many of them unsound. However, if you aspire to become a company executive, then rise above these necessary techniques and concentrate on their meaning, all the while training and developing the line managers to perform the personnel functions. Don't think of yourself as dealing with people but rather dealing with the factors that affect people. There is quite a distinction here. The landscape is the same; the difference is in beholders.

Mystery of Human Personality

Just as there are hucksters in advertising, quacks in medicine, shysters in law, and scoundrels in religion, so also do we have miscreants in personnel. The doctor's mistakes are in the cemetery; the lawyer's mistakes are in jail; the preacher's mistakes may be in hell; and the casualties of misguided personnel practitioners are strewn along the tobacco road of frustration.

The architects can cover their mistakes with ivy, and brides theirs with mayonnaise. But you and I can't do that. We cannot afford to make mistakes. Not as long as we're dealing with something as mysterious and potent as the human personality.

Once we understand, accept, and apply that philosophy to our everyday administrative duties, then personnel management will serve its useful purpose. Then the past will have taught its lessons, the present will offer the proving ground, and the future will be assured.

INDEX

A

B

N

Production, 450-451

Productivity and morale, 46

Productivity in relation to manpower forecasting, 107-109

Professionalism in personnel, 906-915

Profile (test), 186-187

Profit participation bonus, 543

Profit-protection insurance, 707-709

Profit sharing, 112, 543-545, 622, 725-731

Profit-Sharing Research Foundation, 728

Program committee practice, 490-491

Program coordinators, 446

Programmed instruction courses (Du Pont Co.), 347

Programmed learning, 342-347

Projection of manpower needs, 106-113

Project "Total," 445-446

Promoting Cooperation (filmstrip), 309

Promotion—
communicated only by his immediate superior, 463
effective date of accompanying increase, 647
from ranks, 144, 209-214
supervision and management positions, 214-218, 433

Promotions, Transfers, and Training for Responsibility (filmstrip), 309

Property and Liability Insurance Handbook, 205

Psychiatric care, 675

Psychic income, 620-621

Psychological Corporation, The, 184, 199

Psychological testing, 182

Public address system, 462

Public Affairs Council, 831

Public assistance, 259

Public Contracts Division, U.S. Department of Labor, 668

Public Documents Room, U.S. Department of Labor, 733

Public Utility District No. 1, 463-464

Public works projects, 271

Purchasing, 509

Q

Qualifying periods for sick pay, 681-683

Questions asked on applications, 166-167

Quiet hour, 866-867

Quintilian, 338

"Quit Rate" formula, 241-242

R

Race, 167, 262, 271

Radio City Rockettes, 747

Radio-television ads in recruiting, 130

Railroad Retirement Board, 721-724

Railway Labor Act, 781-782

Raises, see Increases

Rand McNally Road Atlas, 320

Ratios of major manpower groups to total manpower, 108-109

Raybestos-Manhattan, Inc., 551-553

Raybestos Savings Club, 551-553

Readers' Guide to Periodical Literature, 320

Reading racks, 475-477, 529

Readings, selected, 377-378

Real Security, The (film), 310

Recall (after layoff), 234

Record retention, 794

Records required by Fair Labor Standards Act, 667

Recreation, 46, 572-576

Recruiting, 47, 67, 81, 119, 121, 144-147, 260

Recruitment brochure, 123

INDEX

United States—(Contd.)
Supreme Court, 783
Treasury Department, 546-548,
596-597, 711
Veterans Administration, 587-588
United States Chamber of Commerce,
73-75, 785
United States Dept. of Labor—
Bureau of Apprenticeship and
Training, 359, 363
contract exemptions, 268
Manpower Administration, 132
notice to employees, 267
Office of Federal Contract Compli-
ance, 271
publications, 87
recordkeeping requirements, 267
Service Contract Act, 269
violations and penalties, 268-269
Wage and Hour and Public
Contracts Div., 269
Walsh-Healey Public Contracts
Act, 269
working conditions, 267
United States Steel Corporation, 425
United Steelworkers, 742
University of California Extension
Div., 327
Unseen Helper, The, 402
Unskilled worker, 313-314
Updating paperwork, 105

V

Vacation pay (unused at separation),
229
Vacation policies, 229, 877-880
Vacillation, 388
Validation study, 195-197
Value engineering, 446-447
Vending machines, 568-571
Verification of age, 798-800
Veterans Administration, 587-588
Veteran's benefits, 586, 587-588
Vetter, Dr. Eric, 106-107
Virginia, University of, 137

Vision, 400
Vista, 236
Visual-aid props, 482
Visual Materials Center, Chicago
Public Library, 716
Vocational Rehabilitation program,
Illinois, State of, 153
Vocational training, 360-363
Vocation of personnel administration,
25-26
Voice, tone, and enunciation, 297
Voluntary employee pension contri-
butions, 711-713, 729
Voting in company groups, 483
Voting time off, 614, 883

W

Wage, minimum, 266
Wage and Hour Division, U.S. De-
partment of labor, 668, 794
Wage and salary administration, 609-
668
Wage assignments, 595-597
Wage differential exceptions, 632-633
Wage freeze of World War II, 673
Wage increase—
automatic, 647, 650
general, 615-650
longevity, 647-650
merit, 616-617, 647-649, 650
procedure, 648
promotion, 647, 650
Wage levels, 242
Wage rate changes, 242
Wage-turnover ratio, 241
Wagner-Peyser Act of 1933, 132, 783
Waiting periods for sick pay, 681-
682, 683
Walker, H. G., 558
Wall Street Journal, 102
Walsh-Healey Act, 629
Washrooms, 861-862

959